AF846327

More information about this series at http://www.springer.com/series/13544

Eurasian Studies in Business and Economics 2/1

Series Editors
Mehmet Huseyin Bilgin, Istanbul, Turkey
Hakan Danis, San Francisco, CA, USA

Representing
Eurasia Business and Economics Society

Mehmet Huseyin Bilgin • Hakan Danis •
Ender Demir • Ugur Can
Editors

Business Challenges in the Changing Economic Landscape - Vol. 1

Proceedings of the 14th Eurasia Business and Economics Society Conference

Springer

Editors
Mehmet Huseyin Bilgin
Faculty of Economics
Istanbul Medeniyet University
Istanbul
Turkey

Hakan Danis
MUFG Union Bank
San Francisco, CA
USA

Ender Demir
Faculty of Tourism
Istanbul Medeniyet University
Istanbul
Turkey

Ugur Can
Eurasia Business & Economic Society
Fatih Istanbul
Turkey

The authors of individual papers are responsible for technical, content, and linguistic correctness.

ISSN 2364-5067 ISSN 2364-5075 (electronic)
Eurasian Studies in Business and Economics
ISBN 978-3-319-22595-1 ISBN 978-3-319-22596-8 (eBook)
DOI 10.1007/978-3-319-22596-8

Library of Congress Control Number: 2015954180

Springer Cham Heidelberg New York Dordrecht London
© Springer International Publishing Switzerland 2016
This work is subject to copyright. All rights are reserved by the Publisher, whether the whole or part of the material is concerned, specifically the rights of translation, reprinting, reuse of illustrations, recitation, broadcasting, reproduction on microfilms or in any other physical way, and transmission or information storage and retrieval, electronic adaptation, computer software, or by similar or dissimilar methodology now known or hereafter developed.
The use of general descriptive names, registered names, trademarks, service marks, etc. in this publication does not imply, even in the absence of a specific statement, that such names are exempt from the relevant protective laws and regulations and therefore free for general use.
The publisher, the authors and the editors are safe to assume that the advice and information in this book are believed to be true and accurate at the date of publication. Neither the publisher nor the authors or the editors give a warranty, express or implied, with respect to the material contained herein or for any errors or omissions that may have been made.

Printed on acid-free paper

Springer International Publishing AG Switzerland is part of Springer Science+Business Media (www.springer.com)

Preface

We are excited to organize our 14th conference on October 23, 24, and 25, 2014, at Hotel Silken Diagonal in Barcelona, Spain. We are honored to have received top-tier papers from distinguished scholars from all over the world. We regret that we were unable to accept more papers than we have. In the conference, 437 papers will be presented and 745 colleagues from 61 countries will attend the conference.

We are pleased to announce that distinguished researchers ***Jonathan Batten*** and ***José-Luis Peydró*** will join the conference as keynote speakers.

Prof. Batten is professor of finance in the Department of Banking and Finance at *Monash University*, Australia. He is a well-known academician who has published articles in many of the leading economics and finance journals and currently serves as the editor of *Emerging Markets Review* and associate editor of the *Journal of Banking & Finance*, *Journal of the Asia Pacific Economy*, and *Research in International Business and Finance*.

Prof. Peydró is a prominent academician specializing in the fields of banking, systemic risk, financial crises, and monetary policy. He is currently professor at *Universitat Pompeu Fabra*, part-time professor of banking and finance at *Cass Business School*, *City University* (London), advisor at *Bank of Spain*, and affiliated professor at *Barcelona Graduate School of Economics*. Previously, he was a visiting scholar at the *University of Chicago* and consultant at the *Federal Reserve Board* and *International Monetary Fund*. He also serves as the associate editor of the *Review of Finance* and associate editor of the *Spanish Review of Financial Economics*. His research has appeared in many of the leading economics and finance journals such as *Econometrica*, *Review of Financial Studies*, *Journal of Finance*, *American Economic Review*, and *Journal of International Economics*.

EBES conferences have been an intellectual hub for academic discussion for our colleagues in the areas of economics, finance, and business. Participants have found an excellent opportunity for presenting new research, exchanging information, and discussing current issues. We believe that our future conferences will improve further the development of knowledge in our fields. In addition, based on the contribution of the paper to the field, the *EBES Award Committee* has selected one of the papers for the ***Best Paper Award***. The Best Paper Award winner will be announced during the conference.

We would like to thank all presenters, participants, board members, and keynote speakers and are looking forward to seeing you all again at the upcoming EBES conferences.

Best regards,

Istanbul, Turkey Ender Demir

Eurasia Business and Economics Society (EBES)

Eurasia Business and Economics Society (EBES) is a scholarly association for scholars involved in the practice and study of economics, finance, and business worldwide. EBES was founded in 2008 with the purpose of not only promoting academic research in the field of business and economics but also encouraging the intellectual development of scholars. In spite of the term "Eurasia," the scope should be understood in its broadest term as having a global emphasis.

EBES aims to bring worldwide researchers and professionals together through organizing conferences and publishing academic journals and to increase economics, finance, and business knowledge through academic discussions. To reach its goal, EBES benefits from its executive and advisory boards which consist of well-known academicians from all around the world. Every year, with the inclusion of new members, our executive and advisory boards became more diverse and influential. I would like to thank them for their support.

EBES conferences and journals are open to all economics, finance, and business scholars and professionals around the world. Any scholar or professional interested in economics, finance, and business around the world is welcome to attend EBES conferences. Since 2012, EBES has been organizing three conferences every year: one in Istanbul (possibly in the early summer) and two in Europe or Asia (possibly in January and in fall).

In 2011, EBES began publishing two academic journals. One of those journals, *Eurasian Business Review—EBR*, is in the fields of industry and business, and the other one, *Eurasian Economic Review—EER*, is in the fields of economics and finance. Both journals are published biannually and we are committed to having both journals included in SSCI as soon as possible. Both journals are published by *Springer* and currently indexed in the *Cabell's Directory, Ulrich's Periodicals Directory, RePEc, EBSCO Business Source Complete, ProQuest ABI/Inform, IBSS: International Bibliography of the Social Sciences*, and *EconLit*. In 2011, EBES also started to publish the *EBES Anthology* annually to give opportunity for the papers presented at the EBES conferences.

Furthermore, in 2014 EBES partnered with Springer which has started to publish EER and EBR, along with a new conference proceedings series: *Eurasian Studies in Business and Economics*. The new series includes selected papers from the EBES conferences and expects its first title to be released early next year. The proceedings are already indexed in the Thompson Reuters Proceedings Index and both EBES and the Springer expect that the series will benefit greatly from the partnership.

On behalf of the EBES officers, I sincerely thank you for your participation and look forward to seeing you at our future conferences. In order to improve our future conferences, we welcome your comments and suggestions. Our improvement is only possible with your valuable feedback and support.

I hope you enjoy the conference and Barcelona!

With my very best wishes,

Jonathan Batten

Contents

Part II Finance and Banking

Part III Economics

EBES Executive Board

- **Jonathan Batten**, Monash University, Australia
- **Iftekhar Hasan,** Fordham University, USA
- **Euston Quah**, Nanyang Technological University, Singapore
- **Peter Rangazas**, Indiana University-Purdue University Indianapolis, USA
- **John Rust**, Georgetown University, USA
- **Alexander Tatarkin**, Russian Academy of Sciences, Russia
- **Marco Vivarelli**, Catholic University of Milano, Italy

EBES Advisory Board

- **Hassan Aly**, Department of Economics, Ohio State University, USA
- **Ahmet Faruk Aysan,** Central Bank of the Republic of Turkey, Turkey
- **Michael R. Baye**, Kelley School of Business, Indiana University, USA
- **Idris Bin Jajri**, Faculty of Economics and Administration, University of Malaya, Malaysia
- **Wolfgang Dick**, ESSEC Business School, France
- **Mohamed Hegazy**, School of Management, Economics and Communication, The American University in Cairo, Egypt
- **Heather Hopfl**, Essex Business School, University of Essex, UK
- **Cheng Hsiao**, Department of Economics, University of Southern California, USA
- **Philip Y. Huang**, China Europe International Business School, China
- **Irina Ivashkovskaya**, State University—Higher School of Economics, Russia
- **Soo-Wook Kim**, College of Business Administration, Seoul National University, Korea
- **Christos Kollias**, Department of Economics, University of Thessaly, Greece
- **Ali M. Kutan**, Department of Economics and Finance, Southern Illinois University Edwardsville, USA
- **William D. Lastrapes**, Terry College of Business, University of Georgia, USA

- **Rita Mårtenson**, School of Business, Economics and Law, Göteborg University, Sweden
- **Panu Poutvaara**, Faculty of Economics, University of Munich, Germany
- **M. Ibrahim Turhan**, Borsa Istanbul, Turkey
- **Wing-Keung Wong**, Department of Economics, Hong Kong Baptist University, Hong Kong
- **Naoyuki Yoshino**, Faculty of Economics, Keio University, Japan

Organizing Committee

Jonathan Batten, PhD, Monash University, Australia
Mehmet Huseyin Bilgin, PhD, Istanbul Medeniyet University, Turkey
Hakan Danis, PhD, Union Bank, USA
Pascal Gantenbein, PhD, University of Basel, Switzerland
Ender Demir, PhD, Istanbul Medeniyet University, Turkey
Orhun Guldiken, University of Arkansas, USA
Ugur Can, EBES, Turkey
Busra Yaman, EBES, Turkey

Reviewers

Sagi Akron, PhD, University of Haifa, Israel
Mehmet Huseyin Bilgin, PhD, Istanbul Medeniyet University, Turkey
Hakan Danis, PhD, Union Bank, USA
Ender Demir, PhD, Istanbul Medeniyet University, Turkey
Pascal Gantenbein, PhD, University of Basel, Switzerland
Orhun Guldiken, University of Arkansas, USA
Peter Harris, PhD, New York Institute of Technology, USA
Gokhan Karabulut, PhD, Istanbul University, Turkey
Davor Labaš, PhD, University of Zagreb, Croatia
Chi Keung Marco Lau, PhD, University of Northumbria, United Kingdom
Gregory Lee, PhD, University of the Witwatersrand, South Africa
Nidžara Osmanagić-Bedenik, PhD, University of Zagreb, Croatia
Euston Quah, PhD, Nanyang Technological University, Singapore
Peter Rangazas, PhD, Indiana University-Purdue University Indianapolis, USA
Doojin Ryu, PhD, Chung-Ang University, South Korea
R. Baris Tekin, PhD, Marmara University, Turkey
Manuela Tvaronavičienė, PhD, Vilnius Gediminas Technical University, Lithuania

Part I
Accounting and Corporate Governance

Use of the Managerial Tools in the Czech Companies

Libuše Svobodová

Abstract The presented article is based on the questionnaire survey, which was conducted in 2014. There were almost 300 Czech enterprises in the study. Questionnaire investigation was focused on the tools used in the managerial accounting in the interviewed enterprises. Specifically, there were questions involved on the monitoring of costs, the use and creation of calculations, plans and budgets, capacity utilization and efficiency, efficiency evaluation and monitoring of economic results and evaluation of financial analysis. In the evaluation there were involved physical persons and also legal entities. It is expected that individuals use less the tools of managerial accounting. It is also expected that SMEs use less the tools of managerial accounting than large companies. The last hypothesis is dedicated to the efficiency of the company. It can be expected that firms that prepare and monitor calculations, plans and budgets are aware of the importance of financial analysis and evaluate it. A detailed research together with the analysis and critical assessment of accessible materials will enable to identify the main objectives in the field of study. The analysis of the initial state will consequently enable to identify the key factors and knowledge.

Keywords Managerial accounting • Survey • Efficiency • Financial analysis

1 Introduction

Managerial accounting is an integral part of the enterprises. Managerial accounting information include: information on the costs of an organization's products and services, calculations, budgets, performance reports and other information which assist managers in their planning and control activities.

A fundamental purpose of managerial accounting is to enhance firm value by ensuring the effective and efficient use of scarce resources. Thus, managerial accounting systems should provide information that improves employees' abilities to make organizationally desirable decisions, thereby enabling employees to

L. Svobodová (✉)
Department of Economics, University of Hradec Kralove, Hradec Králové, Czech Republic
e-mail: libuse.svobodova@uhk.cz

© Springer International Publishing Switzerland 2016
M.H. Bilgin et al. (eds.), *Business Challenges in the Changing Economic Landscape - Vol. 1*, Eurasian Studies in Business and Economics 2/1,
DOI 10.1007/978-3-319-22596-8_1

achieve the organization's goals and objectives (Caplan 1988; Horngren et al. 2000). Additionally, managerial accounting systems should provide information that helps align the interests of employees with owners by directing employee effort and attention to activities that benefit the organization (Atkinson et al. 1997; Lambert 2001). Viewed in this light, the information produced by a managerial accounting system serves two important roles in an organization: to provide some of the necessary information for planning and decision-making, and to motivate individuals (Zimmerman 2000).

In the presented paper there will be not done the detailed description and review of the managerial tools. It is not the main goal of the article (see the details in Sprinkle (2003) and Langfield-Smith (1997)). Coman et al. (2012) focused on Managerial accounting as a source of information for an efficient management in SME. Lazar and Matušková (2012) focused on the variable and fixed costs. Kupkovič and Tóth (2004) focused in their article on Activity Based Costing as on new managerial method of costing, budgeting and accounting system, practice and technic, which represent causal relationship between creation of outputs and activities that would consume enterprise sources. Through the medium this causal relationship can try more accurately allocate costs. Direct costs would direct allocate on individual outputs, indirect costs can through the medium multistage cost allocation base to indirect costs. This calculation method needs the details information about the activities and costs connected to it. Tappura et al. (2015) focused on Cost-based calculations, Balanced Scorecard approach, Payback methods and other management accounting methods for safety-related decision-making. Knápková et al. (2014) and Jirčíková and Remeš (2007) focused on the utilization of balanced scorecard and the effect of its use on the financial performance of companies in the Czech Republic. Janeček and Hynek (2007) firstly focus on the efficiency of firms in a knowledge economy. Janeček and Hynek (2010) focused on the using of indicators counted for various groups of businesses as return on assets, return on sales, level of leverage factor, intensity of capital turnover and mainly return on equity. They compared efficiency of users and non-users Economic Value Added (EVA) concept. Mohelská and Sokolová (2011) focused on the competence and roles of territorial administration. Čámská and Scholleová (2014) concentrate on valuation of entities. Štamfestová (2014) focused in the article on business performance management in manufacturing companies in the Czech Republic. Seidler (2011) wrote about responsible management of the correct way to prosperity companies. Suchánek et al. (2013) presented the article focused on the influence of Quality management on corporate performance. Šiška (2009) wrote How to evaluate economic successfulness of an enterprise.

2 Goals and Used Methods

The article is based on primary and secondary sources. The primary sources are represented more. They are represented by the results from the conducted questionnaire investigation and by ideas of the author. The secondary sources comprise professional literature, information collected from professional press, legal regulations, websites, discussions or previous participations in professional seminars and conferences relating to the chosen subject. Then it was necessary to select, classify and update accessible relevant information from the numerous published materials that would provide the basic knowledge of the selected topic.

3 The Results of the Questionnaire Investigation

3.1 Description of the Project

In 2014, a survey was conducted among nearly 300 businesses. Firstly was conducted pilot testing of questionnaires in spring 2014. Secondly was done the current survey. Concretely were gained 295 questionnaires. Three of them were not possible to use for next evaluation. The partial results will be presented in the article. The survey involved 77 % of SMEs and 23 % of large enterprises from all regions of the Czech Republic. One of questions was focused on the tools that are used in the managerial accounting by the Czech enterprises. Next questions were involved on the monitoring of costs, the use and creation of calculations, plans and budgets, capacity utilization and efficiency, efficiency evaluation and monitoring of economic results and evaluation of financial analysis. The last question was aimed on the utilization of the technologies in the connection with managerial accounting.

3.2 Results from the Questionnaire

In the Fig. 1 there are presented the results from the first question. It was focused on the tools used in managerial accounting by Czech companies. The results are divided on the small and medium enterprises and on the large ones. Into evaluation there were involved: Direct costs, Indirect costs, Type calculation formula, Calculation (full costs), Calculation (variable costs), Activity Based Costing, Controlling, Benchmarking, Balanced Scorecard, Economic Value Added, Market Value Added, Quality Management, Just in Time and Others.

The presented Fig. 1 clearly illustrates and confirms the hypothesis that small and medium-sized enterprises use tools of managerial accounting less than large enterprises. As a result, it may be noted that even individuals are using managerial accounting tools less than large enterprises. The only one tool that small and

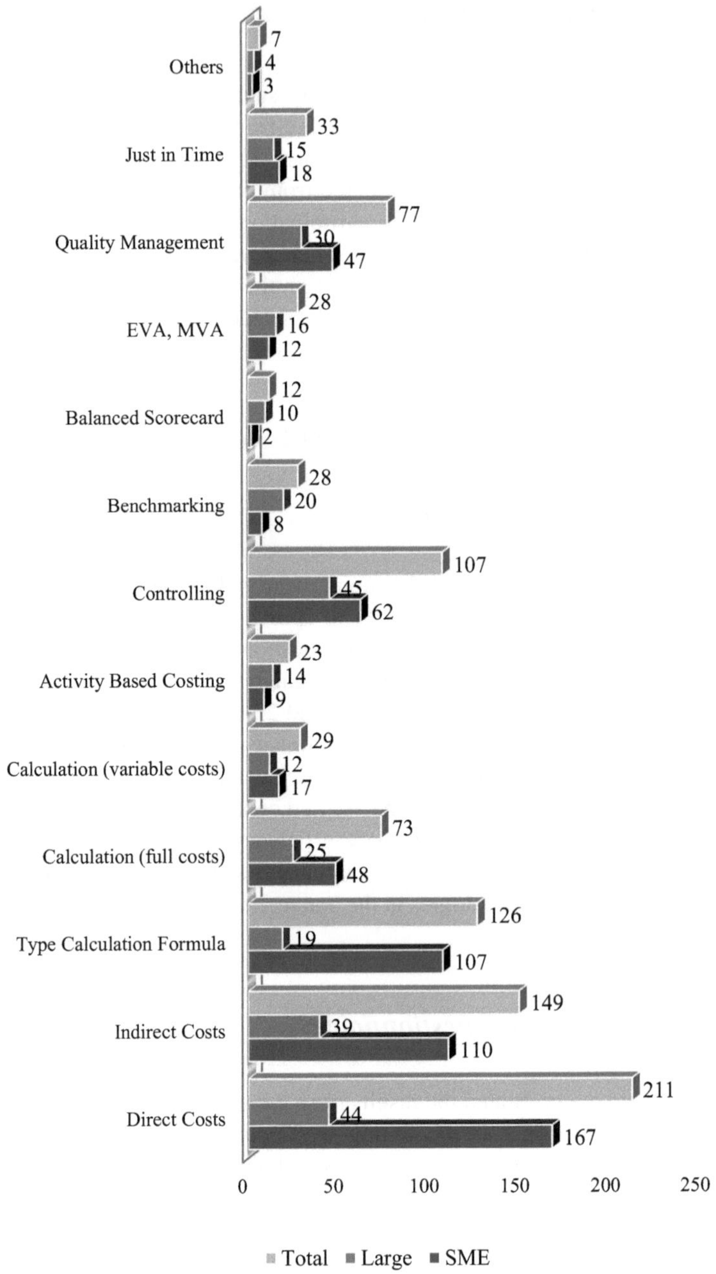

Fig. 1 Tools used in managerial accounting and size of the company

medium-sized companies use more than large businesses is monitoring of the direct costs.

It was expected that SMEs companies will use less the tools of managerial accounting such as Controlling, Benchmarking, Balanced Scorecard, Economic Value Added or Market Value Added, Quality Management or Just in Time than large companies. Balanced Scorecard is the less used managerial tool by the respondents. The reason should be the sophistication of this method. The managers need to classify four perspectives. The first one is financial situation of the company, customer perception, internal business processes and learning and growth of the company. The biggest difference in the results is in the controlling, 39 %. Large companies have mostly the specialists and departments that focused on this field. On the other hand 28 % of the SME use controlling as managerial function like planning, organizing, staffing and directing when control in management means setting standards, measuring actual performance and taking corrective action. The same number of large and SME calculate it. They are represented by 107 respondents in each group. The same can be noted for benchmarking. Each group is represented by 28 companies. It was not expected that SME will calculate the Economic Value Added. The reason should be the information from the financial accounting. The companies that use tax records instead double-entry bookkeeping cannot calculate it, because Economic Value Added is based on financial accounting statements such as balance sheet and income statement. The tax record use other statements based on different data. The calculation of Economic Value Added is not easy due the opportunity costs that are not easy to quantify for a lot of accountants.

When we focus on the calculation, 37 % of large companies used calculation of full costs. On the other hand SME used mostly the type calculation formula. Totally is mostly used the calculation of full costs. It is possible to state that it is mostly the easiest type of calculation in the companies. The calculation of variable costs is used only in the 10 % respondents. The less used calculation method in both groups and also overall is Activity Based Costing with the identification, classification and evaluation of the activities that relate to the object of the calculation.

Table 1 presents the results of tools used in managerial accounting in the percentage of companies. The results are again divided on the SME and large companies and on the overall results.

The Fig. 2 presents the same data from other point of view. One hundred and nine small and medium companies used both, direct and indirect costs. Seventy-four companies used one of the methods. Forty-two SMEs do not used direct and indirect costs. In the large companies used 39 companies both methods, 6 companies used only one of them. It is surprising that 22 large companies do not monitor direct and indirect costs. We can give question whether it is really true. The explanation may be that companies use different terminology for monitoring of costs. Another can be e.g., misunderstanding of question. The next one should be the mistake be rewriting. But it is not expected in such rate. Or it may be a reality.

Both variables show a statistical point of view of dependency (for example by chi-square). The two variables are not statistically significantly independent.

Table 1 Tools used in managerial accounting and size of the company

	Direct costs	Indirect costs	Type calculation formula	Calculation (full costs)	Calculation (variable costs)	Activity based costing	Controlling	Benchmarking	Balanced scorecard	Economic value added, market value added	Quality management	Just in time	Others
SME	74 %	49 %	48 %	21 %	8 %	4 %	28 %	4 %	1 %	5 %	21 %	8 %	1 %
Large	66 %	58 %	28 %	37 %	18 %	21 %	67 %	30 %	15 %	24 %	45 %	22 %	6 %
Total	75 %	53 %	21 %	25 %	10 %	8 %	37 %	10 %	4 %	10 %	28 %	13 %	3 %

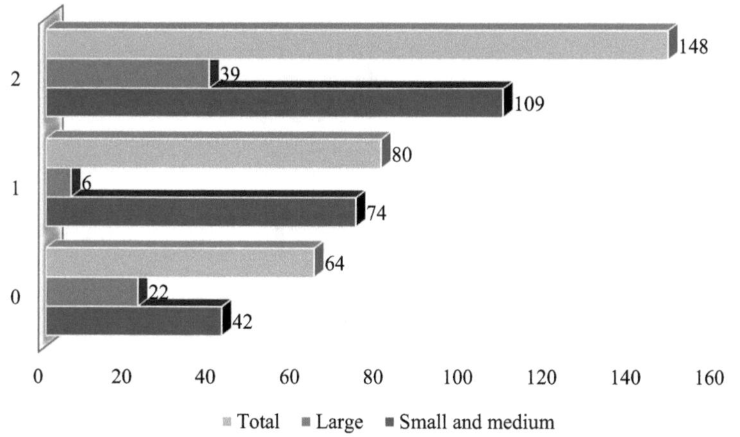

Fig. 2 Number of used methods (direct and indirect costs) in managerial accounting and size of the company

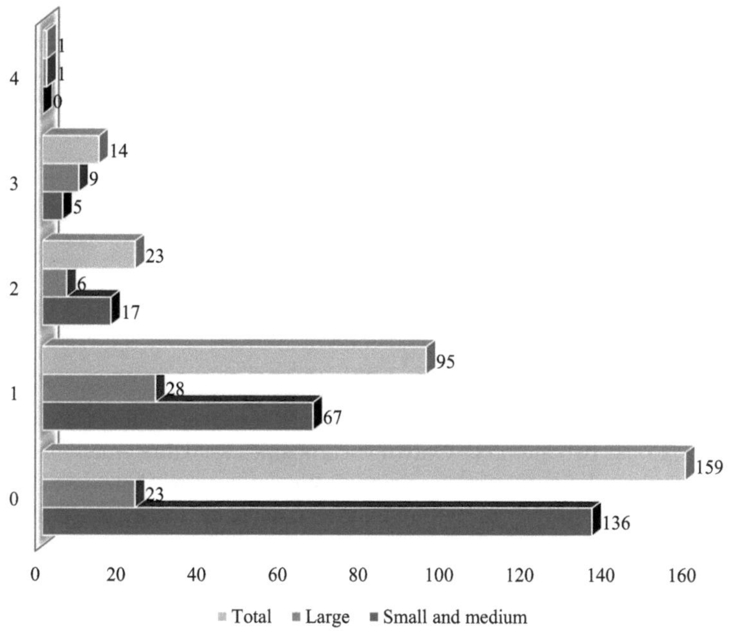

Fig. 3 Number of used calculation methods together (type calculation formula, calculation full and variable costs and activity based costing) in managerial accounting and size of the company

The Fig. 3 presents the number of used calculations methods together (type calculation formula, calculation full and variable costs and activity based costing) in managerial accounting and by size of the company. One hundred and thirty-six

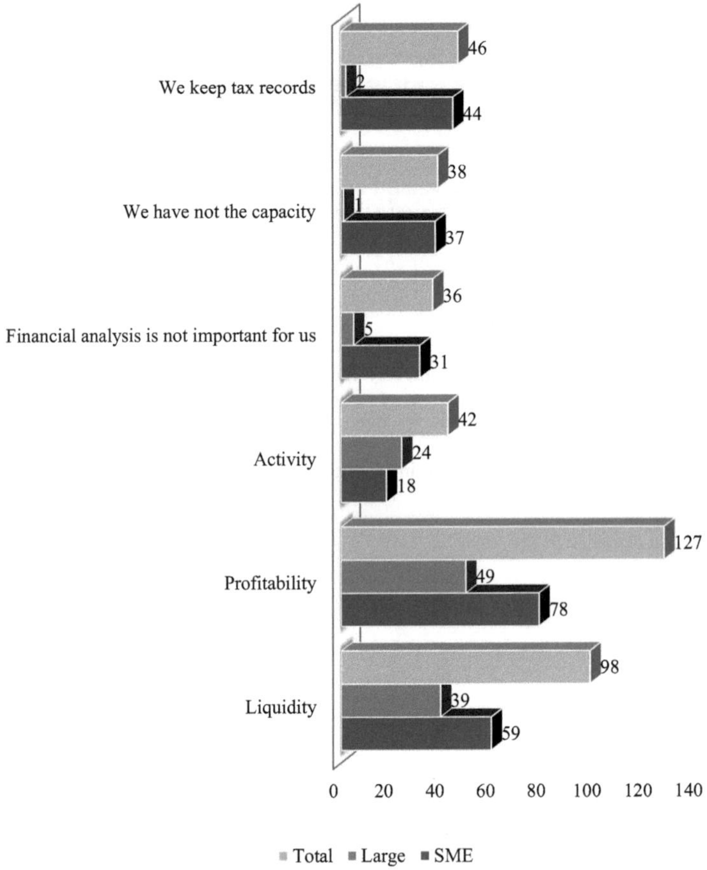

Fig. 4 Indicators used in the financial analysis

SME do not use calculation in their businesses. Sixty-seven of them use one of the method and 17 use two methods. Only five companies used three methods and none used four. The results give a warning signal. We can assume that some companies sell certain products below cost without knowing it. In the large companies there is better situation, as was expected. Twenty-three large companies do not use calculations. Twenty-eight of them use one of the methods, six companies use two methods, nine companies three methods and one company use four methods. It can be stated based on the results that large businesses should use more tools of calculations.

The Fig. 4 and Table 2 presents results from the next question aimed on the financial analysis. The questions were detailed as follows: In the financial analysis we evaluate those indicators: Liquidity, Profitability, Activity. Next group was focused on the reason not doing the results from the financial analysis. It is not important to count the financial analysis in our company. We do not count the financial analysis in our company, we have not the capacity. We do not count the

Table 2 Indicators used in the financial analysis

	Liquidity	Profitability	Activity	Financial analysis is not important for us	We have not the capacity	We keep tax records
SME	26 %	35 %	8 %	14 %	16 %	20 %
Large	58 %	73 %	36 %	7 %	1 %	3 %

financial analysis in our company, we keep tax records. The results are not surprising again.

Large enterprises use more financial analysis tools, which are essential in evaluating the effectiveness of the company. Conversely, some small businesses that keep tax records cannot calculate the financial analysis. In the sample reported that answer 42 companies. Next 37 and 31 SME may keep tax records. A total of 68 SME responded that they do not have the capacity to process financial analysis or the results from the financial analysis are not essential for them. It is possible to expect that some of them use double-entry bookkeeping. The most often used tools by large companies are the assessment of profitability and liquidity. It is the same in the SMEs. Sixteen percent of the SME would like to evaluate the financial analysis but they have no the capacity. Twenty percent of the SME cannot shadow the results from the financial analysis because they keep tax records.

4 Conclusion and Discussion

Other issue that should be solved can be the clusters of the companies. After detailed statistic processing it is possible to present that there are three clusters of the companies. One is compounded mostly from small enterprises. Second two are comprised from all types of the companies. The next results from the questionnaire investigation are aimed for example on the plans and budgets. From the results it is evident that companies that prepare plans and budgets used also tools of financial analysis.

The results of the survey confirmed all three hypotheses. Individuals and small and medium-sized businesses use less tools of managerial accounting than large ones. It may be a lack of capacity, lack of data and difficulties in needed monitoring data. Many small businesses used managerial accounting tools, but they may not fully realize it. The last hypothesis was usage of plans and budgets and financial analysis. Small and medium-sized enterprises use less indicators of financial analysis and they do not so often prepare plans and budgets, as large enterprises.

The managerial tools, budgeting and also financial analysis are very important also in the connection with investment into new equipment, technologies etc. It is necessary to take into account with those investments the budgets, calculations and others. It is also possible recommend to calculate net present value, use payback method, internal rate of return or accounting rate of return when the company prepares the large investment action.

Acknowledgements This paper is written with financial support from specific university research funds of the Czech Republic Ministry of Education, Youth and Sport allocated to the University of Hradec Králové Faculty of Informatics and management, project no. 2111/2014.

References

Atkinson, A. A., Banker, R. D., Kaplan, R. S., & Young, S. M. (1997). *Management accounting*. New Jersey: Prentice-Hall.

Čámská, D., & Scholleová, H. (2014). Valuation of entities operating in creative industries. *International Advances in Economic Research, 20*(2), 229–230.

Caplan, E. H. (1988). *Behavioral accounting research—An overview, behavioral accounting research: A critical analysis* (pp. 3–11). Ohio: Century VII Publishing Company.

Coman, D. M., Coman, M. D., & Boca, I. F. (2012). Managerial accounting a source of information for an efficient management in SME. *Procedia—Social and Behavioral Sciences, 62*, 521–525.

Horngren, C. T., Foster, G., & Datar, S. M. (2000). *Cost accounting: A managerial emphasis*. New Jersey: Prentice-Hall.

Janeček, V., & Hynek, J. (2007). On the efficiency of firms in a knowledge economy. *Ekonomickycasopis, 55*(5), 500–512.

Janeček, V., & Hynek, J. (2010). Incentive system as a factor of firms' efficiency improvement. *Ekonomie a Management, 13*(1), 76–90.

Jirčíková, E., & Remeš, D. (2007). The use of the concept of balanced scorecard to identify the benefits of entering into business cluster. In *Hradec Economic Days 2007—Economic growth and development in the region* (pp. 284–289). Hradec Kralove: Gaudeamus.

Knápková, A., Homolka, L., & Pavelková, D. (2014). Utilization of balanced scorecard and the effect of its use on the financial performance of companies in the Czech Republic. *Ekonomie a Management, 17*(2), 146–160.

Kupkovič, M., & Tóth, M. (2004). Comparison of full absorption costing to Activity Based Costing (ABC). *Ekonomickycasopis, 52*(2), 133–147.

Lambert, R. A. (2001). Contracting theory and accounting. *Journal of Accounting and Economics, 32*(1–3), 3–87.

Langfield-Smith, K. (1997). Management control systems and strategy: A critical review. *Accounting, Organization and Society, 22*(2), 207–232.

Lazar, J., & Matušková, S. (2012). Variable and fixed costs from the economic theory and company management perspective. *Politickaekonomie, 60*(2), 245–264.

Mohelská, H., & Sokolová, M. (2011). The competence and roles of territorial administration: The results of primary research. In *Hradec Economic Days 2011—Economic development and management of regions*. Hradec Králové: Gaudeamus.

Seidler, J. (2011). Responsible management of the correct way to prosperity companies. In *Hradec Economic Days 2011—Economic development and management of regions*. Hradec Králové: Gaudeamus.

Šiška, L. (2009). How to evaluate economic successfulness of an enterprise. In *Hradec Economic Days 2009—Economic development and management region*. Hradec Králové: Gaudeamus.

Sprinkle, G. B. (2003). Perspectives on experimental research in managerial accounting. *Accounting Organizations and Society, 28*(2–3), 287–318.

Štamfestová, P. (2014). Business performance management in manufacturing companies in the Czech Republic with and emphasis on non-financial aspects of business. *Politickaekonomie, 62* (4), 521–541.
Suchánek, P., Richter, J., & Kálová, M. (2013). The influence of quality management on corporate performance. In M. T. Semmelrock-Picej & A. Novak (Eds.), *Proceedings of the 9th European Conference on Management, Leadership and Governance* (1st ed., pp. 266–273). Reading, UK: Academic Publishing International Limited.
Tappura, S., Sievänen, M., Heikkilä, J., Jussila, A., & Nenonen, N. (2015). A management accounting perspective on safety. *Safety Science, 71*, 151–159.
Zimmerman, J. L. (2000). *Accounting for decision making and control*. New York: McGraw-Hill.

[illegible]

Business Processes Intrinsic Accounting Quality Attributes Assessment in Lithuanian Organizations

Kristina Kundeliene

Abstract The most important accelerator in everyday life is rapid growth and development in the area of information technology. Economic efficiency of management decisions is determined by objective and timely information, which must be supplied by the accounting system to the company's managers. Changes in the external surrounding of the business organizations and importance of timely information enforce to recoil and to give special attention to accounting quality of business processes, accounting quality assessment questions. There was performed an empirical research, which gave important findings about business processes intrinsic accounting quality attributes intensity and association between them in Lithuanian organizations. The results of the research highlighted that in several business processes the expression of accounting quality characteristics is different and depends on organization's activity; internal quality characteristics in all business processes aren't the most evident and between these attributes there is only positive correlation.

Keywords Business processes • Accounting quality attributes • Intrinsic quality • Measurement • Evaluation

1 Introduction

In each company the biggest flows of information emerge in the accounting area. Today's business environment, globalization processes, technological progress and other factors determine the necessity to manage it. Company's leaders, managers need timely, actual and relevant information for decision making. Growth and development of information technology is the most important accelerator for every business organization today. Only objective and timely information must be given to the company's managers in order to adopt efficient management

K. Kundeliene (✉)
Accounting Department, School of Economics and Business, Kaunas University of Technology, Kaunas, Lithuania
e-mail: kristina.kundeliene@ktu.lt

© Springer International Publishing Switzerland 2016
M.H. Bilgin et al. (eds.), *Business Challenges in the Changing Economic Landscape - Vol. 1*, Eurasian Studies in Business and Economics 2/1,
DOI 10.1007/978-3-319-22596-8_2

decisions. This is an essential task of the information technology driven accounting system. There is generally accepted that information is vital to the company success and its ability to remain competitive in the market. Over the past years development and expansion of information technology has modified the performance of traditional accounting systems and much more information can be processed, depicted and warehoused quite easily. The use of contemporary accounting systems allowed to reduce the amount of daily routine tasks by automating them; instantly generate reports for decision making process and etc., but also raised challenges, which has not been previously encountered in the traditional accounting systems. Such challenges are the necessity to give special attention to systems maintenance and safety (error retrieval, defense from computer viruses and other invasions, etc.). Indicated changes in the business organizations external and internal surrounding encourages to respond and focus on accounting quality of business processes, accounting quality assessment questions.

Investigations in the accounting quality field were interested in such scientists as Xu et al. (2003), Bushman et al. (2004), Biddle and Hilary (2006), Ruzevicius and Gedminaite (2007), Barth et al. (2008), Bharath et al. (2008), Kundelienė (2009a, b, 2010, 2011), Dumitru (2011, 2012), Fan and Zhang (2012), Rusu 2012), Miculescu and Miculescu (2012), Pascu and Horomnea (2013), Hribar et al. (2014), etc.

Research object—attributes that characterize intrinsic accounting quality in the organization business processes and the association between them.

The research goal—to evaluate the expression of intrinsic accounting quality attributes in Lithuanian organizations' business processes and to determine if the interrelationships between intrinsic accounting quality attributes exists.

Research methods. Empirical research is based on quantitative methodological approach. Results of the empirical research were obtained by applying structural questionnaire, data analysis. Results were processed by using quantitative research methods (correlation, cumulative percent and etc.).

2 Theoretical Background and Hypothesis for Business Processes Intrinsic Accounting Quality Attributes Assessment

The analysis of scientific literature had shown that researchers have different interpretations on the accounting quality and especially in the accounting quality measurement field. Various authors and organizations (Morais and Curto 2008; Chaffey and Wood 2005; Heidmann et al. 2008; Financial Accounting Standards Board 1980; Miculescu and Miculescu 2012; Dumitru 2011) distinguished quite different indicators for the accounting quality measurement and it was stimulus to investigate this question more detailed. There was performed discernment of essential business processes accounting quality attributes with assistance of experts (Kundeliene 2010). The most important attributes for business processes accounting quality assessment were found attributes of intrinsic group, where from 11 attributes presented to evaluate there were selected as the most significant seven of them: correctness, reliability, clarity, understandability, accuracy, objectivity, completeness.

In order to evaluate an expression of intrinsic accounting quality attributes in Lithuanian companies' business processes an empirical research was performed. Executed empirical study is based on two main presumptions:

1. Business processes accounting quality can be assessed using the expression of accounting quality attributes.
2. The expression of accounting systems quality characteristics pertain on the analyzed and evaluated company's business process.

In order to achieve stated research goal there was formulated two research hypothesis which had been tested using appropriate statistical methods. Whereas performed expert research had shown (Kundeliene 2010) that the biggest part of attributes had fallen into the intrinsic quality group, so it is possible, that the expression of these attributes will be on the similar level in all of the organization business processes. On purpose to verify presumption there is formulated the first research hypothesis:

H1: Attributes of the intrinsic quality group have supreme expression in all business processes.

It is probability, that among the accounting quality attributes there are some relation and it should be taken into account by assessing and improving accounting system in the organization, so the second hypothesis is formulated:

H2: There is particular relationship between several accounting quality attributes of business processes in the intrinsic quality group.

For empirical research there were chosen quantitative research method—questionnaire. This structural method was chosen because of the convenience to perform the research (negligible expenses to organize survey, the ability to achieve respondents remotely, comfortable to process the survey results and etc.). In the next section it will be discussed research planning and execution processes.

3 Research Design

In this part of the paper will be disclosed planning and execution process of the performed empirical research in Lithuanian business companies. Three main research design components are survey form, measurement scales used and data collection method.

Content and Layout of a Questionnaire Questionnaire consists of introductory, major and closing parts. At the beginning there is introduced objective of a study, explained how to fill the answers and guaranteed an anonymity of the data. Survey begins with the simple questions about respondents position/role in an organization, responsibility level and accounting system used. Introductory part ends with the question where respondent has to select specific business process and continue to analyze and valuate it in the rest part of the questionnaire. In the main part of the questionnaire there are measured the expression of intrinsic accounting quality attributes in the company's specific selected to evaluate business process. Questions about company's activities, annual turnover, the value of assets, number of employees and etc. are given in the closing part of the survey form.

Measurement Scales Used Nominal, interval and range (Likert) measurement scales are used in the empirical research survey form. Nominal scale is employed to determine type of a company, respondents operating function and in other questions in the introductory and closing parts. While use of interval scale allowed to determine company's annual turnover, assets value and size of the workforce. Exploring the extent of intrinsic accounting quality attributes expression in Lithuanian companies' business processes was used range scale (or Likert scale). There were the possibility to respondent to choose one of five given answers: "fully", "partly", "there is some problems", "problematic area" and "no comments" in the major part of the questionnaire assessing accounting quality of the specific selected business process in an organization.

Data Collection Method The research survey form was distributed via the internet and data was collected in the end of 2009. In the beginning of data collection process there were sent more than 600 invitations to take part in the research by completing given form. Some of forms were filled only partially and were eliminated from the research. Finally 248 forms were suitable for further processing.

4 Results of Business Processes Intrinsic Accounting Quality Attributes Assessment in Lithuanian Organizations

According to general questions about the organization the biggest part of respondents are trade companies—40.30 %, almost equally involved services (25 %) and manufacturing (19.40 %) companies. The rest of the companies didn't specified operating field. In graphic form these results are shown in Fig. 1.

In the introductory part of the research respondents were asked to determine their role in company's accounting system, job functions and responsibility level in an organization. 19 % of respondents pointed out that they need accounting information every day performing their operating activities, about 12 % indicated that they collect and record data and also about 12 % specified that they are supervisors for other employees working with data collection and recording. Besides about 9 % of respondents also stressed that they not only use accounting

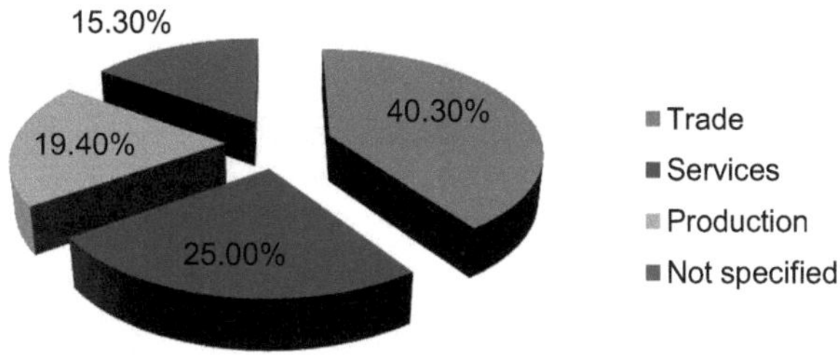

Fig. 1 Distribution of surveyed companies by activity

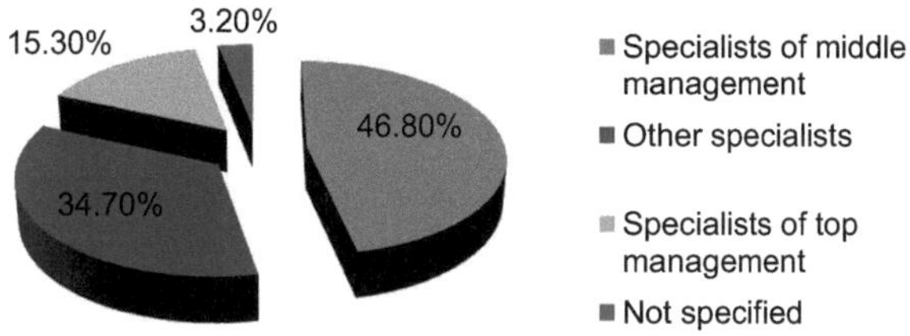

Fig. 2 Distribution of respondents by the responsibility level

information or are managers but as well as inspect and review data in company's accounting system.

According to operational function in a company major part of respondents (about a half) were from management field. 35.5 % of survey participants indicated that they work in accounting or/and finance department and only a small part of respondents were from audit, information technology and other functional departments. Results by the responsibility level in a company are shown in Fig. 2.

The biggest part of respondents by the responsibility level was middle management specialists (46.80 %), 15.30 % were top management specialists and one third of respondents indicated themselves as other specialists (34.70 %). For the evaluation of intrinsic accounting quality attributes there were distinguished and submitted for assessment such business processes: development of commodity/service; resources purchasing planning; procurement; manufacturing; storage; customer/market research; development of sales strategy; sales; management accounting; revenue accounting; non-current assets accounting; payroll accounting; cash management; production capacity management; internal control and tax accounting. Sales were most often valuated business process. About 32.7 % of respondents selected this business process for further analysis and assessment. About 13.3 % of respondents estimated development of commodity/service process, procurement, cash operations management, internal control and management accounting business processes were chosen by 7–11 % of research participants. Others not mentioned business processes valuation frequency fluctuates between 2 and 5 %.

In the Table 1 there is presented results of intrinsic accounting quality attributes assessment in business processes. Numerical values are expressed as a percentage transposing range (Likert) scale values proportionately. Response in range scale "fully" corresponds to 100 %, "partly" corresponds to 75 %, "there is some problems"—50 %, "problematic area"—25 % and answer "no comments"

Table 1 Values of business processes intrinsic accounting quality attributes, percent

	Attributes						
Business processes	Correctness	Reliability	Clarity	Objectivity	Understandability	Accuracy	Completeness
Development of commodity/service	77.27	68.94	68.10	74.14	75.00	78.45	74.14
Procurement	88.89	72.22	63.89	75.00	77.78	77.78	58.33
Manufacturing	75.00	65.00	75.00	65.00	55.00	90.00	80.00
Storage	100.00	75.00	75.00	100.00	100.00	100.00	75.00
Development of sales strategy	75.00	91.67	83.33	75.00	83.33	75.00	41.67
Sales	83.02	74.38	75.62	81.17	77.47	77.78	69.44
Management accounting	66.67	60.42	47.22	44.44	75.00	70.83	66.67
Non-current assets accounting	87.50	87.50	62.50	50.00	62.50	87.50	50.00
Payroll accounting	100.00	75.00	75.00	50.00	75.00	100.00	75.00
Cash management	92.31	76.92	73.08	69.23	76.92	88.46	65.38
Production capacity management	75.00	75.00	75.00	100.00	100.00	100.00	100.00
Internal control	86.11	80.56	44.44	88.89	52.78	75.00	61.11
Tax accounting	50.00	75.00	75.00	75.00	75.00	50.00	75.00

Table 2 Minimax criterion application

Business processes	Group of attributes					
	Intrinsic	Representational	Processing	Contextual	Accessibility	Minimax criterion value
Development of commodity/service	68	**75**	29	**75**	50	75
Procurement	58	42	50	**72**	17	72
Manufacturing	55	10	50	**70**	65	70
Storage	**75**	25	25	0	50	75
Development of sales strategy	42	58	42	**67**	50	67
Sales	**69**	56	41	67	52	69
Internal control	44	50	25	50	**61**	61
Management accounting	44	**69**	46	**69**	63	69
Non-current assets accounting	50	38	25	**75**	50	75
Payroll accounting	50	75	33	**75**	50	75
Cash management	65	65	25	**77**	19	77
Production capacity management	**75**	**75**	**75**	**75**	25	75
Tax accounting	50	0	50	**75**	25	75

Table 3 Values of Spearman's correlation coefficient

	Cor	Rel	Cla	Obj	Und	Acc	Com
Correctness (Cor)	1	0.420**	0.350**	0.376**	0.284**	0.607**	0.383**
Reliability (Rel)	0.420**	1	0.510**	0.357**	0.322**	0.461**	0.228**
Clarity (Cla)	0.350**	0.510**	1	0.376**	0.440**	0.479**	0.321**
Objectivity (Obj)	0.376**	0.357**	0.376**	1	0.344**	0.281**	0.432**
Understandability (Und)	0.284**	0.322**	0.440**	0.344**	1	0.398**	0.321**
Accuracy (Acc)	0.607**	0.461**	0.479**	0.281**	0.398**	1	0.500**
Completeness (Com)	0.383**	0.228**	0.321**	0.432**	0.321**	0.500**	1

**Statistically significant ($p < 0.01$) cases

corresponds to 0 %. After the transposition process there were calculated weighted average of respondents' evaluations and these values are given in the Table 1.

From Table 1, it can be observed the exhibition of intrinsic quality attributes in business processes and how much they differs. In all excluded business processes the difference between minimum and maximum value fluctuates within the pale of 42–100 %.

In order to compare the expression of accounting quality attributes in distinguished quality groups there was created Table 2, where is specified the lowest accounting quality attribute value in separate business process. Then using minimax criterion the maximum value is selected from the least (Drogobickij 2009).

In the Table 2, there is noted an intersection of business process and group of attributes where minimax criterion value is satisfied. Intrinsic group of attributes satisfies criterion in storage, sales and productive capacity management business processes, representational group—product/service development, planning and management accounting and productive capacity management business processes, processing group also in productive capacity management, accessibility group—in internal control. In remaining unmentioned business processes the criterion is satisfied by contextual group attributes. Thus, the analysis in various aspects the expression of accounting quality attributes in business processes leads to the conclusion that the first hypothesis is rejected, i.e., not confirmed.

For the second hypothesis testing there was used Spearman's correlation coefficient. Spearman's correlation coefficient calculation results are presented in Table 3.

Results in Table 3 shows that all intrinsic quality attributes have a positive correlation. Weak correlation was found between these pairs: correctness and understandability, reliability and completeness, objectivity and accuracy (correlation coefficient less than 0.29). While strong correlation (correlation coefficient more than 0.50) is between three pairs of attributes: correctness and accuracy, reliability and clarity, completeness and accuracy. Among other unnamed attribute pairs relationship is average, and the correlation coefficient values ranging from 0.321 to 0.479. Analysis of the relationship among intrinsic accounting quality attributes leads to the conclusions that the second hypothesis can be considered approved. Assessment of intrinsic quality attributes correlation suggests that the attributes are positive interrelated and so they can measure a phenomenon, i.e., business processes intrinsic accounting quality.

5 Conclusions

According to the stated goal there was performed an empirical research, which gave important findings about business processes intrinsic accounting quality attributes intensity and association between them in Lithuanian organizations. The results of the research highlighted that in several business processes the expression of accounting quality characteristics is different and depends on organization's activity.

According to research results the first formulated hypothesis that internal quality characteristics in all business processes are the most evident was dismissed as unfounded. Internal quality characteristics in all business processes aren't the most evident and between these attributes there is only positive correlation.

The second hypothesis that there exists a positive relationship between intrinsic group attributes of business processes accounting quality was confirmed by calculating Spearman's correlation coefficients. Conducted research had shown that the strong relation (relation can be considered as strong if the coefficient is more than 0.50) exists between three pairs of attributes: correctness-accuracy; reliability-clarity; completeness-accuracy; average (correlation coefficient between 0.30 and 0.49)—between 15 pairs of attributes. Correlation was weak (correlation coefficient less than 0.29) among three attributes' pairs: correctness-understandability, reliability-completeness, and objectivity-accuracy.

References

Barth, M. E., Landsman, W. R., & Lang, M. H. (2008). International accounting standards and accounting quality. *Journal of Accounting Research, 46*(3), 467–498.

Bharath, S. T., Sunder, J., & Sunder, S. V. (2008). Accounting quality and debt contracting. *Accounting Review, 83*(1), 1–28.

Biddle, G. C., & Hilary, G. (2006). Accounting quality and firm-level capital investment. *Accounting Review, 81*(5), 963–982.

Bushman, R., Piotroski, J., & Smith, A. (2004). What determines corporate transparency? *Journal of Accounting Research, 42*(2), 207–252.

Chaffey, D., & Wood, S. (2005). *Business information management: Improving performance using information systems*. Harlow/New York: Financial Times/Prentice Hall.

Drogobickij, I. N. (2009). *Sistemnij analiz v ekonomike*. Maskva: Financi i Statistika.

Dumitru, G. (2011). The accounting information quality concept. *Journal of Academic Research in Economics, 3*(3), 559–569.

Dumitru, G. (2012). The accounting information quality concept. *Economics, Management & Financial Markets, 7*(4), 326–336.
Fan, Q., & Zhang, X.-J. (2012). Accounting conservatism, aggregation, and information quality. *Prudence comptable, regroupement et qualité de l'information, 29*(1), 38–56.
Financial Accounting Standards Board. (1980). *Statement of financial accounting concepts no. 2 qualitative characteristics of accounting information* [pdf]. Stamford: Financial Accounting Standards Board. Accessed September 15, 2011, from http://www.fasb.org/cs/BlobServer?blobcol=urldata&blobtable=MungoBlobs&blobkey=id&blobwhere=1175820900526&blobheader=application%2Fpdf
Heidmann, M., Schaffer, U., & Strahringer, S. (2008). Exploring the role of management accounting systems in strategic sensemaking. *Information Systems Management, 25*(3), 244–257.
Hribar, P., Kravet, T., & Wilson, R. (2014). A new measure of accounting quality. *Review of Accounting Studies, 19*(1), 506–538.
Kundelienė, K. (2009a). Apskaitos Kokybė: Kaip Apibrėšime ir Kuo Matuosime? *Economics and management=Ekonomika ir vadyba* [online]. Accessed June 23, 2013, from http://www.ktu.lt/lt/mokslas/zurnalai/ekovad/14/1822-6515-2009-085.pdf
Kundelienė, K. (2009b). *Verslo procesų apskaitos kokybės savybių vertinimas.* Ph.D. Kaunas, University of Technology.
Kundeliene, K. (2010). Assessment possibilities of business processes accounting quality. *Economics & Management, 15*, 972–978.
Kundeliene, K. (2011). Business processes accounting quality attributes assessment: Empirical research in Lithuanian organizations. *Economics & Management, 16*, 66–72.
Miculescu, C., & Miculescu, M. N. (2012). Quality of accounting information to optimize the decisional process. *Annals of the University of Oradea, Economic Science Series, 21*(2), 694–699.
Morais, A. I., & Curto, J. D. (2008). Accounting quality and the adoption of IASB standards—Portuguese evidence. *Revista Contabilidade & Financas-USP, 48*, 103–111.
Pascu, A. M., & Horomnea, E. (2013). Considerations on the quality of information in professional accountant's activity. *USV Annals of Economics & Public Administration, 13*(1), 192–200.
Rusu, A. (2012). National and international perspectives on the quality of accounting information. *Young Economists Journal/Revista Tinerilor Economisti, 9*(18), 70–81.
Ruzevicius, J., & Gedminaite, A. (2007). Business information quality and its assessment. *Inzinerine Ekonomika—Engineering Economics, 2*, 18–25.
Xu, H., Nord, J. H., Nord, G. D., & Lin, B. (2003). Key issues of accounting information quality management: Australian case studies. *Industrial Management & Data Systems, 103*(7), 461–470.

Implementation of Accounting Standards: Financial Reporting in Albania

Sonila Gruda

Abstract Globalization of the today's globe held additionally enhancement of frugal change and internationalization of companies or marketplaces that amplified the demand for the harmonization of accounting standards. The worldwide adoption of the International Financial Reporting Standards is a reflection of the movement towards such globe accounting standards that are vital tendencies that indicates the enhancement of the accounting transparency. Standardization is a demand that imposing a set of rigorous regulations that is demanded uniformly in countless economies that are connected or not. In Albania, commencing from 1 January 2008, business statements demand to comply alongside Regulation No. 9228 "Accounting and Financial Reporting". The regulation defines kinds of Accounting Standards, nationwide or global that demand to be demanded by business entities in Albania. This scrutiny, instituted established on the scrutiny of countless cumulative data, will highlight the present situation of the implementation of accounting regulation and commercial delineating in Albania and indicates facts that scrutiny the Accounting Standards as a brilliant innovation. A number of recommendations will be given, aiming at helping the standardization and harmonization of the present requests of the standards.

Keywords Accounting • Financial describing • Accounting standards

1 Introduction

This introduction presents the authority and objectives of National Accounting Council (following NAC) related with the design and interpretation of National Accounting Standards (following NAS) and also explain the object and authority of National Accounting Standards itself for private and public entities in our country. The introduction must be used as reference for further needed procedures followed during implementation of approved standards from this Council, announced by Minister of Finance. National Accounting Council is a professional, public and

S. Gruda (✉)
Business Administration, Epoka University, Tirana, Albania
e-mail: sgruda@epoka.edu.al

© Springer International Publishing Switzerland 2016

M.H. Bilgin et al. (eds.), *Business Challenges in the Changing Economic Landscape - Vol. 1*, Eurasian Studies in Business and Economics 2/1,
DOI 10.1007/978-3-319-22596-8_3

independent body created based on law nr. 9228, date 29.04.2004 "For Accounting and Financial Statements" (following Accounting Law). NAC performs its activities in accordance with The Accounting Law and other subsidiary acts based on it and its implementation (Phelps and Karremi 2008).

Main objectives of NAC are continuous refinement of accounting legislation, the processing of accounting system in accordance with Accounting Law, drafting of National Accounting Standards, and the incentive of implementation of NAS and International Financial Reporting Standards (IFRS). In order to meet its duties NAC presents to Minister of Finance its proposals for drafting and changing of existing accounting legislation, designs NAC, in accordance with The Accounting Law, designs new rules and regulations in accounting area, gives explanations, interprets and generalizes practical and national accounting standard problems, as accounting instructions, creates specialized commissions, permanent or temporary, and involves experts for development of NAS and legislation and for discussion of problems in accounting area, reviews and express its own opinions over legal and subsidiary draft acts, which contain provisions for accounting and professions, organizes workflow for translation of IFRS, gives recommendations for preparation of accounting specialists in universities, establishes and maintains relations with global accounting organisms (including here Board of International Accounting Standards (BIAS), of European Union and other bodies, which draft these standards in other countries) and involves itself in international activities related with accounting, and creates opportunities for new members to attend professional conferences and seminars in Albania and abroad (Boeva and Prohaska 2002).

The Council of Ministers can release subsidiary administrative and mandatory acts for NAC, in order to accomplish the duties given by Accounting Law and Regulation. NAC is independent in drafting accounting system of NAS and in other accounting regulations.

1.1 Objective of NAC

In order to achieve its duties and objectives, with the support of Albanian Government, through a fund project from Global Bank, being helped by a foreign company "Price Water House Coopers", NAC conducted a set of 14 national accounting standards, which are designed in line with international standards and will be applied by all private and public profit entities by 1 January 2008, without including here big companies, which are included in the list approved by The Council Of Ministers and will fully apply international accounting standards. Based on decree of Minister of Finance nr. 4292, date 15.06.2006, the announcement of 14 national accounting standards has been made, 1 January 2008 is set as their implementation day and as the day to start working with professional trainings from their users and to start announcing these standards.

1.2 Authority of National Accounting Standards in Profit Sector

Every profit entity, based on changed law nr. 9228, date 29.04.2006, "For Accounting and Financial Statements", owes to keep accounting and to prepare and publish Accounting Statements, should take all the needed measures, prepare all the conditions and capacities in order to enforce all the request of these standards. All actual regulations for entities, which have been designed for their internal needs in leading and costs etc., but that are against the trainings and new rules treated in new accounting standards published by NAC, must be rephrased in order to be reconciled with these NAS and with new regulations that NAC published in accounting area. The correct recognition and implementation of these national accounting standards, which are updated and in line with International Accounting Standards and International Financial Reporting Standards (IAS/IFRS), will lead to an important improvement in quality and in general purpose of financial reporting, from public and private profit entities (Boeva and Prohaska 2002). This will make possible the improvement in decision making, in efficient leading and also will increase transparency and will decrease economical informalities in country. The Set of 14 National Accounting Standards is prepared to be applied in 'stated rights' base not in 'cash' base. This requires taking measures for the implementation of this method.

European SMEs share the view that their suppliers, customers and employees are, at most, marginal users of their financial reporting. In all countries included in the study, four main users are reporting financial banks, tax authorities, shareholders and management unit economic. However, significant differences exist between many countries different. In France, the Netherlands, Spain and Germany, the tax authorities are Included in the three main users of financial reporting, namely by 73, 76, 85 and 86 % of the surveyed units.

However, in the UK, only 47 % of the entities involved in the study consider the tax authorities as one of the three primary users. Also banks, which have been identified as the main source of finance SMEs in the six countries considered to be very important users, especially in Italy, Germany and the UK where even been ranked as number 1 among users, with a score of 92 % in Italy, 86 % in Germany, 85 % in Spain, 81 % in the Netherlands, 71 % in the UK and 70 % in France (International Accounting Standards Board 2012).

2 Field of Implementation of Standards

National accounting standards are applied by all the entities of private and public sector, that have profit legal status, or by cost coverage. These standards will not be applied by those entities that will apply international accounting standards and financial reporting (IAS/IFRS), also by those of public sector, which are financed with budgetary funds. The category of public entities will apply special standards for public budgetary sector that are designed by Ministry of Finance, also based in line with international public sector accounting standards (IPSAS) designed and published by IFAC (International Federation Accounting Committee). Any change, improvement, interpretation or in natter need for a new additional standard during the implementation of the standards is an exclusive authority of National Accounting Council. All appearing problems during implementation, all ideas, opinions and possible suggestions should be addressed in writing to National Accounting Council. Approved text of each Accounting standard is that published by NAC and Ministry of Finance in Albanian language. Members of NAC and their supportive staff, are authorized and forced for the preparation of Standard Drafts, published in order to be commented and for approved Standards.

3 Development of Accounting Standards in Albania

The choice of our country to apply the International Financial Reporting Standards (IFRS) is based on our economical conditions, on our objectives to follow the legislation of European countries, and also maintains the traditional accounting practice of the last 50 years. There are still discussions for advantages and disadvantages of this regulation system of accounting, although near a century has passed since the first Accounting Plan and 30 years have passed since the creation of the first uniform Accounting System. The experience of our country for the implementation of national accounting systems and various branches of the economy is not lacking. The history of Accounting in our country starts with the first plan of designed accountings by Jani Vreto, leaded by his own needs in his business, and after the establishment of our independent country there has been found the first structures for identifications of the revenues and expenditures of state budget. Consolidation of state and the establishment of the kingdom brought legal sanction accounting rules and the use of large-scale party double as a basic principle in the accounting records. These regulations date in 1929, when the first Department of Accounting was established in Albania. In the years after liberation accounting, as a technique of recording and identification of economic activities in enterprises in state institutions, was modernize and expand in its area of applying. Organization, functioning and the purpose of the accounting has been adjusted and has been able to respond all the interests of the owner in every level of development in production manner within our country. Modern accounting, literally, although has started since in the kingdom period and continued in socialist period and then has been reaching perfection and improving fast to market economy lately. For 45 years this system has been serving to the centralized economy and to social state and based on the level of accounting technique is rated in a high level. This lead to an easy and low cost application of General Accounting Plan in 1993, because between the techniques of accounting before and after 1993 there was a strong connection, when accounting was reorganized based on commercial companies, and replacing specific accounting based on economic branches, which was an important characteristic of that accounting system. Economical and social conditions, the level of development and the method of economic organization have indicated in the improvement and perfection of accounting system. But a key factor is human factor, with the intelligence, commitment and energies of all the accountants and financiers, who have made possible the realization of this process. In different stages of quality improvements, fortunately our professionals have been oriented to advanced accounting techniques. In the road of development and modernization of accounting were considering world experiences, especially the Italian, Soviet and recent decades it mainly French and continental Europe. These experiences have been adjusted and applied in concrete Albanian economical conditions and have formed a rich accounting tradition, in the bases of which are prepared and worked a whole army of accountants and financiers across the country. New processes of transformation of the Albanian society raised the need for reforms in the field of deep accounting as a discipline which characterized the language of business. If we look back in retro, in 1940s accounting was known as 'the art of registration, classification and summarizing meaningfully the monetary value of transactions' which are at least partially financial character and interpretation of these results, in 1970s this definition has been improved and accounting as a information system is a service activity. The main function of this system is to reassure financial information for entities, in order to make possible a reasonable selection in different ways of undertaking an action. This definition emphasizes more the purpose than the process, more at taking decisions than accounting recording, classification and interpretation, by emphasizing the real role of modern accounting. In a market economy which has entered our country, legal and methodological adjustments have changed profoundly. The variety of entities, free market relations, the role of different economic control, reduction of state intervention and other features made possible the needed change in objectives, role and functions of accounting. In general accounting guidelines were headed by its relations with its partners in the environment where it operates. These adjustments affected the accounting units in several directions: firstly, as a means of measuring the interests of stakeholders such as investors, employees, lenders, suppliers, creditors, etc.; secondly, as a means of state control over the activities of entities within the limits set by national legislation; thirdly, the means of communication with third parties to provide necessary information in economic and financial decision making (Bank of Albania 2012); fourthly, as the means of providing material evidence to resolve conflicts between entities.

These improved accounting adjustments in its entirety. Its continuous evolution gave to interested users a set of information. General Accounting Plan of 1993, which has a sustainable application during these years, was not just a nomenclature or just accounts plan, but also an accounting manual. It contained definitions, concepts, accounting rules and valuation rules. Financial Statements generally gave a structured representation of the financial position and operating performance. The transition to the new accounting standards constitutes a qualitative change for the preparation and reporting of financial statements. With all its difficulties constitutes a necessary step on the path of integration.

4 Corporations Financial Reporting Enhancement Project

Albania has prepared an Action Plan in 2008, which is based on 2006 Report of World Bank (WB) about the Observance of Standards and Codes of Accounting and Auditing in Albania (A&A ROSC). This Action Plan was prepared by National Steering Committee (NSC), consisting of public and private parties, and sets a clear reform program for improvement of Albania legal framework, institutions, accounting and auditing as a profession and culture of accounting, auditing and business as well, in order to realize a high quality financial reporting (Paterson et al. 2009). Corporate Financial Reporting (CFR) is essential for a well functioning market economy as well as the basis for a sound financial system.

Key findings of the Report of WB over (A&A ROSC) in Albania are stated below:

- Enterprise Level: 9 of 10, approximately 40,000 Enterprises are Small and Medium Enterprises (SME). Financial information given by them is not considered credible.
- Regulatory Framework: Legal framework of financial reporting is characterized by a lack of cohesion. Institutional and Professional Capacity: National Accounting Council, developer of accounting standards, in order to fill in its mandate, needs more technical and financial resources.
- Audit Function: The regulatory framework for the audit function has been prepared in accordance with the previous eight directive of EU, which still needs to gain more credibility.
- Education: There needs to be updated the educational curricula, that will be approved and used by Universities and Professional Organizations.
- Rating for A&A ROSC showed that Albania needs to do further steps in order to archive its goal to have a strong framework on financial reporting.

5 Compliance Factors of Accounting

The reason for the change in accounting principles between certain countries may be up because they differ in the level of economic development, legal system, tax system, the intensity of the capital market, the political and cultural features, etc.

Some of the factors that influence the accounting compliance process are identified as follows (also see Fig. 1):

Factors	Anglo-American Model	Continental Europe Model
Legal System	Common laws, Limited numer of regulations	Codified law, heavily influenced by legal concepts
Tax System	Tax System is independent from national accounting requirements	Tax laws define evaluation methods, methods of registration of the entity's transactions and financial statement presentation
Access to capital	Greater extent by shareholders	Greater extent by bank finance and government

Fig. 1 Factors influencing in the financial reporting systems. *Source*: National standard of financial reporting adoption of international financial reporting standards for the first time

(a) Legal system:

This system is identified in two groups:

1. Law based system: The so-called System of common law, typical almost in all European countries, including Albania, except United Kingdom and Japan. According to this law system, laws are defined by Parliament and Accounting Law is very general. It does not contain special rules, but has a general adjustment common for all entities, therefore entities face different problems.
2. Customary Law System: designed with more detailed rules and has more rare cases to contain common rules (USA, Canada, Australia or New Zealand use this kind of system)

(b) Tax System: which affects accounting financial reporting, specifically on accounting measure of elements in financial statements.

The target of NSFR is to ensure that the first financial statements of the entity according NSFR 1 and its interim financial reports, for part of the period covered by these financial statements, that contain information of a high quality, that (Fowler 2004):

(a) is transparent for the users and comparable for all periods presented;
(b) Provides an appropriate start point for accounting according to National Standards of Financial Reporting (NSFR); and
(c) Can be accomplished at a cost that does not exceed the benefits to users

An entity will implement this NSFR in:

1. Its first financial statements according to NSFR 1; and
2. Every interim financial reporting, if it has, that this entity presents, according to IAS 34 Interim Financial Reporting, for part of the period covered by its first financial statements according to NSFR 1. First financial statements of an entity according to NSFR are the annual first financial statements, in which the entity adopts NSFR through an explicit and unreserved statement in these statements, for compliance with NSFR. Financial Statements according to NSFR are the first financial statements of an entity according to NSFR, if for example, the entity:
   (a) Has submitted most recent financial statements:
      (i) According to national requirements that are not in all respects consistent with NSFR;
      (ii) In accordance with NSFR in all aspects, except the fact that financial statements do not contain an explicit and unreserved statement that shows that they are in accordance with NSFR;
      (iii) Contain a clear statement of compliance with some, but not with all NSFR;
      (iv) According to national requirements that are not consistent with NSFR, using some individual NSFR to account elements for which do not exist national requirements; or
      (v) According to national requirements, with a reconciliation of some amounts to the amounts determined according to NSFR;
   (b) Has prepared financial statements under NSFR for internal use only, without making them available to owners of the entity or any other external users;
   (c) has prepared a reporting package under NSFR for consolidation purposes without preparing a complete set of financial statements, as defined in IAS 1 Presentation of Financial Statements; or
   (d) Did not present financial statements for previous periods. NSFR 1 is applied when an entity adopts for the first time NSFR. It is not applied when, for example, an entity:
      (i) Interrupts the presentation of financial statements under national requirements, which it has previously filed, as well as any other financial statement package containing an explicit and unreserved compliance statement with NSFR;
      (ii) Has presented financial statements under national requirements in the previous year, and the financial statements contain an explicit and unreserved compliance statement with NSFR; or
      (iii) In previous year has presented financial statements that contained an explicit and unreserved compliance statement with NSFR, even if the auditors have provided a reserve report on these financial statements NSFR 1 cannot be applied to changes in accounting policies made by an entity that applies NSFR.

These changes are subject to:

(a) Requirements on changes in accounting policies in IAS 8 Accounting Policies, Changes in Accounting Estimates and Errors; and
(b) Transitional specific requirements given in other NSFR.

5.1 Exceptions from Other NSFR

An entity may elect to use one or more of the following exceptions:

(a) Business combinations
(b) Fair value or revaluation of the tried cost
(c) Employee benefits
(d) Cumulative translation differences
(e) Compound financial instruments
(f) Assets and liabilities of subsidiaries, associates and joint ventures
(g) Presentation of previous known financial instruments
(h) Payment transactions based in shares
(i) Insurance contracts
(j) Obsolescence liabilities included in the cost of land, buildings, machinery and equipment
(k) Rents
(l) Measuring the fair value of financial assets and liabilities at initial and
(m) A financial asset or an intangible asset, calculated in accordance with the Service Concession Arrangements (KIRFN)

An entity shall not apply these exemptions by analogy with other elements. Some exemptions below refer to fair value. NSFR 3 Business Combinations explains how to determine the fair value of identifiable assets and liabilities that are acquired in a business combination. An entity uses these explanations, in determining the fair values under this NSFR, unless another NSFR contains more specific guidance regarding the determination of fair values for assets and liabilities in question. These fair values shall reflect conditions that existed at the date for which they were designated.

6 Reporting Needs of Small Units, Medium and Large Units

The size of the entity has some influence on processes but not any impact on the scope or requirements of these processes. Internal Information required in decision making and control of inventories is almost similar in all entities. Thus, databases for all primary units are more or less equally in all its departments. All accounting data required for financial reporting and consolidation transactions with other units are almost the same as for small units of also medium and large ones. Another similarity between the reporting requirements of the small unit's medium and large ones is reasonable rate of return on their investments capital. Investors in large units and units' investors in small and medium are more interested in profit and gain is very important rate return. Small units of medium could not manage their activities and not live long if the rate of return on their investment is consistent with their expectations. On the other hand there are many external similarities between small units of the medium and large ones. First, in both cases, the financial statements are the source key financial information to external users (Brackney 2006). Another common thing of these units is their legal status. Legal rights and obligations for units economic, as small and medium-sized and large ones are determined based on their form, not on the basis of their size but with some exceptions, co-ownership, joint and corporations are corporations. The research discusses some of the differences between large units and small "Big GAAP, Little GAAP: Financial Reporting in the Small Business Environment". The suggestion of determining income and expenses in ways different, according to the size of the entity is one of the differences between units large and small. In Small businesses the importance of investors and creditors can be relatively different compared to those of large businesses. From a study done taken some descriptions when in fact, very few information appears to be essential to the nature of belonging to SMEs and the large, the remainder is mainly related to personal financial interests. Referred financial reporting, we find three differences between SMEs and entities Large: ownership interests in units small and medium; their management and as external stakeholders, creditors, suppliers etc. In this study, there are sufficient explanations to the fact that why owners Small units of medium are less diversified compared to units large. Most investors in large units are considered financially different as they reduce their market risk; they tend to increase portfolio buying their shares in different entities. Therefore, shareholders are mainly focused on that part of the financial information which is valuable for determination of market risk portfolio and less interested periodic information about the overall risk. On the other hand, in most small units of medium, capital is invested by a single person. The key to Success for the growth of a unit, especially the small is a greater commitment Owner financial keep control of the situation. As a result, owners of units Small and medium enterprises are more interested in the overall relative risk with market risk, which is a systematic risk. Many studies have concluded that, as a result of attention to ownership, capital markets for large units are "big" in terms of funding sources for small units of medium. Markets 'small' financial are less efficient and effective as participating parties rely on any accounting information that is likely to provide. In small units of medium, most financial decisions, based on ownership and due to financial reports not very appropriate, changes in ownership can be become frequent. Leaders of local small and medium enterprises are not very dependent on decisions them from formal financial information, compared to larger units, as in Small units of medium one or two individuals can monitor and implement the all management unit. The owner or manager engage in more managerial roles and responsibilities, giving them the opportunity to recognize almost every aspect of activity and thus making them independent in decision making by financial information. In small units of medium, the owner or manager being very active management has more access and the right to use inside information compared with large economic units (Karamanou and Nishiotis 2005). Explanations on accounting decision suggests that in general, Small units of medium entrust him a chartered accountant, which enables 18 synchronization procedures and statements between small units of medium and the creation of a professional standard of businesses that provide accounting services. For consequently, increasing the demand for audit of these statements is not added value the role of banks and other creditors is too short important for small units of medium which do not have easy access to capital markets. These two funds providers need to hold regular information from financial reporting. Thus, referring to all aspects explained above is achieved in concluded that a unit owner of small or medium there is more awareness and general information about management attributes its activity and is rationally informed about where the industry is concentrated but by another much less p.sh information about capital markets and financial or competitive industries promising as happens with large units.

7 Costs and Benefits of IFRS

Adoption of IFRS in Europe generated intense debate in levels of government's terms of discussions on proposed changes in reporting. The reaction of investors to unit's European economy was positive in terms of adoption of IFRS if these latter would provide a financial report with a higher quality, will minimize Information asymmetry, would lower the risk of information between the entity and investor and therefore all the profits will enable these reduction The cost of capital. Application of IFRS reduces the cost of comparative financial statements of unit's different economic environments, thus permitting the European market global capital becomes increase liquidity (Combarros 2011). The only reaction against investors related to the fact that because of regional differences between entities, can decrease the quality of reporting and there is a risk that the costs of implementation and transition IFRS to exceed their benefits. In the study of these four authors, scale entities Low preliminary information on the adoption of IFRS showed a positive reaction related if IFRSs offer investors the benefits of an information stable. It was also proved that there was a positive response from those units Economic having high quality early information on the adoption of IFRS, reaction which was based on the expectation of investors to reduce Information asymmetry. A less positive reaction entities to adoption of IFRS was found in countries 'common law' as in countries with weak accounting standards are some concerns of investors. European Commission (EC) has the right to declare for implementation standards developed by the IASB for their implementation in the European Union. In this Thus, the regulatory authority goes in line with the EC in cases when accept or reject a particular standard or any part thereof. EC pays attention to three criteria when to declare a standard implementation. These criteria are: standard must comply with the principle of reporting really sincere according to the EU; standard must meet the criteria of understandability, reliability, relevance and comparability; adoption of any standard should be in the public interest European.

References

Bank of Albania. (2012). Financial statement legislations. [online] Accessed January 10, 2012, from http://www.bankofalbania.org/web/Legjislacioni_45_1.php

Boeva, B., & Prohaska, M. (2002). *The proper implementation of the accounting standards on financial reporting* (pp. 12–26). Second South-Eastern Europe Corporate Governance Roundtable, Turkey, Istanbul, May 30–31.

Brackney, K. (2006). The European Union's role in international standard setting. *The CPA Journal—Accounting and Finance Audit Harmonization in Balkan Countries, 1*, 17–25.

Combarros, J. (2011). Accounting and finance audit harmonization in the European Union. *European Accounting Review, 9*(4), 643–654.

Fowler, J. (2004). Adapting to a changing world. Financial statement effects of adopting international accounting standards. *European Financial Reporting, 3*, 3–15.

International Accounting Standards Board. (2012). Albanian financial reporting. [online] Accessed January 20, 2012, from www.iasb.org

Karamanou, I., & Nishiotis, G. (2005). *The valuation of firm voluntary adoption of international accounting standards* (University of Cyprus Working Paper, pp. 1–34).

Paterson, I., Fink, M., & Ogus, A. (2009). Economic impact of the regulation of the free professions in several member countries in European Union. *International Journal of Accounting Information Systems, 2*, 24–36.

Phelps, R. W., & Karremi, G. (2008). Report on results of the pilot project on global standardization of the accounting education: Emphasizing regional. *Contemporary Accounting Research, 1*, 21–50.

Principle-Based Agricultural Business Accounting Policy Formation

Neringa Stonciuviene, Danute Zinkeviciene, and Lina Martirosianiene

Abstract The problem which this research is dedicated to prepare a methodology of accounting policy formation of agricultural business subjects which would allow the financial information to best meet the interests of potential investors. The idea of the research has emerged from choosing possibilities provided in the regulations, which form the financial accountancy of agricultural business subjects while evaluating the assets, liabilities, revenue and expenses of agricultural business subject and the asymmetry of provided information, which occur due to these reasons. The accounting policy of agricultural business subjects must be formed based on agency theory, which demands to satisfy the interests of users who employ such information, and signalling theory, which emphasizes the reliability of the information. Factors influencing the formation of accounting policy of agricultural business subjects are the following: chosen view towards the accounting policy; the specifics of activities of agricultural business subjects; possibilities to choose from accounting methods given in accounting regulations; the demands of investors in regards to the financial information in order the investors could make correct and timely management and investment decisions. The model, which reflects the inter-relations between factors, which influence the accounting policy formation of the agricultural business subjects, was prepared.

Keywords Accounting policy • Agricultural business accounting • Decisions of investors

The results, introduced in this paper, are a part of research project supported by the Research Council of Lithuania, grant No. MIP-095/2014.

N. Stonciuviene (✉) • D. Zinkeviciene • L. Martirosianiene
Department of Economics, Accounting and Finance, AleksandrasStulginskis University, Akademija, Lithuania
e-mail: neringa.stonciuviene@asu.lt; danute.zinkeviciene@asu.lt; lina.martirosianiene@asu.lt

© Springer International Publishing Switzerland 2016

M.H. Bilgin et al. (eds.), *Business Challenges in the Changing Economic Landscape - Vol. 1*, Eurasian Studies in Business and Economics 2/1,
DOI 10.1007/978-3-319-22596-8_4

1 Introduction

Recently, literature has increasingly focused on the problem of forming financial information based on defined goals. This also concerns the preparation of agricultural business entities' accounting information and its presentation to the users. Generally, agribusiness accounting policy formation is limited to its suitability for drawing up financial statements without analysing how investors for their decision-making can use this information.

This research analyses the principles, techniques and methods of accounting which are applied in agribusiness accounting policy formation as well as the specific features of the agribusiness branch influencing the choice of such techniques and methods, and investor needs for financial information in order for them to make correct investment decisions.

While analysing agribusiness accounting researchers emphasize agricultural accounting practices adopted by different countries and make their comparative analysis on the international scale. In their research, Fisher and Marsh (2013) and Marsh and Fisher (2013) made a comparison between the US accounting and the requirements laid down in the International Financial Reporting Standards (IFRS). Jack (2006) and Cairns et al. (2011) analysed accounting practices in the UK, Sedlacek (2010)—in Czech Republic, Fisher et al. (2010)—New Zealand. Bohusova et al. (2012) made a comparison between agricultural accounting experiences in France, the UK, the USA and Australia. Agribusiness entities must adhere to the generally accepted accounting principles and regulations at the same time having regard to the peculiarities of this branch of business. This forms the specificity of entering, submitting and interpreting financial information. As emphasised by Athanasios et al. (2010) and Sedlacek (2010), traditional requirements in respect of accounting and presentation of its results do not reflect agricultural peculiarities and their impact on the financial performance of entities in this business.

Researchers' particular interest in agricultural accounting has been noticed after the adoption of the International Financial Reporting Standard 41 *Agriculture* (IAS 41) which requires that a biological asset is measured at fair value less point-of-sale costs. The regulation of application of that exclusive method resulted from the specificity of a biological asset (Van Mourik and Walton 2013). In their research Cairns et al. (2011) have emphasised that the fair value method is hardly applied in the UK, whereas agricultural organisations examined by these authors' measure biological assets applying the method of fair value less point-of-sale costs. Argiles et al. (2012) indicate that agricultural enterprises encounter more problems applying the cost method than the fair value method. Dvorakova (2011) analyses the peculiarities of fair value measurement. Fisher et al. (2010) and Ore (2011) analyse the compliance of financial statements with quality characteristics after the introduction of the International Accounting Standard N 41 *Agriculture* (IAS 41).

However, as correctly noted by Feng and Fu (2012), scientific and perfect accounting system is not only the need to perform the functions of accounting in reflecting and supervising economic activities of agricultural enterprises. Accounting must present authentic and complete information of agricultural enterprises for current and potential owners—investors.

This paper aims to develop an accounting policy formation methodology for agribusiness entities in order for financial information prepared on the basis thereof to best satisfy potential investors' interests. The research object is agribusiness accounting policy formation. We will systemise factors responsible for agribusiness accounting policy formation and develop a model representing their interrelationships.

To meet the goal, the following tasks are solved: (1) to analyse accounting principles, techniques and methods which are material for accounting policy formation; (2) to identify agribusiness peculiarities determining agribusiness accounting policy formation; (3) to analyse the peculiarities of submitting financial information necessary to satisfy the needs of investors in agribusiness; (4) to develop a model showing relationships among factors responsible for agribusiness accounting policy formation.

Agency and signalling theories as well as normative and positive theories substantiating accounting policy formation constitute a methodological basis for research. The research was conducted by analysing previous research works, practical experience and accounting-governing legislation, which determine accounting policy formation at agribusiness entities, and by logically generating conclusions and recommendations. Literature and regulatory documents were theoretically analysed by employing the methods of analysis and synthesis. Research findings are presented by a monographic method.

2 General Principles Behind Accounting Policy Formation

In order to adopt decisions on investment in agribusiness, investors need objective and reliable information. Such information can be obtained from an appropriately formulated accounting policy the choice and implementation of which is the responsibility of the enterprise manager. To explain why managers choose concrete accounting methods and disclosure one or other kind of accounting information, research on accounting generally follows either a normative (Tinker et al. 1982) or a positive (Watts and Zimmerman 1990; Milne 2002; Iatridis and Joseph 2005; Tzovas 2006) theory of accounting. As maintained by Deegan (2006), the normative theory of accounting was developed logically as certain prescriptions, which are important to achieve a certain practice, and therefore has been subject to many criticisms. The analysis of research works leads to the conclusion that explanations for the choice of accounting methods most commonly are based on the positive theory of accounting and have the aim to analyse factors behind the choice of accounting methods. The analysis chiefly concerned the influence on the choice of accounting methods of such factors as enterprise size, financial leverage, profitability, branch of industry or bonuses for managers (Craig and Diga 1998; Tan et al. 2002; Zinkeviciene and Rudzioniene 2005; Ashtami and Tower 2006), but did not the specificity of the branch. However, as noted by Petruk et al. (2013), under current conditions it is not possible to speak of the predominance in the accounting of any single theory since accounting is multi-paradigmatic discipline during the evolution of which is cyclic change fundamental paradigms.

The positive theory of accounting aims to provide explanations and forecasts as information in financial statements must satisfy investor needs. Managers' choices in it are based on an agency theory. From the perspective of this theory, a firm is considered to be a whole of formal and informal contracts between the groups of selfish minded individuals interested in the firm's activity (Deegan 2006; Riahi-Belkaoui 2004; Drever et al. 2007; Scott 2012; Schroeder et al. 2010), while each individual seeks maximising his welfare.

The main objective of investors is to receive maximum return on investments in the firm and therefore they are prone to take bigger risk than company managers who seek to retain their jobs, receive stable salaries, maximise their prestige, etc. Consequently, the manager can choose such accounting methods, which ensure his current personal benefit. Now, both the investors and the managers relate the possibility of obtaining bigger remuneration with the size of profit. The choices of accounting policy in the positive theory of accounting are generally oriented to profit management—decrease or increase—by choosing profit decreasing or increasing accounting methods and procedures or seeking to equalise profit. The essence of the profit increasing accounting policy is to show, by applying certain accounting standards, a higher profit of the reporting period for the account of future periods. Profit decreasing accounting policy is a whole of accounting methods making it possible to defer the profit of the reporting year to future periods. Bowen et al. (1995) argue that in the interests of user needs it is appropriate to choose long-term profit increasing accounting methods the most important of which are those of inventory valuation and depreciation. A straight-line depreciation method and FIFO inventory valuation method allow a firm to increase its profit, while sum-of-the years' digits and declining balance methods of fixed asset depreciation and LIFO inventory valuation method—reduce the profit of the reporting period. In his research, Shaheen (2012) used the assumption that companies in Kuwait also apply profit decreasing accounting methods and has arrived at a conclusion that the obtained results significantly differ from the findings of analogous research done in European states and the USA. In the meantime Ashtami and Tower (2006), having researched individual countries and branches of industry in the Asia-Pacific region, made a conclusion that Indonesian companies normally apply profit decreasing accounting methods, while companies choosing profit increasing accounting methods are characterised by lower financial leverage, smaller equity concentration and broader investment possibilities. Managers can reduce profit if better results are expected in the future or, as maintained by Stolowy and Breton (2003), managers do not want to report large profits as similar performance will be requested from them in the future. Hence, by choosing certain accounting methods it is possible to manipulate profit and thus influence investors' opinion about the company (Degeorge et al. 1999).

Since investors consider that profit fluctuations entail risks they seek to invest only in prospective companies and to obtain steadily growing profit (Riahi-Belkaoui 2004; Scott 2012). In order to be in line with analysts' forecasts or eliminate short-term profit fluctuations accounting methods helping equalise profits are chosen. Research, done by Wang and Williams (1994) has shown that companies with equalised profit data are considered less risky and therefore the equalisation of profit can be useful to both the current owners and the potential investors.

Considering that firm managers can receive such information which is not always available to owners, there emerges some asymmetry of information in respect of investors, while the managers enjoy bigger opportunities to act in a way that is beneficial only for them, and which does not always reflect best owner and investor needs (Tan et al. 2002; Schroeder et al. 2010). As regards investors, information asymmetry can result in an unfavourable choice of investments. Therefore, to avoid the asymmetry of information and reduce representation costs, it is appropriate to shape accounting policies by employing the signalling theory. The idea of this theory is to encourage managers to communicate information by giving certain signals to the users in order for them to adopt correct decisions. In the opinion of Raileanu and Pravat (2008), if investors are not capable of distinguishing between competitive and other companies, a company must use a signalling mechanism in order to show its unique features and capture the attention of investors. As noted by Connelly et al. (2011), generally, the sender of information has to choose whether and how to transmit a signal to the recipient, and the recipient of information—how to interpret the signal. Thus, the transmission of signals is relating with information disclosures in financial statements. As maintained by Leland and Pyle (1977), if firm managers decide to increase their capital shares, this may become an unambiguous signal of investing possibilities. For example, such signals can be borrowing, issuing new shares or increasing profitability. Borrowing signalises that the enterprise's condition allows it to borrow as it generates large cash flows and will be able to meet interest liabilities. Meanwhile the issue of new shares is a bad signal for investors since it shows that share prices are overestimated and then the share price falls (Spence 1973). Consequently, the use of signalling and agency theories in accounting policy formation ensures that the appropriate information is obtained because, as noted by Morris (1987), these theories are consistent theories, in that one set of sufficient conditions of signalling theory is at least consistent with one set of sufficient conditions of agency theory.

In shaping an accounting policy based on the aforementioned theories for investor purposes it is important to evaluate motives for choosing accounting policy:

- Reasonableness. Since most business events are accidental, it is necessary to reasonably understand a possible outcome of the enterprise's activity;
- Content. It is most important to appropriately disclose the essence of an event and its influence on the enterprise's financial performance;

- Materiality. Financial statements must contain such information the omission or misstatement of which might lead to wrong decision-making by investors.

An important element of accounting policy formation is adherence to the Generally Accepted Accounting Principles as all or at least a majority of information users could equally treat only information formed on the basis thereof.

In forming a corporate accounting policy there inevitably arises a question what asset and liability accounting and evaluation methods to choose in order to fairly and correctly reflect the financial position and performance. In choosing the method of evaluation, it is equally important to understand the essence of that method and the possibilities it offers to evaluate the firm's financial position and performance.

The main method of evaluation in a traditional accounting system is historical cost. Other evaluation methods were developed during the transformation of the historical cost method due to micro- and macro-economic factors. When assets and liabilities are evaluated at historical cost they are measured by the amount which had to be paid to acquire the asset or liability in the past (Deegan 2006). The core aim of this method is to fairly value an asset by attributing to its value all main expenses related to its acquisition and production (Zeff 2007; Godfrey et al. 2006). Information on historical prices is based on enterprise's internal data about past events disregarding current external market data (Khurana and Kim 2003), as the assumption of a stable monetary unit is invoked. Under present circumstances, therefore, financial statements drawn up using the historical cost method have lost their relevance, which led to the development of accounting at fair value.

Fair value is described as the price that would be received to sell an asset or paid to transfer a liability in an orderly transaction between market participants at the measurement date (IFRS 13). As noted by Ristea and Jianu (2010), by presenting the fair value of the elements in the balance sheet the entity creates transparency and gives confidence to investors, while Bonaci and Strouhal (2011) argue that the impact of fair value accounting is essential for all users of financial accounting information, especially when considering investment and financial decisions. However, it has been proved in research carried out by Deegan (2006), Godfrey et al. (2006) that information on profit based on the accounting of historical prices (i.e., cost) impacts share prices and is therefore useful for the market and at the same time for investors.

3 Agricultural Activity Peculiarities Having an Influence on Accounting Policy Formation

The accounting policy of agribusiness entities has to be formed taking into consideration the peculiarities of agriculture as an economic branch. As indicated in the international encyclopaedia History of Accounting (Chatfield and Vangermeersch 2014), an agricultural activity poses a lot of challenges to its accountants.

The first specific peculiarity, without doubt, is natural and technological conditions and agricultural activity seasonality. Agriculturalists are the chief managers of terrestrial 'useable' lands (Tilman et al. 2002). Agricultural activity is particularly affected by *force majeure* circumstances such as unpredictable change of weather, climate warming, the excess or lack of humidity, etc. In comparison with other economic entities, it is more difficult for agribusiness entities to change the nature of their activity. This economic branch is particularly affected by natural biological factors, the seasonality of activity and changes in market needs, as it is very difficult to shift to other kind of production, for example, from meat production to milk production (Sedlacek 2010).

However, as noted by Feng and Fu (2012), scientific and perfect accounting system is not only the need to perform the functions of accounting in reflecting and supervising economic activities of agricultural enterprises. In recent decades there has formed a view that agriculture is an economic branch which must not only ensure supply with food products but also preserve the environment (Harris and Roach 2013; Firoz and Ansari 2010). Agriculture is expected to fulfil three important functions: economic, social and environmental (Dumitru et al. 2011) and provide public goods to the society (Banzhaf 2010; Pimentel 2012). The preservation of farming as a way of living can also be attributed to the social function of agriculture. In a broader context, however, this factor is related to territorial limitations, demographic changes, psychological attitudes and a variety of ownership forms.

The activity of agribusiness entities is impossible without biological assets. As noted by Feng and Fu (2012), the objects of agricultural production activities and agricultural production means are animate biological assets. These assets are characterised by a specific life/growth cycle that is inherent in their particular type (Chatfield and Vangermeersch 2014) and differences in products obtained from them. Biological transformation is defined as the process of growth, aging, production, or procreation of the biological asset. Some kinds of biological assets provide more than one product or the biological asset itself can be sold at a certain moment of its growth (Fisher and Marsh 2013; Marsh and Fischer 2013; Sedlacek 2010). Part of produce in a family farm can be consumed for the personal needs of the farmer and his family in a form of food products. This consumption has a direct influence on the family farm's capital. On the other hand, farmers regularly make internal investments—owner contributions to ensure and develop family farm activities.

The analysis of research leads to the conclusion that agricultural activity is unimaginable without grants and subsidies. This determines the necessity to form the specific accounting policy of agribusiness entities. The withdrawal of subsidies linked to production in the EU will take effect from 2005 and leave agricultural businesses more exposed to the fluctuations of commodity markets (Jack 2006). In Greece it is impossible to deal with the problem of the economic inefficiency of agriculture without subsidies to agriculture (Tzouvelekas et al. 2001). Tilman et al. (2002) note that subsidising agricultural business in the United States, EU and Japan redirected to reward sustainable practices.

The result of efforts to reflect agribusiness peculiarities in accounting—*International Accounting Standard N 41 Agriculture (IAS 41) adopted by the International Accounting Standards Committee (IASC) in 2001*. IAS 41 applies to biological assets with the exception of bearer plants, agricultural produce at the point of harvest, and government grants related to these biological assets. Bearer plants were excluded from the scope of IAS 41 in June 2014. This change applies to annual periods beginning on or after 1 January 2016.

IAS 41 (2014) requires that biological assets and agricultural produce at the point of harvest be measured at fair value less estimated costs to sell, even though until then most countries applied the historical cost method. The fair value calculation is based on management assumptions about the likelihood of default, prepayment rates, and discount rates (Dechow et al. 2010). Historical cost is the amount of cash or cash equivalents paid or the fair value of the consideration given to acquire them at the time of their acquisition. Cost should include all: costs of purchase (including taxes, transport, and handling) net of trade discounts received; costs of conversion (including fixed and variable manufacturing overheads); other costs incurred in bringing the inventories to their present location and condition (IAS 2).

On the topic of biological assets, before IAS 41 adoption, current accounting principles typically do not respond very well to the particular characteristics of agricultural business and the information needs of farmers and their stakeholders (Fisher et al. 2010; Goncalves and Lopes 2014). Authors approving of the measurement of biological assets by the fair value method maintain that one of the more positive things about IAS 41 is it should resolve the problem of heterogeneity in valuation, because both measures of sold and unsold production are based on fair value. On the other hand, the overall conclusion reached by Herbohn and Herbohn (2006) is that the approach taken in IAS 41 is too academic and not focused on the practicalities of reporting on biological assets (Fisher et al. 2010), the requirements of the IAS 41 are not theoretically or practically compatible with most of the accounting models (Bohusova et al. 2012).

As an accounting practice analysis has shown, the historical cost method to measure biological assets is applied in the UK, France, Czech Republic, USA (Bohusova et al. 2012), and Romania (Feleaga et al. 2012). This method is also chosen by most agribusiness entities in Lithuania (Jatkunaite et al. 2006), although biological assets and agricultural produce in the latter country can be measured either at fair value less estimated costs to sell or by historical cost. After summarising biological asset accounting experiences in five countries and comparing them with international regulations Bohusova et al. (2012) argue that the historical cost method reflects best natural changes in biological assets during their growth; however, it does not take into consideration the value added created by the biological process. In the meantime the fair value method in contrast to historical cost accounting, puts the risk in the future into the balance sheet (Jiang and Penman 2013).

The main problem related to biological asset valuation at fair value less point-of-sale costs is the determination of fair value. The choice of this valuation method requires the establishment of the internal value of an asset, which is not provided to external information users, and its changes. The fair value of a biological asset varies not only between breeds, classes and varieties, but also between relatively small geographical locations, which is likely to cause the problem of limited comparability between agricultural firms (Fisher et al. 2010). This is particularly important when it is difficult or impossible to use market prices for fair value measurement. International Financial Reporting Standard N13 *Fair Value Measurement* (IFRS 13), intended for the application of fair value method in financial reporting, recommends three fair value measurement approaches: market approach, cost approach and income approach. In researchers' opinion, different methods of fair value measurement are likely to determine unreliable estimate of fair value (Goncalves and Lopes 2014; Muhammad and Ghani 2013; Bohusova et al. 2012).

The separation of bearer plants from biological assets for accounting purposes at agricultural enterprises has led to the situation when part of biological assets is accounted for as biological assets, while another one—as non-current assets. There are some proposals in literature to account for biological assets as three different accounting objects, i.e., non-current assets, inventories and biological assets (Aryanto 2011).

Revenue accounting requires particular attention in agribusiness entities accounting policy formation. Revenues are one of the most common elements of business valuation indicators. Agribusiness entities account for sales, financial, investment and other activity revenues. By its economic origin, the value of biological assets and agricultural produce consumed for farm and personal needs is attributable to revenues.

Accounting concepts used in IAS 41 is the concept of accretion. In this concept, revenues are recognized along with the growth of assets (Aryanto 2011; Marsh and Fischer 2013). According to IAS 41 (2014), agribusiness entities must recognise the specific outcome of biological asset growing. The gain on initial recognition of biological assets and agricultural produce at fair value less costs to sell, and changes in fair value less costs to sell of biological assets during a period, are included in profit or loss (IAS 41, 2014). It is necessary to highlight that change in the value of a biological asset is not recognised as revenue and therefore the costs incurred by the enterprise in connection with biological assets do not have their reflection in the form of the corresponding revenues (Bohusova et al. 2012). For this reason it is more suitable for agribusiness entities to present costs by nature (IAS 1).

The result of change in the value of a biological asset—profit or loss—reflects the physical quantitative or qualitative changes in biological assets and change in the price of their units. It is a complicated indicator in terms of both its calculation and information presentation (IAS 41) requires that reconciliation of changes in the carrying amount of biological assets, showing separately changes in value, purchases, sales, harvesting, business combinations, and foreign exchange differences be presented in notes). Fisher et al. (2010) expressed doubts as to the meaningfulness of such presentation arguing that such transformation of changes in value is not quite clear to users and therefore raises doubts as to the application of the fair value method.

To produce agricultural produce and grow biological assets agribusiness entities buy products and produce them themselves. The use of all of them has a single purpose—to deliver a finished product suitable for the consumer; however, after using self-produced products in production the agribusiness entity himself becomes consumer. Consequently, he has not only to recognise the costs of consumption of these products but also income (sales to oneself). On the other hand, the acquired produce is measured at historical cost, while the self-produced—at fair value less point-of-sale costs. Sedlacek (2010) has referred to such a situation as valuation risk.

Another form of income generation inside an organisation is the possibility granted to agricultural producers of consuming part of the produce for own needs. It is a specific form of income not analysed in literature. In accordance with IAS 1, the total comprehensive income of the period consists of profit or loss and other comprehensive income and therefore it is necessary to consider the possibility of recognising the consumption of agricultural produce for business or personal needs as other income.

From a macroeconomic approach one of the main factors responsible for the preservation of financial stability is subsidising (Nawaz 2010). Agricultural business is a business branch that receives most subsidies. Some of the subsidies are lump sum or periodic payments, intended to compensate for the income foregone or costs incurred; other subsidies are support to investments the economic benefits; and there are also subsidies that support investments the economic benefits whereof future generations will enjoy (Alekneviciene et al. 2013).

IAS 20 *Government Grants and Disclosure of Government Assistance* (IAS 20, 2009) covers subsidies and grants. On the basis of this standard government grants can be disclosed in accounting using two methods: the capital method according to which a grant is recorded in accounting directly as equity or the income method according to which a grant is recorded in accounting as the income of one or several periods.

All grants and subsidies are divided into two groups: grants related to income and grants related to assets. While recording grants related to income in accounting by the income method, the respective reimbursable income of the reporting period is increased or the respective reimbursable expense is decreased. This distorts the cost of produce or services or the amounts of grants are recorded together with the income earned by the enterprise. There are two options for the accounting of grants related to assets: increasing the income of future periods or decreasing the book value of assets. Such reflection of grants in the accounting improves the performance results of an agribusiness entity.

Agribusiness entities in their activities use many items of expensive property, plant and equipment. IAS 16 *Property, Plant and Equipment* (IAS 16), intended for the accounting of such assets, indicates that items of property, plant and equipment must be recorded in accounting at factual historical cost and then carried using one of the chosen models: the Cost model when the asset is carried at cost less accumulated depreciation and impairment, or the Revaluation model—the asset is carried at a revalued amount, being its fair value at the date of revaluation less subsequent depreciation and impairment, provided that fair value can be measured reliably (IAS 16). Furthermore, while formulating the accounting policy for property, plant and equipment several important factors have to be considered. According to Zinkeviciene and Vaisnoraite (2014), the most important of them are determining the value of a non-current asset item, including expenses in the unit cost, choosing the method of depreciation, determining the period of asset use, etc.

Inventory accounting regulations offer many choices. There are several methods to write off used inventories: the FIFO, specific identification of costs, weighted average, LIFO. When inventories are accounted for by the FIFO method, the first entry is processed first. Due to impairment of inventories value and the time value of money the sales cost of a product is lower. Gu (2013) argues that the FIFO method best reflects the actual flow of inventories and the inventory value presented in the balance-sheet best reflects the market value. An analogous opinion is found in works by other researchers (Wanstrom 2012; Jesswein 2010).

Another choice—using the methods of constant or periodic accounting of inventories. The particularity of the constant inventory accounting method lies in the fact that each transaction related to the reception or consumption of inventories is recorded. However, as maintained by Warren et al. (2011), if an enterprise carries out many transactions, this method becomes expensive and time consuming. The essence of the periodic inventory accounting method—it does not require the recording of every facet of product sales/consumption. The balance of inventories is determined during inventory checking carried out at the end of the period. According to this method, however, inventories are not evaluated at the time of their sales or other consumption, which relatively infringes the accrual principle (Warren et al. 2011).

The choice of accounting methods changes entity's financial performance and information submitted to investors.

4 Peculiarities of Presenting Financial Information Aimed at Satisfying the Needs of Investors in Agribusiness

Agriculture is an economic branch that requires enormous material resources and investments that are necessary for its modernization and future development. Under complicated business management and competitive market conditions and in the presence of large information flows business success is guaranteed by precise accounting information presented in a timely manner to current and potential investors. Brozova (2011) has noted that this applies in particular to agricultural enterprises, the position of which is quite exclusive (arising from the production process and market process specificities). Obviously, quality information about enterprise activities can be supplied with the help of a group of indicators.

Information asymmetry between managers and outside capital suppliers can affect how firms finance capital investments. A growing body of evidence indicates that better accounting quality can reduce information asymmetry costs and reduce financing constraints (Beatty et al. 2010). Consistent with this possibility, Biddle and Hilary (2006) document that higher accounting quality reduces the sensitivity of firms' investment to their internally generated cash flows. Verdi (2006) and Biddle et al. (2009) find that accounting quality is positively correlated with investment for firms prone to underinvest and is negatively correlated with investment for firms prone to overinvest. Financial statements' main objective is to give information on the financial position, performance and changes in financial position of the reporting entity, which is useful to a wide range of users in making economic decisions. In order to be useful, financial information must be relevant to the decision-making process of users in general, and investors in particular, meaning that it must have the capacity to influence their economic decisions (Octavian 2012).

In order to improve the usage of financial information in the context of the decision making process, we need to analyse financial statements. Information in financial statements drawn up on the basis of an agribusiness entity's accounting policy must: (1) make it possible to analyse and assess the agribusiness entity's financial position; (2) create preconditions for comparing the results of the analysis of entities' financial position; (3) enable financial statement users to adopt more efficient decisions on the usage and management of resources.

The basic financial statements are the statement of financial position (Balance Sheet) and the Statement of Profit or Loss and Other Comprehensive Income (IAS 1). The analysis of data in these financial statements can be described as the process where we convert data from financial statements into usable information for business quality measurement by different analytical techniques, which are very important in the process of rational management (Zager and Zager 2006). Although absolute measures of these financial characteristics are useful in analysing business performance over time, ratios are more appropriate in comparing one business relative to others since absolute measures are likely to differ by business size. Brigham and Ehrhardt (2010) point out that financial ratios are designed to help evaluate financial statements.

There are still differences between income calculation practices of certain countries, and these deviations result in different incomes. Since the different income categories—differing in name, content and value—do not cover each other, to compare them, investors have to be very careful. There has been observed the basic difference between the income calculation systems: one aims to present the income of the enterprises, while the other wants to express all the income reached by the family—from agricultural and non-agricultural activities, employment, etc. (Orban and Dekan 2013).

Based on accounting standards, agricultural activity is reported in the financial statements in the context of the historical cost and fair view. Investor decisions may be incorrect if the equity capital of the company (through the income statement) increases due to growth in the fair value of the assets, the financial position of the holding improves (however, the improvement may be temporary). This means the company may be, for example, allowed to obtain the necessary financial resources (positive for agricultural holdings) in the context of the historical cost and fair view (Hinke and Starova 2013).

Literature analyses one more problem—different perception of changes in inventories in the operating costs by nature. While the IFRS accounting system considers this item as belonging to adjustment costs, in some countries "changes in inventories" are featured as financial accounting income (Hinke and Starova 2013). It leads to a distorted financial analysis and a quantification of such indicators.

Financial ratios analysis is used to evaluate the performance of an organization: it aims to determine the strong and weak points and it offers solutions by providing appropriate plans. In particular, financial performance measures are characterized by liquidity, solvency, profitability, repayment capacity and financial efficiency (Barry and Ellinger 2012). These five broad categories are intended to be used jointly to explain the financial performance and viability of farm businesses: liquidity is the farm business' ability to meet financial obligations as they become due; solvency is the farm's ability to pay all its debt if the farm were to be sold and all assets used to cover debt; profitability is the difference between the value of goods produced and the cost of the resources used in their production; repayment capacity is the borrower's ability to repay term debt on time; financial efficiency shows how effectively the farm business uses assets to generate income (Splett et al. 1994; Reichert and Posey 2011; Bruce and Katchova 2012).

Most researchers divide the financial ratios into four groups: liquidity ratios, activity ratios, debt ratios and profitability ratios (Ross 2007). Liquidity ratios indicate the organization's ability to pay debt in short term. Activity ratios are used to measure the speed with which various accounts are converted into sales or cash. They are also used to measure how efficiently a company manages its assets. Debt ratios show how effectively the organization uses other people's money and whether it is using a lot of borrowed money; and profitability ratios consist of several measures by which to assess the organization's success in making money (Lasher 2005). In the opinion of Zeddies (1991), Scott and Colman (2008), investors receive the greatest deal of information on the financial position and financial stability of an agricultural enterprise from solvency ratios. In addition to these ratios, the return on investment ratio (Scott and Colman 2008; EEIG Agrosynergie 2011) and the return on assets ratio (EEIG Agrosynergie 2011) are worth to mention. Durguner and Katchova (2007) find that the prior year's working capital to gross farm return, debt-to-asset ratio, and return on farm assets are the most pertinent factors explaining enterprise's attractiveness to investors.

During the calculation of financial indicators, the investor first of all should find out whether in its preparation the company has taken into consideration the IFRS or national business accounting standards. If the company does not apply standards, it is suggested to prepare the list of additional questions in the form of tests, which should be addressed to the owner of small company in order to be sure that the financial information is objective (Kotane and Kuzmina-Merlino 2012). The analysis of the literature leads to the conclusion that due to the specificity of agriculture, as an economic branch, investors generally take a different attitude to the basic financial indicators which determine their decision making. Farm gross investment is positively associated with real sale growth suggesting that farm investment decisions are based on market conditions (Ferto et al. 2011). A growth in sales is measured by calculating the ratio between a change in sales value of the period and invested capital (Ferto et al. 2011) and the return on equity (net income/average total equity) ratio which, according to Isberg and Pitta (2013), can also be broken out into three concepts that measure the impact of profitability, sales volume, and financial policy on the value of a firm. Although a business can operate in the short run on negative returns, profits are necessary in the long run to sustain the business. Hence, a growth in the cash flow of the farm, defined as before tax profits plus depreciation, is another indicator of high importance for investor decisions. In this connection, the cash flow/invested capital ratio and cash flow/sales income ratio are calculated.

Where a big part of assets is financed with loans higher efficiency of enterprise performance and at the same time a larger share of profit per equity can be expected. However, big loans exacerbate the problems of enterprise insolvency. Based on empirical research carried out by Khrawish and Khraiwesh (2010), profitable enterprises generally use a lower level of debts in comparison to less profitable ones. For investors it is important to analyse debt level dynamics and evaluate the main debt indicators. Valladares and Flores (2005) indicate the following debt level ratios: total debt ratio, debt/equity ratio (financial leverage), long-term debt ratio and interest coverage ratio. Fosberg and Ghosh (2006) describe the level of debt by the total debt ratio and financial leverage.

Gross farm investment is positively associated with investment subsidies. Public programmes to support farm investment (investment subsidies) seem to be successful in enhancing investment in short-term, but farms investment behaviour pertaining to investment subsidies is more cautious on long-term (Ferto et al. 2011). A reliable indicator for evaluating agribusiness entity's performance is considered to be the indicator calculated as a ratio between investment subsidies and capital stock plus depreciation in values. In making investment decisions it is necessary to pay attention to the fact that unused subsidies increase the amount of invested capital, whereas used subsidies increase income (or reduce expense) and also increase agribusiness entity's profits.

Sharma (2012) presents a list of criteria which may be used to rate the advantages and disadvantages of measures of the efficiency of the farm business as a unit: (1) the ratio must be selected in view of the objective, (2) the ratio should be easily understood; (3) the ratio should be accurate, precise, and unequivocal; (4) the ratio should be reasonably easy to calculate; (5) it should represent a definite period and be comparable through time; (6) it should measure something over which the farm operator has a significant degree of control; (7) the measure should evaluate only that which it is supposed to measure; (8) it should be: possible to isolate variations in the measure due to the influence of variables other than one being studied; (9) the measure should be one for which accurate and flexible 'standards can be calculated; (10) the data on which the ratio is based should be accurate. In fact, in order to modernize agriculture it is necessary to develop a proper accounting system covering financial, costing and management aspects of the farm affairs.

5 Model of Correlation Between the Factors Responsible for Agribusiness Accounting Policy Formation

Having analysed literature dealing with the issues of accounting policy formation the research authors maintain that the agribusiness accounting policy should be formed considering three groups of factors: general accounting principles, techniques and methods which are material for accounting policy formation; agribusiness peculiarities determining agribusiness accounting policy formation; and the information needs of investors in agribusiness as regards potential investment entities. After generalising the findings of the research, a model was developed to reflect the correlation between the aforementioned factors determining agribusiness accounting policy formation and the peculiarities of agribusiness accounting policy formation (Fig. 1).

Researchers and practitioners hold regular discussions on the principles of assets measurement and their choice. Traditionally, businesses apply the cost concept, which reflects the formation of the value of an asset over the period of its creation and use. Another principle is the principle of fair value, which aims to reflect the current value of an asset taking into account the demand/supply ratio and other market factors.

In forming the accounting policy of agribusiness entities the specific peculiarities of this business branch should not be ignored. The main peculiarities are natural and technological conditions: natural biological factors having an influence on business development and performance, changes in natural conditions, which do not depend on human activities, and the seasonality of activities. Agricultural activity is impossible without a biological asset, its quantitative and qualitative changes, produce from it and the specificity of use thereof. The success of this business is greatly impacted by market changes the influence of which has recently been attempted to mitigate with the help of multi-functionality of activities. New functions—environmental protection and creation of public goods—have been ascribed to contemporary agriculture.

The specificity of using the value added generated by business can also be considered an agribusiness peculiarity. Produce created by an agribusiness entity is not only sold to external consumers but is also consumed for internal business and personal investor needs. At the same time, business owners regularly invest their personal funds or other assets in business. The specificity of agribusiness determines a regular need for grants and subsidies, which may be used to compensate for foregone income or to reduce incurred costs. Quantitative and qualitative changes in biological assets also have an impact on the income earned by an agribusiness entity.

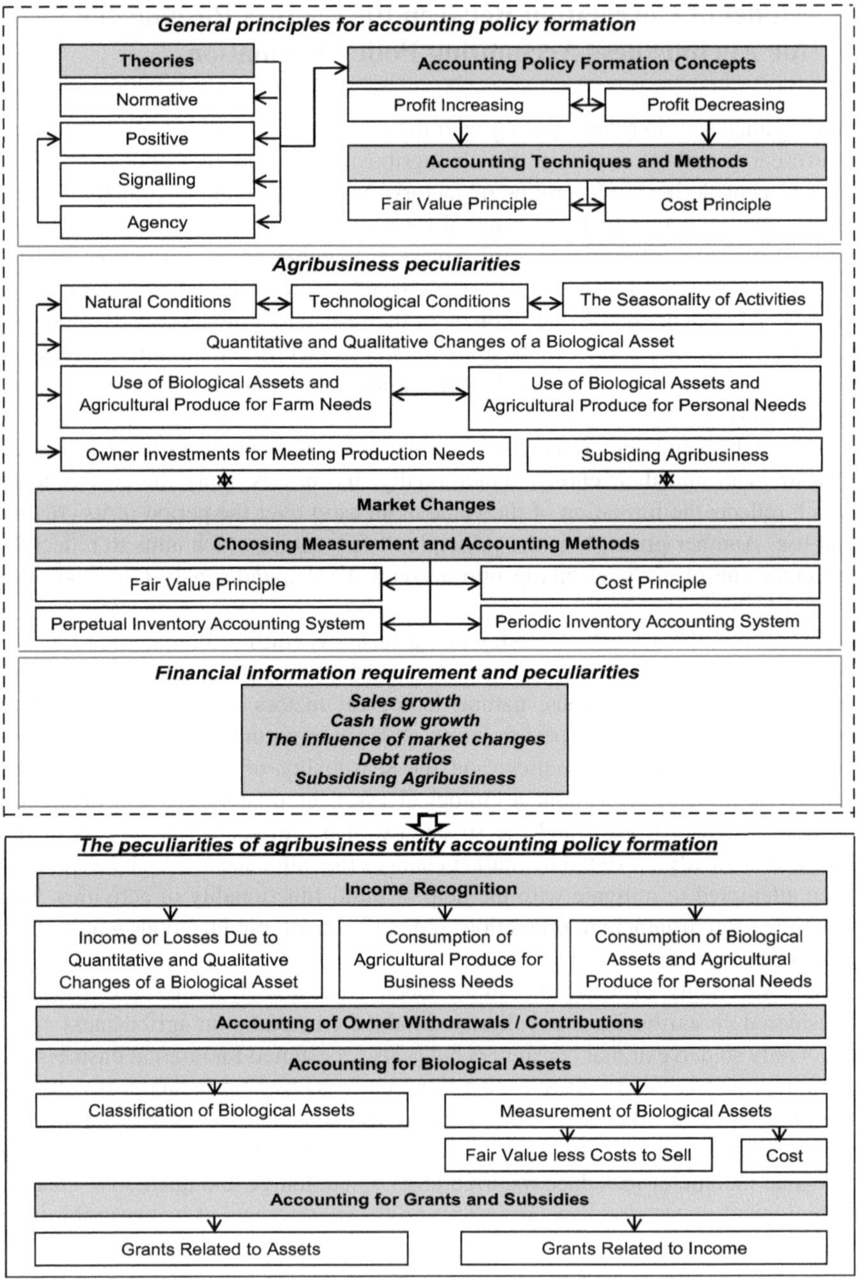

Fig. 1 Model of correlation between the factors responsible for agribusiness accounting policy formation

6 Conclusion

The research is intended for an integrated analysis of factors responsible for agribusiness accounting policy formation.

The methodological basis of research is built on the theories of signalling and agency. The latter determines the choice of the positive theory of accounting. In order to satisfy the different needs of information users, enterprises must endeavour to shape a certain financial image. One of the ways to do so is to choose either profit increasing or profit decreasing accounting methods. Profit equalisation can be useful for both the current owners and the potential investors. Considering that, enterprise managers are in possession of more accurate information in comparison to other information users, in order to supply the relevant information and attract investor attention the enterprise has to use a signalling mechanism. In the interests of fair and correct reflection of the financial position and performance results there are discussions in literature on the usefulness for investors of the fair value and cost methods. Most authors are in favour of the fair value method arguing that it creates transparency and gives confidence to investors.

The agribusiness has its specificity which, naturally, has to be reflected in the information presented to investors and which also has an influence on accounting policy formation. The research has pointed out the following most important characteristics of agricultural business having an influence on the formation of agricultural business organization policy: natural and technological conditions; territorial and social constraints by recognizing business as a way of life; use of the specific asset—biological asset—in activities; direct withdrawals and internal investments in business; business subsidising.

The analysis of accounting methods used for agribusiness accounting has shown that the peculiarities of agribusiness have a direct impact on the accounting of biological assets, income and subsidies. There are many discussions in literature on the issues of biological assets measurement. Most authors are in favour of the method of fair value less costs to sell regulated by IAS 41 maintaining that it reflects continuous qualitative and quantitative changes of these assets better. These changes are reflected as gains or losses in a profit and loss account. Relevant issues in connection with accounting policy formation include the following problem points in agricultural business accounting: separation of part of biological assets—bearer plants—from biological assets; recognition as income of the value of biological assets consumed for business needs and biological assets and agricultural produce taken for personal needs; presentation of grants and subsidies related to income in financial statements.

Under complicated business management and competitive market conditions and in the presence of large information flows business success is guaranteed by precise accounting information presented in a timely manner, while performance indicators create a consistent and systematic relationship for the adoption of both operative and strategic decisions. Good quality of accounting reduces the asymmetry of information, financial constraints and the sensitivity of investment cash flows to uncertainties. Four main groups of ratios are generally analysed in literature and in practice: liquidity (stability), solvency, profitability and operational activity (efficiency). However, the following ones are highlighted as important to investors in agribusiness organisations: growth of sales and cash flows, the influence of market changes on the organisation's financial position, debt ratios, subsidising and its influence on the financial capacity, competitiveness and development of business.

The theoretical benefit of this research is reflected in the designed model for agribusiness accounting policy formation, which shows the correlation between the factors responsible for agribusiness accounting policy formation. It has singled out: factors behind the choice of accounting policy formation direction; factors—agricultural activity peculiarities determining accounting policy formation peculiarities; factors reflecting the needs of investors in agribusiness organisations and the specificity of presenting information for satisfying these needs. The integrity of the impact of these factors is reflected in the peculiarities of agribusiness accounting policy formation.

In practice this model is useful to accounting policy makers as it singles out the factors responsible for accounting policy formation at agricultural enterprises and presents an integrated approach to their influence on the formation of accounting policies at agribusiness organisations and helps ensure presentation of fair and correct information to investors.

References

Alekneviciene, V., Stonciuviene, N., & Zinkeviciene, D. (2013). Determination of the fair value of a multifunctional family farm: A case study. *Studies in Agricultural Economics, 115*, 124–133.

Argiles, J. M., Aliberch, A. S., & Blandon, J. G. (2012). A comparative study of difficulties in accounting preparation and judgement in agriculture using fair value and historical cost for biological assets valuation. *Revista de Contabilidad, 15*(1), 109–142.

Aryanto, Y. (2011). *Theoretical failure of IAS 41*. Accessed July 26, 2014, from http://papers.ssrn.com/sol3/papers.cfm?abstract_id=1808413&download=yes

Ashtami, W. E., & Tower, G. (2006). Accounting-policy choice and firm characteristics in the Asia Pacific region: An international empirical test of costly contracting theory. *The International Journal of Accounting, 41*(1), 1–21.

Athanasios, V., Stergios, A., & Laskaridou, E. C. (2010). The importance of information through accounting practice in agricultural sector-European data network. *Journal of Social Sciences, 6* (2), 221–228.

Banzhaf, H. S. (2010). Economics at the fringe: Non-market valuation studies and their role in land use plans in the United States. *Journal of Environmental Management, 91*, 592–602.

Barry, P. J., & Ellinger, P. N. (2012). *Financial management in agriculture* (7th ed.). Upper Saddle River, NJ: Prentice Hall.

Beatty, A., Scott, L., & Weber, J. (2010). The effect of private information and monitoring on the role of accounting quality in investment decisions. *Contemporary Accounting Research, 27*(1), 17–47.

Biddle, G., & Hilary, G. (2006). Accounting quality and firm-level capital investment. *Accounting Review, 81*(5), 963–982.

Biddle, G., Hilary, G., & Verdi, R. (2009). How does financial reporting quality improve investment efficiency? *Journal of Accounting and Economics, 48*(2–3), 112–131.
Bohusova, H., Svoboda, P., & Nerudova, D. (2012). Biological assets reporting: Is the increase in value caused by the biological transformation revenue. *Agricultural Economics, 58*, 520–532.
Bonaci, C. G., & Strouhal, J. (2011). Fair value accounting and the regulation of corporate reporting. *Economics and Management, 16*, 14–21.
Bowen, R. M., DuCharme, L., & Shores, D. (1995). Stakeholders' implicit claims and accounting method choice. *Journal of Accounting and Economics, 20*(3), 255–295.
Brigham, E. F., & Ehrhardt, M. C. (2010). *Financial management: Theory and practice* (13th ed.). Mason, OH: Cengage Learning.
Brozova, I. (2011). Financial health of agricultural enterprises in the organic farming sector. *Actauniversitatisagriculturaeetsilviculturaemendelianaebrunensis, LIX*(7), 91–96.
Bruce, L. A., & Katchova, A. L. (2012). Financial ratio analysis using ARMS data. *Agricultural Finance Review, 72*(2), 262–272.
Cairns, D., Massoudi, D., Taplin, R., & Tarca, A. (2011). IFRS fair value measurement and accounting policy choice in the United Kingdom and Australia. *The British Accounting Review, 43*(1), 1–21.
Chatfield, M., & Vangermeersch, R. (2014). *The history of accounting: An international encyclopedia.* [e-book] Routledge. Available at: Google books. Accessed July 22, 2014, from http://www.google.lt/books
Connelly, B. L., Certo, S. T., Ireland, R. D., & Reutzel, C. R. (2011). Signaling theory: A review and assessment. *Journal of Management, 37*, 39–67.
Craig, R., & Diga, J. (1998). Corporate accounting disclosure in ASEAN. *Journal of International Financial Management and Accounting, 9*(3), 246–274.
Dechow, P. M., Myers, L. A., & Shakespeare, C. (2010). Fair value accounting and gains from asset securitizations: A convenient earnings management tool with compensation side-benefits. *Journal of Accounting and Economics, 49*(1), 2–25.
Deegan, C. (2006). *Financial accounting theory* (2nd ed.). Sydney: McGraw Hill.
Degeorge, F., Patel, J., & Zeckhauser, R. (1999). Earnings management to exceed thresholds. *Journal of Business, 72*(1), 1–33.
Drever, M., Stanton, P., & McGowan, S. (2007). *Contemporary issues in accounting.* Australia: Wiley.
Dumitru, M., Gorgan, C., Dumitru, V. F., & Gorgan, V. (2011). Computing the cost of the agricultural products: A case study. *African Journal of Agricultural Research, 6*(1), 198–211.
Durguner, S., & Katchova, A. (2007). *Credit scoring models by farm type: Hog, dairy, beef, and grain.* American Agricultural Economics Association Meeting, Portland, OR, July 29–August 1.
Dvorakova, D. (2011). *Developments in fair value measurement: Some IFRS 13 view.* Proceedings of the 3rd World Multiconference on Applied Economics, Business and Development (AEBD '11), Recent researches in applied economics, Iasi, Romania, July 13.
EEIG Agrosynergie. (2011). *Evaluation of income effects of direct support, Final Report.* Accessed July 4, 2014, from ec.europa.eu/agriculture/eval/reports/income/fulltext_en.pdf
Feleaga, L., Feleaga, N., & Raileanu, V. (2012). Theoretical considerations about implementation of IAS 41 in Romania. *Theoretical and Applied Economics, 2*(2), 31–38.
Feng, D., & Fu, G. (2012). Primary investigation in the completeness evaluation model of accounting system in agricultural enterprises. *Accounting and Finance Research, 1*(1), 231–238.
Ferto, I., Bakucs, L. Z., Bojnec, S., & Latruffe, L. (2011). *Investment and financial constraints in European agriculture: Evidence from France, Hungary and Slovenia.* International Congress, Zurich, Switzerland, August 30–September 2. European Association of Agricultural Economists.
Firoz, C. M., & Ansari, A. A. (2010). Environmental accounting and International Financial Reporting Standards (IFRS). *International Journal of Business and Management, 5*(10), 105–112.

Fisher, M., & Marsh, T. (2013). Biological assets: Financial recognition and reporting using us and international accounting guidance. *Journal of Accounting and Finance, 13*(2), 57–74.

Fisher, R., Mortensen, T., & Webber, D. (2010). *Fair value accounting in the agricultural sector: An analysis of financial statement preparers' perceptions before and after the introduction of IAS 41 agriculture*. Accounting and Finance Association of Australia and New Zealand (AFAANZ) conference, Christchurch, New Zealand, July 4–6.

Fosberg, R. H., & Ghosh, A. (2006). Profitability and capital structure of Amex and Nyse firms. *Journal of Business and Economics Research, 4*(11), 57–64.

Godfrey, J. M., Hodgson, A., Holmes, S., & Tarca, A. (2006). *Accounting theory* (6th ed.). Australia: Wiley.

Goncalves, R., & Lopes, P. (2014). Firm-specific determinants of agricultural financial reporting. *Procedia-Social and Behavioral Sciences, 110*, 470–481.

Gu, S. (2013). Research and analysis on issued inventory valuation methods of enterprises. *Balance, 50*, 541–544.

Harris, J. M., & Roach, B. (2013). *Environmental and natural resource economics: A contemporary approach* (3rd ed.). [e-book] ME Sharpe. Available at: Google books. Accessed July 15, 2014 from Google books http://www.google.lt/books

Herbohn, K., & Herbohn, J. (2006). International Accounting Standard (IAS) 41: What are the implications for reporting forest assets? *Small-Scale Forest Economics Management and Policy, 5*(2), 175–189.

Hinke, J., & Starova, M. (2013). Application possibilities and consequences of biological assets and agricultural produce reporting in accordance with IFRS principles in the Czech Republic. *Agris On-Line Papers in Economics and Informatics, 5*(4), 77–89.

Iatridis, G., & Joseph, N. L. (2005). A conceptual framework of accounting policy choice under SSAP 20. *Managerial Auditing Journal, 20*(7), 763–778.

Isberg, S., & Pitta, D. (2013). Using financial analysis to assess brand equity. *Journal of Product and Brand Management., 22*(1), 65–78.

Jack, L. (2006). Protecting agricultural accounting in the UK. *Accounting Forum, 30*(3), 227–243.

Jatkunaite, D., Martirosianiene, L., & Stonciuviene, N. (2006). Case study of the accounting policy formation at agricultural holdings in Lithuania. *Economics and Rural Development, 2*(2), 28–38.

Jesswein, K. R. (2010). The changing LIFO-FIFO dilemma and its importance to the analysis of financial statements. *Academy of Accounting and Financial Studies Journal, 1*(14), 53–62.

Jiang, G., & Penman, S. (2013). A fundamentalist perspective on accounting and implications for accounting research. *China Journal of Accounting Research, 6*(4), 233–245.

Khrawish, A. H., & Khraiwesh, A. H. (2010). The determinants of the capital structure: Evidence from the Jordanian industrial companies. *Economics and Administration, 24*(1), 173–196.

Khurana, I. K., & Kim, M. S. (2003). Relative value relevance of historical cost vs. fair value: Evidence from bank holding companies. *Journal of Accounting and Public Policy, 22*, 19–42.

Kotane, I., & Kuzmina-Merlino, I. (2012). Assessment of financial indicators for evaluation of business performance. *European Integration Studies, 6*, 216–224.

Lasher, W. R. (2005). *Practical financial management* (4th ed.). Mason, OH: South-Western.

Leland, H. E., & Pyle, D. H. (1977). Informational asymmetries, financial structure, and financial intermediation. *The Journal of Finance, 32*(2), 371–387.

Marsh, T., & Fischer, M. (2013). Accounting for agricultural products: US versus IFRS GAAP. *Journal of Business and Economics Research (JBER), 11*(2), 79–88.

Milne, M. J. (2002). Positive accounting theory, political costs and social disclosure analyses: A critical look. *Critical Perspectives on Accounting, 13*(3), 369–395.

Morris, R. D. (1987). Signaling, agency theory and accounting policy choice. *Accounting and Business Research, 18*(69), 47–56.

Muhammad, K., & Ghani, E. K. (2013). A fair value model for bearer biological assets in promoting corporate governance: A proposal. *Journal of Agricultural Studies, 2*(1), 16–26.

Nawaz, A. (2010). Performance of microfinance: The role of subsidies. *Savings and Development, 34*, 97–138.

Octavian, M. V. (2012). Value relevance of group financial statements based on entity versus parent company theory: Evidence from the largest three European capital markets. *Annals of the University of Oradea, Economic Science Series, 21*(1), 949–955.

Orban, T., & Dekan, I. (2013). Methodological aspects of agricultural enterprises' income calculation. *Annals of the University of Oradea, Economic Science Series., 22*(2), 523–529.

Ore, M. (2011). *Problematic aspects of accounting for biological assets* (pp. 204–210). Proceedings of the International Scientific Conference Economic Science for Rural Development, 24, Latvia University of Agriculture, Jelgava.

Petruk, O. M., Legenchuk, S. F., & Koroliuk, N. M. (2013). Development of accounting theory in English-speaking countries: On the way to multi-paradigmatic discipline. *Accounting and Finance, 3*(61), 48–57.

Pimentel, D. (2012). *Food and natural resources.* [e-book] Academic Press. Available at: Google Books. Accessed July 19, 2014, from http://www.google.lt/books

Raileanu, A. S., & Pravat, I. C. (2008). Positive theory of accounting choice—Using accounting choice as signaling variable. *Annals of the University of Oradea, Economic Science Series, 17* (3), 1443.

Reichert, A., & Posey, R. (2011). Using financial ratios and lender relationship theory to assess farm creditworthiness. *Accounting and Taxation, 3*(1), 45–56.

Riahi-Belkaoui, A. (2004). *Accounting theory* (5th ed.). London: Thomson learning.

Ristea, M., & Jianu, I. (2010). *Dynamics of the fair value in accounting.* Accessed July 12, 2014, from http://anale.feaa.uaic.ro/anale/resurse/ctb7ristea.pdf

Ross, S. R. (2007). *Financial management fundamentals in Malaysia.* Malaysia: McGraw-Hill.

Schroeder, R. G., Clark, M. W., & Cathey, J. M. (2010). *Financial accounting: Theory and analysis.* Hoboken, NJ: Wiley.

Scott, W. R. (2012). *Financial accounting theory* (6th ed.). Toronto, ON: Pearson Prentice Hall.

Scott, J., & Colman, R. (2008). *The GPI soils and agriculture accounts: Economic viability of farms and farm communities in Nova Scotia and Prince Edward Island—An update.* Nova Scotia: GPI Atlantic. Accessed June 25, 2014, from www.gpiatlantic.org/pdf/agriculture/farmviability08.pdf.

Sedlacek, J. (2010). The methods of valuation in agricultural accounting. *Agricultural Economics—Czech, 56*, 59–66.

Shaheen, M. A. (2012, January 11). The choice of accounting policy in developing countries: Case of the state of Kuwait (An empirical investigation of the validity of the positive theory). *Social Science Research Network.* Accessed June 28, 2014, from http://papers.ssrn.com

Sharma, R. S. (2012). Ratio analysis in farm management. *International Journal of Recent Research and Review, 1*, 47–50.

Spence, M. (1973). Job market signalling. *The Quarterly Journal of Economics, 87*(3), 355–374.

Splett, N. S., Barry, P. J., Dixon, B. L., & Ellinger, P. N. (1994). A joint experience and statistical approach to credit scoring. *Agricultural Finance Review, 54*, 39–54.

Stolowy, H., & Breton, G. (2003). Accounts manipulation: A literature review and proposed conceptual framework. *Review of Accounting and Finance, 3*(1), 5–66.

Tan, C. W., Tower, G., Hancock, P., & Taplin, R. (2002). Empires of the sky: Determinants of global airlines' accounting-Policy Choices. *International Journal of Accounting, 37*, 277–299.

Tilman, D., Cassman, K. G., Matson, P. A., Naylor, R., & Polasky, S. (2002). Agricultural sustainability and intensive production practices. *Nature, 418*(6898), 671–677.

Tinker, A. M., Merino, B. D., & Neimark, M. D. (1982). The normative origins of positive theories: Ideology and accounting thought. *Accounting, Organization and Society, 7*(2), 167–200.

Tzouvelekas, V., Pantzios, C. J., & Fotopoulos, C. (2001). Economic efficiency in organic farming: Evidence from cotton farms in Viotia, Greece. *Journal of Agricultural and Applied Economics, 33*(1), 35–48.

Tzovas, C. (2006). Factors influencing a firm's accounting policy decisions when tax accounting and financial accounting coincide. *Managerial Auditing Journal, 21*(4), 372–386.

Valladares, E. V., & Flores, J. L. D. (2005). Analysis of financial ratios of an intensive dairy enterprise: a case study in the mexican high plateau. *Vet Mex, 36*(1), 25–40.
Van Mourik, C., & Walton, P. (2013). *The Routledge companion to accounting, reporting and regulation*. [e-book] Routledge. Available at: Google Books. Accessed July 5, 2014, from http://www.google.lt/books
Verdi, R. (2006). *Financial reporting quality and investment efficiency*. Ph.D. thesis, University of Pennsylvania. Accessed July 22, 2014, from https://www.gsb.stanford.edu
Wang, Z., & Williams, T. H. (1994). Accounting income smoothing and stockholder wealth. *Journal of Applied Business Research, 10*(3), 96–110.
Wanstrom, R. (2012). *Moving average-valuation of inventories. An empirical study of four manufacturing companies*. Master thesis. Accessed July 25, 2014, from http://www.diva-portal.org/smash/record.jsf?pid=diva2:536769
Warren, C., Reeve, J., & Duchac, J. (2011). *Financial accounting* (12th ed.). [e-book] South Western Cengage Learning. Available at: Google Books. Accessed June 26, 2014, from http://www.google.lt/books
Watts, R. L., & Zimmerman, J. L. (1990). Positive accounting theory: A ten year prospective. *The Accounting Review, 65*(1), 131–156.
Zager, K., & Zager, L. (2006). The role of financial information in decision-making process. *Innovative Marketing, 2*(3), 35–40.
Zeddies, J. (1991). *Viability of farms*. Luxembourg: Office for official publications of the European communities.
Zeff, S. A. (2007). The SEC rules historical cost accounting: 1934 to the 1970s. *Accounting and Business Research, 37*(1), 49–62.
Zinkeviciene, D., & Rudzioniene, K. (2005). Impact of company's leverage on financial accounting method choice. *Engineering Economics, 45*(5), 25–30.
Zinkeviciene, D., & Vaisnoraite, G. (2014). Factors affecting the choice of tangible fixed asset accounting methods: Theoretical approach. *European Scientific Journal, 10*(10), 199–208.

Transition from Tax Records to Double-Entry Bookkeeping in the Czech Republic

Libuše Svobodová

Abstract The aim of this paper is to describe the process of transition from tax records to double-entry bookkeeping in the Czech Republic. The transfer of tax records on double-entry bookkeeping is not so often used in the Czech Republic. It is expected that it will change. The prerequisite is a change in legislation which has occurred since January 1, 2014. Specifically, the new Law No. 90/2012 Coll. on commercial companies and cooperatives, which replaced the Act No. 513/1991 Coll. Commercial Code. Mostly is the transition done mandatory due crossing sales or the physical person must convert tax records into double-entry bookkeeping in case of change of the status from the physical person on the legal entity. In the article there are described the steps that are necessary to do in the transition. At the end of the article there are the graphs that present the situation in record keeping in the Czech Republic, in Hradec Králové and Pardubice region. A detailed research together with the analysis and critical assessment of accessible materials will enable to identify the main objectives in the field of study. The analysis of the initial state will consequently enable to identify the key factors and knowledge.

Keywords Double-entry bookkeeping • Tax records • Transition • Bridge

1 Introduction

Business performance can be evaluated from many perspectives. One of the most common is assessment of the financial situation of the company. The financial analysis is based on the results of double-entry bookkeeping. Physical persons, however, usually keep tax records, for which it is not possible to carry out a typical financial analysis, because she/he does not smeared data. One of the main differences is monitoring of income and expenses and determine profit for those who keep tax records of revenues and costs for those who keep their accounts. We can still analyse the company's performance for the companies which keep tax records.

L. Svobodová (✉)
Department of Economics, University of Hradec Kralove, Hradec Kralove, Czech Republic
e-mail: libuse.svobodova@uhk.cz

© Springer International Publishing Switzerland 2016

M.H. Bilgin et al. (eds.), *Business Challenges in the Changing Economic Landscape - Vol. 1*, Eurasian Studies in Business and Economics 2/1,
DOI 10.1007/978-3-319-22596-8_5

Table 1 Distinctive characteristics, tax records and bookkeeping

	Physical person keeping tax records	Physical person that use bookkeeping
Basis for identifying tax base	Profit—difference between income and expenses	Profit—difference between revenues and costs
They are subject to tax	Taxable income	Taxable revenues
Against income (revenues) is applicable	Taxable expenditure	Taxable costs
Acquisition of fixed assets	Applicable tax depreciation	Applicable tax depreciation
Acquisition of intangible assets	Applicable in tax expense reimbursement (§ 24.2, n/the Act on Income Taxes)	Applicable tax depreciation
Inventories and valuables	When paying—tax expense	Tax expense on consumption
Buying services	When paying—tax expense	Tax expense for reimbursement, subject to delivery (a liability)
Accrued costs and revenues	Only for lessees under finance leases	Always used (for costs and also for revenues)
Accepted or advances except advances fixed assets	Taxable income or expense when paying	Tax balance sheet operations without affecting on the profit
Invoicing own performance (the debt)	Taxable income only when paid	Taxable revenue while meeting delivery
Is it possible to use legal reserves?	Yes	Yes
Is it possible to use statutory deductions and discounts?	Yes	Yes
Is it possible to apply the statutory provisions for receivables?	No	Yes

Source: Jaroš (2011)

Legislation in the Czech Republic adjusts the evidence, which is currently in European Union usual:

Accounting based on the "accrual basis"—accounting at the moment implementation of accounting transactions, thus accounting for costs and revenues. If is in the article written about accounting is meant double-entry bookkeeping. The double-entry bookkeeping have to lead legal persons and some physical persons.

Records of the so-called "cash basis", where the priority for capture operations is the movement of money (or registered with the revenue and expenditure, the notion of costs and benefits in accounts on a cash basis does not exist). It is acceptable for the so-called micro-enterprises with a simple activity—so for most physical persons.

As is presented in the chapter tax records and accounting in the Czech Republic, Hradec Králové region and Pardubice region, most of the physical persons that filled the "accounting" method, used the tax records, so "cash basis" type of accounting. This method is for the majority of physical persons easier than accounting based on the "accrual basis", called double-entry bookkeeping.

In the double entry-bookkeeping all companies must adjust the economic result to a tax base according to the national tax legislation, which is associated with high administrative, financial, and time-consuming demands. The mutual ratio between the economic result and the tax base also varies in connection with the sector of business activity in which the company operates (Blechová et al. 2013).

Janhuba (2013) argue that accounting as a branch of economic science and research is not in the centre of attention of economists, whether they are focused macroeconomic or Business Administration (microeconomic). Whoever, it is necessary to underline the crucial importance of accounting for the formation of a number of findings from the field of business management, e. g., cost, efficiency and economy of production. Accounting is a branch of science developed in the world and around us in the last 150 years and represents today an accepted part of the microeconomic oriented research and the formation of some theoretical conclusions. Table 1 presents the distinctive characteristics of tax records and bookkeeping.

2 Goals and Used Methods

In this article we will focus on the steps that you need to make in the transition from tax records to double-entry bookkeeping. We will aim on the accounting point of view and also in the matter of tax. Another goal is to publish data on tax records and accounting and transitions between these two methods in two selected regions. The tax records should be also mentioned as single entry bookkeeping. In the presented article will be the term defined as tax records. Transfer from tax records on double-entry bookkeeping was in practice not often occurring situation. With this issue we need to deal quite exceptionally, and then look for sources where we can find the necessary information and procedures on how to make the transition flawlessly.

In the first part of the article there were used primarily secondary sources. The secondary sources are represented by professional literature, information collected from professional press, legal regulations, websites, discussions or previous participations in professional seminars and conferences relating to the chosen subject. Then it was necessary to select, classify and update accessible relevant information from the numerous published materials that would give the basic knowledge of transition. In the last part, tax records and accounting in the Czech Republic, Hradec Králové region and Pardubice region, were used data gained from the competent person from the Ministry of Finance and from individual tax offices in the regions.

3 The Reasons for the Transition from Tax Records to Bookkeeping

3.1 *Optional Transition from Tax Records to Accounting*

The main reasons are either internal requirement of the company, ie, for example, greater awareness, and it is an external requirement, ie, such as the requirement of the bank. As was mentioned above the new legislation Law No. 90/2012 Coll. on commercial companies and cooperatives increased flexibility of the Limited Liability Company and removed limitations that presented a barrier to establishing a company and its activities. The most important changes include waiving the statutory limit of registered capital and decreasing the minimum amount of the deposit, the option of creating various types of shares and the option of expressing the share by a security (see Pokorná and Večerková (2014) for more details). Those changes should motivate physical persons to change the type of the company from the physical person to limited liability company. Entrepreneur may benefit from the change eg. that personal property is not liable for the obligations of the company or firm may gain a better image. If an individual decides to voluntarily keep double-entry accounting, then the charge in double-entry accounting throughout the period (Dušek 2008).

3.2 *Mandatory Transition from Tax Records to Accounting*

Most of the entrepreneurs moving from tax records to double-entry bookkeeping as a result of exceeding the limit of turnover. A substantial change occurs on the amendment to the Accounting Act, Act No. 261/2007 Coll. stabilization of public budgets, have changed the legal limit of CZK 15 million to CZK 25 million today. Keep accounts then starts from the period following the tax year, when he became the entity. In the Czech Republic there are a lot of reasons when the physical person has to use bookkeeping instead of tax records. Table 2 shows in what circumstances the physical person accounts and when he must begin to lead.

Transfer from tax records to bookkeeping is done by 1 January the following year, when are fulfilled the conditions for mandatory or voluntary transition from tax records to bookkeeping.

Table 2 Obligation to leads accounts

I crossed in 2013 sales	Obligation to keep accounts from January 1, 2015
I am a foreign person	Obligation to keep records from the date of commencement of activities
I am a person registered in the Commercial Register	Obligation to keep accounts from date of writing
I am a member of an association whose member is a person entity	Obligation to keep accounts from the next period
Saves me the special accounting rule	Obligation to keep accounts from the start of the activity

Source: Own processing

4 Regulations Governing the Transfer from Tax Records on Double-Entry Bookkeeping

To the end of 2000 was a transfer from tax record to double-entry accounting solved in Annex 2 to Action Ministry of Finance ref. 281/71 702/1995, as amended. The procedure described here deal with the transfer from the perspective of accounting and tax. From 1 January 2001 is already a transfer from the accounting point of view and from the perspective of the tax dealt with separately. Transition from tax records to accounting, reporting anywhere, it is evident from the mandatory attachments of tax return.

4.1 Accounting Rules

Accounting for entrepreneurs from transfer tax accounting to double-entry bookkeeping solves Decree No. 472/2003 coll. § 61b and transitional provisions of Art. II. The transfer method from tax records on double-entry bookkeeping is in § 61b of the Decree 500/2002 to Accounting Act.

The transition from tax records to accounting has two levels. These levels are accounting and tax. In the case of voluntary transition to accounting in the application of deductible expenses and the purchase of the subject leases tax payer will cover the transition to accounting only in financial terms. In these cases, based profit/loss of the physical person under § 7 of the Act of Income taxes, the difference between income and expenditure provided by the fee (Practical adviser in tax issues 12/2010).

4.2 Closing Tax Records

There are used the basic steps of the transition from tax record to accounting: The inventory of all assets and liabilities, an entry on this finding and the adjustment of the tax base of any differences, Preparation of tax returns, Closure of partial records—might be needed regardless of whether there is a change in record keeping or not, and Separation of items that will affect the tax base in the tax period in which it was started posting.

Before opening the books of 1 January 2015 we have to determine the actual condition of assets and liabilities in the tax records of 31 December 2014 and then we will address the accounting for these items. First, perform a physical and book inventory, where we find states of individual components of assets and liabilities, or reserves, revaluation reserve for consideration to the acquired assets and leases of tangible assets, which was not on duty the transition from tax records for bookkeeping still applied in tax base. Part of the expenditure of financial leasing tangible assets, which was applied as a tax expenditure to be shown as opening balance on the Prepaid expenses account. In addition to financial leases are no further accruals. But sometimes it is a very significant amount that we pay in advance, such as rent paid/received in advance for a certain period. This situation can be justified in some cases dealt with under the provisions of § 7, para.2, of the Accounting Act, which allows, in exceptional cases proceed differently. This situation needs to be addressed from the perspective of the tax correctly.

4.3 Mandatory Treatment Tax Base

Adjustments of income tax during the transition from tax records on bookkeeping is affecting only the tax base for the period when the first year we conduct accounting, but it is necessary to deal with these items already in the conclusion of tax records and books of account opening (Pilátová et al. 2014). Specified in Annex 3 to the Act No. 586/1992 Coll. the process of transition from tax records to bookkeeping, in response to specific legislation (Accounting Act) this:

The tax base is the taxable period in which they were initiated bookkeeping increase the value of inventories and valuables, the value of the advances except advances for fixed assets, the value of claims that would have been paid in taxable income. The tax base is the taxable period in which they were initiated accounting, reduced by the amount of advances received, the value of liabilities that would have been paid on expenditure to generate, assure and maintain income. If it is the payer of value added tax, it is understood for the purposes of this procedure value of the liability value exclusive of value added tax. If it has been deducted from the value added tax, value means the value of assets without value added tax, if it was true tax liability on the output. The tax base is the taxable period in which they were initiated bookkeeping, increase the value of the receivables, which would have been paid in taxable income, in the case of claims, which at the time were tax records from the debtor referred to in § 24 para.2 point.y.

When discussing the additional tax returns after the performed inspection is not being blocked by the existing wording of § 38p. para.2 of the Income Accounting Tax the ability of the taxpayer to eliminate the additional tax assessment by making a supplementary tax return and increase the amount of the applied according to § 23 para.14 of the Income Tax Act. According to the nature of this item, it is fundamentally the same category as the reading of tax losses, and the reason in this way to give the taxpayer the option to eliminate the impact of their own shortcomings, which determines the tax during a tax, in calculating the correct amount of tax. The tax base includes the difference between the valuation of a business or part of the business, forming a separate organizational unit, acquired by purchase and the total valuation of the individual components of assets in the accounts of the seller reduced the liabilities assumed. Table 3 contains the presentation of the tax base.

The law is clear on the concepts of income and expenditure. That is, if the payment were in tax record revenues or expenses, the tax must be taken into account. All other cases are for transfer from tax records to accounting tax inefficient. It obviously pays "principle higher tax": to tax expenses or income can give only what concerns business. Moreover, this should not be in the accounting (Dušek 2008).

Adjustment of tax refers to the tax period in which we start accounting. The potential tax effects of the transfer are part of the normal income tax return for the taxable period. It will be no separate tax return from the bridge transferring, or on the date of transmission of the bridge. It is known that a significant number of larger businesses would have switched from tax records to double-entry bookkeeping, if they do not have adverse tax effects caused by high inventory levels and outstanding receivables. If recorded, the date of transfer from tax records to double entry bookkeeping, there were no stocks, no outstanding tax debts and any outstanding tax liabilities, and anything that affects the tax base of the transfer, then the tax effect of zero. Own transfer from tax records to accounting does not affect the income tax in the last year leadership tax records. Tax affects only those cases that are recommended at each step to make closing even in tax records, they are in terms

Table 3 Presentation of the tax base

Items increasing income tax base, line No. 105 of Annex 1 to the individual income tax return	Items decreasing tax base, line No. 106 of Annex 1 to the individual income tax return
+ Inventory	− Advances received
+ Stamps	− Commitments that the payment was tax-deductible
+ Advances (exceptions = advance payments for tangible and intangible assets)	
+ Claims that the payment was taxable income	

Source: Pilátová et al. (2014)

of purity accounting voluntary. Liabilities and assets reflect the tax return regardless of whether they are paid or not. Change of accounting system does not affect the possible utilization of tax losses in the next years.

It is also necessary for management accounting chart of accounts to build, create and compile the Accounting Directives and prepare opening balance sheet. Decree No. 500/2002 Coll., which implements certain provisions of Act No. 563/1991 Coll., on accounting, we stated the classification and identification of individual balance sheet items. According to Annex 1, this Regulation should have the following balance sheet form, which is attached in Annex 3: Structure of balance sheet assets and liabilities.

4.4 *Start of Double-Entry Bookkeeping*

Instructions on how to open the books in the transition from tax records for bookkeeping regulated by § 61b Decree no 500/2002 to Accounting Tax. This paragraph tells us that physical person keeping tax records pursuant to § 7b of the Act on Income Tax, which became the entity has in its records tax records to find out:

- the number of individual components of assets and liabilities,
- reserve,
- adjustment to acquired fixed assets for consideration,
- for financial leasing and subsequent purchase of the leased tangible assets unclaimed portion of the expenditure on the day preceding the first day of the accounting period in which they incurred a duty to initiate accounting.

The individual components of assets and liabilities are valued in accordance with § 24 and § 25 of the Accounting Act. The basic valuation of assets and liabilities are presented also in Table 4.

For fixed assets depreciation schedules shall be established in accordance with § 28, para.6, of the Act on Accounting. At the beginning we need to build an opening balance sheet, because of the known components of state assets, liabilities, reserves and valuation differences on assets acquired for a consideration to the first day of the accounting period converted as the opening balances of the balance sheet accounts. The resulting difference between the total value of assets and liabilities through settlement, and posting an account in the accounting group 49 with that may arise both passive and active balance. In the tax provision process is essential for the transition from tax records to accounting § 5, para.8 of the Income Tax Act, which saves taxpayer to proceed in accordance with Annex 3 to the Income Tax Act. These adjustments are always included in the tax period in which the accounting is initiated, ie, the transition to 1 January 2015 affects 2015.

Table 4 Evaluation components of assets and liabilities

Asset and liability	Valuation
Tangible fixed assets other than inventory, with the exception of fixed assets developed	The acquisition price
Tangible fixed assets other than stocks internally generated	The actual costs
Inventories except for inventories by the company	The acquisition price
Internally developed inventory	The actual costs
Cash and cash equivalents	The nominal value
Shares, securities and derivatives	The acquisition price
Loans and advances in the development	The nominal value
Receivables arising from the acquisition of a fee or deposit	The acquisition price
Liabilities	The nominal value
Intangible assets, other than debts, with the exception of intangible assets developed	The acquisition price
Intangible assets, other than receivables generated internally	The actual costs
Born animals	The actual costs
Assets in cases free of charge, with the exception of the above assets or property in cases where the cost of its own to create custom actions cannot be determined	The replacement cost

Source: Pilátová et al. (2014)

4.5 Minimizing the Tax Effect

There are not many ways how to minimize tax impact, but it can be minimized at least by the following:

- Minimize stocks (no matter whether they are purchased or own, regardless of whether they are paid or unpaid). Be observed only necessary (optimal) operating condition.
- Minimize status of unpaid tax debts—remember to be enforced.
- It is not necessary to minimize the status of unpaid tax liabilities. However, remember that your contractor may also have an obligation to transfer from tax records to accounting and will therefore follow the rule to minimize claims.

5 Tax Records and Accounting in the Czech Republic, in the Hradec Králové Region and Pardubice Region

The first part of this chapter will focus on a nationwide comparison of tax records and accounting. Furthermore, in the chart persons who stated that they are not the entity. 45 % of companies did not specify what accounting lead. By comparison there were included companies from the Hradec Králové and Pardubice Region. We have selected areas that are close to our University. Due to the availability of the data will be reported in this chapter data for 2010. Data were obtained either by reaching a competent person at the Ministry of Finance and in the second part the data were obtained from separate financial authorities.

The Fig. 1 present the physical person that keep tax records and accounting in the Czech Republic. If we compare the available data and focus on physical persons who indicated that keep tax records or accounting, we find that 89.4 % of the respondents keeps tax records and 9.6 % accounting. In Hradec Králové region keeps tax records of almost 93 % and in the Pardubice region of 92 %. Taking into account all respondents 25.2 % of respondents keep tax records and 2.7 % double-entry bookkeeping. As mentioned earlier, 45 % of respondents did not specify how the accounting lead. Due to the overall results may be biased.

5.1 *Hradec Králové Region*

In the Hradec Králové region were addressed all financial authorities. The offices surveyed answered only from a financial office in Hradec Kralove, Jaroměř, Náchod and Trutnov. Not all respondents answered complex questions. Table 5 shows the data obtained in this region.

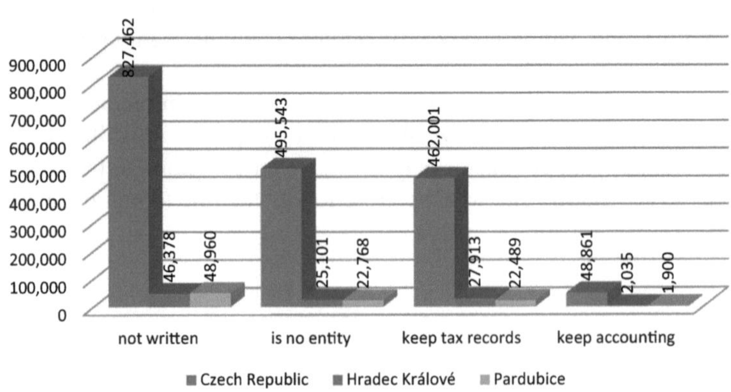

Fig. 1 Physical person that keep tax records and accounting

Table 5 Accounting method used in the Hradec Králové region in 2010

Tax office	Accounting	Tax records	Transition from tax records to accounting	Transition from accounting to tax records
Hradec Králové	600	7305	–	9
Jaroměř	58	1730	0	0
Náchod	2180	4150	–	–
Trutnov	221	2880	–	–
Total	3059	16,065	0	9

Table 6 Accounting method used in the Pardubice region in 2010

Tax office	Accounting	Tax records	Transition from tax records to accounting	Transition from accounting to tax records
Hlinsko	55	3411	–	–
Litomyšl	82	2448	5	
Přelouč	1052	105	2	0
Ústí n/O	196	2766	–	–
VysokéMýto	108	–	1	6
Total	1411	6282	8	6

The majority of business entities use tax records. As is evident from the data available the transition from the tax records to accounting or vice versa in region too often not conducted in 2010. The tax authorities reported that only nine companies done transition from accounting to tax records in Hradec Králové. After again addressing query to tax offices that responded, this is similar in other years.

5.2 *Region Pardubice*

In the Pardubice region were contacted 11 tax offices, which are located in this region. Of those surveyed responded in the county offices of the Tax Office in Hlinsko, LitomyšlPřelouč, ÚstínadOrlicí and VysokéMýto. Again, the answers were not complete. Table 6 shows the data obtained in this region.

As is clear from this table and from the previous table Hradec Králové region, there are leads mostly tax records. In 2010 moved from tax records to accounting, according to available data, eight businesses. On the contrary, the available data passed back from accounting to tax records six businesses. Also from those data is evident that the transition is not so often used.

6 Discussion and Conclusion

The transfer of tax records on double-entry bookkeeping is not a simple matter and, therefore, most trying to make in this situation at all, but do not always succeed and it becomes necessary to transfer, which are then no longer be avoided. Transition from tax records to double-entry bookkeeping for the transition should be to someone better, since we submit accurate accounting and integrated information. The double-entry bookkeeping offers us better control of business, it is also easier to obtain an overview of the state of the business. Yet there is no transition in the Czech Republic frequent used and most ordinary physical person keeps tax records.

When the companies change the tax records on accounting, it is necessary to do the inventory of all assets and liabilities and an entry on this finding and the adjustment of the tax base of any differences. Furthermore, it is necessary to do the tax return for the period in which was the tax records leaded. It has to be done also without the change. Finally, we have to commit the items that will affect the tax base in the tax period in which it was started leading. When the physical person started to use double-entry bookkeeping he or she is still taxed as a physical person (not as a legal person). So there is no change in the taxation of profit and paying of the social and health insurance. The personal tax is now 15 % in the Czech Republic and the corporation tax is 19 %.

Acknowledgements This paper is written with financial support from specific university research funds of the Czech Republic Ministry of Education, Youth and Sport allocated to the University of Hradec Králové Faculty of Informatics and management, project no. 2111/2014.

References

Act No. 261/2007 Coll., Art. II.

Act No. 563/1991 Coll., Accounting tax.

Act No. 586/1992 Coll., Income tax act.

Blechová, B., Janoušková, J., & Sobotovičová, Š. (2013). Analysis of the relationship between financial and tax accounting in the Czech Republic in the context of EU legislation. In *Proceedings of the International Conference Accounting and Management Information Systems AMIS 2013* (pp. 783–797).

Decree No. 472/2003 Coll.

Decree No. 500/2002 Coll.

Dušek, J. (2008). *Transfer from tax records to double-entry bookkeeping* (6th ed.). Praha: Grada.

Janhuba, M. (2013). Accounting and its place in science and teaching in the University of Economics, Prague. *Politickaekonomie, 61*(4), 420–431.

Jaroš, T. (2011). *Taxation of income in 2011*. Praha: Grada.

Pilátová, J., Červinka, T., & Janoušek, K. (2014). *Tax records: A comprehensive solution to the issue of tax records for the entrepreneurs*. Olomouc: ANAG.

Pokorná, J., & Večerková, E. (2014). The limited liability company as a universal legal form of business. *Procedia Economics and Finance, 12*, 533–538.

Practical adviser on tax issues: Magazine of tax and accounting news, comments, advice and examples, 2010.VerlagDashöfer Holding, nr. 12.

Determinants of Corporate Social Reporting in India

Mohammad Talha, Benjamin Christopher, and J. Karthikeyani

Abstract Corporate Social Reporting (CSR), which stems from the root of Corporate Social Responsibility of a corporation, is gaining importance across nations. As a research theme, CSR has attracted the attention of many researchers who have explored the concept from different perspectives. The present paper examines the extent of corporate social reporting and the variables that determine it. Based on market capitalization, the top 100 companies included in BSE 200 of Bombay Stock Exchange, India, have been included in the study. Data required have been obtained from the annual reports of the companies for the period from 2007–08 to 2011–12. Content analysis reveals that companies report extensively on 'community involvement'. The determinants of corporate social reporting have been identified through multiple regression analysis. The variables that have been tested are size, age, nationality, industry type, ownership, liquidity, leverage, profit, dividend, reserves, and gross fixed assets. Corporate Social Reporting Index—constructed based on the number of CSR components a company reports—has been regressed on the select variables. The results indicate that Size, Nationality, Industry Type, Ownership and Leverage determine the level of corporate social reporting of Indian companies.

Keywords Corporate Social Reporting • Corporate Social Responsibility • Stakeholders • Extent of Reporting • Determinants of Corporate Social Reporting

M. Talha (✉)
Department of Accounting and MIS, King Fahd University of Petroleum and Minerals, Dhahran, Saudi Arabia
e-mail: talha@kfupm.edu.sa

B. Christopher
Department of Commerce, NGM College, Pollachi, Tamilnadu, India
e-mail: ben_chris59@hotmail.com

J. Karthikeyani
Department of Commerce with Computer Applications, Kovai Kalaimagal College of Arts and Science, Coimbatore, India
e-mail: karthikeyani_j@yahoo.co.in

© Springer International Publishing Switzerland 2016

M.H. Bilgin et al. (eds.), *Business Challenges in the Changing Economic Landscape - Vol. 1*, Eurasian Studies in Business and Economics 2/1,
DOI 10.1007/978-3-319-22596-8_6

1 Introduction

Corporate Social Reporting (CSR), a by-product of Corporate Social Responsibility of the corporations, has assumed greater importance in recent years. It has become the prime duty of every corporation to perform its socially-relevant duties and communicate them to the stakeholders to justify their meaningful existence. Gray et al. (1996) feel that corporate social and environmental reporting pertains to the process of communicating the social and environmental effects of organizations' economic actions to particular interest groups within the society at large.

Nations have developed primarily because of the growth witnessed in the industrial sector. However, industrialization has brought along with it several environment-degrading effects because of which it becomes essential for the corporations to protect the globe from such adverse impact. Accordingly, many corporations dedicate themselves for the cause of the society and have been taking up many society-oriented programmes the outcome of which is reported through several media like annual report, web site and the like. However, the reliability of such information is still questionable. There are claims, vouching for the quality of information. For instance, Mammatt et al. (2010) feel that there has been a steady increase in the quality of information reported.

Corporate social reporting, as a topic of research, has created enough curiosity that several studies have been carried out. A brief summary of studies, relevant to the present focus of the paper, is presented in the following paragraphs.

2 Review of Literature

Jupe (2005) analyzed the disclosure in the corporate annual reports within the framework of legitimacy theory by selecting 200 large companies from the list of companies of Financial Times UK 500. His study provided broad support for legitimacy theory as an explanatory variable for the disclosures in the separate environmental reports prepared by companies. Ayadi (2007) selected a sample of 82 French firms from a list of 500 large firms for the period 2000. The model he developed using such data revealed that stakeholder theory was more suitable for analysis pertaining to corporate disclosure. He found that variables like reputation of the industry and size influenced the disclosure practice of the firms. Hossain (2008) examined the extent of disclosure practices of banks in India by selecting 38 banks, both public and private, during the year 2002–03. The results indicated that size, profitability, board composition and market discipline influenced the level of disclosure. Hossain and Helmi (2009) found that age, assets, complexity and assets-in-place significantly influenced the level of corporate social reporting of Doha Securities Market-listed companies in Qatar. Cecil (2010) examined the corporate social reporting in the United States by considering all the companies which reported that they were following the standards like GRI (Global Reporting

Initiative) 2002, GRI G3, and AA1000AS (AccountAbility Assurance Standard). The study period spanned from 1991 to 2006. It was found that many US companies had started to bring out stand-alone reports though they were not audited. Rouf (2010) examined the association between corporate characteristics, governance attributes and corporate voluntary disclosure in Bangladesh. He found that corporate social reporting was negatively related with profitability and higher management ownership while it was positively associated with dual leadership structure, size of board, and board audit committee. Hussainey et al. (2011) found that firms in Egypt reported product-related information extensively as opposed to other types of information. They also found that profitability remained the main determinant of corporate social reporting. Kolsi (2012) reported that leverage and profitability influenced the disclosure level. Naser and Hassan (2013) ascertained that firm size, industry type and profitability influenced corporate social reporting. Juhmani (2014) came out with a result that highly levered companies reported more on the environmental information. Marquis and Quian (2014) found that firm size, required disclosure, reporting experience, media exposure and stock market exchange had significant influence on the probability of issuing a corporate social responsibility report. Burgwal and Vieira (2014) concluded that size of a firm influenced environmental disclosure. Jouirou and Chenguel (2014) examined 22 Tunisian firms and found that size of the firm, the independence of the board and the quality of audit firm had a positive and significant influence on the level of voluntary disclosure while a negative relationship was observed between firm age and level of disclosure. Alkababji (2014) investigated the extent and nature of social and environmental reporting in the annual reports of 48 firms listed on the Palestine Exchange (PEX) in 2012 and came to the conclusion that profitability did not have any significant association with disclosure. Thus, several researchers have come out with varied findings after studying different types of business enterprises. The present study focuses on corporate social reporting practices of companies in India wherein only a relatively less number of attempts have been made to explore the determinants of corporate social reporting.

3 Research Methodology

The purpose of this paper is to find out the extent of corporate social reporting as well as to fix the variables that influence the level of such reporting in India. To facilitate this, data from the annual reports of top 100 companies listed in BSE Index 200, maintained by Bombay Stock Exchange of India have been collected for the years from 2007–08 to 2011–12. Market capitalization is the basis for selecting the companies for the purpose of the study. Purposive sampling method has been used to identify the sample companies. Annual reports of the sample companies have been collected from Capitaline database.

Content analysis has been used to examine the extent of corporate social reporting by the selected companies. Words, used to report corporate social responsibilities fulfilled by the companies, are counted to measure the extent of reporting. This method is widely used and preferred to other methods. Measuring the number of words is more detailed than measuring page disclosure (Deegan and Gordon 1996; Ratanajongkol et al. 2006). A measure based on sentences ignores issues like type face size and does not account for different grammar conveying the same thing (Milne and Adler 1999). The present study therefore, has used content analysis to find out words used to report different items under the four broad sections namely, 'Environment', 'Community Involvement', 'Products' and 'Employees'. Twenty one items have been included under these headings. The determinants of corporate social reporting are examined using multiple regression. The dependent variable is 'Corporate Social Reporting Index'—developed by assigning scores to the 21 items included under the above four heads. If an item is reported, then 1 is assigned; otherwise, '0' is assigned. Score for each company has been computed and converted into an index by dividing the actual score by the maximum score (for 21 items, it is 21) and multiplying it by 100. This is the variable regressed on the select independent variables to find out those that influence the level of corporate social reporting.

4 Corporate Social Reporting

Even in the absence of any mandatory guidelines for corporate social reporting in India, still a few companies are publishing information pertaining to their social responsibility activities mostly through the Annual Reports as well through the web sites. A glimpse at how the sample companies report on social activities is presented in Table 1.

Table 1 consolidates the items that are reported by the sample companies over the selected period of study from 2007–08 to 2011–12. The items are classified under four major headings namely 'Environment', 'Community Involvement', 'Products' and 'Employees'. It can be seen that under the environment-related information, the focus of the companies is more on environment action support as around 80 companies out of the selected 100 companies have reported on this. The number of companies disclosing information on this aspect has kept increasing over the study period though the increase is only marginal. Conservation of natural resources is the next popular area on which, on an average, 79 companies have reported.

Community involvement is the next segment of corporate social reporting. This broadly includes society-linked programmes carried out either by the company itself or by the employees with the support of their companies. Community activities executed by the organizations are reported by almost 91 companies across the years. Many companies seem to have lent support to the employees in their endeavor to do service to the society.

Reporting on the safety and how eco-friendly are the products produced has remained the focus for many of the sample companies. Accordingly, it is seen that,

Table 1 Item-wise reporting by sample companies

S. no	Item	Number of companies 2007–08	2008–09	2009–10	2010–11	2011–12	Mean number of companies
A. Environment							
1	Pollution Control	73	73	75	75	77	74.6
2	Prevention of Environmental Damage	60	61	63	65	66	63.0
3	Conservation of Natural Resources	79	78	79	80	81	79.4
4	Environmental Action Support	77	78	80	81	82	79.6
B. Community Involvement							
5	Community Activities	90	89	90	92	93	90.8
6	Health-related Activities	67	65	68	71	71	68.4
7	Education and Arts	73	70	75	77	78	74.6
8	Charitable Donation	45	43	45	45	44	44.4
9	Support to Community Activity of Employees	86	87	89	90	95	89.4
10	Participation in Government Committees	43	46	46	47	49	46.2
C. Products							
11	Safety	78	78	82	83	83	80.8
12	Improvement of Public Interest towards Eco-Friendly Products	52	49	52	53	56	52.4
13	Consumer Affairs Expenditure	52	53	54	53	53	53.0
14	Quality Control	48	47	51	51	50	49.4
D. Employees							
15	Employee Health and Safety	83	83	83	86	85	84.0
16	Employee Training	87	86	87	87	87	86.8
17	Education Facilities	86	85	87	87	87	86.4
18	Leave Facility	19	18	20	21	22	20.0
19	Employment of Women	25	24	24	27	28	25.6
20	Trade Union/Worker Consultation	38	37	37	41	42	40.8
21	Profit Sharing Scheme	44	44	42	44	46	44.0

on an average, 81 companies have reported on product safety. Nevertheless, reporting on other heads falling under 'Products' is not encouraging since the number of companies revealing such information is very few, considering the size of the sample.

The last segment deals with what do the companies do for their employees to make them feel highly motivated as well as to kindle the spirit of morale among them to achieve higher productivity. The prominent aspects on which the corporate India has reported are employee training, education facilities and employee health and safety, in their order. More than 83 companies, on an average, have reported on these during the period under study. It may be noted that the number of companies that have reported on leave facility and employment of women is very less. The reason for only a few companies reporting on employment of women is that in India still the women participation rate in employment is low. It is reported that women participation in employment is 24.8 % in urban area and 14.7 % in rural area (The Economic Times 2014).

Thus, it could be seen that companies in India report on various aspects of corporate social responsibility. 'Community activities', 'Support to community activities of employees', 'Employee training', 'Education facilities' and 'Employee health and safety' are the prominently reported items since on average more than 80 companies have reported on these. 'Leave facilities' and 'Employment of women' are the least reported items. While 'Leave facility' is reported by 20 companies, 'Employment of women' has been reported by 26 companies, on an average.

5 Location of Corporate Social Reporting

Information on corporate social responsibility may be shown in different parts of annual report like 'Chairman's Report', 'Directors' Report', 'Auditors' Report' and 'Corporate Governance Report'. Table 2 shows the location in which the companies report about their social responsibilities.

As shown in Table 2, the most popular place for social responsibility disclosures is the Directors' Report. Nafez Abu-Baker (2000) also came out with a similar finding. No company has used the Auditors' report in the years 2007–08, 2008–09 and 2009–10. Only one company, each in 2010–11 and 2011–12, has selected Auditors' Report—meant for reporting on financial matters—for disseminating information about its social activities. Twenty-three companies have reported in Chairman's Report in the year 2007–08. The number of companies has increased over the years. In the year 2007–08, seven companies have used Corporate

Table 2 Location of corporate social reporting

Location	Number of companies					Mean number of companies
	2007–08	2008–09	2009–10	2010–11	2011–12	
Chairman's Report	23	25	26	26	29	25.80
Directors' Report	100	100	100	100	100	100.00
Auditors' Report	–	–	–	1	1	0.40
Corporate Governance Report	7	8	10	12	14	10.20

Governance Report for reporting on how they have gone in fulfilling the responsibilities. The number has gone up to 14 in 2011–12. Number of companies, which use Corporate Governance Report for showing information on social activities, has consistently increased over the years.

Directors' Report is the most widely used space for mentioning about the activities relating to corporate social responsibility. The other sections in their order are Chairman's Report, Corporate Governance Report and Auditors' Report. Appah (2011) has found out that Directors' report is the most preferred location for social accounting information.

6 Extent of Reporting

In order to examine the extent of reporting, content analysis has been used. Word is considered as the basic measure for assessing the level of reporting. The results of such analysis are consolidated in Table 3.

As can be seen from Table 3, the theme most widely reported in annual report is 'community involvement'. A considerable space in the annual report has been devoted to community activities such as tree plantation, city beautification, scholarships, health-care, sponsoring sports and tournaments, art competitions and concerts. The number of words used by the companies has varied among different sections. The mean words used have increased consistently. Ratanajongkol et al. (2006) came out with a similar finding.

Table 3 Extent of reporting

Section	Number of words					Total words	Mean words
	2007–08	2008–09	2009–10	2010–11	2011–12		
Environment	60,402 (16.48 %)	63,237 (17.25 %)	68,139 (18.59 %)	78,911 (21.53 %)	95,871 (26.15 %)	366,560 (100.00 %)	73,312.0
Community Involvement	74,871 (16.15 %)	84,447 (18.21 %)	90,069 (19.42 %)	103,144 (22.24 %)	111,210 (23.98 %)	463,741 (100.00 %)	92,748.2
Product	64,603 (18.39 %)	70,243 (19.99 %)	70,576 (20.09 %)	71,257 (20.28 %)	74,670 (21.25 %)	351,349 (100.00 %)	70,269.8
Employee Details	64,196 (18.11 %)	68,271 (19.26 %)	67,477 (19.04 %)	75,327 (21.25 %)	79,200 (22.34 %)	354,471 (100.00 %)	70,894.2

7 Variable Choice

The logical connectivity of the select variables with corporate social reporting is explained in the following paragraphs.

7.1 Size

Falkman and Tagesson (2008) are of the view that large organizations come under the scanner of government more than their smaller counterparts. They have a more pronounced effect on the community and therefore, normally have a larger group of stakeholders who influence them. In general, large organizations are also more closely scrutinized by the mass media than the smaller ones. They have further stated that the demand for information from the mass media and the public increase the perceived political pressure on big organizations to deliver information about them.

Using total assets (Naser and Hassan 2013; Jouirou and Chenguel 2014; Juhmani 2014; Mohammed and Islam 2014) or total revenues (Burgwal and Vieira 2014) to represent size of organizations, prior research studies have examined the association between corporate social responsibility disclosure and size of firms. A significant positive association has been reported between the two. Large companies, therefore, are likely to disclose more information than small companies. The rationale behind this conclusion is that large companies receive more attention from the public as these companies are more likely to be diversified across geographical and product market and hence these companies might have larger and more diverse stakeholder groups. Thus, the following hypothesis has been framed:

H_1: There is a positive association between firm size and Corporate Social Reporting

7.2 Age

Age—years since when a company was established—influences the level of disclosure. According to Owusu-Ansah (1998), three factors may be responsible for this—competition, cost of gathering and processing of information and inadequacy of information to be reported since the newly started companies might not have extensively carried out any society-relevant activities. Flamholtz (1986) argues that older companies are well-established and are exposed to less competition and hence are willing to report more on the corporate social responsibility activities.

H_2: Companies of long years of existence report more on society-centric activities than newly-established companies

7.3 Nationality

Corporate social reporting practices are likely to differ across firms operating in different countries. Specifically, multinational companies in India, as compared to Indian companies, always tend to focus more on their social responsibility programmes to justify their presence. Agca and Onder (2007) feel that if a firm's shares are held by a foreign firm it is likely that reporting would be at higher levels in such a firm. Therefore, the following hypothesis is framed:

H_3: Nationality is significantly associated with Corporate Social Reporting

7.4 Industry Type

Firms belonging to different industry groups engage themselves in social responsibility activities of their own choice and therefore there shall be a marked difference in the themes included in their social reports. Ratanajongkol et al. (2006) have found that manufacturing companies reported extensively on 'environment', 'human resource', and 'community'. Service sector companies concentrated less on 'environment' themes though they reported liberally on 'human resources' and 'community'. The level of reporting therefore is bound to be unique and industry-linked. Accordingly, the following hypothesis has been framed:

H_4: Industry Type influences Corporate Social Reporting

7.5 Ownership

Based on ownership, companies can be broadly classified as government companies and private sector companies. Government companies, wherein the government has higher stake, tend to reveal more information pertaining to their commitment to the society. Naser et al. (2006) observe that government-owned companies reveal more through social reports to exhibit how committed is the government towards society-linked issues. To probe further, the following hypothesis is framed:

H_5: Ownership determines Corporate Social Reporting

7.6 Leverage

Corporate leverage is given due attention at the time when the companies sketch their social reports. Highly levered companies, in order to project positive information, tend to report more on social responsibility programmes. Purushothaman et al. (2000) argue that highly levered companies will go for voluntary disclosure so as to mitigate agency cost and cost of capital as well. It becomes imperative, therefore, to explore if there could actually be a relationship between leverage and corporate social reporting. To facilitate this, the following hypothesis is framed:

H_6: Leverage is positively associated with Corporate Social Reporting

7.7 Liquidity

Abd-Elsalam and Weetman (2003) have found that firms with high liquidity report more information through their reports on corporate social responsibility to distinguish themselves from low-liquidity firms. This is usually done to satisfy the information needs of stakeholders. Firms effectively managing their short-term funds, tend to report more. To test the validity of this, the following hypothesis is framed:

H_7: Liquidity is positively associated with Corporate Social Reporting

7.8 Profit

Companies with considerable amount of profit are susceptible to governmental intervention and accordingly they start reporting more about their society-centric activities. Managers of reputed companies, which earn a sizable amount of profit, report about commitment of their companies to the society just to exhibit that the shareholders' funds are put to the best use. Belkaoui and Karpik (1989) and Meek et al. (1995) have found that profitability of a firm positively influences the level of corporate social reporting. Hence, the following hypothesis has been framed:

H_8: There is a significant relationship between level of profit and Corporate Social Reporting

7.9 *Dividend*

Growth firms, as they may have profitable projects, usually declare lesser amount of dividend which in turn forces them to report more on the purpose for retaining the earnings. It is quite usual to expect these firms to spend considerable amount on social responsibility projects too. Naser et al. (2006) have reported that there exists a positive association between dividend and corporate social reporting. To examine if this relationship is possible, the following hypothesis is framed:

H_9: There is an association between dividend and Corporate Social Reporting

7.10 *Gross Fixed Assets*

Butler et al. (2002) argue that firms with a higher percentage of tangible assets have lower agency costs. Reduced agency costs enable firms to report less. Nevertheless, contrary views are held by Chow and Wong-Boren (1987), Hossain et al. (1994) and Raffournier (1995) who have found the relationship between gross fixed assets and Corporate Social Reporting to be insignificant. In order to examine if there is an association between gross fixed assets and corporate social reporting the following hypothesis is framed:

H_{10}: There is a significant association between gross fixed assets and Corporate Social Reporting

7.11 *Reserves*

Firms do save to spend specifically on profitable projects as well as on those activities associated with the society. Higher levels of reserves, therefore, give firms much muscle power to allocate more funds to fulfil social obligations. It is obvious that firms with high amount of reserves would report more on their involvement in social responsibility-related activities. Thus, it becomes imperative to test the following hypothesis:

H_{11}: Positive association prevails between reserves and Corporate Social Reporting

8 Determinants of Corporate Social Reporting

In order to find out the variables that determine the level of corporate social reporting, the selected eleven variables have been regressed on Corporate Social Reporting Index. The following regression equation has been framed:

$$SRI_i = \alpha_0 + \beta_1 SIZ_i + \beta_2 AGE_i + \beta_3 NAT_i + \beta_4 IND_i + \beta_5 OWN_i + \beta_6 LIQ_i$$
$$+ \beta_7 LEV_i + \beta_8 PRO_i$$
$$+ \beta_9 DIV_i + \beta_{10} RES_i + \beta_{11} GFA_i + \varepsilon_i \quad (1)$$

where,

α = Constant
CSRI = Corporate Social Reporting Index
$\beta_1 \ldots \beta_{11}$ = Regression Coefficients
SIZ = Size, measured using net sales
AGE = Age, years of existence since incorporation
NAT = Nationality, Indian or Multinational
IND = Industry Type, Manufacturing or Service sector
OWN = Ownership, Government-owned or owned by private sector
LIQ = Liquidity, measured based on current ratio
LEV = Leverage, measured by debt-equity ratio
PRO = Profit, measured by actual amount of net profit
DIV = Dividend, measured by amount of dividend declared
RES = Reserves, representing free reserves
GFA = Gross Fixed Assets, taken as actual values of assets
ε = Error Term

The variables namely 'Nationality', 'Industry Type' and 'Ownership' have been introduced as dummy variables. In the case of 'Nationality', a score of 1 is assigned if a company is of Indian origin and 0 is assigned if multinational; similarly, 1 is assigned if industry type is 'Manufacturing' and 0 is assigned if it is 'Service', and for 'Ownership', government companies (in which Government of India has a major share) are assigned 1 while the private sector companies are assigned 0. Net sales, Profit, Dividend, Reserves and Gross Fixed Assets have been converted into per share data of Rs.10. This has been done by dividing each item with the value of equity capital and multiplying it by Rs.10, to facilitate uniformity of data. The results of the regression analysis are shown in Table 4. Of the variables taken for consideration, Age, Liquidity, Profit, Dividend, Reserves and Gross Fixed Assets are not found to be significant. Only the variables that influence the Corporate Social Reporting are taken up for discussion.

Table 4 Determinants of corporate social reporting

	Unstandardized coefficients		Standardized coefficients	
Variables	B	Std. error	Beta	t (df = 488)
(Constant)	65.633	2.483		26.434
Size	0.002	0.001	0.129	2.478*
Age	0.014	0.028	0.023	0.507
Nationality	−8.430	1.538	−0.257	−5.479**
Industry Type	5.054	1.724	0.152	2.931**
Ownership	11.434	1.865	0.309	6.132**
Liquidity	0.428	0.481	0.068	0.890
Leverage	−0.090	0.046	−0.150	−1.983*
Profit	−0.015	0.012	−0.089	−1.229
Dividend	−0.037	0.020	−0.101	−1.833
Reserves	−0.001	0.002	−0.017	−0.284
Gross Fixed Assets	0.003	0.002	0.062	1.130
Adjusted R^2: 0.154; R^2: 0.173**; calculated F-value: 9.252*				

*Significant at 5 % level, **significant at 1 % level

8.1 Size

Net sales have been used to classify the companies into different size groups. Usually, bigger firms play an important role in an economy and therefore it is quite common that the stakeholders will expect to have more information from such companies. Cooke (1989) states that larger firms are likely to be entities of economic significance so that there may be greater demands on them to provide information to the customers, suppliers, analysts and governments as well as the general public. The regression coefficient indicates that size of the company highly influences Corporate Social Reporting. The regression coefficient, being positive, indicates that as size increases, the level of reporting also increases.

8.2 Nationality

Multinational companies are expected to disclose more information. The regression coefficient indicates that nationality influences Corporate Social Reporting. Regression coefficient indicates that multinational companies report more as opposed to Indian companies.

8.3 Industry Type

It has been argued that companies in certain industries are politically more visible and exposed to the scrutiny of activists and media (Patten 1992). No doubt, the industry to which a company belongs to influences the level of reporting. The regression coefficient indicates that 'Industry Type' influences Corporate Social Reporting. Manufacturing companies are found to report more compared to service-sector companies.

8.4 Ownership

Government companies tend to report more on their social programmes as they are likely to be exposed to a large group of stakeholders and are under greater scrutiny from activists. The present study finds that Government companies are reporting more about their social activities compared to private sector companies. However, Hossain et al. (1994) have found a negative association between ownership structure and level of voluntary disclosure by Malaysian listed firms.

8.5 Leverage

According to agency theory, monitoring costs would be more for firms that are highly levered. To reduce these costs, firms are expected to disclose more information, i.e. the relationship between leverage and the extent of Corporate Social Reporting is expected to be positive (Bhayani 2012). The regression coefficient indicates that leverage influences reporting. More the leverage less is the reporting. This result, however, is contrary to what has been arrived at by earlier researchers.

To summarize, the level of corporate social reporting is being influenced by five of the selected variables. The value of R^2 is found to be significant at 1 % level. This shows that the regression equation framed is a good fit. The value of R^2 indicates that around 17.3 % of variation in corporate social reporting is due to the selected variables.

9 Variables Prominently Associated with Corporate Social Reporting

To further probe and find out if there could be any order in the variables that influence the level of corporate social reporting, step-wise regression has been carried out. Table 5 consolidates the findings.

Table 5 Prominent variables of corporate social reporting

Step	Constant	Ownership	Nationality	Industry type	Leverage	Dividend	Size	R^2
1	65.210	0.205	–	–	–	–	–	0.042
2	69.850	0.292	−0.272	–	–	–	–	0.108
3	65.092	0.320	−0.232	0.177	–	–	–	0.137
4	66.832	0.352	−0.236	0.121	−0.119	–	–	0.146
5	68.245	0.347	−0.262	0.123	−0.131	−0.104	–	0.156
6	66.550	0.321	−0.251	0.149	−0.105	−0.141	0.118	0.168

In the first step, the variable 'Ownership' has been introduced. This variable contributes 4.2 % to the variation in reporting. 'Nationality' is the second variable introduced in step two. This variable, along with 'Ownership', accounts for 10.8 % of variation in reporting. The contribution has increased by 6.6 %. 'Industry Type', a third variable, has increased the contribution from 10.8 to 13.7 %. The contribution gets further increased by 0.9 % with the introduction of the variable 'Leverage'. 'Dividend' and 'Size' are the other two variables included in step five and six, respectively. The total contribution of the six variables namely, (1) Ownership, (2) Nationality, (3) Industry Type, (4) Leverage, (5) Dividend and (6) Size amounts to 16.8 %. The R^2 value of the multiple regression amounts to 17.3 %. The difference 0.5 % is due to the contribution of other variables. It can be seen that 'Ownership' stands out as the most prominent variable impacting the level of corporate social reporting. This reaffirms the fact that government companies report more as compared privately-held companies.

10 Conclusion

The study has considered some prominent corporate attributes in examining their impact on the level of corporate social reporting. The results of multiple regression analysis reveal that Size, Nationality, Industry Type, Ownership, and Leverage are the variables that significantly influence the level of corporate social reporting. Evidences to these findings are available in the studies conducted earlier. Hossain (2008) has found size to be a variable associated with corporate social reporting. The step-wise regression analysis has shown that there are six prominent variables that dominate the variables which determine Corporate Social Reporting. They are (1) Ownership, (2) Nationality, (3) Industry Type, (4) Leverage, (5) Dividend and (6) Size.

The results have several implications. For instance, it has been found the size is a variable that influences the level of corporate social reporting and only big companies report more as compared to smaller firms. Hence, controlling bodies like Securities and Exchange Board of India may see that even the small companies do also report more on their community-linked programmes. Alternatively, norms may be laid down that even small-sized companies take active part in corporate social responsibility programmes. As for nationality is taken into account, it is seen that the level of corporate social reporting of multinational companies is high prompting that steps need to be taken to encourage the Indian companies to come out with more information on social responsibility activities. It is surprising to note that heavily borrowed companies report less. Hence, appropriate measures are to be initiated to make the highly-levered companies to go in for extensive reporting.

The present study has focused on the top 100 companies listed in BSE 200. Nevertheless, lot of scope exists in extending the present study. Attempts may be made to examine how and why there could be differences in the level of corporate social reporting practices among companies belonging to different regions and managed by different groups of businessmen. Further, practice of companies belonging to financial sector may be explored. Board constitution is another variable that may be considered while finding out the level of corporate social reporting among the companies. The role of the government and other regulatory bodies in enforcing the companies to prepare reports on corporate social responsibility may also be probed into.

Any research work is bound to have some limitations. One of the limitations of the present study is that the analysis relating to assessing the level of corporate social reporting is based on the information as revealed through the annual reports of the companies under focus. There are, nevertheless, many other sources, through which corporate social responsibility-related information may be shown. Such sources are not considered. Further, the sample of the study is confined to those companies included in the BSE 200. Other companies, however popular they may be, therefore, are out of the purview of the analysis.

References

Abd-Elsalam, O. H., & Weetman, P. (2003). Introducing international accounting standards to an emerging capital market: Relative familiarity and language effect in Egypt. *Journal of International Accounting, Auditing and Taxation, 12*, 63–84.

Abu-Baker, N. (2000). Corporate social reporting and disclosure practice in Jordan: An empirical investigation. *Administrative Sciences, 27*(1), 249–260.

Agca, A., & Onder, S. (2007). Voluntary disclosure in Turkey: A study on firms listed in Istanbul Stock Exchange (ISE). *Problems and Perspectives in Management, 5*(3), 241–251.

Alkababji, M. W. (2014). Voluntary disclosure on corporate social responsibility: A study on the annual reports on Palestinian corporations. *European Journal of Accounting Auditing and Finance Research, 2*(4), 59–82.

Appah, E. (2011). A study of social accounting disclosures in the annual reports of Nigerian companies. *Asian Journal of Business Management, 3*(3), 145–151.

Ayadi, S. D. (2007). Determinants of the corporate decision to disclose stakeholder's reports in France. In *27th annual congress of the European Accounting Association*, Halshs-00154181, Version 1-12.

Belkaoui, A., & Karpik, P. (1989). Determinants of the corporate decision to disclose social information. *Accounting, Auditing and Accountability Journal, 2*(1), 36–51.

Bhayani, S. (2012). The relationship between comprehensiveness of corporate disclosure and firm characteristics in India. *Asia-Pacific Finance and Accounting Review, 1*(1), 52–66.
Burgwal, D., & Vieira, R. J. O. (2014). Environmental disclosure determinants in Dutch listed companies. *Revista Contabilidade & Finanças, 25*(64), 60–78.
Butler, M., Kraft, A., & Weiss, I. S. (2002). *The effect of reporting frequency on the timeliness of earnings: The cases of voluntary and mandatory interim reports* (Working Paper Rochastes).
Cecil, L. (2010). Corporate social responsibility reporting in the United States. *McNair Scholars Research Journal, 1*(1), 42–52.
Chow, C. W., & Wong-Boren, A. (1987). Voluntary financial disclosure by Mexican corporations. *The Accounting Review, 62*(3), 533–541.
Cooke, T. E. (1989). Disclosure in the corporate annual reports of Swedish companies. *Accounting and Business Research, 19*(74), 113–137.
Deegan, C., & Gordon, B. (1996). A study of the environmental disclosure practices of Australian corporations. *Accounting and Business Research, 26*(3), 187–199.
Falkman, P., & Tagesson, T. (2008). Accrual accounting does not necessarily mean accrual accounting: Factors that counteract compliance with accounting standards in Swedish municipal accounting. *Scandinavian Journal of Management, 24*(3), 271–283.
Flamholtz, E. (1986). *How to make the transition from entrepreneurship to a professionally managed firm*. London: Jossey-Bass.
Gray, R., Owen, D., & Adams, C. (1996). *Accounting and accountability: Changes and challenges in corporate social and environmental reporting*. Hemel Hempstead: Prentice Hall.
Hossain, M. (2008). The extent of disclosure in annual reports of banking companies: The case of India. *European Journal of Scientific Research, 23*(4), 659–680.
Hossain, M., & Helmi, H. (2009). Voluntary disclosure in the annual report of an emerging country: The case of Qatar. *Advance in Accounting incorporating Advances in International Accounting, 25*, 255–265.
Hossain, M., Tan, L. M., & Adams, M. (1994). Voluntary disclosure in an emerging capital market: Some empirical evidence from companies listed on the Kuala Lumpur Stock Exchange. *The International Journal of Accounting, 29*(4), 334–351.
Hussainey, K., Elsayed, M., & Razik, M. A. (2011). Factors affecting corporate social responsibility disclosure in Egypt. *Corporate Ownership and Control Journal, 8*(4), 432–443.
Jouirou, M., & Chenguel, M. B. (2014). The determinants of voluntary disclosure in Tunisian Stock Exchange. *Journal of Business and Management Research, 4*, 86–97.
Juhmani, O. (2014). Determinants of corporate social and environmental disclosure on websites: The case of Bahrain. *Universal Journal of Accounting and Finance, 2*(4), 77–87.
Jupe, R. (2005). *Disclosures in corporate environmental reports: A test of legitimacy theory* (Working paper, 91). Kent Business School.
Kolsi, M. C. (2012). The determinants of corporate voluntary disclosure: Evidence from the Tunisian Capital Market. *The IUP Journal of Accounting Research and Audit Practices, 11*(4), 49–68.
Mammatt, J., Marx, B., & van Dyk, V. (2010). Sustainability reporting and assurance: The way of the future. *ASA Accountancy Journal*, 22–25.
Marquis, C., & Quian, C. (2014). Corporate social responsibility reporting in China: Symbol or substance? *Organisation Science, 25*(1), 127–148.
Meek, G., Roberts, O. B., & Gras, S. J. (1995). Factors influencing voluntary annual report disclosures by U.S, U.K and Continental European multinational corporations. *Journal of International Business Studies, 3*, 555–572.
Milne, M. J., & Adler, R. W. (1999). Exploring the reliability of social and environmental disclosures content analysis. *Accounting, Auditing and Accountability Journal, 12*(3), 237–256.
Mohammed, S., & Islam, M. (2014). Nonfinancial information disclosure and company characteristics: A study on listed pharmaceutical and chemical companies of Bangladesh. *Pacific Business Review International, 6*(8), 16–24.

Naser, K., Al-Hussaini, A., Al-Kwari, D., & Nuseibeh, R. (2006). Determinants of corporate social disclosure in developing countries: The case of Qatar. *Advances in International Accounting, 19*, 1–23.

Naser, K., & Hassan, Y. (2013). Determinants of corporate social responsibility reporting: Evidence from an emerging economy. *Journal of Contemporary Issues in Business Research, 2*(3), 56–74.

Owusu-Ansah, S. (1998). The impact of corporate attribute on the extent of mandatory disclosure and reporting by listed companies in Zimbabwe. *International Journal of Accounting, 33*(5), 605–631.

Patten, D. M. (1992). Intra-industry environmental disclosures in response to the Alaskan oil spill: A note on legitimacy theory. *Accounting, Organizations and Society, 17*(5), 471–476.

Purushothaman, M., Tower, G., Hancock, P., & Taplin, R. (2000). Determinants of corporate social reporting practices of listed Singapore companies. *Pacific Accounting Review, 12*(2), 101–133.

Raffournier, B. (1995). The determinants of voluntary financial disclosure by Swiss listed companies. *European Accounting Review, 4*(2), 261–280.

Ratanajongkol, S., Davey, H., & Low, M. (2006). Corporate social reporting in Thailand: The news is all good and increasing. *Qualitative Research in Accounting and Management, 3*(1), 67–76.

Rouf, M. A. (2010). Corporate characteristics, governance attributes and the extent of voluntary disclosure in Bangladesh. *Asian Journal of Management Research, 1*(1), 166–183.

The Economic Times. (2014, July 21). Women's participation in workforce is half of men: Government. http://articles.economictimes.indiatimes.com/2014-07-21/news/51831122_1_workforce-participation-urban-india. Accessed 26 Dec 2014.

Board Evaluation in Italian Listed Companies

Franco Rubino, Bronzetti Giovanni, Romilda Mazzotta, Graziella Sicoli, Tenuta Paolo, and Rija Maurizio

Abstract In the last decade performance evaluation of the Board of Directors has become a best practice at national and international level. Italy is an interesting area of analysis given the high concentration of ownership that characterizes companies, including listed companies. In this context the choices of governance that affect the level of disclosure, for which the expectation is to have a low level of disclosure on the practice of BE (Board Evaluation).The first purpose of this paper is to present a résumé on the state of the art in terms of BE for Italian listed companies at 31st December 2012, in terms of presence/absence of the practice of disclosure and its more or less extensive disclosure. The second objective is to highlight the modality of adoption of BE and the third is to analyze the relationship between the quality of BE (measured using as a proxy the disclosure on its setting up) and corporate governance. The results reveal there are few companies that use board evaluation and that there is a relationship between BE adoption and good governance and between the quality of BE and good governance.

Keywords Governance • Performance • Board evaluation

1 Introduction

The issues of corporate governance are now deeply examined in all industrialized countries (OECD 2004). This approach is the result of the belief that good governance improves the level of reliability, transparency and integrity of the business. Good governance improves business performance and therefore the value of the enterprise. A central aspect of the issues of internal governance is the Board of Directors (or board) because it is the ultimate decision-maker of the company and therefore is responsible for the company's performance (Kiel and Beck 2006). Moreover, nowadays there is a growing demand for internal and external accountability, as a result of changes in the relationship between management, directors

F. Rubino • B. Giovanni • R. Mazzotta • G. Sicoli (✉) • T. Paolo • R. Maurizio
Department of Business Science, University of Calabria, Arcavacata, Italy
e-mail: franco.rubino@unical.it; giovanni.bronzetti@unical.it; romilda.mazzotta@unical.it; graziella.sicoli@unical.it; ptenuta@unical.it; m.rija@unical.it

© Springer International Publishing Switzerland 2016

M.H. Bilgin et al. (eds.), *Business Challenges in the Changing Economic Landscape - Vol. 1*, Eurasian Studies in Business and Economics 2/1,
DOI 10.1007/978-3-319-22596-8_7

and shareholders, and enlargement of the number of stakeholders (Ingley and Van Der Walt 2001). This has led in the last decade to the need to evaluate the performance of the Board since such an analysis is possible through improved effectiveness of the board and thus potentially a better performance record on its part.

Also European Commission recommend the introduction of good governance that provide best practices for improving the functioning of the Board and a more appropriate use of its facilities. One of the best practices that can be found at national and international level is the performance evaluation of the Board (Board evaluation or board performance evaluation). Board evaluation (BE) is a process that improves the dynamics and performance of the Board, to maximize the strengths and minimize the weaknesses. Through BE a company tries to detect the presence of internal governance issues and identify ways to solve them, thereby making the changes necessary to avoid business failure. BE, as we shall see, can be conducted in different ways and with different tools, and the choice is determined by the purpose for which the BE is conducted. There is in fact an optimal method for assessing directors for different contexts and purposes that requires specific evaluations of the board. To this is added that the best practice is included in the Code of conduct, and therefore also BE, and together they are primarily adopted by firms as signaling devices for demonstrating positive credentials, with the aim of strengthening corporate reputation and more generally organizational legitimacy (Wright and Rwabizambuga 2006).

There are several studies that seek evidence of a direct relationship between good governance and good performance (Bhagat and Bolton 2008; Brown and Caylor 2003), other studies are more focused on the board and argue that the best board performance is a translational motion in the best governance structure (Shleifer and Vishny 1997; Abdullah 2004; Coskun and Sayilir 2012; Shukeri et al. 2012) and that "understanding the nature of effective board functioning is among the most important areas of management research" (Forbes and Milliken 1999, p. 489). There are few, and these in any case of a purely theoretical type, studies on BE, on its determinants and on the disclosure on how to adopt it. There are no studies that analyze board evaluation with reference to the Italian context. Italy is an interesting area of analysis given the high concentration of ownership that characterizes companies, including listed companies. The high ownership concentration affects, in fact, the choices of governance that, in turn, affect the level of disclosure for which the expectation is to have a low level of disclosure on the practice of BE.

Starting from these assumptions, the first purpose is to present a résumé of the state of the art in terms of BE for companies listed at the Italian Stock Exchange in Milan at 31st December 2012, in terms of presence/absence of the practice of disclosure and on quality of BE (more or less extensive disclosure). The second objective is to highlight the modality of adoption of BE and the third is to analyze the relationship between the quality of BE (measured using as a proxy the disclosure on its setting up) and corporate governance. To achieve these objectives information has been collected on the presence or absence of BE and the modality of its adoption and on the mechanism of internal governance such as board composition and the leadership structure. The information was found in the report on the ownership structure and governance to 31/12/2012.

The results reveal that to date only a limited number of companies carry out board evaluation, as is shown by a different level of detail in the information on this report, on the ownership structure and in the results of the analysis. The results reveal that it would be better to formalize the results of board evaluation as well as to specify better in the same report how BE is conducted. From the perspective of stakeholders, who read the report to obtain information about the company, it would be appropriate to have all the information provided in order to help decision making. The results reveal also that there is a relationship between the adoption of BE and good governance and between the quality of BE and good governance.

The implications of the research are that it extends knowledge on governance and in particular on the prevalence of BE, on the way of its adoption and on its determinants.

2 Italian Code of Conduct and Board Evaluation

Continuous corporate crises lead to the search for new ideas and perspectives focused on how to improve the performance and effectiveness of the Board (Minichilli et al. 2007). Among them there is the demand for a systematic evaluation of the board (Board Evaluation). This is because it is believed that BE can help to prevent business failures and identify performance gaps within the Board of Directors (Kiel and Nicholson 2005).

The need to initiate BE practices emerges from the large international debate on corporate governance (Ingley and Van Der Walt 2002). The BE theme started in America in 1994 when the National Association of Corporate Directors (NACD) published its Blue Ribbon Commission on Performance Evaluation of CEOs, Boards and Directors followed in 2000 by its Blue Ribbon Commission report on Board Evaluation: Improving Director Effectiveness (Long 2006). Subsequently, in 1995, the Toronto Stock Exchange Committee on Corporate Governance outlined the best practice guidelines in the Dey Report and require that Every board of directors should implement a process to be carried out by the nominating committee or other appropriate committee for assessing the effectiveness of the board as a whole, the committees of the board and the contribution of individual directors (Toronto Stock Exchange 1994).

In the same year, the Vienot Committee reviewed the principle issues concerning the membership, powers and operations applied by the boards of directors of listed companies in France and released a set of guidelines intended to strengthen investor confidence in the bodies governing the companies in which they were asked to invest, stating that each board should periodically review its membership, organization and operations, and keep shareholders informed of conclusions and action taken (CNFP and AFEP 1995).

In 2000 the German Panel on Corporate Governance, following an Organisation for Economic Cooperation and Development (OECD) state that "The supervisory board shall subject its activity subject to a regular (for example annual) evaluation to check opportunities for improvements on a continuous basis." (German Panel on Corporate Governance 2000, p. 8). Subsequently, Australia was to enter into the recommendations of the governance is ASX Corporate Governance Council, Principles of Good Corporate Governance and Best Practice Recommendations) stating: The performance of the board and key executives should be regularly reviewed both against measurable and qualitative indicators. Following the recommendation different countries introduced their codes of conduct. Italy did it in 2011 with the revision of the Code of Conduct. At the beginning 1.C.1 g) (Table 1) specifies that the Board should, at least once a year, prepare an evaluation of the functioning of the Board and its committees, as well as of its size and composition. In other words, the Code of Conduct identifies what has to be looked at (operation, the size and composition of the Board and its committees). The same code states that the Board may rely on the work of external consultants and that a corporate governance report

Table 1 BE in the Italian code of conduct

ARTICLE 1—ROLE OF THE BOARD OF DIRECTORS
Criteria
(g) at least once a year, an assessment of the functioning of the Board and its committees as well as on their size and composition, taking into account factors such as the characteristics of professional experience, including managerial, and gender of its components, as well as their length of service. In the event that the board of directors makes use of the work of external consultants for the purpose of self-assessment, the corporate governance report provides information about any additional services provided by such advisors to the issuer or company in a control relationship with the same;
(h) taking into account the results of the assessment referred to in subparagraph g), expresses the shareholders, prior to the appointment of the new board, the professional figures whose presence on the board is considered appropriate;
(i) provide information in the report on corporate governance: (1) on its composition, indicating the status for each component (executive, non-executive, independent) within the role of the board (e.g., president or chief executive officer, as defined Article 2), the main professional characteristics as well as the seniority of the first appointment; (2) on the application of this Article 1 and, in particular, on the number and average duration of the meetings of the Board and the executive committee, if any, held during the year as well as on the percentage of participation of each administrator; (3) the procedures for carrying out the process of the assessment referred to in subparagraph g);
Comments
The board is also required self-assessment, especially with regard to the size, composition and functioning of the organ and of the committees in which it is articulated.
In the evaluation of the composition of the board, you must ensure that they are adequately represented, in relation to work done by the issuer, the different components (executive, non-executive, independent), and professional and managerial skills, including international character, and taking into account the benefits that may result from the presence on the board of several gender, age and length of service.

Source: Corporate Governance Committee (2011)

provides useful information on any additional services provided by such consultants.

Today almost all countries recommend, within their codes of conduct, to indicate whether the board are carrying out BE and this, in conjunction with the information from the practitioner (Kiel et al. 2005; Charan 2009) is driving the BE characteristics to new corporate governance practices also supported by the first evidence. These point out that effective board self-evaluation presented in commitment to performance at the highest level is an insurance policy against leadership changes and times of crisis (Lawler et al. 2002).

3 Literature Review

Despite the importance of BE, studies on governance have dealt little about it (Conger et al. 1998; Ingley and Van Der Walt 2002). The first existing studies on the subject are focused primarily on the content of BE (Lorsch 1995; Conger et al. 1998; Ingley and Van Der Walt 2002) or on the identification of a framework to evaluate the performance of the board (Ingley and Van Der Walt 2001).

Subsequent developments reveal that BE cannot be solved only in the understanding of "what to evaluate" because, for its proper application, it is necessary to design the BE evaluation process properly because each decision (for example in terms of content, method of assessment, actors, subjects evaluated and recipients of the evaluation) is not independent from the other (Kiel et al. 2005; Kiel and Nicholson 2005; Minichilli et al. 2007). Schmidt and Brauer (2006) show that performance evaluation of the Board has increased over time and Long (2006) stated that this process must be built taking into account the entity and its environment, specific factors such as the stage of the life cycle of the company, the corporate structure and board cultures.

Other studies highlight the reasons why the board should evaluate their own performance. At a broader level external pressures (institutional investors, regulators and other external stakeholders, globalization and increased international competitiveness) act on board evaluation that drive to introduce measures such as BE in order to improve the accountability of the board (Ingley and Van Der Walt 2002; Kiel and Nicholson 2005; Belcourt and Kluge 1999; Lawler and Finegold 2005). Such pressures lead to recommendations within the codes of conduct and call for a renewed and effective role of the directors as a premise for better performance and improved professionalism among the members of the Board (Ingley and Van Der Walt 2002; Leblanc and Gillies 2005). At the same time academics point out that the most widely used and investigated variables related to the effectiveness of governance (e.g., board structure, independence of directors, use of committees within the Board) appear to have little explanatory power in predicting the effectiveness of the Board (Tricker 1984). It is therefore important to understand how the components of the boardwork (Clarke and Klettner 2010).

At a corporate level one motivation is that BE can provide benefits at different levels of the company because through it is possible to identify points of strengths and weaknesses of the Board (Conger et al 1998; Kiel and Nicholson 2005); then it allows a better understanding of what is expected from each director (Atkinson and Salterio 2002; Conger and Lawler 2001; Nadler 2004) as well as building the culture of the board (Stybel and Peabody 2005). Then it is also a mechanism of accountability which can improve external trust and reputation. In this sense, the evaluation serves as an informal contract between the members of the Board who have the potential to help improve the effectiveness of the Board. Today the most important reasons to adopt BE, at a corporate level, is that the members of the board are not "pawns" (Lorsch and MacIver 1989) or simple ornaments of the company (Mace 1971) but are subject to involve more and more in business decisions (Hendry and Kiel 2004; Huse 2007; Lorsch 1995; Conger et al. 1998). The adoption of a formal practice and regular assessment of the Board can provide a way to disclose the commitment of the directors through transparency and show the quality of their work (Minichilli et al. 2007). As Sonnenfeld (2002) highlights people and organizations cannot learn without feedback. No matter how good a board is, it's bound to get better if it's reviewed intelligently. An effective BE can improve the working conditions of the Board, in particular the development of the team's ability to perform the roles required of it.

The impact of BE can affect decisions on the composition of the Board. Dulewicz and Herbert (2008) reported that BE influences the decisions of the directors on the confirmation of the directors, and at the same time, Tricker (1984) shows that BE provides a basis for the Chair (or similar) to discuss strategies for staff development with each director separately. The potential benefits are identified in terms of leadership, clarity of roles and responsibilities, improved team work, adoption of improved decision-making, accountability, communication and operation of the board.

4 The BE Process

Businesses have the opportunity to develop BE in different ways (in terms of methodologies and objectives) and they are influenced by the size of the Board, the phase of the life cycle and development of competitive environment. Similarly, the scope of BE will be determined by the problem the Board has to face and the availability of resources necessary for an assessment. The ability to direct BE at different actors consequently highlights the function of the system of BE. A comprehensive system of BE should be built considering four key areas that respond to the following questions "for-whom", "who" (divided in "who evaluate" and "who is evaluated"), "what is evaluated", "how to evaluate" (Minichilli et al. 2007; Nicholson et al. 2012) and "with how to discuss BE".

4.1 *'For Whom' Evaluation*

The first key aspect of the analysis is to identify the target and whether the activity is the result of a legal requirement or a recommendation (by a mere exercise of the same compliance), or if the purpose is to improve the performance of the board. Focusing on the last case, there can be three possible recipients: the board of directors itself, internal stakeholders and external stakeholders. In the first case, the objective is to improve the internal performance of the board through a self-evaluation or external evaluation. If recipients are stakeholders within the company, such as the management and employees, the BE objective might be involvement in setting objectives and determining and shaping the value and corporate identity. In the third case, the objective is to satisfy a demand for accountability through self- or external assessment. In this approach, the evaluation of the recipients is made by persons external to the Board.

When the recipient of the assessment is the Board, the BE system should be guided by the objective of improving internal work structures and processes. When recipients are external actors to the Board, the BE system should be guided by the objective of being transparent. In both cases, the overall aim is to measure the effectiveness and contribution to business performance of the Board (Minichilli et al. 2007).

4.2 *'Who' Evaluation*

A second key aspect of the BE system is the identification of the person who performs the evaluation. The most important decision concerns the choice among external parties (external review) or internal (internal review) the company, or of the figure on which to shift the responsibility for the evaluation. The internal evaluator certainly knows the organization better, has a more intimate relationship with the measured and is inexpensive. On the other hand the external evaluator is generally a person who has specific knowledge and skills, is more independent and transparent. The existing literature highlights the use of internal evaluation as the most common method (Conger et al. 1998; Stybel and Peabody 2005). Self-evaluation is a tool aimed at improving the internal work of the board (Ferguson 2001), when doing self-assessment of the Board, the President or his delegate, as the Lead of Independent Directors (LID), are generally the persons who carry out the analysis (Kiel and Nicholson 2005).

The other way is to appoint an external evaluator, it would solve, in fact, the problem of subjectivity and lack of independence that inevitably occurs when the evaluator is a person inside. The use of an external entity, in general, is when the company has strong demands for transparency and accountability, and/or when the internal components do not have the ability to carry out self-evaluation (Kiel and

Nicholson 2005). The organization can choose as an external consultant either specialized reviewers (specialist consultant) or trust (trusted general advisor).

4.3 Who Is Evaluated and What Is Evaluated

Another aspect linked to the second question is related to the identification of key subjects to be evaluated ("who is evaluated"). There are three main evaluable subjects: the Board of Directors in its complexity (including committees); individual directors and key personnel of the governance corporate (CEO, for example). The latter being choice of those who consider that the analysis depends on the objective it pursues. The evaluation of the board in its complexity is the best choice to become familiar with this new practice, but has the disadvantage of focusing rather more on team performance than on the individual to help solve the problems of governance. In this case BE does not respond to a genuine desire to improve the functioning of the board. The evaluation of the Committees of the Board of Directors, agencies who are delegated certain responsibilities with the aim of increasing the efficiency of decision-making processes, allows the adequacy of their structure to be ensured and the manner of performance of their duties to be controlled with respect to expectations from others, which ensures that committees play a useful and a valid role. The evaluation of individual directors brings the greatest benefits in situations where the performance of the board has problems. The objective of the evaluation is to encourage members to recognize their contribution to the achievement of the assets of the entire Board, promoting future development and improvement. The LID evaluation aims to provide a clear point of reference for the shareholders and the most important corporate stakeholders (Kiel et al. 2005). Another person assessed is the CEO.

That evaluate depends on the goals set for evaluation. This can be subject to evaluation functions of the board and the strategy (such as risks, communication with stakeholders, the appointment of the CEO); the structure and composition of the Board and/or Committees; the process of meeting; the individual directors and their responsibilities (Lorsch 1995; Conger et al. 1998; Ingley and Van Der Walt 2002).

BE can relate to the individual or the Board in its complexity (Conger et al. 1998; Kiel and Nicholson 2005; Leblanc and Gillies 2005).

The evaluation of the Board membership focuses on the characteristics of the different directors and how they contribute to achieving the tasks of the board, individually and collectively (Kiel and Nicholson 2005; Huse 2007). Board membership evaluation includes the evaluation of the characteristics of the directors on the basis of well-defined criteria (O'Neal and Thomas 1996) such as age, gender, professional background, in terms of education, professional experience, skills and independence abilities developed. In other cases, the focus of analysis can be on processes and cultures (Atkinson and Salterio 2002; Huse et al. 2005) or leadership structure.

4.4 'How to' Evaluation

There are several techniques that can be used to conduct BE, including open discussion, self-evaluation in comparison with codes of corporate governance; schedules and questionnaires; interviews and observation. Each of the techniques have strengths and weaknesses and there is no best way to set up BE. One of the most-used techniques is self-evaluation that is based on perception and personal reflection of one's contribution and as such does not have an objective view. The directors have distortions in the image of themselves (Conger et al. 2001) and can reach compassionate judgments on the results achieved (Kiel et al. 2005). From a scientific point of view the reliability of self-assessment is one of the main problems of BE (Carcio 2004; Sonnenfeld 2004) due to the fact that the board tends to be more lenient, less variable, blackberries biased and show less agreement with the judgment ruling of others (Carcio 2004). Still, in situations of not good performance, the directors may unite in order to avoid a negative rating. These problems might diminish rather than improve the board effectiveness. The involvement of external parties that facilitate self-assessment can ensure greater professionalism in the appraisal process but does not solve all problems (like the last). Another technique used is the interview. This mode is particularly useful for analyzing the interactions within the Board, the climate, the cooperation between the components (Kiel and Nicholson 2005). In general, the interview technique is used when the chairman (or a non-executive director) takes on the role of the interviewer. The presence of a person, in addition to the interviewer, in the role of facilitator is common practice, as his presence can reduce the problems of interpretation and improve the categorization of the responses of the analysis.

Another method is the fairly widespread use of questionnaires. All these methods can be combined with a review of key documents (Kiel and Nicholson 2005; Huse 2007). The analysis of key documents can provide insights into the meaning of the board and its members' work. Information can be obtained from the reading of the minutes of meetings, attendance records, and in general all documents of the council. The technique requires a long time for analysis. A combination of techniques can better reflect how the board is performing.

4.5 With Whom to Discuss BE

The results obtained must, finally, be discussed and communicated. The decision of the subjects to be included in the communication of the results of the evaluation process, and the manner in which the final choices is represented, are the last stage of the process. The lack of feedback is self-defeating (Sonnenfeld 2002). The determination of the persons with whom to discuss the data is conditioned by the objectives and the communication is a real demonstration of the seriousness and commitment undertaken by the company in search of improvement as well as an element that strengthens the relationship with the external environment. The final results should lead to a report and discussion and then to an implementation (action plans) according to the results observed. The whole process is useless if people cannot obtain information about the results. If the target of the board is to build a reputation for transparency and develop relationships with external stakeholders, then the results should be communicated. Communicating BE results demonstrates that the Board is attentive to the aspects of governance.

5 Formulation of Hypotheses

The elements that can affect the application of good practice of corporate governance, such as BE, and disclosure/how to adopt it, can be divided into two different levels: macro and micro.

At the macro level the main determinant of BE is identified in the recommendation (of a voluntary nature) on its adoption contained in the Italian Code of Conduct of governance. This is a document outlining best practices regarding the board (Zattoni and Cuomo 2008). Despite their voluntary nature, firms can interpret these recommendations, and therefore BE, as compulsory in order to respond to public expectations (and then to respond to pressure from other organizations or by conformity to regulatory standards established by external institutions) and to prevent any damage to corporate reputation. Therefore, codes of conduct play a role in the competitive market for reputational status among firms, since it can help differentiate an individual firm's reputation from the malpractices of competing firms or clients, and boost their credibility (Fombrun and Shanley 1990).

This is because stakeholders whether they are shareholders, investors, future employees, or community groups of public policy makers, assign reputational status to individual firms based on a comparison of corporate practices adopted by firms (Fombrun and Shanley 1990). In fact, for a stakeholder to be able to express such assessments he needs information, so companies that adopt best practices, must disclose it if they want to obtain the related benefits. This information is part of what is known as a voluntary disclosure. There is evidence of a positive relationship between the adoption of the recommendations of best practices and business value (Klapper and Love 2004; Durnev and Kim 2005). Leaving to others studies the task of analyzing the relationship between BE and firm's value, this research focuses on the determinants at the micro- or firm-specific level.

The mode of adopting BE and its level of disclosure is influenced by firm-specific characteristics, such as special ownership structure on which depends, in turn, the specific structure of corporate governance, in terms of the composition of the Board and the presence or absence of internal committees.

A high concentration of ownership, such as that which characterizes the Italian listed companies (as well as unlisted), has a negative effect on the adoption of good governance practices (Bhatala and Rao 1995; Prevost et al. 2002; Rediker and Seth 1995; Bozec and Bozec 2007) and therefore also on how to implement any information supplied about BE. Good governance mechanisms, identified in the literature and in the Code of Conduct, are for example, an adequate number of independent directors, as they can improve the quality of monitoring (Fama and Jensen 1983; Beasley 1996; Eng and Mak 2003) and encourage voluntary disclosure (Chen and Jaggi 2000; Cheng and Courtenay 2006; Cerbioni and Parbonetti 2007; Lim et al. 2007; Ajinkya et al. 2005; Adams and Hossain 1998; Leung and Horwitz 2004; Abdelsalam and Street 2007); the presence of the Committees of the Board, whose role is essentially to improve the quality of information between principal and agent; the lead independent director (LID) who with his function, as a link between the chairman of the board and the independent directors, contributes to the better functioning of the board's work (e.g. significantly increases the information for the board or the organization of meetings with the management for the study of specific topics for operations). In a system with concentrated ownership, such as in Italy, the LID will be a reference point for the minority shareholders, and especially institutional investors (without, however, replacing the leadership of the company in dealings with shareholders).

The Code of Conduct also states that the efficiency and effectiveness of the work of the board can improve where specific committees (audit committee, remuneration and nomination committee) are constituted with consultative and advisory functions. Empirical studies regarding the presence and the functioning of these committees are limited and focused on the audit committee. Existing studies fail to provide evidence of a positive relationship between the existence of this committee and the quality of accounting and probability that the presence of internal committees is able to prevent opportunistic behavior (Dechow and Sweeney 1996).

On the basis of the empirical literature examined, a positive relationship between the adoption of BE and a good governance structure is assumed in the research. The hypothesis to be tested is:

H1: the adoption of the BE is positively associated with better internal governance structures

Despite the adoption of BE and disclosure being voluntary, it is very likely that it will be adopted and accountable. This, as mentioned earlier, is due to the impact that a failure to adopt, or a low quality of disclosure can have on corporate reputation. In other words, the company adopting best practices is evaluated better than those who do not adopt. At the same time is in the interests of the companies to provide voluntary information (voluntary disclosure) on the practice adopted also in order to differentiate themselves from the others and to be better known by the investors and stakeholders (Bozzolan et al. 2003; Macagnan 2009; Mangena and Pike 2010). It also helps investors and lenders to better assess the company (Levinsohn 2001), reduce the information asymmetry between companies and investors, reduce the risk perceived by market participants and therefore the cost of capital raised (Diamond and Verrecchia 1991; Leuz and Verrecchia 2000). A greater disclosure in the case of BE allows appreciation of how BE has been adopted and then assessment albeit only in the form of its quality. A good BE is better qualitatively if it is conducted by an outside evaluator (more impartial than an in-house counterpart) or when the valuation techniques are more than one. The methods of adoption, and disclosure of these aspects in turn are influenced by the choices of governance, so it is expected that the BE adoption method is the best in the best governed companies. Starting from these premises let's test the following hypothesis:

H2: The quality of BE is positively associated with better internal governance structures.

6 Methodology

To achieve the objectives two indicators of BE were calculated: one dichotomous (BE), expressive of the adoption of BE (which assumes the value of 1 when the company adopts the BE and 0 when not adopted) a second indicator, a sum indicator, obtained by assigning a score to each of the available information on BE in the report on the ownership structure (Table 2). The scoring in the various aspects is defined in view of the importance of placing the assessment can have for stakeholder (a valuation performed by an independent entity inside is less than that carried out by an outside analyst, therefore the use of several analysis techniques is more reliable than using a single technique, the analysis makes sense if it is reflected in terms of results). The companies, in general, provide information on what they do, therefore, if they do not indicate several analysis methods carried out, it is because they do not use more than one. Based on this approach the following scores were assigned (Table 2).

In this way, an indicator (Qual_BE) is obtained whose minimum score is 0 and whose maximum score is five. The two indicators BE and Qual_BE are used as dependent variables in the analysis. The choices of internal governance are measured using as proxies: the ratio of independent (measured by comparing the number of non-executive and independent of the size of the Board (AI)); the presence of LID (P_LID) and at least two committees (D_2COM) are two dichotomous variables that takes the value 1 if the LID is present within the organization and if there are at least two committees within the board, and 0 otherwise.

Table 2 The measurement of quality formal implementation of the BE

Variable	Point	Variable	Point
Valuator		Two or more techniques used	2
Internal Valuator	0		
External Valuator	1	Feedback/results	
Techniques used		Non communicated	0
Non communicated	0	Indicated positive results, effective, neutral	1
Indicated (only one)	1	Communication of results and comparison with other companies	2

To test the hypothesis H1 (the companies that adopt best practices, BE internal governance structures) and H2 (the quality of BE is positively associated with better internal governance structure) the following models were studied respectively:

$$\text{BE} = \beta_0 + \beta_1\,\text{BoardChar} + \beta_2\,\text{FirmChar} + \varepsilon \quad (1)$$

$$\text{Disc\_BE} = \beta_0 + \beta_1\,\text{BoardChar} + \beta_2\,\text{FirmChar} + \varepsilon \quad (2)$$

where:

BE is a dummy variable indicating whether the company carries out BE periodically; **Qual_BE** is instead a proxy for the quality of BE calculated as shown in Table 6.

BoardChar is a vector that contains the characteristics of the board, such as: the incidence in the Independent Director in the Board, the Lead Independent Director presence and, at least, two committees.

FirmChar is instead representative of the control variables. They are identified in the percentage of shares held by the five largest shareholders (Own_5), and the presence of such a BIG4 audit firm (DBIG4).

DBIG4 was chosen because, in line with previous studies, it is believed that the disclosure is wider in those companies in which the auditor is one of the big four auditing firms (Bonson and Escobar 2006; Wang et al. 2008). The variable on the independent auditors (BIG4) is measured using a dichotomous variable equal to 1 if the audit firm is one of the big 4 (KPMG, PricewaterhouseCoopers, Deloitte, Ernst Young) and zero otherwise. The variable related to the concentration of ownership, OWN_5, is included because the literature shows that the greater the ownership concentration the lower the level of corporate disclosure, because the controlling shareholders have direct access to information and develop as a result of lower demand information (Chau and Gray 2002; Mitchell et al. 1995; Haniffa and Hudaib 2006). It is assumed that there is a negative relationship between the BE adoption methods and disclosure and the proportion of shares owned by the five biggest shareholders. Even the variable BIG4 is deemed not to be significant with respect to the adoption of the practice that does not depend precisely on the concentration of ownership in the presence of a BIG4 audit firm, however, it is believed to affect the extent of the quality of BE.

The two measures of BE were regressed on the choice of internal governance, the first (BE dichotomous) with a logit regression and the second (quality BE) with OLS.

From the analysis of the reports information was acquired on corporate governance, adoption or not of the practice of BE and, if adopted, the way of setting up the BE. Specifically, information was sought about those who do the evaluation, the subjects evaluated, the aspects evaluated and techniques used. All data were acquired separately by two of the authors and compared to ensure its reliability.

7 Findings: Descriptive Statistics

7.1 The Sample

The sample consists of all companies listed on the Milan stock exchange (excluding financial assets). For each company 2013 was analyzed, for the year 2012, the report on corporate governance and ownership structure, available online on the website of the Italian Stock Exchange and/or the company website. The universe is represented by 175 listed companies. Sixteen companies were deleted from it for the reasons set out in Table 3, and the analysis sample is therefore represented by 159 companies.

In the following Table 4 the breakdown of the sample as taken from Borsa Italiana. The sample is representative for each sector, including more than 80 % universe. The most consistent sectors are those from Industry (with 50 firms) and consumer goods (37 firms).

7.2 BE Adoption and Subjects Assessed

Italian boards have adopted the BE just, in our opinion, as a fulfillment of a bureaucratic procedures and compliance with self-regulatory codes. Considering the whole sample analysis shows that compared to the 159 companies included in

Table 3 The sample

Universe	175
Companies not included as per a not traditional model of governance	2
Not Italian companies	4
Companies without data	10
Final sample	159

Table 4 Sample for activity sector

Sector	Universe	Sample	%
Oil & Gas	6	6	100
Chemical & Raw Material	4	3	75
Industry	51	50	98
Consumer goods	41	37	90
Health	7	7	100
Consumer services	28	23	82
Telecommunication	3	3	100
Public services	17	15	88
High Technology	18	15	83
Total	175	159	91

the sample, about 80 % engage in practices of BE (Table 5). They are: technology sector enterprises (86.7 %), Health (85.7 %) and consumer goods (81.1 %) that, more than the others adopt this practice. Less disposed to this practice is the chemical sector (33.3 %).

BE can be developed by analyzing subjects (such as the Board of Directors, the executive (AE), the non-executive (ANE), the independent directors (AI), the CEO (AD), the chairman of the board (P), the lead independent director (LID) and the Committees (C) or "aspects", such as the composition, function and size of the Board and its Committees; role and responsibilities of the Board, adequate number of executive, non-executive and independent directors, the presence of minority directors, the adequacy of the Board, the quality of the organization and leadership of the meetings and the frequency of meetings, the relevance of the subjects of the advice, role and competence of the committees (Table 6).

Table 5 Companies with adopt BE

Sector	Sample	Adopt BE	% respect sample
Oil & Gas (O&G)	6	6	100.0
Chemical & Raw Material (C&RM)	3	1	33.3
Industry (I)	50	39	78.0
Consumer goods (CG)	37	30	81.1
Health (H)	7	6	85.7
Consumer services (CS)	23	18	78.3
Telecommunication (T)	3	2	66.7
Public services (PS)	15	12	80.0
High Technology (HT)	15	13	86.7
Total	159	127	79.9

Table 6 Subject assessed

Sector	BE	SCDA (%)	SAE (%)	SANE (%)	SAI (%)	SAD (%)	SP (%)	SLID (%)	SC (%)
O&G	6	100	33.3	33.3	33.3	33.3	50.0	0.0	83.3
C&RM	1	100	100	100	100	0.0	0.0	0.0	100
I	39	78.0	76.0	42.0	42.0	44.0	0.0	2.0	0.0
CG	30	81.1	81.1	10.8	8.1	16.2	2.7	2.7	0.0
H	6	85.7	85.7	0.0	0.0	0.0	0.0	0.0	0.0
CS	18	78.3	73.9	8.7	4.3	8.7	4.3	0.0	0.0
T	2	66.7	66.7	0.0	0.0	0.0	0.0	0.0	0.0
PS	12	80.0	80.0	0.0	0.0	6.7	0.0	0.0	0.0
HT	13	81.3	75.0	0.0	0.0	0.0	0.0	0.0	0.0
Total	127	97.6	23.6	22.0	26.8	3.1	3.9	0.0	89.8

BE number of companies with BE, *SCDA* subject evaluated board, *SAE* evaluated as executive director, *SANE* subject evaluated as non-executive director, *SAI* subject evaluated independent director, *SAD* subject evaluated CEO, *SP* subject evaluated as chairman of the board, *SLID* subject evaluated as lead independent director, *SC* subject evaluated as committee

In most cases, the object of evaluation is the Board (97.6 %) in its complexity accompanied by the evaluation of AI (26.8 %) of AE (23.6 %) and ANE (22 %). The main object of evaluation is the AD (3.1 %) and P (3.9 %). The evaluation of committees is widespread (89.8 %). It thus appears that BE is used by P to evaluate the members of the Board. Analyzing the data by sector seems to indicate a different behavior according to the sector in which they operate. More market-oriented companies, such as the consumer goods sector and consumer services, tend to develop BE considering all the subjects of the Board, including P and AD. Companies in the SPL sector, however, use BE as a tool to evaluate individuals with executive positions, such as chief executive and executive directors. Technology, Telecommunications and Health sectors, adopt BE and use it to evaluate the performance of the executive directors. The Committees, although widespread in all industries, are analyzed only in companies in the Oil & Gas and Chemicals & Raw Materials sectors.

7.3 *What Evaluated, Methodology of Analysis and Evaluator*

An analysis of aspects assessed (Table 7), shows that the most analyzed aspect is the composition, functioning of the board (96 %) and size of the Board (93 %). Following the analysis of the size, composition and functioning of the committees. The appropriate composition of the Board in terms of AE, ANE and AI is not the object of our attention (respectively 18 %, 19 % and 39 %), although differences can be observed according to the sector of activity. In fact, companies in the oil and gas sector and chemical sector, are much more attentive to these aspects (respectively 50 % and 100 % of the companies) companies operating in other sectors are more attentive to the figure of the independent director.

Not all companies that adopt BE practices specify the methodology used (43 %) (Table 8). Focusing on companies that provide information to that effect emerges as one of the most utilized techniques is the questionnaire (on average in 47 % of cases), which is often used as the sole method of analysis. In three sectors (Oil & Gas, Industry, Consumer Goods and SPL) interviews are also used.

The last thing to consider is the type of the evaluator (internal, external or both). The summary data are presented in Table 9.

The evaluator is in 90 % of cases, a person inside and in 2 % of cases is supported by an external party as in the case of Atlantia, Isagro and Autogrill (Table 10). Only in 12 % of cases, is the assessment carried out by external parties, while the percentage drops to 10 % if cases are excluded in which external evaluators are joined by the internal evaluator. It showed two cases of joint internal/external evaluation, two cases are related to the consumer services sector, in one case the leads and the administrative function is involved and three other cases in which the evaluation is carried out by most individuals inside, as the Chairman and social affairs, the Chairman and an independent director, the nomination Committee and the lead (Table 11).

Table 7 Aspects evaluated

	CCdA (%)	CC (%)	FCdA (%)	FC (%)	DCdA (%)	DC (%)	AAE (%)	AANE (%)	AAI (%)	ACdA (%)	R (%)	FR (%)	RCC (%)
O&G	100	83	100	83	100	83	17	50	50	50	0	33	17
C&RM	100	100	100	100	100	100	0	100	100	100	0	0	0
I	92	85	92	87	87	82	13	15	15	36	8	33	23
CG	100	87	100	87	100	87	0	20	20	40	0	40	0
H	100	100	100	100	100	100	17	0	0	17	0	33	17
CS	94	94	100	100	89	89	11	22	28	56	0	56	28
T	100	100	100	100	100	100	0	0	0	0	0	0	50
PS	92	92	92	92	92	92	25	17	17	33	0	25	17
HT	100	100	92	92	92	85	8	8	15	31	0	38	23
Total	96	90	96	91	93	87	10	18	20	39	2	37	17

CCdA board composition, *CC* committee composition, *FCdA* board functioning, *FC* committee functioning, *DCdA* board size, *DC* size committee, *AAE* adequate presence executive director, *AANE* adequate presence non executive director, *AANEI* adequate presence independent director, *ACdA* adequate composition CdA, *R* adequate meeting management, *FR* meeting frequency, *RCC* role and competences of committees

Table 8 Techniques in the BE

Techniques	Questionnaire (%)	Interview (%)	Observation (%)	Analysis documents (%)	Other (%)	Not indicated (%)
O&G	50	33	0	0	17	0
C&RM	100	0	0	0	0	0
I	56	8	0	0	0	36
CG	33	10	0	0	0	57
H	50	17	0	0	0	33
CS	61	0	0	0	0	39
T	50	0	0	0	0	50
PS	33	33	0	0	8	25
HT	31	0	0	0	0	69
Total	46	10	0	0	2	42

Table 9 Evaluator typology

	External evaluator		Internal evaluator		Number of companies with int/ext	
	V.A.	%	V.A.	%	V.A.	%
O&G	2	33	4	67	0	0
C&RM	1	100	1	100	1	100
I	5	13	35	90	1	3
CG	0	0	30	100	0	0
H	0	0	6	100	0	0
CS	1	6	18	100	1	6
T	0	0	2	100	0	0
PS	6	50	6	50	0	0
HT	1	8	12	92	0	0
Total	16	13	114	90	3	2

7.4 Evaluation Effects

BE has as the ultimate goal to improve the operation and therefore the effectiveness of the Board while providing recommendations on how to improve their performance. Among the recommendations are found those that act on the composition of the Board requesting a different composition in terms of gender or a different size (reducing or increasing the number of members of the Board). From other assessments emerge, instead, improvements on organizational issues such as an increase of meetings with thematic focus, a greater involvement of the directors at meetings of the Board, the acquisition of broader skills also open to international, improve the activity of the committees (Table 11). One of the most referred to as the results of the BE is made available to the Board of major papers and on their availability in time for the meeting. Very often the BE ends with the declaration which states that Board and/or Committees are adequate in terms of composition, size and functions, then without any suggestion for an improvement in the performance of the Board.

Table 10 Internal/external evaluator

	nd (%)	LID (%)	C (%)	AD (%)	FI (%)	OA (%)	P/C (%)	E (%)	Pcda (%)	I/E (%)	Tot (%)
O&G	1.57	0.00	1.57	0.00	0.00	0.00	0.00	1.57	0.00	0.00	0.00
C&RM	0.00	0.00	0.00	0.00	0.00	0.00	0.00	0.00	0.00	0.00	0.79
I	18.11	0.79	2.36	0.00	2.36	0.00	0.79	2.36	3.94	0.00	0.00
CG	14.96	0.79	3.94	0.79	1.57	0.79	0.79	0.00	0.00	0.00	0.00
H	0.79	0.00	1.57	0.00	0.79	0.00	0.00	0.00	0.79	0.00	0.79
CS	5.51	1.57	3.94	0.00	0.79	0.79	0.00	0.00	0.79	0.00	0.79
T	0.79	0.00	0.79	0.00	0.00	0.00	0.00	0.00	0.00	0.00	0.00
PS	4.72	0.00	0.79	0.00	0.00	0.00	0.00	3.94	0.00	0.00	0.00
HT	7.87	0.00	1.57	0.00	0.00	0.00	0.00	0.00	0.00	0.00	0.79
Total	54.33	3.15	16.54	0.79	5.51	1.57	1.57	7.87	5.51	0.00	3.15

nd non told, *LID* lead independent director, *C* committee, *AD* CEO; *FI* function internal and internal auditing, *OA* administrative body, *P/C* chairman of advisory board or advisory board, *E* external evaluator, *Pcda* chairman, *I/E* internal evaluator helped by an external evaluator

Table 11 Implication of the analysis

	Implication (%)	No info on implication (%)	Tot (%)
O&G	1.6	3.1	4.7
C&RM	0.8	0.0	0.8
I	8.7	22.0	30.7
CG	6.3	17.3	23.6
H	1.6	3.1	4.7
CS	5.5	8.7	14.2
T	0.0	1.6	1.6
PS	4.7	4.7	9.4
HT	3.9	6.3	10.2
Total	33.1	66.9	100.0

8 Regression Analysis: Adoption and Quality on BE and Governance Choices

To test the relationship between the adoption of the BE and the choices of governance (hypothesis 1) a logit analysis was conducted using the dichotomous dependent variable, which took the value 1 if the company adopts the practice of BE and 0 otherwise. The analysis was conducted with the software Stata 11 and the results of the analysis are presented in the following Table 12.

The value of Prob> chi2 shows that the model is statistically significant. The variables related to the structure of governance are all significant, indicating their influence on the decision whether or not to activate BE. As expected for the control variables do not appear to be significant, indicating that the adoption of the practice is independent of the presence of such a BIG4 audit firm and the high concentration of ownership. The sign of the coefficient of the variable SHAREprimi5 is still negative, indicating the likelihood of an inverse relationship between ownership concentration and adoption of best practices. The results show also that if the independent directors increase by 1 % the probability of the company initiating BE practices increases by 2.49, without prejudice to the other variables. For a better interpretation of the data the odds-ratio was calculated, as shown in Table 13.

The odds ratios indicate the magnitude of an anticipated change when a unit changes in the dependent variables while keeping all other variables constant. The odds of success (presence of BE) are defined as the ratio of the probability of success over the probability of failure. The results show a strong positive relationship with the incidence of independent directors and with the presence of at least two committees and a moderate relationship with the presence of a LID. The concentration of ownership indicates a negative effect on the probability of the company adopting BE. In detail, the odd-ratios show that the adoption of BE is 12 times higher in companies where there is a higher incidence of independent directors than those with lower incidence of independent directors; two times

Table 12 Logit regression

Variable	Coeff.	Std. err.	P > |z|	90 % conf. interval	
Const	−0.243	1.402	0.863	−2.549	2.064
AI	2.489	1.359	0.067	0.254	4.724
P_LID	1.053	0.487	0.031	0.252	1.853
D_2COM	1.456	0.553	0.008	0.546	2.366
D_BIG4	0.351	0.659	0.595	−0.734	1.435
SHAREprimi5	−0.019	0.014	0.158	−0.043	0.003
Prob > chi2	0.0002				
Number of obs	159				

Table 13 Odds ratio for logit regression

Variable	Odds ratio	Std. err.	P > |z|	90 % conf. interval	
AI	12.053	16.378	0.067	1.289	112.653
P_LID	2.866	1.395	0.031	1.287	6.382
D_2COM	4.289	2.373	0.008	1.727	10.655
D_BIG4	1.420	0.936	0.595	0.480	4.200
SHAREprimi5	0.980	0.014	0.158	0.958	1.003
Prob > chi2	0.0002				
Number of obs	159				

Table 14 OLS regression

Variable	Coeff.	Std. err.	P > |t|	90 % conf. interval	
Const	0.168	0.445	0.706	−0.568	0.904
AI	1.641	0.556	0.004	0.721	2.561
P_LID	0.206	0.169	0.223	−0.073	0.486
D_2COM	0.108	0.236	0.646	−0.281	0.498
D_BIG4	0.446	0.185	0.017	0.139	0.753
SHAREprimi5	−0.009	0.005	0.046	−0.018	−0.002
Prob > chi2	0.0002				
Number of obs	159				

higher in companies where there is the LID and four times in the companies that have at least two internal committees of the Board of Directors.

To test the second hypothesis a regression was conducted in which dependent variable is Qual_BE, a non-dichotomy variable calculated as indicated in Sect. 8. The results are present in Table 14.

The VIF (variance inflation factors) are less than 2 for all variables, suggesting the absence a collinearity issues.

As assumed a higher incidence of independent directors in the Board improves the quality of implementation and disclosure on BE. The presence instead of a LID and at least two committees within the Board does not appear significant. The impact of BE on the control variables is assumed significant. The result confirms our hypothesis that BE is influenced by good internal mechanism governance.

9 Final Consideration

At international, as well as Italian level, the code of conduct requires companies to engage in BE practices. In the light of this recommendation, the Italian listed companies have introduced BE. To date, there are few companies that provide additional disclosures about how to set it up. This does not allow an understanding of how it helps to improve the functioning of the organization. The lack of information leads, in fact, to thinking that this is a purely formal adherence to the recommendation, viewed as mere fulfillment. The results of the analysis reveal that in most cases the assessment is conducted by individuals inside the Board, with the obvious limitations due primarily to the limited independence of the evaluator, there is no reference to the recipients of information from the BE; one is generally the technique of analysis and only in a few cases has the evaluation had implications on the composition of the Board. The first thing to do then is to act on a cultural level in order to understand that BE can provide the organization in terms of an objective assessment of how to improve the performance of the Board, the Chairman and individual directors. Second, it could be appropriate to provide for a scheme to be included in the report on the ownership structure that summarizes key issues on what to report, in order to enable the reader to understand the external circumstances and compare it with other companies in the enterprise concerned. The absence of a reference framework has led many companies to write, within the report, the sentence in this code shall, at least once a year, conduct an assessment of the functioning of the Board and its committees, as well as on their size and composition. The results should be read considering the context in which companies operate, the phase of the life cycle, the history, the reference framework, and the type of organization. However, the whole process is determined by these aspects, so BE will be structured on the basis of all these elements, for example if it can be avoided in the initial phase of evaluating the CEO, in subsequent stages it becomes necessary to conduct an annual assessment that can be informal at first but then more formalized.

The study presents as a limit the fact that it only considers the data and information derived from the governance documents that can give cognizance only of the accession to the formal recommendation regarding best practices but that does not allow the effect of BE on the composition of the Board to be known.

The prospects for future research are the same as those to support the analysis of documents and interviews with the directors of the board evaluation analyzing the impact on the composition of the Board.

Another prospective research is to analyze the adoption and the modality of adoption of BE in the future, we believe that tomorrow BE will no longer be a mere formality but should be the desire to build high performance of the board, in order to anticipate and meet the changes that gradually arise. Businesses in other words, must move from a "check the box" approach to the use of BE as a tool for ensuring the company be aligned with its long term strategies.

References

Abdelsalam, O. H., & Street, D. L. (2007). Corporate governance and the timeliness of corporate internet reporting by U.K. listed companies. *Journal of International Accounting, Auditing and Taxation, 16*, 111–130.

Abdullah, S. N. (2004). Board composition, CEO duality and performance among Malaysian listed companies. *International Journal of Business in Society, 4*(4), 47–61.

Adams, M., & Hossain, M. (1998). Managerial discretion and voluntary disclosure: Empirical evidence from the New Zealand life industry. *Journal of Accounting and Public Policy, 17*, 245–281.

Ajinkya, B., Bhojraj, S., & Sengupta, P. (2005). The association between outside directors, institutional investors and the properties of management earnings forecasts. *Journal of Accounting Research, 43*(2), 343–376.

Atkinson, A., & Salterio, S. (2002). Function vs. form. *CMA Management, 76*, 23–27.

Beasley, M. (1996). An empirical analysis of the relation between the board of director composition and financial statement fraud. *The Accounting Review, 71*, 443–465.

Belcourt, M., & Kluge, H. (1999). Measuring board performance. *Ivey Business Journal, 63*, 26–32.

Bhagat, S., & Bolton, B. (2008). Corporate governance and firm performance. *Journal of Corporate Finance, 14*, 257–273.

Bhatala, C. T., & Rao, R. P. (1995). The determinants of board composition: An agency theory perspective. *Managerial and Decision Economics, 16*(1), 59–69.

Bonson, E., & Escobar, T. (2006). Digital reporting in Eastern European: An empirical study. *International Journal of Accounting Information System, 7*, 299–318.

Bozec, Y., & Bozec, R. (2007). Ownership concentration and corporate governance practices: Substitution or expropriation effects? *Canadian Journal of Administrative Sciences/Revue canadienne des sciences de l'administration, 24*(3), 182–195.

Bozzolan, S., Favotto, F., & Ricceri, F. (2003). Italian annual intellectual capital disclosure: An empirical analysis. *Journal of Intellectual capital, 4*(4), 543–558.

Brown, L. D., & Caylor, M. L. (2003). *Corporate governance and firm performance* (Georgia State University Working Paper).

Carcio, W. (2004). Board governance: A social systems perspective. *Academic of Management Executive, 18*, 97–100.

Cerbioni, F., & Parbonetti, A. (2007). Corporate governance and intellectual capital disclosure: An analysis of European biotechnology companies. *European Accounting Review, 16*(4), 791–826.

Charan, R. (2009). *Owing up: The 14 question every board member need to ask*. San Francisco: Jossey-Bass.

Chau, G., & Gray, S. (2002). Ownership structure and corporate voluntary disclosure in Hong Kong and Singapore. *The International Journal of Accounting, 37*, 247–265.

Chen, C. J., & Jaggi, P. B. (2000). Association between independent non-executive directors, family control and financial disclosures in Hong Kong. *Journal of Accounting and Public Policy, 19*, 285–310.

Cheng, E., & Courtenay, S. (2006). Board composition, regulatory regime and voluntary disclosure. *The International Journal of Accounting, 41*, 262–289.

Clarke, T., & Klettner, A. (2010). Board effectiveness and performance. Australian Council of Superannuation Investors Research Paper.
CNFP and AFEP. (1995). *The boards of directors of listed companies in France, Vienot report*. Paris: Conseil National du Patronat Français—Association Française des Entreprises Privées.
Conger, J. A., Finegold, D., & Lawler, E. E. (1998). Appraising boardroom performance. *Harvard Business Review, 76*(1), 136–148.
Conger, J. A., & Lawler, E. E. (2001). Building a high-performing board: How to choose the right members. *Business Strategy Review, 12*, 11–19.
Conger, J. A., Lawler, E. E., & Finegold, D. L. (2001). *Corporate boards: New strategies for adding value at the top*. San Francisco: Jossey-Bass.
Corporate Governance Committee. (2011). *Corporate governance code—Italian code of conduct*. Milan: Corporate Governance Committee.
Coskun, M., & Sayilir, O. (2012). Relationship between corporate governance and financial performance of Turkish companies. *International Journal of Business and Social Science, 3*(14). 59–64.
Dechow, P. R., & Sweeney, S. A. (1996). Causes and consequences of earnings manipulations: An analysis of firms subject to enforcement actions by the SEC. *Contemporary Accounting Research, 13*(1), 1–36.
Diamond, D. W., & Verrecchia, R. E. (1991). Disclosure, liquidity and the cost of capital. *The Journal of Finance, 41*, 1325–1359.
Dulewicz, V., & Herbert, P. (2008). Current practice of FTSE 350 Boards concerning the appointment, evaluation and development of directors, boards and committees post the Combined Code'. *International Journal of Business Governance and Ethics, 4*(1), 99–115.
Durnev, A., & Kim, E. H. (2005). To steal or not to steal: Firm attributes, legal environment and valuation. *Journal of Finance, 60*, 1461–1493.
Eng, L., & Mak, Y. (2003). Corporate governance and voluntary disclosure. *Journal of Accounting and Public Policy, 22*, 325–345.
Fama, E., & Jensen, M. C. (1983). Separation of ownership and control. *Journal of Law and Economics, 26*, 301–325.
Ferguson, W. J. (2001). Performance in the boardroom: How should it be assessed? *Real Estate Finance, 17*, 49–55.
Fombrun, C., & Shanley, M. (1990). What's in a name? Reputation building and corporate strategy. *Academy of Management Journal, 42*, 87–99.
Forbes, D., & Milliken, F. (1999). Cognition and corporate governance: Understanding boards of directors as strategic decision making groups. *Academy of Management Review, 24*, 489–505.
German Panel on Corporate Governance. (2000). *Corporate governance rules for quoted German companies*. Frankfurt: German Panel on Corporate Governance.
Haniffa, R., & Hudaib, M. (2006). Corporate governance structure and performance of Malaysian listed companies. *Journal of Business Finance & Accounting, 33*(7/8), 1034–1062.
Hendry, K., & Kiel, G. C. (2004). The role of the board in firm strategy: Integrating agency and organisational control perspectives. *Corporate Governance, 12*, 500–520.
Huse, M. (2007). *Boards, governance and value creation: The human side of Corporate Governance*. Cambridge: Cambridge University Press.
Huse, M., Minichilli, A., & Schoning, A. (2005). The value of process-oriented boardroom dynamics. *Organizational Dynamics, 34*, 285–297.
Ingley, C. B., & Van Der Walt, N. T. (2001). The strategic board: The changing role of directors in developing and maintaining corporate capability. *Corporate Governance: An International Review, 9*(3), 174–185.
Ingley, C. B., & Van Der Walt, N. T. (2002). Board dynamics and the politics of appraisal. *Corporate Governance: An International Review, 10*, 163–174.
Kiel, G., & Beck, J. (2006). Seven steps to effective board and director evaluations. *Company Secretary*, 588–592.

Kiel, G., & Nicholson, G. J. (2005). Evaluating board and directors. *Corporate Governance: An International Review, 13*, 613–631.
Kiel, G. C., Nicholson, G. J., & Barclay, M. A. (2005). *Board, director and CEO, evaluation*. Sydney: McGraw-Hill.
Klapper, L., & Love, I. (2004). Corporate governance, investor protection and performance in emerging markets. *Journal of Corporate Finance, 10*, 703–728.
Lawler, E. E., & Finegold, D. (2005). The changing face of corporate boards. *MIT Sloan Management Review, 46*(2), 67–70.
Lawler, E. E., Finegold, D., Benson, G., & Conger, J. A. (2002). Adding value in the boardroom. *MIT Sloan Management Review, 43*(2), 92–93.
Leblanc, R., & Gillies, J. (2005). *Inside the boardroom; How boards really work and the coming revolution in corporate governance*. Toronto, ON: Wiley.
Leung, S., & Horwitz, B. (2004). Director ownership and voluntary segment disclosure: Hong Kong experience. *Journal of International Financial Management and Accounting, 15*(3), 235–260.
Leuz, C., & Verrecchia, R. (2000). The economic consequences of increased disclosure. *Journal of Accounting and Research, 38*(3), 91–124.
Levinsohn, A. (2001). FASB weights the value of voluntary disclosure. *Strategic Finance*, 72–74.
Lim, S., Matolcsy, Z., & Chow, D. (2007). The association between board composition and different types of voluntary disclosure. *European Accounting Review, 16*, 555–583.
Long, T. (2006). This year's model: Influences on board and director evaluation. *Corporate Governance: An International Review, 14*(6), 547–557.
Lorsch, J. W. (1995). Empowering the board. *Harvard Business Review, 73*(1), 107–117.
Lorsch, J. W., & MacIver, E. (1989). *Pawns or potentates: The reality of America's corporate boards*. Boston: Harvard Business School Press.
Macagnan, C. B. (2009). Voluntary disclosure of intangible resources and stock profitability, Intangible capital disclosure practices and effects on the cost of equity capital: UK evidence. *The institute of Chartered Accountants of Scotland, Intangible Capital, 5*(1), 1–32.
Mace, M. L. G. (1971). *Directors: Myth and reality*. Boston: Division of Research Graduate.
Mangena, M., & Pike, R. (2010). The effect of audit committee shareholding, financial expertise and size on interim financial disclosures. *Accounting and Business Research, 35*(4), 327–349.
Minichilli, A., Gabrielsson, J., & Huse, M. (2007). Board evaluations: Making a fit between the purpose and the system. *Corporate Governance: An International Review, 15*(4), 609–622.
Mitchell, J., Chia, C., & Loh, A. (1995). Voluntary disclosure of segment information, further evidence in Australia. *Accounting and Finance, 35*(2), 1–16.
Nadler, D. A. (2004). What's the board's role in strategy development?: Engaging the board in corporate strategy. *Strategy & Leadership, 32*(5), 25–33.
Nicholson, G., Kiel, G., & Tunny, J. A. (2012). Board evaluations: Contemporary thinking and practice. In D. Bransons & T. Clarke (Eds.), *THE SAGE handbook of corporate governance* (pp. 285–324). London: Sage.
O'Neal, D., & Thomas, H. (1996). Developing the strategic board. *Long Range Planning, 29*(3), 314–327.
OECD. (2004). *Principles of corporate governance*. Paris: OECD.
Prevost, A. K., Rao, R. P., & Hossain, M. (2002). Board composition in New Zealand: An agency perspective. *Journal of Business Finance & Accounting, 29*, 731–760.
Rediker, K., & Seth, A. (1995). Boards of directors and substitution effects of alternative governance mechanisms. *Strategic Management Journal, 16*(2), 85–99.
Schmidt, S. L., & Brauer, M. (2006). Strategic governance: How to assess board effectiveness in guiding strategy execution. *Corporate Governance: An International Review, 14*(1), 13–22.
Shleifer, A., & Vishny, R. W. (1997). A survey of corporate governance. *The Journal of Finance, 52*(2), 737–783.

Shukeri, S. N., Shin, O., & Shaari, M. S. (2012). Does board of directors; characteristics affect firm performance: Evidence from Malaysian public listed companies. *International Business Research, 5*(9), 120–127.

Sonnenfeld, J. A. (2002). What makes great boards great. *Harvard Business Review, 80*(9), 106–113.

Sonnenfeld, J. (2004). Good governance and the misleading myth of bad metrics. *Academy of Management Executive, 18*, 108–113.

Stybel, L. J., & Peabody, M. (2005). How should board directors evaluate themselves? *MIT Sloan Management Review, 47*, 67–72.

Toronto Stock Exchange. (1994). *Toronto report—Where were the directors? Guidelines for improved corporate governance in Canada*. Toronto, ON: Toronto Stock Exchange.

Tricker, R. I. (1984). *Corporate governance: Practices, procedures, and powers in British companies and their boards of directors*. Aldershot: Gower Press.

Wang, K., Sewon, C., & Claibone, M. C. (2008). Determinants and consequences of voluntary disclosure in an emerging market: Evidence from China. *International Journal of Accounting, Auditing and Taxation, 17*(1), 14–30.

Wright, C., & Rwabizambuga, A. (2006). Institutional pressures, corporate reputation, and voluntary codes of conduct: An examination of the equator principles. *Business and Society Review, 111*(1), 89–117.

Zattoni, A., & Cuomo, F. (2008). Why adopt codes of good governance? A comparison of institutional and efficiency perspectives. *Corporate Governance: An International Review, 16*(1), 1–15.

Corporate Social Responsibility Seen Through Codes of Conduct in Czech Companies

Jaroslav Kacetl and Ilona Semradova

Abstract The paper discusses the relation between social welfare and business profit. Based on the review of relevant literature, it proceeds to a brief history of corporate social responsibility (CSR), which sees profit as one of several—i.e., not the only one—important business values, grouped under three P-terms, namely profit, people, and planet. Then, the paper questions whether the commitment to CSR is voluntary. The code of conduct can be an instrumental gauge of the company's commitment. Especially, whether and how they have created, implemented, and enforced their codes of conduct. The paper includes different theoretical approaches to creating them. In a pilot study, authors carried out a text analysis of tens of different company codes of conduct in order to assess the position of CSR and business ethics in Czech companies. Although results did not correspond fully with the authors' hypotheses, they helped them specify the direction of further research.

Keywords Corporate social responsibility • Code of conduct • Business ethics • Socio-cultural change

1 Introduction

We live in differential world, which shows a lot of signs of socio-cultural imminent change. The most significant changes include a paradigm shift towards mutual communication, an unprecedented advance of new technologies, in particular ICT, and globalization. Globalization brings about new problems as well as new ways of solving them. Consequently, the importance of corporate social responsibility as well as business ethics and company codes of conduct has been growing in relation to this socio-cultural change.

Unfortunately, some companies, organizations and institutions are not always fully aware of that. Others, however, are capable of self-reflection and in concord

J. Kacetl (✉) • I. Semradova
Department of Applied Linguistics, University of Hradec Kralove, Hradec Králové, Czech Republic
e-mail: jaroslav.kacetl@uhk.cz; ilona.semradova@uhk.cz

© Springer International Publishing Switzerland 2016
M.H. Bilgin et al. (eds.), *Business Challenges in the Changing Economic Landscape - Vol. 1*, Eurasian Studies in Business and Economics 2/1,
DOI 10.1007/978-3-319-22596-8_8

with their position in society aspire not only to create their own code of conduct but also to force their employees to follow it. The code of conduct can represent minimum requirements, or essential imperatives related to the given job or profession but it may also set the ideal, vision and philosophy of an activity, company, organization, or institution. The latter implies knowledge of possibilities and theoretical bases needed for creating a quality code of conduct. In the Czech Republic, there has been done little research in this field (Canik 2007). The authors of this paper are planning to do research in the incidence and quality of codes of conducts used by Czech companies. Their pilot study results are presented below.

2 Relationship Between Companies and Society

Economic entities exist only in society, through society, and society. Society as a whole is the prerequisite for their existence and growth. It is common knowledge that economic entities have got hold of a significant share of power, which is why the public call for their stricter control. Another reason for that is the experience from previous decades that witnessed bankruptcies of several companies. A number of financial frauds and other corrupt practices in business added to it. For example, many managers find themselves forced to resort to practices which they acknowledge are shady, but which appear necessary to survive (Porter 2008). Consequently, the position of those who criticize current business practices and support approaches widely known as business ethics, corporate social responsibility (CSR) has been improving. The mentioned approaches aim at deepening the cooperation between companies and society and easier control of their activities.

Even though some authors, among others Fernández and Rajagopal (2014), claim that companies exist in a symbiotic relationship with society, there is no single understanding of the relationship between companies and societies. On the contrary, it is a difficult-to-solve problem. There are a lot of questions to be asked: Is more important the welfare of society or the effort of companies to maximize their profit? (Masaka 2008); should companies be legally bound and institutionally controlled in their relationship to the society or should it be left to them to decide how (or if at all) they would like to support the society?

In the field of corporate social responsibility there are two extreme views. The most significant supporter of the classical view is Milton Friedman, who disapproved of corporate social responsibility. Both Kacetl (2011) and Masaka (2008) mention that according to Friedman, the only justifiable goal of the company is to make profit. Friedman nonetheless believed that companies should use fair practices. According to Branco and Rodrigues (2007), the classical view is justified mainly on the basis of neoclassical economic theory arguments using notions such as the free market, economic efficiency, and profit maximization.

The other extreme view is that of the so-called social activists who support stakeholder theory asserting that companies have social purposes and must therefore also have social goals (Kacetl 2011). According to Branco and Rodrigues

(2007), stakeholder theory asserts that companies have a social responsibility that requires them to consider the interests of all parties affected by their actions. Management should not only consider its shareholders in the decision making process, but also anyone who is affected by business decisions. All in all, the most common view is moderate, slightly closer to the social activists' position even though their position is becoming stronger (Porter 2008).

Porter (2008) states that companies are under the growing pressure to publish annual reports and demonstrate that their activities do not harm the society but support it. We assume that this is the environment that makes more and more companies accept corporate social responsibility as their policy not as their firm conviction but for strategic reasons. Therefore, we claim that with respect to the above mentioned circumstances the acceptance of corporate social responsibility is in many cases an opportunistic act done in order to improve the image of the company and to increase its profit. It is not a result of owners' or managers' efforts to secure welfare of the society. In other words, it is the result of the pressure from the side of the public, government institutions as well as those shareholders who invest in socially responsible companies. Kasparova and Kunz (2013) point out that socially responsible behavior results from the effort of companies to maintain their right to conduct business by means of keeping the social license. Companies first started to publish reports about their environmental activities and then gradually widened the reports to other areas. The problem remains that these reports are of various quality and detail. The most frequently used standard used for making reports about sustainable development of the company is the Global Reporting Initiative (2013).

Kasparova and Kunz (2013) emphasize that the way and scope of reporting are also influenced by the size of the company, the type of ownership and the industry. Companies active in potentially problematic industries (e.g., extracting raw materials, chemical industry, tobacco industry) pay much more attention to corporate social responsibility than companies with relatively lower or less damaging impact on the society and environment.

3 Development of Corporate Social Responsibility

Corporate social responsibility is not new. Both company owners and employees realized they could not focus only on profit maximization. They understood that their company should also follow some tacitly agreed moral rules in order to survive in the long term. Kuldova (2010) maintains that this rule is as old as business itself and even though what we know today as CSR (corporate social responsibility) or SA (social accountability) has never been as easily measurable or quantifiable as profit, costs or salary, the company would find it difficult to survive without it.

Masaka (2008) has it that the quest to make business show its moral face by being socially responsible in its operations and interactions with the environment as well as human society goes back at least as far as the ancient Greece. It was Aristotle who was strongly interested in the ethics of exchange and therefore he can be called the first business ethicist. Aristotle criticized profit-motivated trade, which he believed was lacking in virtue. He thought such trade was exploitation and even regarded those who traded purely for profit as "parasites". Furthermore, Aristotle suggested that one should think of oneself as a member of human community and strive to bring out what is best for oneself as well as for humanity. He believed that what is best for businesspeople is in turn defined by the larger community. Consequently, there is no real contradiction between individual self-interest and the greater public good. Moreover, Masaka (2008) continues that Aristotle was not the only ancient source of such opinions as the Old Testament also contains references to the need for both individuals and corporate organizations to be socially responsible.

Nonetheless, the real beginning of systematic CSR research dates back to the 1950s, which marks the modern era of this concept. Bowen (2013) is largely credited not only with coining the phrase 'corporate social responsibility' but also with providing the first definition of CSR: "it refers to the obligations of businessmen to pursue those policies, to make those decisions, or to follow those lines of action which are desirable in terms of the objectives and values of our society" (ThinkingShift 2007). This definition emphasizes the fact that businessmen have to take into account the interconnectedness between their companies and the society and environment where they operate. CSR definitions expanded during the 1960s as well as the 1970s. The CSR theory was further elaborated by K. Davis, who defined CSR as referring to "businessmen's decisions and actions taken for reasons at least partially beyond the firm's direct economic or technical interest"(ThinkingShift 2007). Davis thus clearly appeals to businessmen to take into account the fact that business does not exist in the void but in human society.

Both the above mentioned definitions propose the opinion that profit is not the only value in business. After all, in the late 1970s Carroll (1979) discerned four parts of corporate social responsibility, namely economic, legal, ethical and philanthropic and he determined their ratio as 4:3:2:1. The 1980s saw fewer new definitions but more empirical research. It was particularly the stakeholder theory that helped widen the actual corporate social responsibility. Davis, among others, found out that CSR contributes to the company's development and growth (Madrakhimova 2013). In the 1990s, CSR was already generally accepted and in the new century it is considered by most businesspeople to be a vitally important from the strategic point of view.

4 (In)voluntary Corporate Social Responsibility

If we accept that corporate social responsibility is strategically important, then we can agree with Rolny and Lacina (2001) who discuss that the characteristic feature of this epoch is ethics itself but its utilitarian (ab)use in the world of business. Is it therefore possible to say that the companies that embrace CSR behave in a utilitarian way? If so, then it is against CSR definitions. For instance, "Business Leaders Forum (n.d.) and its member companies define corporate social responsibility as a voluntary commitment of companies to behave responsibly towards the environment and society in which they operate."

It is commonly understood that companies that accepted CSR behave ethically, decrease their negative impact on the environment, contribute to sustainable development, strive to increase the quality of life of their employees and their families, and support local community. We usually talk about three facets or levels of CSR, namely, PROFIT (economic aspect), PEOPLE (social aspect) and PLANET (environmental aspect). As a result, we talk about the 3P. Is it really so, though? Can we label this commitment as voluntary?

There is another pressure on companies, the SRI, or socially responsible investment. There are various indices assessing investments on the bases of economic results as well as the willingness of companies to solve environmental and social problems. Shareholders can consequently decide to support those companies, which embrace CSR. Masaka (2008) argues that companies are forced to accept CSR and repeatedly prove their interest in society and environment. Therefore, their acceptance of CSR is neither voluntary, nor sincere. In fact, it is not their goal but a means to an end, which is to improve their image and increase profit. Similarly, Branco and Rodrigues (2007) believe that companies accept CSR in order to some get competitive or other economic advantage. Masaka (2008) uses Kantian argumentation to emphasize that it is immoral to enforce corporate social responsibility. He is convinced that moral actions must be done for their own sake. They must not be justified by any reasons or possible consequences. Corporate social responsibility therefore cannot be considered as moral because it brings about something favorable to society. Enforced corporate social responsibility is devoid of moral value if it is seen as prescribed by external bodies and not based on the sense of duty. As a result, corporate organizations should show social concern because they believe it is the right thing to do. On the other hand, corporate social responsibility done in order to get benefit is in fact immoral. In other words, we can talk about moral acceptance of corporate social responsibility only in case the company accepts it voluntarily and unconditionally.

5 Codes of Conduct as a Dimension of CSR

One way of manifesting CSR in companies is to formulate, accept, launch, and follow a code of conduct. It is however important to realize that there are a lot of approaches to creating one. Semradova (2009) listed attitudes to formation of codes of conduct with reference to Nida-Rümelin (1996).

Nida-Rümelin (1996) thinks of the company code of conduct as a set of rules, rights and duties related to the company, its employees, job performance, and to the wider social environment, including the ecological dimension. Company codes of conduct may result from the dialogue between two worlds, that of economic issues and that of ethical demands of both the society and individuals. There are various approaches to creating company codes of conduct, including the following ones: operational, intentionalist, socio-economic, pragmatic, and social-ethical.

Nida-Rümelin (1996) explains that the operational approach refers to ethical dilemmas arising when an economically advantageous solution to a problem is compatible with legal requirement. Nevertheless, it is often perceived as unethical and against good manners. If this is the case, it is recommended to conduct an ethical discourse in order to reach a consensus. The consensus ought to be an expression of the will of all affected parties and it should conciliate them. Another attitude is intentionalist. It understands companies as moral persons and states that these persons have the same privileges, rights and duties as if they were individuals. Company philosophies, principles, values, standards, norms and objectives are defined, which influences the whole social environment of these companies. Social-economic approach is also frequently applied. It denies a simplified neo-classical idea that desire to own land and property is the basic driving motive of human behavior. On the other hand, human beings are influenced in their decision-making and behavior not only by economic and business objectives but also by their longing for respect and for social approval of their behavior. Pragmatic approach strives to introduce business ethics into university curricula and into job performance. It also helps constitute research, education, as well as meetings in companies which are meant to improve company codes of conduct: analyses of immoral behavior, summary and evaluation of problem solving case studies; analyses of current business practice; justification of widely accepted values in a democratic society; analyses of partial problems of economic behavior; etc. Last but not least, social-ethical approach, which is present above all in Christian social teaching, emphasizes the need to balance social responsibility and individual freedom.

Neo-Aristotelian attitude teaches that economics, ethics, and political science should not be separated as they are mutually related disciplines. They are considered to be complementary in what is known as practical philosophy. Its objective is the synthesis of economic, ethical and political theories in what would be a renewed link to the Aristotelian intellectual tradition. Philosophy and ethics deal with three mutually related areas of theoretical reflection: philosophy of culture as a positive part of ethical economy looks into business culture, which is not morally relevant, and its goal is to explain economic behavior; business ethics is a normative part of ethical economy, which explores ethical-cultural attitudes in society and formulates moral norms that regulate economic behavior; economic ontology is interested in economic, manufacturing, business and similar activities that belong to the area of Being.

In partial areas of ethics applied in business, i.e., in marketing, management and economic decision-making, there are enforced following principles: respect to the law (as the minimum of morality); principle of responsibility for products, advertisement, company procedures, processes, values, consequences, and behavior that may trespass the given legal framework; communication not only when solving dilemmas; an elaborated institutional dimension related to the performance of individuals in various positions; transparency of objectives, values, norms with respect to employees and company representatives as well as in relation to clients, the public and other companies; motivation as well as sanctions in the code of conduct; company education, social-psychological training; reflection and self-reflection of one's behavior, or ethical auditing.

Codes of conduct aim at fairness, honesty, respect for the law, quality of job performance, health and safety at workplace. Company codes of conduct treat conflicts of interest, corruption, etc. and they may be categorized into aspirational, educational, regulatory or combined. The aspirational codes testify to objectives, ideals and the general philosophy of the company. Educational codes form basic principles and rules of expected behavior, they provide comments and interpretations. Regulatory codes determine sets of detailed rules of professional behavior and serve as a reference in case a complaint must be solved. Frequently used combined codes include all the above mentioned aspects.

Codes of conduct are a source of public assessment, express professional socialization, may act as a prevention in relation to unethical behavior, they may improve the image of the company, increase its trustworthiness and be a basis for rectification in case of a fault.

6 Contents of Codes of Conduct: A Pilot Study

Most existing researches looking into codes of conduct in the first decade of twenty-first century, Canik (2007) mentions a Study of Code of Conduct Application done by Transparency International in cooperation with the University of Economics, Prague in 2005 and 2006, focused on the incidence of code of conduct existence in companies, organizations and institutions and the relation between their size and origin and their having their own code of conduct. It was also researched how long the company codes of conducts were—from one-page list of basic rules to brochures 10-plus pages long—and whether they were public or only restricted only to the company's employees.

The authors of this contribution would like to continue in these studies of codes of conduct. As the above mentioned study was done almost 10 years ago, it would be interesting to compare the development in this area in the Czech Republic in the last 10 years. The authors are only at the beginning and therefore have only conducted a pilot study so far.

The pilot study consisted of two analyses. The first one looked into 20 randomly selected companies with codes of conduct available to the public on the Internet while the latter analyzed codes of conduct (if there were any) of top 20 companies in the 2013 EVA (Economic Value Added) TOP 100 ranking of the most significant Czech companies. All available codes of conduct were thoroughly studied. In both parts of the pilot study the authors were trying to find answers to a premeditated set of questions. Later, the number of questions was limited to the following four queries:

1. Does the code of conduct have a relevant theoretical basis based on one of the above listed attitudes (see Sect. 5)?
2. Does the code of conduct include formulations related to corporate social responsibility, in particular its social and environmental parts?
3. Does the code of conduct respects human rights?
4. Are in the code of conduct explicitly included formulations related to customer satisfaction, or even their protection?

Four hypotheses (H) were proposed to be tested:

H_1: Most (i.e., more than 10 out of 20) of the examined codes of conduct are not based on any relevant business ethics theory.

H_2: Most of the examined codes of conduct apply corporate social responsibility in relation to environmental issues.

H_3: Most of the examined codes of conduct include references to observing human rights.

H_4: Most of the examined codes of conduct contain explicit formulations relating to customer satisfaction, or even to their safety.

Concerning the 20 randomly selected companies, the requirement was the existence of a publicly available code of conduct on the Internet. Therefore, the incidence of code of conduct existence in companies, organizations and institution was not the point here. The authors focus on the questions listed above.

Nevertheless, in the second part of the pilot study it was possible to determine how many of the top 20 EVA TOP 100 ranking companies have a publicly accessible code of conduct on the Internet. The incidence was 80 % as the authors did not find any reference to a code of conduct in case of four companies. Even so, it is a good result if compared with the Transparency International study figures, where the figures were 8.4 % (104 out of 1240) for the first half of 2006 and 10.3 % (59 out of 574) for the latter half of 2005.

In the case of 20 randomly selected companies only H1 was confirmed as there was only one company whose code of conduct was based on a relevant business ethics theory. H2, H3, and H4 disproved (Table 1).

In the case of the top 20 EVA TOP 100 ranking companies, 16 of them have a code of conduct although two of them share one (i.e., there were found and studied 15 different codes of conduct) and another company do not have its own code of conduct as it accepts a professional code of conduct created by a state institution. Concerning the hypotheses, H1 and H2 were confirmed. H3 would have been confirmed if only existing codes of conduct had taken into account as human rights

Table 1 Results of the pilot research—randomly selected sample of 20 companies

Relevant theoretical basis	Environment protection	Human rights protection	Customer satisfaction	Customer safety	Quality of services and solving complaints	Appointed ethics committee
1	9	4	10	5	4	1

Table 2 Results of the pilot research—EVA 100 TOP 20 companies

Relevant theoretical basis	Environment protection	Human rights protection	Customer satisfaction	Customer safety	Quality of services and solving complaints	Appointed ethics committee
0	11	10	6	6	3	0

were mentioned in 10 out of 16 (or rather 9 out of 15) codes of conduct. H4 was disproved even though some companies do not sell their products and services to individuals but rather corporate customers (Table 2).

7 Conclusion

Mature companies are aware of the fact that the ethical part of their performance is vital and include ethical education into their training programs. The most frequently formulated objectives of ethical education in companies are the following ones: stimulation of moral imagination; development of the ability to discern and anticipate ethical problems; development of analytical abilities; forming the sense of moral duty; support to the effort to understand others in case of disagreement; creating the environment that encourages faith in fair play and the sense of duty; strengthening the sense for norms of rightness so that the employees could behave in concord with the right norm and their conviction.

The pilot study suggests, though, that Czech companies still have much to improve. Of course, the pilot study sample was not representative but helped point out several interesting facts and problems to be studied and elaborated on in the years to come.

It was also very instrumental to compare various codes of conduct. It brought some noteworthy outcomes. The studied codes varied from very short, basic lists of 10 or so rules to very well-structured brochures divided into several relevant chapters embellished with pictures, tables and figures illustrating the contents. Further studies of the format and contents of company codes of conduct may bring interesting results. It also seems to be promising to look for cases of good practice in creating company codes of conduct. Consequently, the authors have been planning to focus on the following problem areas:

- Incidence of codes of conduct in Czech companies, organizations and institutions;
- Origin of codes of conduct: created by the company itself; adopted from its mother company; adopted from another company, organization, institution
- Contents of existing codes of conduct: solved problems (as suggested in the pilot study) and their division into chapters or individual rules; depth of proposed

solutions; FAQ (frequently asked questions); types of advisory or control bodies (ombudsman for ethics, outside consultants, ethical or assistance helpline)

- Format of company codes of conduct: short list of rules; structured text document; one-page poster; brochure with pictures, graphs, etc.
- Size of codes of conduct: up to one page; two to ten pages; more than ten pages

The results of the pilot study proved there is enough space for further study of this area. The authors are planning to start the main part of their research in the course of 2015.

References

Bowen, H. R. (2013). *The social responsibilities of the businessman*. Iowa City: University of Iowa Press.

Branco, M. C., & Rodrigues, L. L. (2007). Positioning stakeholder theory within the debate on corporate social responsibility. *Electronic Journal of Business Ethics and Organisation Studies EJBO, 12*(1), 5–15.

Business Leaders Forum. (n.d.). *What is CSR*, [online] Available at http://www.csr-online.cz/en/what-is-csr/. Accessed 26 Nov 2013.

Canik, P. (2007). *Eticky kodex: Ani alfa, ani omega, ale uzitecny nastroj* [Code of conduct: Neither an alpha, nor an omega, but a useful tool], [online] Available at http://www.canik.cz/2007/11/18/eticky-kodex-ani-alfa-ani-omega-ale-uzitecny-nastroj/. Accessed 21 Jan 2014.

Carroll, A. B. (1979). A three-dimensional conceptual model of corporate performance. *The Academy of Management Review, 4*(4), 497–505.

Fernández, A. M. L., & Rajagopal. (2014). Convergence of corporate social responsibility and business growth: An analytical framework. *International Journal of Business Excellence, 7*(6), 791–806.

Global Reporting Initiative. (2013). *G4 sustainability reporting guidelines*, [online] Available at https://www.globalreporting.org/resourcelibrary/GRIG4-Part1-Reporting-Principles-and-Standard-Disclosures.pdf. Accessed 27 Jan 2014.

Kacetl, J. (2011). *Obchodni a podnikatelska etika* [Business ethics]. Hradec Kralove: Gaudeamus.

Kasparova, K., & Kunz, V. (2013). *Moderní pristupy ke spolecenské odpovednosti firem a CSR reportování* [Modern approaches to corporate social responsibility and to CSR reporting]. Praha: Grada Publishing.

Kuldova, L. (2010). *Spolecenska odpovednost firem: Eticke podnikani a socialni odpovednost v praxi* [Corporate social responsibility: Ethical entrepreneurship and social responsibility in practice]. Plzen: OPS.

Madrakhimova, F. S. (2013). Evolution of the concept and definition of corporate social responsibility. *Global Conference on Business and Finance Proceedings, 8*(2), 113–118.

Masaka, D. (2008). Why enforcing corporate social responsibility (CSR) is morally questionable. *EJBO Electronic Journal of Business Ethics and Organization Studies, 13*(1), 13–21.

Nida-Rümelin, J. (Hrsg.). (1996). *Angewandte Ethik. Die Bereichsethiken und ihre theoretische Fundierung* [Applied ethics: Professional ethics and its theoretical basis] (pp. 290–344). Stuttgart: Kröner Verlag.

Porter, B. A. (2008). *The role of the tripartite audit function in securing corporate accountability*, [online] Available at http://papers.ssrn.com/sol3/papers.cfm?abstract_id=2046347. Accessed 23 Feb 2015.

Rolny, I., & Lacina, L. (2001). *Globalizace—etika—ekonomika* [Globalisation—Ethics—Economics]. Boskovice: Albert.

Semradova, I. (2009). Ethical aspects of corporate culture. *E + M Economics and Management, 4*, 69–76.

ThinkingShift. (2007). *The evolution of CSR*, [online] Available at http://thinkingshift.wordpress.com/2007/03/27/the-evolution-of-csr/. Accessed 26 Nov 2013.

Part II
Finance and Banking

Profits and Risks of Foreign Exchange Mortgage Loans: Case of Poland

Michał Buszko

Abstract This paper describes phenomenon of using of foreign currency mortgage loans for housing purposes in Poland. Such phenomenon appeared also in other developing countries of CEE (e.g., Hungary, Romania, Croatia, Serbia, Bulgaria) but at different scale, scope and consequences. The aim of this paper is to present the major issues of foreign currency mortgage loans in Poland, the conditions and reasons of their spreading, their relative benefits and costs and characteristics of risk created by such loans for whole banking system in Poland. In the paper, the author will enclose the results of data analysis for Polish financial system, mortgage loans market, as well as foreign exchange rates. The paper will contain also the author's analysis of effectiveness of repayment of fx mortgage loans (CHF and EUR) in Poland versus PLN loans. The results of the author's research in general demonstrate that foreign exchange mortgages benefits depends primarily on the exchange rate on the date of taking the loan. The main conclusion from the research is that foreign currency mortgage loans are relatively beneficial but they create significant potential risk to the economic safety of the Polish households as well as whole banking system.

Keywords Foreign currency loans • Exchange rate • Risk

1 Introduction

Fast growing Polish economy, increasing employment and a raise of salaries as well as good financial results of Polish commercial banks allowed engaging unusual value of debt in financing of development of Polish real estate market. The safety, stability and good funding access of Polish banking sector led to easing off credit policy and reduction of credit spreads. Such conditions convinced households to take loans to buy new apartments or build new houses. The major problem of financing real property purchase in Poland at that time was a relatively high level of

M. Buszko (✉)
Department of Financial Management, Nicolaus Copernicus University in Toruń, Toruń, Poland
e-mail: mibus@econ.umk.pl

© Springer International Publishing Switzerland 2016

M.H. Bilgin et al. (eds.), *Business Challenges in the Changing Economic Landscape - Vol. 1*, Eurasian Studies in Business and Economics 2/1,
DOI 10.1007/978-3-319-22596-8_9

nominal as well as real interest rates for Polish zloty (PLN). This phenomenon was rather typical for emerging markets with fast-developing but inflated economies. Simultaneously, it raised the cost of loans and hindered development of mortgage loans market. At the same time one could observe significantly lower interest rates on euro (EUR), Swiss franc (CHF) or Japanese yen (JPY) but also quick appreciation of the Polish zloty versus such currencies. As the commercial banks in Poland had good access to the international interbank market, mostly through foreign parent companies, they started to sell intensively loans denominated or indexed in foreign currencies (predominantly in CHF). The peak period for such loans occurred in second and third quarter of 2008 when Swiss currency and euro reached historical minimum pricings in PLN. Within 3 years foreign currencies denominated mortgage loans had dominated mortgage loans segment as well as total assets of the banking sector in Poland. At the same time stability and profitability of Polish commercial banks started to be strongly dependent on the condition of international interbank market as well as exchange rate of CHF/PLN and EUR/PLN. The foreign currency risk of foreign currency mortgage loans was materialized just in July 2008, when the 4-years PLN appreciation trend had reverted. Due to abrupt increase of the value of Swiss franc and euro, foreign currency denominated loans installments have increased significantly transforming partially foreign currency risk into credit risk and exposing whole banking sector in Poland to the systemic risk thanks to the scale and number of banks engaged. The major problem for Polish borrowers and creditors was primarily an extraordinary increase of LtV ratio, which have reached levels strongly over 100 % and thus determined potential immediate bankruptcy in case of delays with repayment of such loans. This negative condition was partially compensated by a strong decrease of interest rates in Switzerland and Eurozone (and hence LIBOR CHF and EURIBOR), which led to reduction of interest paid on loans. In fact, such reduction helped to lower the monthly installments of loans and keep them at the level possible to carry by most of the borrowers. Nonetheless, the young age of the portfolio of foreign currency mortgage loans, long maturity of loans (25–30 years), excessive value of loans with LtV $>$ 100 %, strong dependence on international interbank market have created risk to the whole banking sector.

The aim of the paper is to characterize the specificity of Polish foreign exchange mortgage loans market, to present the role, influence and conditions of granting such loans, as well as to characterize their benefits and risks from the point of view of borrowers and creditors.

2 Literature Review

The problem of foreign exchange loans risks was quite commonly described and analysed in Poland and CEE countries by many professionals. As in many countries in Europe the consequences of subprime crisis led to disruption of local borrowing markets due to excessive use of foreign currencies to finance mortgage loans, this problem was also investigated by academics and researchers. Ranciere et al. (2010) analysed currency mismatch and investigated its influence onto systemic risk and economic growth at macro and micro level. Yesin (2013) described the problem of foreign currency loans in different countries in Europe, presenting differences in currency mismatch level between Western Europe and CEE countries. Szpunar (2012) and Szpunar and Głogowski (2012) indicated the dependencies between foreign exchange loans and systemic risk as well as current consequences of foreign currency borrowing in chosen countries. Buszko (2013a, b) presented the problems of foreign exchange loans hedging in Poland and an analysis of their profitability. Brzoza-Brzezina et al. (2014) investigated how foreign currency loans affect the transmission of monetary policy and their impact on effectiveness of macroprudential policy. Brzoza-Brzezina et al. (2010) analysed potential of substitutability between domestic and foreign currency loans in four biggest Central European countries. The bank-level perspective of foreign currency lending was analysed by Brown and De Haas (2010). The determinants of foreign currency borrowings by private sector in the new EU member states and the different patterns of such borrowings were investigated by Rosenberg and Tirpak (2008).

3 Methodology

In the first part of the paper the author explains the conditions and reasons of using foreign currency loans, specially focusing on Polish banking sector. An interest disparity and an influence on developing CHF and EUR mortgage loans in Poland are presented here. Then, upon using banking data, one conducts descriptive analysis of the role and significance of the foreign currency mortgage loans, as well as analyses time, maturity and LtV parameters. Then the paper characterizes conditions of an exchange of Polish zloty for CHF and EUR, i.e., most important currencies in mortgages in Poland. The author presents the exchange rate trends and calculates relative cost-effectiveness of loans on account of variable exchange rates. Finally, the paper contains the costs and benefits of foreign currency mortgage loans upon repayment analysis prepared by the author. The results are compared with the expenditures related to PLN mortgage loans. At the end of the paper the author presents conclusions.

4 The Findings

4.1 Foreign Currency Loans

Foreign currency denominated loans are granted by commercial banks mostly to finance and hedge the transactions of foreign trade, to support foreign investments of domestic companies, to refinance operating activities of foreign subsidiaries or to provide liquidity to other banks. Primarily such loans are destined to companies conducting international operations. In recent years foreign currency loans proliferated also amongst the individuals. In Europe foreign currency loans, especially in CHF, were commonly sold by Austrian banks, which offered them to Austrian citizens working and getting incomes in Switzerland in CHF. Due to interest rates disparity this type of loans become more and more widespread. As Austrian banks started conducting intensive expansion in CEE countries, they also started to sell foreign currencies loans in emerging markets like Poland (Szpunar 2012). At present, in many countries of CEE domestic households instead of companies predominantly use foreign currency loans to purchase, build, or renovate apartments or houses. The major reason for such loans is to reduce cost of installments due to lower interest rates of major European currencies against emerging markets currencies. In modern history of Poland neither central bank nor interbank interest rates have been lower comparing to that in Eurozone or Switzerland (Fig. 1).

Analyzing Polish financial market one may say that the primary factor determining the foreign currency borrowing is general level of interest rates as well as disparity of such rates versus local currency. Due to scope of disparity for Swiss franc, ranging between 2 and 6 p.p. as well as the general extremely low interest rate level in comparison to other European currencies, Swiss franc became prime long-term borrowing currency in Poland. Generally, it was used for mortgage loans of households, however there was also noted some minor use by non-financial companies as well as by consumers to finance e.g., a purchase of cars. EUR denominated loans were used mostly for financing export–import activities of companies.

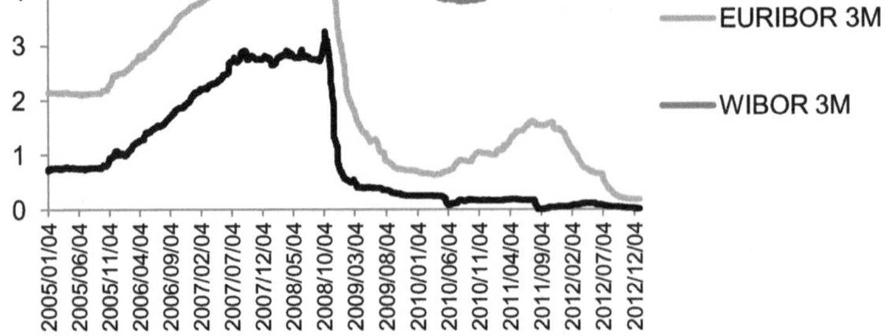

Fig. 1 Interbank interest rates in Poland, Eurozone and Switzerland (in %)

4.2 Foreign Currency Mortgage Loans in Poland

Due to very good economic condition of the whole banking sector, its stability and improving macroeconomic situation in Poland due to joining EU, as well as easy access to the international interbank market, very attractive interest rates of foreign currencies and competitive pressures led majority of banks in Poland to sell mortgages in Swiss franc. At the same time, to enlarge their market share, they eased policy of credit rating of borrowers as well as reduced credit spreads, leveling them off with the Polish zloty mortgages. Because most of banks in Poland were foreign owned, they could get favorable funding and refinancing facilities in CHF or EUR (Table 1). The dominant share of foreign banks in local banking sectors is a typical phenomenon for CEE countries, and hence it influenced the foreign currency borrowing in most countries of the region (Szpunar and Głogowski 2012).

Apart from mentioned factors, the condition, which strongly backed up the development of foreign currency loans in Poland and other countries of CEE, was strong appreciation of local currencies 2004–2008. Falling installments value was convincing Poles to borrow Swiss francs or less frequently euros instead of Polish zloty.

Having a good access to foreign funding (from parent companies or interbank market) most of commercial banks in Poland focused on mortgage loans in foreign currencies, which dominated mortgage market. In period 2005–2008 very few commercial entities offered mortgages exclusively in Polish zloty. The premises for which banks decided to promote foreign currencies loans were: getting additional profits due to currency exchange, creating artificially creditworthiness of borrowers and hence increasing value of the loans as well as getting higher profits from sales of insurance of foreign currency loans. As the lowest interest rate currency in Europe during the considered period was Swiss franc, which in 2005–2008 was strongly depreciating versus Polish zloty and was not particularly volatile or unpredictable in pricing, it became dominant foreign currency used for mortgages. Despite close connections of Polish economy with euro zone countries euro was used marginally until 2010. Apart from bank pressure on selling CHF loans, the dominance of CHF on Polish mortgage loans came from clients demanding CHF-denominated loans as there was a substantial difference in installments' value between Swiss franc and Polish zloty. In case of an average 20-years mortgage loan of approx. €62.5K with credit spread of 2 p.p. taken in August 2008, i.e., (during the lowest rate of CHF), the installment of a mortgage in PLN was approx. 23 % higher in the moment of taking the loan than in Swiss currency (Buszko 2013a). At the same time use of other foreign currencies for credits was

Table 1 Share of assets of banking sector in Poland controlled by foreign entities

Year	2005	2006	2007	2008	2009	2010	2011	2012
Share	70.0 %	69.6 %	70.9 %	72.3 %	68.1 %	66.2 %	65.0 %	63.6 %

Source: Polish Financial Supervision Authority

minor if not exceptional. Due to small interest rates disparity and significant level of other credit costs such as fx spreads, mortgage loans in euro were more expensive than in Polish currency and hence they were not used until late 2008 (Table 2).

Considering development of foreign mortgage loans in Poland the most intensive increase of number and value of loans was noted in years 2006 and 2008. In the year 2007 one could observe lower increase both the number and value of new loans what was mostly caused by implementation in July 2006 Recommendation S of Polish Financial Supervision Authority (KNF), which imposed on banks additional requirements when giving mortgage loans denominated or indexed in foreign currencies. From 2012 foreign mortgage loans were severely limited due to regulations of KNF giving possibility to grant loans only to persons earning money in foreign currencies (euro).

Table 2 Fx mortgage loans against other bank assets in Poland (bln €, %)

	2005	2006	2007	2008	2009	2010	2011	2012
Fx mortgage loans for households	8.1	12.5	16.3	34.0	35.5	42.3	49.5	44.6
CHF	nd	nd	nd	33.0	33.2	36.9	40.9	36.2
EUR	nd	nd	nd	0.7	1.9	4.9	8.0	7.8
Fx loans in total	17.2	22.6	27.1	51.8	52.8	63.2	76.7	69.0
Share of fx mortgage loans in total fx loans	46.9 %	55.3 %	60.1 %	65.7 %	67.3 %	67.0 %	64.5 %	64.6 %
Mortgage loans for households in total	12.7	19.6	29.4	48.8	54.5	66.9	79.7	80.5
Share of fx mortgage loans in total mortgage loans	63.5 %	63.9 %	55.3 %	69.7 %	65.2 %	63.3 %	62.0 %	55.4 %
Loans in total	64.6	80.7	106.9	163.4	178.5	196.9	227.8	233.8
Share of fx mortgage loans for households in total loans	12.5 %	15.5 %	15.2 %	20.8 %	19.9 %	21.5 %	21.7 %	19.1 %
Total assets of banking sector in Poland	146.6	170.5	198.9	259.8	265.2	289.9	323.7	338.2
Share of fx mortgage loans for households in total assets of banking sector in Poland	5.5 %	7.3 %	8.2 %	13.1 %	13.4 %	14.6 %	15.3 %	13.2 %

Note: All data expressed in € are converted from Polish zloty at an average rate for 2005–2012 EUR/PLN = 4.00. *Source*: Polish Financial Supervision Authority

The mortgage loans in foreign currencies were mostly taken to buy medium and high value real property, thus their average value per loan was considerably higher comparing for Polish zloty loans. Until the end of 2012 the average value per loan for mortgage loans in CHF, EUR and PLN reached respectively: €62.3K, €69.1K and €35.4K. Considering the value of a single loan the most often were given mortgage loans in PLN up to €25K (approx 47 % of loans) and such tendency were also observed in case of loans in foreign currencies, however the share was considerably lower (approx. 27.3 % of loans). Taking into account the total value of loans, for PLN the biggest share had mortgages of a value €25–50K (approx 30.6 % of value of all loans in PLN) while for foreign currencies the dominant were loans of a value €125K and more (33.3 % of all loans in foreign currencies). Small value foreign currency loans are then less frequent than loans in Polish currency, and they are usually taken for high-value investments (dominance of a value of large loans). Analyzing the maturity of mortgage loans in Poland, both loans denominated in PLN and in foreign currencies are taken most often for 25–30 years (30.9 % of all loans in PLN and 27.4 % of all loans in foreign currencies). They concentrate respectively 43.4 % of total value of loans in PLN and 34.3 % of total value of loans in foreign currencies. One should also note that foreign currencies loans usually have very long maturities, in majority exceeding maturity of loans in PLN. Apart from that, either for loans in Polish currency or foreign currencies one may find loans with maturity more than 30 years. Loans in CHF and EUR usually repaid in period exceeding 30 years concentrated in 2012 10.4 % all loans in foreign currencies, and 16.4 % of total value of such loans. Loans in Polish zloty represented respectively 5.2 % and 9.2 %. The prolonged period of borrowing (30 years or more) was quite often proposed by commercial banks in Poland to reduce the value of monthly installments and hence artificially raise creditworthiness of the borrowers.

Very important feature of Polish mortgage foreign exchange loans is a relation of the loan to the value of the credited real property, expressed by LtV ratio. In this area, loans given in foreign currency differ significantly from loans in local currency. In case of PLN approx. 7.9 % of all loans was given with LtV ratio exceeding 100 %, while 23.3 % of all foreign currencies mortgage loans exceeded such ratio. Considering total value of loans with $LtV > 100$ % Polish currency borrowings got a share 13.4 % while foreign currencies loans 38.2 %. Thus, one may find mortgage loans market in Poland as not properly collateralized and risky in case of default of borrowers. Such excessive value of loans in relation to credited real property value was caused by two main factors, i.e., internal credit policy of banks, which were eager to lend money up to 130 % of LtV when the real property prices were quickly increasing in Poland in 2005–2008 as well as changes of foreign exchange rate of CHF/PLN which made banks to translate loans in CHF into PLN at inflated rate (after February 2009).

4.3 Foreign Currency Mortgage Loans and Exchange Rates

A major problem of mortgage loan market given in foreign currencies is a variable exchange rate of Polish zloty toward other currencies. Since 12 April 2000 a floating foreign exchange rate regime is applied in Poland and the exchange rates of CHF/PLN and EUR/PLN for period 2005–2012 presents Fig. 2.

From the point of view of stability of banking sector and whole financial system in Poland the biggest concern is about the loans taken in 2008, when the pricing CHF/PLN reached historical minimum and when the highest volume and value of foreign exchange loans took place. As majority of foreign currency loans (both in CHF and EUR) in Poland are serviced in Polish zloty, i.e., they were paid out and are being repaid in Polish zloty, the exchange rate at the beginning of the borrowing period as well as its change until maturity determines the total costs of borrowing. During the period of low pricing of foreign currency the borrower has to take higher value of a loan to get sufficient amount in local currency to purchase the real estate.

If we assume that fundamental long-term exchange rate for EUR and CHF is a median value of the daily rates for a long period, i.e., whole period of floating exchange rate regime in Poland (12.04.2000–31.12.2012) and the long-term mortgage loans will be paid at rates oscillating around median value, we may determine relative cost-effectiveness of borrowing in foreign currencies. Subtracting median value from the spot rate and division by median value indicates the relative benefit or loss due to the exchange rate in the moment of taking a mortgage loan. As in Poland majority of CHF loans were taken in period 2006–2008, when Swiss currency was low priced against Polish zloty, such borrowings generate relative losses (additional costs) due to a change of exchange rate. Particularly, the loans

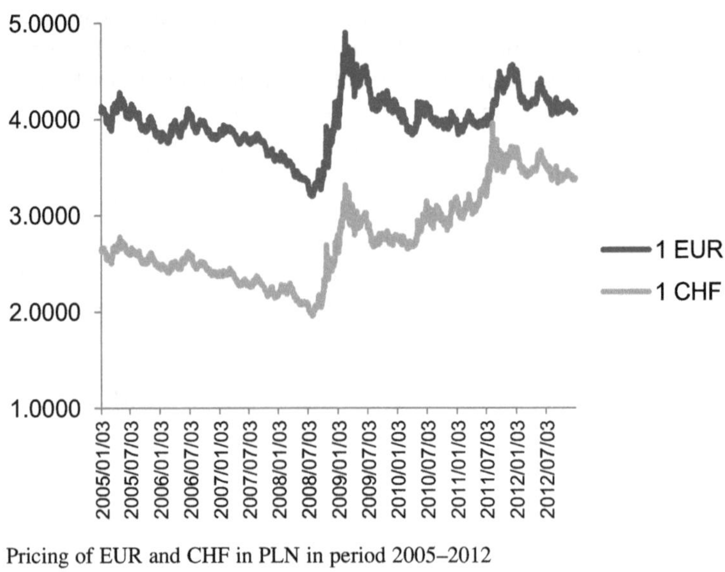

Fig. 2 Pricing of EUR and CHF in PLN in period 2005–2012

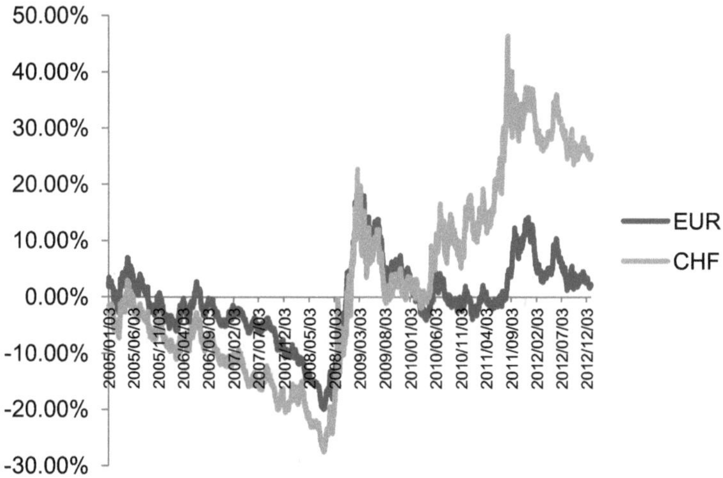

Fig. 3 Relative cost-effectiveness of borrowing in foreign currencies

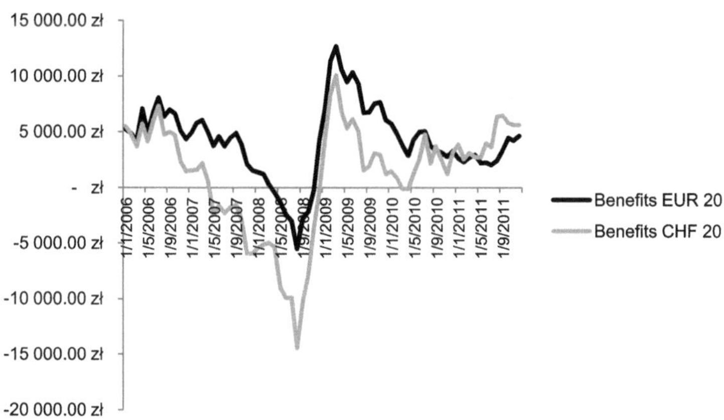

Fig. 4 Total benefits of 20-years foreign currency loans

given at the end of July 2008, i.e., when Swiss franc in Poland fall to the historical minimum, are prone to highest loss (approx. 27.5 %) (Fig. 3).

In case of EUR-denominated loans, their substantial part was created in 2010 and 2011 what has made them relatively neutral to the banking system considering potential change of EUR/PLN exchange rate and the change of LtV. The Fig. 4 indicates that the best periods for taking loans in CHF and EUR were February 2009 and August 2011, however during both periods availability of Swiss franc financing was already strongly limited.

The borrowers taking loans in CHF in period 2006–2008 were particularly exposed to the change of exchange rate, as they got payment of the loan counted

Table 3 Statistics of CHF/PLN and EUR/PLN exchange 2005–2012

	Range (%)	St. dev.	Coefficient of variation (%)	St. dev. of daily returns (%)	Average daily return (%)	Max daily return (%)	Min daily return (%)
CHF	101.89	0.4541	16.38	0.95	0.70	5.84	−7.51
EUR	53.00	0.2782	6.99	0.70	0.51	4.06	−4.49

at a very low rate CHF/PLN. The foreign exchange risk materialized quite soon, i.e., in February 2009, when Swiss currency value increased its price by approx. 69.3 % and then in August 2011 when CHF was even more expensive (by 101.9 %) in comparison to July 2008. The volatility of exchange rate of euro against Polish zloty was considerably lower and not particularly hit Polish borrowers. Nonetheless in 2012 banks ceased giving mortgage loans in euro to retail clients. Table 3 presents major characteristics of CHF and EUR in relation to Polish Zloty.

The problem of materialization of an exchange rate risk and its influence on the borrowers in Poland (and similarly in other CEE countries) started to be a subject of many concerns and discussions due to lack of hedging instruments which would be accessible and safely implemented by individuals or households to protect against unwanted movements of currency prices. Apart from CHF/PLN futures contracts on Warsaw Stock Exchange, which can be used practically by professional investors, there are no either financial or legal instruments allowing private borrowers in Poland to manage the risk of foreign exchange rate as well as foreign interest rate change (Buszko 2013b).[1]

4.4 *Benefits of Foreign Currency Mortgage Loans*

To assess relative benefits of foreign currencies mortgage loans against loans in Polish zloty and to find their global effectiveness from the point of view of borrowers, the author of this paper proposed mathematical model of repayment of both types of loans. The model features are as follows:

Relative benefits of foreign currency (FC) mortgage loan = Total repayment of PLN mortgage loan in PLN—Total repayment of FC mortgage loan in PLN

where

Total repayment of PLN mortgage loan = Sum of monthly installments in PLN repaid from the date of taking the loan until 30.06.2014

[1] As a rule borrowers do not have the access to the fx derivatives such as forwards. That means majority of foreign exchange loans are unhedged and prone to both type of risks. Just minor part of euro mortgage loans is partially covered by euro denominated earnings of borrowers or members of their families working in Eurozone countries.

Total repayment of FC mortgage loan = Sum of monthly installments in FC multiplied by exchange rate of PLN repaid from the date of taking the loan until 30.06.2014

Monthly installments were calculated using formula[2]:

$$Installment = \frac{\text{loan balance} * \text{monthly rate}}{1\text{-}\ (1 + \text{monthly rate})^{\text{- number of payments}}} \quad (1)$$

To investigate the effectiveness of foreign currency against domestic borrowings the author calculated value of installments upon actual market interest rates as well as currency exchange rates and then found total repayment values for both types of loans on the day 30.06.2014. The calculation was made for 100,000 PLN (approx. €25,000) of loans taken out in period December 2005—December 2011. The benefits and losses of foreign currency loans were calculated upon exchange rates EUR/PLN and CHF/PLN on the day of the payment of each installment. As the installments of mortgage loans are usually paid at the beginning of each month, hence the author assumed an average from the first 6 days of each month as the exchange rate to convert value of foreign currencies installments into PLN. The average rate was further adjusted by bid-offer currency spread of 7 %, which is a common spread used by banks in Poland. All the calculations were made with assumption of variable interest rate CHF LIBOR 3M, EURIBOR 3M, WIBOR 3M plus fixed credit spread 2 p.p. A variable reference rate plus fixed credit spread is a typical formula of calculation of mortgage loans installments in Poland. The author's analysis was conducted for borrowings with maturity of 20 and 30 years, which are most common chosen periods for crediting residential real estates in Poland. The benefits were assessed also with use of LtV ratio, i.e., a value of remaining debt on 30.06.2014 in relation to initial amount of loan.

Considering the total benefits from foreign currency mortgage loans taken in 2006–2011 and measured as a difference between cash outflows due to repayment of Polish zloty loan and foreign currency loan (EUR or CHF) we may distinguish three subperiods. The first one is a period of a surplus of foreign exchange loans, the second is a subperiod of losses and the third is again a period of a surplus. In case of 20-years loans the first one lasted until April 2007 for CHF borrowings and to March 2009 for EUR. The second period, in which loans taken by borrowers have been generating losses, lasts until December 2008 for EUR borrowings and January 2009 for CHF. After those dates borrowers taking loans in foreign currencies were obtaining benefits (cash savings) due to lower installments comparing to PLN loans. The worst period for taking currency loan was in case of both currencies July 2008 and the best February 2009. It's worth noting that EUR borrowers obtained higher benefits (12,725 zł on each 100,000 zł of loan) than CHF borrowers (10,090 zł on each 100,000 zł of loan) for loans taken in February 2009. Also, EUR

[2] Each quarter installments were recalculated according to the change of the reference rates (WIBOR 3M, LIBOR 3M, EURIBOR 3M) to reflect actual crediting conditions in Poland.

loans taken in July 2008 brought lower global losses comparing to CHF (−5516 zł vs. −14,466 zł) (Fig. 4).

From the point of view of borrowers 30-years loans were more beneficial than those with maturity of 20 years. Firstly, for CHF borrowings the period of losses begins in may 2008, i.e., 1 year later than for 20-years loans, what in turns increases the number of borrowers having cheaper loans than loans in PLN. Secondly, 30-years EUR borrowings on 30.06.2014 do not generate relative losses at all. The repayment value is in their case lower than for PLN loans independently on time of starting the borrowing. Similarly to 20-years loans, the best period for taking 30-years loans was January 2009, while the worst July 2008 for both currencies. The sum of benefits obtained by EUR borrowers taking loan in January 2009 were 13,086 zł vs. 12,239 zł for CHF and the sum of losses for those starting with a loan in January 2009 was −4351 zł (only CHF) (Fig. 5).

The average level of benefits obtained by borrowers which took loans from 12.2005 to 12.2010 was for 20-years EUR loans 4173 zł and for CHF loans 1162 zł. In case of 30-years borrowings the corresponding amounts were 6693 zł for EUR and 6053 zł for CHF.

Figures 6 and 7 present benefits and losses for 20 and 30-years loans obtained per installment according to the period of taking the loan.

As foreign exchange loans can be beneficial financial solutions for Polish borrowers with, one has to note that the majority of such loans, especially denominated in CHF were taken just in the period of losses (2007–2008). Upon the presented analysis of total benefits one may find that Swiss currency loans turned out to be less profitable than EUR borrowings, which until 2009 had been rarely used. The crucial factor determining the decision about currency of mortgage loan was then a value of installment at the moment of taking the loan, which in the period of losses was the lowest for CHF products, but not the possibility or potential of installment's change.

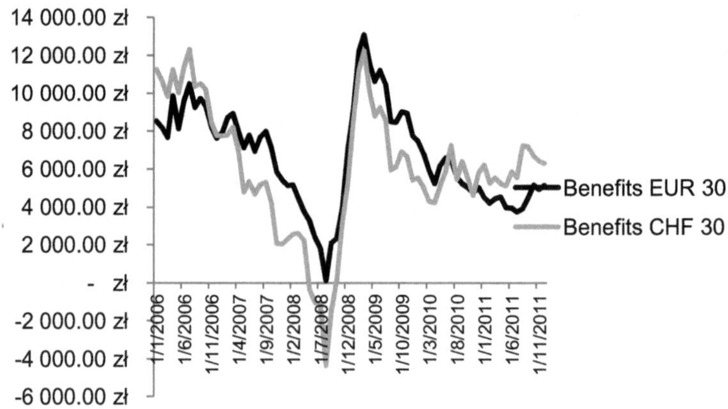

Fig. 5 Total benefits of 30-years foreign currency loans

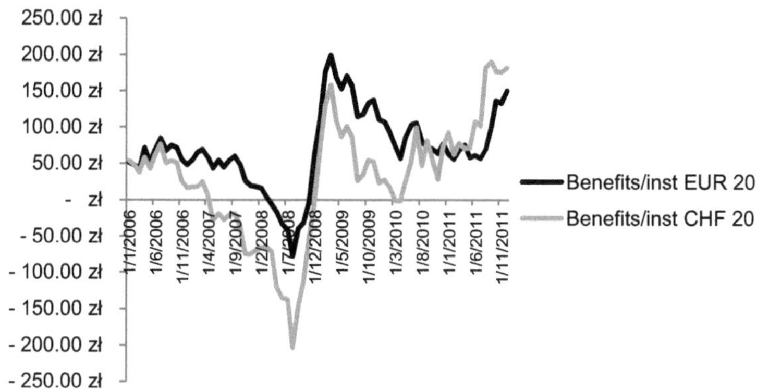

Fig. 6 Benefits per installment of 20-years foreign currency loans

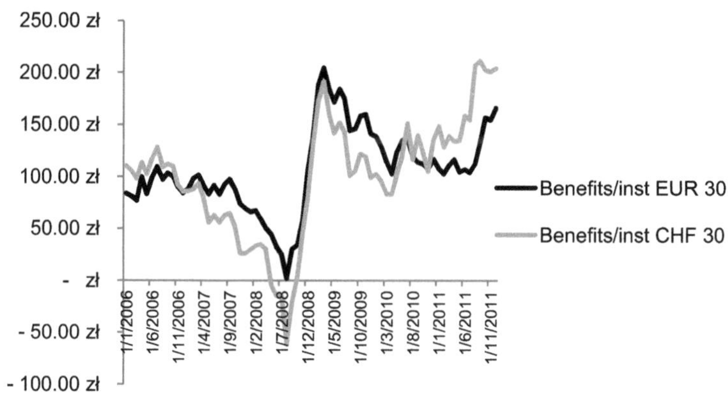

Fig. 7 Benefits per installment of 30-years foreign currency loans

When analyzing the benefits of foreign currency loans, it's worth to investigate also the general level of debt remaining to repay. In case of currency loans its value is usually primarily dependent on the exchange rate. Thus, one may expect relatively high volatility of debt to repay during increased volatility of the currency, and then increased risk of the credit ability of the borrower.

In case of both 20 and 30-years loans one can observe high level of LtV for CHF loans, which are derived from borrowings starting during the low pricing of EUR and CHF (at the historical minimal rate of CHF/PLN). In case of 20-years CHF loans borrowers taking a loan in July 2008 had to repay on 30.06.2014 130 % of the initial value of the loan. The euro borrowers had to repay 99.4 %. At the same time, lowest level of LtV and hence total repayment risk had PLN loans, where the debt to repay on 30.06.2014 constituted approx. 77 % of the initial value from July 2008. Nonetheless, in case of foreign currency loans one could find in time ratio LtV below the PLN loans. E.g. such situation took place at the beginning of 2009 i.e., when mortgages were taken during maximal pricing of euro (Fig. 8).

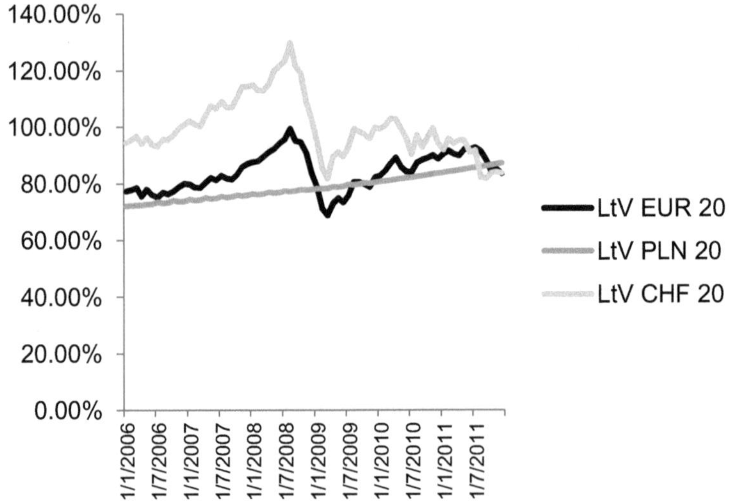

Fig. 8 LtV for 20-years loans

When analysing 30-years loans, one can find much higher LtV level for currency borrowings, especially CHF. Certainly, the increased period of loan repayment keep elevated level of debt as the dominant part of the installment takes interest. Therefore, a higher level of debt is dependent on exchange rate risk. In case of 30-years borrowings, as in the previous case, the most risky turned out to be 30 years CHF loans taken in August 2008, which on 30.06.2014 were requiring to repay 154 % of initial value of the loan. The euro-denominated loans reached approx. 117 % of LtV at the same time. Borrowers taking euro loans at the beginning of 2009 got on 30.06.2014 lower LtV ratio than Polish zloty borrowers (Fig. 9).

4.5 Foreign Currencies Mortgage Loans and the Risk

As it was stated before, the foreign currency mortgage loans are primarily exposing households onto the exchange rate and, to a lesser extent, foreign interest rate risk. Apart from borrowers, foreign currency loans substantially expose crediting banks onto different types of risk, e.g., indirect credit risk, concentration risk, funding risk, refinancing risk, foreign currency liquidity risk, operational risk, leverage risk, legal risk, tax risk, reputation risk or socio-political risk (Pann et al. 2010). Such risks may arise simultaneously and in case of a large share of foreign mortgage loans in the sector's portfolio they may lead to the failure of the whole banking sector. In fact, risks related to foreign currencies make domestic banking sector more prone to the conditions of international interbank market and more dependent on the international hedge instruments. At the same time domestic banks become

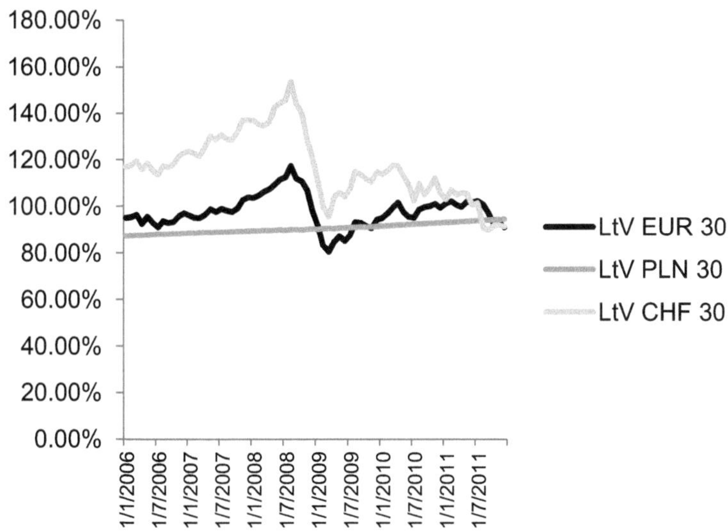

Fig. 9 LtV for 30-years loans

less dependent of monetary policy and supporting instruments of domestic central bank. Hence, we may find systemic influence of the foreign currency mortgage loans.

In contrary to most of them Polish banks and borrowers are exposed primarily on the CHF exchange risk (as Hungary). As Swiss currency deposits are not available in Poland, such loans (mortgages) are primarily financed on the interbank market (from the parent banks). Despite Polish banking sector keeps more assets in Swiss franc than liabilities, what partially hedges it against credit risk of foreign currency loans and brings profits during the increasing pricing of Swiss currency, such assets are consisting mostly of loans to unhedged households. That makes polish banking sector particularly vulnerable to the change of exchange rate of CHF. Moreover, the risk of exchange rate is reinforced through the fact that substantial part of the currency mortgage loans (47.5 % of total volume and 28.8 total value at the end of 2012) had been given to the borrowers of low and medium incomes (up to €1000 per household). That part of loans may become not-performing when exchange rates of foreign currencies go up and remain at inflated level during medium or long period.

Until now a share of non-performing mortgage loans in foreign currencies remains low and stable. At the end of 2012 it was 1.85 % against 4.14 % for loans in Polish currency. In both cases non-performing loans are not strongly influencing condition of banking sector in Poland. In fact, a major condition of a low level of non-performing loans in foreign currencies in Poland is a consequence of linking foreign exchange mortgage loans costs directly to market interest rates on a basis variable reference rate plus fixed spread (e.g., CHF LIBOR 3M + spread). Therefore, the strong appreciation of Swiss currency toward Polish zloty was substantially compensated by a fall of market interest rates (from 3.25 % to 0.0033 %). Such fall helped to service better foreign currency loans. Different situation was in Hungary, where due to a different credit pricing regime, Hungarian banks set unilaterally the interest rates in separation to the market conditions. The fall of EUR and CHF interest rates was not reflected in fall of installments paid by Hungarian borrowers leading to substantial share of non-performing loans (Szpunar 2012).

5 Summary and Conclusions

Foreign exchange mortgage loans which in Polish banking sector are substantially responsible for systemic risk were given in several previous years (2005–2010). The main risk factor is the increased volatility of Swiss currency and the high debt level originating from the high valuation of franc. In case of appearance of any circumstances leading to a cease of the repayment, the borrowers would not be able to repay them due to excessive rate of LtV and hence to continue normal economic existence. As most of the loans have very long maturity (25–30 years), they will be prevalent in polish banking sector long in the future. The major condition reducing their risk is a fall of exchange rate of CHF. In such circumstances the debt burden will fall and some part of the loans will be converted into Polish zloty.

The dominance of the CHF loans is unfavorable in Polish banking sector due to the higher volatility and exchange risk of Swiss currency in relation to Polish zloty. A very high increase of the value of the Swiss currency between July 2008 and September 2011 (approx. 100 %) did not raise a share of non-performing loans in francs. A majority of loans in foreign currency was taken when CHF/PLN rate was about historical minimal value, what makes such loans less profitable then in Polish zloty. The notable effect of rising price of Swiss currency in Poland is substantial increase of the ratio of LtV, which for most loans is now exceeding 100 %. That makes most of the CHF loans practically impossible to repay if the contracts are going to be denounced.

The value of the equity in banking sector in Poland does not cover foreign currency exposures. In case of default of borrowers it would strongly influence functioning of all banks in Poland. Due to foreign exchange mortgage loans Polish banking sector is less dependent on monetary policy and financial support of National Bank of Poland. The borrowers cannot translate currency of the loans due to high pricing of CHF against EUR and PLN, hence they have to keep the risk of exchange rate of Swiss currency. Due to lack of earnings in Swiss currency Polish borrowers cannot use the natural hedge for CHF exchange rate risk. National Bank of Poland as well as Polish Financial Supervisory Commission actively support reduction of foreign exchange mortgage loans in Poland. The systemic risk is related to the foreign currency loans, especially mortgages, require complex instruments of measurement, taking into account the exchange rate regime (floating vs. fixed), volatility of the currency, and concentration of loans in the banking sector.

References

Brown, M., & De Haas, R. (2010). *Foreign currency lending in emerging Europe: Bank-level evidence* (Working Paper, No 122). European Bank For Reconstruction and Development.

Brzoza-Brzezina, M., Chmielewski, T., & Niedzwiedzinska, J. (2010). *Substitution between domestic and foreign currency loans in Central Europe. Do central banks matter?* (Working Paper Series, 1187). European Central Bank.

Brzoza-Brzezina, M., Kolasa, M., & Makarski, K. (2014). *Monetary and macroprudential policy with foreign currency loans* (NBP Working Paper, No. 184). National Bank of Poland, Economic Institute.

Buszko, M. (2013a). Walutowe kredyty mieszkaniowe we franku szwajcarskim—zagrożenie czy źródło korzyści kredytobiorców? [Foreign currency mortgage loans in Swiss franc—A threat or source of benefits for borrowers]. *Copernican Journal of Finance and Accounting, 2*(2), 27–43.

Buszko, M. (2013b). Ograniczanie wydatków z tytułu spłaty walutowych kredytów mieszkaniowych [Limiting of repayment expenditures of foreign currency mortgage loans]. *Annales Universitatis Mariae Curie-Skłodowska Sectio H: Oeconomia, 47*(3), 77–88.

Pann, J., Seliger, R., & Ubeleis, J. (2010). Foreign currency lending in Central, Eastern and Southeastern Europe: The case of Austrian banks. *Financial Stability Report, 20*, 56–76.

Ranciere, R., Tornell, A., & Vamvakidis, A. (2010). Currency mismatch, systemic risk and growth in emerging Europe. *Economic Policy, 25*(64), 597–658.

Rosenberg, B. C., & Tirpak, M. (2008). *Determinants of foreign currency borrowing in the new member states of the EU* (IMF Working Paper, WP/08/173).

Szpunar, P. (2012). System risk lessons from FX loans in Central and Eastern Europe. [online]. Accessed April 16, 2014, from http://www.centralbanking.com/central-banking-journal/feature/2175181/risk-lessons-loans-central-eastern-europe

Szpunar, P. J., & Głogowski, A. (2012, December). Lending in foreign currencies as a systemic risk. *Macro-prudential Commentaries*, European Systemic Risk Board, Issue no 4.

Yesin, P. (2013). Foreign currency loans and systemic risk in Europe. *Federal Reserve Bank of St. Louis Review, 95*(3), 219–235.

Graphs in Annual Reports of Banks: Trustworthy or Not?

Laivi Laidroo and Nele Tamme

Abstract The objective of this paper is to analyse the graph use in annual reports of Central and Eastern European (CEE) banks during 2006–2011 and to determine the extent of impression management strategies employed. The results reveal distinct differences in CEE banks' graph use compared to other types of companies covered in previous studies. These include lower levels of graph use, differences in identified key financial variables (KFVs), and more extensive use of activity and macroeconomic indicator graphs. There is quite strong support for impression management in banks' graph use in the context of selectivity. Weaker support was found for the existence of favourable measurement distortions. Still, compared to previous research, weaker links exist between KFV graph use and banks' profit performance. Although the proportions of materially distorted graphs remain lower than reported in previous studies, the results do indicate that annual report users should pay more attention to sudden disappearance of certain graphs and cross-check graphed KFVs with numerical data presented in audited financial reports.

Keywords Disclosure • Impression management • Graphs • Banks

1 Introduction

For decades companies' stakeholders have considered annual reports as the most important medium for learning about the company's performance (for a review see Hines 1982; Vergoossen 1993). Although more recent surveys indicate decreasing role of annual reports,[1] their relevance should not be underestimated. First, unlike

[1] 2008 survey by Abt SRBI (http://www.sec.gov/pdf/disclosuredocs.pdf) conducted in US indicates that only 13 % of investors obtain company's annual report and from those almost half rarely, very rarely or never read these reports. The main reason for not reading was mainly that these were considered hard to understand or too long. Similarly, 2011 BoX IR's Financial Market survey (http://www.slideshare.net/BoxIR/financial-market-survey-2011-summary) conducted in Sweden indicates that less than half of the investors considered annual reports important or very important.

L. Laidroo (✉) • N. Tamme
Finance and Economics, Tallinn University of Technology, Tallinn, Estonia
e-mail: laivi.laidroo@ttu.ee; nele@planet.ee

© Springer International Publishing Switzerland 2016

M.H. Bilgin et al. (eds.), *Business Challenges in the Changing Economic Landscape - Vol. 1*, Eurasian Studies in Business and Economics 2/1,
DOI 10.1007/978-3-319-22596-8_10

other mediums, annual reports are independently verified by auditors and there through enable the stakeholders to validate previously released information (Hines 1982). Second, despite the decreasing importance of annual reports as information asymmetry reduction tools, this medium remains important as a legitimacy and impression management device (Hooghimestra 2010; Ditlevsen 2012). The latter has been supported by several longitudinal studies which have tended to support the increasing length of annual reports accompanied with increasing trends in voluntary disclosures, use of graphs and pictures (e.g., Lee 1994; McKinstry 1996; Graves et al. 1996; Beattie et al. 2008).

Annual report graphs provide an easy to grasp alternative to text. They may improve report users' decisions, because visual information may be easier to process (Vessey and Galletta 1991). This is especially important considering that 38 % of annual report readers spend up to 9 min and 60 % up to 30 min reading the annual report.[2] However, as the disclosure of information through graphs is not regulated and audited, companies could distort graphs to bias stakeholder evaluations of companies' performance. According to the impression management theory, managers may employ concealment strategies to influence the report users' perceptions (Merkl-Davies and Brennan 2007). In the context of disclosed graphs these are expected to lead to selectivity in graph use and/or presence of measurement distortions. Understanding the extent of such practices would provide valuable insight to different users of annual reports. This is especially important in the context of banks, as the credibility of their disclosures is considered an important determinant of banking crises (Tadesse 2006). Also the fact that banks' activities are under greater public scrutiny may create significant pressures for managing their disclosures. Therefore, the objective of this paper is to analyse graph use in annual reports of Central and Eastern European (CEE) banks during 2006–2011 and to determine the extent of impression management strategies employed. The sample covers 33 commercial banks from seven CEE countries: Estonia, Latvia, Lithuania, the Czech Republic, Slovakia, Hungary and Slovenia.

There exists quite extensive empirical research on graph use (see Appendix for references). This paper contributes to this strand of research in several respects. First, this paper focuses exclusively on commercial banks. Previous studies have, with the exception of Beattie and Jones (1994), focused simultaneously on companies from different industries. As banks' activity is more interlinked with the overall macroeconomic developments and their financial reporting also exhibits significant differences compared to other types of companies, their inclusion in samples covering other industries may hinder the possibilities to accurately capture bank-specific graph disclosure phenomena. Second, although several previous papers have used a longitudinal research design (e.g., Courtis 1997; Beattie and Jones 1998, 2000; Frownfelter-Lohrke and Fulkerson 2001; Beattie et al. 2008; Muiño and Trombetta 2009; Dilla and Janvrin 2010), the reports used in these studies end with 2005. The annual reports used in this paper cover the time period of

[2] 2008 survey by Abt SRBI http://www.sec.gov/pdf/disclosuredocs.pdf

2006–2011. Therefore, to the knowledge of the authors, it represents the first attempt to investigate graphs' disclosure patterns surrounding the 2008 financial crisis. Crisis periods are expected to be associated with significant changes in disclosure patterns, as shown in the context banks' sustainability disclosure narratives in Laidroo and Ööbik (2014). Third, previous research has mainly focused on Anglo-Saxon countries, with limited attention being paid to emerging markets (with the exception of Frownfelter and Fulkerson 1998; Frownfelter-Lohrke and Fulkerson 2001). However, to the knowledge of the authors, previous papers have not considered graph use in any of the CEE countries. This setting provides especially good testing ground for the impression management theory, as these countries' economies, financial systems and banks were severely adversely affected in the course of the recent financial crisis.

The paper is divided as follows. The theoretical and empirical background is discussed in Sect. 2 and data and methodology in Sect. 3. Section 4 presents the results and discussion. Finally, Sect. 5 concludes.

2 Theoretical and Empirical Background

Discretionary disclosure of information can take various forms covering narratives and graphs. Previous theoretical literature on discretionary disclosure can, according to Merkl-Davies and Brennan (2007), be divided into two schools: incremental information and impression management. The former covers numerous economics-based models categorised in Verrecchia (2001) as discretionary-based disclosure. These models assume semi-strong or strong-form market efficiency and rely heavily on disclosure preparers' and users' rationality (Merkl-Davies and Brennan 2007). Economics-based models explain the existence of reporting bias, however, their applicability in real life setting remains constrained by modelling assumptions and inefficiency of voluntary disclosure (Verrecchia 2001). Similarly, Merkl-Davies et al. (2011) claim that economics-based models' ability to consider social constraints remains poor. Therefore, impression management may provide a richer theoretical context and this perspective is also chosen in this paper.

Impression management is a concept developed in social psychology. According to Leary and Kowalski (1990, p. 34): "impression management refers to a process by which individuals attempt to control the impressions others form of them". In the context of company disclosures it can be considered managers' attempt to "control and manipulate the impression conveyed to users of accounting information" (Clatworthy and Jones 2001). In accounting context this issue has deserved attention since the development of positive accounting theory (Watts and Zimmermann 1978, 1990). In this vein Revsine (1991) proposed that selective financial misrepresentation in financial reporting occurs because it benefits different constituents of the firm. Although initially most of the attention was paid to the detection of accounting manipulations, like earnings management (e.g., Schipper 1989), in time the focus has broadened to the management of corporate disclosures (Gibbins et al. 1990). Recently, Merkl-Davies et al. (2011) have employed the social psychology view of impression management in the context of corporate reporting. They introduce ex post accountability as a driver of impression management.

According to Leary and Kowalski (1990) impression management is determined by two interlinked discrete processes: impression motivation and impression construction. Impression motivation relies on the goal relevance of impressions, value of desired goals and discrepancy between the desired and current image (Leary and Kowalski 1990). As this paper focuses on the disclosure preparer's perspective, the motivation for impression management is driven mainly by factors arising from agency relationships. Impression construction in the context of this paper will occur in the form of graphs. The possibilities to use graphs as impression management tools relate to graphical perception theory (Kosslyn 1985, 1989; Cleveland and McGill 1987). The latter is based on cognitive psychology and its extensions enable to determine the biases in graph use (for further discussion see the methodology section).

There exist numerous empirical papers focusing on impression management through graphs included in companies' reports (see Appendix). The first comprehensive studies were conducted by Steinbart (1989) and Beattie and Jones (1992). Overwhelming majority of the studies have focused on annual reports. Still, the more recent literature includes papers concentrating on IPO prospectuses (Mather et al. 2000), proxy statements (Bannister and Newman 2006) and sustainability reporting (Jones 2011; Cho et al. 2012). The use of longitudinal data has also increased with several papers focusing on graphing patterns over a period of 4–11 years (e.g., Courtis 1997; Beattie and Jones 1998, 2000; Frownfelter and Fulkerson 1998; Frownfelter-Lohrke and Fulkerson 2001; Beattie et al. 2008; Muiño and Trombetta 2009; Dilla and Janvrin 2010). Regional focus has mainly lied with UK, US and Australia with emerging markets being covered only in Frownfelter and Fulkerson (1998) and Frownfelter-Lohrke and Fulkerson (2001) in the form of Philippines and Mexico. Empirical research has mostly concentrated on the use of key financial variable (KFV) graphs defined as graphs depicting 4–5 most frequently depicted financial indicators of the company. The companies included in the samples have been mainly determined based on the biggest existing or the biggest listed firms. This indicates that most of the samples have included companies from very different industries. Only Beattie and Jones (1994) focused exclusively on fund-raising charities. This paper extends the empirical research on graph disclosure by focusing on emerging CEE countries in longitudinal context (time period 2006–2011) and by concentrating only on annual reports of commercial banks.

Managers may employ concealment strategies for impression management. Concealment may be achieved in two ways: emphasising positive outcomes or obfuscating negative outcomes (Merkl-Davies and Brennan 2007). In the context of graphs, emphasising positive outcomes can be linked to selectivity in graph use. The impact of that activity would be very similar to framing effects (Tversky and Khaneman 1981) as it would enable to alter the meaning of information provided to annual report users. Such selective disclosure would mean that improved performance is emphasised through more extensive use of KFV graphs. Therefore, the first hypothesis to be tested in this paper is:

H1: Individual bank's KFV graph use will be related positively to the direction of change in individual bank's performance.

It should be noted that firm's performance can be measured either by focusing on changes in graphed variable or on changes in some general performance indicator. Both perspectives are considered in this paper while testing H1. Previous empirical papers have tended to support the view that there exists selectivity in graph use with improved profit or earnings per share (EPS) numbers being reflected in increased use of KFV graphs (e.g., Steinbart 1989; Beattie and Jones 1992, 1997, 1999, 2000; Frownfelter and Fulkerson 1998; Mather et al. 2000; Beattie et al. 2008; Dilla and Janvrin 2010). Fewer studies, testing the impact of change in KFVs themselves, have similarly shown that the improvement in KFV is positively related to the use of that variable on graphs (e.g., Beattie and Jones 1992, 2000; Beattie et al. 2008; Dilla and Janvrin 2010).

Concealment of information (e.g., because of poor performance) may be achieved also through obfuscation. According to the obfuscation hypothesis (Adelberg 1979), managers prefer to communicate in a way that they hide bad news. In the context of graphs one possibility to do that is to alter their visual representation through the creation of measurement distortions (for discussion see methodology). Therefore, additional hypotheses to be tested in this paper include the following:

H2: Measurement distortion is likely to give a more, rather than less, favourable portrayal of bank's performance.

H3: Favourable measurement distortion is more likely to occur in the annual reports of banks with "bad", rather than "good", performance in terms of the variable graphed.

Most of the previous empirical papers tend to support a positive (favourable) measurement distortion bias in annual report graphs (e.g., Beattie and Jones 1992, 1999; Mather et al. 1996; Beattie et al. 2008). Still, in the context of IPO prospectuses Mather et al. (2000) find negative (unfavourable) distortion bias for key financial indicators after 1991. When the companies are divided into two groups based on their performance, then most of the results indicate no significant differences in the positive measurement distortion bias (e.g., Beattie and Jones 1992, 1999). Steinbart (1989), however, supports greater positive measurement distortion bias for poorly performing firms.

3 Data and Methodology

This paper focuses on 2006–2011 annual reports issued by commercial banks operating in seven CEE countries: Estonia, Latvia, Lithuania, the Czech Republic, Slovakia, Hungary and Slovenia. The initial set of CEE countries was bigger, however, only for the abovementioned seven it was possible to create a sample of banks covering more than 50 % of each country's total banking sector assets. The average banking sector coverage of the final sample is 70 %. The banks included in the sample were selected based on the following criteria. First, the market share of each bank had to be higher than 5 %. Second, annual reports disclosed in English had to be available on the bank's web-site. The final sample includes in total of 33 banks (2–7 banks per country) and 197 annual reports.[3]

Banks' financial indicators were taken from BankScope database. Data related to and depicted on graphs was collected from banks' annual reports obtained from banks' web-pages. Annual reports were read and during this process the indicators graphed were recorded and measurement distortion determined and entered into a special database.

Hypotheses tests focus mainly on key financial variables (KFVs). These are defined in this paper as the most frequent financial indicators being present in at least 25 % of the reports including graphs. Banks' overall performance is measured in terms of net profit as this reflects the amount available for distribution to shareholders. H1 is tested using a Chi2 test to determine whether the proportions of graph use differ across banks with "good" and "bad" performance. "Good" performance is considered to occur if bank's KFV or net profit of the current year increased compared to that of the previous year and "bad" otherwise.

Measurement distortions refer to situations where the numerical values of the variables graphed do not coincide with the representation of numbers on the surface of the graph. These can be measured through Tufte's "lie factor" (Tufte 1983). In this paper the measurement distortion is calculated only for time series graphs[4] and by using the graph discrepancy index (GDI) developed in Taylor and Anderson (1986):

$$GDI = \left(\frac{a}{b} - 1\right) \times 100 \tag{1}$$

Where

[3] Lithuanian bank Bankas Snoras went bankrupt and, therefore, no 2011 annual report for that bank has been issued.

[4] Similarly to many previous papers the measurement distortions on pie charts are not considered as these require slightly different measurement distortion detection approach (see Beattie and Jones 1994). This indicates that the number of KFV graphs available for GDI calculation is smaller than the total count of KFV graphs.

a—percentage change depicted on graph (percentage change in the height of the first and last column);
b—percentage change in data.

If no measurement distortion is present, GDI is equal to 0. Positive GDI indicates exaggeration and negative understatement of values. As suggested in Tufte (1983), most of the previous empirical papers classify as material distortions the situations where GDI is greater than 5 % in absolute terms. Still, the experiments conducted by Beattie and Jones (2002) indicate that measurement distortion in excess of 10 % in absolute terms tends to alter the users' perceptions. Therefore, in this paper both 5 and 10 % thresholds are used in defining material distortions. The main drawback of GDI is that if there is no change in the underlying variable, GDI cannot be calculated, and if the variable on the graph does not change (although the underlying variable might), GDI would be −100 %. To overcome the limitations of GDI, some empirical papers (e.g., Muiño and Trombetta 2009; Jones 2011; Cho et al. 2012) have used relative graphs discrepancy index (RGDI) developed in Mather et al. (2005). However, RGDI is not used in this paper, because as noted in Jones (2011) RGDI tends not to be highly correlated with GDI due to significant measurement differences, the interpretation of RGDI is more cumbersome and comparative evidence from previous empirical research is almost lacking.

Binomial test is used to determine whether favourable and unfavourable material distortions ($GDI > 5\,\%$ or $GDI > 10\,\%$) are equally likely (H2). Favourable measurement distortions occur in case there is an exaggeration of a positive trend (KFV increases and GDI is positive) or understatement of a downward trend (KFV increases and GDI is negative). Unfavourable distortions occur in case downward trend is exaggerated or positive trend understated. In order to provide more accurate results in testing this hypothesis, the following distorted graphs are excluded from H2 testing. First, distorted graphs with reversed axis (years presented in decreasing order) in case the reversal could be easily detected from the figure's title. Second, the trend varied within the depicted timeframe and at the same time, non-zero axis or broken vertical axis was used.

In order to test H3, banks are divided annually into two performance groups: "good" and "bad". "Good" performance occurs if respective bank's variable graphed on that year was above the median of the same bank for the whole period of 2006–2011 and "bad" otherwise. The Chi2 or Fisher's exact test is used to determine whether the proportions of graphs with favourable measurement distortion differ across groups of banks with "good" and "bad" performance.

4 Results and Discussion

4.1 Graph Use in Annual Reports of CEE Banks

The analysis covers 1620 graphs included in annual reports of banks. The average number of graphs per report is 8.2. This is rather similar to 8.6 reported in Uyar (2011) for Turkish companies and in line with results reported for developed countries before 2000s (Beattie and Jones 1996, 1997, 1999; Frownfelter-Lohrke and Fulkerson 2001). Still, it does remain below 16.0 reported for Spain in Muiño and Trombetta (2009). 140 reports (71 %) include at least one graph. In previous studies the proportion of reports including graphs has been higher ranging mostly between 75 and 90 % (e.g., Steinbart 1989; Beattie and Jones 1992, 1997, 1999; Mather et al. 1996). From the most recent studies Beattie et al. (2008) have even referred to a 99 % level for UK firms and Muiño and Trombetta (2009) to 92 % in Spanish companies. The only paper that has included and reported separate results for UK financial firms, Beattie and Jones (1992), showed that 78 % of reports included at least one graph. The abovementioned statistics indicate that the graph use in CEE banks' annual reports remains slightly lower than previously reported in financial sector context and in the context of more recent studies covering other industries in developed countries.

When looking at the variables graphed, it is possible to distinguish three main indicator groups: financial variables, activity indicators of banks and macroeconomic indicators (see Table 1). 28 % of graphs depict at least one of the four most commonly graphed financial variables including loans, total assets, deposits or net profit. These are considered as key financial variables (KFVs) in this paper[5] and most of the following discussion will focus on these variables. In previous studies, concentrating on other types of companies, the list of KFVs has been rather different including mainly sales, various profit indicators, earnings per share (EPS), dividends per share (DPS) or dividends. In fewer instances equity, assets or cash flow indicators have been amongst the list of KFVs (e.g., CICA 1993; Beattie and Jones 2001). This shows that the activity profile of banks tends to create very significant differences in financial variable graphing practices. Compared with previous studies the only common indicator in the list of KFVs is net profit. This refers to the importance of excluding financial firms from samples including other types of companies in graph disclosure studies.

As shown in Table 1 at least one KFV graph is included in 49 % of reports including graphs. Although the KFVs in Beattie and Jones (1992) were turnover, profit before tax, EPS and DPS, they reported exactly the same result for financial firms. In previous empirical papers covering companies from other industries the

[5] Obligations group has slightly higher count of graphs than profit, however, the former topic includes several different subcategories which are significantly more heterogeneous. Therefore, obligations are not included amongst KFVs in this paper.

Table 1 Graph use statistics by themes

	Graphs		Reports including graphs	
	No.	% of total	No.	% of total
Any graphs	**1620**	**100.0**	**140**	**71.1**
Key financial variables (KFVs)	**457**	**28.2**	**97**	**49.2**
Incl. loans	189	11.7	68	34.5
Incl. total assets	118	7.3	79	40.1
Incl. deposits	80	4.9	53	26.9
Incl. net profit	70	4.3	50	25.4
Other financial variables	**393**	**24.3**	**98**	**49.7**
Incl. obligations	76	4.7	56	28.4
Incl. share price	44	2.7	27	13.7
Incl. income and costs	40	2.5	33	16.8
Incl. capital	34	2.1	22	11.2
Incl. cost to income ratio	31	1.9	28	14.2
Activity indicators	**590**	**36.4**	**92**	**46.7**
Incl. market share	94	5.8	31	15.7
Incl. number of employees	66	4.1	45	22.8
Incl. number of customers	61	3.8	34	17.3
Incl. number of transactions	58	3.6	30	15.2
Macroeconomic indicators	**180**	**11.1**	**60**	**30.5**
Incl. GDP	44	2.7	41	20.8
Incl. inflation	28	1.7	27	13.7
Incl. country level loans	23	1.4	17	8.6

graphing rates of KFVs have ranged between 60 and 75 % (Steinbart 1989; Beattie and Jones 1992, 1994, 1999; Beattie et al. 2008).

Similarly to KFVs, banks graph quite extensively other financial variables and activity indicators. Other financial variables include different liability items, banks' share price, income and costs, capital, cost to income ratio, risk indicators, financial indicators of the whole banking group etc. Graphed activity indicators are mainly dominated by variables characterising banks' market share and the number of employees. One third of reports including graphs contain at least one macroeconomic indicator graph. The most popular macroeconomic indicator graphed is the GDP being present in 21 % of reports including graphs. Other macro variables graphed include inflation, exchange rates, banking sector indicators, interest rates etc. Previous studies focusing on other sectors (e.g., Beattie and Jones 1997; Beattie et al. 2008) have reported only one macroeconomic indicator stock market index and even this has been present in very few reports. This difference could be explained by the fact that unlike in the case of other types of firms, banks' activities are more closely linked to the countries' macroeconomic conditions and to the developments on global financial markets. Therefore, banks' performance can be better explained in the macroeconomic context.

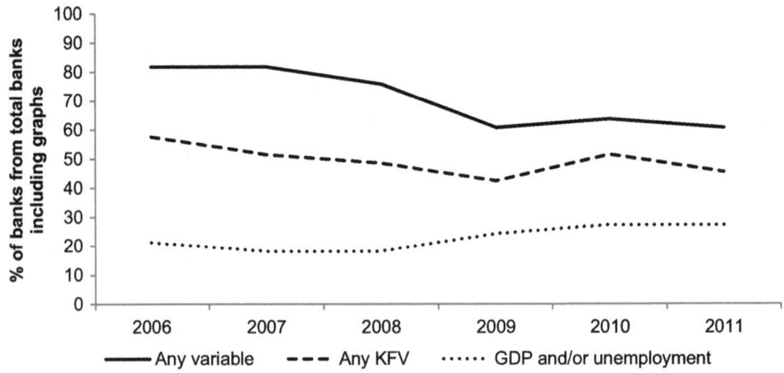

Fig. 1 Main trends in CEE banks' graph use during 2006–2011

The abovementioned results tend to refer to the possibility that graph use in banks' reports compared to nonfinancial firms is more versatile in terms of graphed variables and less concentrated on KFVs. The authors did observe that banks, which graphed a variable, tended to use more than one graph to do it. This on the other hand may mean that the benefits of topic versatility in banks' graph use may be downplayed by the noise which extensive repeated graphing inevitably creates. The latter aspect may require additional attention in future studies.

The main trends in graph use across years are depicted on Fig. 1. There has been a decreasing trend in graph use with the proportion of banks including any graph in their report declining from 2006 82–61 % by 2011. During the same period the average number of graphs per report decreased from 9.8 to 7.5. These decreases relate to declining graph use in most countries except for banks in the Czech Republic and Slovenia. Especially dramatic decrease in graph use has occurred in Estonian and Latvian banks, where none of the banks have graphs in their annual reports starting from 2009. These results contradict with the findings of a longitudinal study by Beattie et al. (2008) which showed that in UK firms the graph use increased from 1989 79 % to 99 % by 2004. One potential reason for declining graph use in CEE banks' context may relate to bank ownership. Company ownership's significant impact on its disclosure practices has been widely documented in previous disclosure research (for a review see Laidroo 2009). Considering that the banks covered in this paper are foreign-owned, the interest of their parent banks to issue rich-coloured annual report documents in English may be decreasing, e.g., parent banks' disclosure policies may have a major role to play in graphing decisions. In the context of this paper, the authors did observe a tendency that banks belonging to the same banking group (Unicredit, SEB and Swedbank) have similar graphing practices across countries. In order to verify this tendency, future studies could focus on graphing patterns of international banks operating on developed markets and focus more closely on group's influence on graph disclosure.

As shown on Fig. 1, the decrease in KFV graph use has been lower than in the context of all graphs decreasing from 2006 58 % to 45 % in 2011. Similar tendencies have been reported in Beattie et al. (2008) and Dilla and Janvrin (2010). These have been mainly attributed to increasing use of other types of graphs, but in the context of this paper tend to confirm the overall decreasing trend in graph use. An opposite trend has occurred in the context of graphs depicting GDP or unemployment indicators the use of which has increased from 2006 21 % to 27 % in 2011.

As shown in Table 2, there exist quite significant differences in graph use across banks' home countries. The most extensive use of graphs occurs in Slovenian banks, followed by banks from the Czech Republic and the least extensive in Estonia and Latvia. These may relate partly to differences in bank sizes with banks from the Czech Republic, Slovenia, Slovakia and Hungary being bigger than those from the Baltics (Estonia, Latvia and Lithuania). Considering the lower graphing indicators characterising banks from the Baltics and also the potential regional differences, the selectivity testing is run both on the whole sample and on a reduced sample excluding Baltic banks. Due to the problems with the sample size, the possibilities to split the sample by countries and years remains rather limited, leading to the use of pooled indicators.

As can be seen from Table 2, the most common graph type is a column chart which accounts for 49.1 % of graphs, followed closely by pie charts 18.3 % and line charts 16.7 %. Rather similar results have been reported in previous studies for other types of companies (e.g., Beattie and Jones 1992, 1997, 1999; Courtis 1997; Frownfelter-Lohrke and Fulkerson 2001; Beattie et al. 2008). The graph types across countries are rather similar with the exception of Slovakian banks, which tended to use line charts the most frequently. However, if only KFV graphs are considered, even Slovakian banks use column charts the most frequently. No significant differences in graph type preferences across years are observed. This indicates that graphing techniques employed by banks are rather uniform and highly comparable to those of other types of companies.

Table 2 Graph use statistics across countries

Country	No. of banks	Total no. of graphs	Average no. of graphs per report	% of banks graphing			The most frequent graph	
				Any variable	Any KFV	GDP and/or unemployment	Type	Type from total graphs (%)
SI	5	628	20.9	100.0	96.7	46.7	Column	42.2
CZ	4	278	11.6	100.0	45.8	4.2	Column	53.2
LT	6	233	6.7	72.2	63.9	2.8	Column	60.9
HU	7	228	5.4	61.9	35.7	26.2	Column	65.8
SK	5	176	5.9	90.0	43.3	53.3	Line	37.5
EE	2	39	3.3	25.0	25.0	16.7	Column	41.0
LV	4	38	1.6	16.7	16.7	2.5	Column	50.0
Total	33	1620	8.2	71.1	49.2	33.8	Column	49.1

4.2 Impression Management Using Graphs

Banks' tendencies to conceal information by emphasising positive outcomes are likely to be manifested in selective use of key financial variable (KFV) graphs. The Chi2 tests tend to support the employment of such a strategy in the context of most KFVs (see Table 3). The results show that an increase in bank loans, deposits, profit and any KFV is associated with increased use of respective graphs. This conclusion supports H1 and is in line with previous research (e.g., Beattie and Jones 1992, 2000; Beattie et al. 2008; Dilla and Janvrin 2010). However, in the context of bank's assets, H1 is not supported. The latter result can be explained by the fact that total assets are more of a measure of bank size, meaning that banks may consider its graphs almost obligatory components of the report. Also assets as such do not capture bank performance as well as loans or deposits and, therefore, there is no reason to use such graphs for impression management purposes.

When graph use is linked with the change in banks' net profit, H1 is not supported for most of the KFVs (with the exception of net profit). Most of the previous research linking KFV use with earnings measures (mainly EPS) has tended to provide stronger support to selectivity in similar context (e.g., Beattie and Jones 1992, 1997, 1999, 2000; Frownfelter and Fulkerson 1998; Beattie et al. 2008; Dilla and Janvrin 2010). The differing results of this paper can be explained by the fact that an increase in bank's loans, assets and deposits cannot be readily linked with bank's net profit, while in the context of other types of firms their sales, profit, EPS and DPS are closely associated with EPS. These results seem to indicate that selectivity testing is more fruitful if the KFVs remain closely linked with the performance measure employed, i.e., industry-specific differences need to be considered in selectivity testing.

Bank managers may conceal poor performance also by obfuscating outcomes. In the context of graphs it may take the form of measurement distortions. Table 4 Panel A presents the GDI indicators calculated for all KFV graphs. If GDI $> 5\,\%$ 34 % of graphs are materially distorted, and if GDI $> 10\,\%$, the proportion of materially distorted graphs falls to 29 %. These proportions vary less than 5 percentage points across KFVs, with the exception of asset graphs which tend to

Table 3 Selectivity in KFV graph use (H1) tested with Chi2 test

	Whole sample				Whole sample excl. the Baltics			
Variable	Year-on-year change in variable itself		Year-on-year change in net profit		Year-on-year change in variable itself		Year-on-year change in net profit	
Loans	11.85	***	1.28		3.02	*	0.50	
Total assets	1.70		0.04		0.08		0.57	
Deposits	8.96	***	0.03		4.20	**	0.04	
Net profit	3.77	*	3.77	*	2.96	*	2.96	*
All KFVs	22.22	***	0.02		7.40	***	0.03	

Notes: Chi squared test statistics, statistical significance ***$p<0.01$, **$p<0.05$, *$p<0.1$

Table 4 KFV graph measurement distortion statistics and binomial tests (H2)

Panel A. GDI indicators across all graphs

GDI range %			No. of graphs: Loan	Assets	Deposits	Net profit	Total	Total graphs by GDI range as % of total
...	< GDI ≤	−50	19	18	14	4	55	17
−50	< GDI ≤	−25	2	2	2	3	9	3
−25	< GDI ≤	−10	1	2	1	2	6	2
−10	< GDI ≤	−5	0	5	1	0	6	2
−5	< GDI ≤	5	80	45	46	48	219	66
5	< GDI ≤	10	3	2	3	1	9	3
10	< GDI ≤	25	5	3	2	0	10	3
25	< GDI ≤	50	4	2	1	2	9	3
50	< GDI ≤	100	2	1	0	1	4	1
100	< GDI ≤	...	3	1	0	2	6	2
Total			119	81	70	63	333	100
Mean GDI			−14.7 %	−21.9 %	−38.7 %	0.2 %	−15.7 %	

Panel B. Material distortions excluding reversed axis

	No. of graphs: Loan	Assets	Deposits	Net profit	Total
Material distortions at GDI > 10 %					
No. of favourable distortions	13	11	6	5	35
No. of unfavourable distortions	9	11	5	9	34
Binomial test p-value	0.119	0.168	0.226	0.122	0.095
Material distortions at GDI > 5 %					
No. of favourable distortions	16	16	9	6	47
No. of unfavourable distortions	9	13	6	9	37
Binomial test p-value	0.061	0.126	0.153	0.153	0.048

exhibit slightly higher level of distorted graphs. Still, the material distortion proportions are in line with results reported in most previous research before 2000s (Steinbart 1989; Beattie and Jones 1992, 1997, 1999; Mather et al. 1996). It does appear that the more recent papers have tended to report higher material distortion levels ranging between 44 and 64 % of graphs (e.g., Mather et al. 2000; Beattie et al. 2008). This may refer to the possibility that CEE banks have either been behind in using graph distortion techniques employed in developed countries or that banks in general have been less eager to obfuscate outcomes by distorting graphs. To clarify the potential reasons for the observed differences, future studies could focus on banks operating on developed markets.

Quite strikingly the mean GDI indicators reported in this paper for all KFVs (with the exception of net profit) are negative, meaning that understatement of trends is more common than overstatement. Most previous papers have shown positive mean GDI indicators ranging mainly between 5 and 17 % (e.g., Steinbart 1989; Beattie and Jones 1992, 1994, 1997; Mather et al. 1996). One of the reasons for differing results in this paper relates to some banks' very frequent use of time series graphs with reversed axes. Namely, one thirds of all materially distorted graphs include such distortions. Another very common distortion accounting for roughly 24 % of material distortions is the use of non-zero vertical axis. Other types of distortions are significantly less common.

The picture somewhat changes, once the graphs with reversed axes are eliminated and material distortions are divided into favourable and unfavourable ones (see Table 4 Panel B). In the context of most KFVs (with the exception of net profit at 5 and 10 % level and assets at 10 % level), favourable distortions are more likely than unfavourable ones. The binomial tests support this finding at the 10 % GDI level for all KFVs ($p < 0.1$) and at the 5 % GDI level for loans and all KFVs ($p < 0.1$ and $p < 0.05$ respectively). This indicates that quite strong support for H2 is found for all KFVs combined and at lesser extent for loans. This result is in line with previous research which has tended to support the existence of positive measurement distortion bias (e.g., Beattie and Jones 1992, 1999; Mather et al. 1996; Beattie et al. 2008).

When banks are divided into two groups based on their respective KFV performance, there is support for H3 only in the context of asset graphs at 10 % GDI level (Fisher's exact test gives $p < 0.1$). The results indicate that while 70 % of banks with "bad" asset performance use favourably distorted asset graphs, only 33 % of banks with "good" performance do the same. Although at the level of all KFVs H3 is rejected, the proportions of KFV graphs being favourably distorted are 10–20 percentage points higher for "bad" performance group. When bank performance is defined in terms of net profit, H3 is supported only for deposits. This means that favourable distortion in deposit graphs is more common if bank's net profit performance has been poor (Fisher's exact test gives $p < 0.1$ for both) with 83 % of banks with "bad" profit performance distorting deposit graphs compared to 20 % with "good" profit performance doing the same. The latter finding refers to the possibility that banks use the distortion of deposit graphs with the hope of improving their overall performance outlook. These results indicate weak support to the expectation that the deterioration in KFVs is likely to lead to their more favourable presentation on graphs. In the context of other types of companies similar result has been reported in Steinbart (1989). Although Beattie and Jones (1992, 1999) failed to find statistically significant support to the hypothesis, they also showed that favourable distortions tended to be more common in poorly performing firms.

The authors also considered the distribution of materially distorted graphs across years. It could be assumed that deteriorating bank performance during crisis years increased banks' desire to distort graphs. Unfortunately, the number of material measurement distortions per year remains below 20 and no clear pattern emerges. The use of bigger sample of banks might provide further insight into this issue.

The abovementioned results show that during the period of 2006–2011 CEE banks' graphing decisions have tended to be influenced by impression management strategies. Quite strong support is found for selectivity in KFV graph use (H1) and weaker evidence for the employment of measurement distortions (H2, H3). Unlike in other types of firms, the selectivity in banks' KFV graph use has weaker links with banks' profit performance. Proportions of materially distorted graphs in CEE banks' reports have also been slightly lower than reported in previous studies. These results indicate that better understanding of impression management in banks' graph disclosure practices is needed. Considering that this paper focuses only on CEE banks and there is a shortage of previous research on financial firms, an important research avenue for future research would be the investigation of graphing practices of banks operating in developed countries. The univariate results also indicate that in order to better explain some of the observed phenomena a multivariate setting could provide deeper insight into factors affecting banks' graphing decisions.

Taking into account the signs of impression management reflected in CEE banks' annual report graph use, annual report users should pay more attention to the graphical material they use in making their decisions. The existence of selectivity in graph use refers to the importance of detecting the lack of graphs of some KFVs, as this could potentially indicate problems with the respective indicator. The existence of favourable measurement distortions may be caused by bank managers' deliberate impression management attempts. Still, part of the measurement distortions may also be related to bank personnel's unfamiliarity with the graphical design principles. This may create situations where they unintentionally construct biased graphs. Some support for this additional factor is provided by the fact that unfavourable misrepresentations also existed and some banks were too eager to constantly use graphs with reversed axes. Irrespective to the cause of the measurement distortion, report users should not rely solely on the graphical presentation of data and should in the context of KFVs cross-check it with numerical data presented in audited financial reports.

5 Conclusion

The objective of this paper was to analyse the graph use in annual reports of Central and Eastern European (CEE) banks during 2006–2011 and to determine the extent of impression management strategies employed.

The results revealed that there existed some distinct differences in banks' graph use compared to other types of companies covered in previous studies. First, there was a declining trend in CEE banks' graph use across years and the proportion of reports including graphs was below the numbers presented in the most recent empirical research covering other types of companies. Second, the list of KFVs differed significantly, the only common indicator being the net profit. The remaining KFVs included loans, deposits and total assets which are performance indicators specific to banks. Third, unlike other types of companies, banks graphed quite extensively different non-financial activity indicators as well as macroeconomic variables.

Quite strong support was found for impression management in banks' graph use in the context of selectivity. In line with expectations (H1) the increase in KFVs was associated with increased use of respective graphs (with the exception of total assets). Weaker support was found for the existence and preference towards favourable measurement distortions (H2 and H3). Despite the fact that the abovementioned results confirm the findings in previous empirical research, some surprising differences emerged. First, unlike in other types of firms, the selectivity in banks' KFV graph use (H1) indicated weaker links between banks' profit performance and the use of KFV graphs. Second, the proportions of materially distorted graphs in CEE banks' reports tended to be lower than those reported in previous studies.

The main limitation of this paper is the focus on CEE banks. This has set limits to the sample size and the interpretations remain limited to the selected developing countries. Therefore, in order to verify the results reported, the extension of research in the context of banks operating in developed countries is needed. Another important implication for future research, arising from the results, which deviate from previous findings, is the need to investigate banks' graph disclosures separately from that of other types of companies. Third, the results presented in this paper are based on univariate tests which limit the possibilities to control for different bank- and country-specific factors. Therefore, in order to uncover the factors driving banks' graphing decisions, the future research should focus on using multivariate approaches.

Overall, the results presented in this paper indicate that the users of CEE banks' annual reports should remain wary of impression management attempts made through graphs. This means that more attention should be paid to sudden disappearance of certain graphs and the trends of some key indicators, observed on graphs, should be cross-checked with numerical data presented in audited financial reports.

Acknowledgements The authors are grateful for the financial support provided by the Estonian Ministry of Education and Research to projects SF0140059s12 "Economic Fluctuations in Central and Eastern Europe: Causes, Consequences and Challenges". This paper represents the work conducted in connection with this project. The funding providers had no role in the research process from study design to submission.

Appendix

Overview of empirical papers on graph disclosure

Reference	Medium	Region	Period	No. of companies
Steinbart (1989)	Annual report	US	1986	319
Beattie and Jones (1992)	Annual report	UK	1989	240
Green et al. (1992)	Annual report	Ireland	1989	240
Beattie and Jones (1993)	Annual report	UK	1989	240

(continued)

Reference	Medium	Region	Period	No. of companies
CICA (1993)	Annual report	Canada	1991	200
Beattie and Jones (1994)	Charity report	UK	1990	47
Mather et al. (1996)	Annual report	Australia	1991/1992	187
Beattie and Jones (1996)	Annual report	Australia, France, Germany, Netherlands, UK, US	1991/1992	300
Beattie and Jones (1997)	Annual report	UK, US	1990	176
Courtis (1997)	Annual report	Hong Kong	1992–1995	116–140
Beattie and Jones (1998)	Annual report	UK	1988–1992	137
Frownfelter and Fulkerson (1998)	Annual report	12 countries	1984–1994	74
Beattie and Jones (1999)	Annual report	Australia	1991	89
Beattie and Jones (2000)	Annual report	UK	1988–1992	137
Mather et al. (2000)	IPO prospectus	Australia	Pre 1991 and post 1991	N/A
Beattie and Jones (2001)	Annual report	Australia, France, Germany, Netherlands, UK, US	1992	300
Frownfelter-Lohrke and Fulkerson (2001)	Annual report	12 countries	1984–1994	74
Bannister and Newman (2006)	Proxy statement	Global	1993	141
Beattie et al. (2008)	Annual report	UK	1965, 1978, 1988, 1989, 2004	25–240
Muiño and Trombetta (2009)	Annual report	Spain	1996–2002	67
Dilla and Janvrin (2010)	Annual report	US	1999–2005	184
Jones (2011)	Social and environmental report	UK	2005	63
Uyar (2011)	Annual report	Turkey	2006	96
Cho et al. (2012)	Corporate sustainability report	UK, US, France, Germany, Italy, Spain	2006	120

References

Adelberg, A. H. (1979). Narrative disclosures contained in financial reports: Means of communication or manipulation? *Accounting and Business Research, 9*(35), 179–190.

Bannister, J. W., & Newman, H. A. (2006). Disclosure biases in proxy performance graphs: The influence of performance and compensation committee composition. *Review of Accounting and Finance, 5*(1), 30–44.

Beattie, V., Dhanani, A., & Jones, M. J. (2008). Investigating presentational change in U.K. annual reports. *Journal of Business Communication, 45*(2), 181–222.

Beattie, V., & Jones, M. J. (1992). The use and abuse of graphs in annual reports: Theoretical framework and empirical study. *Accounting and Business Research, 22*(88), 291–303.

Beattie, V., & Jones, M. J. (1993). Information design and manipulation: Financial graphs in corporate annual reports. *Information Design Journal, 7*(3), 211–226.

Beattie, V., & Jones, M. J. (1994). An empirical study of graphical format choices in charity annual reports. *Financial Accountability and Management, 10*(3), 215–236.

Beattie, V., & Jones, M. J. (1996). *Financial graphs in corporate annual reports: A review of practice in six countries* (Research Report). London: Institute of Chartered Accountants in England and Wales.

Beattie, V., & Jones, M. J. (1997). A comparative study of the use of financial graphs in the corporate annual reports of major U.S. and U.K. companies. *Journal of International Financial Management and Accounting, 8*(1), 33–68.

Beattie, V., & Jones, M. J. (1998). *Graphical reporting choices: Communication or manipulation* (Research Report 56). Chartered Association of Certified Accountants, Certified Accountants Educational Trust.

Beattie, V., & Jones, M. J. (1999). Australian financial graphs: An empirical study. *Abacus, 35*(1), 46–76.

Beattie, V., & Jones, M. J. (2000). Changing graph use in corporate annual reports: A time-series analysis. *Contemporary Accounting Research, 17*(2), 213–226.

Beattie, V., & Jones, M. J. (2001). A six-country comparison of the use of graphs in annual reports. *International Journal of Accounting, 36*(2), 195–222.

Beattie, V., & Jones, M. J. (2002). Measurement distortion of graphs in corporate reports: An experimental study. *Accounting, Auditing and Accountability Journal, 15*(4), 546–564.

Cho, C. H., Michelon, G., & Patten, D. M. (2012). Enhancement and obfuscation through the use of graphs in sustainability reports: An international comparison. *Sustainability Accounting, Management and Policy Journal, 3*(1), 74–88.

CICA. (1993). *Using ratios and graphics in financial reporting* (Canadian Institute of Chartered Accountants Research Report, pp. 1–222).

Clatworthy, M., & Jones, M. J. (2001). The effect of thematic structure on the variability of annual report readability. *Accounting, Auditing and Accountability Journal, 14*(3), 311–326.

Cleveland, W. S., & McGill, R. (1987). Graphical perception: The visual decoding of quantitative information on graphical displays of data. *Journal of the Royal Statistical Society. Series A (General), 150*(3), 192–229.

Courtis, J. K. (1997). Corporate annual report graphical communication in Hong Kong: Effective or misleading? *Journal of Business Communication, 34*(3), 269–288.

Dilla, W. N., & Janvrin, D. J. (2010). Voluntary disclosure in annual reports: The Association between magnitude and direction of change in corporate financial performance and graph use. *Accounting Horizons, 24*(2), 257–278.

Ditlevsen, M. G. (2012). Revealing corporate identities in annual reports. *Corporate Communications: An International Journal, 17*(3), 370–393.

Frownfelter, C. A., & Fulkerson, C. L. (1998). Linking the incidence and quality of graphics in annual reports to corporate performance: An international comparison. *Advances in Accounting Information Systems, 6*, 129–151.

Frownfelter-Lohrke, C., & Fulkerson, C. L. (2001). The incidence and quality of graphics in annual reports: An international comparison. *Journal of Business Communication, 38*(3), 337–358.

Gibbins, M., Richardson, A., & Waterhouse, J. (1990). The management of corporate financial disclosure: Opportunism, ritualism, policies, and processes. *Journal of Accounting Research, 28*(1), 121–143.

Graves, O. F., Flesher, D. L., & Jordan, R. E. (1996). Pictures and the bottom line: The television epistemology of U.S. annual reports. *Accounting, Organizations and Society, 21*(1), 57–88.

Green, P., Kirk, R., & Rankin, C. (1992, November). Graphs: The use and abuse. *Certified Accountant*, p. 34.

Hines, R. D. (1982). The usefulness of annual reports: The anomaly between the efficient markets hypothesis and shareholder surveys. *Accounting and Business Research, 12*(48), 296–309.

Hooghimestra, R. (2010). Letters to the shareholders: A content analysis comparison of letters written by CEOs in the United States and Japan. *International Journal of Accounting, 45*(3), 275–300.

Jones, M. J. (2011). The nature, use and impression management of graphs in social and environmental accounting. *Accounting Forum, 35*(2), 75–89.

Kosslyn, S. M. (1985). Graphics and human information processing: A review of five books. *Journal of the American Statistical Association, 80*(391), 499–512.

Kosslyn, S. M. (1989). Understanding charts and graphs. *Applied Cognitive Psychology, 3*(3), 185–226.

Laidroo, L. (2009). Association between ownership structure and public announcements' disclosure quality. *Corporate Governance: An International Review, 17*(1), 13–34.

Laidroo, L., & Ööbik, U. (2014). Banks' CSR disclosures—Headquarters versus subsidiaries. *Baltic Journal of Management, 9*(1), 47–70.

Leary, M. R., & Kowalski, R. M. (1990). Impression management: A literature review and two-component model. *Psychological Bulletin, 107*(1), 34–47.

Lee, T. (1994). The changing form of the corporate annual report. *Accounting Historians Journal, 21*(1), 215–232.

Mather, D., Mather, P., & Ramsay, A. (2005). An investigation into the measurement of graph distortion in financial reports. *Accounting and Business Research, 35*(2), 147–160.

Mather, P., Ramsay, A., & Serry, A. (1996). The use and representational faithfulness of graphs in annual reports: Australian evidence. *Australian Accounting Review, 6*(12), 56–63.

Mather, P., Ramsay, A., & Steen, A. (2000). The use and representational faithfulness of graphs in Australian IPO prospectuses. *Accounting, Auditing and Accountability Journal, 13*(1), 65–83.

McKinstry, S. (1996). Designing the annual reports of Burton Plc from 1930 to 1994. *Accounting Organizations and Society, 21*(1), 89–111.

Merkl-Davies, D. M., & Brennan, N. M. (2007). Discretionary disclosure strategies in corporate narratives: Incremental information or impression management. *Journal of Accounting Literature, 26*, 116–196.

Merkl-Davies, D. M., Brennan, N. M., & McLeay, S. J. (2011). Impression management and retrospective sense-making in corporate narratives. *Accounting, Auditing and Accountability Journal, 24*(3), 315–344.

Muiño, F., & Trombetta, M. (2009). Does graph disclosure bias reduce the cost of equity capital. *Accounting and Business Research, 39*(2), 83–102.

Revsine, L. (1991). The selective financial misrepresentation hypothesis. *Accounting Horizons, 5* (4), 16–27.

Schipper, K. (1989). Commentary on earnings management. *Accounting Horizons, 3*, 91–102.

Steinbart, P. J. (1989). The auditor's responsibility for the accuracy of graphs in annual reports: Some evidence of the need for additional guidance. *Accounting Horizons, 3*(3), 60–70.

Tadesse, S. (2006). *The economic value of regulated disclosure: Evidence from the banking sector* (William Davidson Institute Working Paper No. 875).

Taylor, B. G., & Anderson, L. K. (1986). Misleading graphs: Guidelines for the accountant. *Journal of Accountancy, 162*(4), 126–135.

Tufte, E. R. (1983). *The visual display of qualitative information*. Cheshire, CT: Graphic Press.

Tversky, A., & Khaneman, D. (1981). The framing of decisions and the psychology of choice. *Science, 211*(4481), 453–458.

Uyar, A. (2011). Firm characteristics and voluntary disclosure of graphs in annual reports of Turkish listed companies. *African Journal of Business Management, 5*(17), 7651–7657.

Vergoossen, R. G. A. (1993). The use and perceived importance of annual reports by investment analysts in the Netherlands. *European Accounting Review, 2*(2), 219–243.

Verrecchia, R. E. (2001). Essays on disclosure. *Journal of Accounting and Economics, 32*(1–3), 97–180.

Vessey, I., & Galletta, D. (1991). Cognitive fit: An empirical study of information acquisition. *Information Systems Research, 2*(1), 63–84.

Watts, R. L., & Zimmermann, J. L. (1978). Towards a positive theory of the determination of accounting standards. *Accounting Review, 53*(1), 112–134.

Watts, R. L., & Zimmermann, J. L. (1990). Positive accounting theory: A ten year perspective. *Accounting Review, 65*(1), 131–156.

Ecological Evolution of Financial Market: Ecologically Responsible Investment

Leszek Dziawgo and Ewa Dziawgo

Abstract The international financial market is significantly influenced by ideas of Corporate Social Responsibility/Environmental-Social-Governance. As it is commonly known—CSR/ESG-ideas contain also crucial ecological components. Nowadays, a lot of leading financial institutions in Europe keep or gain clients thanks to using environmental aspects. The aim of the elaboration is to indicate and analyse the problem of implementation of environmental rules in financial business, especially Ecologically Responsible Investment (ERI). The considerations are based on selected cases of business practice of Polish financial market and surveys conducted in the period of 2009–2014 on a representative sample of Polish society. Poland is one of the most important and promising emerging markets hosting key financial players such as Deutsche Bank, Commerzbank, Citigroup, BNP Paribas, UniCredit, Millennium, Raiffeisen Bank, ING, and also Banco Santander. The results clearly show that problem of ecological adjustment of financial institutions to public requirements concerning ecological standards really exist. The growing and consistent engagement of financial business for natural environment protection is a fact. ERI is a clear evidence of that. The results could be also useful for creating responsible financial business in modern economy. However, the implementation of environmental rules on financial market is not only inspiring, but also questionable. Undoubtedly, the ecological challenge in financial business is an important subject of scientific research.

Keywords Ecology • Corporate social responsibility • Financial market

L. Dziawgo (✉)
Department of Financial Management, Nicolaus Copernicus University, Toruń, Poland
e-mail: ldziawgo@econ.umk.pl

E. Dziawgo
Department of Econometrics and Statistics, Nicolaus Copernicus University, Toruń, Poland
e-mail: dziawew@umk.pl

© Springer International Publishing Switzerland 2016

M.H. Bilgin et al. (eds.), *Business Challenges in the Changing Economic Landscape - Vol. 1*, Eurasian Studies in Business and Economics 2/1,
DOI 10.1007/978-3-319-22596-8_11

1 Introduction

The international financial market evolves to CSR/ESG including ecological criteria. Nowadays, a lot of leading financial institutions over the World keep or gain clients thanks to using environmental aspects. The rapidly growing and widely diversified ecological engagement of financial institutions is clearly visible. This process could be even called ecological evolution of financial market.

Also in Poland "ecologization" of financial business is noticeable. It means that not only on developed but also on developing financial markets the CSR/ESG—ideas including crucial ecological aspects are in progress. The case of Poland is very impressive. The Polish financial market is one of the most important and promising emerging markets hosting key financial players.

The elaboration is focused on indicating and analysing the problem of implementation of environmental rules in financial business—especially the use of financial products related to natural environment protection (ERI—Ecologically Responsible Investment). The problem is presented in two aspects: theoretical and empirical. Empirically, the considerations are based on selected cases of business practice of International and Polish financial market and surveys conducted in the period of 2009–2014 on a representative sample of Polish society.

The results show really wide engagement of financial business for natural environment protection. Ecological evolution of financial market is a fact.

2 Research Methodology

To describe and analyse the problem of "ecologization" of financial market the following research methods have been used: critical analysis of literature and financial data, comparison method, induction method and questionnaire method. The surveys on a representative sample of Polish society in the period 2009–2014 have been conducted with support of Polish NCN (National Centre of Science) and Santander Universidades. The last survey was financed within a research project titled 'Ecological Evolution of the Financial Market (EcoFin)' supported by Bank Zachodni WBK under Santander Universidades programme. The surveys have been created, ordered and supervised by the Author and conducted by the Millward Brown SMG/KRC and GfK Polonia. For selected data analysis the IBM SPSS Statistics software has been used. The statistical error is ±3.1 %, with confidence interval 95 %.

3 "Ecologization" of the International Financial Market

3.1 Proecological Activities

The term "ecologization of financial market" means the adjustment of financial institutions to ecological requirements within the frames of CSR/ESG concepts (for other specialized term used to describe such investments see Staub-Bisang 2012). For years, many leading financial institutions have supported natural environment in the following ways: financing proecological NGO's, saving resources, implementing procedures for ecological risk assessment in loan business, offering financial products and services related to financing natural environment in business/ economy (Fig. 1) (Dziawgo 2003).

The first two mentioned proecological activities are commonly used in business, but saving resources in financial business is something special. Financial institutions have a relatively very low direct environmental impact. However, to be more ecologically friendly, commercial financial institutions begin to save: power energy, heating energy, water, and paper. It is important to reduce even the number and length of business trips due to the greenhouse effect (Dziawgo 2014).

The last two mentioned activities are very specific for financial institutions. The assessment of ecological risk has become an integral part of credit risk assessment (Hawkins 2006). However, what is more inspiring, is offering special financial products and services related to natural environment protection. This kind of proecological activities is not widely known. Yet, there are a lot of ecological diversified investment offers in financial business and their number is growing (Werner 2009). That is exactly why Ecologically Responsible Investment (ERI) deserves wider presentation and advanced scientific research.

All proecological activities mentioned above are undertaken due to legal regulations, risk avoidance, profitability, and the pressure of shareholders, customers and public (Moszynski and Wieckowska 2014). The main aim of all these activities is not only to create ecological image and to be clearly distinguished from other competitive financial institutions. Also, reducing risk and costs is also very important in financial business.

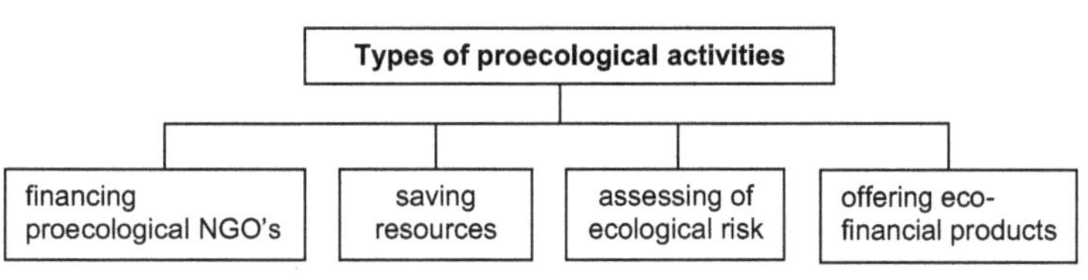

Fig. 1 Types of proecological activities of financial market institutions

3.2 Critical Aspects of "Ecologization"

The ecological engagement and achievements of financial business should be really appreciated. However, it is also possible to indicate some important controversial aspects concerning ecological activities. The aim of the criticism is not to discredit, but to explain these and, in result, to improve the process of ecological evolution of financial market. There is a wide range of critical aspects: from some minor doubts to serious and robust critical arguments. In many cases this criticism is really well-founded and concerns both theoretical and practical areas of ecologization. In the both above mentioned areas, criticism concerns the following aspects (Fig. 2):

- real motives of ecological rules implementation,
- scope of ecological activities,
- scale of ecological activities,
- effectiveness of ecological activities (Dziawgo 2014).

The adequate criticism is of a fundamental importance for quality of "ecologization" process on financial market. There are a lot of questions concerning critical aspects. There is absolutely no certainty about the main reason of ecological rules implementation: supporting sales, saving costs or real conviction to protect natural environment. None of the above motives exclude each other, but doubts still exist. The same problem concerns other aspects such as: scope, scale and effectiveness of all ecological activities in financial business (Dziawgo 2014).

The ecological engagement of financial institutions comparing to their huge business potential does not look great and diversified enough. Moreover, many financial institutions undertake some single or superficial ecological initiatives instead of systematic approach. The reason of such activities is creating positive ecological image in the easiest way. Unfortunately, on the financial market there are even some examples of abuse of ecological image (Deml and Blisse 2011).

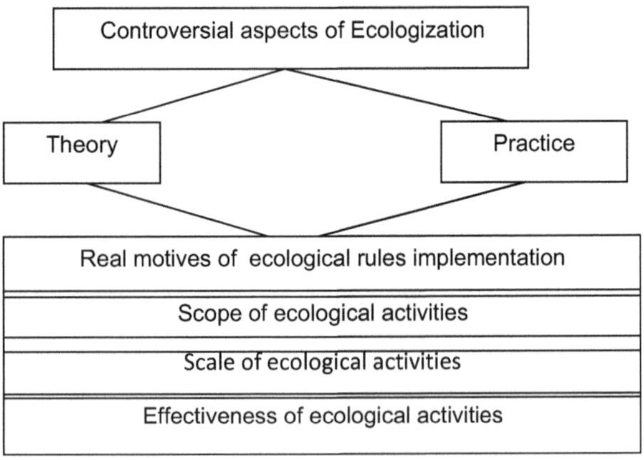

Fig. 2 Controversial aspects of "Ecologization"

4 International Financial Market: Ecologically Responsible Investment—Selected Examples

On the international financial market a lot has been done for natural environment. There are numerous of proecological initiatives of local, regional and international dimension. Many leading financial institutions co-ordinate their activities in the frame of UNEP-FI (United Nations Environment Programme—Finance Initiative), EPFI (Equator Principles Financial Initiative), PRI (Principles for Responsible Investment), WBCSD (World Business Council for Sustainable Development) or GRI (Global Reporting Initiative). It is also necessary to indicate an internal proecological initiative such as German VfU—Verein fuer Umweltmanagement und Nachhaltigkeit in Finanzinstitutionen e.V. (Association for Ecological Management and Sustainability in Finance, www.vfu.de), and others.

Also interesting are Investor Relations or Public Relations activities of financial business oriented on CSR, ESG including ecology (Dziawgo 2012). A perfect example of this is annually organized by Financial Times and IFC (International Financial Corporation) international contest for "Sustainable Bank of The Year".

Concluding, financial institutions widely support natural environment in all the ways mentioned in Sect. 3.1. However, special attention should be paid to financial products and services related to natural environment. Certainly, creating this part of financial offer requires from financial business greater proecological engagement than saving resources or financing proecological NGO's exclusively.

According to a reliable estimation already billion euros all over the world are invested in respect to social criteria. A crucial part of it is invested in respect to ecological criteria (Upgang 2009; Gabriel 2007; Rotthaus 2009). The financial business offers a lot of possibilities of proecological investments. Below, some selected examples of Ecologically Responsible Investments are presented: deposits, loans, bonds, shares, structured products, investment funds, asset management, private banking/wealth management, private equity.

Moreover, Ecologically Responsible Investment is supported by use of specialized capital market indices such as: Dow Jones Sustainability Index, FTSE4Good, FTSE KLD Global Climate, Nasdaq Clean Edge Index, S&P Global Clean Energy Index, S&P Global Water Index. CSR profiled indices facilitate indicating appropriate investment objectives and measuring their effectiveness (Dziawgo 2014; Perez 2007).

The subject of Ecologically Responsible Investment can be considered in many scopes. Two of them are described below. The institutional approach is presented on the example of German bank. In turn, instrumental approach is presented on the example of investment units of investment funds.

Some financial institutions are really deeply involved in Ecologically Responsible Investment offering a wide range of financial products. As a good example German bank Deutsche Bank can be presented. The bank offers numerous specialized products in different business lines such as: Asset Management, Wealth Management, Investment Funds and others. In 2013 the total value of asset under

Table 1 CSR/ESG—investment funds in German-speaking Europe 2014

Specification	Number	Amount (million euros)
Equity funds	108	15,125
Bond funds	37	4719
Mixed funds	18	2292
ETF	7	597
Money market funds	2	119
Fund of funds	9	129
Total	181	22,981

management invested in respect to ESG criteria was over 5100 million euros. The bank is also engaged in "Green Bond Principles", in 2014 as Lead Manager for "Climate Awareness Bond" issued by European Investment Bank (350 million CHF). The number of all pro-ecological activities provided by Deutsche Bank in domestic and international dimension is really high. The latest mentioned activity is one of the newest international initiatives. The "Green Bond Principles" enables capital raising and investment for projects with environmental benefits.

Considering ERI, it is also adequate to present the instrumental approach focused on different financial instruments used to support natural environment in business. One of them is investment unit in investment funds. In the international financial market operate already hundreds of so called ethic-ecological investment funds (CSR/ESG investment funds) and they are becoming very popular (Ulshoefer and Bonnet 2009). Recently, German speaking Europe represents very dynamic market for this kind of investment (Deml and May 2005; Deml and Blisse 2011). The value of this market is over 23,000 million euros (Table 1). Moreover, many of ethic-ecological investment funds belongs to the leading financial institutions, which create standards in financial sector.

Concluding, the above mentioned specific examples of ERI on financial market can be treated as clear evidence of advanced and diversified pro-ecological engagement of financial business in natural environment protection in business activities. There are a lot of possibilities to invest capital according to ecological standards.

5 Ecologically Responsible Investment on Polish Financial Market

Also the Polish financial market evolves to CSR/ESG including ecological criteria. Poland has already been permanently presented in the acknowledged European SRI Study since 2010 edition. Obviously, Ecologically Responsible Investment represents only a part of Polish SRI investment. On Fig. 3 some examples of proecological financial products are indicated and some selected ones are described below.

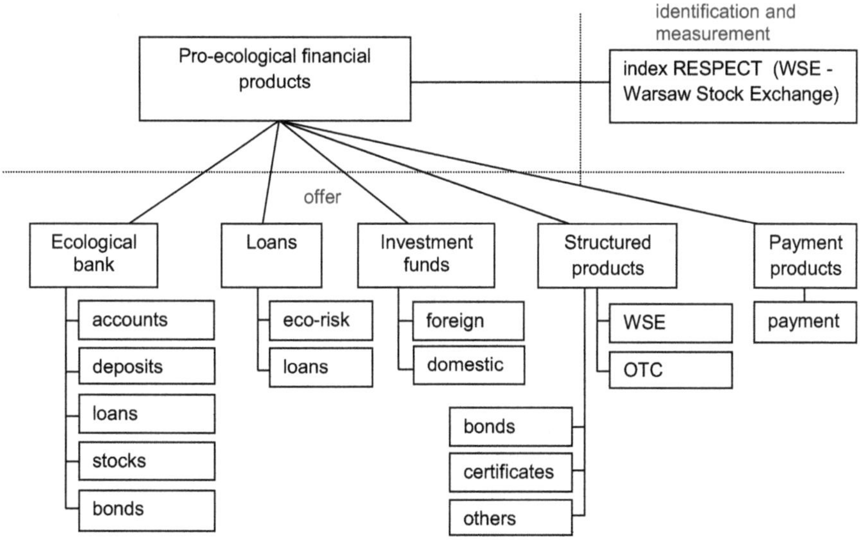

Fig. 3 Financial products related to natural environment protection (Poland 2008–2014)

The Polish Bank Ochrony Srodowiska BOS (Bank of Natural Environment Protection) is an excellent example of a combination of ecological and commercial criteria. This is a universal commercial bank specializing in financing eco-friendly business undertakings. A general assumption of "ecological bank concept" is an entire subordination of all business activities to ecological rules based on economic calculations. The bank offers a wide range of financial products related to ecology: deposits, loans, bonds and stocks.

Especially interesting are certain deposits connected with protection of selected endangered animal species. This is really unique. Such products have been used for protection of: stork, wolf, owl, wildcat, buzzard, gopher, moose and wizard. Moreover, the bank is also listed on the Warsaw Stock Exchange (WSE). A clear ecological strategy of the bank is an important advantage on competitive financial market.

The next example of positive social and ecological changes on Polish financial market is Index "RESPECT" launched on Warsaw Stock Exchange (WSE) in 2009 as the first CSR Index in Eastern and Central Europe (Dziawgo 2014). The name "Respect" is an acronym of words: Responsibility, Ecology, Sustainability, Participation, Environment, Community, and Transparency. WSE-Index "RESPECT" is constantly developing and already includes shares of the best 22 public companies from the ecological, social and also economic point of view (among others seven financial companies). What is also important, this part of the capital market represents approximately 30 % stock market capitalization.

On the Polish financial market also some special financial products related to ecology were or still are available such as: bonds, investment certificates and structured products. In the last mentioned category should be indicated: "Good

Energy", "Green Energy", "Alternative Energy", "Forestry", "Climate Protection", "Water", "Friendly Planet", "New Energy". The specialized products are offered by mBank, BZ WBK Santander Group, Barclays and Raiffeisen.

Another example of Ecologically Responsible Investment is an activity of ethical & ecological investment funds. On the Polish capital market operate foreign and domestic specialized investment funds: Allianz EcoTrends, Investor Climate Change, BGF New Europe, BNP Paribas L1 Green Tigers, Arka BZ WBK Energia, SKOK Etyczny 1, SKOK Etyczny 2, PZU Energia Medycyna Ekologia and still others.

The next examples of proecological activities are payment cards issued in association with recognized ecological organizations such as WWF—World Wide Fund for Nature. Millennium Bank offers affinity payment card of MasterCard. In turn BZ WBK offers some payment cards with ecological motives.

Financial institutions engaged in CSR/ESG inform the public in scope of PR and IR publishing specific information and specialized reports about their ecological activities, using also GRI standards. The company website is used widely for that purpose, as well.

The above mentioned facts about Ecologically Responsible Investment and other proecological activities lead to the conclusion that new ecological trend is visible also on the Polish financial market.

6 Surveys: Public Opinion in Poland 2009–2014

Public support and recognition by customers are very important success sources in modern financial business. The ecological engagement of financial institutions based on public ecological sensitivity clearly seems a very useful activity to gain public and customers attention which then can be used to compete on the market. For that reason, eco-activities of financial institutions are widely presented to the public opinion by their Investor Relations and Public Relations services. However, a question rises whether these eco-activities are really recognized by public opinion and customers.

The aim of the surveys conducted by the Author on representative sample of the Polish society is to recognize public opinion on and assessment of the proecological adjustment of Polish financial sector. Already the surveys in 1997 and 2002 provided the first evidence of symptoms that the significance of eco-activities of financial institutions for society is probably overestimated or the quality of PR and IR services is not satisfactory. The latest surveys were conducted in 2009 and 2014. All the surveys were based on questionnaire method and were created and supervised by the Author and conducted by a specialized institute (2009—Millward Brown SMG/KRC, 2014 GfK Polonia). In selected cases the PASW Statistics software was used for the data analysis.

Below are presented only several selected questions and answers to gain a general view of the problem. The presented results should be treated with caution.

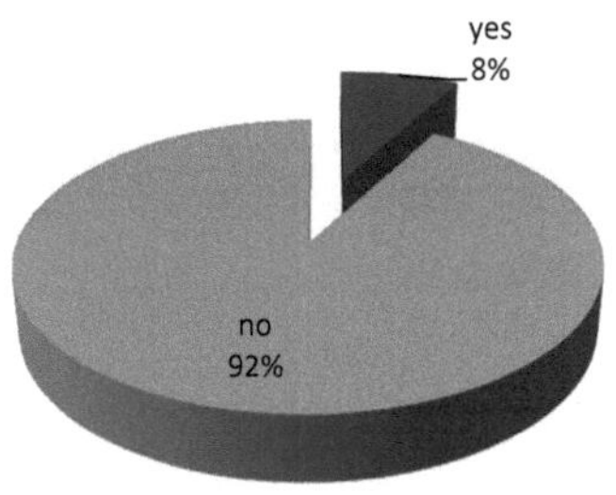

Fig. 4 The range of answer to the question: "Have you heard about CSR?" (%)

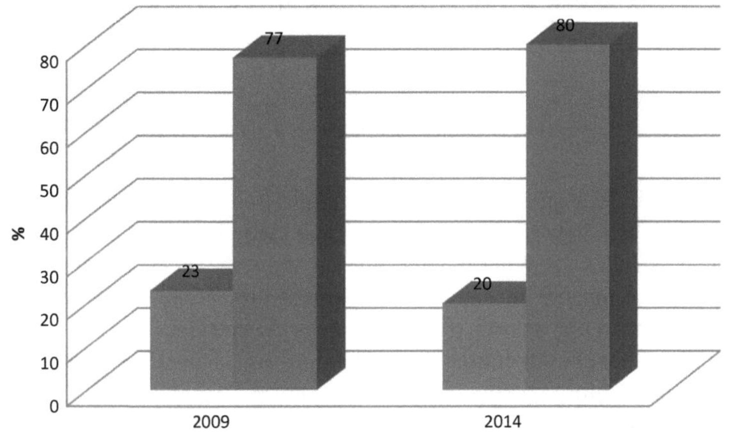

Fig. 5 The range of answers to the question: "Do you know any banks, financial institutions or stock quoted companies involved in protecting natural environment?"

The first question was asked only in 2014 and was formulated as follows: "Have you heard about CSR?" The respondents have answered as illustrated in Fig. 4.

The result is, of course, unsatisfactory. Many managers and activists who are engaged in greater CSR implementation in modern business and society are wrong, believing that the CSR—idea is widely known. Unfortunately, this is an unreal picture of the situation. The presented results seem a very pessimistic starting point to analyse the next questions. Also, some relationships connected with the answer were tested. The influence of respondents' education, sex or place of residence on the given answers is very weak. Below the results: education: test Czuprov's T 0.15; sex: test Czuprov's T 0.07; place: test Cramer's V 0.14.

The next two questions were asked in 2009 as well as 2014. The first of them was formulated as follows: "Do you know any banks or stock quoted companies involved in protecting natural environment?" Only 20–23 % respondents indicated the positive answer. The majority chose the "no" answer—77–80 % (Fig. 5). The best recognized financial institution supporting natural environment in Poland according to results of the surveys was Polish Ecological Bank—BOS: 2009—7.4 % answers; 2014—9 % answers.

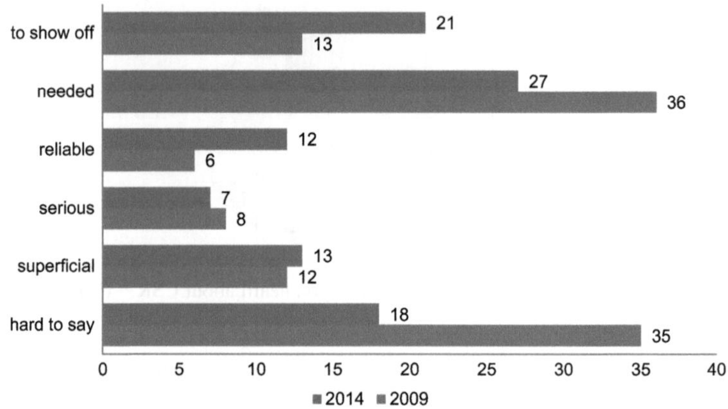

Fig. 6 The range of answers to the question: 'What is your opinion about the engagement of banks, financial institutions and stock quoted companies in natural environment protection?' (%)

With the previous question corresponds a question related to the social opinion on ecological activities of financial sector and capital market. The question was formulated as follows: "What is your opinion about the engagement of banks and stock quoted companies in natural environment protection?" (It was possible to indicate more than one answer from a few possible entries).

The most often chosen entries were: "hard to say"—35–18 %, "to show off"—13–21 %, and, unfortunately, "reliable"—6–12 %, "serious"—8–7 %, "superficial"—12–13 %, but as many as "needed" 36–27 % (Fig. 6). The public expectations related to greater business engagement for natural environment protection are relatively high, but the public assessment of the quality of this engagement is very low. Also, the answers to this question were statistically tested. In case of sex of respondents achieved the following result: Chi-square test = 11.2; df = 8; p = 0.19. There are no grounds to reject null hypotheses: the sex of respondents has no influence on given answer. There is no relationship between sex and the given answer. In turn, in case of place of residence: test Cramer's V = 0.125; education: test Czuprov's T = 0.11. Concluding, the influence of education and place of residence of respondents on the given answers is very weak.

The last question was asked in 2014 and dealt with public expectations concerning ecological engagement of companies from financial and capital market. The question was formulated as follows: what do you expect from banks or stock quoted companies involved in protecting natural environment? Below are presented the most common answers (Fig. 7).

Public expectations concerning ecological engagement of entities of financial and capital market are really not too high. As many as 58 % respondents answered "hard to say". From enormous financial business is mostly required only financial support for natural environment protection (15 %) or at least saving paper (4 %) or saving energy (3 %). The results seem deeply disappointing, but answers given to the first question should prepare anyone for this situation.

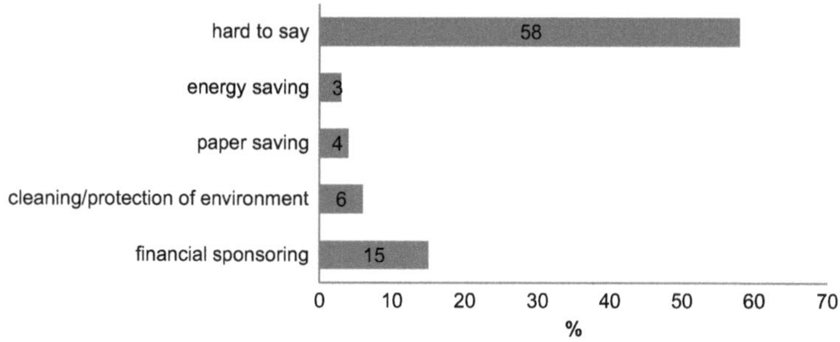

Fig. 7 "What do you expect from banks or stock quoted companies involved in protecting natural environment?"

Moreover, some respondents expect from financial institutions even cleaning or protecting forest and rivers and also afforesting (6 %), but the problem is in which way: financing this kind of activity or undertaking direct activity?

7 Conclusions

Based on the presented facts it is possible to draw conclusions. The conclusions can be divided into two parts:

- universal conclusions adequate for international as well as Polish financial market,
- specific conclusions adequate for Polish financial market exclusively.

The universal conclusions:

- a social and ecological evolution of financial market is a fact,
- a significant part of this evolution is also offering financial products related to natural environment protection (ERI—Ecologically Responsible Investment).

The specific conclusion: significance of eco-activities of financial institutions for society is overestimated or the quality of PR and IR services related to these activities is unsatisfactory.

The financial market evolves according to social and ecological criteria. There are a lot of more or less significant signs of positive changes. Ecologically Responsible Investment is a very important part of this positive evolution of modern financial business. However, criticism is highly required for proper assessment of this promising process—in developed as well as in developing countries.

Creating a new prosocial and proecological model of functioning of modern economy we still face a number of challenges. One of them is to use adequately, effectively and trustworthily the huge potential of financial market to support natural environment in everyday business. For this purpose public awareness and support are also highly needed. The results of the surveys may be useful in this mission.

References

Deml, M., & Blisse, H. (2011). *Gruenes Geld* [Green money]. Stuttgart: Hampp Verlag.
Deml, M., & May, H. (2005). *Gruenes Geld* [Green money]. Stuttgart: Balance.
Dziąwgo, L. (2003). *Eco-offers of banks and investment funds. Poland and international trends.* Torun: UMK.
Dziawgo, D. (2012). Investor relations and importance in the global financial market. *Equilibrium, 7*(2), 59–76.
Dziawgo, L. (2014). Greening financial market. *Copernican Journal of Finance and Accounting, 3* (2), 9–23.
Gabriel, K. (2007). *Nachhaltigkeit am Finanzmarkrt* [Sustainability on financial market]. Munich: oekom Verlag.
Hawkins, D. E. (2006). *Corporate social responsibility*. New York: Palgrave Macmillan.
Moszynski, M., & Wieckowska, M. (2014). Evolution of ecological financial market from the perspective of institutional economics. *Copernican Journal of Finance and Accounting, 3*(1), 121–133.
Perez, O. (2007). *The new universe of green finance: From self-regulation to multi-polar governance* (Bar-Ilan University, Working Paper No. 1-07, pp. 1–33).
Rotthaus, S. (2009). *Erfolgreich investieren in gruene Geldanlagen* [Effective investing in green financial assets]. Frankfurt: Campus Verlag.
Staub-Bisang, M. (2012). *Sustainable investing for institutional investors*. Singapore: Wiley.
Ulshoefer, G., & Bonnet, G. (2009). *Corporate Social Responsibility auf dem Finanzmarkt* [Corporate social responsibility on financial market]. Wiesbaden: VS Verlag fuer Sozialwissenschaften.
Upgang, M. (2009). *Gewinn mit Sinn* [Profit with sense]. Munich: oekom Verlag.
Werner, T. (2009). *Oekologische Investments* [Ecological investments]. Wiesbaden: Gabler.

Common Characteristics of Financial Development in Balkan Region Economies

Erinda Imeraj

Abstract Balkan countries' economies have different backgrounds due to the political regimes they have been through, but studies have realized that in the first phase of transition progress, the initial conditions have the major impact. Restructured Reform and new policies are the major impacts on the progress and development of the Balkan countries economies. Balkan countries, being in transition economic period, have implemented same reforms in the financial systems which are monitored by international institutions. This study aims to analyze key financial developments in the Balkan countries, and to highlight joint characteristics of this sector. Countries considered in this study are Albania, Bulgaria, Bosnia-Herzegovina, Macedonia, Montenegro, Romania and Serbia. Firstly the study will go through the origin of the development of financial system and the key indicators of a common origin. Based on official statistics of the World Bank, the study will compare economies of Balkan while setting together the common ones. In conclusion the common characteristics of the financial development of Balkan countries would be originated from the banking system used by the former regime and the same reforms implementation.

Keywords Balkan • Transition • Financial development • Characteristics

1 Introduction

Balkan region economies have different backgrounds depending on political regimes that have been through, but has been studied that, only in the first steps of the transition, the initial conditions have the major impact on the progress. Then, almost the whole impact on the transition effect has been due to the policies pursued by the reforms undertaken. Reform of the transition has been different in many developing countries, but based on the latest report of the European Bank for Reconstruction and Development (EBRD), financial sector reforms adopted in early 2008–2009 crisis have shown more resilience than other sectors.

E. Imeraj (✉)
Department of Banking and Finance, EPOKA University, Tirana, Albania
e-mail: eimeraj@epoka.edu.al

© Springer International Publishing Switzerland 2016

M.H. Bilgin et al. (eds.), *Business Challenges in the Changing Economic Landscape - Vol. 1*, Eurasian Studies in Business and Economics 2/1,
DOI 10.1007/978-3-319-22596-8_12

The situation that the policymakers face in the transition countries and economies as the Balkan countries is very difficult and asks for a lot support. Despite the effort undertaken in years for the developed countries and the Internationals to improve the financial sector and the macroeconomic environment it is believed that financial markets and system yet is underdeveloped. The situation has hampered the policymaker's job through the financial reform development and bigger issues have been brought through their agendas and their studies (Torre et al. 2007).

This study aims to analyze key financial developments in the Balkans, and separate common characteristics in this sector. Initially, the study will look at some of the many studies that different authors have done exactly on financial system development in developing countries, including also Balkan countries, which matched the economic transition period, or and implementation of various reforms, specifically financial reform. Recent studies have paid special attention to the decisive origin of financial development in different countries, and the key determinant affecting balanced developing. Part of this study includes a summary of these determinants, from which it could be verified that the Balkan countries originate from rough financial development, and therefore can be studied their common characteristics.

In order the study to be complete and oriented toward the main goal, the next section will present indicators of financial system development in the Balkans for years, respectively in 1998–2011 and the inclusion of initiatives or reforms of international development institutions. Based on current statistics, the records of the EBRD in its latest report in 2013 and the records of the World Bank, this study will present the development of indicators and financial imbalances that have these financial systems. The first indicator presented is Deposits Money Bank assets to GDP percentage for every country selected in this paper for the Balkan region, which claims on domestic real nonfinancial sector by deposit money banks as a share of GDP. The study will continue with Net Interest Margin in percentage form, which serves as a measurement of a country's banking efficiency. Then there will be an overview of the data of the same Balkan countries on Banking Return on Equity and Banking Return on Capital. A basic measure of bank profitability that corrects for the size of the bank is the return on assets (ROA). There exists some absences through some years in two of the countries studied, Bosnia-Herzegovina and Montenegro. The forth financial indicator taken into consideration is Liquidity Risk, which covers the study of national statistics on loan-deposit ratio. Liquidity of a bank is specifically covered from the ability of it to meet obligations in the time needed through the increase of its assets.

Finally, the study will conclude the main objective response of which are the joint characteristics of the financial system in the Balkan countries, which exactly will go through banking system and its performance. Banking Sector Indicators are the main and common factors in the development of the financial system of the Balkan countries.

2 Literature Review

The Balkan economies have been and continue to be part of various studies related to many different concepts or economical sides. The main features of the studies made highlighted the transition influence and the fact that for some countries the process took too long time while the others are on the right path. As economies they have been stated as similar because of the past joint policy and systems, these reasons made the research part of the common characteristics on comparing their development. Gorton and Winton (1998) showed a link between the size of the banking system and economic stability of countries in transition, which the Balkan countries are included. Banks in these countries have a large amount of bad loans inherited from the previous central bank. The study shows that when bank regulator imposes higher capital requirements and tries to impose market discipline, banks will come out from the industry and new banks would be inclined to failure. Thus, the banking system will become small and inefficient. They call the idea that the banking system will be smaller than normal in transition economies, "the effect on economies in transition."

Golubovic and Golubovic (2005) conclude from the study on the reform of the financial system in the Balkans, the main goal of this sector for the countries in transition is to change the role of the financial system. This means that the financial sector should have an active role in the mobilization, concentration and distribution of limited financial resources. Changes in the reformation of the banking system in these countries have not resulted in the expected levels. Instead, financial sector reform should include changes harmonized in all its segments: banking, insurance, capital markets, institutional investor's position and supply of financial instruments. Only the changes synchronized successfully in all these segments can create an efficient financial system.

Through a study regarding the banking development in transition economies of Dow et al. (2008) it is summarized a four stage approach implemented on transition economies in former Soviet Union (FSU). The authors concluded on shock results of the primer policies that these economies had implemented in 1990, which resulted in difficult financial problems as hyperinflation, macroeconomic chaos and a general public loss of trust in the banking system. So this increased and made every product of the bank less credible and the function of it more difficult. In this situation the first stage to go through for these transition economies was the institution—building process strongly cash—based. Parallel to the gain of the public confidence the banking system has to go smoother in its transition from a mono-bank system to the market-based two-tier system. Without these policies the transition of the sector analyzed would be much more difficult.

Most Balkan countries in transition have reached a point in their development where the financial sector is an effective determinant of the general economic growth. However, the impact of various financial institutions like banks or financial markets, legal and regulatory environment, changes strongly amongst the states (Djalilov and Piesse 2011).

3 Origin of Financial Development

In recent studies on the development of financial systems, the definition of some indicators of potential determinant has occupied an important role. This section will present some possible determinants, which fit well with some financial development determinants in the Balkan countries. Firstly, countries are institutions that are part of determinants, especially legal institutions. According to Huang (2010), a legal and regulatory system that includes protection of property rights, contract enforcement and accounting best practices has been identified as crucial to financial development. Based on this conclusion, the research states that the Balkan countries, respectively, highlighting the Western Balkans (Albania, Macedonia, Serbia, Montenegro, Bulgaria, Romania etc.), also taking into account their history, are places with little development of these key points or have absence in the normal development of the legal system. The study also argues that the legal origin of the code significantly affects the treatment of creditors and shareholders, and the efficiency of contract enforcement.

Following determinants as the origin of financial developments can highlight also the Policies of the particular countries. Study made on the undertaken policy emphasizes the importance of macroeconomic policies, the opening of markets for goods and financial liberalization, or financial development. Some important macroeconomic policies are assessed as favorable as that of maintaining low inflation or increased investment. To compare the studies done for other countries, the same can be said also for the Balkan countries. These countries are part of many macroeconomic policies, some of them already part of the European Union, and the rest inspirits to be part of the EU. Based on the research states that the Balkan countries undertake policies related to such purposes.

Fewer studies have been addressed as a determinant on the geographical position, by not giving the required importance to the institutions or the implemented policies. But in the case of this study it deals with countries with a similar geographical position by emphasizing other aspects. Initially Balkan countries have a small area, and this fact in Huang (2010) is stated as a relation with financial development. Also national resources as an aspect of the geographical position brings the same reasoning for the Balkan countries, countries with considerable economic resources but the policies are in slower development stage.

Other aspects determining the financial development are: gross domestic product per person, interest rates and savings, loans and deposits of banks, foreign investment etc. These indicators will be analyzed more precisely in the next parts of the study, based on official data from the World Bank of the Balkan countries.

4 Statistics and Evaluations

4.1 *Financial Development in Terms of Banking Sector*

Table 1 shows some data on the ratio of the Deposits Money Bank assets to GDP percentage for every country selected in this paper for the Balkan region, which Claims on domestic real nonfinancial sector by deposit money banks as a share of GDP. It is easily observed the absence of the data for Montenegro and Bosnia-Herzegovina in the years 1999–2005. What is observed by the data and by converting them into real charts covers a positive and similar change for the countries selected. So the banking sector has a slow development but the increase of the banking sector assets has a higher percentage to GDP from 1999 to 2011. The correlation and the similarity on the growing motion start basically from the 2001 year. So it can be considered as a joint financial indicator for the economies selected for the study.

4.2 *Net Interest Margin*

Table 2 shows the data for the country selected on the Net Interest Margin in percentage form. Net Interest Margin serves as a measurement of a country's banking efficiency. But must be remembered that his landing, not always signal an improvement in efficiency. It is observed from the data the constant trend of growth, highlighting again Montenegro to the absence of complete data. Basically as a second financial data observed, again it is the year 2001 which makes the difference for a more similar trend of growth of the data for the selected countries. The trend in the data is observed to be similar and in same motion, which would consider this indicator as similar for the economies considered.

4.3 *Bank ROA and Bank ROE*

Table 3 gives an overview of the data of some Balkan countries on Banking Return on Equity and Banking Return on Capital. A basic measure of bank profitability that corrects for the size of the bank is the return on assets (ROA), which divides the net income of the bank by the amount of its assets. ROA is a useful measure of how well a bank manager is doing on the job because it indicates how well a bank's assets are being used to generate profits (Mishkin and Serletis 2011). These data are showed in the Table 3 Panel A for the countries of the Balkan region. It is easily observed the similar trends except of the Montenegro and Bosnia-Herzegovina countries which seems that have had many difficulties during the financial crises of the last years. There has to be specified that the years 1999–2003 which seem to

Table 1 Deposit money bank assets to GDP (%)

Year	Albania	Bulgaria	Bosnia-Herzegovina	Macedonia	Montenegro	Romania	Serbia
1999	32.45	16.3		19.03		14.92	28.2
2000	32.4	15.62		20.21		11.59	33.54
2001	32.1	16.82		21.45		10.85	35.14
2002	33.63	21.36		21.01		12.35	22.83
2003	33.27	27.02		20.65		13.8	18.42
2004	35.27	34.65		22.25		15.5	21.43
2005	38.29	41.04		24.66		18.47	26.33
2006	43.82	45.85		29.25	29.02	22.56	29.53
2007	50.44	54.8	45.35	33.66	56.17	29.3	31.36
2008	55.21	68.42	50.03	40.08	81.05	35.62	37.03
2009	58.76		53.23	45.38	87.23	45.62	46.94
2010	58.77		53.67	46.46	74.84	49.14	55.31
2011	61.29		61.13	47.58	65.99	48.56	59.87

Source: World Bank Financial Development and Structure Dataset

Table 2 Net interest margin (%)

Year	Albania	Bulgaria	Bosnia-Herzegovina	Macedonia	Montenegro	Romania	Serbia
1999	3.58	4.51	5.68	6.92		16.81	8.91
2000	3.86	5.52	6.32	5.6		9.07	4.27
2001	3.64	4.66	5.99	4.7		9.78	6.39
2002	3.35	4.79	6.4	4.94		8.43	7.1
2003	3.63	4.64	6.04	5.67	14.52	7.15	8.13
2004	3.95	5.77	5.09	5.46	8	8.75	7.09
2005	4.4	5.12	4.83	5.07	5.72	6.67	7.69
2006	4.69	5.55	4.69	4.73	4.07	5.55	8.46
2007	5.65	5.26	4.72	5.89	3.74	3.89	7.85
2008	4.74	5.12	4.13	5.3	3.34	4.99	7.94
2009	4.33	4.42	4.26	5.19	4.25	5.7	6.95
2010	4.52	4.53	4.39	4.46	3.33	6.29	5.67
2011	4.45	4.11	4.52	4.31	5.43	5.02	5.4

Source: World Bank Financial Development and Structure Dataset

Table 3 Bank ROA and Bank ROE

Year	Albania	Bulgaria	Bosnia-Herzegovina	Macedonia	Montenegro	Romania	Serbia
Panel A: Bank ROA							
1999	14.76	2.41	−0.36	0.82		3.35	0.6
2000	1.96	3.92	0.71	0.59		2.85	3.1
2001	0.83	1.86	−1.86	−1.02		2.85	−0.15
2002	0.66	2.27	0.61	0.32		1.96	−1.07
2003	1.08	2.39	1.24	1.49	3.36	0.83	1.92
2004	0.81	2.27	0.82	1.7	2.02	2.96	−1.52
2005	1.61	1.94	0.79	1.41	0.18	1.95	0.54
2006	1.28	1.92	1.03	1.97	0.68	1.74	1.95
2007	1.55	2.63	0.99	2.26	0.5	1.12	1.89
2008	1.46	2.24	0.47	1.52	−0.29	1.83	1.65
2009	1.06	1.04	0.24	0.81	0.33	0.82	0.72
2010	1	0.87	−0.57	0.98	−2.91	0.69	0.83
2011	1	0.76	0.98	0.39	−0.9	0.3	0.97
Panel B: Bank ROE							
1999	21.63	11.6	−2.01	4.49		22.29	5.95
2000	21.03	19.12	3.89	3.17		16.73	16.05
2001	8.83	10.77	3.4	−5.76		15.98	−0.92
2002	7.19	15.24	5.06	1.85		11.42	−5.73
2003	12.86	16.65	9.91	8.06	16.64	5.29	8.79
2004	11.18	18.71	7.17	9.51	10.54	22.29	−7.54
2005	22.65	17.8	7.6	8.69	1.13	16.78	3.06
2006	18.59	18.63	10.35	13.22	5.81	17.21	10.56
2007	21.82	24.87	10.48	16.53	6.14	12.61	9.12
2008	17.4	20.11	4.91	11.57	−3.85	21.14	7.31
2009	10.58	8.56	2.32	6.37	3.6	8.93	3.27
2010	9.4	6.74	−5.01	8.25	−25.6	6.87	4.26
2011	8.96	5.82	7.73	3.31	−7.54	2.75	4.97

Source: World Bank Financial Development and Structure Dataset

be problematic for Montenegro in all the indicators considered, where some difficult years for the country not only financial but also political ones.

Although ROA provides useful information about bank profitability, it is not what the bank's owners (equity holders) care about most. They are more concerned about how much the bank is earning on their equity investment, an amount that is measured by the return on equity (ROE), the net income per dollar of equity capital. Bank ROE is showed in the Table 3 Panel B. It also seems to have the same motion of growth for the countries selected and specifically the same countries are observed with the lowest rates due to the financial crises happening. Despite the more highlighted differences in these two indicators for the countries selected, they can be considered as joint indicators for the main characteristics that the study aims to specify.

4.4 *Liquidity Risk*

One way to study Liquidity risk is the study of national statistics on loan-deposit ratio. Table 4 gives data on the selected Balkan countries on this report. Liquidity of a bank is specifically covered from the ability of it to meet obligations in the time needed through the increase of its assets. The important role and function of the bank is the transformation of the deposits in loans and manage to transform without causing gaps which would take the bank to the liquidity risk. Each bank has an important sector that has a duty of managing the liquidity risk. There is a general downward trend of this ratio in every country which leads us to the improvement of the liquidity. Albania is distinguished by a slightly lower ratio. Bosnia-Herzegovina, Macedonia and Serbia can be easily distinguished for the high ratios which continue to be high despite the decrease through the years. It is observed a similarity through Bulgaria, Romania and Macedonia but again the differences are considerable.

5 Conclusions

Financial system development is one of the main focuses for every country, specifically for countries which are not yet part of EU and inspired to have the accession. After the many crises and strong flows of the economies on Balkan countries the stages in the transition are very difficult and not all the reforms made the situation easier. Firstly the economies are faced on strong deviations of financial indicators which mainly were similar not for Balkan countries but probably in all transition economies. This study aimed the identification of common characteristics of financial development in the Balkan countries. A group of countries of the Balkan region was part of this study, Albania, Bulgaria, Bosnia-Herzegovina, Macedonia, Montenegro, Romania and Serbia. These countries were selected

Table 4 Bank credit to bank deposits

Year	Albania	Bulgaria	Bosnia-Herzegovina	Macedonia	Montenegro	Romania	Serbia
1999	8.61	53.93	729.4	154.1		37.72	324.5
2000	10.67	53.95	598.2	119.8		36.17	349.3
2001	12.74	53.17	129.8	68.17		44.41	257.9
2002	14.26	65.92	143.2	79.31	71.48	48.68	113.8
2003	16.3	82.73	144.8	71.83	94	70.66	108.6
2004	19.46	94.85	126.8	74.33	109.6	71.34	116.7
2005	29.2	95.33	129.8	76.47	79.94	80.35	122.3
2006	38.75	88.59	123.9	78.68	87.31	93.52	103
2007	47.96	107.3	128.2	82.76	121.2	114.5	98.14
2008	61.64	129.2	155	98.6	168.8	130.7	120.6
2009	63.52		140.1	95.25	157.8	119.8	111.5
2010	59.01		134.5	90.03	139.6	119.8	121.9
2011	58.43		115.7	89.39	119.3	121.1	118.1

Source: World Bank Financial Development and Structure Dataset

mainly from the similarities between them through other aspects rather than the financial one. Under the main determinants, which has been studied as the origin of the same development of countries, this study concludes that policies in the Balkan countries, legal institutions, reforms and geographical are common leading indicators. Based on official statistics and the stud of each of them, the banking sector indicators make the largest set of the joint determinants of the financial development in the Balkan countries selected.

References

Djalilov, K., & Piesse, J. (2011). Financial development and growth in transition countries: A study of Central Asia. *Emerging Markets Finance and Trade, 47*(6), 4–23.

Dow, S. C., Ghosh, D., & Ruziev, K. (2008). A stages approach to banking development in transition economies. *Journal of Post Keynesian Economics, 31*(1), 3–33.

Golubovic, S., & Golubovic, N. (2005). Financial sector reform in the Balkan countries in transition. *Facta Universitatis: Economics and Organization, 2*(3), 229–236.

Gorton, G. B., & Winton, A. (1998). Banking in transition economies: Does efficiency require instability? *Journal of Money, Credit and Banking, 30*, 621–650.

Huang, Y. (2010). *Determinants of financial development*. New York: Palgrave Macmillan.

Mishkin, F., & Serletis, A. (2011). *The economics of money, banking, and financial markets*. Toronto: Pearson Addison Wesley.

Torre, A., Gozzi, J. C., & Schmukler, S. (2007). Financial development: Maturing and emerging policy issues. *The World Bank Research Observer, 22*(1), 67–102.

The Determinants of Formal and Informal Household Loan Selection: Evidence from China

Chen Xue

Abstract The study investigates the relationship between household factors and the choice of Loan channels in the household borrowing decision. Using the survey data from the 2010 China Family Panel Studies (CFPS 2010), this paper finds that the households with better education and higher income are likely to get loans from formal financial institutions such as commercial banks, while middle-aged households show more probability to get loans from banks and private money lenders. But the household with less income and poor education background are more reliable to be financed by their social relationships such as friends and relatives. The house-ownerships play different roles in such selection. The household investors are less likely to turn to their social relationships. Comparatively, the house renters are harder to get money from banks as lack of collateral. Moreover, the household with the ownership of house for investment, would increase their risk preferences to increase amount of money financed by such channel and even afford a higher interests.

Keywords Household finance • Informal loan • Social circles • Private lending • House-ownership

1 Introduction

A growing body of research on credit supply in developing countries, especially in the household finance, which shows that the structure of the finance system in developing countries is different from the developed countries (Agenor and Montiel 2008). The households get access to formal financial system to attain their objectives is not as easy as the developing countries, so the informal financial sector flourishes and serves many households. So the formal and informal financial sectors coexist.

An alternative hypothesis is that the informal financial institutions play a complementary role to the formal ones by serving the credit demanders who cannot

C. Xue (✉)
School of Management, Shenzhen University, Shenzhen, PR China
e-mail: chenxue@szu.edu.cn

© Springer International Publishing Switzerland 2016
M.H. Bilgin et al. (eds.), *Business Challenges in the Changing Economic Landscape - Vol. 1*, Eurasian Studies in Business and Economics 2/1,
DOI 10.1007/978-3-319-22596-8_13

access the formal service as the lack of good credit ratings due to the information asymmetry problems. But the informal lenders hold a monitoring advantage over the formal lenders as the peer monitoring view (Stiglitz 1990) and operating different enforcement mechanism from formal ones to screen borrowers.

Allen et al. (2005) suggest that China is an example which is rely on alternative financing channels rather than formal external finance especially for private firms. Ayyagari et al. (2010) find the determinants of the Chinese firms to access to bank loans is the ability to post collateral but not the performance of firms. To the personal credit need, another kind of informal finance also is dominant in the Chinese culture, which is the dependence on their social circles, especially to the households having fewer resources to qualify the commercial banks requirement than others on average (Georgarakos and Pasini 2011). Furthermore for such households with poorer social circles resources to satisfy their credit need, the might turn to the private money lenders who function like banks but charge very high interest rate (Ferrer-i-Carbonell 2005).

So this is the first paper I classify the channels for the household getting credit into commercial banks which is the formal channel and the other two informal channels are their social circles such as friends or relatives and the private money lenders and discuss household credit choice on the formal and informal financial institutions using the survey data from the 2010 China Family Panel Studies (CFPS 2010).

I find that the commercial banks in China actually to deal with the potential default risks via controlling the loan applicators backgrounds such as age, income, education background and sufficient collateral such as houses. And the household with less income and poor education background are more reliable to be financed by their social circles such as friends and relatives. The house-ownerships play different roles in such selection. The household investors are less likely to turn to their social circles. Comparatively, the house renters are harder to get money from banks as lack of collateral. Private money lenders are poor at acquiring qualified borrowers with a good background about the income or education or house-ownership but they don't favour to finance the aged people.

This paper is organized as follows: Sect. 2 gives a literature review of household decision on the loan selections. Section 3 describes the data and the empirical model, Sect. 4 shows the empirical results and Sect. 5 concludes the paper.

2 Literature Review and Hypotheses

Both informal and formal finance have their strengths and weaknesses (Allen et al. 2013). The formal financiers they lack mechanisms for collecting the required soft information but the hard information just like the income, wealth and so on. Comparably, Informal finance relies on relationships and reputation implying that information asymmetries between informal lenders and their borrowers are less acute, the informal sources have superior information through social networks or business relations hence reduce moral hazard or adverse selection problems. Especially Furthermore, informal financiers are often better positioned to efficiently monitor and enforce repayment when legal enforcement is difficult and time-consuming as in the case of China (Allen and Qian 2009). Based on the reasoning, we propose the following set of hypotheses.

H1: Informal and formal household financiers complement each other.
H2: Formal household financiers could screen borrowers with better backgrounds.

However, there are also informal financing sources that are not confined to direct business or social relations, Tsai (2004) documents a broad set of informal sources used by Chinese through rich field interviews: interpersonal lending, trade credits, money lenders, loan sharks, rotating savings, credit organization, pawnshops, indigenous banks, money houses, mutual assistance societies, especially the lending agencies or loan brokers working for underground financial institutions, as they don't have the soft information about the borrowers, they may charge high interest and fees to cover the extreme risk in their business. I classify informal financing into two types based on whether there exists a soft information advantage which are the social circles and private money lenders.

H3: Social circle household financiers rely less often on collateral than formal ones.
H4: Private household financiers rely less background information than the other two kinds of Financiers.

3 Data and Variables

3.1 Data and Samples

We use the data from the China Family Panel Studies (CFPS) in 2010 investigated by the Social Sciences Research Center of Peking University. CFPS 2010 tracks approximately more than 6000 households living in almost all the cities in China. The households with non-borrowing behavior and total income are less than 1000 RMB in the previous year has deleted. So there are 3526 households included in my sample.

3.2 Variables

Table 1 describes three dependent variables and other independent variables with definition.

IFbankloan, *IFrelationloan* and *IFprivateloan* standing for the household selections on the types of the loan channels. *IFbankloan* equals 1 if the family get loan from banks, 0 otherwise. *IFrelationloan* equals 1 if the family get loan from their

Table 1 Definition of variables

Variable	Definition
IFbankloan	1 if the family get loan from banks last year, 0 otherwise.
IFrelationloan	1 if the family get loan from social circles last year, 0 otherwise.
IFprivateloan	1 if the family get loan from private money lenders last year, 0 otherwise.
Bankloanr	The percentage of loan the family gets from banks last year.
Relationloanr	The percentage of loan the family gets from social circles last year.
Privateloanr	The percentage of loan the family gets from private money lenders last year.
Age	The average age of adults in the family.
Income	The average income of the family member last year, denominated in 1000 Yuan.
IFinvesthouse	1 if the family buys multiple houses for investment, 0 otherwise.
IFrenthouse	1 if the family has no houses but rent house for living, 0 otherwise.
IFBachelor	1 if the family's highest degree is bachelor or higher (including the master and Ph.D.), 0 otherwise.

friends or relatives, 0 otherwise. And *IFprivateloan* equals 1 if the family get loan from private money lenders, 0 otherwise. Other dependent variables are *Bankloanr, Relationloanr, Privateloanr* which are the share of loan the family get from the banks, social relationships and private money lenders in the previous year.

Age stands for the average age of adults in the family. Income is measured as the average income of all adult members in the family last year, denominated in Yuan RMB by thousands. House-ownership shows in two types, the first is IFinvesthouse, which means that the household who could buy more than one house as they would invest in house to gain benefits from appreciation or renting. And the other one is the IFrenthouse, which stand for the household whether have ownership of their living space. If not they might be regarded as lack of collateral. IFBachelor is used to indicate whether the family's highest degree is above bachelor (including the master and Ph.D.).

As dependent variables *IFbankloan, IFrelationloan* and *IFprivateloan* are binomial variable, the binary logistic models are used in my study. The ordinary least squares regression was used for the continuous dependent variable *Bankloanr, Relationloanr, Privateloanr*.

3.3 Descriptive Statistics and Comparisons

Table 2 shows descriptive statistics for the variables On average, about 26.38 % of the households in the sample has got financial assistance from commercial banks in the previous year, the ratio are 68.93 % and 3.77 % for the informal channels which are social relationships and private money lenders. And loan from relationships plays an important role in the Chinese household borrowing. More than 70 % of the

Table 2 Descriptive statistics (N = 3526)

Variable	Mean	Std. Dev.	Min	Max
IFbankloanloan	26.38 %	44.08 %	0	1
IFrelationloan	68.93 %	46.29 %	0	1
IFprivateloan	3.77 %	19.05 %	0	1
Bankloanr	24.75 %	40.59 %	0	1
Relationloans	71.97 %	42.25 %	0	1
Privateloanr	3.27 %	16.71 %	0	1
Age	43.22	10.44	16	88
Income	7.89	17.42	0	500.05
IFinvesthouse	3.82 %	19.18 %	0	1
IFrenthouses	3.17 %	17.68 %	0	1
IFBachelor	5.34 %	22.49 %	0	1

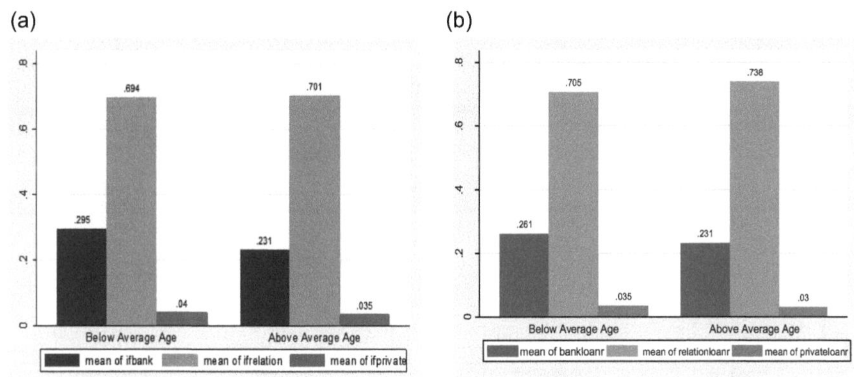

Fig. 1 Mean comparison of the dependent variables groups divided by average age. (**a**) Binomial variables: *IFbankloan, IFrelationloan* and *IFprivateloan*. (**b**) Continuous variables: *Bankloanr, Relationloanr, Privateloanr*

loans are financed by the relationships averagely and banks take a quarter of the loan. The private money lender only takes more than 3 % of the household loan.

The average age for the household adults in our sample is 43.22. Moreover, the average income of the household is 7.89 thousand Yuan per year on average while the maximum is 5 million Yuan. There are 3.82 % of households in the sample having more than one house ownership and only 3.17 % living in the renting house. 5.34 % of the household includes university graduates.

In order to compare the backgrounds information of the households to choose different financial channels and percentage of loan getting from these financiers, Figs. 1, 2, 3, 4, and 5 shows elder ages, less income, no ownership of the houses for investment and living, lack of education would increase the possibility and percentage of loan getting from the informal channels.

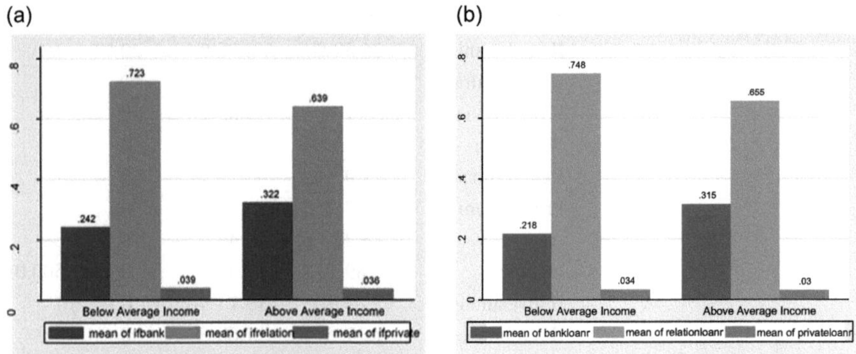

Fig. 2 Mean comparison of the dependent variables groups divided by average income. (**a**) Binomial variables: *IFbankloan, IFrelationloan* and *IFprivateloan.* (**b**) Continuous variables: *Bankloanr, Relationloanr, Privateloanr*

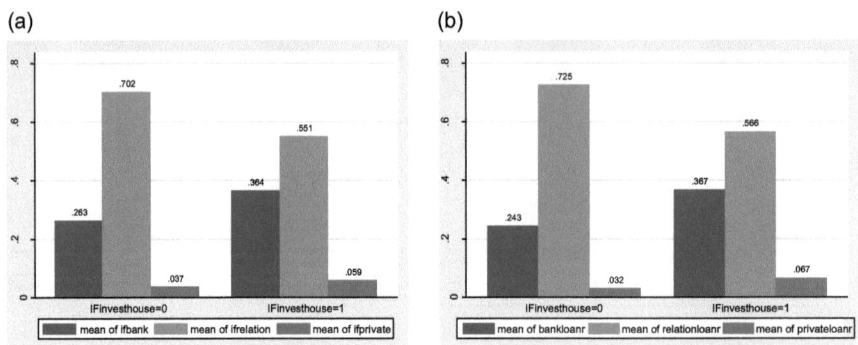

Fig. 3 Mean comparison of the dependent variables groups divided by IFinvesthouse. (**a**) Binomial variables: *IFbankloan, IFrelationloan* and *IFprivateloan.* (**b**) Continuous variables: *Bankloanr, Relationloanr, Privateloanr*

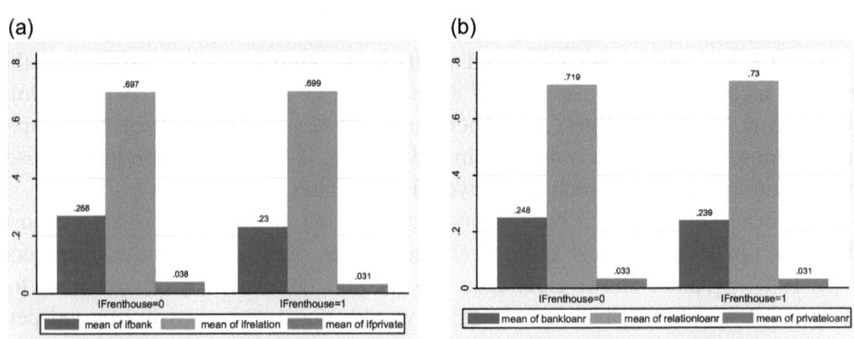

Fig. 4 Mean comparison of the dependent variables groups divided by IFrenthouse. (**a**) Binomial variables: *IFbankloan, IFrelationloan* and *IFprivateloan.* (**b**) Continuous variables: *Bankloanr, Relationloanr, Privateloanr*

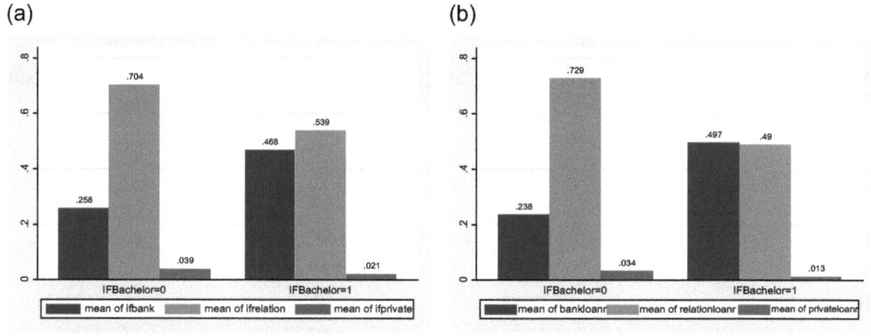

Fig. 5 Mean comparison of the dependent variables groups divided by IFBachelor. (**a**) Binomial variables: *IFbankloan, IFrelationloan* and *IFprivateloan.* (**b**) Continuous variables: *Bankloanr, Relationloanr, Privateloanr*

4 Regression Results

Table 3 predicts the probability of the Chinese household loan selection. The results of logistic regression of *IFbankloan* are depicted in column (1) of Table 3. The likelihood of choosing banks would increase if the household are elder but such effect would decrease to a certain point which means too old are not people are not preferred by the banks as they might retired from the labor market. Moreover, the household with higher income and better education are inclined to get credit from the banks. But renting a house is related with the household choice the formal loans provided by the commercial banks. The odds of choosing banks would decrease by 0.35 as depicted if they are living in the rental houses as they are lack of collateral.

Comparably, as depicted in column (2), the odds of choosing the social circles to get credit would decrease significantly if they can get a higher income and better education backgrounds. And also the multiple house owners who has already invested in the house are not refer to this channel as they might not be troubled in dealing with the lack of money. So we can get the clues that the social circle are a better supplement channel of formal loan services as the friends or relatives are not judged the loan seekers by age, income education background and house-ownership. Additionally, another informal loan are provided by private money lenders, Column (3) shows only the coefficients of Age and the square of the Age are significant here. The elder households are preferred but if they are too old, the incentive for getting such private loan would shrink.

After running a linear regression to examine factors associated with the share of loan getting Channel. I find the results are depicted in Table 4. Column (1) shows the share of loan getting from bank is higher for households with older age, but such effect would decrease to a certain point which means too old people don't increase their bank loan. Moreover, the household with higher income and better education would increase the percentage of loan getting from banks.

Table 3 Regression results for binomial variables

Variable	(1) IFbankloan	(2) IFrelationloan	(3) IFprivateloan
Age	0.0666**	−0.0347	0.1338*
	(2.341)	(−1.425)	(1.752)
Age-square	−0.0009***	0.0004	−0.0017*
	(−2.882)	(1.487)	(−1.956)
Income	0.0116***	−0.0115***	−0.0033
	(3.676)	(−3.684)	(−0.423)
IFBachelor	0.5967***	−0.3724*	−0.6515
	(3.103)	(−1.937)	(−1.065)
IFinvesthouse	0.1836	−0.4006**	0.6265
	(0.873)	(−2.011)	(1.541)
IFrenthouses	−0.3523*	0.1379	−0.1825
	(−1.900)	(0.815)	(−0.426)
Constant	−2.2497***	1.6540***	−5.6979***
	(−3.552)	(2.972)	(−3.421)
Observations	3526	3526	3526
Pseudo R-squared	0.0182	0.0094	0.0098

Note: z-statistics in parentheses
***$p < 0.01$, **$p < 0.05$, *$p < 0.1$

Table 4 Regression results for continuous variables

Variable	(1) Bankloanr	(2) Relationloanr	(3) Privateloanr
Age	0.0108**	−0.0141***	0.0033*
	(2.4981)	(−3.1298)	(1.8131)
Age-square	−0.0001***	0.0002***	−0.0000**
	(−2.7904)	(3.5110)	(−2.0623)
Income	0.0025***	−0.0024***	−0.0001
	(6.2410)	(−5.7198)	(−0.6515)
IFBachelor	0.1844***	−0.1609***	−0.0235
	(4.9919)	(−4.1773)	(−1.5027)
IFinvesthouse	0.0519	−0.0940**	0.0421**
	(1.3396)	(−2.3267)	(2.5722)
IFrenthouses	−0.0365	0.0362	0.0002
	(−1.1927)	(1.1359)	(0.0190)
Constant	0.0054	1.0250***	−0.0304
	(0.0547)	(9.8932)	(−0.7238)
Observations	3485	3485	3485
Adjusted R-squared	0.0279	0.0260	0.0026
F-stat	17.64	16.49	2.52

Note: z-statistics in parentheses
***$p < 0.01$, **$p < 0.05$, *$p < 0.1$

As the Column (2) shows the share of loan getting from social relationships are increased by the younger or elder household. The hard backgrounds such as income, education and ownership of invest house are negatively correlated with the ratio of relationship loan. However, the percentage of loan provided by private money lenders shows in Column (3). Only the coefficients of Age and the square of the Age are significant here. The elder households are preferred but if they are too old, the incentive for getting such private loan would shrink. And if they have the ownership of house for investment, the percentage for getting financed by the private money lender would increase the risk preference for these household in the total sample and they would lending money to afford a higher interests.

5 Conclusions

This paper advocates the formal and informal channels of household loan selection are determined by the credit resources they may supply to the financiers. I find that the commercial banks in China actually deal with the potential default risks via controlling the loan applicators hard backgrounds such as age, income, education background and sufficient collateral like houses while the household with less income and poor education background are more reliable to be financed by their friends and relatives. Because their social circles might get more soft information about the borrowers and this kind way of getting access to loan plays important role in the Chinese household finance selections as more than half of our sample declare they have refer to their social circle when lack of money. So we can say the commercial banks and social circles complement each other properly. And Private money lenders are poor at acquiring qualified borrowers with a good background about the income or education or house-ownership and they only don't favor to finance the aged applicants, but the household with the ownership of house for investment, would increase their the risk preferences to increase amount of money financed by such channel and even afford a higher interests.

References

Agenor, P. R., & Montiel, P. J. (2008). *Development macroeconomics*. Princeton, NJ: Princeton University Press.

Allen, F., & Qian, J. (2009). *Comparing legal and alternative institutions in finance and commerce* (Wharton Financial Institutions Center Working Paper 08-26).

Allen, F., Qian, J., & Qian, M. (2005). Law, finance, and economic growth in China. *Journal of Financial Economics, 77*(1), 57–116.

Allen, F., Qian, M., & Xie, J. (2013). *Understanding informal financing*. Accessed January 1, 2014, from http://abfer.org/docs/track2/track2-understanding-informal-financing.pdf

Ayyagari, M., Demirgüç-Kunt, A., & Maksimovic, V. (2010). Formal versus informal finance: Evidence from China. *Review of Financial Studies, 23*(8), 3048–3097.

Ferrer-i-Carbonell, A. (2005). Income and well-being: An empirical analysis of the comparison income effect. *Journal of Public Economics, 89*(5), 997–1019.

Georgarakos, D., & Pasini, G. (2011). Trust, sociability, and stock market participation. *Review of Finance, 15*(4), 693–725.

Stiglitz, J. E. (1990). Peer monitoring and credit markets. *The World Bank Economic Review, 4*(3), 351–366.

Tsai, K. S. (2004). Imperfect substitutes: The local political economy of informal finance and microfinance in rural China and India. *World Development, 32*(9), 1487–1507.

Households Financial Behavior: Selected Aspects at the Time of Turbulence

Danuta Dziawgo

Abstract In the modern global financial market investment safety is extremely significant. Therefore, the article focuses on trust in the financial market of average citizens which is a crucial element for saving and investing money. This is the first stage for further implementation of other criteria during the decision making process such as CSR. The aim of the elaboration is to draw attention to selected aspects of the problem of activating individual investors as exemplified by Poland, which can be viewed as an important market concerning the number of citizens, the size of the market and the European Union membership. In the article, description, comparison and questionnaire methods were used. The theory aspect was complemented with selected survey results on a representative sample of Polish citizens. The survey was conducted on the basis of the author's project and requested by an agency specializing in research of this type on a representative sample of the Polish society in 2014.

Keywords Household • Citizens • Investment • Trust • CSR

1 Introduction

As the last two financial crises have shown, trust seems to be a crucial element for saving and investing money. It is also an important feature for future market development and economy stabilization. Undoubtedly, citizens and their activity as well as behavior influence the condition of world economy. This can be also exemplified by Poland, which can be viewed as an important country due to the number of citizens, the size of the market and the European Union membership. Therefore, in the article are presented results of the questionnaire survey to identify public feelings concerning financial market and behavior towards savings.

Collecting resources by households is necessary due to income fluctuations. Therefore, for keeping a relatively stable level of consumption, resources are allocated in real estates, currencies, bank deposits, securities, and others. The

D. Dziawgo (✉)
Department of Accounting, Nicolaus Copernicus University, Toruń, Poland
e-mail: ddziawgo@umk.pl

© Springer International Publishing Switzerland 2016
M.H. Bilgin et al. (eds.), *Business Challenges in the Changing Economic Landscape - Vol. 1*, Eurasian Studies in Business and Economics 2/1,
DOI 10.1007/978-3-319-22596-8_14

proportion between such allocations depends, among others, on the preferences of individual households, on the quality of savings allocation mechanism and on the household life cycle (Du and Kamakura 2006; Brown and Gray 2014).

It should also be mentioned that finally all economic subjects are owned by individual investors in the direct way (by possessing shares) or indirect way (by investment funds, pension funds, asset management companies, and others). So, individual investors are the most important link in this process; it's their capital and their activity which influence the condition of the world economy.

2 Theoretical Background

The theory of economics assumes that households are a key part of economy (Le Blanc et al. 2014). This stems from the fact that households are final consumers, supply human capital, generate savings which are the basic source of capital for company investment and, in consequence, they influence the economic development and, finally, the level of society's wealth. The investing of households as individual investors on the securities markets has a significant impact in the macroeconomic, microeconomic and social spheres (Dziawgo 2004).

When we expose the macroeconomic point of view, we should point out e.g.:

- reallocation of capitals and ownership rights in domestic and international economies,
- facilitating stock exchanges to fulfil their functions, especially in the rational pricing, effective capital allocations and liquidity,
- development of financial markets,
- wider public involvement in economic processes through capital and ownership engagement,
- increase of the level of citizens wealth.

Due to transactions made on the financial markets by individual subjects, reallocation of capital takes place from subjects which temporarily have capital surplus to those with temporary lack of capital. Also, the reallocation of capital within the group of subjects in need of capital, occurs; not all the issues of securities are successful and not always are they possessed as a whole. Investors analyze the investment risk, the price for lent capital, the liquidity of invested capital, and finally they make an investment decision—positive or negative. The capital flows from entities which can effectively put capital in working order, where the gap between benefit and expense, including risk, is the biggest, in investors' opinion. It should also be pointed out that capital reallocation is made not only within one country but also internationally. If the capital transfer takes place through a financial instrument called share then along with the capital transfer occurs the transfer of owners' rights, e.g. the right to decide about the way of using the assets. When we consider the examples of microeconomic importance of individual investors investment, we should particularly point out collected capital by issuers, companies value management, owners' supervision (as an element of corporate government), and impact on certain attitude and behavior of companies.

Shareholders influence company's value in the direct and indirect way (Useem 1996). The direct influence is at the moment of buy/sell transactions through share price and when orders with price limits are placed. The indirect influence on company value happens through participation (or lack of participation) in the Annual General Meeting and voting for companies executive and non-executive directors. Those bodies should secure such company development which satisfies shareholders, which in turn, should influence the increase of companies' market value.

In the framework of value management a concept of active owner's supervision called corporate government was created. The idea is that owners could and should effectively control the level of main goal achievement, which increases company value. The essence of corporate government is to settle pro-development balance between goals of all subjects engaged in company activity through appropriate law and economic institutions (Mallin 2010). There is no doubt that the owner's right is met by individual shareholders, who act individually or in a group and whose fulfilment should be viewed as fulfilment of a part of a gap in the functioning of the owner's right in public companies. The gap is when the right incorporated in shares possessed by individual investor is ignored because it is dispersed. The ownership vacuum will be reduced.

Also, it should be pointed out that more often investors pay attention to social (also called ethical or ecological) consequences of their decisions on investment. It is assumed that support, for example for environmental protection, cannot be effective without certainty how invested money works. In consequence, individual investors and their organization take activities to make pressure on companies to modify their behavior. It can be viewed as a profit for the society resulting from a wider engagement of individual investors on the securities markets. The so-called corporate social responsibility is more clearly accepted especially in the context of the process of globalization. Corporate social investment is understood as an obligation for a subject to take action in order to achieve positive influence on society or, at least, minimize the negative results of its activity (Bochenek 2003). The social aspect of individual investment is, among others, related to the development of financial responsibility of citizens. The responsibility connected with the financial protection of people in the future in the long perspective can result in a decrease of dependence on government services (Brazier et al. 1999). This is particularly important in societies where negative birth-rate occurs and/or they grow old.

The securities market is suitable for citizens' capital and ownership engagement. Educating numerous citizens who can consciously invest, calculate investment effectiveness, identify risk associated with different forms of potential investment and enforce their rights, is not easy, but it seems crucial (Fernandes et al. 2014). Individual investors prepared to invest consciously are crucial for financial market functioning. Also, they are exceptionally important for economy because, in consequence, their investment will be more effective and it may result in more effective capital and ownership reallocations in the whole economy. In effect, it could result in the increase of citizens' wealth.

The more often claimed idea is a change of a society into an 'investors society' and an achievement, to a high degree, of coordination of economic and social goals with a reduction of the significance of administrative bodies in this scope. The phrase 'investors society' emphasizes the importance of individual investors for the development and effective functioning of companies, for international financial markets, and also, in the social scope, for households being a consequence of educational aspect coming from savings and investment.

3 Polish Public Opinion on Investment: Survey Results

3.1 Aim of the Survey

Identifying the status quo is the starting point for each discussion. However, it cannot be identified without finding out the opinion of average citizens. Thanks to that, it would be easier to identify whether trust is a barrier stopping or making the increase of participation of the Polish society in opportunities offered by the financial market, and, in particular, the capital market.

Since there has never been conducted a similar research in Poland, it has a unique character. The aim of the survey was an introductory analysis of behavior and preferences of households which can be perceived as potential individual investors in Poland. The results of research presented below may serve in an introductory indication of the opinion of Poles on the topic of investing on the financial market and an introductory indication of the level of education on investing of the Polish society. Among others, the following problems are presented: the saving structure of Poles, the public trust in public quoted companies, the readiness to take some CSR elements into consideration.

3.2 Samples

The questionnaire was conducted by a firm specializing in the research of this type, GfK Polonia, on the basis of the author's project and at the author's request. The survey was financed within a research project titled 'Ecological Evolution of the Financial Market (EcoFin)' supported by Bank Zachodni WBK under Santander Universidades programme. A face-to-face questionnaire on a nation-wide representative sample of 1000 Polish citizens over 15 years old was conducted between August 7 and 11, 2014. The statistical error is ±3.1 %, with confidence interval 95 %.

Moreover, in the article some previous results obtained in the author's surveys were presented for comparison purpose. Those surveys were also conducted on the representative sample of the Polish society. One of the surveys made between April, 5 and 8, 2002, was conducted by CBOS—The Public Opinion Research Centre (sample of 1044 Polish citizens). The other survey made between September 17 and 30, 2009, was conducted by the institute Millward Brown SMG/KRC (sample of 1012 Polish citizens). Both of them were created, ordered and supervised by the author and based on the questionnaire method. The surveys were financed by the Polish Ministry of Science and Higher Education (Dziawgo 2010a). Questions in the questionnaires were formed in the simplest possible way so that they would be comprehensible for respondents from the representative sample of society. It was necessary in order to conduct the survey at such a wide social range. Note that in one question respondents could give more than one answer, therefore the total percentage does not equal 100. The characteristics for the last survey of respondents of nation-wide sample and ranges in which they were grouped were presented in Appendix.

3.3 *Selected Results*

The presented results of the questionnaire survey enable to evaluate the state of the Polish capital market from the perspective of citizens who are customers and potential individual investors. The results of the questionnaire survey are presented with a short comment and supplemented by additional analytical data related to the distribution of answers in the sample structure.

3.3.1 The Structure of Financial Investments

The matter of using particular instruments of the financial market in investments by individuals is a crucial problem. The answers obtained to this question are presented in Table 1. The question asked was of a closed type with a possibility of multiple-choice answers.

In the representative sample a very low indicator of using in investment such financial instruments as shares (only 1 %), bonds (only 1 %) and units in investment funds (only 2 %) occurs. From the point of view of long-term economic development, a very high indicator of persons declaring a lack of savings, as many as 67 %, is also very alarming. In Polish society, bank deposits are still most frequently used in investing: 12 % of respondents possessed them. The percentage of respondents holding money at home is also relatively high (10 %). Perhaps this is still the effect of the uncertainty due to the last financial crises and the current situation in Ukraine.

The structure of the value of financial means invested in particular kinds of investments requires further research. An analysis of answers to this question would certainly create interesting conclusions. The percentage of respondents holding

Table 1 The range of answers to the question: 'What do you invest your money in? Please, indicate all ways of investing money you use'

Specification	Percentage of answers		
	2002	2009	2014
Shares	3	1	1
Bonds	1	1	1
Bank deposits	**10**	**8**	**12**
Derivative instruments	0	0	0
Investment funds	1	1	2
Currencies	1	1	0
Real estates	4	2	2
Others[a]	1	1	1
I have savings but I do not invest, I keep my savings at home	**4**	**12**	**10**
I do not have any savings therefore I do not invest	**79**	**70**	**67**
Refuse to answer	0	5	8

[a]Others include gold, insurance with investment part, numismatic coins

shares increases along with the level of education (from 0 % of respondents with elementary education and vocational to 2 % with university degree). Also within the group which considers their wealth position as very good, the percentage of those holding shares is 15 %. Other characteristic are not significantly different.

In case of bonds, the percentage of respondents holding bonds is higher among highly educated managers and administration officers (4 %), those whose net income is in the highest scope (3 %), living in cities over 500,000 inhabitants (8 %), with wealth self-assessment as very good (9 %). Bank deposits and saving accounts belong to the most popular forms of investing of financial means. A higher than average possession of bank deposits was declared by respondents over 60 years old (15 %), in households which consist of three (16 %) or five and more family members (15 %), with university (24 %) and college degree (16 %), with the highest income (17 %), living in the biggest cities (35 %), with very good (16 %) and good (22 %) wealth self-assessment. At the same time, a lower level than average for bank deposits were for those with primary education (1 %), the smallest net income (6 %), farmers (1 %), the unemployed (8 %), living in the villages (8 %), with worst wealth self-assessment (1 %).

In the case of respondents who declare they keep money at home, the percentage was as high as 10 %. Higher than average were the following groups: at the age between 40 and 49 years (14 %), with higher education (15 %), the highest income (15 %), managers and owners (27 %), with good (23 %) and very good (16 %) wealth self-assessment. In turn, in the group of persons declaring a lack of savings, one can observe that the percentage of indications is clearly correlated with the level of education and income. The figures are: 83 % of answers of respondents from the scope of persons with elementary education and lowest net income level, as well as the unemployed (87 %) and bad wealth self-assessment (89 %).

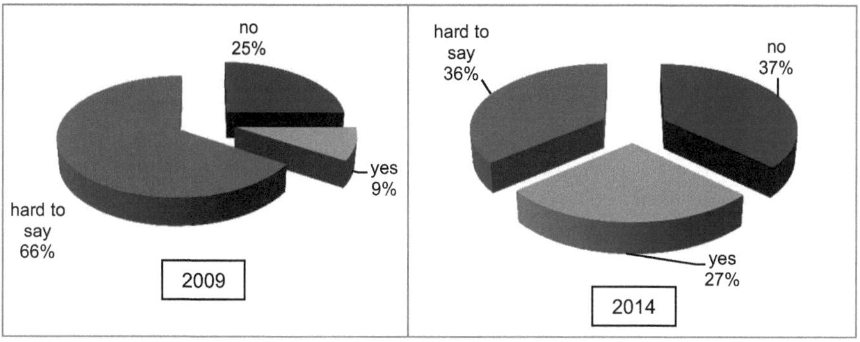

Fig. 1 The range of answers to the question: "Do you think stock quoted companies deserve for 'public trust company' status?"

3.3.2 Public Trust to Public Companies

At the beginning, the level of trust of the wide Polish nation sample to stock quoted companies should be estimated: are they viewed as a symbol of the best part of economy with their high status? Unfortunately, it seems it does not take place in Poland. Figure 1 presents that only 27 % Poles agree that stock quoted companies deserve 'public trust company' status. Meanwhile, 37 % disagree and 36 % do not have an opinion on that. What also seemed interesting was checking cross-tabulation between the trust to public companies and form for investing money in (Table 2).

The results for 2014 inquiry were compared with results obtained in 2009 survey. Although the public trust to stock quoted companies significantly increased from 9 to 27 %, still 1/3 level is unsatisfactory. As an important factor we can emphasize the reduction of undecided group—the answer 'hard to say' was shifted from 66 to 36 %. Unfortunately, at the same time the group of people who is against trusting stock quoted companies increased from 25 to 37 %. We can interpret this as a kind of erosion of general trust to information generated in the financial market.

3.3.3 Inclusion of CSR Concept

In the world in highly-developed countries since the 1970s a movement, which originated in the US trend as the so-called CSR—'Corporate Social Responsibility' or SRI—'Socially Responsible Investment', has been gaining more and more significance (Sparkes 2002). In Europe, though, and particularly in Great Britain, the movement is referred to as 'ethical investment'. A very important factor within the frames of CSR is environmental protection. It is reflected in a more and more often encountered modification of the term 'ethical investment' into 'eco-ethical investment' for stressing the importance of environmental protection in the modern world (Dziawgo 2010b).

Table 2 Cross-tabulation for form of saving and investing trust to stock quoted companies

Specification		Do stock quoted companies deserve for 'public trust company' status?			Total
		Yes	No	Hard to say	
Ways of investing money	Shares	4	2	1	7
	Bonds	5	5	0	10
	Bank deposits	48	19	37	104
	Derivative instruments	0	2	0	2
	Investment funds—open end	0	5	0	5
	Investment funds—close end	0	7	0	7
	Currencies	0	0	1	1
	Real estates	7	3	4	14
	I keep my savings at home	34	24	40	98
	I do not have any savings	157	267	248	672
Total		255	334	331	920

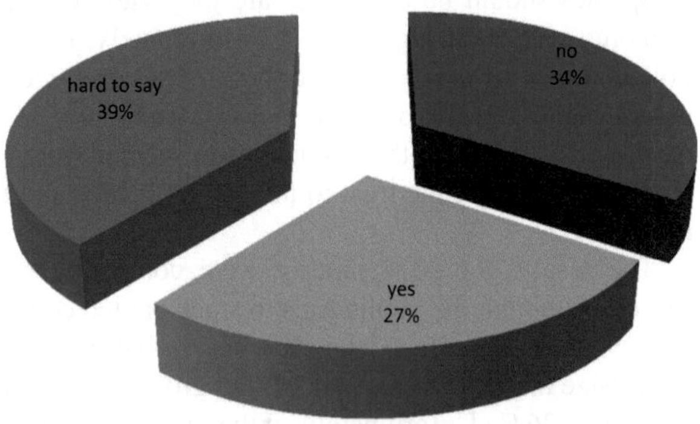

Fig. 2 The range of answers to the questions: "At the moment of doing shopping or taking a decision about saving or investment, do you choose goods/services of the company which you view as ethical/ecological?"

An increasing importance of the CSR movements in the world results, among others, from the fact that pension funds, as well as a part of investment funds, invest their financial resources according to the principle of SRI (Dziawgo 2014). It seemed important to ask respondents from a representative sample of Polish society a question if, apart from financial criteria, they also consider other elements in the process of making consumer and investment decisions due to doubts: 'Do consumers really care?' (Devinney et al. 2010) (Fig. 2).

In the analysis with regard to the social cross-section of respondents from the representative sample an attention should be paid to the fact that readiness for preferred goods and services of the company which they viewed as ethical/ecological is the highest among respondents with the highest net income (30 % answer yes to 34 % no) and the lowest in the group of the lowest net income (24 % yes to 35 % no). The group which is not aware of ethical/ecological aspects of their spending and investing money are pupils & students (16 % yes vs. 39 % no) and farmers

(18 % yes vs. 31 % no). Those who are open to CSR idea are managers & owners (37 % yes vs. 32 % no), administrative officers (32 % yes vs. 39 % no), also those living in small cities (up to 50,000 inhabitants) (35 % yes vs. 26 % no) and with good wealth self-assessment (38 % yes vs. 33 % no).

The analysis of respondents in reference to their level of education is also interesting. One can observe that together with the increasing level of education, the level of positive answers in each bracket (from 18 % for education on the basic level to 32 % for university degree) grows and, simultaneously, the percentage of negative indications grows smaller, as well as the percentage of indications "hard to say" grows smaller (respectively from 45 % to 34 %).

What seemed interesting was checking if there is a relationship between the trust to stock quoted companies and the readiness to prefer goods and services of the company which they view as ethical/ecological (CSR). On the basis of made calculations null hypotheses should be rejecting in favor of its alternative. We may conclude that this relationship is statistically significant. The Pearson chi-square is 159,944 and p-value lower than 0.01. Further analysis of cross-tabulation allows us to drawn a conclusion that the trust to stock quoted companies significantly influences the decision about ethical/ecological choices (Tables 3, 4, and 5).

Commenting the results obtained, one should indicate a high level of awareness of stockholders as consumers: as many as 27 %. However, simultaneously, a high level of negative indications (34 %) is striking (they do not include the CSR concept

Table 3 Cross-tabulation for trust to stock quoted companies prefer goods/services of ethical/ecological company

Specification		Do you choose goods/services of the company which you view as ethical/ecological?			Total
		Yes	No	Hard to say	
Do stock quoted companies deserve for 'public trust company' status?	Yes	132	69	71	272
	No	65	185	118	368
	Hard to say	71	83	206	360
Total		268	337	395	1000

Table 4 Chi-square tests

Specification	Value	df	Asymp. Significance (2-sided)
Pearson chi-square	159,944[a]	4	0.000
Likelihood ratio	149,449	4	0.000
Linear-by-Linear association	84,509	1	0.000
N of valid cases	1000		

[a]0 % units (0) has expected count less than 5. An expected frequency is 72.90

Table 5 Symmetric measures

Specification		Value	Approx. significance
Nominal by nominal	Phi	0.400	0.000
	Cramer's V	0.283	0.000
	Contingency coefficient	0.371	0.000
N of valid cases		1000	

while shopping and investing). Undoubtedly, this problem should be investigated in more depth. We can say that an average citizen has two powerful tools which they should be aware of and consciously use. The tools are used during elections (voting) and during shopping or saving & investing—deciding to whom and for what the money will flow. And those decisions should be made knowingly and intentionally.

4 Conclusion

Nowadays, the quality of financial market functioning is being discussed worldwide. In this article the attention was drawn to the trust of average citizens to financial products and generally to financial market. The trust influences the willingness to save money and the structure of money investment. Unfortunately, over time around 70 % Polish society declare the lack of savings. But among those who own savings, as many as 10 % keep them at home so they mistrust banks and other financial agents. Only 12 % representative sample declare having bank deposits, and from more advanced financial products only 1 % Poles profit. But looking forward, the perspective of living without any savings or on credit should worry not only economists, but also politicians. Nevertheless, what is optimistic here, some citizens do not rely only on the government and they build up their future financial stability themselves. They also construct their portfolio using different products not only from financial markets.

It needs to be emphasized that those people who save and invest their resources are more resourceful, they less rely on government help, are more flexible on the labor market, enlarge their wealth which, in consequence, increases national wealth.

Modern society is more and more conscious of its rights and position as citizens, investors, clients, and consumers. Also, its economic and financial education increases. Therefore, the present society formulates more and more precise expectations towards companies, including those quoted on stock exchanges. As it can be seen in survey results, Warsaw stock quoted companies have to substantially raise the standard of market communication.

However, the most important fact is that citizens still trust companies' generated information and that trust is increasing. The loss of the capital of trust could evoke catastrophe not only in the capital market but in the financial market in general. And that scenario would be the worst.

Appendix

Characteristics of respondents from representative sample (1000 people)

Household net income		Age (years)		Savings possessors		Place of residence		Socio-professional group	
Up to 2000 PLN	24 %	15–29	24 %	Yes	26 %	Village	39 %	Managers, private entrepreneurs	6 %
2000–2999 PLN	22 %	30–39	19 %	No	67 %	Towns up to 50,000	24 %	Administration officers	17 %
3000–4499 PLN	27 %	40–49	15 %	Refuse to answer	7 %	Towns 50,000–500,000	26 %	Physical workers	25 %
4500 PLN and more	25 %	50–59	17 %			Towns over 500,000	11 %	Farmers	8 %
		Over 60	25 %					Housewives	6 %
								Pupils and students	9 %
								Old-age pensioners	22 %
								Unemployed	7 %

Household size		Sex		Education		Self-assessment of wealth position		T1
Only respondent	9 %	Female	52 %	Elementary	18 %	Very good	1 %	
2 persons	18 %	Male	48 %	Vocational	34 %	Good	27 %	
3 persons	21 %			Secondary and college	35 %	Average	55 %	
4 persons	23 %			University degree	13 %	Bad	17 %	
5 and more	29 %							

References

Bochenek, M. (2003). Ecological management and rationality. In D. Dziawgo & L. Dziawgo (Eds.), *Finance and natural environment* (pp. 33–58). Torun: TNOiK. [online] Accessed November 11, 2014, from https://repozytorium.umk.pl/bitstream/handle/item/1102/Finance__Natural_Environment.pdf?sequence=1.

Brazier, A., Greener, K., Jarvis, T., Roll, J., & Wilson, W. (1999). *Welfare reform and pensions bill.* [online] Accessed December 10, 2014, from www.parliament.uk/briefing-papers/RP99-19.pdf

Brown, S., & Gray, D. (2014). *Household finances and well-being: An empirical analysis of comparison effects* (IZA Discussion Papers 8530).

Devinney, T. M., Auger, P., & Eckhardt, G. M. (2010). *The myth of the ethical consumer.* Cambridge: Cambridge University Press.

Du, R. Y., & Kamakura, W. A. (2006). Household life cycles and lifestyles in the United States. *Journal of Marketing Research, 43*(1), 121–132.

Dziawgo, D. (2004). *Stowarzyszenia indywidualnych inwestorow i kluby inwestycyjne na rynku papierów wartosciowych* [Association of individual investors and investment clubs on the securities market]. Torun: UMK.

Dziawgo, D. (2010a). Saving and investing money among Polish society—Discussion starting point. *Culture and Education, 5*(79), 154–166.

Dziawgo, L. (2010b). *Zielony rynek finansowy* [Financial market in green]. Warsaw: PWE.

Dziawgo, L. (2014). Greening financial market. *Copernican Journal of Finance and Accounting, 3* (2), 9–23.

Fernandes, D., Lynch, J. G., & Netemeyer, R. G. (2014). Financial literacy, financial education and downstream financial behaviors. *Management Sciences, 60*(8), 1861–1883.

Le Blanc, J., Porpiglia, A., Teppa, F., Zhu, J., & Ziegelmeyer, M. (2014). *Household saving behavior and credit constraints in the Euro area* (DNB Working Paper No. 428, pp. 1–33). [online] Accessed December 12, 2014, from http://papers.ssrn.com/sol3/papers.cfm?abstract_id=2462103

Mallin, C. A. (2010). *Corporate governance* (3rd ed.). Oxford: Oxford University Press.

Sparkes, R. (2002). *Socially responsible investment. A global revolution.* West Sussex: Wiley.

Useem, M. (1996). *Investor capitalism.* New York: Basic Books.

The Relationship Between CSR Engagement and Firm Risk in Polish Public Companies

Ewa Chojnacka

Abstract The paper deals with the influence of Corporate Social Responsibility (CSR) on firm risk. The first part of the study concentrates on theoretical descriptions of the relationship between CSR and firm risk in the light of former research concerning this issue. The second part of the paper presents our own analysis of the situation of Polish public companies listed on Warsaw Stock Exchange. For quite a long time, CSR engagement of firms has been an important issue in developed markets whereas in Poland this problem has not been sufficiently examined so far. The econometric model used in the article is the result of our study of the extant accounting and finance literature as well as of data availability. The results show that CSR engagement is not significantly related to firm risk in the Polish public companies we analyzed. Perhaps the data that we used were not sufficient to construct a reliable model. It is also possible that the CSR idea itself is not important enough on the Polish market when it comes to evaluating firm risk. Thus, it must be emphasized that the present paper is only a preliminary study and the problem requires further analysis.

Keywords Corporate social responsibility • Firm risk

1 Introduction

The idea of Corporate Social Responsibility (CSR) has been developing during the last two decades. It has become increasingly important, especially in developed countries, and resulted in many theoretical and practical publications concerning this issue. Moreover, a growing number of financial institutions interested in CSR have developed on different markets and companies started to issue additional CSR reports.

As far as developing markets are concerned, the importance of CSR idea is growing, but not to the same extent as in developed markets in Western Europe and the United States. In Poland, CSR has only been developing since the beginning of

E. Chojnacka (✉)
Department of Accounting, Nicolaus Copernicus University, Toruń, Poland
e-mail: echoj@umk.pl

© Springer International Publishing Switzerland 2016
M.H. Bilgin et al. (eds.), *Business Challenges in the Changing Economic Landscape - Vol. 1*, Eurasian Studies in Business and Economics 2/1,
DOI 10.1007/978-3-319-22596-8_15

the twenty first century. This difference concerning the importance of CSR in developed countries and in Poland is due to several reasons. First of all, it is only recently that Poland began to follow certain trends which could be observed in more developed markets for quite a long while. It is also connected with the inflow of many foreign investors to Poland within the last few years (Ministry of Economy 2010). Finally, the increased interest in CSR idea stems from the fact that, in May 2004, Poland joined the European Union whose strategy promotes the CSR idea (Pośpiech 2013).

Generally, in Poland, the CSR idea can be observed only in largest companies, as well as in entities based on foreign capital. Unfortunately, in the case of numerous small- and medium-size enterprises, many CSR-type initiatives are one-time actions which are not connected with firm strategy. In reports, they are known as "unconscious CSR". In 2011 and 2013, the KPMG Company conducted a survey concerning the rate of corporate responsibility reporting across 41 countries. This research explored the percentage of companies reporting on CSR among the 100 largest companies in each country. Table 1 presents the results for selected countries including Poland. In 2013, only 56 % of the 100 largest companies in Poland presented reports on CSR and this was one of the lowest results among EU members included in the survey (KPMG 2013).

The CSR idea is still developing in Poland. In 2009, a new index of socially responsible companies was created, concerning only companies listed on the Warsaw Stock Exchange Main List. It is called RESPECT Index and includes companies which fulfill certain obligations given in the Management Board resolution no. 871/2013. According to WSE standards, social responsibility is understood as "a management strategy and approach to the concept of conducting business, which involves building a good and lasting relationship based on mutual understanding and RESPECT expectations of the wider business environment (i.e., with all stakeholders: employees, suppliers, customers, community, shareholders and envisaging the care of natural environments)". The Index name, RESPECT, is an acronym of CSR components, such as Responsibility, Ecology, Sustainability, Participation, Environment, Community and Transparency.

The development of CSR idea in Poland, as well as the availability of RESPECT Index data enables us to investigate the impact of CSR on the situation of companies. In theoretical and empirical research, different benefits of CSR engagement for the financial situation of companies are taken into account. Due to the fact that different analyses often showed contradictory results, Deutsche Bank Climate Change Advisors (DBCCA) decided to study and compare 56 papers published within the last 15 years which they considered as most valuable. As a result, three groups of studies were identified and analyzed (Deutsche Bank Climate Change Advisors 2012). The classification was based on the type of problems analyzed in each study and included papers concentrating on the relationship between CSR and the corporate cost of capital, papers analyzing the relationship between CSR and financial results of companies, and papers studying the relationship between CSR and financial results of investment funds.

Table 1 The percentage of companies reporting on CR in the 100 largest companies in selected countries

	France	Denmark	UK	USA	Canada	Spain	Finland	Sweden	Hungary	Romania	Belgium	Germany	Slovakia	Poland	Greece
2011	94	91	100	83	79	88	85	72	70	54	X	62	63	X	33
2013	99	99	91	86	83	81	81	79	78	69	68	67	57	56	43

Source: KPMG (2013)

As far as the first problem is concerned, papers included in DBCCA research investigated the correlation between company's CSR rating and the corporate cost of capital (both equity and debt). Generally, companies with high CSR index have a lower cost of capital. Moreover, socially responsible companies have a higher valuation and a lower risk.

The purpose of this paper is to study the relationship between CSR engagement and firm risk in Polish public companies. Firm risk is a combination of market risk (or so-called systematic risk) and unique risk (also called unsystematic or firm-specific). Market risk is undiversifiable and stems from the fact that there are perils on the market which are a threat to all businesses. Unique risk, on the other hand, is a diversifiable one and stems from the fact that some perils are connected with particular companies (Brealey and Myers 2000). The first part of the study concentrates on theoretical descriptions of the relationship between CSR and firm risk in the light of former research concerning this issue. The second part of the paper presents our own analysis of the situation of Polish public companies listed on Warsaw Stock Exchange.

2 CSR Research in Business Literature

A significant part of business literature concentrates on the relationship between firms' CSR and their financial performance or cost of capital. A good financial standing lowers firm risk, whereas a reduced cost of capital could be the result of reduced risk. Thus, findings regarding the relationship between CSR and financial performance or cost of capital may be taken into consideration in analyzing the relation between CSR and firm risk. In this respect, two main theoretical streams may be observed in business studies.

On one hand, a number of studies expect a negative relationship between CSR engagement and firm risk. Their assumptions are based on the fact that some benefits of CSR engagement could cause a reduction in firm risk. According to Sharfman and Fernando (2008), it can be connected with environmental risk management, which also results in a reduction of the cost of capital. CSR engagement also improves transparency. It reduces informational asymmetries between the company and investors, as a consequence of additional reports which need to be published (Jensen and Meckling 1976; Dhaliwal et al. 2011). Improved transparency might allow for easier access to financial market. Finally, risk reduction obtained thanks to CSR engagement (in environmental, social and governance issues) should positively influence on the company's cash flow.

On the other hand, a certain authors point out to a possible positive relationship between CSR engagement and firm risk. According to neoclassical economics, CSR initiatives increase company's cost and decrease its profits, which might also increase the firm-specific risk (Friedman 1970; Jensen 2001).

The relationship between CSR engagement and firm risk has been presented in many practical analyses. Most of them focused on developed markets. These studies used different measures of CSR as well as different measures of risk.

McGuire et al. (1988) analyzed the relationship between CSR and firm's financial performance, taking into consideration stock-market returns, accounting-based measures and measures of risk. The latter included beta and standard deviation of total return (i.e., market risk measures), as well as debt to assets ratio, operating leverage and standard deviation of operating income (i.e., accounting-based measures of risk). The results show that measures of risk are closely associated with the perceptions of firm's social responsibility. According to recently conducted research, CSR engagement inversely affects firm risk. Also, the effect of risk reduction through CSR engagement is more significant in controversial industry firms (such as e.g., alcohol, tobacco or gambling) (Jo and Na 2012). Salama et al. (2011) examined the relationship between corporate environmental performance and firm risk in rated UK companies. Theirs results prove that the company's environmental performance is inversely related to its systematic financial risk. An increase of 1.0 in the community and environmental responsibility rankings gives a 0.028 reduction in financial risk measured by company's beta. Oikonomou et al. (2012) found out that "CSR is negatively but weakly related to systematic firm risk and that corporate social irresponsibility is positively and strongly related to financial risk". These authors point out to the fact that overall volatility conditions of the financial markets are also very important as far as the relation CSR-risk is concerned.

The relationship between CSR and firm risk can also be related to the cost of capital (both equity and debt) and access to finance. According to previous research, companies with better CSR scores reach cheaper equity financing (Ghoul et al. 2011). Companies with superior social responsibility performance that decide to initiate disclosure of their CSR activities gain a subsequent reduction in the cost of equity capital. These companies also attract dedicated institutional investors and analyst coverage and achieve lower absolute forecast errors and dispersion (Dhaliwal et al. 2011). As far as cost of debt is concerned, Bauer and Hann (2010) found out that the credit standing of borrowing companies depends on legal, reputational and regulatory risks associated with environmental incidents. Their study of U.S. public corporations showed that proactive environmental practices are associated with a lower cost of debt. Better CSR performance also leads to lower capital constraints (defined as market friction that may cause that a firm would resign from undertaking a positive net present value investment). It can be attributed to reduced agency costs due to enhanced stakeholder engagement, as well as reduced information asymmetry due to increased transparency (Cheng et al. 2014).

3 CSR Engagement and Firm Risk in Polish Public Companies

3.1 Data and Measurement

The influence of Corporate Social Responsibility (CSR) on firm risk is a problem examined is many papers. Yet, none of them have taken into consideration the situation in Poland. The sample population for this study included Polish public companies listed on WSE Main List between 2010 and 2013. The period of study was determined by the existence of RESPECT Index that was chosen as reputation data for CSR. The base date for this index was December 31, 2009. We used a dummy variable to specify that a company is or is not a participant in RESPECT Index within the analyzed period, which was an indicator whether a company is or is not perceived as socially responsible. Financial data were obtained from Notoria Servis database. All calculations were carried out using GRETL (an open source software package for econometric analysis).

We obtained an unbalanced panel data with observations for 279 listed companies over different periods of time varying from 1 to 4 years within the period of 2010–2013. The model was estimated using OLS regression as well as models for panel data, i.e., random and fixed-effects models. We used White's test to verify the problem of heteroskedasticity, Wald's test to choose between OLS regression and fixed-effects model, Breusch-Pagan's test to choose between OLS regression and random-effects model and Hausman's test to choose between fixed-effects model and random-effects model.

Our panel was based on a number of additional assumptions listed below.

1. Companies which debuted on WSE in 2012 and 2013 were not included in the panel.
2. Companies which debuted on WSE in 2010 or 2011 were included in the panel but the first financial data were gathered for the year following the debut.
3. Companies with poor financial standing (negative shareholder's equity) were not included in the panel.

As far as variables are concerned, the dependent variable in the model is firm risk measured by the total risk composed of market risk and firm-specific risk. It is measured by the standard deviation of daily stock returns in the current year (VOLATILITY[1]). The main explanatory variable taken into consideration in this analysis is the fact that the company is perceived as a socially responsible entity, which is indicated by a dummy variable mentioned above (CSR). Additionally, following the finance literature and former studies, we included some financial variables that characterize companies and may affect firm risk. Variable

[1] Variables indicated with capital letters are those included in the actual model.

Table 2 Variable descriptions

Variable name	Description
VOLATILITY	Firm risk measured by the standard deviation of daily stock returns in current year (the mean value)
CSR	Takes the value 1 to indicate that company is included in RESPECT Index and is perceived as a socially responsible entity, the 0 value in opposite situation
MV_BV	Market value of assets to book value
SIZE1	Size of the company measured by the log of total assets
SIZE2	Size of the company measured by the log of net revenues from sales
GEAR	Capital gearing measured by total debt divided by total capital
ROA1	Profitability of the company measured by operating profit before depreciation divided by total assets
ROA2	Profitability of the company measured by the operating return on assets (operating profit divided by total assets)
LIQU1	Liquidity of the company measured by the relation of net cash flow from operating activities to total assets
LIQU2	Liquidity of the company measured by the current ratio
GROW1	Growth of the company measured by $(TA_t - TA_{t-1})/TA_{t-1}$, where TA is the book value of total assets
GROW2	Growth of the company measured by $(NR_t - NR_{t-1})/NR_{t-1}$, where NR is the net revenues from sales

descriptions are presented in Table 2. In the case of four explanatory variables, we used two alternative methods of calculation.

Let us now comment on the expected influence of each explanatory variable on the dependent variable. Following empirical studies, we would expect the relationship of market value of assets to book value (which defines the future growth potential of the company) to have a negative impact on firm risk. Also, large firms are presumed to be less risky, so a negative relation between firm size and firm risk is expected. Moreover, a positive relationship between debt level and firm risk is predicted due to the fact that larger debt causes higher risk of default. The higher the profitability, the lower the risk, so the relation between profitability and firm risk should be negative. As far as liquidity is concerned, a negative relation is also expected: the higher the liquidity, the lower the firm risk. We also expect a negative relation between firm risk and asset growth (Salama et al. 2011).

Table 3 presents the correlation analysis between the dependent variable VOLATILITY and the explanatory variables, i.e., CSR and other company characteristics. The Spearman correlation analysis was used in this study.

Based on Spearman correlation coefficients, we have chosen the following variables for the model: CSR, MV_BV, SIZE1, GEAR, ROA2, LIQU1, GROW2. The coefficient for CSR variable (which is of greatest interest for this study) equals −0.26 and is significantly different from zero at 1 % level. This negative relation is consistent with the theory stating that CSR strategy in a company reduces firm risk. Other company characteristics, such as market to book ratio, firm size, the level of debt, profitability, liquidity and growth of company also have significant correlation

Table 3 Spearman correlation coefficients

Symbol	Spearman correlation coefficient between explanatory and dependent variable
CSR	**−0.26413051**
MV_BV	**−0.34126923**
SIZE1	**−0.44432091**
SIZE2	−0.43729916
GEAR	**0.07511595**
ROA1	−0.25452805
ROA2	**−0.26504911**
LIQU1	**−0.15882517**
LIQU2	0.02769657
GROW1	−0.05745309
GROW2	**−0.06750385**

The bold values are statistically significant.

Table 4 Descriptive statistics of CSR and non-CSR companies in the panel

	VOLATILITY	MV_BV	SIZE1	GEAR	ROA2	LIQU1	GROW2
Descriptive statistics for CSR companies							
Mean	0.0211	1.7635	15.320	0.4167	0.0543	0.0631	0.0289
Median	0.0213	1.5394	15.046	0.3924	0.0374	0.0507	0.0387
SD	0.0041	0.8201	1.6898	0.1962	0.0757	0.0659	0.1902
Descriptive statistics for non-CSR companies							
Mean	0.0297	1.7080	12.293	0.4020	0.0338	0.0503	0.2439
Median	0.0268	1.4424	12.149	0.3838	0.0353	0.0404	0.0508
SD	0.0174	1.0259	1.3692	0.1945	0.0919	0.1007	2.1421

coefficients with the dependent variable (company growth is significantly different from zero at 10 % level).

Table 4 presents selected descriptive statistics of analyzed companies, which we divided into two groups. The first one includes companies regarded as a socially responsible, i.e., those listed in RESPECT Index. The second one consists of other companies not listed in the index. Taking into consideration those statistics, we can see that in general, companies considered as socially responsible are larger and have a higher profitability and a slightly better liquidity rate.

Model specification

The model used in the study is as follows:

$$VOLATILITY_{i,t} = a + b_1 CSR_{i,t} + c_1 MV\_BV_{i,t} + c_2 SIZE1_{i,t} + c_3 GEAR_{i,t} + c_4 ROA2_{i,t} + c_5 LIQU1_{i,t} + c_6 GROW2_{i,t} + \varepsilon_{i,t} \quad (1)$$

The variables below marked with capital letters should be defined as follows:

$VOLATILITY_{i,t}$	standard deviation of daily stock returns in current year
$CSR_{i,t}$	0–1 variable indicating that the company is included in RESPECT Index
$MV\_BV_{i,t}$	market to book ratio—market value of assets to book value of assets
$SIZE1_{i,t}$	the log of total assets
$GEAR_{i,t}$	book value of debt divided by total assets
$ROA2_{i,t}$	operation profit before depreciation divided by total assets
$LIQU1_{i,t}$	net cash flow from operating activities divided by total assets
$GROW2_{i,t}$	net revenues from sales growth rate from year t−1 to t
$a, b_1, c_1, c_2, c_3, c_4, c_5, c_6$	structural parameters of the model
$\varepsilon_{i,t}$	the error term.

3.2 *Empirical Results*

Table 5 presents the regression results of the model. OLS and random-effects model are reported for the sample within the period of 2010–2013. The dependent variable is VOLATILITY.

As we can see from the table, CSR turned out to be an insignificant variable both in OLS-regression and in random-effect model CSR. Thus, participation in RESPECT Index, considered here as a CSR indicator, is not significant in reducing firm risk. Moreover, not all of additional financial variables are statistically significant for determining firm risk. Variables which turned out to be significantly associated with depended variable, both in pooled model and in random-effect model, include MV_BV and SIZE1. Additionally, ROA2 turned out to be significant in the pooled model. The negative relationship between firm risk and variables such as predicted growth of the company, size of the company and profitability confirms financial theory.

The results of our analysis differ significantly from those of studies conducted for developed markets. However, we should be aware of certain weak points of the present research. First of all, one of the serious limitations of the analysis was connected with data availability. We were able to use data starting from 2009, the year when RESPECT Index (considered here as CSR reputation index) was established. This may be a serious constraint for the study, due to the fact that CSR engagement is supposed to have a positive impact on firm financial performance in a long-term perspective. What is more, foreign studies also used larger samples. Finally, analyses concerning developed markets used different methods of calculating the CSR variable was. Their authors had access to more specific data, i.e., more detailed firm rankings based on more sophisticated criteria determining

Table 5 Results of the model

Independent variables		Pooled model	Random effects model
Intercept	Coefficient	0.0562668	0.0585135
	p-value	2.92e-022***	2.80e-015***
CSR	Coefficient	−0.00219107	−0.00148901
	p-value	0.4313	0.6588
MV_BV	Coefficient	−0.00172707	−0.00178621
	p-value	0.0093***	0.0144**
SIZE1	Coefficient	−0.00192903	−0.00206245
	p-value	1.61e-05***	0.0004***
GEAR	Coefficient	0.00221321	−0.000366341
	p-value	0.4961	0.9268
ROA2	Coefficient	−0.0162883	−0.00689533
	p-value	0.0351**	0.3184
LIQU1	Coefficient	−0.00617809	−0.00122982
	p-value	0.3644	0.8306
GROW2	Coefficient	0.000262842	0.000111554
	p-value	0.3764	0.6436
R^2		0.074602	
Adjusted R^2		0.065654	
Number of observations		732	732
Number of companies		269	269

Note: ***, **, * indicate statistical significance at 1 %, 5 % and 10 % level respectively

how socially responsible a company is. Therefore, the results of their studies may turn out to be more accurate.

4 Conclusion

CSR is still a topic of interest both for theoretical and empirical studies. In Poland, the idea of CSR has only been developing for few years. Former studies have mainly been conducted concerning the United States and developed members of the European Union. Therefore, the main purpose of this study was to contribute to literature concerning CSR by empirically investigating the relationship between CSR engagement and firm risk in Polish public companies. Based on results obtained in other studies, we expected a negative relationship indicating that CSR engagement (measured by the fact that a given company is included in RESPECT Index) decreases the firm risk. The results show that CSR engagement is not significantly related to firm risk in the Polish public companies we analyzed. This may have several explanations. As we mentioned above, the data that we used were perhaps not sufficient to construct a reliable model. It is also possible that the CSR idea itself is not important enough on the Polish market when it comes to evaluating firm risk. Thus, it must be emphasized that the present paper is only a preliminary study. The problem requires further analysis which could be based on longer periods or take into consideration more advanced measures of CSR engagement for the Polish market.

References

Bauer, R., & Hann, D. (2010). *Corporate environmental management and credit risk*. (Working Paper [pdf] SSRN). Accessed May 20, 2014, from http://ssrn.com/abstract=1660470

Brealey, R. A., & Myers, S. C. (2000). *Principles of corporate finance* (6th ed.). New York: Irwin McGraw-Hill.

Cheng, B., Ioannou, I., & Serafeim, G. (2014). Corporate social responsibility and access to finance. *Strategic Management Journal, 35*(1), 1–23.

Deutsche Bank Climate Change Advisors. (2012). *Sustainable investing. establishing long term value and performance*. [pdf]. New York: Deutsche Bank Group. Accessed May 20, 2014, from https://institutional.deutscheawm.com/content/_media/Sustainable_Investing_2012.pdf

Dhaliwal, D. S., Li, O. Z., Tsang, A., & Yang, Y. G. (2011). Voluntary nonfinancial disclosure and the cost of equity capital: The initiation of corporate social responsibility reporting. *The Accounting Review, 86*(1), 59–100.

Friedman, M. (1970, September 13). The social responsibility of business is to increase its profits. *New York Times Magazine*, pp. 122–126.

Ghoul, E. S., Guedhami, O., Kwok Ch, C. Y., & Mishra, D. R. (2011). Does corporate social responsibility affect the cost of capital? *Journal of Banking and Finance, 35*(9), 2388–2406.

Jensen, M. C. (2001). Value maximization, stakeholder theory, and the corporate objective function. *Journal of Applied Corporate Finance, 14*(3), 8–21.

Jensen, M., & Meckling, W. (1976). Theory of firm: Managerial behaviour, agency costs, and capital structure. *Journal of Financial Economics, 3*, 305–360.

Jo, H., & Na, H. (2012). Does CSR reduce firm risk? Evidence from controversial industry sectors. *Journal of Business Ethics, 110*(4), 441–456.

KPMG. (2013). *The KPMG survey of corporate responsibility reporting 2013*. [pdf]. s.l.: KPMG. Accessed May 15, 2014, from http://www.kpmg.com/Global/en/IssuesAndInsights/ArticlesPublications/corporate-responsibility/Documents/corporate-responsibility-reporting-survey-2013.pdf

McGuire, J. B., Sundgren, A., & Schneeweis, T. (1988). Corporate social responsibility and firm financial performance. *Academy of Management Journal, 31*, 854–872.

Ministry of Economy. (2010). *Corporate social responsibility in Poland*. [pdf]. s.l.: Ministry of Economy. Accessed June 5, 2014, from http://www.mg.gov.pl/files/upload/10892/CSR_ENG.pdf

Oikonomou, I., Brooks, C., & Pavelin, S. (2012). The impact of corporate social performance on financial risk and utility: A longitudinal analysis. *Financial Management, 41*(2), 483–515.

Pośpiech, D. (2013, September 27). Moda na CSR. *Media i Marketing Polska*.

Salama, A., Anderson, K., & Toms, J. S. (2011). Does community and environmental responsibility affect firm risk? Evidence from UK panel data 1994–2006. *Business Ethics: A European Review, 20*(2), 192–204.

Sharfman, M. P., & Fernando, C. S. (2008). Environmental risk management and the cost of capital. *Strategic Management Journal, 29*, 569–592.

Internal Innovativeness and Management of Current Finances of Enterprises in Poland

Małgorzata Okręglicka

Abstract Innovativeness is today one of the basic determinants of success achieved by economic entities. It determines the changes in forms and ways of managing an enterprise. One of basic areas of a company management is management of current finances, and one of basic categories of current finances is financial liquidity. The aim of this paper is to identify the influence of an enterprise's innovativeness on management of its current finances and maintenance of financial liquidity. The main thesis is: Financial liquidity of enterprises and ways of managing current finances depend on the level of innovativeness of enterprises. The verification of this hypothesis has been based on the results of questionnaire empirical studies conducted in 2014 on a group of 380 enterprises in Poland. The character of the studies was mainly qualitative, therefore statistical dependences were examined using: Spearman's rank correlation coefficient as a measure of correlation between ordinal variables and Pearson's Chi-squared test and CramØr's V as a measure of association between nominal variables. The studies resulted in finding statistical dependencies that show the influence of innovativeness on the management of current finances of an enterprise, e.g., degree of management formalisation, competences, professionalization of employed methods.

Keywords Innovativeness • Liquidity • Current finances • Enterprises • Poland

1 Introduction

Whole process of the enterprise's management is an outcome of many factors, which may condition the success of an organization (Lemańska-Majdzik 2009). One of them is innovativeness which plays a significant role in this process. Innovation tends to be considered a major driver of both economic growth and the competitiveness of companies and industries. Enterprise's innovativeness not only influences production of new goods and services but also results in changes of forms and methods of management. Innovation activities affect firm performance in

M. Okręglicka (✉)
Faculty of Management, Czestochowa University of Technology, Częstochowa, Poland
e-mail: m.okreglicka@wp.pl

© Springer International Publishing Switzerland 2016

M.H. Bilgin et al. (eds.), *Business Challenges in the Changing Economic Landscape - Vol. 1*, Eurasian Studies in Business and Economics 2/1,
DOI 10.1007/978-3-319-22596-8_16

terms of value added, sales, employment and profitability, etc. (Loof and Heshmati 2006; Aralica et al. 2008). Surely, innovative approach is applied in various activity areas but some of the dependences are not sufficiently identified.

According to Drucker (2004), innovation constitutes a tool for entrepreneurs which helps them to use the change as a possibility to implement another business or service. According to Crespell and Hansen (2008), innovation is a change, but not every change is innovation. A tendency to innovation results in changes which are characterized by unconventionality or originality. Such changes are also hazardous since not every innovation will be beneficial.

One of the areas, which are changing under the influence of entrepreneur or manager's innovation, are current finances. It is said that the biggest change was implemented in the current finances since the entrepreneurs use financial innovations such as new electronic payment methods. It is emphasized that information availability and administrative cost savings are just as valuable as float savings. However, it was entrepreneurs' tendency to innovations that decided about the scale and the speed of using modern payment system within the enterprise's finances (Sartoris and Hill 1989; Rauf and Khan 2012). Cash management is only one of the areas in the current finances management. Financial decisions regarding receivables management or stock management are equally significant. The question is if, also in these areas, the tendency to innovations results in better, more effective and more professional management. Improvement of the effectiveness in every area of current finances positively influences financial liquidity of the enterprise and the stock of working capital. Therefore, the analysis of the impact of internal innovativeness on particular aspects of current finances is an interesting research problem.

2 Review of Literature

2.1 Innovations and Enterprises

Nowadays, innovation is a prime subject. In business and government, innovations are held to be essential in the face of the massive and complex problems and the rapid pace of change in contemporary society. Innovation is also thought to be the way to harness the creative potential of humanity in order to survive, to progress, and to prosper (Gow 2014). Special importance of innovation refers to the economic operators and is identified with the firm's willingness to adopt new ideas (Menguc and Auh 2006). It has also been identified as a useful capability in adapting to changes in markets, technology, and competition (Kock et al. 2011). Innovation encompasses different organizational mechanisms such as experimentation, creativity, novelty, and a company tendency to support new ideas for achieving competitiveness in a dynamic business environment (Ryan and Tipu 2013). Firm innovativeness stimulates innovative behaviors that may yield new products, services, or processes (Dibrell et al. 2011; Hurley and Hult 1998). It helps translate tangible and intangible resources into innovative product or services. This in turn leads to a sustainable competitive advantage (Alarcón and Moisés 2014). Thus, business innovation has been acknowledged as a key driver of firm growth and productivity (Ganotakis 2012; Slaper et al. 2011). A firm that can introduce an innovation faster than its rivals may achieve greater success (Mumford and Gustafson 1988).

Innovation plays an important role in firms' survival (Cefis and Marsili 2006). A number of theoretical arguments suggest a positive link between innovativeness and subsequent survival. Often it is indicated that: innovativeness enhances firms' market power (Schumpeter 1934), improve the ability to escape competition (Porter 1980), reduce their production costs (Cohen and Klepper 1996), improve dynamic capabilities (Teece et al. 1997), and lead to enhanced absorptive capacity (Zahra and George 2002).

Most organizations innovate only when necessary because many business models assume that delivering profits dominate other goals, including development of new products or services (Miller and Friesen 1982). Besides, innovations are expensive, risky, and time consuming and do not always provide advantages. It is even more difficult to estimate the impact of innovation on the functioning of the company.

2.2 *Maintaining Liquidity and Short Term Financial Management*

Mcmenamin (2005) defines the main financial aims of a company, such as being profitable, pursuing liquidity and sustaining a proper capital structure. It can be concluded, that maintaining liquidity is one of the priorities of the company, and one of the main objectives of short-term financial management of the company.

Corporate liquidity is a short-term characteristic that measures the ability of a company to pay its obligations on time (Gryglewicz 2011). Maintaining liquidity requires that an enterprise possess not only cash and transferable assets, but also an optimal share of liabilities with a long maturity (Kusak and Kowalczyk 2006). The liquidity of a company is an important aspect of its financial soundness for clients, suppliers, creditors, equity holders, employees and other stakeholders (Mramora and Valentincic 2003).

According to Brealey et al. (2008), there is still little knowledge about the ideal liquidity level, understood as current assets, in order to maximize company value. Insufficient liquidity can lead to reputation loss and bankruptcy (Dunn and Cheatham 1993). On the other hand, too much liquidity can be detrimental to firms' profitability. The higher the inventories and trade credit, the less money is available to the enterprise for profitable investment (Ding et al. 2013). Thus, this area requires the effective current financial management.

Management of the risk of liquidity loss can bring an enterprise a lot of benefits. Strengthening liquidity risk management can circulate business funds, speed up cash flow, reduce business risk, and enhance the competitiveness of the company (Chang and Chen 2014). At the same time it can significantly affect the growth of the organization (Gorzeń-Mitka 2013). Short-term financial management has been used to focus attention on all decisions of an enterprise that affect cash flow in the short term—usually less than the year (Sartoris and Hill 1989). This entails considering two related problems: managing the firm's investment in current assets and managing the firm's use of current liabilities (Toby 2005). Opler et al. (1999) report several findings consistent with the precautionary motive for cash holdings. Specifically, they find that observed cash balances are positively related research and development (R&D) expenditures.

3 Data and Methodology

In order to examine hypotheses concerning relations between internal innovativeness of the enterprise and the management of particular areas of current finances, the researcher conducted studies in 380 enterprises from southern regions of Poland.[1] The studies in form of a direct questionnaire were carried out in the first half of 2014. Despite the fact that the studies referred to enterprise's finance, they had a qualitative character. This resulted from the fact that there were microenterprises in the study group which conduct limited financial reporting; therefore, an access to the quantitative data was restricted. The studies had pilot character and constitute the basis for the preparation of extended quantitative and qualitative research in the future.

Due to the qualitative character of obtained research material, the statistical analysis was conducted on the basis of Spearman's rank correlation coefficient as a measure of correlation between ordinal variables and Pearson's chi-squared test and Cramér's V as a measure of association between nominal variables. Although range of the studies is wide, detailed results was presented only in case of statistically significant relations (significance $p < 0.05$).

The aim of the studies is to confirm the relations between the level of enterprises' innovativeness (evaluated in the nominal scale 1–5 by the entrepreneurs), the level of enterprises' financial liquidity and methods of management of current finances. Therefore, the main hypothesis of the author is: *Enterprises' financial liquidity and methods of management of current finances are dependent on the level of enterprises' innovativeness*. In the course of research proceedings, the main hypothesis was divided into two detailed hypotheses:

H1: Level of financial liquidity is dependent on internal innovativeness of the enterprise.

[1] The study group consisted of 68.9 % of microenterprises, 21.8 % of small enterprises, 5.3 % of medium enterprises and 3.9 % of large enterprises.

H2: Enterprises with higher internal innovativeness manage current finances more professionally than enterprises with lower level of internal innovativeness.

4 Empirical Results

Enterprises' innovativeness is determined with various measurements such as level of expenditures on studies and development or the number of registered patents etc. Such an approach to the innovativeness is usually reliable in case of large enterprises, whereas it is rarely used in case of microenterprises or small enterprises which mainly realize organizational and marketing innovations (Okręglicka 2007). Hence, the level of enterprises' innovativeness was evaluated indirectly, i.e., through opinions of entrepreneurs (self-evaluation). Thus, the study group was divided into subjects with different level of innovativeness.[2]

One of the most important conditions for functioning of the enterprise is maintaining the financial liquidity. Problems with prompt regulation of the liabilities contribute to the loss of company's credibility and may even lead to its bankruptcy. The focus of the author was to check if the enterprise's innovativeness has a direct impact on its financial liquidity. The analysis of the statistical material, conducted with Spearman's rank correlation coefficient, indicated moderate statistical dependence. The majority of the enterprises declared an average level of financial liquidity. However, one may notice that the enterprises, which determined themselves as more innovative, were characterized by a higher level of financial liquidity (Table 1).

To confirm the credibility of opinions regarding the level of financial liquidity, it is necessary to verify the methods which were used to measure the liquidity.

Table 1 Evaluation of enterprise's financial liquidity and the level of internal innovativeness, according to the assessment of surveyed entrepreneurs

	Innovativeness of enterprises					
	Very low (%)	Low (%)	Average (%)	High (%)	Very high (%)	Total (%)
High liquidity	28.6	3.4	13.3	23.0	63.2	20.3
Average liquidity	57.1	62.7	72.0	9.8	34.2	65.8
Low liquidity	14.3	32.2	12.7	5.6	2.6	12.4
Lack of liquidity	0.0	1.7	2.0	1.6	0.0	1.5

Spearman's rho correlation coefficient = −0.364, p = 0.000

[2] Level of innovativeness (% of enterprises): very low—1.8 %, low—15.3 %, average—39.5 %, high—33.4 %, very high—10.0 %.

Table 2 Used measures of liquidity and the level of internal innovativeness in the assessment of surveyed enterprises

	Innovativeness of enterprises					
	Very low (%)	Low (%)	Average (%)	High (%)	Very high (%)	Total (%)
Economic formulas, e.g., a formula for current liquidity or increased liquidity	0.0	3.4	8.0	18.3	50.0	14.7
Regular assessment based on possessed cash, receivables from customers and liabilities	100.0	96.6	92.0	81.7	50.0	85.3

Chi-square = 51.520, p = 0.000, Cramér's V = 0.368

Table 3 Methods of management of current finances and the level of internal innovativeness

	Innovativeness of enterprises					
	Very low (%)	Low (%)	Average (%)	High (%)	Very high (%)	Total (%)
Formalised (there are procedures/principles in place)	0.0	20.3	30.7	49.2	76.3	39.2
Not formalised (intuitive, used as needs arise, without clearly defined principles)	100.0	79.7	69.3	50.8	23.7	60.8

Chi-square = 45.155, p = 0.000, Cramér's V = 0.345

Generally, it may be indicated that a vast majority of studied companies did not analyze its financial liquidity with mathematical formula. It resulted from the fact that microenterprises and small enterprises, which constituted the majority of studied companies, usually do not have developed finance and accounting departments (Table 2). Thus, this is an estimation rather than a precise measurement of the financial liquidity.

In the course of the studies, there was a moderate dependence diagnosed between the innovativeness and the method of financial liquidity examination. The results show that innovative companies use professional measures of liquidity more often than companies with low level of innovativeness do. Precise determination of the financial liquidity level opens up the possibility to manage this area effectively, therefore, it may be stated that the innovativeness will foster the improvement of the quality and professionalism in finance management.

The impact of the innovativeness on current finances management is confirmed by the data from the Table 3. Although the innovativeness is often associated with creativity and unconventionality, innovative enterprises manage the finances in more formalized way, basing on rules and procedures. In turn, low innovativeness encourages an intuitive approach to the management, which is commonly used by small business, but may constitute a threat when it comes to lack of necessary knowledge and information in making appropriate decisions.

Table 4 Methods of management of trade receivables and the level of internal innovativeness

	Innovativeness of enterprises					
	Very low (%)	Low (%)	Average (%)	High (%)	Very high (%)	Total (%)
Very professional, in accordance with theoretical knowledge about the management	0.0	0.0	2.7	7.1	10.5	4.5
Professional, we have established policy in relation to the recipients or their groups	14.3	18.6	36.0	54.8	50.0	40.5
Ad hoc (incidental), we deal with receivables when it is needed	85.7	81.4	61.3	38.1	39.5	55.0

Chi-square = 51.520, p = 0.000, Cramér's V = 0.238

The studies comprised also the relations between the innovativeness and the risk taken in the management of current finances. In this case, separate dependences were not statistically significant. The area within the current finances, which is mostly related to enterprise's innovativeness, is the management of trade receivables. Nelson Jr. (1977) also emphasized that accounts receivable is an area of great potential for liquidity improvement. Studies in this area confirmed also that the higher innovativeness of the enterprise is, the more professional management it has—in this case, management of trade receivables (Table 4). Full professionalism of the receivables management was declared by merely 4.5 % of the companies, among which there were no enterprises with the innovativeness below the average. The subjects with limited innovativeness managed the receivables in an ad hoc manner, which suggests lack of the mid-term or long-term policy.

Companies with low accounts receivable and high sales do not need much cash, as customers tend to pay immediately (Kling et al. 2014). Normally, however, the sale entails granting trade credit. Nowadays enterprises work with ever longer payment periods, which means significantly longer-term trade credits than before. It means, that companies should be able to finance those longer timeframes (Fenyves et al. 2014).

Statistical dependence, but with a weak concentration, was also found in the length of commercial credit granted to the recipients. The majority of the enterprises used periods of invoice payment amounting from 8 to 30 days. The subject with average or increased innovativeness used longer payment periods than the subjects with low level of innovativeness or very innovative subjects (Table 5). The length of the trade credit was analyzed in relation to the management of receivables recovery (results below).

There are some accuracies in the analysis of reasons for contractors' delay in invoice payment (Table 6). Innovative companies often struggled with dishonest trading partners, whereas they dealt less often with payment gridlocks on market. The enterprises with low level of innovativeness were afraid that they would not collect trade receivables in relation to the deteriorating financial situation of the contractor and his problems with receivables recovery.

Table 5 Length of the period of invoice payment granted mainly to the recipients and the level of internal innovativeness

	Innovativeness of enterprises					
	Very low (%)	Low (%)	Average (%)	High (%)	Very high (%)	Total (%)
Cash sales	14.3	18.6	12.0	5.6	34.2	13.2
To 7 days	14.3	25.4	21.3	18.3	10.5	19.7
8–14 days	42.9	37.3	32.7	34.1	23.7	33.2
15–30 days	14.3	13.6	29.3	27.0	26.3	25.5
31–90 days	14.3	5.1	4.7	13.5	5.3	7.9
More than 90 days	0.0	0.0	0.0	1.6	0.0	0.5

Chi-square = 41.380, p = 0.003, Cramér's V = 0.165

Table 6 Main reason for contractors' delay in invoice payment and the level of internal innovativeness

	Innovativeness of enterprises					
	Very low (%)	Low (%)	Average (%)	High (%)	Very high (%)	Total (%)
Contractor has problems with the recovery of his own receivables	42.9	23.7	30.0	23.8	15.8	25.8
Contractor is in the deteriorating financial situation	28.6	33.9	18.7	29.4	10.5	23.9
Contractor is not afraid of the consequences in relation to the delay i.e., to the penalty interests	14.3	15.3	16.0	17.5	18.4	16.6
Contractor is dishonest	0.0	6.8	11.3	6.3	36.8	11.3
In Poland there is a social consent to make the payments after due date	14.3	20.3	24.0	23.0	18.4	22.4

Chi-square = 39.760, p = 0.001, Cramér's V = 0.162

In course of the studies, the researcher found dependences related to the recovery of trade receivables and the collateral for due repayment of the receivables. The management is professional if the company applies the recovery policy, which means that it uses some methods to discipline the debtors. The analysis indicated that there is a relatively weak statistical dependence between the innovativeness of the enterprise and the frequency of charging the penalty interests for delayed payments (Table 7). The companies with low level of innovativeness are the subjects which rarely charged unfair contractors with penalty interests since they were afraid that they would lose them. It may be assumed that the enterprises with low development potential were anxious about losing the clients, as opposed to the innovative enterprises which were more prone to reach new markets and clients.

Although the majority of enterprises in Poland do not require any collateral for trade liabilities, it may be seen that there is a variety of such collaterals in case of

Table 7 Charging the penalty interests for the delay in invoice payments and the level of internal innovativeness

	Innovativeness of enterprises					
	Very low (%)	Low (%)	Average (%)	High (%)	Very high (%)	Total (%)
Yes, always	14.3	6.8	9.3	7.9	36.8	11.3
Yes, in some cases	14.3	22.0	28.0	35.7	34.2	30.0
No, never	71.4	71.2	62.7	56.3	28.9	58.7

Spearman's rho correlation coefficient = −0.205, p = 0.000

Table 8 Collaterals required in case of delivery of wares with deferred payment period and the level of internal innovativeness

	Innovativeness of enterprises					
	Very low (%)	Low (%)	Average (%)	High (%)	Very high (%)	Total (%)
Promissory note	42.9	10.2	6.7	6.3	7.9	7.9
Pledge	0.0	3.4	2.0	0.0	28.9	4.2
Suretyship	0.0	10.2	8.7	8.7	13.2	9.2
Bank guarantee	0.0	3.4	8.0	13.5	7.9	8.9
We do not require collaterals	57.1	72.9	74.7	71.4	42.1	69.7

Chi-square = 86.726, p = 0.000, Cramér's V = 0.239
Source: Own research—survey 2014

Table 9 Use of insurances in case of contractors' insolvency and the level of internal innovativeness

	Innovativeness of enterprises					
	Very low (%)	Low (%)	Average (%)	High (%)	Very high (%)	Total (%)
Yes, always	0.0	3.4	5.3	11.9	47.4	11.3
Yes, but only in case of the largest orders	0.0	5.1	11.3	15.9	7.9	11.3
Only in exceptional cases	14.3	15.3	16.7	23.0	13.2	18.2
Never	85.7	76.3	66.7	49.2	31.6	59.2

Spearman's rho correlation coefficient = −0.316, p = 0.000

innovative enterprises (Table 8). They apply both property and personal collaterals, but as one may assume, only in some cases.

Other methods of limiting the market risk are collaterals in the event of the insolvency of the contractors (Table 9). The majority of studied companies have never used the collaterals which reduce the risk of contractor's insolvency. Thus, it is difficult to talk about active management. Among the enterprises which declare they use collaterals, there are more enterprises with the innovativeness above the

Table 10 Level of inventory balance and the level of internal innovativeness

	Innovativeness of enterprises					
	Very low (%)	Low (%)	Average (%)	High (%)	Very high (%)	Total (%)
High level of inventory balance	0.0	8.5	11.3	18.3	26.3	14.5
Sufficient (average) level of inventory balance	100.0	64.4	76.7	71.4	63.2	72.1
Low level of inventory balance	0.0	27.1	12.0	10.3	10.5	13.4

Spearman's rho correlation coefficient = −0.175, p = 0.001

average. Almost the half of the companies with a high level of innovativeness insures themselves in case of the insolvency of the recipients, what confirms that the management in this area is professional.

Another area of current finances management is the management of stocks. According to Blinder and Maccini (1991), larger inventories can reduce supply costs and price fluctuations and prevent interruptions in the production process and loss of business due to scarcity of products. Maintenance of high inventory balance requires a high level of working capital. If stocks are too low, it increases the risk of current activity of the enterprise what may result in temporary interruptions in production or sale.

In the study, the majority of the enterprises declared to have an average level of stocks (Table 10). In addition, statistical analysis did not reveal any significant relations with the innovativeness of the company. Generally, it can be noticed that innovative companies had increased inventory balance, whereas the companies with low innovativeness tended to lower the level of stocks (although this fact requires further research).

When analyzing the methods of making financial decisions regarding the stock management, the enterprises indicated the statements which they identify themselves with. The aim of this task was to examine professionalism in stock management (Table 11). Similarly to other areas of current finances management, the enterprises with low level of innovativeness more often make decisions intuitively and ad hoc, whereas the subjects with higher innovativeness apply more professional methods and instruments of stock management, such as implementation of computer systems or application of stock optimization models.

The studies conducted by the author had a pilot character and were supposed to indicate the areas for more detailed analysis. Among 26 studied dependences between the innovativeness of the enterprise and particular aspect within current finances management, the statistical significance was noticed in 11 cases. It constitutes an opportunity to scrutinize and specify the studies in the future.

Table 11 Techniques of stock replenishment and the level of internal innovativeness

	Innovativeness of enterprises					
	Very low (%)	Low (%)	Average (%)	High (%)	Very high (%)	Total (%)
Having a predetermined stock level and we make an order if the stock differs from this level	28.6	32.2	34.0	35.7	21.1	32.9
Using a computer system in order to control the stock and on this basis we make a decision	14.3	8.5	13.3	24.6	15.8	16.6
Applying an economic model to determine the optimal stock level	0.0	1.7	2.7	0.8	31.6	4.7
Following the market practice in relation to the stock level (our inventory balance is similar to the inventory balance of our competitors)	0.0	6.8	9.3	4.8	7.9	7.1
Making decisions Ad hoc—we act intuitively, without particular analyses	42.9	37.3	31.3	24.6	15.8	28.7
Other	14.3	13.6	9.3	9.5	7.9	10.0

Chi-square = 84.041, p = 0.001, Cramér's V = 0.235

5 Conclusion

Currently, innovativeness of the enterprise constitutes one of the major determinants of its development. The tendency to innovativeness is a necessary feature for the enterprise which wants to achieve a competitive edge. Innovativeness influences many areas of the company's operations such as finances. As long as the relations between the innovativeness and long-term finances seem to be natural (implementation of innovativeness often constitutes a part of investment activity of the company), dependences between innovativeness and current finances management require constant analysis and verification. In the course of the studies, the author endeavored to confirm abovementioned dependences. It may be assumed that this confirmation is relatively general since the studies had a pilot character and were supposed to detail the assumptions for proper studies.

In the article, the author adopted two research hypotheses. Statistical analysis of the questionnaire results confirmed the hypothesis H1. The author diagnosed a moderate dependence between the increase of financial liquidity level and a higher level of enterprise's innovativeness. Due to imprecise methods of examining the liquidity level, in case of considerable part of studied enterprises, it is necessary to scrutinize the analysis. The analysis of the results confirms partially the hypothesis H2. The dependence between the level of innovativeness and professionalism in current finances management was diagnosed both generally and in relation to the management of receivables and stocks; these dependences were characterized by weak or moderate concentration. Partial confirmation of the hypothesis H2 results from the fact that some of studied dependences were not statistically significant so they were not considered in the conclusion. Conducted studies turned out to be significant, owing to the fact that they indicated the areas in which more detailed analyses may be carried out.

References

Alarcón, O., & Moisés, A. (2014). Innovation and internationalization as a single strategy of the firm: A unification of theories. *International Journal of Management and Marketing Research (IJMMR), 7*(1), 73–84.

Aralica, Z., Račić, D., & Radić, D. (2008). Innovation propensity in Croatian enterprises: Results of a community innovation survey. *South East European Journal of Economics and Business, 3* (1), 77–88.

Blinder, A. S., & Maccini, L. J. (1991). The resurgence of inventory research: What have we learned? *Journal of Economic Surveys, 5*(1991), 291–328.

Brealey, R. A., Myers, S. C., & Allen, F. (2008). Brealey, Myers, and Allen on valuation, capital structure, and agency issues. *Journal of Applied Corporate Finance, 20*(4), 49–57.

Cefis, E., & Marsili, O. (2006). The role of innovation in firms' survival. *Research Policy, 35*, 626–641.

Chang, Q., & Chen, K. (2014). The research of liquidity risk management based on EVA improvement. *Academy of Accounting and Financial Studies Journal, 18*(3), 63–75.

Cohen, W. M., & Klepper, S. (1996). A reprise of size and R&D. *Economic Journal, 106*, 925–951.

Crespell, P., & Hansen, E. (2008). Managing for innovation: Insights into a successful company. *Forest Products Journal, 58*(9), 6–17.

Dibrell, C., Craig, J., & Hansen, E. (2011). Natural environment, market orientation, and firm innovativeness: An organizational life cycle perspective. *Journal of Small Business Management, 49*(3), 467–489.

Ding, S., Guariglia, A., & Knight, J. (2013). Investment and financing constraints in China: Does working capital management make a difference? *Journal of Banking and Finance, 37*(5), 1490–1507.

Drucker, P. F. (2004). *Natchnienie i fart czyli innowacja i przedsiębiorczość [Inspiration and luck or innovation and entrepreneurship]*. Warsaw: Studio EMKA.

Dunn, P., & Cheatham, L. (1993). Fundamentals of small business financial management for start-up, survival, growth, and changing economic circumstances. *Managerial Finance, 19*, 1–13.

Fenyves, V., Tarnóczi, T., & Vörös, P. (2014). Financial indicators in managerial decision-making. *Annals of the University of Oradea, Economic Science Series, 23*(1), 893–904.

Ganotakis, P. (2012). Founders' human capital and the performance of UK new technology based firms. *Small Business Economics, 39*, 495–515.

Gorzeń-Mitka, I. (2013). Zarządzanie ryzykiem we wzroście wartości organizacji [Risk management in the value growth of the organization]. In: B. Ziółkowska (Ed.), *Wybrane problemy z teorii i praktyki zarządzania wartością w przedsiębiorstwie* (pp. 21–32). Częstochowa: Sekcja Wydawnicza Wydziału Zarządzania Politechniki Częstochowskiej.

Gow, J. I. (2014). Public sector innovation theory revisited. *Innovation Journal, 19*(2), 2–22.

Gryglewicz, S. (2011). A theory of corporate financial decisions with liquidity and solvency concerns. *Journal of Financial Economics, 99*, 365–384.

Hurley, R. F., & Hult, G. T. M. (1998). Innovation, market orientation, and organizational learning: An integration and empirical examination. *Journal of Marketing, 62*(3), 42–54.

Kling, G., Paul, S. Y., & Gonis, E. (2014). Cash holding, trade credit and access to short-term bank finance. *International Review of Financial Analysis, 32*, 123–131.

Kock, A., Gemünden, H. G., Salomo, S., & Schultz, C. (2011). The mixed blessings of technological innovativeness for the commercial success of new products. *Journal of Product Innovation Management, 28*(s1), 28–43.

Kusak, A., & Kowalczyk, J. (2006). *Płynność finansowa: analiza i sterowanie [Financial liquidity analysis and control]*. Warsaw: C.H. Beck.

Lemańska-Majdzik, A. (2009). *Czynniki sukcesu firm powstałych w wyniku samozatrudnienia [Business success factors resulting from self-employment]*. Częstochowa: Sekcja Wydawnicza Wydziału Zarządzania Politechniki Częstochowskiej.

Loof, H., & Heshmati, A. (2006). On the relationship between innovation and performance: A sensitivity analysis. *Economics of Innovation and New Technology, 15*, 317–344.

Mcmenamin, J. (2005). *Financial management*. London: Routledge.

Menguc, B., & Auh, S. (2006). Creating a firm-level dynamic capability through capitalizing on market orientation and innovativeness. *Journal of the Academy of Marketing Science, 34*(1), 63–73.

Miller, D., & Friesen, P. H. (1982). Innovation in conservative and entrepreneurial firms: Two models of strategic momentum. *Strategic Management Journal, 3*, 1–25.

Mramora, D., & Valentincic, A. (2003). Forecasting the liquidity of very small private companies. *Journal of Business Venturing, 18*, 745–771.

Mumford, M. D., & Gustafson, S. B. (1988). Creativity syndrome: Integration, applications, and innovation. *Psychological Bulletin, 103*, 27–43.

Nelson, R. E., Jr. (1977). Liquidity improvement: A management approach. *Business Horizons, 20* (5), 54–60.

Okręglicka, M. (2007). Innovation activities in the microenterprise sector–selected aspects. In J. T. Duda (Ed.), *Information technologies in economics and innovative management* (pp. 162–168). Krakow: AGH.

Opler, T., Pinkowitz, L., Stulz, R., & Williamson, R. (1999). The determinants and implications of corporate cash holdings. *Journal of Financial Economics, 52*(1), 3–46.

Porter, M. E. (1980). *Competitive strategy: Techniques for analyzing industries and competitors*. New York: The Free Press.

Rauf, S. A., & Khan, M. S. M. (2012). The effect of financial innovation on cash demand. *Journal of Business and Economics, 4*(1), 89–105.

Ryan, J. C., & Tipu, S. A. A. (2013). Leadership effects on innovation propensity: A two-factor full range leadership model. *Journal of Business Research, 66*(10), 2116–2129.

Sartoris, W. L., & Hill, N. C. (1989). Innovations in short-term financial management. *Business Horizons, 32*(6), 56–64.

Schumpeter, J. A. (1934). *The theory of economic development*. London: Oxford University Press.

Slaper, T. F., Hart, N. R., Hall, T. J., & Thompson, M. F. (2011). The index of innovation: A new tool for regional analysis. *Economic Development Quarterly, 25*(1), 36–53.

Teece, D. J., Pisano, G., & Shuen, A. (1997). Dynamic capabilities and strategic management. *Strategic Management Journal, 18*(7), 509–533.

Toby, A. J. (2005). Empirical survey of corporate liquidity management practices of Nigerian–quoted manufacturing enterprises. *Journal of Financial Management and Analysis, 18*(2), 41–56.

Zahra, S. A., & George, G. (2002). Absorptive capacity: A review, reconceptualization, and extension. *Academy of Management Review, 27*(2), 185–203.

Private Equity/Venture Capital Sector Specifics in Certain Clusters of Countries Within Europe

Elzbieta Grzegorczyk

Abstract Development of private equity/venture capital market (PE/VC) is an opportunity for economic growth, as it partially complements the equity gap affecting companies from the SME sector, which cover a significant portion of the total number of enterprises. The main goal of this work is to define the characteristics of the PE/VC sector in particular groups of European countries, distinguished using taxonomic analysis based on their convergent traits. In the study, special emphases are on identifying: the size of the market, its financing structure and the split of capital between sectors. The article is based on: broad literature, latest statistical data collected by EVCA, as well as, the latest research reports on the PE/VC market. Proper specification of this market is extremely important as it allows a better understanding of the mechanisms affecting the analysed sector.

Keywords Private equity • Venture capital • PE/VC specifics • Taxonomy • Clusters

1 Introduction

Most reports regarding PE/VC market describes the individual countries separately, or combine them into subgroups usually for geographic location e.g., CEE countries, western countries, etc. There is no, however, an appropriate grouping depending on the level of development of the market. The main goals of this work are thus to identify the particular groups (clusters) of European countries, distinguished based on their convergent traits and specify its PE/VC sector characteristics. Special emphasis is put on identifying: the size of the market expressed as GDP share (which elements have a big influence on the PE/VC market), the PE/VC financing structure and the split of capital between different sectors. To examine private equity/venture capital market, which is a part of the total

E. Grzegorczyk (✉)
Department of Finance and Accounting of SMEs, University of Lodz, Lodz, Poland
e-mail: el.li.grzegorczyk@interia.pl

© Springer International Publishing Switzerland 2016

M.H. Bilgin et al. (eds.), *Business Challenges in the Changing Economic Landscape - Vol. 1*, Eurasian Studies in Business and Economics 2/1,
DOI 10.1007/978-3-319-22596-8_17

investment, the analysis must take into account some specific features of the study area. For the purpose of the following analysis there were collected the statistical data published by EVCA (European Private Equity and Venture Capital Association) in the Yearbook 2014 (European Private Equity Venture Capital Association 2014b) and by European Commission in Eurostat statistics (European Commission 2014).

Before starting strictly analytical part of this research, previously there will be described PE/VC market characteristics, which may have a significant impact on the results obtained. Depending on the phase of the companies' development, different types of funding can be distinguished. Companies located in seed or start-up stage, are usually looking for contacts with business angels, especially when they do not require excessive amounts of capital, as this early phase development is the primary object of BA's interest. The situation is different in the case of venture capital or private equity. Mainly the interest to VC funds is grabbed by developed companies in their transformation phase. In contrast, developed company with fairly stable position on the market usually seek the source of financing in private equity funds (Mikolajczyk and Krawczyk 2007).

EVCA defines private equity as equity capital provided to enterprises not quoted on a stock market. However, going into details, private equity includes the following few investment stages such as: venture capital, growth capital, replacement capital, rescue/turnaround and buyouts, so on the real market the range is much more extensive, than only the balanced growth. Private equity also aims to achieve capital growth in the long term.

When it comes to venture capital, it is a part of private equity. These are investments made in the early stages of business development, for launching a company or its expansion. These funds, in the form of 'interest-free' capital is mainly invested in innovative projects especially for a relatively long period of time, which in practice is 5–10 years. The provider of the capital resigns from current profits for higher guarantee of the future success of the project, by improving the structure of liabilities of the company. This has also an indirect positive impact on the possibility of obtaining further support from other sources such as additional bank loan (Janasz 2004). PE/VC providers are not interested in current profits but are focussed to maximize the growth of the company in the future. Therefore, the support of the company is held not only by providing financial resources, but also by the know-how in the management field.

It is worth noting that investing in private equity/venture capital is an alternative to investing available cash in commercial banks or insurance companies (Weclawski 1997). This capital is an important source of fundraising companies with high growth potential, particularly in the area of new technologies (Karpinska 2014).

2 Identification of Clusters of Countries According to the Level of Development of the Private Equity/ Venture Capital Market

To identify clusters of countries based on the level of development of PE/VC market taxonomic analysis has been used. Taxonomic analysis is an estimation of the level of differentiation of objects described by a set of statistical characteristics. This leads consequently to identify clusters of objects with similarities in their development and to obtain homogeneous groups upon they exhibit properties (Kopczewska et al. 2009). This type of research can further expand the knowledge base of enriching our knowledge of the objects under consideration. It gives the opportunity to assess the level of participation of each object in the development of the whole community, to make a graphic visualization of the problem and the coherence, internal homogeneity and stability of the resulting clustering (Mlodak 2006). The creator of multidimensional comparative analysis is Professor Zdzislaw Hellwig (1968).

2.1 *Identification of Factors in the Hellwig Analysis Method*

Hellwig's method allows constructing a synthetic indicator of development, built on the basis of partial measures reflecting different aspects of its development. To analyse the level of development of the PE/VC in Europe, using the linear ordering of taxonomic methods (cluster analysis), it is necessary to identify factors describing the evolution of this market. It will allow establishing a hierarchy of objects and sorting them, from the ones being highest in the hierarchy to the ones in its lowest. Therefore are groups of similar objects will be created, when the elements are described by more than one feature.

Proper identification of factors is essential for the study. Firstly, it should take into account factors which have a strong influence on the PE/VC market in Europe, and which have been identified by estimation analysis[1] and add these features-elements that characterize the market itself such as: the size, structure, dynamics of development, etc. Objects finally used in the study were therefore

[1] The survey estimation method conducted was Classical Least Squares Method—CLSM (not yet published). This included cross-sectional data for 31 European countries (Austria, Bulgaria, Belgium, Croatia, Czech Republic, Cyprus, Denmark, Estonia, Finland, France, Greece, Spain, Netherlands, Ireland, Iceland, Liechtenstein, Lithuania, Luxembourg, Latvia, Germany, Norway, Poland, Portugal, Romania, Slovakia, Slovenia, Sweden, Switzerland, Hungary, United Kingdom, Italy) in 2011. Of the eight factors identified as potentially liable to affect the formation of the size of PE/VC investments, only three have proven to be important: the number of patent applications, the density of the population of human resources employed in technology and science, the level of trade balance.

- size of the PE/VC investments (in thousands of euros)
- an increase in PE/VC investments (compared to the previous year)
- the number of PE/VC companies
- the number of companies in which PE/VC invests
- the share of PE/VC investments in GDP (in percent)
- the number of patent applications
- population density of human resources employed in technology and science

Due to the extremely and disproportionately strong impact on the level of the trade balance achieved results, this variable was removed from the analysis. In order not to deprive from the analysis the factor that images the level of the economy development and its obvious impact on the level of development of the analysed sector, in the study there were used the rate of GDP per capita. All elements of the analysis mentioned above were considered in the study as stimulants.[2]

In the taxonomic analysis, it is important to harmonize the level of variability of characteristics, to ensure their comparability. In order to bring the traits studied for comparability, subjected to standardization based on the formula:

$$Z_{ij} = \frac{x_{ij} - \overline{x}_j}{S_{xj}} \tag{1}$$

where:

x_{ij}—the empirical value of the j-th diagnostic variable for i-th object,
$\overline{x}_j$—the arithmetic average in the distribution of the diagnostic variable x_j,
S_{xj}—standard deviation in the distribution of variable diagnostic x_j.

On the basis of the variables after standardization an exemplary synthetic variable is achieved, i.e., 'development pattern': $P_{0j} = [z_{01}, z_{02}, \ldots, z_{0k}]$, where:

$z_{0j} = \max(z_{ij})$ for variables which are stimulants,
$z_{0j} = \min(z_{ij})$ for variables which are destimulants.[3]

The next step is to determine (for each tested object) Euclidean distance from the pattern of development P_{0j}:

$$d_{i0} = \sqrt{\sum_{j=1}^{k} \left(z_{ij} - z_{0j}\right)^2}, \quad i = (1,2\ldots,\mathrm{m}), \; j = (1,2\ldots,\mathrm{k}), \tag{2}$$

where: z_{ij}—normalized j-th diagnostic variable for i-th object,

[2] Stimulant is a diagnostic variable, where the higher the value, the better the situation of the object.

[3] Destimulant is a variable that high values indicate unfavourable position of the object.

z_{0j}—normalized variable of development pattern for j-th diagnostic variable.

Variable d_{i0} is a subject of normalization process (calculated relative taxonomic measure of development for individual objects) and takes on values in the range [0:1]. The higher the value, the test object is closer to the pattern and the better is his situation. Result close to zero indicates a very unfavourable situation of the analysed object. On the basis of the taxonomic development measure the arrangement of objects due to the level of the analysed phenomenon is possible to be conducted.

Using the arithmetic average and standard deviation of the relative measure of development allows the identification of four categories of countries (clusters), which were assigned to four assessments from very good to unsatisfactory. Clusters are as follows:

Cluster I—very good rating	$\overline{z} + S_z < z_i$
Cluster II—good rating	$\overline{z} < z_i \leq \overline{z} + S_z$
Cluster III—sufficient rating	$\overline{z} - S_z < z_i \leq \overline{z}$
Cluster IV—insufficient rating	$z_i \leq \overline{z} - S_z$

where: $\overline{z}$—the arithmetic average of the relative measure of development,
S_z—the relative standard deviation of the measure of development.

It should be noted that the proposed evaluation are relative, i.e., are based on the available diagnostic variables of the analysed countries in a specified period of time.

2.2 *The Results of the Hellwig Analysis*

The taxonomic analysis of clusters for the 5 year period 2009–2013 brought the results outlined in the Table 1 placed below. Countries are ranked according to the received metrics, from the countries with the best of the condition of PE/VC market, to those in which the market is underdeveloped. In addition, there was conducted a grouping of countries in accordance with the aforesaid rules. Colours, according to legend placed below, marked with the appropriate group membership.

Analysing the results received it is obvious that the undisputed leaders in the European PE/VC market are Germany, United Kingdom and France. It is not surprising, especially as these three countries are the fundament of venture capital investments, comprising over 70 % of all VC investment in Europe. Moreover, also in accordance with the International Innovation Index, these countries followed in the top 20 countries with the highest level of innovation (Dutta and Lanvin 2013) and the Innovation Union Scoreboard is placing them as 'innovation followers' (Hollanders and Es-Sadki 2014). The level of innovation in the economy has in fact

Table 1 Ranking of European countries according PE/VC market development based on Hellwig analysis (clusters distinguished using colours)

No.	2009		2010		2011		2012		2013	
	Country	Metric	Country	Metric	Country	Metric	Country	Metric	Country	Metric
1	Germany	0.450	United Kingdom	0.600	Germany	0.623	Germany	0.534	Germany	0.610
2	United Kingdom	0.401	Germany	0.572	France	0.582	United Kingdom	0.487	United Kingdom	0.554
3	France	0.393	France	0.549	United Kingdom	0.532	France	0.423	France	0.516
4	Luxembourg	0.324	Sweden	0.450	Sweden	0.448	Sweden	0.374	Norway	0.392
5	Sweden	0.295	Netherlands	0.392	Netherlands	0.413	Switzerland	0.329	Netherlands	0.382
6	Belgium	0.288	Norway	0.381	Luxemburg	0.356	Belgium	0.296	Denmark	0.378
7	Czech Republic	0.270	Switzerland	0.367	Denmark	0.346	Norway	0.293	Sweden	0.345
8	Finland	0.259	Spain	0.354	Switzerland	0.344	Netherlands	0.286	Spain	0.311
9	Netherlands	0.259	Austria	0.324	Finland	0.343	Denmark	0.271	Belgium	0.310
10	Switzerland	0.246	Finland	0.306	Italy	0.322	Spain	0.268	Luxemburg	0.304
11	Italy	0.243	Ireland	0.301	Spain	0.319	Finland	0.262	Switzerland	0.302
12	Norway	0.241	Belgium	0.297	Belgium	0.310	Bulgaria	0.237	Austria	0.302
13	Ireland	0.240	Italy	0.293	Norway	0.308	Italy	0.233	Italy	0.280
14	Spain	0.229	Denmark	0.277	Austria	0.262	Austria	0.226	Finland	0.275
15	Denmark	0.211	Luxemburg	0.255	Portugal	0.258	Luxemburg	0.225	Ireland	0.234
16	Austria	0.193	Baltic countries	0.250	Ireland	0.256	Other CEE[a]	0.222	Greece	0.231
17	Bulgaria	0.184	Poland	0.242	Hungary	0.244	Ireland	0.218	Portugal	0.227
18	Other CEE[a]	0.174	Czech Republic	0.195	Baltic countries	0.243	Greece	0.210	Baltic countries	0.225
19	Portugal	0.146	Other CEE[a]	0.188	Poland	0.228	Poland	0.174	Poland	0.221
20	Greece	0.134	Bulgaria	0.187	Other CEE[a]	0.198	Baltic countries	0.170	Czech Republic	0.203
21	Hungary	0.134	Portugal	0.187	Czech Republic	0.194	Portugal	0.163	Other CEE[a]	0.179
22	Poland	0.132	Hungary	0.175	Greece	0.172	Hungary	0.153	Romania	0.174
23	Romania	0.117	Greece	0.174	Romania	0.155	Czech Republic	0.151	Hungary	0.167
24	Baltic countries	0.110	Ukraine	0.166	Bulgaria	0.145	Romania	0.109	Bulgaria	0.139
25	Ukraine	0.058	Romania	0.160	Ukraine	0.136	Ukraine	0.100	Ukraine	0.128

Source: Own based on analysis conducted

Notes:

Cluster 1	Very good ranking
Cluster 2	Good ranking
Cluster 3	Sufficient ranking
Cluster 4	Insufficient ranking

[a]Central and Eastern Europe

a very strong influence on the rate of PE/VC market development, as the capital, by its definition, is invested primarily in innovative solutions. Interestingly, the United Kingdom, which manages more than 40 % of the market, only in the 2010, metrics places it in the first place. This is mainly due to far more dynamic development of German technology and patents, as well as, the predominance of the number of projects, which German fund managers are willing to invest in. It is worth noting that in the period 2010–2012 Sweden, which covers about 2–3 % of the total European PE/VC market, was in the first group, but fell in 2013 to the second group. This happened mainly due to decrease in the volume of PE/VC investments in Sweden by more than 67 % compared to 2012.

The second group/cluster, also considered to be ‘good’, consists of: Belgium, Netherlands, Luxembourg, Denmark, Sweden, and Switzerland. Since 2010, Spain was also found in this group. Sometimes Finland, Norway, and Austria appeared in the concentration, in the examined period. Although depending on the year, countries changed places within this group, the overall structure seems to be stable. These countries, it is also the state of the top 20 countries with the highest International Innovation Index.

The third cluster includes countries for which the level of development of PE/VC market is assessed as ‘satisfactory’. This group includes, among others: Ireland, Portugal, Austria (except 2010 and 2013), the Baltic countries (Lithuania, Latvia, and Estonia), other CEE countries (Croatia, Slovakia, and Slovenia) and Poland (since 2010). Since 2012 also Italy (decrease from position in second cluster) and Greece (raising its rating from cluster 4) joined the ranks of the group. In the case of the third group, the situation is not as stable as in the two previous ones. Here happens a strong mixing between ratings depending on the year. This is due to the fact that in the case of markets with weaker position, where the value of investments, number of patents, etc. are not significant, any positive signal from the market (a slight increase investment, increase of the number of patents and the number of PE/VC firms) by even a unit, strongly influences on the final index of a country. Hence the countries which are on the border of clusters also change their group assignments.

The last group, with the weakest rating assesses of the level of PE/VC market development consists of the following countries: Romania, Ukraine and Grace (2009–2011). By 2010, Hungary also had belonged to this group. These countries (except Hungary) followed by the last places International Innovation Index for European countries (Dutta and Lanvin 2013) as well as, is treated as ‘modest innovators’ by Innovation Union Scoreboard (Hollanders and Es-Sadki 2014).

An interesting case, with unstable configuration is Bulgaria, which from third cluster in 2009–2010 fell to group 4 in 2011. In 2012, its rating positioned it as a strong element of cluster 2, so that in the next year to fall back to the most vulnerable group of countries. This sudden improvement happened due to a strong increase in PE/VC investments in 2012 (more than tenfold increase in the value of investments compared to the previous year). Similarly unstable situation was presented by Luxembourg, which changed its position passing successively each year from the second to the third group. It should be remembered, however, that the smaller the market, the stronger the impact of changes in the values.

It is also worth to pay attention to the Polish PE/VC sector. It is among the countries with the “sufficient” assessment, growing in 2010 from fourth cluster to the third one, where its position seems to stabilize. This can be read as a good sign for the future of this sector. Stabilization means that the market is becoming more well-known inside the country (which encourages domestic investors) and more visible outside, attracting foreign capital. Unless, in the subjective assessment of investors often Polish PE/VC market is perceived as interesting, still the level of innovation the economy does not prove that (in a study of a group of European countries, in 2013, Poland was on 49 place ranked third position from the end, just before Greece and Ukraine (Dutta and Lanvin 2013)). Also the Czech market seems to be in a similar situation, though in his case in 2010, the rating dropped dramatically, moving the country from a group of 2–3 concentration, where is stabilizing its position.

When analysing separately the group of countries of Central and Eastern Europe—CEE, Baltic States and Poland have the strongest position in terms of the level of development of the PE/VC market. The fact that Poland is in the group is not surprising taking into account that the Polish PE/VC sector covers more than 50 % (58 % in 2013) of the Central and Eastern Europe market and is assessed by investors from abroad as interesting—in 2013 years more than 62 % of the investment capital of PE/VC investments abroad. CEE and Balkan countries include 7 % and 9 % of the market in Central and Eastern Europe. In the case of the Balkan countries plays a strong role of good scientific base in CE Europe, where in 2013 more than 44 % of the workforce was employed in science or technology. CEE countries, in turn, are characterized by a relatively high (for this part of Europe) number of PE/VC companies. The Czech Republic (representing approximately 20 % of the analysed sector), depending on the year, have a relatively high position in the market, despite the small number of PE/VC companies operating in the local market and a small number of projects in which these companies have invested their capital. Other countries like Ukraine, Bulgaria, Romania and Hungary have much weaker ratings.

3 Analysis of PE/VC Sector Specifics in Designated Clusters of Countries

Overall investments in European companies remained stable in 2013. More than 5000 companies were backed as in previous year. Equity investments decreased by 3 % to 35.7 billion euros. What is more, over 40 % of the companies that received investments in 2013 were backed for the first time (European Private Equity Venture Capital Association 2014a).

Based on the analysis of statistical data for the previously separated clusters of countries (Fig. 1), some of the characteristics of the specificity of the PE/VC sector can be identified. Due to the volatility of the markets, especially in the last decade and crisis situation, the greatest emphasis was placed on the most recent data—including especially year 2013.

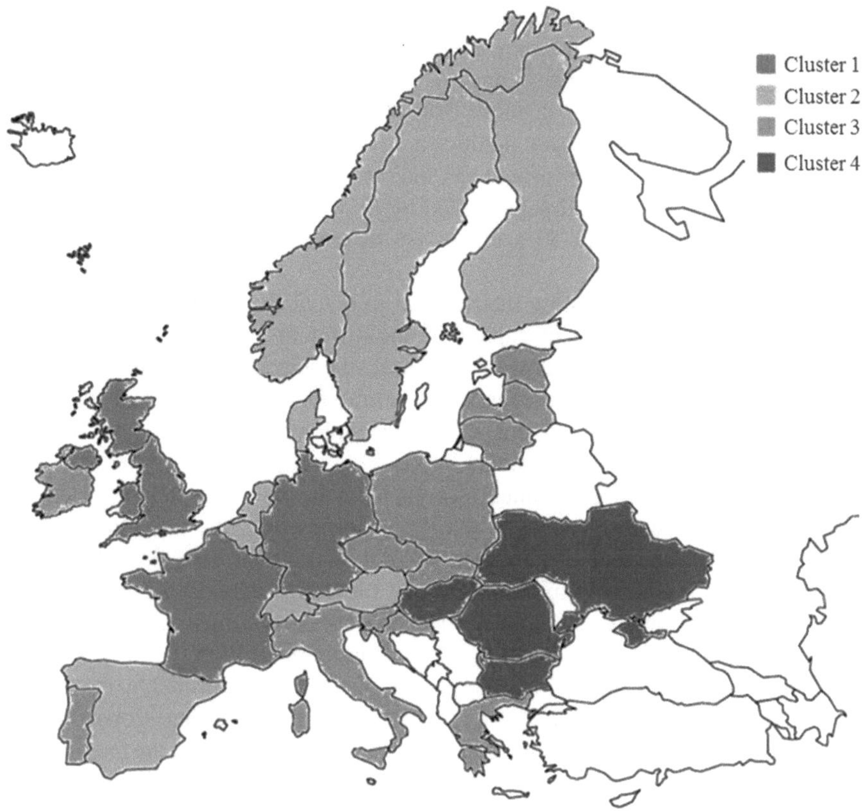

Fig. 1 Map of Europe with analysed clusters indicated

To characterize the market, in addition to the data used in the analysis of the level of development, there also were used: the information on the industry in which the funds are invested in, the development stage of companies in which capital providers are willing to inject funds and the source from which the venture capital comes. For the study, it will be called an analysis of the "4-S analysis" (Size of the PE/VC market, Source of the capital, Stage of the company, Sector of the PE/VC market). As per 4-S analysis data are taken from EVCA statistics (as per the extensive volume of the data, they are available in Appendix under Tables 3, 4, 5, and 6).

3.1 *First Cluster: Germany, United Kingdom, France*

This group includes countries whose share in the overall size of the market for venture capital investments exceeds 10 %, which is associated both with a relatively high proportion of PE/VC investments in gross domestic product (from 3 to 5 % of GDP). Thus, at the same time they are characterized by a large number of PE/VC companies investing in many projects (the national average of more than 200 PE/VC firms investing in more than 900 companies). On the level of this market also has the influence a significant advantage over other countries for the number of patents in patent offices (as indicated by the three countries together cover more than 61 % of all patents filed by European countries[4]). The relatively high proportion, because 45–53 % of workers are employed in the field of science or technology.

PE/VC Investors are putting their capital in practically all branches (Table 4). There is a large dispersion of capital among different branches. Most capital is attracted by: business and industrial products, life sciences, and consumer goods and retail and communications; least likely to grab funds are: agriculture, construction and the real estate. Investments in high technology constitute about 5–10 % of the total venture capital investments.

As for the phase of companies' development in which capital providers are willing to invest venture capital (Table 5), countries from the first cluster invest primarily in phase buyout[5]—more than 70 % of total investments. Also the growth step is seen as a relatively investors interest (approximately 10 %). Investors, in turn, are not at all interested in the seed[6] phase or rescue/turnaround.[7] This stands somewhat in contradiction with the original assumption of PE/VC, which says that it is risk capital, therefore, it finance organizations not yet unverified by the market, which affects the high riskiness of investments while providing scope for high return rates. Here, investors reduce their risk by investing capital in the final stage of the company, at the same time hoping to relatively high rates of return. But it appears that the there is a PE/VC market trend in investing increasing amounts in the final phases of companies life.

The funds mainly come from pension funds—from 11 to 41 % depending on the country. Also Insurance companies and private individuals invest relatively large sums, respectively 17 % and 14 %.

[4] Eurostat data for 2013 (Germany 21,724.39; France 8740.58; United Kingdom 4745.45).

[5] Financing provided to acquire a company. It may use a significant amount of borrowed money to meet the cost of acquisition. This category includes: MBI, MBO, LBO, Public-to-Private or other type of buyout transaction.

[6] Financing provided to research, assess and develop an initial concept before a business has reached the start-up phase.

[7] Financing made available to an existing business, which has experienced trading difficulties, with a view to re-establishing prosperity.

3.2 Second Cluster: The Benelux Countries, Scandinavia, Switzerland, Austria and Spain

Value of PE/VC sector investments in this group of countries is at a relatively high level, representing an average of 2–4 % of GDP (Table 3). The number of companies investing in venture market is in the range of 18–130 depending on the country.[8] In turn, the number of projects in which the funds are invested PE/VC fundus is an average of 150 projects (Luxembourg is an exception investing in 2013 only eight companies, as in previous years). The level of technological knowledge in this cluster is relatively high: the average country from this group in 2013 reported about 1500 patents. Important is the fact that on average about 51 % of employees in the national economy works in science or technology. This is a strong factor for the development of the country and certainly reflected in the number of licenses and patents. This means as well that these countries' aim is to develop quickly and to reach the level of 'top' countries rapidly.

When it comes to analysis called for this study '4-S analysis', this market in the second group is characterized (similarly as in the first group) by a significant diversification of industries in which PE/VC capital providers invest. As well similarly, the greatest interest in 2013 was attracted by life sciences and consumer goods and retail industry, as well as, business and industrial products (Table 4). Sectors such as real estate and financial services sectors are the least interesting for venture capitalists. In contrast to first group, slightly greater interest is in the sector of agriculture, particularly in Norway. For this group of countries it is interesting and at the same time distinctive (from the first cluster), that a much greater investment goes to the so-called high technology. Size of investment in high-tech depending on the country varies between 5.1 % (Austria) and 26 % (Switzerland). Exception is Denmark—42 %. This may result from the fact that the entities operating in these markets, for raising the competitiveness and the effectiveness of the solutions, in new technologies they see the creative solutions. It is also to strengthen the position of the country.

The main capital providers are here: the government agencies and fund of funds (Table 6). In most countries of this cluster, depending on the country, capital from government agencies reach a value of 13 % (in the Netherlands) up to 76 % (in Austria). In turn, the financial resource of the fund of funds amounts at about 10–40 % of the total (with the exception of Austria and the Netherlands, where in 2013 it was 0 %). A slightly different structure of financing for the Scandinavian countries is worth mentioning. In these countries, the largest shares, in addition to the fund of funds, have pension funds that provide up to 35 % equity. In turn, academic institutions and capital markets does not actually participate in the PE/VC market.

As for the analysis of the investment, depending on the phases of the enterprise (Table 5), also the biggest part of the investment is placed in the phase of the buyout

[8] Excluding Netherlands—18 PE/VC firms.

(average for a group of approximately 48 %). In turn, an average of about 14 % of the PE/VC capital is invested, similarly to cluster 1, in the growth stage. However, in countries of this concentration, about 5–20 % of PE/VC funds are invested in start-up[9] phase, which is in an early stage of company's development. The other initial phases such as the seed (average 1.5 %) and later stage venture (average 13 %) gain capital providers in this group of countries.

3.3 Third Cluster: Italy, Greece, Portugal, Ireland, Baltic Countries, Poland, Czech Republic, CEE

Third group of contains a particular part of the countries of Central and Eastern Europe and the countries of the eastern Mediterranean basin. These are the countries where the level of development of the PE/VC sector is assessed as satisfactory. These countries are characterized by low participation of PE/VC investments in GDP value. It is usually about 1–2 % (Table 3). In Europe, there is a widespread view that venture investments are beneficial for the innovativeness of the economy, so too low percentage in relation to GDP is inadvisable because it reduces the possibility of a more rapid development of the economy (European Private Equity Venture Capital Association 2014c). In 2013, an average of about 55 PE/VC firms[10] financed approximately 67 companies.[11] In this group, from 28 to 50 % of the employees are qualified employees hired in technology or science. Not significant difference when it comes to comparison to the previous cluster. On average, the countries of this group report about 700 patents to the Patent Offices.[12]

Venture capital in this cluster comes mainly (31–58 %) from government agencies, both indirectly and directly, in the form of quasi-funds, recapitalization of seed funds or throughout various funds of funds (Table 6). Depending on the country the funds are flowing, to some extent, from the banks (if there are no strong restrictions on the banking policy) and the corporate investors.

When the distribution of resources between industries is being concerned (Table 4), in this group there is no longer visible such diversification as in the previous two clusters. All countries are focused mainly on 2–3 branches in a given year, and they draw from about 60 % up to 90 % of the total value of PE/VC investments. For each of the countries, however, other sectors such are interested. E.g. for Polish there are: consumer goods and retail (26 %), Business andindustrial services (17 %) and transportation (16 %); for the Czech Republic—communications (33 %), financial services (31 %) and computer and consumer electronics

[9] Financing provided to companies for product development and initial marketing. Companies may be in the process of being set up or may have been in business for a short time, but have not sold their product commercially.

[10] Exceptions: Greece—230 firms and Czech Republic—6 firms.

[11] Exceptions: Greece—3 companies in portfolio and Czech Republic—14 companies.

[12] Exception: Italy—4434 patent applications in 2013.

(16 %), and for Italy: business and industrial products and services (45 % of the products plus 26 % of services) and consumer goods and retail (20 %). The remaining industries attract capital only in minimum size. When it comes to investing in high technology, it is about 1–13 % of total investment financed high-tech (in 2013 except for the Baltic countries 41 % and Ireland 55 %).

In the third cluster of countries, on average, approximately 66 % of capital[13] is invested in buyout phase (Table 5). In turn, from 5 % up to 50 % in some countries is invested in a growth phase. Here, as in second group, the early phase of development gain in importance, as it is often the company in these stages, that have the greatest difficulty in obtaining funding for the development. At the same time, these particular enterprises (SMEs) are the driving wheel of economies that want to catch up with more developed countries. Hence the strong interest of governments and the EU to support these phases through the capital for seed, start-up and growth. Thanks to this, the average level of investment in these phases in third cluster is: seed—2 %, start-up—10 % and later stage venture—3 %.[14] Although the values tend to be insignificant, the fact that investments in these company's development stages are associated with the greatest risk for the investor should be taken into account. Amount of expenditures, however, still is considered to be insufficient, because it must be remembered that this is a 15 % share of the relatively low value of PE/VC capital operating in these countries.

3.4 *Fourth Cluster: Romania, Bulgaria, Hungary, Ukraine*

The countries included in this group are characterized by a very low share of the size of PE/VC investments in GDP, less than 1 %. Venture sector is here at a very low level of development: an average of about six PE/VC firms invests in less than 20 companies (Table 3). In this case, as in other clusters, it can be seen that the funds in all EU countries prefer large investment projects. This means that the sector made investments are becoming lower (Gieroczynska 2006). Only 25–35 % of workers are employed in science and high technology. The average number of patent applications for specific countries was about 70 in 2013. An exception is Hungary, where the number of patents is about 200 in the same year.

For the analysis of sources of capital in the countries of forth cluster (Table 6), the vast majority of PE/VC capital—70–73 %, comes from government agencies. Other, depending on the country of origin is provided by private individuals (Bulgaria) and pension funds (Romania). In this group of countries there is no dissipation of capital, on the contrary, are strongly clustered around public funds—governmental and 1–2 other sources.

[13] Exceptions: Baltic Countries—2.8 % in buyout.

[14] Cluster 1: Seed—0.3 %, Start-up—5 %, Later stage venture—4 %; Cluster 2: Seed—2 %, Start-up—13 %, Later stage venture—8 %.

In addition to Bulgaria, where in 2013, 99 % of venture capital financed computer and consumer electronics, in other countries, as in the case of second group, PE/VC funds were concentrated primarily around three major industries, different for each country, e.g.: Romania are transportation (42 %), chemicals and materials (26 %) and communications (18 %) and for Ukraine: business and industrial services (42 %), communications (40 %) and financial services (15 %). In total, about 85–95 % equity goes to the selected sectors. What is more, in the case of this group it is difficult to assess distinctive level of investments in high technology: in 2013—Romania 0 %, Ukraine 4 %, Hungary 12 % and Bulgaria to 100 %. Additionally this level is very strongly fluctuating, depending on the year of analysis.

For this group of countries, it is not a major phase of buyout investing (Table 5). This involves certainly a low level of development of the market yet, in comparison with the countries of the previous groups. Majority of the investments here concerns the initial phases of life of the enterprise, where it is pressed more than 60 % of the PE/VC capital (seed 0.8 %, start-up 40 %; later stage 21 %). Buyout absorbs on average 30 % of the venture funds.

4 Summary

Table 2 consists the data collected on the characteristics of the individual designated in the study groups as the summary of the taxonomic and descriptive analysis conducted in this paper. The data are presented as a numerical (or percentage) value averages for groups, where the countries are similar, or on the basis of range values when there is a relatively stronger misalignment between the data. In some cases there were used both ways of characterizing (the split and the average) to make the view more clear. Each cluster is specified by few indicators precisely commented previously in this paper.

Summarizing, there is a significant difference between the first and the last cluster. These groups can be easily recognized by it's characteristics, as there is a homogeneity within each group. When it comes to second and third cluster, however, some countries are quite similar in some aspects regardless the cluster indicated. Thus we cannot be sure that these countries are associated properly to the groups. To be able to uniquely determine whether in fact there is such a dependency, the analysis should be again raised to verify assumptions for subsequent periods. It may turn out that such coupling occurs only in the examined time period (characteristic as per of the recent economic downturn), and it may occur that in next years the connections between countries will change.

This study may, however, constitute a point of reference for subsequent analysis on the venture capital market in Europe, in particular, that the apparent convergence is motivated not only geographically (as most of the reports stand). What is more it can also be the ground for the other taxonomy methods (e.g., Ward's analysis) for further recognition and verification.

Table 2 The summary of the indicated clusters characteristics

	Cluster 1	Cluster 2	Cluster 3	Cluster 4
Countries	Germany, United Kingdom, France	Belgium, Netherlands, Luxembourg, Scandinavian countries, Switzerland, Austria, Spain	Italy, Greece, Portugal, Ireland, Baltic countries, Poland, Czech Republic, CEE countries	Romania, Bulgaria, Hungary, Ukraine
Percentage of PE/VC investments in GDP	3–5 %	2–4 %	1–2 %	Less than 1 %
Total number of PE/VC firms	52–380 (av. 230)	18–130 (av. 75)	6–260 (av. 55)	2–12 (av. 6)
Total number of companies with PE VC capital invested in	av. 917	av. 150	av. 67	av. 17
Human resources in science and technology as a share of labour force	45–53 % (av. 49 %)	40–58 % (av. 51 %)	28–50 % (av. 38 %)	25–35 % (av. 30 %)
Number of patent applications regardless if there were granted	4700–21,700 (av. 11,700)	83–3200 (av. 1510)	23–4400 (av. 704)	12–202 (av. 72)
Main sources of PE/VC capital	Highly diversified-pension funds: 20 % Insurance companies: 17 % Private individuals: 14 %	Government agencies: 13–76 % Fund of funds: 10–40 % Pension funds: 35 %	Government: 31–58 % Corporate investors, banks	Government: 70–73 %
Most popular market sectors	Business and industrial products; life sciences; Consumer goods and retail; communications	Life sciences; consumer goods and retail; Business and industrial products	Not diversified—three main sectors 60–90 %	Not diversified—three main sectors 85–95 %
Level of investments in high-tech	5–10 %	5–26 %	1–13 %	Diversified, not stable
Stage of the company grabbing most of the PE/VC capital	Buyout: 70 % Growth: 10 % Early stages: 9 %	Buyout: 48 % Growth: 14 % Early stages: 23 %	Buyout: 66 % Growth: 5–50 % Early stages: 15 %	Early stages: 60 % Buyout: 30 %

Appendix

Table 3 Data for 2013 collected from Eurostat and EVCA database

Country	Total PE/VC investment	PE VC growth according previous period	Total number of PE–VC firms	Total number of companies with PE VC capital invested in	Percentage of PE VC investments in GDP (%)	Number of patent applications regardless if there were granted	Human resources in science and technology as a share of labour force (%)
Austria	539,854	0.91	50	140	0.02	1577.08	41.90
Baltic countries	60,404	1.04	22	53	0.01	23.24	44.33
Belgium	1,029,095	−0.27	61	174	0.03	1414.54	50.30
Bulgaria	11,098	−0.87	2	4	0.00	12.20	32.60
Czech Republic	134,339	0.27	6	14	0.01	268.17	36.50
Denmark	1,841,562	1.14	46	90	0.07	1337.80	52.90
Finland	791,032	0.30	24	211	0.00	1164.95	53.70
France	6,442,859	0.22	52	812	0.04	8740.58	48.10
Germany	4,927,533	−0.26	270	1316	0.03	21,724.39	45.70
Greece	4833	−0.86	260	3	0.02	75.97	34.20
Hungary	56,827	−0.45	12	43	0.00	202.55	35.40
Ireland	170,582	−0.36	21	97	0.01	353.56	50.50
Italy	1,538,238	0.15	30	120	0.01	4423.56	34.40
Luxembourg	155,025	1.28	95	8	0.01	83.30	58.60
Netherlands	2,371,972	0.72	18	336	0.03	3206.01	52.20
Norway	1,657,336	0.71	125	149	0.04	407.05	55.30
Other CEE	49,351	−0.64	48	18	0.00	74.99	35.87
Poland	380,033	−0.20	25	89	0.02	305.22	37.70
Portugal	321,123	0.41	25	143	0.02	108.42	28.70
Romania	70,099	1.54	3	15	0.00	39.98	25.70
Spain	1,969,208	−0.02	135	141	0.02	1454.12	40.60
Sweden	813,725	−0.68	136	390	0.02	2865.14	52.60
Switzerland	755,133	−0.59	58	95	0.02	2951.58	55.60
Ukraine	18,933	−0.56	6	4	0.00	35.02	25.00
United Kingdom	9,616,015	−0.04	378	624	0.05	4745.45	53.10

Table 4 Data for 2013 on percentage of PE/VC investments in market sectors—'Sector', collected from EVCA database

Country	Agriculture (%)	Business and industrial products (%)	Business and industrial services (%)	Chemicals and materials (%)	Communications (%)	Computer and consumer electronics (%)
Austria	0.0	14.5	1.3	13.1	15.5	13.2
Baltic countries	0.5	22.7	1.9	0.3	9.3	18.5
Belgium	0.2	19.4	6.0	1.6	3.1	4.0
Bulgaria	0.0	0.0	0.0	0.0	0.3	99.7
Czech Republic	0.0	15.0	0.0	0.0	32.6	16.0
Denmark	0.0	7.0	1.0	0.1	2.2	7.1
Finland	0.0	0.0	0.0	0.0	1.0	1.6
France	5.6	9.6	13.3	0.1	5.5	7.1
Germany	0.0	38.1	4.9	4.2	12.0	7.1
Greece	0.0	38.1	4.9	4.2	12.0	7.1
Hungary	0.0	0.0	0.0	0.0	100.0	0.0
Ireland	0.0	3.4	14.8	0.0	14.1	6.2
Italy	0.0	0.5	3.5	0.6	11.8	45.7
Luxembourg	0.0	25.5	45.2	2.2	0.9	0.2
Netherlands	0.0	14.6	0.0	0.0	14.3	23.0
Norway	2.7	15.4	15.5	3.8	2.3	6.8
Other CEE[a]	15.6	14.3	5.5	0.0	1.0	8.1
Poland	0.0	4.6	16.7	0.0	3.2	6.4
Portugal	0.0	13.7	0.1	1.0	1.9	5.3
Romania	0.0	0.0	0.5	25.8	18.4	0.0
Spain	2.7	5.3	6.3	6.3	42.4	7.6
Sweden	0.0	7.1	5.6	0.1	8.8	6.4
Switzerland	0.0	9.2	3.9	0.1	25.0	8.0
Ukraine	0.0	0.0	42.4	0.0	39.7	0.0
United Kingdom	1.3	5.8	7.0	0.4	9.9	8.3

Country	Construction (%)	Consumer goods and retail (%)	Consumer services (%)	Energy and environment (%)	Financial services (%)	Life sciences (%)
Austria	4.3	10.8	6.1	2.4	0.3	16.8
Baltic countries	0.3	31.2	4.8	2.3	2.0	3.6
Belgium	13.6	26.1	8.7	7.4	0.0	9.0
Bulgaria	0.0	0.0	0.0	0.0	0.0	0.0
Czech Republic	5.0	0.0	0.0	0.0	31.4	0.0
Denmark	0.0	13.4	0.8	4.6	0.2	49.9
Finland	0.0	22.1	6.8	31.8	0.0	36.7
France	0.7	16.6	8.8	7.4	1.8	10.5
Germany	0.7	7.2	2.2	11.8	0.5	7.9
Greece	0.7	7.2	2.2	11.8	0.5	7.9

(continued)

Table 4 (continued)

Country	Construction (%)	Consumer goods and retail (%)	Consumer services (%)	Energy and environment (%)	Financial services (%)	Life sciences (%)
Hungary	0.0	0.0	0.0	0.0	0.0	0.0
Ireland	0.0	8.5	6.7	4.6	0.4	24.5
Italy	0.0	0.1	0.4	0.2	0.4	36.7
Luxembourg	0.8	19.8	1.9	2.0	0.6	0.7
Netherlands	0.0	6.1	3.1	0.0	0.0	18.3
Norway	0.1	17.7	17.9	3.4	2.0	12.1
Other CEE[a]	1.9	4.6	0.0	43.0	0.3	5.7
Poland	7.5	25.9	4.9	8.5	2.9	4.0
Portugal	1.3	14.7	2.5	9.1	0.2	4.4
Romania	1.7	0.5	4.1	0.0	7.2	0.0
Spain	4.2	7.4	5.8	0.5	0.1	4.1
Sweden	2.6	18.7	13.4	17.5	0.1	17.2
Switzerland	2.5	7.3	14.6	2.1	0.8	26.1
Ukraine	0.0	0.0	0.0	0.0	13.7	4.2
United Kingdom	0.3	16.3	13.4	3.5	12.4	17.0

Country	Real estate (%)	Transportation (%)	Unclassified (%)	Total (%)	High-tech (in total) (%)
Austria	0.0	0.9	0.9	100.0	5.1
Baltic countries	0.0	2.8	0.0	100.0	41.9
Belgium	0.2	0.8	0.0	100.0	6.5
Bulgaria	0.0	0.0	0.0	100.0	100.0
Czech Republic	0.0	0.0	0.0	100.0	2.3
Denmark	0.0	13.7	0.0	100.0	42.9
Finland	0.0	0.0	0.0	100.0	7.3
France	0.2	1.6	11.3	100.0	0.1
Germany	0.0	3.2	0.1	100.0	0.1
Greece	0.0	3.2	0.1	100.0	5.7
Hungary	0.0	0.0	0.0	100.0	0.0
Ireland	0.0	11.3	5.4	100.0	12.0
Italy	0.0	0.0	0.2	100.0	55.4
Luxembourg	0.0	0.2	0.0	100.0	1.7
Netherlands	0.0	20.6	0.0	100.0	35.3
Norway	0.0	0.1	0.2	100.0	11.4
Other CEE[a]	0.2	0.0	0.0	100.0	7.3
Poland	0.0	15.4	0.0	100.0	0.7
Portugal	3.6	3.9	38.4	100.0	13.4
Romania	0.0	41.8	0.0	100.0	0.0
Spain	0.0	7.2	0.0	100.0	5.3
Sweden	0.1	2.5	0.0	100.0	0.1
Switzerland	0.0	0.4	0.1	100.0	26.0
Ukraine	0.0	0.0	0.0	100.0	4.2
United Kingdom	0.6	3.8	0.0	100.0	6.3

[a]Central and Eastern Europe

Table 5 Data for 2013 on percentage of PE/VC investments in stage of companies' development—'Stage', collected from EVCA database

Country	Seed (%)	Start-up (%)	Later stage venture (%)	Growth (%)	Rescue/ Turnaround (%)	Replacement capital (%)	Buyout (%)
Austria	12.7	7.7	11.1	30.4	0.4	10.8	26.8
Baltic countries	9.0	24.7	10.5	53.0	0.0	0.0	2.8
Belgium	0.1	6.4	5.0	18.8	4.2	4.4	61.1
Bulgaria	0.0	76.2	23.8	0.0	0.0	0.0	0.0
Czech Republic	0.7	2.1	0.0	10.7	0.0	0.0	86.5
Denmark	0.3	7.1	6.2	2.5	0.1	0.0	83.7
Finland	0.0	21.2	1.6	23.9	21.4	0.0	32.0
France	0.2	4.7	5.7	9.1	0.8	1.7	77.9
Germany	0.9	8.0	5.4	7.1	0.8	0.8	77.1
Greece	0.7	6.0	4.4	5.9	0.3	1.4	81.2
Hungary	0.0	0.0	100.0	0.0	0.0	0.0	0.0
Ireland	2.5	37.2	38.8	6.7	0.0	0.0	14.8
Italy	1.4	74.0	19.2	5.4	0.0	0.0	0.0
Luxembourg	0.2	2.8	1.0	5.8	0.6	2.9	86.7
Netherlands	0.0	43.6	15.8	11.8	7.1	9.8	11.9
Norway	0.4	9.2	5.6	18.3	5.0	3.3	58.2
Other CEE	0.2	5.0	3.9	26.6	0.2	0.0	64.0
Poland	0.4	1.4	4.6	22.0	0.0	7.2	64.5
Portugal	2.1	6.8	2.3	20.8	0.0	3.9	64.1
Romania	0.0	7.2	0.0	14.7	0.0	9.9	68.1
Spain	0.4	4.8	5.5	19.9	0.0	2.9	66.5
Sweden	0.6	11.8	16.0	13.5	0.0	0.1	57.9
Switzerland	1.3	22.9	11.3	9.0	1.5	20.1	34.0
Ukraine	0.0	4.4	0.0	57.8	0.0	0.0	37.8
United Kingdom	0.0	3.4	2.4	11.8	1.0	2.2	79.3

Table 6 Data for 2013 on structure of sources of capital—'Source', collected from EVCA database

Countries	Academic institutions (%)	Banks (%)	Capital markets (%)	Corporate investors (%)	Endowments and foundations (%)	Family offices (%)	Fund of funds (%)
Austria	0.0	0.0	0.0	0.0	0.0	0.0	0.0
Belgium	4.4	0.0	0.0	0.0	0.0	0.0	0.0
Bulgaria	0.0	0.0	0.0	3.7	0.0	0.0	0.0
Czech Republic	0.0	14.6	0.0	29.1	0.0	0.0	0.0
Denmark	0.0	9.2	0.0	0.0	0.0	0.0	29.4
Other CEE	0.0	0.0	0.0	0.0	0.0	0.0	0.0
Finland	0.1	0.4	0.0	3.3	8.0	4.0	9.6
France	0.2	4.5	0.0	4.1	0.6	4.2	2.9
Germany	0.0	1.1	0.0	0.3	6.0	10.6	14.5
Greece	0.2	4.5	0.0	4.1	0.6	4.2	2.9
Hungary	0.0	0.0	0.0	0.0	0.0	0.0	0.0
Ireland	0.0	20.6	0.0	0.0	0.0	0.0	0.0
Italy	0.0	4.3	0.0	6.4	4.7	0.0	20.3
Luxembourg	0.0	0.0	0.0	0.0	0.0	0.0	0.0
Netherlands	0.0	2.8	0.0	2.0	0.0	32.4	22.1
Norway	0.0	7.5	0.0	0.0	9.1	3.7	13.4
Poland	0.0	0.0	0.0	2.5	0.1	1.0	23.6
Portugal	0.0	37.2	0.0	13.2	0.0	0.0	0.0
Romania	0.0	0.0	0.0	0.0	0.0	0.0	0.0
Spain	0.0	13.1	0.0	5.6	0.0	11.9	11.2
Sweden	0.0	5.1	4.6	2.1	2.0	4.2	20.1
Switzerland	0.0	8.0	0.0	14.6	1.3	3.9	40.2
Ukraine	0.0	0.0	0.0	0.0	0.0	4.5	0.0
United Kingdom	0.1	0.8	0.9	0.9	4.1	2.1	9.8

Countries	Insurance companies (%)	Other asset managers (%)	Pension funds (%)	Private individuals (%)	Sovereign wealth funds (%)	Unclassified (%)	Total (%)
Austria	0.0	0.0	0.0	18.3	0.0	5.1	100
Belgium	7.4	23.5	0.0	5.9	0.0	0.0	100
Bulgaria	0.0	0.0	0.0	26.3	0.0	0.0	100
Czech Republic	0.0	0.0	0.0	1.9	0.0	0.0	100
Denmark	9.2	18.4	9.2	0.0	0.0	24.5	100
Other CEE	0.0	0.0	0.0	0.0	0.0	42.1	100
Finland	0.1	0.4	21.5	1.7	0.0	15.4	100
France	31.3	0.6	13.4	9.4	2.4	8.4	100
Germany	13.7	0.5	11.8	29.5	0.0	9.8	100

(continued)

Table 6 (continued)

Countries	Insurance companies (%)	Other asset managers (%)	Pension funds (%)	Private individuals (%)	Sovereign wealth funds (%)	Unclassified (%)	Total (%)
Greece	31.3	0.6	13.4	9.4	2.4	8.4	100
Hungary	0.0	0.0	0.0	0.0	0.0	30.0	100
Ireland	25.9	0.0	0.0	0.0	0.0	0.0	100
Italy	2.1	0.5	2.3	7.6	0.0	35.2	100
Luxembourg	0.0	0.0	0.0	0.0	0.0	100.0	100
Netherlands	3.9	4.7	6.4	4.4	2.7	4.9	100
Norway	10.9	0.5	31.6	0.5	1.5	11.9	100
Poland	2.5	1.1	9.1	5.7	0.5	12.2	100
Portugal	0.0	0.0	0.0	0.0	0.0	18.9	100
Romania	0.0	0.0	27.3	0.0	0.0	0.0	100
Spain	0.1	0.0	13.0	15.4	0.0	3.7	100
Sweden	5.1	2.9	35.0	1.1	16.2	0.6	100
Switzerland	3.8	0.0	12.9	8.0	0.0	6.0	100
Ukraine	0.0	44.4	0.0	2.2	0.0	0.0	100
United Kingdom	5.8	5.7	41.4	3.3	12.6	11.3	100

References

Dutta, S., & Lanvin, B. (Eds.). (2013). *The Global Innovation Index 2013: The local dynamics of innovation*. Geneva: Cornell University, INSEAD, WIPO.

European Commission. (2014). *Eurostat statistics*. [online] Accessed September 12, 2014, from http://epp.eurostat.ec.europa.eu/portal/page/portal/statistics/search_database

European Private Equity Venture Capital Association. (2014a). *European Private Equity Activity: Statistics on fundraising, investments and divestments*. [online] Accessed August 20, 2014, from http://www.evca.eu/media/142790/2013-european-private-equity-activity.pdf

European Private Equity Venture Capital Association. (2014b). *EVCA Yearbook 2014—Europe, country tables*. [online] Accessed August 28, 2014, from https://www.google.pl/url?sa=t&rct=j&q=&esrc=s&source=web&cd=1&cad=rja&uact=8&ved=0CCAQFjAA&url=http%3A%2F%2Fwww.evca.eu%2Fmedia%2F165475%2Fyearbook-2014europecountrytablesfinal.xlsx&ei=__QNVLS9A8v4yQOaYK4Cg&usg=AFQjCNFn80DU84RqgtqTlMfAGR2SYtTC3A&bvm=bv.74649129,d.bGQ

European Private Equity Venture Capital Association. (2014c). *EVCA Central and Eastern Europe Statistics 2013: An EVCA special paper*. [online] Accessed August 28, 2014, from http://www.evca.eu/media/259990/_evca_bro_sp_cee2013.pdf

Gieroczynska, E. (2006). Efektywne wykorzystanie private equity i venture capital [eng. Effective utilization of the private equity and venture capital]. *Biuletyn Analiz UKIE, 16*, 99–116.

Hellwig, Z. (1968). Zastosowanie metody taksonomicznej do typologicznego podziału krajów ze względu na poziom ich rozwoju oraz zasoby i strukturę wykwalifikowanych kadr [eng. Application of the taxonomic method in typological dividing of countries due to their level of development as well as their resources and the structure of qualified staff]. *Przegląd Statystyczny, 4*, 307–326.

Hollanders, H., & Es-Sadki, N. (2014). *Innovation Union Scoreboard 2014*. Maastricht: Maastricht Economic and Social Research Institute on Innovation and Technology.

Janasz, W. (2004). *Innowacje z rozwoju przedsiębiorczości w procesie transformacji* [eng. Innovation in the development of entrepreneurship in the process of transformation]. Warszawa: Difin.

Karpinska, N. (2014). *Venture capital—kapitał dla innowacyjnych* [eng. Venture capital—capital for innovatives] Forum Edukacji Biznesowej Uniwersytetu Ekonomicznego we Wrocławiu. [online] Accessed August 15, 2014, from http://feb.ue.wroc.pl/86,venture_capital_kapital_dla_innowacyjnych.html

Kopczewska, K., Kopczewski, T., & Wojcik, P. (2009). *Metody ilościowe: Aplikacje ekonomiczne i finansowe* [eng. Quantitative methods: Economic and financial implementations]. Warszawa: CeDeWu.

Mikolajczyk, B., & Krawczyk, M. (2007). *Aniołowie biznesu w sektorze MSP* [eng. Business Angels in the SME sector]. Warszawa: Difin.

Mlodak, A. (2006). *Analiza taksonomiczna w statystyce regionalnej* [eng. The taxonomic analysis of regional statistics]. Warszawa: Difin.

Weclawski, J. (1997).*Venture capital. Nowy instrument finansowania przedsiębiorstw* [eng. Venture capital. The new instrument of corporate financing]. Warszawa: Wydawnictwo Naukowe PWN.

Part III
Economics

The Role of Institutions in Socio-Economic Development

Alise Vitola and Maija Senfelde

Abstract The aim of the paper is to quantitatively evaluate the impact of institutions on the socioeconomic development on a global scale and in factor-driven, efficiency-driven and innovation-driven economies. We define institutions as socially approved behavior models that restrict the rationality of an individual and constrain or encourage specific behavior and classify institutions into three groups—economic institutions, political institutions and value institutions. The regression analysis confirms that institutions play an important role in socioeconomic performance. But the importance of specific institutions depends on the socioeconomic development level of the economy. Results of the research can be applied to global development policies for less developed countries, as well as regional development policies for geo-political regions, e.g., the European Union.

Keywords Institutions • Institutional arrangements • Governance • Values • Economic development

1 Introduction

There is a wide discussion on the causes of differences in economic performance around the world. As Rodrik et al. (2004, p. 1) put it: "it is hard to think of any question in economics that is of greater intellectual significance or of greater relevance to vast majority of the world's population". A recent body of literature argues that the institutions are the fundamental cause of differences in economic development. Institutions, according to the Nobel prize laureate D.C. North, are "the rules of the game in society" that consist of formal, public-order institutions as laws and constitutions and informal, private-order institutions as values, norms and beliefs (North 1990, p. 4).

Following the theoretical assumptions of new institutional economics, the aim of the paper is to quantitatively evaluate the impact of institutions on the socioeconomic development on a global scale and in factor-driven, efficiency-driven and

A. Vitola (✉) • M. Senfelde
Faculty of Engineering Economics and Management, Riga Technical University, Riga, Latvia
e-mail: alise.vitola@rtu.lv; maija.senfelde@rtu.lv

© Springer International Publishing Switzerland 2016
M.H. Bilgin et al. (eds.), *Business Challenges in the Changing Economic Landscape - Vol. 1*, Eurasian Studies in Business and Economics 2/1,
DOI 10.1007/978-3-319-22596-8_18

innovation-driven economies. In order to evaluate the role of institutions, we define institutions as socially approved behavior models that restrict the rationality of an individual and constrain or encourage specific behavior. We also classify institutions into three groups—economic institutions, political institutions and value institutions. Moreover, we assume that high quality institutions encourage an efficient use of limited production resources in order to fulfill the needs of society. Detailed evaluations of institutions are especially important for relatively new democracies and developing countries that are transposing not only legislation, but also values and norms that are crucial for a smooth operation of market economy.

The methods of the study are: document analysis and data analysis by using correlation and regression analysis. The authors focus on the latest findings in the particular field. The analysis confirms that institutions play an important role in socioeconomic performance. But the importance of specific institutions depends on the socioeconomic development level of the economy. It should be taken into account when designing development policies.

2 Literature Review

At the end of twentieth century economic thought has returned to the analysis of institutional environment. It has been acknowledged that market will not function effectively unless the institutions (both public and private) form an environment that fosters productive action. This shift has been influenced by the collapse of communism, the transition from socialism to capitalism in post-soviet countries and China, as well as the persistent underdevelopment in the Third World.

Institutional economics argue that institutions are the fundamental cause of differences in socioeconomic development. Institutions are "the rules of the game in society"; the social infrastructure that determines the economic environment within which individuals accumulate skills, and firms accumulate capital and produce output (North 1990; Hall and Jones 1999). Institutions are defined as the "the humanly devised constraints that shape human interaction", "the rules of the game in society" (North 1990, pp. 3–4). They are the "non-technologically determined constraints that influence social interaction and provide incentives to maintain regularities and behavior" and "are complemented by self-enforcing constraints generated through interactions within these rules" (Greif 1998, p. 80).

Institutions consist of (1) formal, public-order institutions as laws and constitutions and (2) informal, private-order institutions as values, norms and beliefs (North 1990, 1994). Large literature focuses on the formal institutions, most often—the property rights and rule of law, but it is only the most visible part. Also culture, religion, legal origins and even historical events long after they have passed play an important role in economics.

Institutions affect investment in physical and human capital as well as the organization of production (North 1990). In order to reach high level of output per worker, social infrastructure should provide an environment that supports productive activities, encourages capital accumulation, skill acquisition, invention and technology transfer (Hall and Jones 1999). However, institutions are strongly influenced by path dependence. Therefore countries might stay underdeveloped due to inappropriate institutional environment (Acemoglu et al. 2005; North 1994).

The role of institutions in socioeconomic performance has been analyzed using qualitative and quantitative research methods. Qualitative research focuses on economic history by analyzing the role of institutions in industrial revolution and the modern economic regime. Literature shows that institutions played an important role in facilitating technological progress and thus overcoming Malthusian stagnation. The interaction of economic power and economic and political institutions created the circumstances in which industrial revolution could happen thus leading the world into the modern economic regime. The decrease in transaction costs led to an expansion of markets, urbanization and international trade. That created further incentives to improve institutions and to exchange knowledge and innovation, leading to the modern economic regime (Crafts and Mills 2009; Galor and Weil 2000; Hansen and Prescott 1998; Bogart et al. 2010; Persson 2010; Acemoglu et al. 2005; Acemoglu and Robinson 2006).

Quantitative research measures the impact of institutions, based on numerous indicators. For example, Rodrik et al. (2004) show that institutional quality outweighs geography and trade. By using a large number of indicators of geography, integration and institutions in a sample of 80 and 140 countries to measure the effects of institutions, geography and trade on income, they found that the institutional quality accounts for the most part of differences in income. Moreover, Hall and Jones (1999) analyzed data on 127 countries and measures on physical capital stock, primary languages spoken, distance from the equator, trade share, openness to trade, educational attainment and mining share of GDP and an index of government anti-diversion policies. They found that differences in institutions account for much of the differences in output per worker, because countries with good social infrastructure have high physical and human capital, as well as high productivity.

3 Data and Methodology

In order to perform a quantitative analysis, we designed a conceptual model of the interaction among institutions and socioeconomic performance (Fig. 1). We define institutions as socially approved behavior models that restrict the rationality of an individual and constrain or encourage specific behavior and assume that high quality institutions encourage an efficient use of limited production resources in order to fulfill the need of society. Moreover, we classify institutions into three groups—economic institutions, political institutions and value institutions.

The most important economic institutions are the structure of property rights and the presence and perfection of markets. They should provide incentives for investment in human and physical capital. Economic institutions are characterized by the extent of the rule of law and the quality of the regulatory framework, as well as the

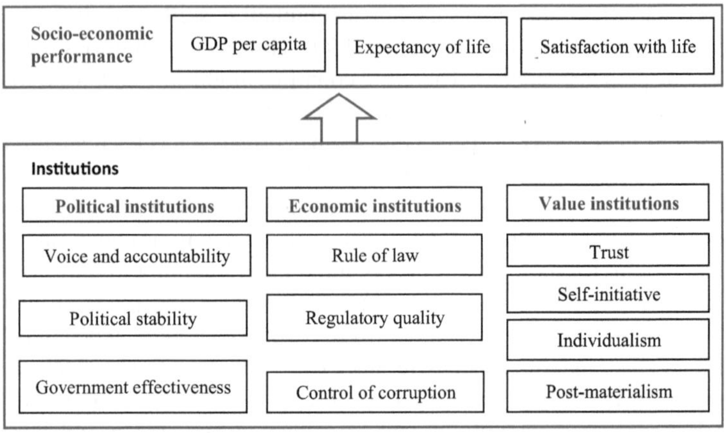

Fig. 1 Institutions and socioeconomic performance—a conceptual model

level of corruption, because corruption distorts the operation of markets by limiting fair competitiveness.

The most important political institutions are the form of government and the extent of constraints on politicians. Political institutions should ensure political stability in order to encourage investment and at the same time have a decent level of political competitiveness to facilitate political action that brings benefits to the majority of society, not only the political elite. Also a professional and politically independent bureaucracy plays an important role, as it is more long-run productivity oriented that politicians because of the job security and a need for a reputation (Williamson 1995).

Also the values of society impact the use of production resources. Higher trust promotes sharing knowledge and other resources thus decreasing production costs and encouraging innovation. Initiative raises economic and social activity leading to higher rates of employment, entrepreneurship and non-governmental activity. Individualism decreases the need to conform to common rules and norms thus facilitating innovation and rational behavior. Last but not least, post-materialism encourages civic activity and political participation thus promoting democracy and increasing the constraints on political elites.

In order to perform a quantitative analysis we used correlation analysis and multiple linear regression analysis that covers 54–108 countries on the world scale depending on the data availability. To measure the level of socioeconomic performance in a comprehensive way we used such indicators as the GDP per capita and the life expectancy at birth from the World Bank World Development Indicators and the satisfaction with life from the World Value Survey. These indicators include objective and subjective evaluation of the quality of life.

To measure the quality of institutions we used the World Bank Worldwide Governance Indicators: for economic institutions—regulatory quality, rule of law and control of corruption; for political institutions—voice and accountability, government effectiveness and political stability and absence of violence. Last but not least, to measure values we used results from the World Value Survey—the post-materialism and individualism indexes, as well as indicators developed by the authors using Likert scale and the answers to the questions about general trust and responsibility of state versus individual (the self-initiative).

We used 10-year (2000–2011) average indicators from the World Development Indicators and World Governance Indicators (World Bank 2012a, b), and the average indicators from World Value Survey rounds in 1999–2002 and 2005–2008 (World Values Survey Association 2012). The multiple linear regression analysis was performed in two rounds. First round of analysis covered all countries in the sample and the second round was performed in three groups of countries—factor-driven economies, efficiency-driven economies and innovation-driven economies. The classification of countries is based on the methodology used in the World Competitiveness Reports (The World Economic Forum 2012).

4 Results

Firstly, we used correlation analysis to identify coherence among socioeconomic performance and institution indicators. GDP per capita strongly correlates with satisfaction with life and expectancy of life. Also the satisfaction with life correlates with the expectancy of life but to a lesser extent (Table 1).

Regarding the institutions, individualism correlates with post materialism and to lesser extent—with trust; trust is also linked with self-initiative. Such value institutions as trust and self-initiative strongly correlate with economic and political institutions, but we don't see significant linkage in the case of individualism and post-materialism values, except from government effectiveness, which correlates with individualism (Table 2). Moreover, political and economic institutions strongly correlate with each other (all correlation coefficients are higher than 0.7 with $p < 0.01$).

Secondly, we used multiple linear regression analysis to determine the relationship among institutions and socioeconomic performance indicators. We follow the assumption that institutions are the cause of socioeconomic development (Formula 1).

$$Y[socioeconomic\ performance] = a + b[institutions] \tag{1}$$

Table 1 Correlations among socioeconomic performance indicators

Indicator	GDP per capita (n = 93)	Expectancy of life (n = 93)
Expectancy of life (n = 93)	0.560***	
Satisfaction with life (n = 90)	0.622***	0.412***

Note: ***p < 0.01, **p < 0.05, *p < 0.10

Table 2 Correlations among institution indicators

Indicator	Trust (n = 90)	Self-initiative (n = 90)	Individualism (n = 88)	Post-materialism (n = 69)
Value institutions				
Trust (n = 90)		0.360***	0.239**	0.117
Self-initiative (n = 90)			0.144	0.205
Individualism (n = 88)				0.391***
Political institutions				
Voice and accountability (n = 47)	0.283**	0.349***	0.122	0.097
Political stability (n = 47)	0.397***	0.291**	0.084	−0.080
Government effectiveness (n = 47)	0.418***	0.330***	0.270**	0.077
Economic institutions				
Regulatory quality (n = 47)	0.280**	0.289**	0.119	0.022
Rule of law (n = 47)	0.405***	0.274**	0.179	0.095
Corruption control (n = 47)	0.336***	0.274**	0.070	0.081

Note: ***$p < 0.01$, **$p < 0.05$, *$p < 0.10$

Table 3 Results of the regression analysis on the impact of value institutions on socioeconomic performance (n = 69)

Indicators	GDP per capita	Expectancy of life	Satisfaction with life
Constant	−27,011.702 (15,763.854)	16.419 (7.552)	42.345 (10.101)
Trust	589.830*** (117.079)	−0.063 (0.056)	0.246*** (0.075)
Initiative	355.643* (190.619)	−0.124 (0.091)	0.484*** (0.122)
Individualism	−151.103 (236.877)	−0.034 (0.113)	−0.422*** (0.152)
Post-materialism	426.188 (256.328)	0.053 (0.123)	0.490*** (0.164)
R^2	0.460	0.090	0.458

Note: Standard deviation in brackets; ***$p < 0.01$, **$p < 0.05$, *$p < 0.10$

In the first round we performed the analysis on the world scale; the number of observations depends on the data availability and is indicated in the data tables. Analysis shows that institutions have a significant impact on such socioeconomic development aspects as income (GDP per capita) and the satisfaction with life. It explains 45–65 % of variation among income and around 45 % of variants among satisfaction with life (Tables 3 and 4).

Table 4 Results of the regression analysis on the impact of political and economic institutions on socioeconomic performance (n = 90)

Indicators	GDP per capita	Expectancy of life	Satisfaction with life
Constant	−13,851.628 (3099.901)	59.076 (2.976)	50.063 (2.309)
Political institutions			
Voice and accountability	195.249** (85.075)	−0.021 (0.082)	0.113* (0.063)
Political stability	135.680 (86.245)	−0.014 (0.083)	−0.018 (0.064)
Government effectiveness	197.065 (206.836)	0.307 (0.199)	0.243 (0.154)
Economic institutions			
Regulatory quality	−286.058* (166.916)	−0.014 (0.160)	−0.128 (0.124)
Rule of law	265.760 (197.311)	−0.078 (0.189)	−0.227 (0.147)
Corruption control	31.489 (193.295)	0.007 (0.186)	0.277* (0.144)
R^2	0.648	0.200	0.448

Note: Standard deviation in brackets; ***$p < 0.01$, **$p < 0.05$, *$p < 0.10$

The level of income (objective well-being) is determined by such institutions as trust and voice and accountability, as well as initiative, but with a lower statistical significance. These results correspond to the theoretical assumptions about the role of social capital in innovation economy because higher level of social capital provides quicker, cheaper and higher quality exchange of information and knowledge (Malecki 2012), as well as encourages economic agents to cooperate in order to achieve common targets (Emery and Trist 1965; Feldman and Zoller 2012). They also support the presumption that constraints on politicians positively influence economic development, because it improves decision-making process and brings benefits to a wider society (Acemoglu et al. 2005).

On the contrary to the expected, higher regulatory quality has a negative impact on the income level. It could be explained by a strict environmental and social legislation that balances economic, social and environmental goals and impedes a further rise of income in developed countries. Satisfaction of life (subjective well-being) is determined by all value institutions—trust, initiative, post-materialism and, contrary to the theoretical assumptions (e.g., Greif 2000), not individualism, but collectivism values. It could be explained by the fact that collectivism values provide feelings of safety and thus positively influences the satisfaction with life. It might also imply that in the contemporary society (at least in the developed countries) traditional values are less harmful to the creation of innovation. Also, voice and accountability and corruption control increases the satisfaction with life, but with a lower statistical significance. The positive impact of corruption control indicates that corruption not only distorts market, but has also a negative social impact.

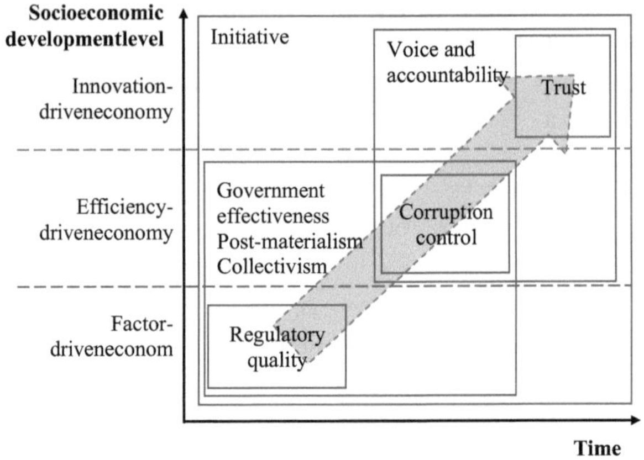

Fig. 2 Results of the regression analysis on the impact of institutions on socioeconomic development in factor-driven, efficiency-driven and innovation-driven economies

The results of the regression analysis on a world scale confirm that institutions significantly influence such socioeconomic development indicators as GDP per capita and the satisfaction with life, but they don't have a significant impact on the life expectancy at birth. To conclude, most crucial institutions for socioeconomic development are trust, initiative and voice and accountability that impact objective and subjective well-being—income level and the satisfaction with life. For the subjective well-being important role is played also by other value institutions (collectivism and post-materialism), as well as such economic institutions as corruption control.

In the second round we performed the regression analysis in three groups of countries—factor-driven economies, efficiency-driven economies and innovation-driven economies. The results are given in a graphical form (Fig. 2). Analysis shows that in factor-driven economies important role is played by institutions that shape formal conditions of the economy such as private sector regulation and government effectiveness; both institutions have a statistically significant impact on the income level. Also such values as post-materialism, collectivism and initiative influence the socioeconomic performance by increasing the satisfaction with life. These results approve that well established property rights and efficient markets are fundamental preconditions for socioeconomic development because they encourage investment in capital and human resources.

In efficiency-driven economies an important role is played by such governance dimensions as corruption control and voice and accountability. Corruption control increases the efficiency of markets, as well as decreases costs for economic agents because corruption acts as an additional tax. Whereas voice and accountability increases the participation of economic agents and other parties in decision making thus shaping legislation that supports and encourages socioeconomic development. Also government effectiveness, post-materialism, collectivism and initiative have a significant impact on the socioeconomic performance in this stage of development.

Last but not least, in innovation-driven economies a critical role is played by such informal institutions as trust, initiative and voice and accountability. Results suggest that once formal institutions are in place informal institutions play the most important role in socioeconomic development.

5 Conclusions and Suggestions

Analysis confirms that institutions play an important role in socioeconomic performance by influencing the use of production factors. But the importance of specific institutions depends on the socioeconomic development level of the economy; it should be taken into account when designing development policies in a specific territory. Thus research results can be applied to global development and regional development policies for geo-political regions, e.g., the European Union.

Institutions influence the behavior of every individual and organization. Therefore public, private and non-governmental sector should pay more attention to the evaluation of institutions by measuring institutional indicators and taking into account institutional environment in public and private decision-making. Public sector should also focus on shaping policies that improve the quality of institutions. Further research is needed to identify policies that help to raise the quality of institutions. Last but not least, evaluation methodologies should be improved to capture the state-of-art and future perspectives of institutions in an innovative and consistent yet simple and informative way.

References

Acemoglu, D., Johnson, S., & Robinson, J. A. (2005). Institutions as a fundamental cause of long run growth. In P. Aghion & S. N. Durlauf (Eds.), *The handbook of economic growth* (Vol. 1, pp. 385–472). North-Holland: Elsevier.

Acemoglu, D., & Robinson, J. A. (2006). Economic backwardness in political perspective. *American Political Science Review, 100*(1), 115–131.

Bogart, D. M., Drelichman, M., Gelderblom, O., & Rosenthal, J. L. (2010). State and private institutions. *The Cambridge Economic History of Modern Europe, 1*, 70–95.

Crafts, N., & Mills, T. C. (2009). From Malthus to Solow: How did the Malthusian economy really evolve? *Journal of Macroeconomics, 31*(1), 68–93.

Emery, F. E., & Trist, E. L. (1965). The causal texture of organizational environments. *Human Relations, 18*, 21–32.

Feldman, M., & Zoller, T. D. (2012). Dealmakers in place: Social capital connections in regional entrepreneurial economies. *Regional Studies, 46*(1), 23–37.

Galor, O., & Weil, D. N. (2000). Population, technology, and growth: From Malthusian stagnation to the demographic transition and beyond. *The American Economic Review, 90*(4), 806–828.

Greif, A. (1998). Historical and comparative institutional analysis. *The American Economic Review, 88*(2), 80–84.

Greif, A. (2000). The fundamental problem of exchange: A research agenda in historical institutional analysis. *European Review of Economic History, 4*, 251–284.

Hall, R. E., & Jones, C. I. (1999). Why do some countries produce so much more output per worker than others? *The Quarterly Journal of Economics, 114*(1), 83–116.

Hansen, G. D., & Prescott, E. C. (1998). *Malthus to Solow* (National Bureau of Economic Research Working Papers 6858).

Malecki, E. J. (2012). Regional social capital: Why it matters. *Regional Studies, 46*(8), 1023–1039.

North, D. C. (1990). *Institutions, institutional change, and economic performance*. Cambridge, MA: Cambridge University Press.

North, D. C. (1994). Economic performance through time. *The American Economic Review, 84*, 359–368.

Persson, K. G. (2010). *An economic history of Europe. Knowledge, institutions and growth, 600 to present*. Cambridge, MA: Cambridge University Press.

Rodrik, D., Subramanian, A., & Trebbi, F. (2004). Institutions rule: The primacy of institutions over geography and integration in economic development. *Journal of Economic Growth, 9*, 131–165.

The World Economic Forum. (2012). *The global competitiveness report 2011–2012*. Geneva: The World Economic Forum.

Williamson, O. E. (1995). The institutions and governance of economic development and reform. In *Proceedings of the World Bank Annual Conference on Development Economics*. Washington, DC: The World Bank.

World Bank. (2012a). *World development indicators*. [online]. Accessed November 1, 2012, from http://data.worldbank.org/indicator

World Bank. (2012b). *World governance indicators*. [online]. Accessed November 1, 2012, from http://info.worldbank.org/governance/wgi/index.asp

World Values Survey Association. (2012). *World values survey*. [online]. Accessed November 1, 2012, from http://www.worldvaluessurvey.org/

Exchange Rate Volatility Exposure on Corporate Cash Flows and Stock Prices: The Case of Poland

Lucie Tomanova

Abstract Exchange rate volatility may influence the expected cash flows and thus the firm value; however, previous empirical work finds mixed results and rarely considers Central and Eastern European markets. To examine the economic significance of the exchange rate to firm value relation, this paper analyses the foreign exchange rate exposure on the value of publicly listed companies in Poland on the basis of stock prices and more than 6000 large, medium sized and small firms on basis of corporate cash flows. The analysis covers post-transformation period, from 2003 to 2012, respectively to 2014 in case of stock prices, using panel regression and orthogonalized exposure regressions. With Eurozone countries as one of the most important trade partners, a large number of transaction settlements are conducted in euro, therefore, the analysis focuses on the PLN/EUR exchange rate using monthly data. Results show that significant number of these firms, especially small and medium sized is exposed. The measuring of exchange rate risk and hedging is therefore crucial for reduction of the firms' uncertainty, especially in case when firms have limited access to currency derivatives.

Keywords Exchange rate exposure • Cash flows • Stock prices

1 Introduction

Companies that engage in foreign trade are influenced by exchange rate movements regarding different payment timing which leads to transaction exposure. Additionally, firms with foreign operations also face translation exposure when these are consolidated and notionally converted into the domestic company's currency. Economic currency exposure is a broader concept that includes both transaction and translation exposure effects but also takes account of changes in the relative competitive position of firms resulting from unanticipated currency movement. Foreign exchange rate risk increases with the volume of foreign markets production

L. Tomanova (✉)
Department of Finance, Silesian University in Opava, Opava, Czech Republic
e-mail: tomanova@opf.slu.cz

© Springer International Publishing Switzerland 2016

M.H. Bilgin et al. (eds.), *Business Challenges in the Changing Economic Landscape - Vol. 1*, Eurasian Studies in Business and Economics 2/1,
DOI 10.1007/978-3-319-22596-8_19

and with the volume of purchased materials from abroad. Managing and measuring exchange rate risk is therefore crucial for reduction of the firms' uncertainty concerning exchange rate fluctuations, which could affect value of assets, cash flow and profit margins. Exchange rate movements affect corporate expected cash flows, and hence stock returns, by causing changes in the domestic currency denominated revenues and the terms of competition for firms operating in international market. Although there are financial instruments which can prevent the changes in cash flows resulting from the currency volatility, smaller firms have usually limited resources to hedge. It implies that the firm's value is rather sensitive to exchange rate uncertainty (Bodnar and Marston 2002). Some firms are also able to reduce the risk by using lagging, leading or netting strategy. However, these strategies are feasible between multinational companies with subsidiaries in foreign countries. Other strategies are currency matching, which involves pairing suitably a multinational firm's foreign currency inflows and outflows with respect to amount and timing and invoicing in domestic currency, which reduces transaction risk primarily related to exports and imports. When exports are invoiced in domestic currency, the exchange rate risk is transferred to the importer. Polish zloty as a currency is however not preferred as a settlement currency, since the vast of exports flow to euro area countries and settlement is conducted in euro. One of the benefits of a single currency zone is that foreign exchange risk is eliminated for the trade and investment amongst the countries that form monetary union which significantly reduces the uncertainty of firms. Poland is the biggest European Union economy outside the Eurozone (besides Britain and Sweden) which is bound to a commitment of adopting euro as a single currency. However, Poland has committed to adopting the euro, though without setting a date. Regarding Maastricht criteria, Poland already meets two of the entry criteria. Of the remaining, one relates to the budget deficit, which it is on track to meet by 2015, and the other is the ERM-2 requirement. Polish monetary policy authorities consider free-floating regime as the most appropriate nowadays and also highlight its function as a strong shield against the global financial crisis.

Estimating both cash flow and stock price exposures offers a new perspective and provides new evidence on the foreign exchange rate exposure of nonfinancial firms in a post-transformation country. This paper also contributes to a gap of empirical findings of exchange rate volatility and its effects on firm value in the case of post transformation economy. Although some papers concern exchange rate exposure in emerging markets, there is a lack of literature concerning Central and Eastern European countries. In this paper, internal cash flow data of more than 6000 firms are used. Studies of foreign exchange rate exposures thus generally use stock returns to proxy for changes in cash flows. In this paper, both approaches are used due to a complex view. It allows us to understand the effect and measurement of exchange rate risk which is then essential for possible hedging strategies.

The paper focuses on exposures of Polish zloty to Euro exchange rate fluctuations of small, middle sized and large companies in Poland and aims to examine the exchange rate exposure on the basis of stock prices and corporate cash flows. The exchange rate sensitivity is estimated for small, middle sized and large companies selected according to the industry using the technique pioneered by Jorion (1990) that has become standard in the exchange exposure literature, involving a time-series regression of changes in the exchange rate against the return on a firm's stock or cash flows, while controlling for market effects in case of the stock prices analysis. The results suggest that significant number of publicly listed companies is exposed. Regarding the cash flow exposures, large, middle sized and small companies of different industries are exposed. However, cash flow exposures diverge from stock prices exposure, indicating that accounting measures are worse proxies for economic exposure.

The paper is organized as follows. The literature related to exchange rate volatility and its influence on a firm is covered the second section. The third section specifies model and describes the concepts of cash flows exposure and stock prices exposure. Fourth section provides information about dataset. The exposure results and the robustness of these results are discussed in the fourth section. The paper is concluded by a summary of results.

2 Literature Review

The exchange rate exposure itself can be interpreted as the sensitivity of a firm's market value to a change in exchange rate. It is generally held view that exchange rate fluctuations are an important factor causing macroeconomic uncertainty and thus it probably has a significant impact on firm value, regardless of whether the firm operates in domestic market or is engaged in international activities (Shapiro 1975). Most of the studies follow the approach of Adler and Dumas (1984) who define the extent of exchange rate exposure as the elasticity between changes in firm value and an exchange rate. The exposure coefficient is obtained by running a linear regression of stock returns on an exchange rate change, whilst some researchers add macroeconomic control variables, such as the returns of a market index. The empirical evidence concerning exchange rate exposure provides mixed results. While some studies have found strong evidence of exposure (Allayanis and Ofek 2001), other empirical studies present rather weak relationship between firms' stock prices and exchange rate volatility (Dominguez and Tesar 2006; Griffin and Stulz 2001; Bartram and Bodnar 2012).

However, some studies show that the effect of exchange rate uncertainty on the firm value depends on variety of firm characteristics, including percentage of foreign sales (Jorion 1990), firm size (Dukas et al. 1996) or industry concentration (Bartram and Karolyi 2006). Starks and Wei (2004) find that the magnitude of exchange rate exposure is related to proxies for probabilities of financial distress, growth opportunities and product uniqueness. The mixed results are explained by using different methodology in the papers and also different proxy for foreign exchange rate movements. Some papers use a single currency exchange rate, whereas others have employed weight indices of exchange rates (Bartov and Bodnar 1994; Jorion 1990).

Regarding the cash flow exposures, the evidence is limited and usually conducted on a basis of case studies of individual firms. The majority of studies on the impact of exchange rates on firm performance assess the exposure of non-financial firms, typically by regressing exchange rate changes on contemporaneous stock returns in the presence of control variables. The seminal work on exchange rate exposure is by Adler and Dumas (1984) who have presented a single factor model to estimate foreign exchange rate exposure by estimating the elasticity of firm stock returns to exchange rate changes. According to them, the market value of a firm is constructed as the present value of future cash flows, thus the exposure can be obtained using market data which simplifies the estimation. They argue that insignificant exposure can be explained by well managed foreign exchange risks. Jorion (1990) added a variable for market movements to the model and analyzed foreign exchange rate exposure of 287 U.S. multinationals over the period from 1971 to 1987. Using OLS method and monthly basis data, he finds out that only 5.2 % of companies are significantly exposed at the 5 % level. Choi and Prasad (1995) in the latter paper use similar two-factor model, but they orthogonalized the exchange rates to the market factor and found out that 14.9 % (61 out of 409) of the individual firms in U.S. are significantly exposed at the 10 % level. Chung and Zhou (2012) used two-factor and multi-factor nonparametric models and found out that in recent years, large number of U.S. firms has been significantly affected by exchange rate fluctuations. Muller and Verschoor (2006) analyze the exposure of 817 - European multinational firms using OLS to estimate two-factor model by Jorion (1990), with euro's bilateral exchange rate with alternatively the US dollar, UK pound and Japanese yen as explaining variables. They used the OLS method to estimate two-factor model or the GARCH (1, 1) method in case when residuals of a particular regression exhibit time-varying heteroskedasticity. Their results suggest that about 13 % of the multinational firms experienced significant exposure effects to the Japanese yen, 14 % to the US dollar and 22 % to the UK pound.

Some empirical studies show a significant exposure of firms in emerging countries. Kiymaz (2003) analysed the exposure of Turkish firms traded in Istanbul Stock Exchange over the period 1991–1998 using monthly orthogonalized market return and a foreign exchange basket of US dollar and ECU. The results show that 61 % of firms were highly exposed to exchange rate risk, especially those operating in textile, machinery, chemical and financial industries. Bartram and Bodnar (2012) analysed exposure of non-financial firms in 37 countries around the world, not including the countries of Central and Eastern Europe. According to their results, 30–40 % of firms in open and emerging market countries are significantly exposed. Chue and Cook (2008) estimated the exchange rate exposure in 15 emerging economies using GMM-IV and OLS method, excluding transition economies from their analysis. They have found that depreciations had negative impact on emerging market stock returns during 1999–2002; however, this impact significantly faded during 2002–2006. By using OLS method, about 40 % of firms have shown significant exposure.

3 Exposures of Stock Prices and Cash Flows

To examine the importance of exchange rate exposure for stock returns, the sensitivity of each firm's return to the change of, exchange rate is estimated. According to the seminal paper by Adler and Dumas (1984), the exposure elasticity can be obtained as the change in the market value of the firm resulting from a unit change in the exchange rate. Among other studies, the advantage of this approach relies in the ability to estimate elasticity of exposure from the coefficient on the exchange rate variable. Classical framework of the exposure to exchange rate risk employs regression analysis. Foreign exchange rate exposures have been frequently estimated by the following two-factor model introduced by Jorion (1990) which also controls for stock market portfolio:

$$R_{i,t} = \alpha_i + \beta_i RM_t + \delta_i R_{S,t} + \varepsilon_{i,t} \tag{1}$$

where $R_{i,t}$ denotes the monthly stock return of a company i in period t, RM_t represents the monthly return on a market portfolio index in period t, and $R_{S,t}$ denotes the local currency return on a foreign currency exchange rate variable S in period t, δ_i represents the sensitivity of an i-th company's stock returns to exchange rate movements. Under this definition it reflects the change in returns that can be explained by movements in exchange rate after conditioning on the market return. Given that the exchange rate is measured in direct quotation, the estimated coefficient measures the exposure to a depreciation of the local currency. Exporters are expected to have positive exposure coefficient, while importers are expected to have negative exposure. Positive value of δ_i indicates that a depreciation of Polish zloty corresponds to an increase in the stock prices of a firm and vice versa for a negative coefficient. Coefficient α_i is a constant, $\varepsilon_{i,t}$ is the residual error term with zero mean and constant variance. Equation (1) is extended regression of the original model which controls for market movements used in empirical studies. The estimates of exposure coefficients could be biased due to omitted variables (Priestley and Odegaard 2007), this problem thus motivated to include a stock market portfolio RM in the regression. The inclusion contributes to improvement in the precision of the exposure estimates. Market portfolio is an aggregation of the individual firms' stocks. If the individual firms' stocks are exposed, it can be assumed that the market stock will be exposed, too. This corresponds with a view that foreign exchange rate movements are more likely to influence stock market than vice versa. The evidence of this issue was provided in Dumas and Solnik (1995) who showed that cross-country aggregate stock returns are affected by currencies. However, possible multicollinearity problem can be eliminated by orthogonalizing the market returns. Following Priestley and Odegaard (2007), orthogonalization of the return of market portfolio on a set of exchange rates can be done by estimating the following regression:

$$RM_t = \alpha_i R_{S,t} + \upsilon_{m,t} \quad (2)$$

where $\upsilon_{m,t}$ is an error term which is defined as the orthogonal market return which is not correlated with the exchange rate movements. Therefore this variable will be used in Eq. (1) as proxy for the market returns.

As an alternative to the traditional approach, a firm's cash flows measures are used. The availability of internal cash flow data of 6109 firms during the period 2003–2012 allows conducting an exposure analysis using the following regression as suggested in Bartram (2007):

$$RCF_{i,t} = \alpha_i + \delta_i R_{S,t} + \varepsilon_{i,t} \quad (3)$$

where *RCF* denotes changes in corporate cash flows of a company group *i* in period *t*, $R_{S,t}$ denotes the percentage change of currency *S* in period *t*, The regression coefficient δ captures the sensitivity of the respective cash flow to an exchange rate change and, thus, represent a measure of foreign exchange rate exposure of *i*-th group of firms.

Similarly, changes in corporate cash flow variables are regressed on contemporaneous and lagged exchange rate changes in Oxelheim and Wihlborg (1995). Firms with higher and significant coefficients δ will indicate larger exposures. With regard to firm size, larger firms might be more exposed thanks to the possibility of operating on global international markets, but they also might have more resources to hedge against the exchange rate risk. Larger firms may also be more geographically diversified. It is assumed that smaller firms will tend to be more exposed. The advantage of cash flow regression consists of the fact that the estimated effects of the exchange rate risk on corporate cash flows are independent of the perception of market participants (Bartram 2007). Another advantage relies in the fact, that only a fraction of Polish companies are publicly listed.

If exposures of firms differ depending on their operations, then categorizing firms according to various attributes could potentially lead to more powerful and interesting results. Therefore, we estimate exchange rate exposure of large, medium-sized and small firms separately, also categorized by the operating industry because the exposure varies across industries. It is assumed that more exporting industry will be also more exposed to foreign currency volatility. While firms in retail business might act more on domestic market, transportation firms are more likely to operate worldwide. The sample comprises of 6109 large, medium-sized and small Polish non-financial firms which represent nine industries: Accommodation and food service activities, agriculture, forestry and fishing; construction; electricity, gas, steam and air conditioning supply; information and communication; manufacturing; mining and quarrying; transportation and storage; wholesale and retail trade. The total number of 1247 companies belongs to the large companies' group. Medium-sized group consists of 3054 companies and small firms' data consist of 1808 firms. More detailed specification is provided in Table 1.

Table 1 Panel data overview—number of firms

Industry	Large	Medium sized	Small
Accommodation and food service activities	11	44	70
Agriculture, forestry and fishing	246	125	130
Construction	58	353	249
Electricity, gas, steam and air conditioning supply	62	37	11
Information and communication	63	115	199
Manufacturing	325	735	409
Mining and quarrying	22	13	7
Transportation and storage	38	158	87
Wholesale and retail trade	422	1474	646
Total	1247	3054	1808

Source: Own elaboration

4 Data

The sample comprises of non-financial firms operating in Poland with data available for the period 2003–2012 in case of cash flow exposure estimation and publicly listed companies with data available for the period 1/2003–5/2014. The data were obtained from different sources. Data of stock prices are from Patria Finance historical database, cash flows data are from the Amadeus database and the exchange rates from European Central Bank's database. The proxy for exchange rate changes is represented by changes in PLN/EUR (in direct quotation) nominal bilateral exchange rate (average of observations through period), since the majority of the transactions are settled in euro. The stock prices data are on monthly basis (average of observations through period) from January 2003–May 2014 and the sample includes companies publicly listed in the Warsaw Stock Exchange. As a proxy for market returns, returns of Warsaw Stock Exchange's index are used. Corporate cash flow data were available only on annual basis for the period from 2003 to 2012. Unfortunately, the limitations lie in unavailability of longer period data.

Equation (2) is used for regression of the changes in exchange rate against market portfolio returns and the estimated orthogonal market return. The returns of Warsaw Stock Exchange's index are used as proxy for market returns. The orthogonalized market returns are then used in Eq. (1) to estimate the firms' stock prices exposure coefficient. Equations (1) and (3) are estimated using Ordinary Least Squares (OLS) regressions, whereas cash flow exposure analysis comprises of panel data regressions with fixed effects.

5 Estimation Results

In the following sub-sections, the estimates of orthogonalized linear exposure and cash flow exposure to exchange rate fluctuations are reported. The results differ across the industries and also groups of small, medium and large companies. Significantly different results are present in the case of stock prices exposure analysis, where about 27 % of the companies seem to be exposed at 10 % significance level.

5.1 *Stock Prices Exchange Rate Exposures*

The individual company regressions were estimated in three periods: beginning in January 2003 and ending in July 2014 and then in two sub-periods from 01/2003 to 12/2006 and from 01/2007 to 05/2014 to test for the persistency of exchange rate exposure. The period under the investigation is between 01/2003 and 05/2014, which also offers the opportunity to analyze exposure during different economic stages. Estimation results are presented in Table 2. The regressions yield a percentage of 18.9 % of the sample firms with significant foreign exposure at the 10 % significance level. In the second sub-sample, number of significantly exposed companies is significantly higher than in the period from 2003 to 2006. This can be explained preferably by the development at financial markets and higher volatility of Polish zloty to euro during the years 2007–2009. During the period from 2007 to 2014, total of 27.3 % of all companies seem to be exposed at 10 % significance level.

During the early sub-period, there are substantially more firms with negative exchange rate exposure than in the whole period. Number of significantly exposed firms is only 6.7 %, smaller percentage than in the following sub-period, mainly caused by less liquid stock market and also due to the fact that companies with good resources to hedge against exchange rate risk participated in stock market and the currency was rather less volatile. Nevertheless, also in the following sub-period companies surely used hedging strategies. However, the situation in the global economy was rather less predictable. The mean exposure coefficient for all periods remained negative. Most of the companies show negative exposure coefficient,

Table 2 Exchange rate exposure estimation results

	Sample size	Mean exposure coefficient	Standard deviation	Significant exposure[a] (%)
Full sample	35	−0.2199	1.5710	18.9
2003–2006	22	−0.0108	0.5578	6.7
2007–2014	33	−0.2410	1.9127	27.3

[a]Denotes significance at 10 % level

therefore depreciation of domestic currency corresponds with a decrease of firm's stock returns. Results are consistent with other studies using orthogonalizated model. Some authors obtained results claiming that higher percentage of firms are exposed, i.e., Kiymaz (2003), Priestley and Odegaard (2007) who analyzed exposure of firms in emerging market economies.

5.2 Cash Flows Exchange Rate Exposures Estimation

Although theory suggests a number of channels through which firms and industries may be exposed to exchange rate risk, in the final analysis theory provides us with little guidance as to which firms are most likely to be exposed. The firms were thus segmented according to their size and operating industry because firm size, industry affiliation and degree of internationalization are all factors that may influence whether a firm or industry is exposed. However, the precise linkage between those factors and the direction of the exposure is unclear. The estimation of cash flows exposure has resulted in 27 panel data regressions with fixed effects. Results from estimating the exposure to PLN/EUR fluctuations are reported in Table 3. In the sample of 6109 firms examined over the period 2003–2012, we find that the response of cash flows to exchange rate fluctuations is mostly positive. However, large companies' data in case of four industries show negative exposure coefficient. This is consistent with our expectations that the exposure coefficient might be either positive or negative for large companies due to international activities and better access to hedging instruments. It implies that these four industries would suffer from the depreciation of Polish zloty against euro; nevertheless, the large companies' panel data groups show insignificant coefficients of exposure. A positive exposure coefficient means that a depreciation of the domestic currency goes together with an increase of a firm's cash flow. For the significantly exposed firms with negative exposure coefficient it implies that depreciation of Polish zloty decreases a firm's cash flow. The exposure coefficients are positive and negative within the industries, implying heterogeneity across firms' exposure.

The cash flow regressions take more of a corporate point of view where the exposure is important information for risk management in a company. The exposures of cash flows and stock prices are related via the present value. The stock prices are measure of corporate performance as the present value of cash flows; however, the stock market in Poland is rather less liquid compared to some developed countries, thus the cash flow exposure estimation is essential to complete the analysis. Regarding the entire sample of more than 6000 firms, only five industries show significant exchange rate exposure. The coefficient of determination R-squared is generally quite low; however, this is consistent with most of the studies using similar approach.

The significant cash flow exposure is present in a group of large firms operating in manufacturing industry and in transportation and storage industry both significant at 5 % level. The coefficients in these cases are positive, meaning that the

Table 3 Cash flow exposure estimations

Size	Industry	Intercept α	Prob.	Exposure coefficient δ	Prob.	R-squared
Large	Accommodation and food service activities	0.7023	0.0547	−0.0316	0.4978	0.1620
	Agriculture, forestry and fishing	0.6935	0.0200	0.0363	0.4688	0.1417
	Construction	0.4628	0.0272	−0.0034	0.8752	0.1699
	Electricity, gas, steam and air conditioning supply	0.8631	0.0000	−0.0109	0.5162	0.7601
	Information and communication	0.4862	0.1244	−0.0206	0.5384	0.2933
	Manufacturing	**2.2579**	**0.0042**	**0.2506**	**0.0146**	**0.2266**
	Mining and quarrying	0.9243	0.0873	0.0301	0.5852	0.3109
	Transportation and storage	**1.5738**	**0.0447**	**0.3202**	**0.0026**	**0.2291**
	Wholesale and retail trade	0.5038	0.0000	−0.0071	0.6179	0.2856
Medium	**Accommodation and food service activities**	**0.6302**	**0.2079**	**0.1166**	**0.0533**	**0.1844**
	Agriculture, forestry and fishing	0.7983	0.1079	0.0764	0.3852	0.1413
	Construction	0.8439	0.0000	−0.0218	0.3149	0.6758
	Electricity, gas, steam and air conditioning supply	0.3950	0.0067	−0.0040	0.8310	0.1428
	Information and communication	0.5911	0.0001	−0.0199	0.2589	0.3018
	Manufacturing	1.4279	0.0121	−0.0211	0.7899	0.1965
	Mining and quarrying	0.6808	0.1901	0.0064	0.9281	0.2018
	Transportation and storage	0.5748	0.0005	0.01309	0.5417	0.2545
	Wholesale and retail trade	0.6577	0.0000	−0.0429	0.4416	0.1893
Small	Accommodation and food service activities	0.6995	0.1134	0.0410	0.3793	0.2272
	Agriculture, forestry and fishing	0.4758	0.0000	−0.0156	0.3129	0.2486
	Construction	**1.3410**	**0.0002**	**−0.0635**	**0.0683**	**0.2104**
	Electricity, gas, steam and air conditioning supply	3.4229	0.2621	0.0262	0.9428	0.2961
	Information and communication	0.1293	0.8782	0.0849	0.3300	0.1468
	Manufacturing	0.1649	0.7010	−0.0067	0.9017	0.1772
	Transportation and storage	0.4532	0.0487	−0.0144	0.6750	0.2850
	Wholesale and retail trade	**0.2835**	**0.1557**	**−0.0703**	**0.0096**	**0.2559**

Source: Author's calculations based on data from Amadeus and ECB
The bold values are statistically significant.

depreciation of Polish zloty is connected with an increase in company's cash flow. The positive exposure is also present in case of medium sized firms in accommodation industry, significant at 10 % level. Regarding the group of medium sized companies, the results are not robust in most cases, except the accommodation and food service activities industry. Small firms, particularly in construction and wholesale and retail trade industry, seem to be significantly exposed. However, the coefficient is negative. Unlike large and middle sized firms, this means that small firms usually don't benefit from the exchange rate depreciation. According to the results, large firms operating in the transportation industry are exposed the most, followed by large firms operating in the manufacturing industry. In conclusion, few industries in each category of firm size have statistically significant exposure coefficients. As is suggested by some papers, the larger firms should be better prepared for the exchange rate risk than smaller firms and therefore it is more likely they will use hedging strategies. The results could mean that the firms benefited from the exchange rate development which resulted in higher export revenues. However, we also observe insignificant exchange rate exposures. This fact might be explained by other factors determining the exposure of a firm. The percentage of foreign sales is also likely a further important factor that determines whether a firm has a big or small exposure. It would be also advantageous to obtain cash flow data on higher frequency due to possible higher robustness of results.

6 Conclusion

Measuring and managing currency risk exposure are important functions in reducing a firm's vulnerabilities from major exchange rate movements. Regarding hedging strategies, currency derivatives market is rather young and instead of using costly derivatives, firms may rely more on internal hedging methods, such as leading and lagging or pricing policy. In contrast to the literature that typically uses stock returns as a measure of firm performance to assess the effect of foreign exchange rate risk on non-financial firms, an alternative approach is taken in this paper by estimating the foreign exchange rate exposure of a sample of non-financial firms on the basis of corporate cash flows and on the basis of stock prices. The exchange rate exposure of firms was estimated by investigating the effect of changes in PLN/EUR exchange rate on cash flows and stock returns during the period 2003–2012 and January 2003—May 2014 resp. As the stock prices exposure analysis showed, a significant number of publicly listed companies are exposed to exchange rate fluctuations, particularly 27 % companies are significantly exposed during the period 2007–2014. However, the stock market in Poland is rather less liquid and it is necessary to examine this matter further with application to smaller companies. Unfortunately, for this group, the cash flow data are on yearly basis. The higher frequency could lead to more interesting results. The firms were divided according to size and operating industry and 27 panel regressions were estimated. Only five categories of large, middle sized and small firms in some industries showed significant exposure to exchange rate risk. In case of small firms, it is mostly construction and wholesale and retail trade, accommodation and food service activities industry in case of middle sized firms and manufacturing and transportation and storage industry in case of large firms. Theoretically, the number of statistically significant exposure coefficients is limited implying that either firms are successful in hedging activities or do not participate extensively in international trade and thus do not have significant exposure. However, the results are consistent with previous researches taking cash flows in account, proving that the accounting proxies are worse variables than market variables.

Giving the high percentage of trade flows aiming to Eurozone markets, these results have implications for corporate finance, risk management and asset pricing. Investors should be aware of the fact that exchange rates are an important risk factor. Although the financial derivatives markets are not that easily accessible by medium sized and small firms which, by the time of euro adoption, the hedging against exchange rate risk would result in more effective protection of the firm value. The results show that companies in Poland currently underestimate the economic foreign exchange rate risk.

Acknowledgements Publication of this paper was supported by the Student Grant System of Silesian University (project SGS/7/2013). The support is gratefully acknowledged.

References

Adler, M., & Dumas, B. (1984). Exposure to currency risk: Definition and measurement. *Financial Management, 13*(2), 41–50.

Allayanis, G., & Ofek, E. (2001). Exchange rate exposure, hedging and the use of foreign currency derivatives. *Journal of International Money and Finance, 20*(2), 273–296.

Bartov, E., & Bodnar, G. M. (1994). Firm valuation, earnings, expectations, and the exchange-rate exposure effect. *The Journal of Finance, 49*(5), 1755–1785.

Bartram, S. M. (2007). Corporate cash flow and stock prices exposures to foreign exchange rate risk. *Journal of Corporate Finance, 13*(5), 981–994.

Bartram, S. M., & Bodnar, G. M. (2012). Crossing the lines: The conditional relation between exchange rate exposure and stock returns in emerging and developed markets. *Journal of International Money and Finance, 31*(4), 766–792.

Bartram, S. M., & Karolyi, G. A. (2006). The impact of the introduction of the euro on foreign exchange rate risk exposures. *Journal of Empirical Finance, 13*(4–5), 519–549.

Bodnar, G. M., & Marston, R. C. (2002). Exchange rate exposure: A simple model. *International Finance Review, 3*(2002), 107–115.

Choi, J. J., & Prasad, A. (1995). Exchange risk sensitivity and its determinants: A firm and industry analysis of U.S. multinationals. *Financial Management, 24*(3), 77–88.

Chue, T. K., & Cook, D. E. (2008). Emerging market exchange rate exposure. *Journal of Banking and Finance, 32*(7), 1349–1362.

Chung, Y. P., & Zhou, Z. G. (2012). The pricing of exchange rate risk in the stock market: A nonparametric approach. *Studies in Nonlinear Dynamics and Econometrics, 16*(1), 1558–3708.

Dominguez, K. M. E., & Tesar, L. (2006). Exchange rate exposure. *Journal of International Economics, 2006*(68), 188–218.

Dukas, S. D., Tavakkol, A., & Fatemi, A. M. (1996). Foreign exchange exposure and the pricing of exchange rate risk. *Global Finance Journal, 7*(2), 171–192.

Dumas, B., & Solnik, B. (1995). The world price of foreign exchange risk. *Journal of Finance, 50* (2), 445–479.

Griffin, J. M., & Stulz, R. M. (2001). International competition and exchange rate shocks: A cross-country industry analysis of stock returns. *Review of Financial Studies, 14*(1), 215–241.

Jorion, P. (1990). The exchange-rate exposure of US multinationals. *The Journal of Business, 60* (3), 331–345.

Kiymaz, H. (2003). Estimation of foreign exchange exposure: An emerging market application. *Journal of Multinational Financial Management, 13*(1), 71–84.

Muller, A., & Verschoor, W. F. C. (2006). European foreign exchange risk exposure. *European Financial Management, 12*(2), 195–220.

Oxelheim, L., & Wihlborg, C. G. (1995). Measuring macroeconomic exposure: The case of Volvo cars. *European Financial Management, 1*(3), 241–263.

Priestley, R., & Odegaard, B. A. (2007). Linear and nonlinear exchange rate exposure. *Journal of International Money and Finance, 26*(6), 1016–1037.

Shapiro, A. C. (1975). Exchange rate change, inflation and the value of the multinational corporation. *Journal of Finance, 30*(2), 485–502.

Starks, L. T., & Wei, K. D. (2004). *Foreign exchange rate exposure and short-term cash flow sensitivity* (University of Texas at Austin and Binghamton University Working Paper). [online] Accessed July 12, 2014, from http://papers.ssrn.com/sol3/papers.cfm?abstract_id=405521

Reshoring as a Modern Form of Economic Competition Between Developed and Developing Countries

Larisa Shahovskaya and Yana Matkovskaya

Abstract Developed countries are still trying to overcome the consequences of the global financial economic crisis. The BRICS countries are doing this better as they have cheap resources at their disposal, on the one hand, and develop their hi-tech manufacturing via foreign investments, which strengthens the competitive power of these countries on the global market. Trying to prevent this situation, developed countries are applying such a form of a competitive struggle as returning their offshored assembly plants from developing countries to their own locations—this process was called reshoring. Using the examples of China and Russia, the authors discuss the following questions: What will developing countries do in the reshoring conditions and which measures will they take to protect their domestic markets?

Keywords Reshoring • Reindustrialization • Competition • Financial economic crisis • Commercialization of innovation

1 Introduction

The economy of developed countries is still under the pressure of the consequences of the global financial economic crisis. At the same time, the economies of developing countries—the BRICS countries (Brazil, Russia, India, China, and South America) are still being successfully developed. Although the global economic crisis has also affected these countries with a slowdown in economic growth, especially in Russia, these countries possessing cheap resources are in a better position than developed ones. Based on foreign investments, they are developing their own manufacturing, especially resource exploration and assembly production based on new technologies, thus gaining extra competitive power on the global market in comparison with developing countries. At the same time, in the process of global trading, prices for resources are gradually becoming balanced while transporting expenses are constantly growing.

L. Shahovskaya • Y. Matkovskaya (✉)
Volgograd State Technical University, Volgograd, Russia
e-mail: mamol4k@yandex.ru; yana.s.matkovskaya@gmail.com

© Springer International Publishing Switzerland 2016

M.H. Bilgin et al. (eds.), *Business Challenges in the Changing Economic Landscape - Vol. 1*, Eurasian Studies in Business and Economics 2/1,
DOI 10.1007/978-3-319-22596-8_20

Many European and American scientists and politicians have been discussing how profitable it is to maintain the production of their own brands in developing countries under post-crisis conditions, thus strengthening the competitive power of these countries? One of the key announcements in respect of this situation is the article by Álvaro Santos Pereira (Portugal), José Manuel Soria (Spain), Corrado Passera (Italy), Arnaud Montebourg (France) and Philipp Rösler (Germany)—the ministers of the EU countries—entitled "The EU's new industrial policy" and published in the Wall Street Journal. The article expresses their concerns about the increased influence on the proper functioning of the chains of values by developing countries, which also start to dictate the rules of the game. This article gives its estimate to the power and possibilities of the EU's economy and encourages to reshore and produce goods by means of the European capacity (Soria et al. 2013). In his report at the World's Economic Forum and in his further interviews recorded by Veronica Cruz on the same issue in Market Business News, David Cameron stated: "There is a chance for Britain to become the reshore nation. Europe needs to act now to seize the opportunities of reshoring"; "It is the same dystopian vision. The East wins while the West loses; the workers lose while the machines win. I don't believe it has to be this way". D. Cameron directly pointed at the fact that it is hardly reasonable in respect of developed countries (Cruz 2014). As a reaction to this statement, the process of returning assembly production to the home location of high technologies, which is referred to as either industrialization in the EU or reshoring in the USA, has taken place. Developed countries derive benefit from this return through a larger number of the employed in their homeland, a reduced number of the unemployed, raised income, and sustained economic growth. Increase in prices for famous brands, related to this return, keeps their availability in developed countries and, at the same time, limits it in developing countries, impairing the national quality of life.

2 Analysis

It is essential to point out that the process of reshoring has practically been in progress for several years. It is evidenced by the American Internet resource "The Reshoring Initiative" (http://www.reshorenow.org), founded by Harry Moser in 2010. As cited in the homepage, the mission of this initiative institution is "to bring good, well-paying manufacturing jobs back to the United States by assisting companies to more accurately assess their total cost of offshoring, and shift collective thinking from offshoring is cheaper to local reduces the total cost of ownership." Besides, The Reshoring Initiative, being non-commercial organization, provides a free software tool—the Total Cost of Ownership Estimator—enabling one to estimate the efficiency of offshoring.

Moreover, in 2012 The Boston Consulting Group (BCG) conducted a research which showed 37 % of American large businesses being ready and launching the process of manufacturing return to its home locations from other countries, first and foremost from the PRC. 48 % large companies from other countries have declared that they do have the same plans. The BCG's research, released on November 15, 2012, also gives the results of the survey amongst consumers, showing that: firstly, more than 80 % of American consumers and over 60 % of Chinese consumers are willing to pay more for products made in the USA than for those made in China. The surveys among German and French consumers demonstrated the same results; secondly, about two-thirds of U.S. consumers are willing to pay a premium for 10 key product categories that were tested in the USA—from baby food to electronics and apparel—and the premium that Chinese consumers are willing to pay ranges from about 10 % to almost 80 %. The BCG concludes that the U.S. has improved its cost competitiveness compared with China and the EU. And as a result of reshoring, U.S. exports would create 2.5 million to 5 million new U.S. jobs (Boston Consulting Group 2014).

Actually, European economists associate the implemented strategy of reshoring basically with the possibility to prepare industrial capacities for R&D dislocation while American economists associate it also with the possibility to gain extra income from using the word combination "Made in USA".

In this context, the article entitled *The Reshoring Trend is Good for U.S. Engineers and America* gives the examples of the executed reshoring projects (Robinson 2014):

Thus, the facts prove that 250 American companies have undertaken reshoring, which shows its profit as it enables one to minimize expenses related to shipping, increase in wages in developing countries, a stable low confidence in the label "Made in China" and a high confidence in "Made in USA". It is high time to estimate the efficiency of both the value chains of American manufactures and the reshoring of their manufactures to the USA. This issue is thoroughly discussed by some American economists as a current trend in the industrial policy of developed countries (Robinson 2014).

Europeans in turn associate reshoring with a potential decline of unemployment as from 2008 till 2013 the EU saw a liquidation of 3 million jobs in and a 10 % decrease in industrial manufacture was decreased by 10 % (Soria et al. 2013). One should also take into account a more severe unemployment and a further decline of manufacturing, which are coming to the EU due to imposing sanctions against Russia, to understand that reshoring (reindustrialization) is not a phenomenon of the distant future but a real process that is taking place these days and that is expected to speed up because of many reasons.

3 Common Trends of the US and the EU Giving Reasons for Reshoring (Reindustrialization)

The first reason is energy; i.e., domestic prices for gas are decreased in the U.S. due to the exploration of shale deposits, and the state need new markets. The U.S. believes that Europe and China are potential consumers of this gas and that developing partnership programs on building regasification terminals with these countries is strategically important for weakening the competitive position of Russia being the leading gas country. Moreover, selling the American shale gas produced by it in Europe would provoke the reorientation of energetic dependency of the EU countries from the RF to the U.S., which is currently proved by their booming political activity in the Ukraine!

The second reason deals with the economic safety of the U.S. and the EU (read: the NATO) related to the increased influence of the BRICS countries (particularly the PRC being the world's largest creditor of the U.S.) on the global economy and on the international policy, being strengthened after the BRICS's convergence with Russia.

The third reason is associated with a vital necessity to revive national economy after the financial crisis and to embark upon a new phase of its development, which, in the current conditions for the U.S., could be based only on waging and maintaining local conflicts around the whole world (Afghanistan, Iraq, Libya, Syria, Palestine, the Ukraine. . .Who is the next one?)

The fourth reason is raised incomes in China and other developing countries, as well as raised prices for shipping. According to H. Moser's data, the president of the Reshoring Initiative, the wage of a Chinese employer is annually increased by 15–18 % in comparison with a 3 % growth of an American employer's wage; at the same time, American labour productivity is many times higher than that of China (Moser 2014). And according to the BCG, in 2000 Chinese median hourly earnings were 50 cents, and in 2015 these earnings are predicted to average USD 4.5 (Berger 2009).

Table 1 shows that the American reshoring project is aimed at the PRC, giving a reason to find out which measures China took to overcome possible negative consequences of this process. We accept that its experience could be valuable for Russia if the USA or European countries will launch the reshoring (reindustrialization) process in relation to its economy.

4 Chinese Actions to Address Negative Consequences of Reshoring (Reindustrialization)

Analyzing this problem, a dual situation is revealed. The matter of fact is that foreign funds have been taking the leading position in the Chinese economy. This made the Chinese government take measures to protect its economy from the prevalence of foreign funds and their monopolization of the national economy. For this reason, special actions were undertaken, e.g., a so-called economic constitution that entered into force in 2008 and provided for limiting mergers and acquisitions performed by transnational corporations and damaging the Chinese economy and fair competition. Since the 90s, the PRC's society has been discussing whether it is reasonable to create conditions which are better for foreign investors

Table 1 Reshoring companies in the United States

Company	Product	Reshoring from	Reshoring to
Apple	Computers	China	USA
Digital Innovations	Electronic devices	China	USA, California, Middle West
Electrolux	Appliances	China	USA, Tennessee
Farouk Systems	Equipment	China	USA, Taxes
Foxconn	LCD TVs	China, Taiwan	USA, California, Michigan
GE	Appliances	China	USA, Kentucky
Google	Phones	China	USA, California
Lenovo	PCs	Asia	USA, California
Lightsaver Technologies Inc.	Emergency illumination	China	USA, California
Morey Corp.	Printed circuit boards	China	USA, California
NCR	Teller machines	China, India, Brazil	USA, Georgia
Neutex	Illumination	China	USA, Taxes
NV3	Chargers	Asia	USA, Maryland
Seesmart	Illumination	China	USA, California
Suarez Corp (SCI)	Equipment, electrical appliances	China	USA, Ohio
Whirlpool	Appliances	China	USA, Ohio

Source: (Robinson 2014)

than for domestic ones. The PRC's government has begun thinking of activating the processes of both obtaining technological knowledge and manufacturing products on this basis by Chinese producers, and has taken adequate measures.

In other words, this is not always the case when the Chinese economy gains profit from the presence of foreign funds; moreover, according to some estimations, 40 % of the market was controlled by foreign funds in 9 out of 40 industries existing in China and over 50 % of the market in 4 industries, including communication equipment, computers and other electronic devices (83.5 %); professional and office equipment (66.9 %); cultural and household goods and sports goods (61.4 %); furniture (55.4); leathers and furs (52.9 %) (Berger 2009; ChinaPRO 2013).

Nevertheless, China is experiencing foreign capital inflows mostly by Asian countries rather than European ones while American and European funds are gradually reduced year by year. The decrease in investment volumes in the PRC's economy by the USA and the EU started in 2011—a 26 % decline from the USA and a 3.6 % decline from the EU. However, foreign investments from other countries that geographically refer to Southeast Asia are rising on the contrary (Belpolitics 2012).

Thus, in the situation of decreased investment volumes from the USA and the EU, foreign gross investments continue their growing (Cniru 2014). In early 2014, according to the PRC's Ministry of Commerce, the amount of foreign investments was raised by over 16 % in comparison with the same period in 2013 and was USD 10.763 billion: a 57 % growth of foreign investments in servicing and almost a 22 % growth of foreign investments in manufacturing. In January 2014, USD 369 million was funded to the PRC by the USA and USD 482 million was invested by the UN, but, as in 2011, these indexes are declining (Shahovskaya and Matkovskaya 2010).

Therefore, while not denying foreign investments in the economy, the PRC's government will reorient borrowings from the USA and the UN to Russia, Asian and other developing countries, which became obvious after the BRICS summit. We believe that such a change in the direction of attracting foreign investments is the answer of China to reshoring (reindustrialization) as a new form of competitive struggle that is able to limit economic growth and close their access to new technologies in developing countries.

5 Russian Actions to Address Reshoring (Reindustrialization)

It is necessary to point out that negative consequences of reshoring (reindustrialization) will be less painful for Russia than for the PRC. And there exist several reasons. First, the Russian economy doesn't have so many joint ventures with the American business as China do, thus making losses from reshoring be insignificant for the RF.

Second, Russia has much more joint ventures with the UN than those with the USA, including generally assembly manufacturing in automotive industry. The losses of such manufacturing resulted from reindustrialization won't be high for Russia as it can be easily changed by the domestic automotive.

Third, the vast majority of Russian joint ventures with foreign businesses are in extractive industries. Siphoning off their assets from such ventures, European businesses will lose their share of extracted natural resources, which they receive as a participant of such ventures in accordance with the Law on Production Sharing. So, the question that arises then is who will be suffering huger losses due to a decline of investments by the UN to Russia's economy?

In the context of the current global competition, Russia's economic growth is dependent from economic sanctions limiting this growth rather than from reshoring (industrialization) itself. Purely economic methods (i.e., prices, quality, diversity of product range, improved selling conditions, and after sales servicing) were implemented to remove competitors 15–20 years ago; nowadays, a competitor can be simply called "bad" (and the reason doesn't matter) to implement economic sanctions against him without waiting for investigation results. A change of the economic forms of competition to the political ones isn't associated with a definite country. In the present conditions of global competition, this can become a challenge of any country in any continent and even a group of countries and their regional alliances. Another question that arises then is what Russia can do to protect its economy in the epoch of global competition?

First of all, Russia should resume development activities in the real economy, i.e., the national industry, which must become a basis for not only introduction but also a much more important creation of new innovative technologies. This task must become urgent for both the state and Russia's business community. For this purpose, it is necessary to use all possibilities of public-private partnership when the national industrial policy is combined with external economic challenges and internal needs for products, and is supported by businesses as the main manufacturer of these products. Undoubtedly, this should be based on a certain agreement that is institutionalized in the form of regulatory legal acts (Matkovskaya 2014). We can't discuss all details of such institutionalization in the present article; however, it is essential to pay attention to some directions of such development.

The first direction deals with realizing the industrial policy as a kind of assistance to renovate manufacturing funds. This can be specified through implementing the development policy of those economic sectors, in which Russia's manufacturing is competitive in relation to domestic and external markets (e.g., aircraft, space technologies, agricultural production), as well as through developing those industries that create the country's strategic and economic safety (pharmacy, banking, etc.). In other words, Russia's economy should develop clusters, implementing the market approach in creating them in the RF's regions. Orienting primarily to the geographic criterion in creating clusters, researchers usually ignore the objective factor of the territorial capacity of consumer markets, thus underestimating the efficiency of distribution channels to realize products, which is especially important for such a country as Russia. It is not mere chance that large manufactures offshore assembly production to regions closely located to consumers of their products, which significantly increases their sales [for further details, see (Shahovskaya and Matkovskaya 2010).

The second direction is associated with creating the national institutional, legal and financial environment to form innovative economic segments, as well as with creating conditions, in which it becomes profitable both for the country's citizens to produce and consume competitive products and for enterprises to introduce innovations. Obviously, there is a need for market methods to stimulate the process of commercializing innovations accompanied by developing the fiscal policy that stimulates innovative processes and supports real investing process. At the same time, business initiative to commercialize innovations should be non-financially stimulated, thus creating a positive image of Russian products abroad (a successful example deals with a new Russia fly-by-wire jet "SukhoiSuperjet 100"). It is also essential to improve economic institutional structure, taking measures to weaken the state influence on the economy, which will provoke a decrease in corruption and develop public-private partnership in forming economic market infrastructure.

These are only a few of the actions that will help Russia not to lose its positions while the reshoring (reindustrialization) process are being reinforced due to introducing new sanctions and while traditional markets are being cut in number due to a severe global competitions well as in case of the execution of the largest American project on selling shale oil to the EU and China. In general, these processes are closely connected and remind Russia that it is high time to actively develop innovative technologies and manufacturing.

6 Contradictions or New Reality?

Analyzing both the official position of the USA and the EU and some concerns of the Chinese leadership about reshoring, it is possible to conclude that these processes impose a real danger on China's economy. This view is already shared by the West, the "Heavenly Empire", and Russia. But if to trace to the original source, i.e., the official statistical data on international investments in China and the Chinese investments abroad and the data of the trade balance, we can see that, on the one hand, China's positions is being reinforced in both issues (the investments and trade surplus), and, on the other hand, these processes point to two trends. First, the new conditions of global competition are occurring; second, the situation that currently exists and is described by the West as the process of reshoring/reindustrialization is the natural process of the development of capital imports and exports between countries. In this context, the reshoring and reindustrializing plans are still not being executed to the full extent, and the USA's reports on the scale of reshoring are exaggerated and contradict the reality. Even if this should be the case, the contemporary world economy is obviously ready for a qualitative transfer to a new step of globalization that features both a more dynamic capital transition between countries and the states' will to keep their industrial integrity.

The authors of this article consider the second variant as more true-to-life. To prove this view, let us introduce some new facts that allow destroying the myth of the possible problems affecting China due to reshoring/reindustrialization. The following data gives a clear evidence for China's position in the world economy, the specificity of its trade activity, its domestic and international investments, and its key business partners.

The first thing proving the transformation of the current situation in the present world is that China is the world's leader in export volumes. According to Statista (2014b), China ranked first in an export volume of 2209.63 billion US dollars, which was 1.4 times higher than the export volume (1578.97 billion US dollars) of the USA ranking second and 1.5 times higher than that of Germany (1452.8 billion US dollars). By the way, Russia was the 10th ranked country with an export volume of 523.33 billion US dollars, and the UAE ranked 17th (365 billion US dollar) (Statista 2014b). The same data are represented by China's General Administration of Customs—China accounted for 12.0 % of world trade in 2013 (+0.7 as compared with 2012), 13.7 % of world export (+1.5), and 12.1 % of world import (+1.7) (Ministry for Economic Development of the Russian Federation 2014b).

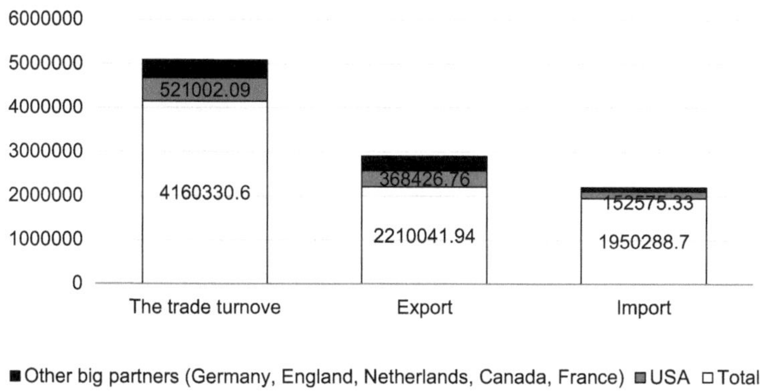

Fig. 1 China's trade turnover with the main foreign trade partners in 2013, million US dollars. *Source*: Built by the authors in accordance with the: (Ministry for Economic Development of the Russian Federation 2014c)

Second, the USA continues being one of China's main partners in international trade (Figs. 1 and 2).

Moreover, the American economy shows 1.4 times higher volumes of import from China than those of export to China (368426.76/152575.33 billion US dollar) (Ministry for Economic Development of the Russian Federation 2014c), and it depends on China's economy. This dependence grew between 2004 and 2013 (Fig. 2).

Third, China doesn't supply low-quality materials and commodities, but supplies machinery and transport equipment (1119983.89 million US dollars in 2013), which accounts for 50.68 % of exports, and chemical goods (229693.32 million US dollars—10.40 %), although a large export volume belongs to commodities. Machinery import is valued at 818315.83 million US dollars (41.94 %); mineral fuel, oil, oil products—314978.28 million US dollars (16.4 %), chemical goods—190448.21 million US dollars (9.74 %). Furthermore, service exports are constantly growing. In 2013, the volume of international service trade accounted for 539.6 billion US dollars (+14.7 %), including export volumes of 210.6 billion US dollars (+10.6 %) and import volumes of 329.0 billion US dollars (+17.5 %) (Ministry for Economic Development of the Russian Federation 2014b).

It is very essential to point out that China's export volumes features the growth of financial service exports (+54.2 %), consulting service exports (+21.2 %), IT and information service exports (+6.8 %), insurance service exports (+20.0 %), and tour service exports (+3.3 %, up to 51.66 billion US dollars). A special place in China's export volumes is occupied by building supplies and contracting services abroad (137.14 billion US dollars in 2013), in the same year China sent more than half a million workers abroad to execute projects (Ministry for Economic Development of the Russian Federation 2014b).

These trends are kept in 2014—according to the data of the first quarter of 2014, exports to the USA accounted for 112.15 billion US dollars, showing a 4.1 %

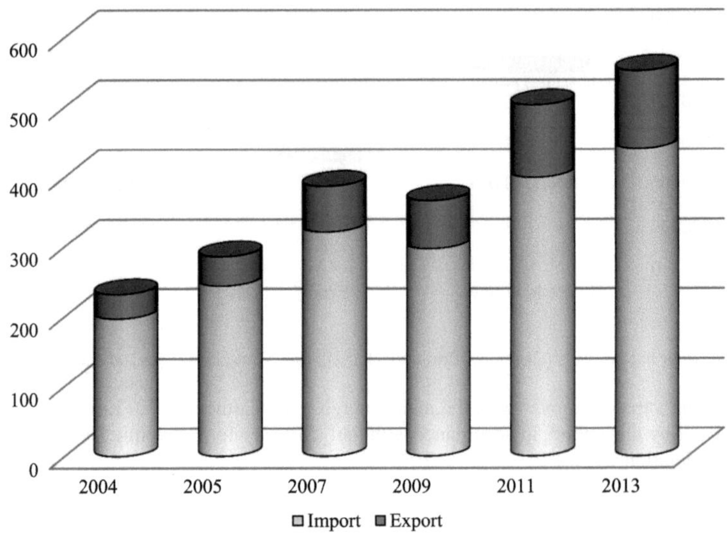

Fig. 2 The ratio of exports and imports of U.S. trade in goods with China, billion USD, 2004–2013. *Source*: Built by the authors in accordance with the: (Statista 2014a)

growth as compared with the same period of 2013; exports to Germany were 21.74 billion US dollars (+8,6 %); exports to England was evaluated at 15.85 billion US dollars (+14 %) (Ministry for Economic Development of the Russian Federation 2014d).

Forth, in 2013 the investments to China by the USA and the EU countries grew immensely, and Chinese companies became active investors on the markets of the USA and the EU. According to the Xinhua News Agency, at the end of 2013 the total amount of investments by Chinese companies into the countries of Central and Eastern Europe was more than 3.5 billion US dollars. Throughout the entire year, the USA and the EU countries experienced the "investment boom" provoked by Chinese private companies via purchasing businesses in these countries and merging. E.g., the Chinese meet processor Shuanghui merged the USA largest meat producer Smithfield Foods; Fosun International bought the sky-scriber One Chase Manhattan Plaza in New-York. Chinese investors are also interested in foods and real estates. This is evidenced by the report of the American consulting company Rhodium Group, according to 2013 saw the highest volumes of investments into the USA (14 billion US dollars) and into England (9.84 billion dollars). The development of the Chinese activity to invest abroad is being prevented by raising barriers. In response to this, Chinese companies started to build their factories in South-Eastern Asia and the USA. Concerning the USA, according to the Rhodium Group, Chinese companies created more than 70 thousand work places at the end of 2013 (i.e., a 7 times growth as compared with 2007). The Xinhua News Agency forecasts the volume of Chinese investments amounting to 500 billion US dollars in the nearest 5 years (CRI 2014).

Moreover, in 2013 the factual investments into China also grew in comparison with the same period of 2012. E.g., the investments from the USA were 3.04 billion US dollars (+12.4 %) resulting in 905 new enterprises, and those from the EU increased up to 6.40 billion US dollars, which was evidenced by a 22.26 % growth and 1216 new enterprises. More investments were directed into the Chinese economy by Japan (6.46 million US dollars), Singapore (5.23 %), Taiwan (4.45 million US dollars), and the leader Hon-Kong (63.46 million US dollars). In 2012–2013, the amount of foreign investments into China totaled 97025.9 million US dollars, including processing industries (38291.62 million US dollars); real estates (22496.70 million US dollars); wholesale and retail trade (9687.73 million US dollars); leasing and trade services (8960.58 million US dollars); transport services, warehousing and postal services (3427.91 million US dollars); information services, computing, software (2524.40 million US dollars); scientific research, technical services and geological exploration (2157.84 million US dollars) (Ministry for Economic Development of the Russian Federation 2014a).

Thus, it is obvious that the trends of capital relationships are still kept, and the processes of reshoring become less evident than the development of investments into China and the growth of Chinese investments into the USA, the EU and other countries. This happens as the Americans launch businesses as national ones in China, and private investors from China purchase American and European companies. This situation proves that the contemporary world economy is obviously ready for a qualitative transfer to a new step of globalization that features both a more dynamic capital transition between countries and the states' will to keep their industrial integrity.

7 Conclusion

Thus, the globalization of the world economy changes the rules and forms of a competitive struggle; i.e., economic methods of competition between definite companies—even the largest ones such as transnational corporations (TNC)—on different types of the market are changed with those of competition between definite countries and alliances of countries united by shared economic and political interests. The rules of a competitive struggle are also changing, and the current competition itself deals neither with the struggle of everyone against everyone as it used to be in late XIX not with the struggle between TNCs for material sources and distribution markets, but the struggle between definite groups of countries and their alliances aimed at preventing new participants from entering any global market segments.

In other words, in early XXI developed countries are not willing to participate in any economic competition with each other and especially with those new fast-growing economies being abundant with own resources. This reluctance is provoked by the fear to lose both their advantages in developing high-tech manufacturing and the right to dictate to other countries which way and what participants to ally with, which products to manufacture, and what prices to set.

Keep the status quo, new industrial countries are still being given a purely raw-exports role by developed countries which are trying to make these countries serve as material sources and distribution markets for their own manufacturing. This situation means that reshoring (reindustrialization) is being transferred from economic competition to political one—at least, this could be evidenced by the current decisions to reshore (reindustrialize), which are replacing offshoring.

References

Belpolitics. (2012). China set a record for attracting foreign capital. *Belta*, [online] Available at http://belpolitics.org/news/world/7276-kitaj-ustanovil-rekord-po-privlechennomu-inostrannomu-kapitalu.html. Accessed 15 Apr 2014.

Berger, Y. M. (2009). *The economic strategy of China*. Moscow: Publishing House "FORUM".

Boston Consulting Group. (2014). *U.S. and Chinese consumers willing to pay more for made in USA products, 2014*, [online] Available at http://www.bcg.com/media/PressReleaseDetails.aspx?id=tcm:12-121840. Accessed 24 Mar 2014.

ChinaPRO. (2013). In China act 442,000 enterprises with foreign capital. *Business Journal ChinaPRO*, [online] Available at http://www.chinapro.ru/rubrics/1/9637/. Accessed 14 Aug 2013.

Cniru. (2014). *Website of products of Chinese enterprises*, [online] Available at http://www.cniru.ru/index.php?m=content&c=index&a=show&catid=9&id=1833. Accessed 19 Feb 2014.

CRI. (2014). The analytical overview: A new structure of China's foreign trade contributes to Chinese investments entering foreign markets. *Xinhua Agency*, [online] Available at http://russian.cri.cn/841/2014/01/16/1s497963.htm. Accessed 16 Dec 2014.

Cruz, V. (2014). Seize reshoring opportunities, David Cameron tells Europeans. *MBN: Market Business News*, [online] Available at http://marketbusinessnews.com/seize-reshoring-david-cameron-tells-europeans/10371. Accessed 24 May 2014.

Matkovskaya, Y. S. (2014). Clusters: Analysis of the origin, the modern forms of its institutionalization and mathematical models. *Financial Analytics: Science and Experience, 203*(17), 2–12.

Ministry for Economic Development of the Russian Federation. (2014a). On the situation in the investment field in China in October 2013. *The Portal on foreign economic information of the RF's Ministry of Economic Development*, [online] Available at http://www.ved.gov.ru/files/images/country/China/On%20the%20situation%20in%20the%20investment%20field%20in%20China%20in%20October%202013%20g.pdf. Accessed 16 Dec 2014.

Ministry for Economic Development of the Russian Federation. (2014b). The brief analytical overview of China's international trade in 2013. *The Portal on foreign economic information of the RF's Ministry of Economic Development*, [online] Available at http://www.ved.gov.ru/files/images/country/China/2014/August/Overview%20of%20China's%20foreign%20economic%20activity%20for%202013.pdf. Accessed 16 Dec 2014.

Ministry for Economic Development of the Russian Federation. (2014c). The brief overview of China's international trade in 2013. *The Portal on foreign economic information of the RF's Ministry of Economic Development*, [online] Available at http://www.ved.gov.ru/files/images/country/China/2014/August/Overview%20of%20China's%20foreign%20economic%20activity%20for%202013.pdf. Accessed 16 Dec 2014.

Ministry for Economic Development of the Russian Federation. (2014d). The overview of China's international trade, April 2014. *The Portal on foreign economic information of the RF's*

Ministry of Economic Development, [online] Available at http://www.ved.gov.ru/exportcountries/cn/about_cn/ved_cn/. Accessed 16 Dec 2014.

Moser, H. (2014). How will China's labor turmoil and rising wages impact reshoring? *Industry Week*, [online] Available at http://www.industryweek.com/ask-expert-reshoring/how-will-chinas-labor-turmoil-and-rising-wages-impact-reshoring. Accessed 14 May 2014.

Robinson, A. (2014). *The reshoring trend is good for U.S. Engineers and America*, [online] Available at http://cerasis.com/2013/09/25/reshoring/. Accessed 25 Sep 2013.

Shahovskaya, L. S., & Matkovskaya, Y. S. (2010). The institutionalization of the commercialization of innovations in Russia as a condition for innovative breakthrough. *National Interests: Priorities and Security, 81*(24), 9–15.

Soria, J. M., Pereira, A. S., Passera, C., Montebur, A., & Rösler, Ph. (2013). The new industrial policy for Europe. *Expert Online*, [online] Available at http://expert.ru/expert/2013/07/novaya-industrialnaya-politika-evropyi/. Accessed 15 Apr 2014.

Statista. (2014a). *Total value of U.S. trade in goods with China*, [online] Available at http://www.statista.com/statistics/277679/total-value-of-us-trade-in-goods-with-china-since-2004/. Accessed 15 Dec 2014.

Statista. (2014b). *Top 20 export countries worldwide in 2013 (in billion U.S. dollars)*, [online] Available at http://www.statista.com/statistics/264623/leading-export-countries-worldwide/. Accessed 14 Dec 2014.

The European Economic Crisis: The Continental Threats for the System of Higher Education in Europe

Irina Morozova and Tatiana Litvinova

Abstract Currently Europe is passing through the very complex and interesting stage of its development. Low levels of socio-economic development of many countries in the European Union clearly demonstrate the necessity for essential changes in the most important areas of European society's life. The article is devoted to analysis of the current economic crisis in the European Union in 2008–2013 and its negative influence on the higher education system in Europe. The key continental threats and the possible ways of their diminution through the private–public partnership mechanism are described in the research. The author examines the key challenges to be faced by the higher education system in Europe in the near future: the search for alternative sources of financing, demand reduction, geographical restructuring of demand. The article describes the most promising market segments of higher education, taking into account the complex social and economic trends in the European Union. The main directions, which modern universities have to focus on to transform the mentioned challenges in additional opportunities, are given in the article.

Keywords The continental threats • The system of higher education • The European Union • Private–public partnership • Domestic austerity program

1 Introduction

The economic situation in many European countries, particularly in the South and East of Europe, suggests the existence of the crisis tendencies of economic development in the territory. The paper briefly describes the main ones because in the coming period the complex trends that are typical for the financial and social

I. Morozova (✉)
Department of Global Economy and Economics Department, Volgograd State Technical University, Volgograd, Russia
e-mail: morozovaira@list.ru

T. Litvinova
Department of Management, Volgograd State Agricultural Academy, Volgograd, Russia
e-mail: litvinova1358@yandex.com

© Springer International Publishing Switzerland 2016

M.H. Bilgin et al. (eds.), *Business Challenges in the Changing Economic Landscape - Vol. 1*, Eurasian Studies in Business and Economics 2/1,
DOI 10.1007/978-3-319-22596-8_21

systems of Europe, will shape the environment in which the higher education institutions have to operate.

The aim of this study is to analyze the nature of the impact and consequences of the economic crisis in the European Union on the system of higher education in Europe and to find out effective financing instruments of modern universities development. The analysis of macroeconomic indicators of European countries development, statistics on demographics and migration trends in the European Union allowed to the author to present a possible scenario of European higher education system growth, as well as to highlight and explore the three most important challenge faced by European universities in the medium term in detail. Search for alternative sources of funding, reducing demand, geographical restructuring of demand are among these challenges. As the result of the study it have been identified that the most promising directions of neutralization of the possible negative effects of the economic crisis on the European system of higher education is the active development and implementation of large-scale regular projects through public–private partnerships between universities, national governments and major industry corporations. The author proves that the European universities, which will be able to provide themselves with a lot of reliable financial partners from the commercial sector in the near future and the institutions that will achieve the support of state structures, will surely survive the tough times, and also will receive the opportunity to take the new market niches vacated by less agile competitors. The article is justified precisely which segments of the educational market will be the most promising in the post-crisis period, and how higher education institutions will be able to refocus on these segments with minimal cost.

2 The European Economic and Social Situation: Challenge or Chance?

The current crisis erupted on the territory of the European Union now cannot be called just an economic one. The depth and duration of its after-effects in various spheres of the European society's life allow to characterize it as a social and political crisis. Some analysts try to explain the existence of such a long-term recession in the EU through the "hangover" by reason of the financial difficulties in 2008. However, the careful disquisition of the current crisis anatomy completely disproves this theory. The financial crisis in 2008 had the global nature and affected many countries in the world. Some of them are quite recovered and show moderate but positive GDP dynamics. For instance, the growth of the national economy in the United States at the beginning of 2013 was 1.9 %, and the unemployment rate was the lowest for the last 4 years (see Figs. 1 and 2) (Delors 2013).

The acute social and economic crisis manifested itself in different ways in Europe. It is necessary to review the main ones briefly, as in the near future the negative trends that appear in the financial and social systems in Europe will shape

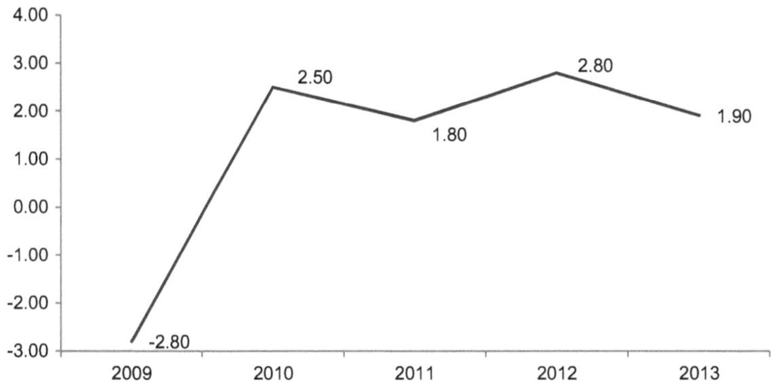

Fig. 1 GDP growth of the USA in 2009–2013 (in percent). *Source*: The World Bank

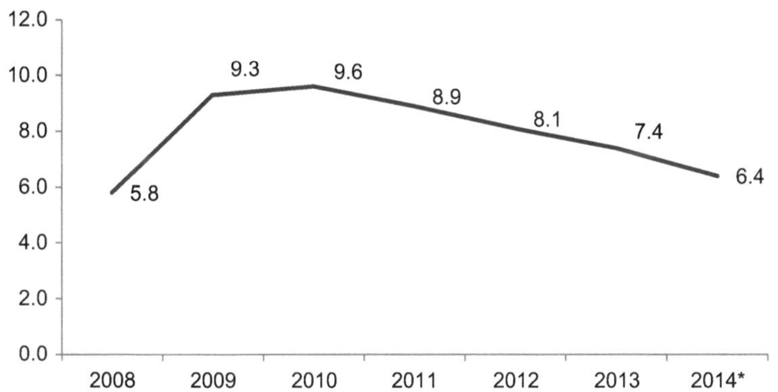

Fig. 2 The average unemployment rates in the USA in 2008–2014 (annual %) *Anticipated level (calculated data from January to July of 2014). *Source*: The United States Department of Labor (http://www.bls.gov/news.release/empsit.nr0.htm)

the environment where institutions of higher education will have to operate. It is in the outcomes of the current recession that the sources of the threats and challenges, which the European educational system will face in the foreseeable future, should be looked for. These threats can change the basic principles of the European higher education significantly.

The current crisis in Europe is characterized by austerity policy, restriction of the interchange fees, absence of a clear and sound strategy of the national markets stimulation, growing imbalance in the economic position of the "Center" (e.g., Germany, Sweden) and "the Province" of the EU (the Southern European countries), rising unemployment and the negative migration trends, destabilizing role of the euro as common currency, growing people's distrust of the national authorities, centrifugal forces pulling the European Union apart.

The austerity domestic program as a method to resolve the current crisis has been proposed by Germany. The national authorities are forced to carry out the budget

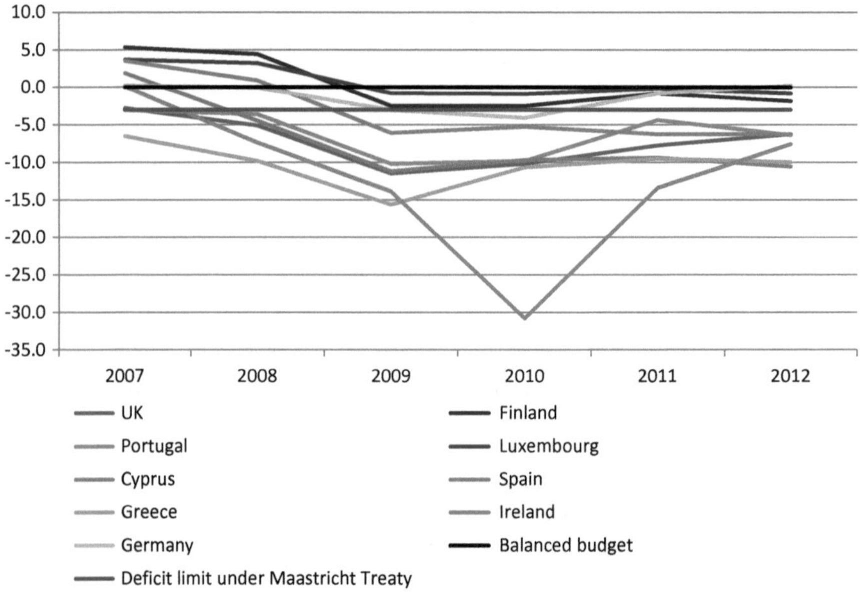

Fig. 3 The European governments deficit or surplus (annual growth, %). *Source*: Eurostat

cuts in terms of annual invariable GDP fall: in Greece—by 5.3 %, Portugal—by 3.9 %, Cyprus—by 4.1 %, Italy—by 2.3 % Spain—by 2 % (Bouras 2013). Recently the group of stagnant economies has been supplemented by France which showed a near-zero growth of GDP in 2013 and was forced to reduce the spending on social sphere dramatically trying to escape the budget deficit. In 2014 France plans to reduce the health care expenses by 6 billion euros. At the same time, in 2013 GDP growth in Germany, which is the main financial donor to the European Union now, has exceeded 6 %, thus, distinguishing Germany sharply from other European countries and creating additional conjunctural benefits (Shedlock 2012). Figure 3 demonstrates vividly the damage to the EU caused by the global financial crisis in 2008. It also shows that the attempts of the EU's periphery economies to come out of the crisis—except Germany, Finland and Luxembourg—are still not very successful.

Taking into consideration the absence of elaborate and efficient strategy of national market stimulation in the countries of Southern Europe, the strategy of domestic spending reduction doesn't seem promising enough. Apparently, in the long term, without looking for supplementary reserves and economic recovery means, with lack of state and public support for small businesses, the European Union will inevitably face total exhaustion of domestic resources, not only within the national economies but also in the European Union in general. When it is nothing more to save in the European Union, the existing disintegrative tendencies will intensify vastly (Popkova et al. 2013b). Today the working population of developed countries like Germany reveals the dissatisfaction with the necessity to continue the financial support of stagnating economies within the EU at the taxpayers' expense. Despite the fact that the Christian Democratic Party has recently won the German elections, the support that the German population gave to the party of eurosceptics, which had been created a few months before the elections, showed the growing trend of discontent in the country. In 2013 the University of Hohenheim and the ING-DiBa bank held the poll which showed that Germany's population did not trust the honesty of the authorities in terms of the official media write-ups of the status quo and the development prospects of the European social and economic crisis. Among the 1000 respondents only 11 % of citizens believe that the government informs the population without fear of favor, fully and authentically (Delors 2013).

3 Impact of Euro and Euroscepticism

It seems unexpected but the euro has a bad aggregative impact on the development of the situation in the Eurozone. The need to carry out all internal and external payments in euros deprives countries with deep budget deficit of an opportunity to reduce the exchange rate of the national currency against the euro and, thus, to cut the production expenses and revitalize domestic markets, at least in the short term. That is why France is in a more difficult position than the UK, which can take advantage of the fractional devaluation of the pound to provide the competitiveness of export goods (Popkova et al. 2013a).

The current economic crisis reveals the obvious inhomogeneity of the European Union and draws a sharp distinction between the levels of development of the Center and the Periphery. While Germany produces high-tech goods exporting them to the Southern Europe and other emerging markets, implements a large-scale investment policy and subsidizes the European Union's budget, other countries have to come back to the help of the International Monetary Fund and the European Union again and again having no chance of the national debt redemption.

4 Social Pressure and Unemployment

The depressing atmosphere of economic recession escalates the social problems of the European society. Unemployment and migration are the most important among them. The austerity measures taken by Portugal in 2011 have led to the increase of domestic unemployment level by 5.3 % for the last 2 years, at the same time the budget deficit of the country has not only diminished but even risen by 1.1 %. In 2013 the external debt has exceeded 123 % of GDP. For the last 2 years, 2.5 % of Portugal working population have left the country preferring to look for a job in Angola, Brazil, etc. (Bouras 2013). Historically, the social sphere of Portugal, that operates within the confines of the "Iberian social" model, strongly depends on the

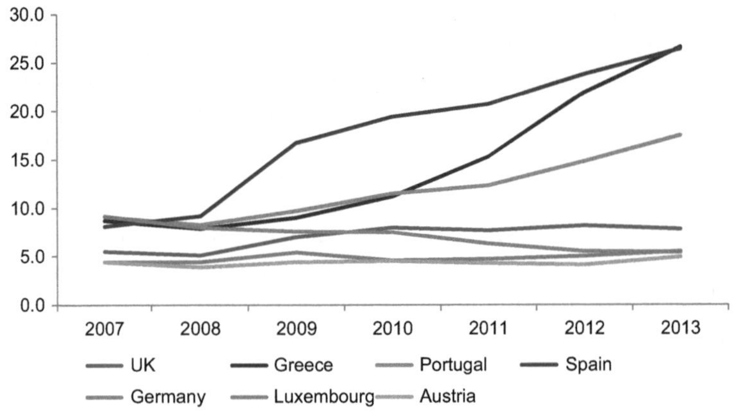

Fig. 4 Unemployment rate in the European Union (growth in Q1 of each year, %). *Source*: Eurostat

external sources of financing and sometimes disagrees with the available capabilities of the national budget. However, before the initiation of austerity measures the unemployment in the country had been growing slower. In 2009 it was near 10.6 %, in 2010—12.0 %, in 2011—12.7 % (Yakovlev 2012). High unemployment is also observed in Greece and Spain. In the framework of modern economic policy of Brussels it will be difficult for these countries to change significantly the situation in labor market (see Fig. 4).

Now many countries implementing socially unpopular course of economic reforms face the situation when the non-systemic opposition begins to take shape and become more powerful, the very model of the citizens' social behavior changes and the mass protests occurs more often. Despite the declarations of EU's senior management about the desire and forward motion to the final formation of a political union in Europe, the long-term integrity of the EU is questionable.

5 Key Challenges for the Higher Education System in Europe

In such conditions the European system of higher education has to fight for the preservation of its fundamental principles and the general stability of the education market. The European universities should be prepared to take the early measures to respond to the new challenges posed by the protracted economic crisis in the European Union. Such challenges are quite numerous, but three of them are the most likely and, consequently, dangerous.

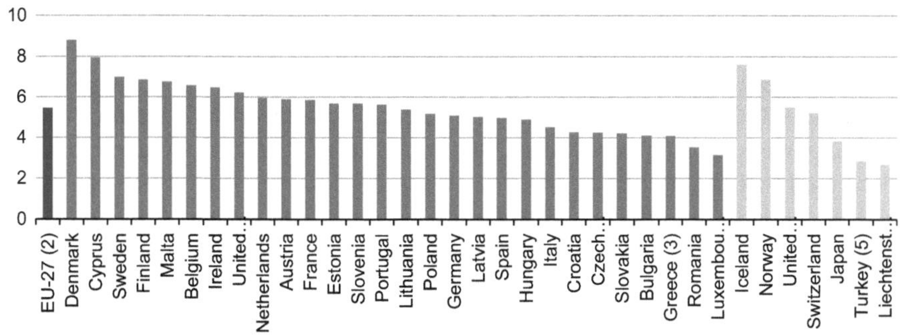

Fig. 5 Public expenditure on education in the EU in 2010 (% of GDP). *Source*: Eurostat

5.1 *Searching of the Alternative Funding Sources*

During the recession, the endowment funds of many European universities have decreased or have been staying in limbo concerning their future financial receipts. If the existing tendency remains and the government expenses on social sphere including education continue to wane in many European countries, higher education institutions are jeopardized of finding themselves in a difficult financial situation. In 2010 the UK authorities increased tuition fees in British universities by 3 times at the legislative level, which reduced significantly the potential effective demand for educational services of the country. Also in 2012 the UK government decreased the public expenses on education by 20 %. The general trend of economic stagnation that leads to the relative fall in business activity of national enterprises and cutting down the demand for the commercial research and universities' projects complicates the situation. Universities have to rely more and more on students financing their own resources, but in this sphere the crisis after-effects are even more evident. In the meantime, active investment in higher education is a powerful tool for social development. Higher education increases productivity and stimulates economic growth, it can reduce social inequality and makes a significant contribution to personal development. High-quality higher education system increases the average level of intellectual capital of a country. Figure 5 illustrates the government expenses in Europe on education in percent of GDP in 2010.

5.2 *The Effective Demand Reduction*

European students often use educational loans or work hard trying to earn enough to pay for study in the next semester. The systematic unemployment and cutback of the average wages in Europe constrict significantly the opportunities of the population to purchase rather expensive educational services (Vught 2009). On the one hand, an unemployed person has enough time and motivation to receive new knowledge; on the other hand, he is short of cash. In June 2013 in France there were more than 3.27 million unemployed people, that is by 11.2 % more than at the same period in 2012 (Delors 2013). By April 2013 in the UK the number of the unemployed has reached 2.56 million, the actual wages were reduced for 70 % of the employees, in the period from 2008 to 2013 the average salary in the country decreased by 6 %.

These crisis after-effects negatively influence the total volume of the market of educational services in Europe causing a significant drop in purchasing power of the population. Geographical restructure of demand. The demand for higher education is closely connected with two key factors—the birth rate and the population mobility. Today the highest growth of birth rate occurs in developing and poorest countries of the world. Europe, on the contrary, is going through the difficult times of a demographic crisis and population ageing.

This means that in the next few decades the greater part of young people will be concentrated not in the European countries but in India, China, Indonesia, the USA, Brazil, Pakistan, Nigeria and so on (Coiffait 2012). Today the dynamic development of the majority of these countries leads to the fact that many students choose to pursue higher education at home, especially as modern distance learning technologies provide the possibility of receiving high-quality educational services comparable to those in Europe (Belgium, and Centre, 2014).

Due to the described global demographic situation, in a couple of decades the bulk of the young population will be concentrated not in the European countries, but in India, China, Indonesia, the USA, Brazil, Pakistan, Nigeria and so on. To preserve the market position, the European universities have to focus considerable efforts on attracting foreign students. Today, the significant part of entrants of the universities in the UK is made up of students from India (16 %), Nigeria (42 %), Malaysia (22 %), Pakistan (26 %), Saudi Arabia (15 %) and Sri Lanka (18 %) (Coiffait 2012). The total contribution to the UK economy made by foreign students in 2010 was 8.25 billion Pounds (Anyangwe 2012). However, today the active development of the majority of Asian countries and the BRICS leads to the fact that many students choose higher institutions in their home country. Furthermore, modern distance learning technology gives the possibility of obtaining high-quality educational services, not worse than the European ones. Also it is possible to study in network universities around the world without having to travel abroad. In the US, for example, more than 25 % of students were enrolled in distance education courses in 2012 (see Table 1).

Taking into the consideration all above, the measures of British government concerning the higher education system are doubtful. The Government attempts to restrict the influx of unwanted migrants who exacerbate the crisis in such complex social spheres as employment and social security. For that reason it have tightened the visa regime for foreign students and increased the requirements for initial educational attainment of immigrants. In these conditions strong competition on the part of universities of the USA and Australia can lead to a significant reduction of the European market of educational services.

Table 1 Number and percentage of students enrolled in distance education courses in the USA, 2012

	Students enrolled exclusively in distance education courses		Students enrolled in some but not all distance education courses		Students not enrolled in any distance education courses	
Number	%	Number	%	Number	%	
Students	2,642,158	12.5	2,809,942	13.3	15,694,955	74.2
Total	21,147,055 = 100 %					

Source: National Center for Education Statistics (http://nces.ed.gov/pubs2014/2014023.pdf)

6 Conclusion

During the crisis the effective demand is sharply reduced. Two price segments become especially popular with consumers: a low-cost services because of their availability and the premium ones due to the prestige. The higher education market is not an exception. During the economic "storms" in Europe, the most promising market segment of higher education will be inexpensive short rounded educational programs using distance learning technologies. They allow students to save considerably. In addition to this, such educational programs is a good variant for professional retraining of specialists who lost their jobs because of the crisis.

In the time of crisis another promising segment of the education market in Europe is the high-quality educational programs of the most prestigious and expensive European universities. Committing money in education at Cambridge, Oxford, Imperial College London (UK), Swiss Federal Institute of Technology (Switzerland), University of Edinburg (Scotland), University of Munich (Germany), people believe what they are doing safe investments which assuring their future career and professional prosperity. During the crisis the modern European universities should take advantage of these features of demand in the education market.

Further, the anti-crisis policy of university should be combined with the previous image and reputation of the university, and not to go much beyond the already established pricing policies. So, the medium universities of the second-tier which have not yet earned the title of "the educational giant" and cannot offer exclusive educational programs and world-wide worth diplomas, could partially revise some existing curricula to reduce the time of learning, optimize and minimize the cost of them. So they would be able to attract more potential entrants and use economies of scale to strengthen their financial position. So they would be able to attract more potential entrants and use economies of scale to strengthen their financial position. Large top-level universities can also take advantage of the proposed strategy. However, they should not be too enthusiastic about dumping, even if in the short term there will be a slight decrease in demand for their educational programs. The thing is that the going down in the low-price segment and increase of the availability of elite education can reduce the uniqueness and the high status of their diplomas. The up-market higher education is the same luxury as diamonds.

And the pricing strategy should be the same. During the crisis, to avoid losing potential students, the prestigious European universities should focus on building up a valid system of communication with the target audience and work with partners and benefactors, who are able to support the University finances in difficult times.

The universal recommendation for universities in Europe can be public–private partnership. The main means of reducing the negative after-effects of the economic crisis in the European system of higher education is intensive development and implementation of various large-scale regular projects through the mechanism of public–private partnership between higher education institutions, national governments and largest industrial corporations. No doubt, one of the top-priority goals is for high-net-worth individuals to support the endowment funds and commercial research of the most prospective universities in Europe, because in periods of deep recession small businesses can only care about their own survival on the market. In the near future European universities, secured reliable financial partners from the commercial sector as well as gained government support, will not only survive hard economic times, but also will occupy the market niches vacated by less prosperous competitors.

References

Anyangwe, E. (2012, January 23). Higher education in 2012: A global perspective. *The Guardian's blog,* [blog]. Available at http://www.theguardian.com/higher-education-network/blog/2012/jan/23/internationalisation-in-2012. Accessed 5 June 2014.

Bouras, S. (2013, September 19). Greece: Extremism and austerity. *The Wall Street Journal blog,* [blog]. Available at http://blogs.wsj.com/eurocrisis/2013/09/19/greece-extremism-and-austerity/. Accessed 4 June 2014.

Coiffait, L. (2012, May 9). HE policy blog: The five big trends shaping higher education-2012. *The Pearson Think Tank blog,* [blog]. Available at http://thepearsonthinktank.com/2012/the-five-big-trends-shaping-higher-education/. Accessed 2 June 2014.

Delors, L. (2013). Why Europe's solution for economic crisis is actually the problem. *GlobalVoices.* [online] Available at http://globalvoicesonline.org/2013/07/13/how-europes-solution-for-economic-crisis-is-actually-the-problem/. Accessed 2 Aug 2014.

Popkova, E. G., Akopova, E. S., Alekhina, E. S., Dubova, Y., Popova, J. N., AvdeevaI, A., et al. (2013a). Methodology of development of strategy of development of economic systems. *World Applied Sciences Journal, 26*(4), 489–493.

Popkova, E. G., Shachovskaya, L. S., Romaniva, M. K., & Dubova, U. I. (2013b). Bases of transition of the territory to sustainable development: Modern city. *World Applied Sciences Journal, 23*(11), 1499–1507.

Shedlock, M. (2012, August 14). Germany 6 % current account surplus a "Threat to the Continent" says EU Commission; solution is gold coupled with eurozone breakup. *Mish's Global Economic Trend Analysis blog,* [blog]. Available at http://globaleconomicanalysis.blogspot.ru/2012/08/germany-6-current-account-surplus.html. Accessed 1 June 2014.

Vught, F. (2009). *The EU innovation agenda: Challenges for European higher education and research.* [pdf] European Centre for Strategic Management of Universities (ESMU), Belgium, and Centre for Higher Education Policy Studies (CHEPS) University of Twente the

Netherlands. Available at http://www.utwente.nl/mb/cheps/publications/publications%202009/eu%20innovation%20agenda%20f%20vanvught.pdf. Accessed 1 June 2014.

Yakovlev, P. (2012). *Crisis in Southern Europe: Spain and Portugal in the grip of austerity.* Centre for Research and analytics Historical Perspective Foundation, Prospects. [online] Available at http://www.perspektivy.info/oykumena/ekdom/krizis_na_juge_jevropy_ispanija_i_portugalija_v_tiskah_zhestkoj_ekonomii_2012-06-13.htm. Accessed 1 Aug 2014.

Overcoming the 'Underdevelopment Whirlpools' on the Basis of Ecologically Pure Industrial Production

Elena Popkova

Abstract The authors analyze the problems of industrial regions, calculate 'underdevelopment whirlpools' for five large industrial regions of Russia on the basis of the suggested methodology, develop methodology of evaluating competitiveness of large industrial regions of Russia in regard of indicator of ecologically pure industrial production development in 2013, analyze the development trend of ecologically pure industrial production of large industrial regions of Russia in 2003–2013, work out the conception of ecologically oriented anti-crisis management of industrial production development.

Keywords 'Underdevelopment whirlpools' • Ecologically pure industrial production • Industrial region • Economic development

1 Introduction

Economic development causes a lot of ecological problems. This is connected with the fact that technological progress together with increasing human needs lead to endless expansion of nomenclature of goods and services. Volumes and types of natural resources, involved in industrial production, are growing. Variety of negative impacts, produces by industry, their cumulation and multiplicative effect destroy natural cycles of reproduction of biological resources and abiotic components of natural environment.

In the second half of twentieth century acid rains, ozone holes, greenhouse effect, pole ice melting, photochemical smog formation in megalopolises, desertification, loss of biodiversity and other negative events led to global ecological crisis: exhaustion of natural ecosystems, depletion of regenerative capacity of environment and degradation of its main components to a level, which is dangerous for physical health of people. That is why nowadays relevant is transition to

E. Popkova (✉)
Department of World Economy and Economic Theory, Volgograd State Technical University, Volgograd, Russia
e-mail: 210471@mail.ru

© Springer International Publishing Switzerland 2016
M.H. Bilgin et al. (eds.), *Business Challenges in the Changing Economic Landscape - Vol. 1*, Eurasian Studies in Business and Economics 2/1,
DOI 10.1007/978-3-319-22596-8_22

conception of ecology oriented development, based on extensive consumption of natural resources and high technogenic environmental load (Popkova et al. 2013a).

In the course of ecology oriented development it is possible to satisfy needs of all member of the society on the basis of increasing efficiency of functioning, stability and ability to resist destroyable impact of environment. Such development does not bring global civilization outside economical capacity of biosphere and does not cause destroying and degradation of biosphere, provides its preservation and stage-by-stage renewal of environment integrity, balance between nature potential and needs of people of all generations (Popkova 2014). However, in the market economy the process of industrial production is cyclic: periods of growth give place to periods of recession, etc.

Environmental problems are relevant all the world over, but the most important these problems are for industrial regions. Forming system of crisis management of industrial production by the principles of ecology oriented development, directed on overcoming 'underdevelopment whirlpools', allows to provide constant 'green' growth in such regions, which is the aim of this research (Popkova et al. 2013b).

2 'Underdevelopment Whirlpools' in Industrial Regions

'Underdevelopment whirlpools' can be defined as a loss of opportunities for development by certain country in the connection with the time lag and the need to resist the negative impact of globalization. The mechanism of dragging into 'underdevelopment whirlpool' is described on the Fig. 1.

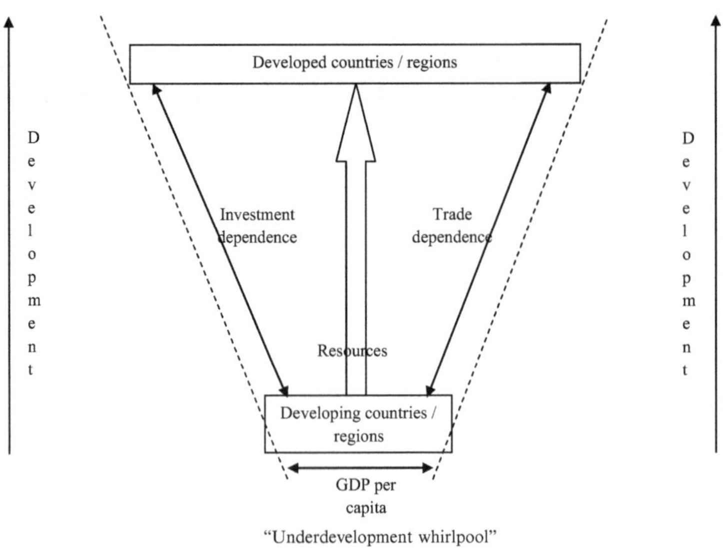

Fig. 1 Mechanisms of dragging into 'underdevelopment whirlpool'

The essential analysis of such phenomenon as 'underdevelopment whirlpools' requires the definition of its parameters: the depth and speed of dragging. The depth of the 'whirlpool' can be measured by the time lag of the country from developed countries, while the speed of getting in the whirlpool—by measuring the increase or reduce of the time lag for a certain period of time. Calculation of 'underdevelopment whirlpools' in industrial regions of Russia is represented in Table 1. For analyzing five large industrial regions of Russia were chosen. The analysis is performed by comparing with the level of economic development of the USA.

Calculation of 'underdevelopment whirlpool' in industrial regions of Russia showed, that the biggest economic lag between industrial regions of Russia and the USA is typical for Irkutsk Region—it constituted 43 years in 2013. The smallest lag is observed in Volgograd Region and constitutes 29 years.

3 Dependence of Economic Growth of Industrial Regions on Development of Ecologically Pure Production

Development of ecologically pure production influences profit of industrial enterprises. In order to determine this influence the authors of this research worked out mixed multifactorial deterministic model (Ashokhov 2008):

$$P = \frac{LP*NS*CLR}{IDr} - K*\frac{C}{IDp}, \tag{1}$$

where P is the profit of production of ecological pure products, LP is the labor productivity of industrial enterprise's stuff, NS is the number of staff of industrial enterprise, CLR represents capital-labor ratio of industrial enterprise, IDr is index deflator of realization of ecologically pure products; K is the coefficient of demand of ecologically pure products, C shows the costs of production of ecologically pure products and IDp is the index deflator of production of ecologically pure products.

Development of ecologically pure production in industrial regions encourages increase of quality of life in regions, because it improves ecological situation. In this connection, the indicator of ecologically pure production development should be included in the system of indicators of industrial regions competitiveness evaluation. The authors of given research worked out an author's methodology of evaluating competitiveness of industrial regions in regard of ecologically pure production development. The main indicators of competitiveness of industrial regions are Social sphere, Natural resources, Production potential, Labor resources, Investment attractiveness, Innovation potential, Market Infrastructure, and Development of ecologically pure production (Popkova et al. 2014).

Listed indicators are evaluated by using expert method. With the help of developed author's methodology of evaluating competitiveness of industrial regions with regard of factor of ecologically pure production development index of region competitiveness is calculated as an arithmetic mean of denoted indicators

Table 1 Calculation of 'underdevelopment whirlpool' in industrial regions of Russia

Region	Economic lag in 2003	Depth	Speed	Economic lag in 2005, years	Depth	Speed	Economic lag in 2007, years	Depth	Speed	Economic lag in 2009, years	Depth	Speed	Economic lag in 2013, years	Depth	Speed
Chelyabinsk region	31	31	0.3	24	24	−0.1	28	28	−0.1	29	29	0.1	29	29	0.1
Yekaterinburg region	26	26	0.3	27	27	0.1	26	26	−0.1	29	29	0.2	30	30	0.2
Irkutsk region	37	37	0.4	40	40	0.2	42	42	0.2	44	42	0.2	43	43	0.2
Volgograd region	26	26	0.2	28	28	0.0	25	25	−0.1	27	27	0.0	28	28	0.1
Kemerovo region	35	35	0.4	34	34	−0.2	33	33	0.0	36	36	0.3	37	37	0.1

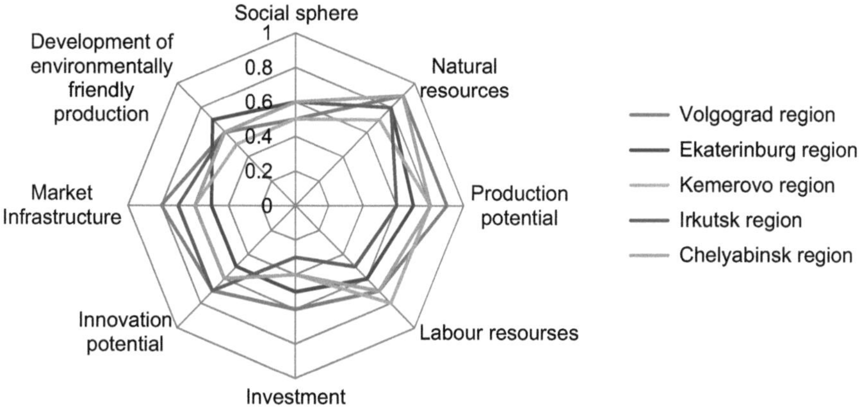

Fig. 2 Evaluation of competitiveness of large industrial regions of Russia with regard of indicator of ecologically pure production in 2013

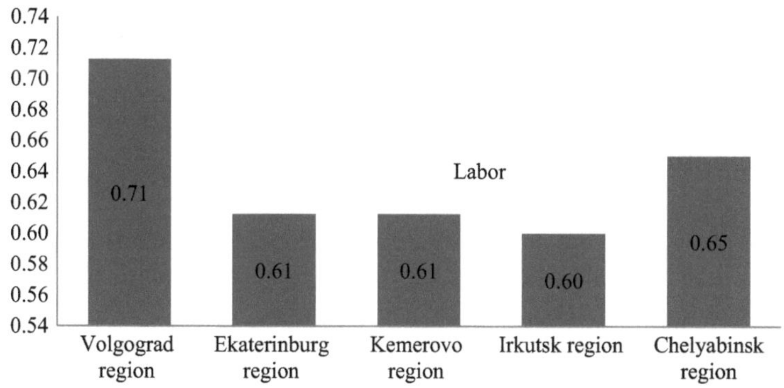

Fig. 3 Index of competitiveness of large industrial regions of Russia with regard of indicator of ecologically pure production development in 2013

(Popkova 2013). By the use of developed methodology the authors of given research evaluated competitiveness of five large industrial regions of Russia (Fig. 2).

The index of competitiveness of large industrial regions of Russia with regard of indicator of ecologically pure production development in 2013 is presented on Fig. 3.

As it is seen from Fig. 2, the biggest value of index of competitiveness of large industrial regions of Russia with regard of indicator of ecologically pure production development in 2013 within the framework of conducted research is observed in Volgograd Region, though the indicator of ecologically pure production development in Volgograd Region is not the highest (Fig. 4).

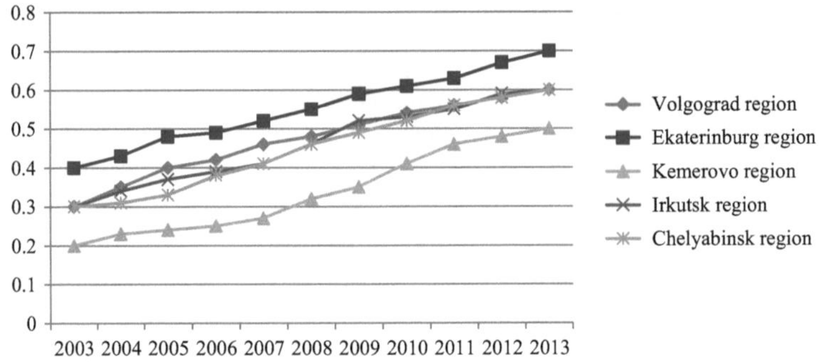

Fig. 4 Dynamics of indicator of ecologically pure production development of large industrial regions of Russia in 2003–2013

As it is see from Fig. 4 the biggest value of ecologically pure production development of large industrial regions of Russia in 2013 is observed in Yekaterinburg Region.

4 Conception of Ecologically Pure Production Development in Industrial Regions

This work gives a conception of anti-crisis development of industrial production, which allows to perform qualitative transition of national economy to the model of sustainable development (Fig. 5).

The developed conception of ecology oriented anti-crisis management of industrial production development includes recommendations about providing stable work of industry on the basis of continuous ecology oriented technological progress and development of the market of 'green' innovations. Within the framework of this conception the following is defined:

- Priority approaches to overcoming disadvantages of industrial production, based on the principles of ecologically safe nature management;
- Main stages of rational state impact on development of industrial production aim on:
  - Smoothing of cycles amplitude, providing controllability;
  - Evolutional changes of technological platform of management and institutional rules of nature management;
  - Ecologization of life cycle of industrial production end product.

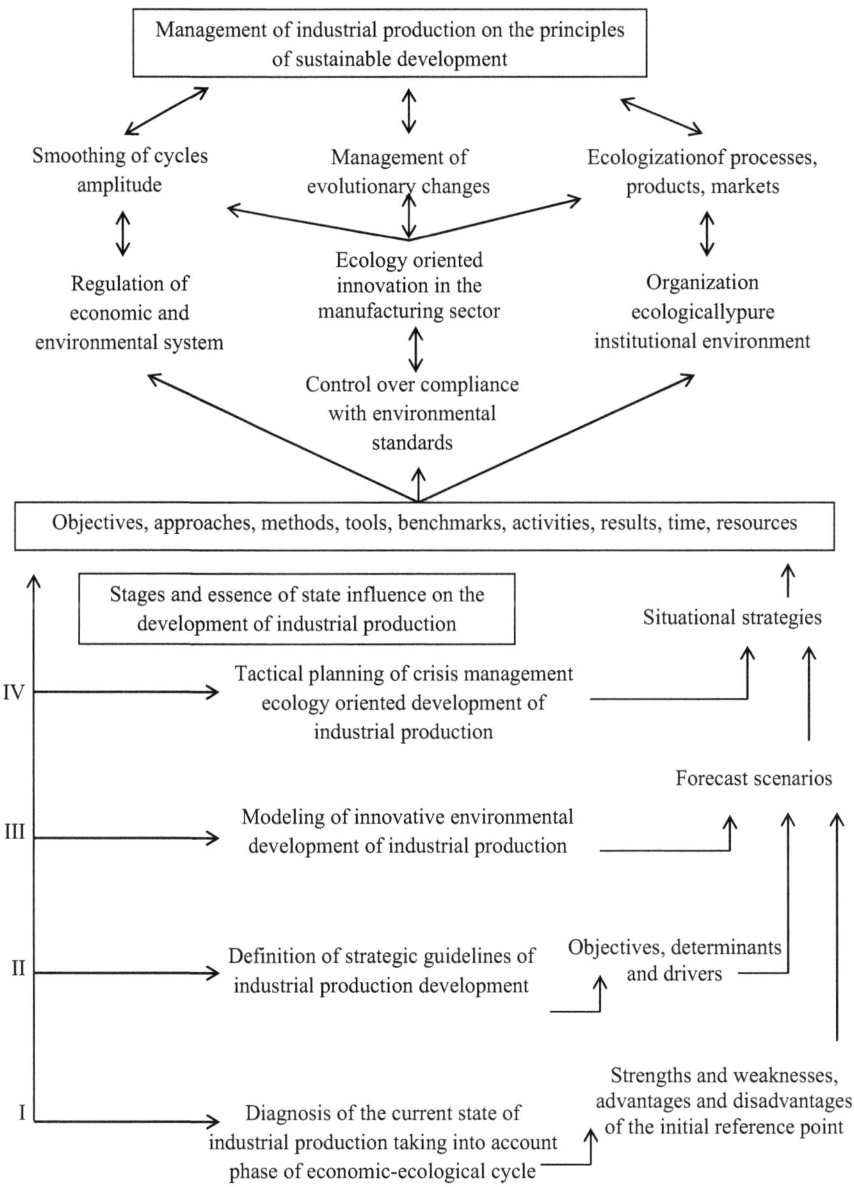

Fig. 5 Conception of ecology oriented anti-crisis management of development of industrial production

5 Conclusion

Development of ecologically pure production in different branches of national economy becomes one of the main orienteers of the ecological policy in the world economy. Ecological goods, services and technologies, which were in circulation in the world market in 2013, are estimated at $675 billion. It is expected that in 2020 this sum will constitute more than $1200 billion, 15 % of which would be for developing countries and countries with transition economies (Popkova 2014).

Pure production has particular potential in agriculture too, because the demand for ecologically pure food is expanding. Solution for this problem demands development of fundamentally new approaches to forming technologies of industrial products producing. In order to protect the environment form pollution such technologies should consider (Aja et al. 2013):

- Using of up-to-date technologies of industrial production;
- Improving the system of environmental protection measures in industrial regions.

In accordance to these requirements, we find it rationally to use both variants of technologies in agriculture.

The first variant: ecologically safe technologies, representing a system of organizational economic measures and technological operations, providing complex use of biological, agrotechnical and chemical means with priority of biological methods, directed on producing maximum quantity of high commercial quality production while preserving ecological balance of the environment and guaranteeing high profitability of production.

Ecologically safe technologies represent natural development of intensive technologies by improving technical, chemical and other means with replacement of dangerous instrument by technical methods (Casey 2014).

The second variant: ecologically pure technologies represent a system of measures, operation and means, excluding use of potentially dangerous chemicals, with replacement of them by biological and agrotechnical production factors, which provide producing normalized quantity of products, safe for human health, in the absence thereof negative influence on the environment, and guaranteeing acceptable income.

Ecologically pure technologies represent special technologies, aimed for using in ecologically vulnerable zones and producing biologically pure products. Realization of mentioned technologies demands creation of organization economic mechanism, which allows enterprises to organize and operate ecologically pure and profitable production under the conditions of strict ecological limitations. The most important, in our opinion, components of this mechanism are the next:

1. Generating regional system of ecological monitoring. Service of ecological monitoring, being dominant in the structure of economic mechanism of management, becomes the determinating factor of ecologically pure production operating, performed in crisis ecological situation.

2. Grounding prices on ecologically pure products. Such prices would depend on chosen variant of technologies, and deeper differentiation of them would be defined by qualitative parameters of product and market segment, which would be such product offered to. In this case, taking into account mentioned parameters, three-level differentiation of price can be suggested.
3. Determining system of privileges in the sphere of taxation and crediting commodity producers, providing operation of ecologically pure production. So, for example, it becomes possible to set land tax breaks, to reduce profit tax in the case of ecological investments.
4. Improving forms of payment for labor for producers, providing ecologically safe production.

Realization of considered but not the completed list of economic instruments of regulating ecologically pure productions would encourage solving environmental tasks in industrial regions, their economic development and overcoming 'underdevelopment whirlpools'.

Acknowledgements Work is executed with financial support of the Ministry of Education and Science of the Russian Federation within the limits of a base unit of the state task (the project # 2797).

References

Aja, A., Bustillo, D., Darity, W., Jr., & Hamilton, D. (2013). Jobs instead of austerity: A bold policy proposal for economic justice. *Social Research: An International Quarterly, 80*(3), 781–794.

Ashokhov, Z. (2008). Increasing of efficiency of ecologically pure production output under the conditions of intensification of management forms. *Russian Economic Journal, 22*(1), 134–138.

Casey, B. H. (2014). From pension funds to piggy banks: (Perverse) consequences of the stability and growth pact since the crisis. *International Social Security Review, 67*(1), 27–48.

Popkova, E. G. (2013). Marketing strategy to overcome the "Underdevelopment Whirpool" of the Volgograd region. *11th EBES Conference, Ekaterinburg (Ekaterinburg, Russia): Proceedings* (pp. 52–61). Istanbul: The Institute of Economics Ural Branch of Russian Academy of Sciences.

Popkova, E. G. (2014). New prospects of economic growth in context of underdevelopment whirlpools phenomena. *Applied Econometrics and International Development, 14*(1), 5–20.

Popkova, E. G., Chashhin, V. V., & Bogdanov, D. V. (2013a). Implementation of the concept of personnel marketing in modern Russia. *World Applied Sciences Journal, 22*(3), 389–395.

Popkova, E. G., Dubova, U. I., & Romanova, M. K. (2013b). Designing the territorial marketing strategy on the principles of cluster policies. *World Applied Sciences Journal, 22*(4), 571–576.

Popkova, E. G., Romanova, M. K., & Kukaeva, L. I. (2014). Formation of the regional meat cluster development strategy in Russia. *Regional and Sectoral Economic Studies, 14*(1), 105–114.

The Development of Unemployment in the European Union's Labour Market Due to the Recent Economic Crisis, Using Cluster Analysis

Tomáš Pavelka and Tomáš Löster

Abstract The recent economic recession has had a significant impact on the labour markets of the Member States of the European Union. The overall unemployment rate from low pre-crisis levels increased significantly during the crisis. The impact on different groups of the labour force, however, was not uniform. Youth unemployment in particular has become a key problem. The continuing economic problems have led to a rapid increase of long-term unemployment. The aim of this paper is, in addition to the basic description of unemployment in the European Union due to the economic recession, to find groups of similar states of the European Union in the period before, during and after the global economic crisis. A cluster analysis was used to find such groups. Individual clusters were compared in terms of labour market characteristics, especially the overall unemployment rate, the unemployment rate of young people, and long-term unemployment. Another objective of this paper is to compare how the global economic crisis impacted the composition of these groups, so in other words, to explore how individual countries responded to the economic crisis, in terms of the labour market and employment.

Keywords Economic recession • Labour market • Unemployment • Cluster analysis

1 Introduction

Member countries of the European Union have recently come through the economic cycle, which of course has also impacted the labour market. After a relatively high growth rate of real GDP and falling unemployment in the period 2004–2007,

T. Pavelka (✉)
Department of Microeconomics, University of Economics, Prague, Czech Republic
e-mail: pavelkat@vse.cz

T. Löster
Department of Statistics and Probability, University of Economics, Prague, Czech Republic
e-mail: losterto@vse.cz

© Springer International Publishing Switzerland 2016
M.H. Bilgin et al. (eds.), *Business Challenges in the Changing Economic Landscape - Vol. 1*, Eurasian Studies in Business and Economics 2/1,
DOI 10.1007/978-3-319-22596-8_23

the European Union was also hit by economic crisis, which had its roots in the financial crisis in the United States associated with problems in the local mortgage market. In the European Union, this crisis has been deepened by debt crises in some member countries (e.g., Greece, Spain and Portugal). Inappropriately strong restrictive governments' response of some member countries deteriorated the economic situation even further. In general it could be said that after 2008 there was a growth of unemployment and a decline in employment in most member countries of the European Union.

When evaluating the labour market, it is not enough to consider only the actual overall unemployment rate and employment rate, but it is necessary to look at the labour market comprehensively, i.e., to evaluate some partial indicators. In this article, the unemployment rate among young people, the unemployment rate of people with the lowest levels of education and the incidence of long-term unemployment are taken into account.

The aim of this paper is, in addition to the basic description of unemployment in the European Union due to the economic recession, to find groups of similar states of the European Union in the period before, during and after the global economic crisis. A so called cluster analysis is used for finding these groups.

Cluster analysis is a multivariate statistical method, which aims to create a group of objects, called clusters. Its principle is based on the creation of groups of objects in such a way that objects in one group are the most similar and two objects form two different groups should be the least similar. Different methods and different metrics can be used for the formation of clusters.

For all the above mentioned criteria, two periods are compared within the cluster analysis. The first period is the pre-crisis period, which is defined by the years 2004–2007. The second period is the crisis and post-crisis period, which is defined by the years 2008–2013. All data that are used in this article come from the Eurostat database. In the case of gross domestic product, data are used that are in line with the ESA95 methodology because some EU countries have yet to recalculate gross domestic product data according to the new ESA 2010.

2 Descriptions of Chosen Variables

In this part of the article, the indicators within the cluster analysis that will be used in the next section will be briefly described.

2.1 Gross Domestic Product

The first indicator is the real gross domestic product, or more precisely its annual growth. The average growth of real gross domestic product in the European Union (EU 28) is shown in Fig. 1. This indicator is used here mainly because it is necessary to distinguish between the pre-crisis and crisis and post-crisis periods.

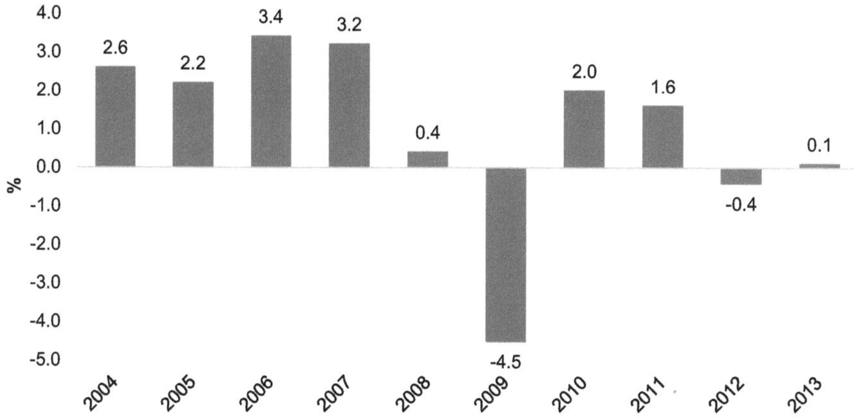

Fig. 1 Development of real gross domestic product in EU 28. *Source*: Eurostat

From Fig. 1 it is evident that a decline in gross domestic product occurred in 2009. From a closer look, however, it is clear that the crisis emerged in 2008, when gross domestic product fell in 10 European Union Member States. In other countries, there was a slowdown of gross domestic product. The only exception was Romania, since the gross domestic product showed a higher growth rate in 2008 than it did in 2007. Therefore in this article the pre-crisis period is defined as 2004–2007 and the crisis and post-crisis period as 2008–2013.

In the pre-crisis period the Baltic States and Slovakia had the highest growth rate of gross domestic product. However, in 2009 the Baltic States also had the deepest slump in gross domestic product, which was in the double-digits. On the other hand, a relatively quick recovery can be observed in these countries in the coming years. The only country in which gross domestic product did not decline in 2009 was Poland. The second phase of the recession happened in 2012, when gross domestic product fell in 14 European Union Member States.

Below are 5 indicators that characterize the development of the labor market.

2.2 *Overall Unemployment Rate*

In Fig. 2, the development of overall unemployment can be seen. The overall unemployment rate expresses the share of unemployed in the total labor force (here expressed for the population aged 15–74 years). The unemployment rate in the European Union declined until 2008, when the average rate was only 7.0 %. The Netherlands, Denmark, Cyprus and Austria had the lowest unemployment rate in that year. Conversely, Spain had the highest rate, followed by Croatia. In the crisis and post-crisis period, the unemployment rate in a number of Member States of the European Union reached double-digit values. The highest unemployment rates

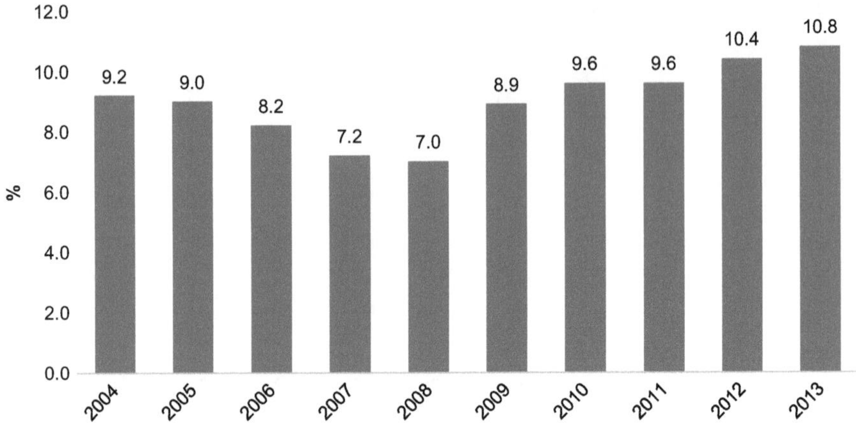

Fig. 2 Total unemployment in EU 28. *Source*: Eurostat

were reached by Greece and Spain, while the Netherlands and Austria had the lowest levels.

2.3 Unemployment Rate of Young People

One of the groups most affected by economic crisis is the group of young people. Youth unemployment has become the most serious problem of the European labour market. The European Commission, in cooperation with Member States, adopted a series of steps aimed at reducing unemployment among young people (see e. g., European Commission 2013). Unemployment among young people is linked to serious social problems. It should be noted that these young people are usually people who have never had any job, so these people can lose hope for finding a job, and there is also a high risk of radicalization of these people.

The average youth unemployment rate in the European Union is shown in Fig. 3. The youth unemployment rate depicts the unemployment rate of persons aged 15–24 years.

The development of unemployment among young people is similar to the development of the overall unemployment rate; the difference is in the amount. The unemployment rate of young people is more than double in comparison with the overall unemployment rate. In the crisis and post-crisis period the unemployment rate among young people exceeded 50 % in Greece, Spain and also Croatia. Conversely, the Netherlands, Austria and Germany had low unemployment rates among young people.

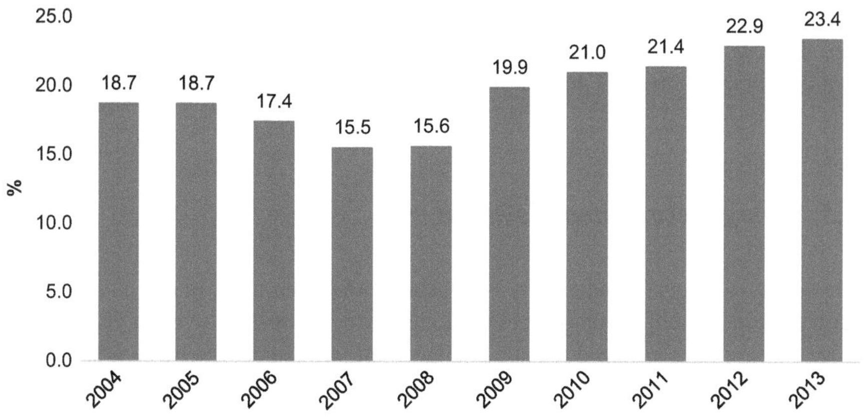

Fig. 3 Unemployment rate of young people in EU. *Source*: Eurostat

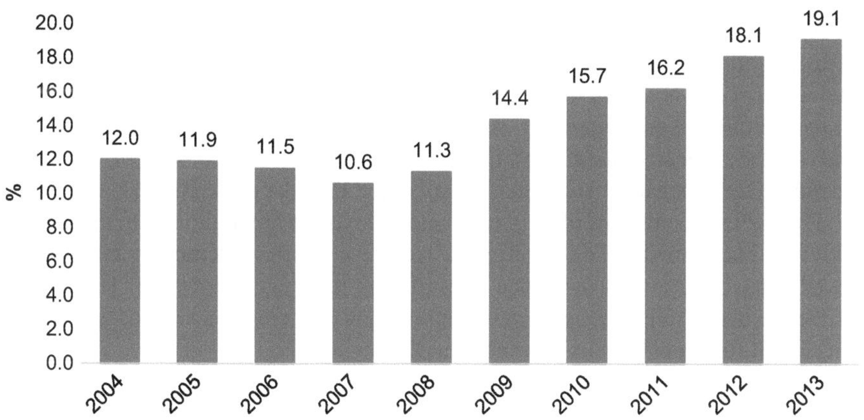

Fig. 4 Unemployment rate of people with the lowest level of education in EU. *Source*: Eurostat

2.4 Unemployment Rate of People with the Lowest Levels of Education

Another group of people that was significantly hit by the economic recession is the group of people with the lowest levels of education, i.e., level 0–2, according to the International Standard Classification of Education. These people usually have the biggest problem with finding a job and during a crisis are very often the first to be dismissed.

The average unemployment rate of people with the lowest levels of education in the European Union is shown in Fig. 4.

As can be seen from Fig. 4, the unemployment rate of those persons declined in the pre-crisis period only slightly, but in the crisis and post-crisis period, its increase was significant. In the crisis and post-crisis period, Romania and the Netherlands had the lowest unemployment rates of people with the lowest levels of education, and conversely, Slovakia and Lithuania had the highest ones.

2.5 *Long-Term Unemployment*

The negative effects of unemployment grow with its duration. In this context long-term unemployment is very often mentioned, which is unemployment lasting more than 1 year. This article does not use the long-term unemployment rate, but the incidence rate of long-term unemployment, which indicates the share of long-term unemployed to total unemployed.

The average incidence rate of long-term unemployment in the European Union is shown in Fig. 5.

The European Union had the lowest incidence rate of long-term unemployment in 2009, which was the year of the highest decline in gross domestic product. In this year, the number of unemployed significantly increased, but as is clear from the definition of the incidence of long-term unemployment, its value had to fall in 2009. In the following years, however, some newly unemployed did not find a new job, and so they became long-term unemployed. The incidence rate of long-term unemployment began to increase gradually (see Pavelka et al. 2011).

The highest incidences of long-term unemployment are traditionally recorded in Slovakia and Croatia. Conversely, the Nordic countries, Denmark, Finland and Sweden have the lowest incidence rates of long-term unemployment. The amount of the incidence rate of long-term unemployment is often used as a measure of the success of the employment policies of a country.

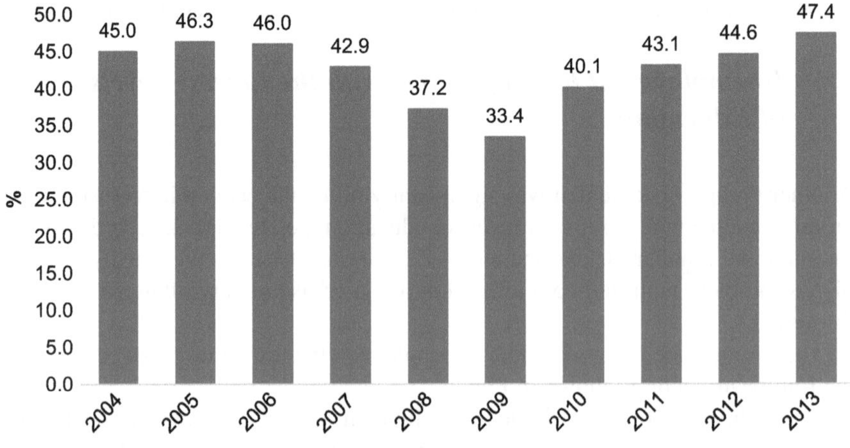

Fig. 5 Incidence of long-term unemployment in the EU. *Source*: Eurostat

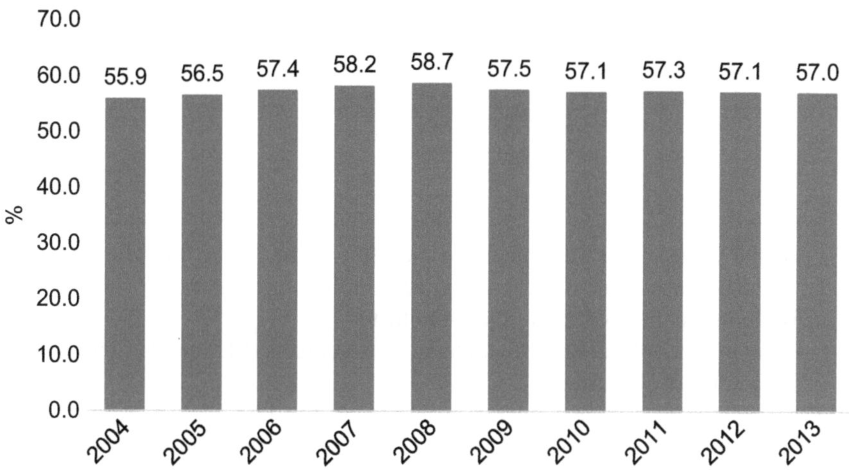

Fig. 6 Employment rate in EU. *Source*: Eurostat

2.6 Employment Rate

The employment rate is the last indicator that characterizes the labour market. The employment rate expresses the share of employed in the total population (expressed here for the population aged 15–74 years). An increase of the employment rate is one of the objectives of the European strategy EU 2020. Under this strategy, the employment rate of the population aged 20–64 should increase to at least 75 % (European Commission 2010).

The average employment rate in the European Union is shown in Fig. 6.

The employment rate in the European Union increased until the outbreak of the economic recession in 2008. The employment rate decreased slightly due to the economic recession. Some Member States have high employment rate, some low. The economic recession has essentially no effect on this division. Austria, the Netherlands, the Nordic countries (Denmark, Finland and Sweden), but also Germany and the United Kingdom have the highest rates of employment. Conversely, Croatia, and Greece due to the crisis, have low employment rates.

3 Methodology

A hierarchical cluster analysis was used to create clusters of objects (EU member countries). Ward's method solves the principle of clustering by minimizing heterogeneity of clusters, i.e., clusters are created using maximization of intragroup homogeneity (see Gan et al. 2007). This method was chosen because it provides the best results in many cases (see Gan et al. 2007). The degree of homogeneity of the clusters is the intragroup sum of squared deviations from the average values of the clusters, denoted by G1, called Ward's criterion, and is calculated according to the formula:

$$G_1 = \sum_{h=1}^{k} \sum_{i=1}^{n_h} \sum_{t=1}^{m} (x_{hit} - \overline{x}_{ht})^2 \tag{1}$$

Where:

x_{hit} is the value of the i-th object and the t-th variable in the h-th cluster,
$\overline{x}_{ht}$ is the average value of the t-th variable in the h-th cluster,
n_h is the number of objects in the h-th cluster,
m is the number of variables that characterize objects (EU member countries),
k is the number of clusters.

The criterion for joining clusters is based on the idea that at every step of clustering there was a minimal increase in G1, thus the expression (2) is minimized.

$$\Delta G_1 = \sum_{i=1}^{n_g} \sum_{t=1}^{m} (x_{git} - \overline{x}_{gt})^2 - \left(\sum_{i=1}^{n_h} \sum_{t=1}^{m} (x_{hit} - \overline{x}_{ht})^2 + \sum_{i=1}^{n_{h'}} \sum_{t=1}^{m} (x_{h'it} - \overline{x}_{h't})^2 \right) \tag{2}$$

Ward's method and this criterion are used only in conjunction with the square of the Euclidean distance. A calculation of this measure of the distance D between the i-th and the j-th object is based on the Pythagorean Theorem, i.e.,

$$D(\mathbf{x}_i, \mathbf{x}_j) = \sum_{t=1}^{m} (x_{it} - x_{jt})^2 \tag{3}$$

Where: x_i represents the i-th object, and where x_j is the j-th object.

Several techniques have been used to determine the optimal number of clusters; firstly, based on the knowledge of economic theory, and secondly on the basis of appropriate criteria. Among the criteria that are used to determine the optimal number of clusters can be included the CHF coefficient, the Davies-Bouldin index and the Dunn coefficient (see Gan et al. 2007).

Davies-Bouldin index DB is a measure whose values do not depend on the chosen method of clustering (see Davies and Bouldin 1979). The dispersion of the h-th cluster S_h must be defined to determine the Davies-Bouldin index. The degree of similarity between the h-th and the h′-th clusters is denoted by $A_{hh'}$; and is based on the dispersion of the h-th and the h′-th clusters and must meet certain conditions (see Davies and Bouldin 1979). The degree of similarity between the h-th and the h′-th clusters, $A_{hh'}$, is calculated according to the formula:

$$A_{hh'} = \frac{S_h + S_{h'}}{D_{hh'}} \tag{4}$$

A maximum degree of similarity between the clusters h and h′ is denoted as A_h, that is:

$$A_h = \max_{h, h \neq h'} A_{hh'} \tag{5}$$

The final Davies-Bouldin index is calculated as the arithmetic mean of the maximum rates of similarities, A_h, as according to the formula:

$$I_{\mathrm{DB}}(k) = \frac{\sum_{h=1}^{k} A_h}{k} \tag{6}$$

According to the Davies-Bouldin index, the best distribution of such objects into clusters is when the value of this index is minimized. Individual clusters are compact and well separated at small values of this index.

As the optimum number of clusters is considered the value k*, for which the value of Davies-Bouldin index is minimal within a predetermined maximum number of clusters, i.e.,

$$I_{\mathrm{DB}}(k^*) = \min_{2 \leq k \leq n-1} I_{\mathrm{DB}}(k) \tag{7}$$

Dunn separation index is used to find compact and well-separated clusters (Dunn 1974). The distance between the h-th and the h′-th clusters is defined as the minimum distance of two objects from these various clusters, so:

$$D_{hh'} = \min_{\mathbf{x}_i \in C_h, \mathbf{x}_j \in C_{h'}} D(\mathbf{x}_i, \mathbf{x}_j) \tag{8}$$

$diam_h$ is defined as the maximum distance of two objects from the same cluster, so:

$$diam_h = \max_{\mathbf{x}_i, \mathbf{x}_j \in C_h} D(\mathbf{x}_i, \mathbf{x}_j) \tag{9}$$

The Dunn index is defined as:

$$I_{\mathrm{D}}(k) = \min_{1 \leq h \leq k} \left\{ \min_{1 \leq h' \leq k} \frac{D_{hh'}}{\max_{1 \leq h \leq k} diam_h} \right\} \tag{10}$$

High values of the Dunn separation index indicate compact and well-separated clusters. The inter-cluster distance is maximized and intra-cluster distance is minimized for these values. The maximum value Dunn separation index within a predetermined number of clusters is sought by determining the optimal number of clusters k*, or:

$$I_{\mathrm{D}}(k^*) = \max_{2 \leq k \leq n-1} I_{\mathrm{D}}(k) \tag{11}$$

CHF index (also called pseudo F index) was suggested by Calinski and Harabasz (1974), and it was further elaborated by Maulik and Bandyopadhyay (2002). The CHF index is defined as a share of the average inter-cluster and average intra-cluster variability, i.e., according to the formula:

$$I_{\mathrm{CHF}}(k) = \frac{\dfrac{SS_{\mathrm{B}}}{k-1}}{\dfrac{SS_{\mathrm{W}}}{n-k}} = \frac{(n-k) \cdot SS_{\mathrm{B}}}{(k-1) \cdot SS_{\mathrm{W}}} \tag{12}$$

Where for individual sums of squares is true:

SS_{B} = the sum of squares between clusters (characteristics of inter-cluster variability),

SS_{W} = the sum of squares within clusters (characteristics of intra-cluster variability),

SS_{T} = the total sum of squares (characteristics of the total variability).

$$SS_{\mathrm{W}} = \sum_{h=1}^{k} \sum_{\mathbf{x}_i \in C_h} \sum_{t=1}^{m} (x_{it} - \overline{x}_{ht})^2 \tag{13}$$

$$SS_{\mathrm{T}} = \sum_{i=1}^{n} \sum_{t=1}^{m} (x_{it} - \overline{x}_t)^2 \tag{14}$$

$$SS_{\mathrm{B}} = SS_{\mathrm{T}} - SS_{\mathrm{W}} \tag{15}$$

The CHF index is used to determine the optimal number of clusters. High values of this index represent well separated clusters, i.e., the maximum value of this index is sought, which indicates the optimal number of clusters k*, i.e.,

$$I_{\mathrm{CHF}}(k^*) = \max_{2 \leq k \leq n-1} I_{\mathrm{CHF}}(k) \tag{16}$$

For the determination of the above mentioned coefficients, the twelfth version of SYSTAT was used.

As is apparent from the Fig. 7, three clusters of EU Member States were selected as the optimum.

The above-described indicators are included in the cluster analysis. Besides the development of gross domestic product, which is used to describe the economic cycle, there are 5 indicators that characterize the labor market itself, including the overall unemployment rate, the unemployment rate of young people, the

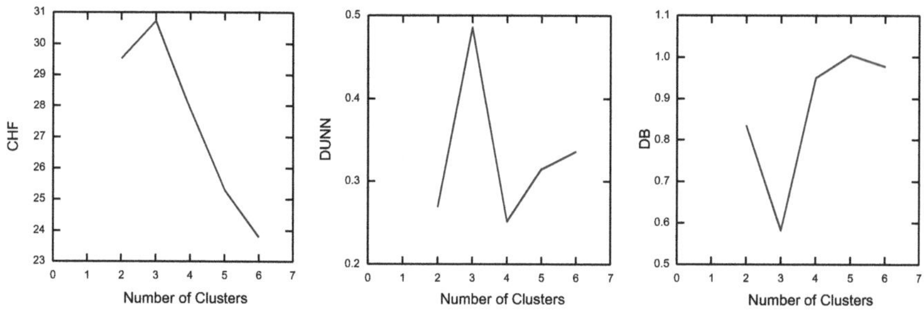

Fig. 7 Evaluating criteria for setting the optimal number of clusters. *Source*: Own calculation, SYSTAT system

unemployment rate of people with the lowest levels of education, the incidence of long-term unemployment and the employment rate.

As already mentioned, the EU Member States are divided into three clusters. For the pre-crisis period, the average value of these indicators for the period 2004–2007 are used. For the crisis and post-crisis period the average values of indicators for the period 2008–2013 are used.

The composition of clusters for the pre-crisis period and for the crisis and post-crisis period is shown in Table 1. The numerical designation of clusters does not simply represent the order of countries from best to worst or vice versa. It is necessary to look at individual clusters in detail. The basic characteristics of individual clusters in the pre-crisis period are shown in Table 2, and the crisis and post-crisis period are shown in Table 3.

In the pre-crisis period, we can say that the best characteristics of the labour market are shown by cluster 2 despite weaker average growth in gross domestic product. Countries contained in cluster 2 show a pre-crisis average of growth 0.8 percentage points lower than countries in cluster 1 and 3.8 percentage points lower than the country in cluster 3 (respectively, compared to Slovakia, because in the pre-crisis period, cluster 3 is only formed by one country, Slovakia). But in all characteristics of the labour market, cluster 2 has a better value compared to the other two clusters. In the pre-crisis period, the countries in cluster 2 show on average an overall unemployment rate of almost 3 percentage points lower than the countries in cluster 1 and 9.2 percentage points lower than in Slovakia. Regarding youth unemployment, the countries in cluster 2 have on average a rate 6.3 percentage points lower than the countries included in the cluster 1. Slovakia has more than double the rate of unemployment among young people than the countries in cluster 2 in the pre-crisis period. Among people with the lowest levels of education, the countries in cluster 2 have on average a pre-crisis level of unemployment 4.9 percentage points lower than the countries in cluster 1 and 40.8 percentage points lower than the country in cluster 3. With regard to long-term unemployment, cluster 3 shows the highest value in the pre-crisis period, on average 21.7 percentage points higher than the countries in cluster 1 and 44.1 percentage points higher than the countries in cluster 2. The countries included in

Table 1 Composition of clusters for pre-crisis and crisis and post-crisis period

Pre-crisis period			Crisis and post-crisis period		
1	2	3	1	2	3
Belgium	Denmark	Slovakia	Belgium	Denmark	Greece
Bulgaria	Ireland		Bulgaria	Germany	Spain
Czech Republic	Spain		Czech Republic	Estonia	Croatia
Germany	Cyprus		Estonia	Cyprus	Italy
Estonia	Luxembourg		Ireland	Luxembourg	
Greece	Netherlands		France	Netherlands	
France	Austria		Latvia	Austria	
Croatia	Slovenia		Lithuania	Slovenia	
Italy	Finland		Hungary	Finland	
Latvia	Sweden		Malta	Sweden	
Lithuania	United Kingdom		Poland	United Kingdom	
Hungary			Portugal		
Malta			Romania		
Poland			Slovakia		
Romania					

Table 2 Clusters characteristics for pre-crisis period

Ward's method		N	Minimum	Maximum	Mean	Std. deviation
1	Total_unemp	16	6.90	15.10	8.6688	2.21230
	Youth_unemp	16	13.60	32.10	19.6938	5.40499
	Low_edu_unemp	16	7.40	24.30	13.7938	5.33922
	Long_unemp	16	36.90	58.40	49.9125	6.08406
	Employment	16	48.10	62.00	54.3500	4.38117
	GDP	16	1.60	10.00	4.7375	2.65050
2	Total_unemp	11	4.10	9.30	5.7000	1.76692
	Youth_unemp	11	7.20	20.70	13.3545	5.07393
	Low_edu_unemp	11	5.50	15.10	8.8545	2.92348
	Long_unemp	11	15.80	48.90	27.5182	9.32050
	Employment	11	56.40	69.10	62.8636	3.99256
	GDP	11	2.40	5.30	3.9364	1.01614
3	Total_unemp	1	14.90	14.90	14.9000	
	Youth_unemp	1	27.50	27.50	27.5000	
	Low_edu_unemp	1	49.70	49.70	49.7000	
	Long_unemp	1	71.60	71.60	71.6000	
	Employment	1	53.70	53.70	53.7000	
	GDP	1	7.70	7.70	7.7000	

cluster 2 have the highest rate of employment, on average 8.5 percentage points higher than the countries in cluster 1 and 9.2 percentage points higher than cluster 3.

In the crisis and post-crisis period, compared with the pre-crisis period, there are relatively significant changes in the composition of the clusters. Again, the

Table 3 Clusters characteristics for crisis and post-crisis period

Ward method		N	Minimum	Maximum	Mean	Std. deviation
1	Total_unemp	14	6.50	14.60	10.1714	2.64355
	Youth_unemp	14	13.30	30.20	23.3143	4.44779
	Low_edu_unemp	14	7.00	42.40	20.5857	9.27062
	Long_unemp	14	35.80	65.50	45.2071	7.37860
	Employment	14	50.10	59.90	55.4714	2.83343
	GDP	14	−1.30	3.10	0.3857	1.26786
2	Total_unemp	10	4.40	8.50	6.6100	1.47983
	Youth_unemp	10	8.10	23.30	15.5400	5.53919
	Low_edu_unemp	10	7.20	16.40	11.4600	3.18685
	Long_unemp	10	16.90	47.30	28.6600	10.03208
	Employment	10	58.20	67.80	62.9000	3.02802
	GDP	10	−1.00	1.10	−0.1100	0.71095
3	Total_unemp	4	9.10	20.20	14.6750	4.81690
	Youth_unemp	4	29.80	43.10	36.8750	5.82144
	Low_edu_unemp	4	11.40	27.50	17.6250	7.01017
	Long_unemp	4	35.70	61.40	49.6250	10.57651
	Employment	4	46.50	52.70	49.7000	2.54558
	GDP	4	−4.40	−1.00	−2.1500	1.52862

countries contained in cluster 2 show the best labour market characteristics, and countries included in cluster 3 show the worst. As regards the growth rate of gross domestic product, on average, only the countries included in the cluster 1 show positive growth. The countries contained in cluster 3 show a larger average drop in gross domestic product than countries included in cluster 2.

EU Member States involved in the crisis and post-crisis period in cluster 2 show on average only a slight fall in real gross domestic product, which was more than 2 percentage points lower than the average drop for the countries in cluster 3. Cluster 1, however, shows positive growth in gross domestic product during the crisis and post-crisis period (by an average of 0.4 %). The overall unemployment rate in Cluster 2 during the crisis and post-crisis period is 3.56 percentage points lower than in cluster 1, and 8.1 percentage points lower than in cluster 3. In the case of unemployment among young people, the countries included in cluster 2 show on average a rate 7.8 percentage points lower than countries included in cluster 1, and 21.3 percentage points lower than the countries in cluster 3. In cluster 2, the unemployment rate among people with the lowest levels of education during the crisis and post-crisis period is 9.1 percentage points lower than cluster 1, and 6.2 percentage points lower than in cluster 3. The incidence of long-term unemployment in cluster 2 is on average 16.5 percentage points lower than in cluster 1, and 21 percentage points lower than in cluster 3. The countries included in cluster 2 also show better values of the employment rate than do the other two groups. Cluster 2 has an employment rate 7.4 percentage points higher than cluster 1, and 13.2 percentage points higher than cluster 3.

In the pre-crisis period only Slovakia belongs to cluster 3, which was the worst with regard to labour market indicators. In the crisis and post-crisis period, four countries show the worst values: Greece, Spain, Croatia and Italy. In all these countries, real output in the post-crisis period decreased, and the employment rate also declined. Conversely, the rate of total unemployment, the unemployment rate among young people, the unemployment rate of people with the lowest levels of education and the incidence of long-term unemployment often increased greatly.

Due to the improvement in almost all the indicators of the labour market, Slovakia shifts from cluster 3 during the pre-crisis period to cluster 1 in the crisis and post-crisis period. During this period, Slovakia shows a 1.9 percentage point lower overall unemployment rate, a 7.3 percentage points lower unemployment rate of persons with the lowest education level, a 6.8 percentage points lower incidence of long-term unemployment and a 1.1 percentage point higher employment rate. Only in the case of unemployment among young people did Slovakia deteriorate in the crisis and post-crisis period, and it increased by 2.7 percentage points (always compared with the average values of the pre-crisis period).

After the outbreak of the crisis, Germany and Estonia moved from cluster 1 to cluster 2. Conversely, Ireland moved from cluster 2 to cluster 1. Germany had on average positive growth of gross domestic product even after the outbreak of the crisis, despite its decline in 2009, when its gross domestic product also fell (−5.1 %). Germany, however, succeeded in the crisis and post-crisis period compared to the pre-crisis period, in the reduction of the overall unemployment rate by 3.7 percentage points, the reduction of unemployment among young people by 4.2 percentage points, the reduction of the unemployment rate of people with the lowest levels of education by 4.3 percentage points, the reduction of the incidence of long-term unemployment by 7.2 percentage points and the increase of the employment rate by 4.6 percentage points. Estonia, despite a significant decline in real gross domestic product in 2009 (a decrease of 14.1 %) eventually managed to maintain a slightly positive growth in the period 2008–2013. Compared to the pre-crisis period, the rate of total unemployment in Estonia was 3.9 percentage point higher, the unemployment rate among young people increased by 6.6 percentage points and the unemployment rate of people with the lowest levels of education increased by 8.1 percentage points. The incidence rate of long-term unemployment during the crisis and post-crisis period, however, was by 7.7 percentage points, and the employment rate declined only slightly by 0.4 percentage points.

4 Conclusion

European labour market was strongly influenced by the economic recession that hit the European Union in 2008. The fall of the product was associated with an increase in unemployment. Unemployment among young people has become one of the main problems of the European labour market. The economic recession had also negative impact on the unemployment rate of people with the lowest level of education and long-term unemployment.

Using cluster analysis, the European Union Member States were divided into three groups, which have similar characteristics of labour market. Labour market has been unfavourable affected notably in some southern states, Greece, Spain, but also in Italy and Croatia. German labour market, despite of the crisis, developed positively. Labour markets of Austria, the Netherlands and the Nordic countries (Denmark, Finland and Sweden) show traditionally good results.

The results of the analysis showed that the economic recession had different impacts on unemployment in individual countries. This confirms that the impact of the recession on the labour market is influenced by many factors (e.g., labour market flexibility, social system, etc.), whose parameters vary by country.

Acknowledgment This paper is the one of the outputs of the grant No. 6/2013 "Evaluation of results of cluster analysis in economic problems" that is financed by the Internal Grant Agency of University of Economics, Prague.

References

Calinski, T., & Harabasz, J. (1974). A dendrite method for cluster analysis. *Comunications in Statistics, 3*(1), 1–27.

Davies, D., & Bouldin, D. W. (1979). A cluster separation measure. *IEEE Transactions on Pattern Analysis and Machine Intelligence, 1*(4), 224–227.

Dunn, J. (1974). Well separated clusters and optimal fuzzy partitions. *Journal of Cybernetics, 4*(1), 95–104.

European Commission. (2010). *EUROPE 2020. A strategy for smart, sustainable and inclusive growth.* [pdf] European Commission. Available at http://eur-lex.europa.eu/LexUriServ/LexUriServ.do?uri=COM:2010:2020:FIN:EN:PDF. Accessed 28 Dec 2014.

European Commission. (2013). *Working together for Europe's young people. A call to action on youth unemployment.* [pdf] European Commission. Available at http://ec.europa.eu/social/main.jsp?catId=1036. Accessed 28 Dec 2014.

Gan, G., Ma, C., & Wu, J. (2007). *Data clustering theory, algorithms, and applications.* Philadelphia: ASA.

Maulik, U., & Bandyopadhyay, S. (2002). Performance evaluation of some clustering algorithms and validity indices. *IEEE Transaction on Pattern Analysis and Machine Intelligence, 24*(12), 1650–1654.

Pavelka, T., Loster, T., Makovsku, P., & Langhamrová, J. (2011). *Dlouhodobá nezaměstnanost v České republice* [Long-term unemployment in the Czech Republic]. Slaný: Melandrium.

Attitudes to Income Inequality and Preferences for Redistribution in Turkey

Ayfer Karayel

Abstract We estimate the determinants of individuals' inequality aversion and preferences for redistribution in Turkey using the 2007 and 2011 World Values Survey data. Our results show that factors as predictors of opposing inequality and supporting redistribution in both surveys are dissatisfaction with the financial situation of the household, being on the left side of the political scale, belief that hard work brings a better life, and the opposite of this belief as well. According to the 2011 survey, being woman, being self-employed, belonging to lower class, living in poorer East Central Anatolia region and in Central Anatolia are associated with increased opposition to inequality and support for redistribution. The odds of supporting redistribution decrease for people living in the Aegean region according to both the surveys. For 2007, being in the highest income category relative to the middle is associated with a decreased opposition to inequality and support for redistribution. As for the impact of living in a specific region, besides Aegean region, for 2007, coefficients indicate a decrease in the odds for the following regions: North Eastern Anatolia, Eastern Marmara, Central Anatolia and Western Black Sea.

Keywords Redistribution preferences • Inequality aversion • World values

1 Introduction

The concepts of inequality aversion and inequity aversion are sometimes used interchangeably in game theory and experimental economics literature implying that inequality of a distribution is an inequitable outcome (Fehr and Schmidt 1999; Fehr et al. 2006). Perceptions of unfairness and injustice are indeed among the most remarkable predictors of inequality averse preferences in empirical studies.

Over the past decade, a growing body of literature has inferred the determinants of preferences for redistribution and attitudes toward income inequality. Those researchers employing the survey approach have used data from surveys such as

A. Karayel (✉)
Department of Economics, Galatasaray University, Istanbul, Turkey
e-mail: ayferkarayel@yahoo.com

© Springer International Publishing Switzerland 2016

M.H. Bilgin et al. (eds.), *Business Challenges in the Changing Economic Landscape - Vol. 1*, Eurasian Studies in Business and Economics 2/1,
DOI 10.1007/978-3-319-22596-8_24

International Social Survey Programme, The Gallup Poll Social Audit, European and World Values Surveys, US General Social Surveys, UK British Social Attitudes Surveys, The Euro-barometer Surveys, and Life in Transition Surveys.

Motivations behind inequality averse attitudes and support for redistribution have been previously examined mostly by cross-section studies from a multi-country perspective, but only few studies have investigated them from a single-country perspective. This paper examines for the first time the determinants of individuals' inequality aversion and preferences for redistribution in Turkey using the 2007 and 2011 World Values Survey (WVS) data, respectively from the last two 2005–2008 and 2010–2013 waves. The paper is organized as follows. Section 2 summarizes the most relevant factors motivating individuals to be inequality averse and to prefer redistribution, and describes briefly public opinion about inequality in Turkey. Section 3 presents the methodology applied, data and variables. Section 4 presents the results of the empirical analysis, and the last section concludes.

2 Relevant Factors for Income Inequality Aversion and Preferences for Redistribution

A large number of papers review more or less comprehensively theoretical discussions and available evidence on preferences for redistribution and inequality aversion (for example, Alesina and Giuliano 2009; Guillaud 2013; Neher 2012). In this section, impact factors most frequently observed in empirical research are stated with references in a non-exhaustive manner.

- Personal history, endowments, and economic factors such as:
  - Current income; the poor are more inequality averse and pro-redistribution, although the pattern is the opposite in the United States (Corneo and Grüner 2002; Alesina et al. 2004; Alesina and Giuliano 2009; Neher 2012),
  - Education; less educated individuals are more inequality averse and pro-redistribution (Verme 2007; Neher 2012),
  - Marriage status: married individuals are supposed to prefer lower redistribution since marriage provides insurance against income risks and unemployment (Fong 2001),
  - Risk aversion; more risk averse individuals are also more inequality averse and pro-redistribution (Ferrer-i-Carbonell and Ramos 2010; Guillaud 2013),
  - Prospect of upward mobility (POUM); individuals expecting or having experienced upward social mobility oppose redistribution (Bénabou and Ok 2001; Alesina and La Ferrara 2005; Corneo and Grüner 2002; Alesina and Giuliano 2009; Guillaud 2013),
  - Subjective social class; the feeling of belonging to a lower social class than the middle makes individuals inequality averse and pro-redistribution (Macunovich 2011; Guillaud 2013),

- Perceptions of the causes of poverty or beliefs about success factors, perception of unfairness; other things equal, individuals who believe more in effort favor less redistribution (Fong 2001; Piketty 1999; Alesina and Angeletos 2005; Corneo and Grüner 2002; Cojocaru 2011),
- Cultural factors, evidenced in the specific contexts of the immigrants in the USA and in reunified Germany (Alesina and Giuliano 2009; Luttmer and Singhal 2011),
- Subjective political orientation; left-wing people are more inequality averse, although the reverse causality problem may occur (Kaltenthaler et al. 2008; Verme 2007),
- Gender; women are more inequality averse and pro-redistribution (Alesina and Giuliano 2009; Guillaud 2013; Neher 2012),
- Religious denomination; religion may act as a substitute for social insurance (Scheve and Stasavage 2006), protestants and catholics tend to oppose redistribution (Guillaud 2013),
- Active union membership: in developing countries union members are found to oppose redistribution to the poor (Haggard et al. 2013).
- Size of the city of residence: while evidence is mixed (Gaeta 2012), living in a big city may boost pro-redistributive preferences (Haggard et al. 2013).

Cross-country analyses point to country-specific factors probably affecting preferences of individuals for redistribution rendering separate analysis for each country useful. Nonetheless, as noted by Gaeta (2012, p. 2385), "while country characteristics also affect individual preferences, it is very difficult to distinguish the effects on individual attitudes determined by (i) the institutional context (ii) the national culture and (iii) the economic context."

In The Life in Transition Survey (LiTS) and several waves of the WVS, Turks appear to be highly averse to income inequality, and inclined to redistribution by the state. According to 2006 LiTS data (World Bank 2010), 85.4 % of the population strongly agreed or agreed with the view that "the gap between the rich and the poor in society should be reduced" which is the highest proportion for the 29 Eastern European and Central Asian countries where LiTS surveys were conducted. Three-quarters of the Turkish population think that poverty is due to factors beyond the control of individuals, and two-thirds of them view injustice in society as the main reason. At the same time, just over three-quarters of the population agree with the view that success is due to efforts, hard work, intelligence or skills. A smaller percentage of the population (22.2 %) attribute economic success to political connections or criminal or corrupt ties. Since, economic failure and deprivation is seen as the result of an unjust system or bad luck, but the rich are considered as deserving of their position, "Turkish attitudes would appear to be 'American upwards', but 'European downwards" (Ferreira et al. 2010, p. 4).

Data of the Turkish sample of the WVS corresponding to the years 2007 and 2011 reveal also similar attitudes to income inequality and preferences for redistribution. Individual attitude towards the desired level of income inequality is measured through the answer given to a scaled question on the desired level of income inequality where 1 = Income should be made more equal and 10 = We need larger income differences as incentives for individual effort. Table 1 reports rankings of mean scores for preferences of societies for the periods 2005–2009 and 2010–2014.

Research on attitudes and preferences based on social surveys assumes that individuals are sincere revealers of their preferences. Yet, it is possible that inequality aversion scores might be upwardly biased in the case of Turkey. A research on the estimation of tax morale score for the Aegean Region, for example, considers that tax morale score for Turkey is above 90 % according to data from

Table 1 Ranking of societies' attitudes to income inequality according to 2005–2009 and 2010–2014 WWS data

Mean 2010–2014		Mean 2005–2009	
3.37	Russia	3.59	Switzerland
3.48	Slovenia	4.17	Iran
3.48	Cyprus	4.53	Germany
3.5	Chile	4.59	Hungary
3.51	Ukraine	4.66	Romania
3.79	Estonia	4.69	Slovenia
4.08	Germany	4.72	Chile
4.27	Rwanda	4.78	Hong Kong
4.3	Egypt	4.79	India
4.45	China	4.91	Iraq
4.49	Turkey	4.97	Finland
4.59	Uzbekistan	5.01	Turkey
4.77	Australia	5.07	Norway
4.87	Belarus	5.12	France
4.88	Sweden	5.24	Cyprus
5	Morocco	5.27	Argentina
5.03	Colombia	5.35	Morocco
5.11	Uruguay	5.35	Uruguay
5.14	Spain	5.36	Great Britain
5.16	New Zealand	5.43	New Zealand
5.2	Japan	5.5	Colombia
5.31	Iraq	5.54	South Africa
5.33	Kazakhstan	5.65	Spain
5.36	Mexico	5.66	Australia
5.47	Netherlands	5.67	Brazil
5.55	Ecuador	5.67	Netherlands
5.58	United States	5.69	Bulgaria
5.74	Singapore	5.8	Moldova
5.76	Peru	5.82	Canada
5.84	Armenia	5.94	Italy
5.89	Taiwan	5.97	China
5.95	Lebanon	5.97	Rwanda

(continued)

Table 1 (continued)

Mean 2010–2014		Mean 2005–2009	
5.97	Tunisia	5.98	Viet Nam
6.01	Palestine	6.08	United States
6.05	Romania	6.1	Serbia and Montenegro
6.07	Azerbaijan	6.11	Mexico
6.12	Kyrgyzstan	6.11	Sweden
6.3	Philippines	6.12	Andorra
6.32	Poland	6.15	Japan
6.36	Yemen	6.42	Russia
6.44	Nigeria	6.47	South Korea
6.45	South Korea	6.61	Ethiopia
6.55	Algeria	6.66	Malaysia
6.57	Kuwait	6.7	Taiwan
6.66	Malaysia	6.79	Egypt
6.79	Qatar	6.81	Poland
6.82	Ghana	6.82	Jordan
6.84	Pakistan	6.87	Georgia
6.84	Zimbabwe	6.94	Ukraine
6.91	Libya	7.02	Guatemala
6.98	Trinidad and Tobago	7.07	Thailand
7.15	Jordan	7.07	Burkina Faso
		7.25	Trinidad and Tobago
		7.37	Indonesia
		7.5	Peru
		7.53	Mali
		7.76	Ghana

Source: http://www.worldvaluessurvey.org

WVS and cannot reflect reality (Tosuner and Demir 2008)[1]. Pro-inequality preferences seem to be less risky to reveal than tax avoidance and evasion revelations, but individuals may prefer to respond in a way they think to be socially desirable (Corneo and Grüner 2002; Alesina et al. 2004), and the fact that Turkey's interpersonal trust scores are one of the lowest among all countries surveyed might boost this tendency. This may be a reason why the number of missing answers are high to the question about political orientation of the respondents.

[1] For example, for the year 2006, public tax auditors reported that 65.3 % of due direct taxes had been evaded and/or avoided (http://arsiv.sabah.com.tr/2007/05/03/haber).

3 Methodology, Data and Variables

Econometric estimations are made with a standard logit model. For this purpose, the dependent variable has been transformed to a dichotomous one and a binary logistic regression has been run.

For the binary logistic regression, the question mentioned in the previous section on the attitude towards reducing income inequality is transformed to a binary response variable in which individuals holding strong redistributionist views are distinguished from all other responses (neutral and opposition views). Thus, values of 1 and 2 of the above WVS variable are equalized to 1, and values from 3 to 10 are equalized to 0. We label this variable INCOMEEQUAL and use it as the dependent variable capturing both inequality aversion and preferences for redistribution, bearing in mind that this question "omits explicit reference to government action" (Haggard et al. 2013, p. 120) and "is more a question on the preference for income equality than for income redistribution" (Neher 2012, p. 10).

Given that the original variable has 10 categories, one could ask why an ordered logit or ordered probit model is not used to exploit data fully. First, the proportional odds assumption or parallel lines assumption underlying ordered logistic and ordered probit regressions is usually violated for a number of variables, therefore using at least a partial generalized ordered logit model becomes necessary which is computationally demanding and time consuming[2]. Second, a binary logistic regression is more helpful to discern the preferences of those who have strong opposition to income inequality and those who do not. We also remark that estimates have also been made with an ordered logit model and have been found similar to estimates made with a binary logit model with a different specification of the binary dependent variable.[3]

Personal face-to-face interview respondents are between 18 and 82 years of age in the 2007 sample, and 18–86 years of age in the 2011 sample. For stratification (selection of blocks), NUTS-1 level was used, and there are 12 NUTS-1 regions in Turkey[4]. The original samples are representative with each stratum having the number of cases proportional to its population.

Our selection of the independent variables was conditioned by data availability. In WVS, no data were available to measure subjective social mobility of

[2] "One of the assumptions underlying ordered logistic (and ordered probit) regression is that the relationship between each pair of outcome groups is the same. This is called the proportional odds assumption or the parallel regression assumption. Because the relationship between all pairs of groups is the same, there is only one set of coefficients (only one model). If this was not the case, we would need different models to describe the relationship between each pair of outcome groups." If the proportional odds assumption is violated, the model needs to be run as a generalized ordered logistic model (Institute for Digital Research and Education (idre) UCLA: Statistical Consulting Group 2012, accessed 20 December 2012).

[3] By equalizing values from 1 to 5 of the dependent variable to 1, and values from 6 to 10 to 0. These results are available upon request.

[4] Technical Specifications for Turkey of the WVS, available at: http://www.wvsevsdb.com.

respondents. Again, data relative to size of the city of residence were not available in the case of Turkey. Therefore our explanatory variables do not include subjective social mobility and city size variables. We take into account most of the relevant variables however. Explanatory variables used in the estimation are presented below with variable labels in parenthesis. Reference (or base) categories for the variables are also given below, since the coefficients are interpreted relative to the reference category. Also, Table 2 displays the summary statistics of the variables.

Table 2 Summary statistics of variables

Variable	Obs. 2011	Min	Max	Obs. 2007
INCOMEEQUAL	1570	1	2	1319
1: Incomes should be made more equal	440			371
0: We need larger income differences as incentives	1130			948
MARITAL	1605	0	1	1346
0: Not married	562			454
1: Married	1043			892
RELIGIOUS	1575	0	1	1321
0: Not relig./atheist	261			237
1: Religious	1314			1084
FINANCIAL	1584	1	3	1341
1: Dissatisfied	74			104
2: Relatively neutral	1299			1105
3: Satisfied	211			132
POLITICAL	1453	1	3	1143
1: Left	134			135
2: Moderate views	1032			758
3: Right	287			250
HWORK	1568	1	3	1318
1: Brings success	461			417
2: Relatively neutral	988			735
3: Does not bring success	119			166
EDUCATION	1605	1	4	1346
1: No education	154			160
2: Lower	491			519
3: Middle	649			503
4: Upper	311			164
EMPLOYMENT	1605	1	8	1346
1: Full time	429			308
2: Part time	100			37
3: Self employed	136			181
4: Retired	174			127
5: Housewife	542			462
6: Students	140			119
7: Unemployed	77			82
8: Other	7			30

(continued)

Table 2 (continued)

Variable	Obs. 2011	Min	Max	Obs. 2007
UNION	1600	0	1	1344
1: Active	31			13
0: Inactive/Non member	1569			1331
SEX	1605	1	2	1346
1: Male	780			675
2: Female	825			671
AGE6CATEGORIES	1605	1	6	1346
1: 18–30	555			589
2: 31–40	424			278
3: 41–50	296			259
4: 51–60	178			129
5: 61–70	101			60
6: 71–86	51			31
SOCIALCLASS	1579	1	4	1277
1: Upper class	31			27
2: Middle class	1089			849
3: Working class	391			333
4: Lower class	68			68
INCOMESCALE	1571	1	3	1319
1: Lowest step	75			635
2: Middle step	1392			628
3: Highest step	104			56
REGION	1605			1346
İstanbul	282			190
Western Marmara	89			58
Aegean	243			179
Eastern Marmara	136			114
Western Anatolia	211			130
Mediterranean	182			175
Central Anatolia	108			84
Western Black Sea	56			98
Eastern Black Sea	65			63
North Eastern Anat.	51			50
East Central Anat.	55			75
South Eastern Anat.	127			132

Source: http://www.worldvaluessurvey.org

To indicate marital status (MARITAL), two dummies are coded: "1. Married; 0. Not married. "Not married" is the base or reference category.

Satisfaction with the financial situation of the household (FINANCIAL) is used as a proxy variable to capture respondents' household income. Originally, answers range on a 10-steps scale where: "1 = Dissatisfied" and "10 = Satisfied". This variable is recoded in three dummies where the first two categories are assigned the value 1 and labelled “Dissatisfied”, categories 3–8 are assigned the value 2 and labelled “Relatively neutral”, and the last two categories are assigned the value 3 and labelled “Satisfied”. The second category is the base.

For self-positioning on a political scale (POLITICAL), respondents choose one of the answers ranging from “1 = Left” to “10 = Right”. This variable is also recoded in three dummies where the first two categories are assigned the value 1 and labelled “Left”, categories 3–8 are assigned the value 2 and labelled “Moderate views”, and the last two categories are assigned the value 3 and labelled “Right”. The second category is the base

To measure the opinions about whether hard work brings success or not (HWORK), answers are ranged on a scale from one to ten where: “1 = In the long run, hard work usually brings a better life” and “10 = Hard work doesn’t generally bring success—it’s more a matter of luck and connections”. Similarly, this variable is recoded in three dummies where the first two categories are assigned the value 1 and labelled “Brings success”, categories 3–8 are assigned the value 2 and labelled “Relatively neutral”, and the last two categories are assigned the value 3 and labelled “Does not bring success”, with the second category being the base.

“Religious denomination” cannot be used as an independent variable, since 99.9 % of the population is muslim, and the remaining 0.1 % are considered as “other”. Therefore, only “religious person or subjective religiosity” variable (RELIGIOUS) is used. In the Turkish case, “subjective religiosity” seems to be more relevant than the “Religious services attendancy” variable used in some studies, as in Turkey, most women stay at home to pray rather than praying at mosque. Originally, respondents choose one of the three categories of answers to the following question: “Independantly of whether you go to ‘church’ or not, would you say you are: 1. A religious person; 2. Not a religious person; 3. A convinced atheist”. Since the number of atheists is very few, this variable is recoded in two dummies: 1. Religious; 0. Not religious or atheist. The reference category here is “Not religious or atheist”.

Sex variable (SEX) takes the values:”1 = Male; 2 = Female” . “Male” is the reference category.

We have coded the age variable in six categories (AGE6CATEGORIES): 1 = 18–30, 2 = 31–40, 3 = 41–50, 4 = 51–60, 5 = 61–70 and 6 = 71–86. The first category is the reference.

Highest educational level attained (EDUCATION) is recoded in four categories. Originally, it was measured on a scale from one to nine where: “1. No formal education” and “9. University-level education with degree”. EDUCATION variable is recoded as follows: 1 = No education (original categories 1 and 2); 2 = Lower education (original categories 3 and 4), 3 = Middle education (original categories 5, 6 and 7), 4 = Upper education (original categories 8 and 9). The fourth category is the base.

Employment status (EMPLOYMENT) variable has eight categories and is used as a proxy for risk aversion. Self-employed workers are supposed to be less risk-averse than average (Alesina and La Ferrara 2005; Guillaud 2013). Public employees, who are supposed to be more risk averse than average are included in the more general "Full time" category. The eight categories are: "1. Full time; 2. Part time; 3. Self employed; 4. Retired; 5. Housewife; 6. Students; 7. Unemployed; 8. Other". The first category is the reference.

Active Labor Union Membership (UNION) is recoded in two categories: "1. Active union members; 2. Inactive union members and non-members". The second category is the base.

Subjective social class (SOCIALCLASS) is recoded into four groups: "1. Upper class; 2. Middle class (includes upper middle and lower middle classes); 3. Working class; 4. Lower class". The reference category is "Working class".

Region where the interview was conducted (REGION) is indicated by one of the 12 NUTS-1 regions in Turkey: "1. Istanbul; 2. Western Marmara; 3. Aegean; 4. Eastern Marmara; 5. Western Anatolia; 6. Mediterranean; 7. Central Anatolia; 8. Western Black Sea; 9. Eastern Black Sea; 10. North Eastern Anatolia; 11. East Central Anatolia 12. South Eastern Anatolia". "Istanbul" is the reference.

Household income scale (INCOMESCALE) is measured originally with a 10-steps scale where: "1 = Lower step" and "10 = Tenth step". This variable is recoded into three steps where the first two steps are assigned the value 1, steps 3–8 are assigned the value 2, and the last two steps are assigned the value 3. The reference category is the second (middle) step.

4 Results

In Table 3, results are displayed as odds ratios. "It is the ratio, given a one-unit increase in the independent variable, of the odds of being in a higher rather than a lower category. Odds ratios are exponentiated coefficients, and have the following interpretation:

odds (if the corresponding variable is incremented by 1)/odds (if variable not incremented) and the odds of an event is: $o = p/(1-p)$ where p is the probability of an event." (Stata Technical Bulletin 2000, p. 24).

For each categorical variable, odds ratios are interpreted relative to the reference category. When the odds ratio is greater than 1, the odds of the outcome increases as the predictor increases, when the odds ratio is less than 1, the odds of the outcome decreases as the predictor increases, and if the odds ratio is equal to 1, the odds of the outcome would not change when the predictor changes.

Coefficients giving odds ratios are non-significant for any of the years for MARITAL, RELIGIOUS, UNION and EDUCATION variables.

Results obtained for satisfaction with the financial situation of the household (FINANCIAL) indicate significant coefficients for the first category and are very similar in both years. The first category "dissatisfied" support income equality and redistribution: in 2007, the odds increase by 87 % relative to the reference category "neutral", and by 85 % in 2011.

Table 3 Logit estimation results reporting odds ratios

	2007	2011
Dep. var.: ıncomeequalıty	Odds ratio (std. error)	Odds ratio (std. error)
MARITAL		
Married	0.778 (0.163)	0.893 (0.153)
Ref. Categ.: 0 = "Not married"		
FINANCIAL		
1	1.869** (0.524)	1.853* (0.613)
Ref. Categ.: 2="Relat. Neutral"		
3	1.119 (0.285)	0.895 (0.193)
POLITICAL		
1	2.233*** (0.530)	2.973*** (0.673)
Ref. Categ.: 2="Moderate views"		
3	1.039 (0.204)	1.521** (0.267)
HWORK		
1 = "Brings success"	3.275*** (0.554)	3.806*** (0.571)
Ref. Categ.: 2="Relat. Neutral"		
3 = "Does not bring success"	1.536* (0.380)	2.015*** (0.492)
RELIGIOUS		
Religious	1.076 (0.233)	1.011 (0.201)
Ref. Categ.: 0 = "Not relig./atheist"		
SEX		
Female	0 .901 (0.221)	1.482** (0.282)
Ref. Categ.: 1 = "Male"		
AGE6CATEGORIES		
Ref. Categ.: 1 = "18–30"		
31–40	1.092 (0.250)	0.669** (0.133)
41–50	1.223 (0.290)	0.897 (0.199)
51–60	1.333 (0.442)	0.735 (0.216)
61–70	1.283 (0.601)	0.920 (0.320)
71–86	1.621 (0.895)	0.607 (0.292)
EDUCATIONAL		
1	0.598 (0.237)	0.586 (0.197)
2	0.683 (0.206)	0.805 (0.190)
3	0.849 (0.234)	0.852 (0.161)
Ref. Categ.: "4 = Upper education"		
EMPLOYMENT		
Ref. Categ.: 1="Full time employed"		
2	0 .626 (0.329)	0.942 (0.299)
3 = "Self employed"	1.155 (0.312	2.312*** (0.591)
4	1.001 (0.351)	1.309 (0.397)
5	1.229 (0.383)	0.963 (0.241)
6	0.764 (0.250)	0.679 (0.203)
7	0.686 (0.253)	1.021 (0.341)

(continued)

Table 3 (continued)

	2007	2011
Dep. var.: ıncomeequalıty	Odds ratio (std. error)	Odds ratio (std. error)
8	0 .476 (0.276)	1.541 (1.269)
UNION		
Active	1.998 (1.299)	0.862 (0.391)
Ref. Categ.: 0 = "Inactive/non member"		
SOCIAL CLASS		
1 = "Upper class"	0.827 (0.510)	0.577 (0.325)
2	1.163 (0.212)	0.650*** (0.104)
Ref. Cat.: 3 = "Working class"		
4	0.752 (0.280)	1.988* (0.802)
REGION		
Ref. Categ.: "1 = Istanbul"		
Western Marmara	0.804 (0.351)	0.276*** (0.110)
Aegean	0.317*** (0.110)	0.536** (0.141)
Eastern Marmara	0 .532* (0.181)	0.851 (0.251)
Western Anatolia	0.966 (0.277)	1.392 (0.343)
Mediterranean	1.312 (0.353)	0.710 (0.196)
Central Anatolia	0.379*** (0.142)	2.320*** (0.659)
Western Black Sea	0.339*** (0.147)	0.934 (0.317)
Eastern Black Sea	0.919 (0.369)	0.904 (0.309)
North Eastern Anatolia	0.133*** (0.087)	0.964 (0.438)
East Central Anatolia	1.643 (0.565)	2.840*** (1.206)
South Eastern Anatolia	1.073 (0.317)	1.137 (0.355)
INCOMESCALE		
1	1.060 (0.194)	1.022 (0.360)
Ref. Categ.: 2 = "Middle step"		
3	0.256*** (0.132)	0.923 (0.295)

Note: *, **, *** mean significantly different from zero at the 0.10, 0.05, 0.01 significance level

For the year 2007, only the first category of the POLITICAL variable has a significant coefficient, indicating that left wing voters are 123 % more likely to support income equality than those having moderate views. For 2011, both categories of this variable are significant. Being on the left side of the political scale increases the odds of supporting income equality and redistribution by 197 %, while being on the right also increases the odds by 52 %.

Coefficients for the believers in hard work are highly significant and very similar in both 2007 and 2011 data. The 2007 odds ratio indicates that the belief in hard work for success is associated with a 228 % increase in the odds of opposing inequality and supporting redistribution relative to neutral people, and the odds ratio for the believers in luck and connections indicates also a 54 % increase. The 2011 odds ratios are higher in magnitude indicating a 281 % increase in the odds for the believers in hard work and a 101 % increase for the believers in luck and connections. Given that the evidence for international data implies reversed order of the categories, i.e., a lower coefficient associated with the belief in hard work, Turkish attitudes may be qualified as atypical.

Sex variable's coefficient is non-significant in 2007, but significant in 2011. The odds of supporting redistribution increase by 48 % for women according to the 2011 data.

Only the coefficient for the 31–40 years of age is significant in 2011. Odds ratio decreases by 33 % for the 31–40 years old, but increases again as the age group gets older, remaining nonetheless lower than 100 %. To test our choice of age categories which may seem arbitrary, we have also run additional regressions where age and its squared value are included as numerical variables. Results are again non-significant for any of the years.

Results obtained for EMPLOYMENT indicate non-significant coefficients for 2007, but a highly significant coefficient for the self-employed for 2011, indicating that the odds of supporting redistribution by the self-employed increase by 131 % relative to full time employees. This result implies that self-employment cannot be supposed as a proxy for risk-taking in the case of Turkey.

SOCIALCLASS coefficients are only significant in the 2011 data, for the middle and lower classes. Accordingly, a 35 % drop in the odds by individuals belonging to middle class, but a 99 % increase in the odds by those belonging to lower class relative to working class is indicated.

For household income scale (INCOMESCALE), the highest income step has a highly significant coefficient for 2007 and none of the coefficients is significant for 2011. Hence, for 2007, a drop by 74 % in the odds for the highest income categories relative to the middle is indicated.

Turkey's regional development pattern, is characterized by eastern spatial peripherality, and rich provinces are located in the west and south coast (Gezici 2006). On the question of regional inequalities, results of spatial data analysis of regional inequalities based on NUTS-1 regions between 1980 and 2001 reveal that within regional inequalities in rich regions are relatively higher (Gezici 2006). Pearson correlation coefficient between regional gross value added per capita and regional ginis is respectively 0.155 and −0.10 for 2007 and 2011, thus confirms Gezici's results only in 2007. For 2007, significant coefficients relative to the REGION variable indicate all a decrease in the odds. Highly significant coefficients for the Aegean and North Eastern Anatolia regions, show a drop respectively by 68 % and 87 % in the odds relative to Istanbul region. Other significant coefficients belong to Eastern Marmara, Central Anatolia and Western Black Sea regions, and show a drop respectively by 47 %, 62 % and 66 %. For 2011, result is similar—in fact nearly identical—only in the case of the Aegean region with a drop by 66 % in the odds. The odds also decrease for Western Marmara region by 72 %. Unlike 2007, the odds increase for Central Anatolia by 132 %. The odds also increase by 184 % for East Central Anatolia region.

To detect the possibility of relationship between preferences for redistribution and regional income, we have replaced regional dummies by regional gross value added per capita. The odds ratio obtained is almost equal to 1 (0.999) and significant at 5 % level, indicating no impact of regional income levels on individual preferences.

The relationship between preferences for redistribution and regional income distribution is also detected by replacing regional dummies by regional gini coefficients. In this case, the odds ratio obtained is 56.03 but non-significant ($p = 0.145$).

5 Conclusion

Assuming that respondents are sincere revealers of their preferences, for Turkey, the most relevant factors for opposing inequality and supporting redistribution in both 2007 and 2011 surveys are the belief in hard work for success, being on the left side of the political scale and being dissatisfied with the financial situation of the household. The evidence that the belief in hard work for success is associated with an increased odds of supporting redistribution is atypical, and this result is combined with the positive and less strong association between the belief in luck and connections for success and increased support of redistribution. Also, with a lower magnitude than the left-wing voters' case, being on the right side of the political scale also increases the odds of supporting redistribution in 2011.

Results relative to sex, self-employment, and subjective social class are non-significant for 2007, but significant for 2011. Accordingly, being woman, being self-employed, and feeling to belong to lower class are associated with increased opposition to inequality and support for redistribution. The 2011 coefficient for the self-employed is highly significant indicating that the odds of supporting redistribution by the self-employed increase relative to full time employees. This result may be due, at least partly, to the effect of the global economic crisis felt mostly in 2009 and implies that self-employment cannot be supposed as a proxy for risk-taking in the case of Turkey. Social class coefficients indicate a decrease in the odds by individuals belonging to middle class, but an increase in the odds by those belonging to lower class relative to working class.

For 2007, being in the highest income category relative to the middle is associated with a decreased opposition to inequality and support for redistribution.

As for the impact of living in a specific region, the odds of supporting redistribution decrease in the Aegean region in both surveys. Besides the Aegean region, for 2007, all other significant coefficients indicate a decrease in the odds for the following regions: North Eastern Anatolia, Eastern Marmara, Central Anatolia and Western Black Sea regions. Unlike 2007, the odds increase for Central Anatolia in 2011. The odds also increase for East Central Anatolia region, but decrease for Western Marmara region in 2011.

Acknowledgements This research was financially supported by the Galatasaray University Scientific Research Projects Fund under the Project code 14.103.001.

References

Alesina, A., & Angeletos, G. M. (2005). Fairness and redistribution. *The American Economic Review, 95*(4), 960–980.
Alesina, A., Di Tella, R., & MacCulloch, R. (2004). Inequality and happiness: Are Europeans and Americans different? *Journal of Public Economics, 88*, 2009–2042.
Alesina, A., & Giuliano, P. (2009). *Preferences for redistribution* (NBER Working Paper 14825), [online] Available at http://www.nber.org/papers/w14825. Accessed 20 Sep 2012.
Alesina, A., & La Ferrara, E. (2005). Preferences for redistribution in the land of opportunities. *Journal of Public Economics, 89*, 897–931.
Bénabou, R., & Ok, E. (2001). Social mobility and the demand for redistribution: The POUM hypothesis. *Quarterly Journal of Economics, 116*, 447–487.
Cojocaru, A. (2011). *Inequality and well being in transition economies: A non-experimental test of inequality aversion* (Working Papers 238). ECINEQ, Society for the Study of Economic Inequality.
Corneo, G., & Grüner, H. P. (2002). Individual preferences for political redistribution. *Journal of Public Economics, 83*(1), 83–107.
Fehr, E., Naef, M., & Schmidt, K. M. (2006). Inequality aversion, efficiency, and maximin preferences in simple distribution experiments: Comment. *The American Economic Review, 96*(5), 1912–1917.
Fehr, E., & Schmidt, K. M. (1999). A theory of fairness, competition, and cooperation. *Quarterly Journal of Economics, 114*(3), 817–868.
Ferreira, F. H. G., Gignoux, J., & Aran, M. (2010). Inequality of economic opportunity in Turkey: An assessment using asset indicators and women's background variables. *State Planning Organization of the Republic of Turkey and World Bank Welfare and Social Policy Analytical Work Program Working Paper No. 3.*
Ferrer-i-Carbonell, A., & Ramos, X. (2010). *Inequality aversion and risk attitudes* (IZA Discussion Paper no. 4703).
Fong, C. (2001). Social preferences, self-interest and the demand for redistribution. *Journal of Public Economics, 82*, 225–246.
Gaeta, G. L. (2012). In the mood for redistribution. An empirical analysis of individual preferences for redistribution in Italy. *Economics Bulletin, 32*(3), 2383–2398.
Gezici, F. (2006). New regional definition and spatial analysis of regional ınequalities in Turkey related to the regional policies of EU. *Australasian Journal of Regional Studies, 12*(1), 10–32.
Guillaud, E. (2013). Preferences for redistribution: An empirical analysis over 33 countries. *Journal of Economic Inequality, 11*(1), 57–78.
Haggard, S., Kaufman, R. R., & Long, J. D. (2013). Income, occupation, and preferences for redistribution in the developing world. *Studies in Comparative International Development, 48*(2), 113–140.
Institute for Digital Research and Education (idre) UCLA: Statistical Consulting Group. (2012). *Stata data analysis examples, ordered logistic regression*, [online] Available at http://www.ats.ucla.edu/stat/stata/dae/ologit.htm. Acccsscd 20 Dcc 2012.
Kaltenthaler, K., Ceccoli, S., & Gelleny, R. (2008). Attitudes toward eliminating ıncome ınequality in Europe. *European Union Politics, 9*(2), 217–241.
Luttmer, E. F. P., & Singhal, M. (2011). Culture, context, and the taste for redistribution. *American Economic Journal: Economic Policy, 3*(1), 157–79.
Macunovich, D. J. (2011). *A note on ınequality aversion across countries. Using two new measures* (IZA Discussion Paper no. 5734).
Neher, F. (2012). *Preferences for redistribution around the world.* Freie Universitat Berlin School of Business and Economics Discussion Paper, Economics 2012/2.
Piketty, T. (1999). *Attitudes toward ıncome ınequality in France: Do people really disagree?* Seminar notes no. 9918, C.E.P.R.E.M.A.P.

Scheve, K. A., & Stasavage, D. (2006). Religion and preferences for social insurance. *Quarterly Journal of Political Science, 1*(3), 255–286.
Stata Technical Bulletin. (2000). *STB-53*. Texas: Stata Corporation.
Tosuner, M., & Demir, İ. C. (2008). Ege Bölgesi'nin Vergi Ahlak Düzeyi. *Afyon Kocatepe Üniversitesi İİBF Dergisi*, [online] Available at http://www.iibfdergi.aku.edu.tr/pdf/10_2/18.pdf. Accessed 27 Jan 2013.
Verme, P. (2007). Happiness and ınequality aversion worldwide. *Conference Paper*, [online] Available at http://www.isid.ac.in/~planning/ConferenceDec07/Papers/PaoloVerme.pdf. Accessed 5 Nov 2012.
World Bank. (2010). *Report No: 48627-TR*. Washington, DC: World Bank.

Application of Stochastic Cooperative Games in the Analysis of the Interaction of Economic Agents

Pavel V. Konyukhovskiy and Alexandra S. Malova

Abstract This article deals with the development of the theory of stochastic cooperative games. The authors deliberate on the possibilities for the future directions and practical applications of this class of games. The principal feature of the proposed approach to the study of stochastic cooperative games is that it is based on the definition of the imputation as a vector, providing the conditions of individual and group rationality with (given) probability α. It differs from previous approaches that consider the imputation in stochastic cooperative games as fixed proportions, according to which the full utility of the coalition, which as a random variable, is distributed among its members. The approach, proposed by the authors of this article, introduces the concept of α to the core of the game (core with probability α), and a number of problems that can be formulated with respect to the properties of this object.

Keywords Stochastic cooperative games • Imputation • Alfa-core • Economic agents interaction

1 Introduction

In today's economy studies of regularities of formation and subsequent behavior of the coalition of economic entity associations are becoming more and more important. At the same time, despite the extremely wide range of forms and extent of those associations, they have a number of similarities and fundamental characteristics. Multiple studies show the co-operative regularities and parameter coalition behavior of enterprises, companies, and other economic actors undoubtedly relevant in both theoretical and applied aspects.

Typical examples of cooperative behavior—commonly known as investors' cooperation—are a series of goals to implement large investment projects, or associations under a public-private partnership (PPP). Note that this organizational structure is becoming an increasingly popular and effective tool for solving

P.V. Konyukhovskiy (✉) • A.S. Malova
Faculty of Economics, St-Petersburg State University, St Petersburg, Russia
e-mail: p.konyukhovskiy@spbu.ru; a.malova@spbu.ru

© Springer International Publishing Switzerland 2016

M.H. Bilgin et al. (eds.), *Business Challenges in the Changing Economic Landscape - Vol. 1*, Eurasian Studies in Business and Economics 2/1,
DOI 10.1007/978-3-319-22596-8_25

complex infrastructure tasks. On the one hand, the partnership helps demonstrate the responsibility of the state, and on the other, the business objectives of private firms and companies.

The main problem jointly faced by the public and private sectors, is the problem of the distribution of wealth between the parties. The distribution largely dictates the choice of instruments, which must be of an adequately multifaceted nature for complex objects like PPP. In this regard, very fruitful and attractive approaches are based on the theoretical methodology of cooperative games. This quantifies are presentation of potential partnerships in the form of classical cooperative games with transferable utility.

A game theoretic model of the PPP can be divided into two categories:

- models in which the state acts as one of the players, along with other potential participants in partnership—private companies;
- models in which the state is not an active player, but is regarded as an external force, which may have an impact on the characteristic function of the game.

The solution to the problem of income distribution from the PPP-project tasks or cost sharing between its members can be found in the basics of traditional concepts. For example, in the nucleolus or the kernel of the Shapley value.

In the latter, the ε–core theory can be applied. The ε–core for games with transferable utility is defined as:

$$C_{\varepsilon}(v) = \left\{\mathbf{x} \in R^m \middle| x(I) = v(I);\;\; (\forall S \subset I,\;\; S \neq \not\subset\,,\;\; S \neq I)\;\; x(S) \geq v(S) - \varepsilon\right\}.$$

The variable ε is generally interpreted as some spending on the coalition education ($\varepsilon > 0$) or as a bonus in the amount $(-\varepsilon)$ of the resulting coalition by the fact of its occurrence (at $\varepsilon < 0$). The modeling of the relationship of PPP $(-\varepsilon)$ can be used to estimate the stimulating effect of the state. The weak side of these models greatly complicates their practical application as the assumption that the value ε is the same for all coalitions $S \subset I$.

At the same time, one of the key problems encountered in the implementation of game-theoretic approaches in modeling PPP becomes the problem of constructing the characteristic features of the game. In particular, the possibility of describing the potential winnings of potential coalitions of alleged members of PPP projects using deterministic values is highly controversial. While a hypothesis about their random nature may be much more realistic and attractive, we lose the ability to directly use the tools of classical cooperative games. One possible way of overcoming this problem becomes a stochastic adaptation to the instruments of cooperative games.

2 Literature Review

The term stochastic cooperative games has a long history in professional game-theoretic literature. However, it should be emphasized that various authors define it differently.

Two of the first papers devoted to stochastic cooperative games were Charnes and Granot (1973, 1977). They introduced the hypothesis that the values of the characteristic function of a cooperative game are random variables, and proposed a two-step procedure for constructing the imputation of the income distribution of a full coalition. To begin with, the so-called fair payoffs are formed. Typically, these distributions are interpreted as market expectations of players. In the second stage occurs a posteriori adjustment of promised values of imputation in accordance with the factual imputation of the realized value of payoff. The focuses of these papers are devoted to the tasks of correcting the imputations in the second stage.

Another essential step in the development of the theory of stochastic cooperative games is based on a series of publications in the late 1990s, by Jeroen Suijs (Suijs and Borm 1999; Suijs 1999a; Suijs et al. 1995, 1998, 1999). The main difference between Suijs and Charnes and Granot was the introduction of assumptions about how to set preferences in relation to stochastic payoffs for all players; as well as an extended version of the game model which provides a choice of different options for coalitions.

A problem arising from both Suijs and Charnes and Granot was the construction of analogues for the superadditivity and convexity concepts for stochastic games. Problems also arose in regards to its core and the definition of the conditions of its existence. The authors introduced the concept of certainty equivalents for stochastic games and formulated statements regarding the relationship of superadditivity, convexity, and non-emptiness in the core of the original game and the game-deterministic analog. The dissemination of the concept of nucleolus to stochastic cooperative games has been developed in the later works of Suijs' (1999a, b).

In some papers (Suijs et al. 1998) practical aspects of stochastic cooperative games were considered and stochastic cooperative games were applied to problems of insurance and reinsurance. As an example, the later works of Jeroen Suijs and his coauthors (Zuofeng et al. 2008) are devoted to the spread of the classical concept of the Shapley value to stochastic cooperative games.

Another relatively independent and intensively developing feature of game-theoretic studies is the concept of differential games with stochastic parameters. This aspect of stochastic cooperative games has been explored by Yeung, Petrosyan and Zenkevich (Yeung and Petrosyan 2004, 2006; Zenkevich and Kolabutin 2007). This theory is best described as the development of the theory of differential games with their integration into their stochastic parameters. Mathematical models of these specific types of practical applications, such as the formalization of the dynamic process management of joint ventures, where the results of this joint venture are subject to further distribution between independent economic entities.

The technology change in this joint venture operation is described by the Ito differential equation.

A common feature of the Yeung, Petrosyan, and Zenkevich studies (Yeung and Petrosyan 2004, 2006; Zenkevich and Kolabutin 2007) are that they determine the imputation and concepts of stochastic games, and show how they are guided by the values of the expectations of utilities or the values of characteristic function. With this approach, the parameters which were originally declared random at a very early stage of the analysis are replaced by their nonrandom substitutes. This undoubtedly distorts the objective stochastic nature of the simulated situation. In this paper, we will develop an alternative concept, suggesting directly binding definitions and sharing solutions to probabilistic characteristics of the random parameters of the game, not to their expectations.

3 Stochastic Cooperative Games with Random Parameters

The baseline definition and parameters of a *stochastic cooperative game* (SCG) is a pair of sets $\Gamma = (I, \ \widetilde{v})$ where

- $I = \{1..m\}$—set of participants
- $\widetilde{v}(S)$—random variables with known density functions $p_{\widetilde{v}(i)}(x)$, which are interpreted as income (utility, payoffs), and are received by the corresponding coalitions $S \subset I$.

Consider in more detail issues relating to the approach to defining of imputation in stochastic cooperative games. In usual non-stochastic games (I, v) the imputation refers to vector $\mathbf{x} \in R^n$, where $m = |I|$ satisfies the following conditions:

(a) individual rationality

$$(\forall \ i \in I) \ \ x_i \geq v_i, \tag{1}$$

(b) group rationality

$$\sum_{i=1}^{m} x_i = v(I). \tag{2}$$

One possible approach to the definition of the imputation concepts in stochastic cooperative games is built on the principle that fulfillment of the analogues of conditions (1) and (2) with the probability α (Zuofeng et al. 2008). Later in the stochastic cooperative game, imputation is a vector $\mathbf{x}(\alpha) \in R^n$ satisfying:

(a)

$$(\forall i \in I) \quad \mathbf{P}\{x_i(\alpha) \geq \widetilde{v}(i)\} \geq \alpha \tag{3}$$

—stochastic analog of individual rationality (1),

(b)

$$\mathbf{P}\left\{\sum_{i=1}^{m} x_i(\alpha) \leq \widetilde{v}(I)\right\} \geq \alpha \tag{4}$$

—stochastic analog of group rationality (2).

Note that condition (3) essentially means that the imputation $\mathbf{x}(\alpha)$ ascribed to the i-player, with a probability not less than α, should be greater than the value of the random variable of the player's individual win. In (3), the ith value and the imputation vector $\mathbf{x}(\alpha)$ is compared with the α-quintile of $F_{\tilde{v}\,(i)}(x)$—the distribution function of the random variable $\widetilde{v}(i)$. For further compactness, we introduce the following notation

$$v_\alpha(i) = F^{-1}_{\tilde{v}\,(i)}(\alpha) \tag{5}$$

for the particular i-player and

$$v_\alpha(S) = F^{-1}_{\tilde{v}\,(s)}(\alpha) \tag{6}$$

for the particular coalition $S \subset I$. Then condition (3) can be rewritten as

$$(\forall i \in I) \quad x_i(\alpha) \geq v_\alpha(i). \tag{7}$$

The transformation of condition (3)–(7) can be justified on the basis of the properties of non-decreasing distribution functions. Indeed, the condition $x_i(\alpha) \geq \widetilde{v}(i)$ holds that the probability for level α will be carried out for all $\alpha^{'} > \alpha$.

In classical cooperative games, group rationality condition (2) fills the need for full utility distribution for a large or full coalition within the imputation. A modification of the stochastic game (4) means that the large coalition is able to win with a probability of not less than α to ensure the implementation of the imputation. Note that condition (4) is equivalent to

$$\mathbf{P}\left\{\sum_{i=1}^{m} x_i(\alpha) \geq \widetilde{v}(I)\right\} \leq 1 - \alpha. \tag{8}$$

From (8) we get the result $\sum_{i=1}^{m} x_i(\alpha) \leq v_{1-\alpha}(I)$, if we mark as $v_\alpha(I) = F^{-1}_{\tilde{v}\,(I)}(\alpha)$ the α-quintile of the $F_{\tilde{v}\,(I)}(x)$ distribution function.

These alterations can lead to significant differences within stochastic games. If in the conventional cooperative games group rationality condition is defined as strict equality, and thus defines a hyperplane in m–dimensional space; the approach proposed here takes the form of inequality and defines a half-space in an m–dimensional space. Thus, the nature of $\mathbf{x}$ vectors satisfying the definition of (3) and (4) differs significantly from the nature of imputations in their classical interpretation. Sometimes in order to classify such objects, the term allocation is used.

Separately, we note that the group rationality formulating strict equality provides TU-cooperative games with a set of positive properties that greatly simplifies the process of their analysis as a set in R^m. However, it is impossible not to recognize that the adoption of this assumption significantly changes the properties of the simulated real objects for which the condition less or equal is definitely more appropriate. These theses are a weighty argument in favor of developing our approach to the definition of group rationality.

As a result, the system conditions which determine the imputation in a stochastic game, take the following forms:

(a)

$$(\forall i \in I) \ \ x_i(\alpha) \geq v_\alpha(i), \tag{9}$$

(b)

$$\sum_{i=1}^{m} x_i(\alpha) \leq v_{1-\alpha}(I). \tag{10}$$

The naming of variables $v_\alpha(i)$ in modern risk management has steadily entrenched the term value at risk (VaR); best explained in the articles Jorion (2006a, b). Thus, among the advantages of approaches (9) and (10) to the definition of the concepts of stochastic imputations in cooperative games can be attributed the fact that it connects the values of imputation with the values of the VaR in the random parameters of the game. This potentially opens up opportunities for meaningful interpretation of the subsequent results of studies and the properties of this class of games and the concepts which determine their outcomes.

For example, in the studies that develop the theory of cooperative games according to Sujis interpretation originally introduced the concept of allocation.

Under the distribution of payoff $\widetilde{v}(S)$ of the random coalition S produces the vector $(\mathbf{d}, \mathbf{r}) \in R^{|S|} \times R^{|S|}$, for example

$$\sum_{i \in S} d_i \leq 0; \ \ (\forall i \in S) \sum_{i \in S} r_i = 1, \ \ r_i \geq 0.$$

When the first player wins in accordance with the regulations of the imputation (**d**, **r**) correlates to $d_i + \widetilde{v}(S) \cdot r_i$. Accordingly, the terms of individual rationality (for a coalition S) are formulated as

$$(\forall i \in S) \ \ d_i + \widetilde{v}(S) \cdot r_i \geq \widetilde{v}_i.$$

With this definition, the utility that the imputation promises to i th player is a random variable. It consists of:

- $d_i \leq 0$—a priori determined absolute values;

- $r_i \cdot \widetilde{v}(S)$—regulation component, that is determined as a share of factual coalition utility, the condition $\sum_{i \in S} r_i = 1, r_i \geq 0$ provides the distribution of this amount without a rest.

Value d_i defines the preliminary rules of distribution of expected utility between the players. The coefficient r_i determines the mechanism of a posteriori redistribution (taking into account actually achieved values). In other words, imputation in this approach promises a player a fixed share from an unknown or random result. Or vice versa, definitions (3) and (4) assume the initial announcement of a nonrandom absolute value of utility or payoff, which is received by the player with the specified level of probability.

Important specific feature of stochastic cooperative games has substantial modification superadditivity concepts in them. For conventional or non-stochastic TU-cooperative games, a situation in which the union of the two coalitions S and T leads only to a simple summation of their utilities

$$v(S \cup T) = v(S) + v(T),$$

This appears trivial, and the association looks meaningless. At the same time the stochastic game provides a similar amount

$$\widetilde{v}^{+}(S \cup T) = \widetilde{v}(S) + \widetilde{v}(T)$$

which is also a random variable. So, the general equation balances out as

$$v_{\alpha}^{+}(S \cup T) \neq v_{\alpha}(S) + v_{\alpha}(T).$$

Note the studies of the relationship between patterns of a quintile sum of random variables and sums of quintiles diverge in relation to probability theory, not game theory.

Thus, in stochastic cooperative games even simple intercoalitional agreements on the summation of income (utility) can bring additional effects. In connection with the circumstances in this class of games it makes sense to distinguish between two types of utility coalition of associations:

- the usefulness of combining coalitions S and T into the coalition $S \cup T$ as a new random variable $\widetilde{v}(S \cup T)$ with the distribution function $F_{\widetilde{v}\,(S \cup T)}(x)$ generates a meaningful specificity of simulated situation. Though, we have a similar situation in the case of classical cooperative games, and when the values $v(S)$ and $v(T)$, on the one hand, and $v(S \cup T)$, on the other hand, are considered exogenous;
- the usefulness of the joint coalition $S \cup T$ in the sum of $\widetilde{v}^{+}(S \cup T) = \widetilde{v}(S) + \widetilde{v}(T)$. A situation with a content point of view of interest solely in the context of stochastic cooperative games.

These properties can be used in the construction of solution concepts for stochastic cooperative games. In particular the analysis of rationality or acceptance for imputation in some of the coalitions, we may have to consider not only the occasional payoff $\widetilde{v}\ (S)$ received by coalition S as characterized by VaR $v_\alpha(S) = F^{-1}_{\widetilde{v}\,(S)}(\alpha)$, but the amount of random players in $S \subset I$ utilities

$$\widetilde{v}^{+}_{\alpha}(S) = \sum_{i \in S} \widetilde{v}(i)), \tag{11}$$

that are characterized by VaR $v^{+}_{\alpha}(S) = F^{-1}_{\widetilde{v}^{+}(S)}(\alpha)$.

In this case the conditions of coalition rationality become

$$x(\alpha, S) \geq v_\alpha(S), \ \ x(S) \geq v^{+}_{\alpha}(S), \tag{12}$$

where $x(\alpha, S) = \sum_{i \in S} x_i(\alpha)$. Note that these issues have been considered in more detail by Konyukhovskiy (2012).

Traditionally, the core in the classical cooperative is defined as the set of non-dominated imputations, which is equivalent to the condition

$$(\forall S \subset I, \ \ S \neq \not\subset, \ \ S \neq I) \quad x(S) \geq v(S), \ \ x(I) = v(I). \tag{13}$$

We note that despite the external similarity designation $x(S)$ should be distinguished from $\mathbf{x}(\alpha)$ by content. In the former ($x(S)$) the amount prescribed by the imputation to the coalition S, i.e., scalar quantity, while in the later ($\mathbf{x}(\alpha)$) the stochastic vector corresponds to a certain level of probability α.

In developing the proposed approach, we can similarly introduce the concept of α–core,[1] and define it as the set of imputations. For Example, vectors $(I, \widetilde{v})$ satisfy (9) and (10), which supports the following statements

$$(\forall S \subset I, \ \ S \neq \not\subset, \ \ S \neq I) \quad x(\alpha, S) \geq v_\alpha(S) \tag{14}$$

or

$$C_\alpha(\widetilde{v}) = \left\{ \mathbf{x} \in R^m \middle| \ \ \forall S \subset I, \ \ S \neq \not\subset, \ \ S \neq I: \ \ \begin{array}{l} x(\alpha, S) \geq v_\alpha(S); \\ x(\alpha, I) \leq v_{1-\alpha}(I) \end{array} \right\}. \tag{15}$$

In other words, the division that belongs to α–core prescribes to any coalition a share not less than the VaR utility of this coalition for a given level α. In this division, imputation reach is provided by the conditions in accordance with the share prescribed by imputation for a great coalition, as long as it does not exceed VaR and its utility.

[1] The core of the game $(I, \widetilde{v})$ for probability level α.

Due to the fact that the distribution functions of random variables $F_{\tilde{v}(S)}(x)$ are incremental, an increase in α implies an increase in value $v_{\alpha}(S)$, or a decrease in value $v_{1-\alpha}(I)$, by which we obtain

$$\alpha^{'} < \alpha^{''} \Rightarrow C_{\alpha'}(\widetilde{v}) \subset C_{\alpha''}(v), \tag{16}$$

indicating, payment for implementation, when α–core is more likely to decrease its size.

Moreover, there may be situations in which a sufficiently large $\alpha\alpha$–core is empty. Based on property (16) we can identify the problem of *selecting the highest probability level in which there is a non-empty α–core.*

Another natural problem posed by property (16) is determining the dependence of the size α–core based on the choice of α. This in turn gives rise to the problem of choosing a measure of volume. Objective complexity of its solutions are defined in such a way that a change in α can cause a change the dimension of the α–core.

One possible—and promising—solution to these problems is the spread of the concepts of coalition excesses in stochastic cooperative games.

Recall that for non-stochastic cooperative games the excess of the coalition is defined as

$$e(S, \mathbf{x}) = v(S) - x(S). \tag{17}$$

In terms of content, value (17) reflects the degree of dissatisfaction with the coalition S of the shares, which it is provided by the imputation $\mathbf{x}$.

By analogy, the excess of coalition S in a stochastic cooperative game to determine the level of probability α can be defined as

$$e(S, \mathbf{x}, \alpha) = v_{\alpha}(S) - x(S). \tag{18}$$

Accordingly, a characteristic of α–cores obtained at different levels of the probability α may use the following value

$$\varepsilon_0(\widetilde{v}) = \max_{S \neq I, \varnothing} \{e(S, \mathbf{x}(\alpha), \alpha)\}, \ \ \mathbf{x}(\alpha) \in C_{\alpha} \tag{19}$$

ormaximal dissatisfaction with the imputation. α–core forms the various coalitions defined as $S \neq \not\subset, I$. Of course, (19) is only a singular example in a very broad set of measures that can be designed based on the notion of the excess.

More detail is required when analyzing a number of specific aspects of the transition from the classical procedure of cooperative games with transferable utility to their stochastic counterparts. In essence, we must resolve the issue of technology transition from deterministic $v(S)$ to stochastic $\widetilde{v}(S)$ utilities. Consider a relatively simple but realistic situation, in which $\widetilde{v}(S)$ can be considered as random variables distributed according to the normal law

$$\tilde{v}(S) \in N\left(\overline{v}(S),\ \sigma_S^2\right). \tag{20}$$

Hypothesis (20) is the basic logical development of traditional approaches. As a rule, the process of constructing the characteristic functions for specific applications of cooperative game-theoretic models provides a way to replace indicators which objectively have a random nature to their deterministic counterparts. It's a different method for averaging operations, in which the $v(S)$ latently is identified with $\overline{v}(S)$. In this case, we abandon this simplification and do not lose additional characteristics of random variables with the variation σ_S^2. Also note that the structures of models that are based on hypothesis (20) have serious structural advantages. It allows visual comparison of the results of their analysis with the results obtained in the framework of deterministic model counterparts.

Of course, the hypothesis relating to the distribution of the value $\tilde{v}(S)$ for normal law is inherently arguable. Moreover, its defense is only possible in cases where the provision is a concrete specification of the simulated object. However, at that level of generality, in which we present the problems of stochastic cooperative games, we can resort to general considerations concerning the merits of the normal distribution as a typical representative of a universal and continuous distributions.

By assuming $\tilde{v}(S) \in N\left(\overline{v}(S),\ \sigma_S^2\right)$, the following VaR equation is possible

$$v_\alpha(S) = \overline{v}(S) + \sigma_s \cdot \Phi^{-1}(\alpha) \tag{21}$$

where $\Phi(x) = \frac{1}{2\pi} \cdot \int\limits_{-\infty}^{x} e^{-\frac{t^2}{2}} dt$—also known as the Laplace integral.

If we take into account $\sigma_s > 0$ and $\Phi^{-1}(\alpha) > 0$ with $\alpha > 0.5$, we calculate

$$v_\alpha(S) > \overline{v}(S)$$

for all probability levels where $\alpha > 0.5$. Further, comparing condition (13), which must be completed by imputations belonging to core in non-stochastic games, with condition (14), we determine that they belong to α–core in stochastic game. Therefore, we conclude that

$$x(S, \alpha) > x(S).$$

where $x(S, \alpha) = \sum_{i \in S} x_i(\alpha)$ is the amount, distributed between members of coalition S by the imputation $\mathbf{x}(\alpha)$, $x(S) = \sum_{i \in S} \overline{v}_i$.

The problem of determining the maximum level of probability α, on which there exists a non-empty α–core for stochastic games based on the premise that (20) takes the form of

$$\Phi^{-1}(\alpha) \to \max, \quad \text{where} \tag{22}$$

$$C_\alpha(\overline{v}) = \left\{\mathbf{x} \in R^m \middle| \ \forall S \subset I,\ S \neq \not\subset,\ S \neq I: \ \sum_{i \in S} x_i \geq \overline{v}(S) + \sigma_s \cdot \Phi^{-1}(\alpha); \right.$$
$$\left. \sum_{i \in I} x_i \leq \overline{v}(I) - \sigma_I \cdot \Phi^{-1}(\alpha) \right\} \neq \varnothing. \tag{23}$$

Let's illustrate the properties described above with a concrete example. Table 1 contains a description of four cooperative games $(m = 3)$ including one basic non-stochastic and three stochastic games. The values of the characteristic functions in the stochastic games are random variables distributed according to the normal law (see (20)), where $\overline{v}(S)$ coincides with the corresponding values of the characteristic function of the basic non-stochastic game. Differences in the parameters σ_S^2 from a content point of view reflect differences in the degree of risk entailed in obtaining the possible outcome (utility) for different players and coalitions.

Table 1 also demonstrates the problems of (22) and (23), as seen in rows x_1^*, x_2^*, x_3^*,[2] $\Phi^{-1}(\alpha^*)$ and α^*. In particular, in game III it is easy to notice that player 3 has a higher degree of risk $(\sigma_3 = 0.5 > 0.3 = \sigma_1 = \sigma_2)$, as compared with players 1 and 2. So the utility of pair coalitions in which player 3 participates are riskier. The consequence of this is the increase in player's 3 share in the imputation, solving problems caused in (22) and (23).

Table 1 Example of difference between stochastic and non-stochastic games

Coalition	Basicnon-stochasticgame, $\overline{v}(\{S\})$	Stochasticgame I, $\sigma(\{S\})$	Stochasticgame II, $\sigma(\{S\})$	Stochasticgame II, $\sigma(\{S\})$
$\{1\}$	1	0.1	0.3	0.3
$\{2\}$	1	0.1	0.4	0.3
$\{3\}$	1	0.1	0.5	0.5
$\{1,2\}$	3	0.5	0.6	1.1
$\{1,3\}$	3	0.5	0.7	1.2
$\{2,3\}$	3	0.5	0.8	1.4
$\{1,2,3\}$	5	0.3	0.2	0.9
x_1^*	5/3	1.62	1.60	1.58
x_2^*	5/3	1.62	1.64	1.62
x_3^*	5/3	1.62	1.68	1.64
$\Phi^{-1}(\alpha^*)$		0.476	0.400	0.182
α^*		0.683	0.655	0.572

[2] In the column "Basic non-stochastic game" data rows contain values of nucleolus.

4 Conclusion

Stochastic cooperative games—in addition to the concept of solving the basis of the stochastic α–cores, discussed in the framework of our paper—take into account the risks and uncertainties in the process of modeling and studying the cooperative interaction of economic agents with additional flexibility. This is consistent with a tendency to increase the requirements for adequacy of tools that reflect the random effects of the environment.

In particular, based on the concept of α–cores, we are able to objectively exclude from consideration the stochastic ineffectiveness of a number of options of income distribution between the parties of the coalition including associations of economic entities.

These examples reflect the properties that the stochastic cooperative games have. Taking into account that these properties can significantly affect the adjustment of traditional decision-making mechanisms, as well as in strategic management and organization of ongoing activities of coalitions, alliances, and partnerships of diverse economic actors.

In particular, cooperative stochastic models allow us to take into account the asymmetry of the potential partnership provisions regarding risks and uncertainties. This further enhances the level of accuracy and adequacy of the generated stimulating effects. Including measures aimed at bringing together the joint efforts of both public and private companies, businesses, and corporations in large-scale investment projects requiring significant accumulation of material resources.

References

Charnes, A., & Granot D. (1973, October 18–19). Prior solutions: Extensions of convex nucleolus solutions to chance-constrained games. *Proceedings of the Computer Science and Statistics Seventh Symposium* (pp. 1013–1019). Ames, IA: Iowa State University.

Charnes, A., & Granot, D. (1977). Coalitional and chance-constrained solutions to n-person games, II: Two-stage solutions. *Operation Research, 25*(6), 1013–1019.

Jorion, P. (2006a). *Value at risk.* Boston, MA: McGraw-Hill.

Jorion, P. (2006b). *Value at risk: New benchmark for managing financial Risk* (3rd ed.). New York: McGraw-Hill.

Konyukhovskiy, P. V. (2012). The application of stochastic cooperative games in studies of regularities in the realization investment projects. *VestnikSPbU: Economics, 4*, 134–143.

Suijs, J. P. M. (1999a). *A nucleolus for stochastic operative games. Cooperative decision-making under risk* (pp. 152–181). Boston: Kluwer Academic Publishers.

Suijs, J. P. M. (1999b). *Cooperative decision-making under risk.* Boston: Kluwer Academic Publishers.

Suijs, J., & Borm, P. (1999). Stochastic cooperative games: Superadditivity, convexity, and certainty equivalents. *Games and Economic Behavior, 27*(2), 331–345.

Suijs, J. P. M., Borm, P. E. M., De Waegenaere, A. M. B., & Tijs, S. H. (1995, September). *Cooperative games with stochastic payoffs* (pp. 193–205). Tilburg University Discussion paper. Center of Economic Research No. 1995-88.

Suijs, J. P. M., Borm, P. E. M., De Waegenaere, A. M. B., & Tijs, S. H. (1999). Cooperative games with stochastic payoffs. *European Journal of Operational Research, 113*(1), 193–205.

Suijs, J. P. M., De Waegenaere, A. M. B., & Borm, P. E. M. (1998). Stochastic cooperative games in insurance and reinsurance. *Insurance: Mathematics & Economics, 22*(3), 209–228.

Yeung, D. W. K., & Petrosyan, L. A. (2004). Subgame consistent cooperative solutions in stochastic differential games. *Journal Optimization Theory and Applications, 120*(3), 651–666.

Yeung, D. W. K., & Petrosyan, L. A. (2006). *Cooperative stochastic differential games.* New York: Springer.

Zenkevich, N. A., & Kolabutin, N. V. (2007). Quantitative modeling of dynamic stable joint venture. *In: Preprint Vol. of the 11th IFAC Symposium "Computational Economics and Financial and Industrial Systems"* (pp. 68–74). IFAC, Dogus University, Istanbul, Turkey.

Zuofeng, G., Wei, L., Jiang, N., & Guo, L. (2008). The shapley value for stochastic cooperative game. *Modern Applied Science, 2*(4), 76–80.

The Use of Simulation Modelling in the Analysis of the Economic Aspects of Diseases in Old Age

Petra Maresova, Hana Tomaskova, and Kamil Kuca

Abstract In the coming decades, the size and age-structure of Europe's population will undergo dramatic changes due to low fertility rates and continuous increases in life expectancy. These changes also bring significant impacts on the economies of these countries. The impacts are a shortage of workers, chronic and degenerative diseases, increased government spending on health care and pensions. The more precise idea of the economic impacts countries have, the better they can over time develop strategies to deal with the situation. The aim of this paper is to present a dynamic simulation modelling as a tool to illustrate the economic aspects of population aging. The purpose of the simulation model is to simulate the behavior of the real system. The simulation model mimics when they run the substantial sites of the modelled system. The key to creating a simulation model is to understand the relationships and constraints of the modelled object. In the context of the research the simulation model is used for diseases in old age, particularly dementia. A tool for the simulation model is a software called STELLA, which meets the requirements for this area. The created and proposed model shows a number of benefits that are important for the expression of the economic aspects of diseases in the old age. These benefits are not included in standard statistical methods for predicting future development and other economic analyses used for this purpose.

Keywords Aging population • Simulation • Model • Disease

P. Maresova (✉)
Faculty of Informatics and Management, Department of Economics, University of Hradec Kralove, Hradec Králové, Czech Republic
e-mail: petra.maresova@uhk.cz

H. Tomaskova
Faculty of Informatics and Management, Department of Information Technologies, University of Hradec Kralove, Hradec Králové, Czech Republic
e-mail: hana.tomaskova@uhk.cz

K. Kuca
Faculty of Informatics and Management, Center of Basic and Applied Research, University of Hradec Kralove, Hradec Králové, Czech Republic
e-mail: kamil.kuca@uhk.cz

© Springer International Publishing Switzerland 2016

M.H. Bilgin et al. (eds.), *Business Challenges in the Changing Economic Landscape - Vol. 1*, Eurasian Studies in Business and Economics 2/1,
DOI 10.1007/978-3-319-22596-8_26

1 Introduction

Over the next few decades, countries in the developed world will experience unprecedented growth in the number of people of advanced years. Demographic aging of population is one of the most recent threats to the economy, plus it is a change in the evolution of mankind. The changes in the age-structure not only bring about negative economic impacts but also new opportunities. People have longer, healthier lives, resulting in extended working years, and different capacities and needs. The key is adaptation on all levels: individual, organizational, and societal. Among frequently quoted negative economic impacts belong the following (Jowit 2013; WHO 2012): higher savings for pensions may reduce capital investment, shortage of workers, chronic and degenerative diseases, higher taxes and increased government spending on health care and pensions. Negative impacts are related to the changing size of the labor force, ageing associated diseases and the consequent higher dependence on support and care (Maresova et al. 2014, 2015).

Evidence from the multi-country Global Burden of Disease project and other international epidemiologic research shows that health problems associated with wealthy and aged populations affect a wide and expanding swath of world population. Over the next 10–15 years, people in every region of the world will suffer more death and disability from such non-communicable diseases as heart disease, cancer, and diabetes than from infectious and parasitic diseases (NIH 2011). Expected development of these diseases in 2030 is shown in Fig. 1.

Chronic diseases are the main contributors to the total burden of disease and mortality in the EU. If chronic diseases remain highly prevalent or their burden increases, EU countries will be challenged by reduced country productivity and competitiveness, increased financial pressures on health systems, reduced health and well-being along with threats of poverty and inequity for patients and their families.

Figure 2 shows the evolution of the causes of death in Europe from 2004 to 2010. The figures clearly show that all fields except diseases of the nervous system experienced a decrease. Diseases of the nervous system are often associated with older age, therefore we cannot assume a spontaneous reduction of such deaths in the coming years. This type of disease will mean a heavy burden for economies in future years.

Figure 3 shows the number of deaths per 100,000 inhabitants in 2010 due to diseases of the nervous system. A relatively high number of these deaths occur in Nordic countries and in economies that are considered to be more prosperous within the EU.

Diseases of the nervous system in the aging population represent a serious problem for the future. Forecasts of the future development are already arising at the present time. For this purpose mainly tools and methods of statistical analysis are used. The aim of this paper is to introduce Stella, a dynamic simulation tool for use in the field of diseases associated with the aging population, specifically with diseases of the nervous system (different types of dementia).

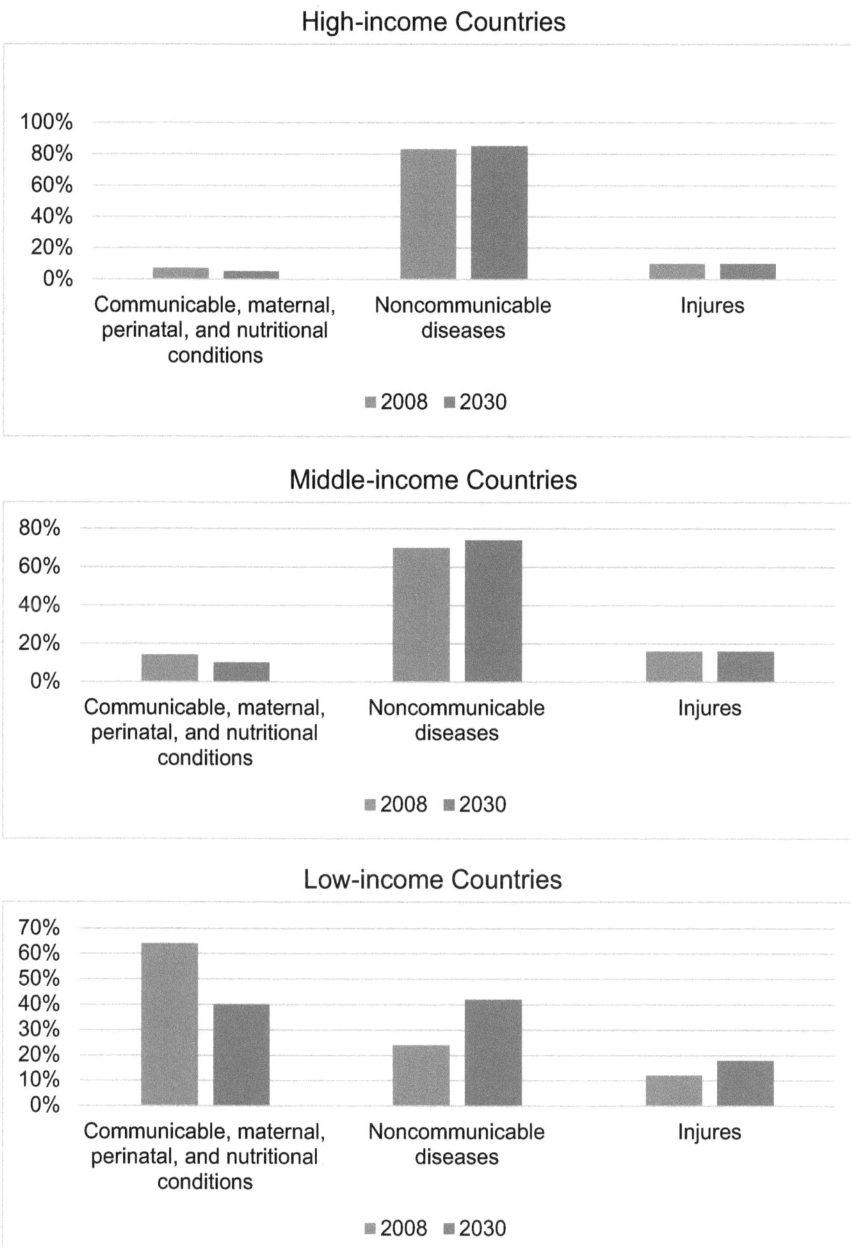

Fig. 1 Chronic disease in 2008 and 2030. *Source*: NIH (2011)

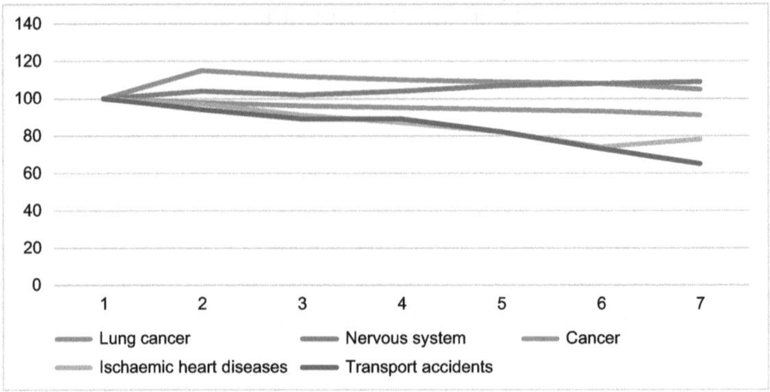

Fig. 2 Death in Europe from 2004 to 2010. *Source*: Eurostat

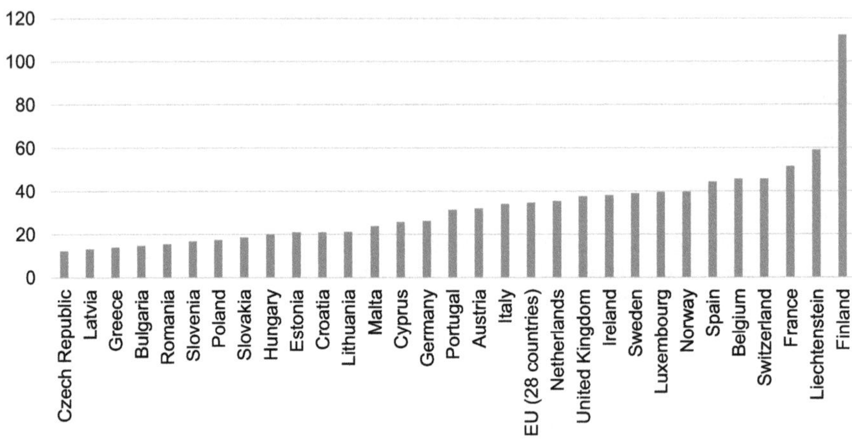

Fig. 3 Number of deaths per 100,000 inhabitants in 2010 due to diseases of the nervous system. *Source*: Eurosat

2 Forecasting Methods

Prediction and forecasting are crucial activities in many areas and serve as a basis for decision-making concerning the future development. Long-term forecasting primarily evaluates what happens in the environment and how it will affect a company (or the whole economy), if their current strategy does not significantly change. Table 1 lists some of the most commonly used forecasting methods.

The most promising methods of forecasting activities include system models. Forecasting system models use both objective as well as subjective methods for expressing future as a structure in which all the sub-elements are interrelated and interacted. A system approach is a way of understanding reality, which does not change the basic methodological forecasting tools. The system approach for forecasting is an effective organizing principle, which contributes to comply the

Table 1 Basic forecasting methods

Statistical methods	Subjective methods	Technological forecasting methods
Analysis of trends and cycles Correlation analysis Mathematical models Structural analysis	Subjective estimate of probability Delphi method Reviews of a seller Comparative method (analogous judgments) Analysis of documents Prescriptive method brainstorming	Morphological research Extrapolation of technology trends

Source: BusinessInfo.cz (2009), He and Bechhoefer (2008), Uckun et al. (2008), Mosallam et al. (2013), Roemer et al. (2013)

forecasts and the actual development. The system models are therefore chosen as a suitable tool for the representation of the potential consequences of an aging population, in relation to the number of patients with diseases of the nervous system, specifically the dementias.

2.1 Simulation Modelling

Modelling or simulation is a frequently used method in professional and scientific practice in many fields of human activity. In practice, the aim is to understand the observed phenomena, to mimic the behavior of the examined system. The application area includes modelling of natural systems or human systems in order to gain insight into their functioning (Guloglu and Tekin 2012). Other contexts include technology simulation for performance optimization, safety engineering, testing, training and education. Modelling is used not only for solving practice problems, but it is also intended for the implementation of various researches and experiments or for the simulations of societal phenomena (Dlouhy et al. 2005; Kvasnicka and Pospíchal 2005; Powell et al. 2006).

The basic concept in the context of simulation modelling is the system, which is the object of the modelling. Compositional definition states that the system is a complex of elements along with the relationships between them and their attributes (Bures 2011; Pokorny 1996). The structure of the system consists of elements and links. It is therefore a way that inputs and outputs of system elements are connected (Bures 2011; Pokorny 1996). By displaying the structure we can obtain, for example, fast orientation on the structure of the reference system, we can create the conditions for defining sub-systems, identify and locate major irregularities in the structure of the system and finally use economic-mathematical methods and computer technology for analysis of the system structure.

The structure and behavior of the system create an integral part and the relationship between them is determined as follows. Certain system structure corresponds to a particular system behavior, but that behavior of the system is identical with a class of the structures, which is defined by the behavior (Bury 2007). A model is a representation of an object or system, conceived from a certain angle. Modelling is the process of creating models, in which during the conventional approaches the mathematical–physical analysis and experiments are used. The model is defined as the appearance of the existing pages of the real system. Identification is a process of identifying the model with the object (Pokorny 1996).

With the development of information technologies in recent years, their use is automatically assumed also in this area. Computer models allow to move the scope and accuracy of mental models. The following points were described in (Sterman 1991). Computer models are explicit and easy to understand. Their assumptions are described in the documentation and enables simple control by others. Reliably calculate the logical consequences of assumptions of models. They are complex and can connect many aspects at once.

The use of simulation models for the experiments brings many benefits (AnyLogic 2014; Gallerani and Sanchez 2012). We can mention, for example, return on investment thanks to the reusability of, the accuracy or the possibility to simulate without the use of real resources. The time aspect, when it is possible to hasten the processes, or to predict the future. Appropriately used simulation containing causality and mutual relations can be used for the control of the company's development, the search for solutions to problems or proposals for improvements and new approaches in the company. A simulation model based on the description of the relations and elements in the system may not contain such a high level of abstraction such as mathematical modeling and optimization, but we can also use the qualitative relations. This allows us to move closer to the simulation more realistic, tested a wide range of experiments and predictions, without receiving any real resources and the consequences.

3 Application of System Dynamics Using Stella Software in Disease Problems in Old Age

The simulation model in STELLA software allows to capture the structure of the system and simulates its evolution in time. The basic elements used in Stella software include:

- Stock—rectangle shape = tank = "stock" it is a modelling element, where the modelled units accumulate until the condition determining the outflow is followed. In other words, until the subsequent outflow opens.
- Conveyor—striped rectangle shape. Special kind of Stock element, which can hold units for a certain, predetermined time. An example could include the incubation period. If we know that a disease takes hold after 3 years, then we can use a conveyor element with a time limit of 3 years.
- Flow (inflow, outflow, bi-flow)—double arrow shape with a cap. It is an element constituting entrant, effluent or bi-directional flow of the units.
- Converter—Circle—The element contains a degree or coefficient.

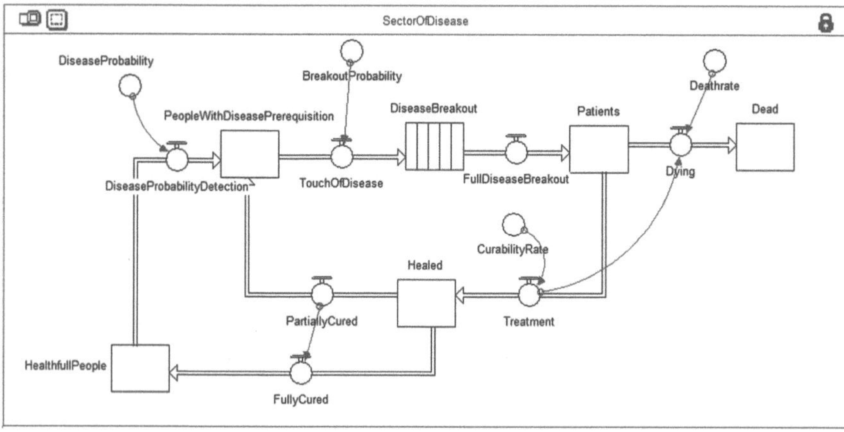

Fig. 4 Population with disease of the nervous system

Figure 4 shows the general level of possible links to characterize a population with disease of the nervous system.

Links in the picture can be described in the following way: there is the basic population of healthy people Stock—“HealtfullPeople”, the probability of disease determines how many people will be transmitted from Stock “HealtfullPeople” into Stock “PeopleWithDiseasePrerequisition”, based on “BreakoutProbability” there will be a manifestation of the disease, and such individuals are then separated in the Conveyor “DiseaseBreakout” for the determined time interval until their disease fully begins. Subsequently they are moved to Stock “Patients”. From the Stock “Patients” units can drain based on Converter “CurabilityRate” to Stock “Healed” or on the basis of Converter “DeathRate” people die of disease and human units move to Stock “Dead”. From Stock “Healed” the units can drain based on the treatment success either to outflow “PartiallyCured” into Stock “PeopleWithDiseasePrerequisition” or outflow “FullyCured” to “HealtfullPeople”.

4 Conclusion

Demographic aging of the population currently affects most developed countries. The issue of the impacts of the demographic aging of the population was opened in the middle of the last century and has become increasingly topical. There are National programs to promote positive aging of population and a variety of measures in the form of pension reforms and various researches.

The central issue are the spheres in this context, which will be really poignant in the context of population aging. They include the estimated increase of persons with diseases of the nervous system. This trend could be seen in the recent years.

The second important issue is the impact analysis of such phenomena. The aim of this paper was therefore to present Stella, a dynamic simulation tool for use in the area of diseases associated with aging of population, specifically with diseases of the nervous system (different types of dementias). The paper presented the initial model created in a Stella system, which could be the basis for forecasting and the subsequent impact analysis of the increasing number of patients with diseases of the nervous system. The model will be tested first on data available for the Czech Republic, then if necessary, it will be adjusted and used in the wider context.

Acknowledgments This paper was supported by the research project SPEV—Economic and Managerial Aspects of Processes in Biomedicine, University of Hradec Kralove, Faculty of Informatics and Management, 2014.

References

AnyLogic. (2014). *Use of simulation modeling. Multimethod simulation software,* [online] Available at http://www.anylogic.com/use-of-simulation. Accessed 22 July 2014.

Bures, V. (2011). *Systémové myšlení pro manažery* [Systems thinking for managers]. Praha: Professional Publishing.

Bury, A. (2007). *Teorie systému a řízení* [Theory and system management]. Ostrava: Vysoká škola bánská, Technická univerzita.

BusinessInfo.cz. (2009). *Predikce vývoje prostředí a proces strategické analýzy* [Prediction of the development environment and process of strategic analysis], [online] Available at http://www.businessinfo.cz/cs/clanky/predikce-prostredi-strategicka-analyza-2803.htnajít. Accessed 22 July 2014.

Dlouhy, M., Fabry, J., & Kuncova, M. (2005). *Simulace pro economy* [Simulation for the economy]. Praha: VŠE.

Gallerani, A., & Sanchez, H. (2012). Method for simulating complex systems in e.g., economics field, involves integrating non-subscripted and subscripted system dynamics models. *Korean Journal of Chemical Engineering, 29*(4), 444–451.

Guloglu, B., & Tekin, R. B. (2012). Panel causality analysis of the relationship among research and development, innovation, and economic growth in high-income OECD countries. *Eurasian Economic Review, 2*(1), 32–47.

He, D., & Bechhoefer, E. (2008). Development and validation of bearing diagnostic and prognostic tools using HUMS condition indicators. *Proceedings of the IEEE Aerospace Conference,* Big Sky, MT.

Jowit, J. (2013). Ageing population will have huge impact on social services. *The Guardian,* [online] Available at http://www.theguardian.com/society/2013/feb/24/britain-ageing-population-lords-inquiry. Accessed 22 July 2014.

Kvasnicka, V., & Pospíchal, J. (2005). *Informatika pre sociálne vedy* [Informatics for social sciences]. Bratislava: Univerzita Komenského.

Maresova, P., Kacetl, J., Stemberkova, R., & Kuca, K. (2015, January 22). Care For Czech Republic's ageing population. *Conference of Modern and Current Trends in the Public Sector Research,* Brno Slapanice.

Maresova, P., Mohelska, H., & Kuca, K. (2014). Economics aspects of ageing population. *3rd World Conference on Business, Economics and Management. Procedia—Social and Behavioral Sciences.*

Mosallam, A., Medjaher, K., & Zerhouni, N. (2013). Nonparametric time series modelling for industrial prognostics and health management. *The International Journal of Advanced Manufacturing Technology, 69*(5), 1685–1699.

NIH. (National Institute on Aging). (2011). *New disease patterns*, [online] Available at http://www.nia.nih.gov/research/publication/global-health-and-aging/new-disease-patterns. Accessed 12 July 2014.

Pokorny, M. (1996). *Umělá inteligence v modelování a řízení* [Artificial intelligence in modeling and control]. Praha: BEN—technická literatura.

Powell, J. D., Franklin, G. F., & Naeini, A. E. (2006). *Feedback control of dynamic systems* (5th ed.). Upper Saddle River, NJ: Prentice Hall.

Roemer, M., Byington, C., Kacprzynski, G., & Vachtsevanos, G. (2013). An overview of selected prognostic technologies with reference to an integrated PHM architecture. *Proceedings of the First International Forum on Integrated System Health Engineering and Management in Aerospace* (pp. 1–9). Barcelona, Spain.

Sterman, J. D. (1991). *A skeptic's guide to computer models*, [online]. Available at http://www.systemdynamics.org/conferences/1985/proceed/sterm852.pdf. Accessed 2 July 2014.

Uckun, S., Goebel, K., & Lucas, P. J. F. (2008, May 23). Standardizing research methods for prognostics. *International Conference on Prognostics and Health Management (PHM08)*, IEEE, Denver.

WHO. (2012). *Global health and aging*, [online] Available at http://www.who.int/ageing/publications/global_health.pdf. Accessed 29 Sep 2014.

Education Affects Health: Empirical Evidence from Turkey

Furkan Besel and Fatih Yardimcioglu

Abstract This study examines whether there is a relation between education index and government health expenditures for Turkey between 1980 and 2012 using the Kapetanios Unit Root Test based on structural breaks, the Maki Cointegration Test and Causality Analysis based on Vector Error Correction Model. Empirical practices in the study showed that series were stationary in first differences and there is a long-term relation between them. As a result of the causality analysis, unidirectional causality was determined from education to health.

Keywords Education index • Health expenditures • Kapetanios unit root test • Maki cointegration test

1 Introduction

Education and health are the factors that increase total factor productivity and economic growth by contributing to the increase of human capital accumulation of the individual. At the same time these services also have positive effects on income distribution. Therefore, education and health services and expenditures are an important element of affecting one another in terms of both macro and micro aspects (Yardimcioglu 2013).

Through different channels education has a positive impact on attitudes and behaviors of people and society in health and contributes to increased levels of life expectations of people. As well as reducing the habits of using harmful substances to health, education also contributes to the protection of physical health and reduces the risk of obesity, and contributes to protection of mental and spiritual (mental) health. In addition, by having an effect on increasing the susceptibility to infectious diseases and acquiring the habit of doing regular sport, education contributes to the reduction of the mortality rate, as well as the increase in life expectancy at birth. Also through contributing to the improvement of the economic factors, education brings out a positive externality on the health. Health produces similar effects on

F. Besel (✉) • F. Yardimcioglu
Public Finance, Sakarya University, Sakarya, Turkey
e-mail: fbesel@sakarya.edu.tr; fyoglu@sakarya.edu.tr

© Springer International Publishing Switzerland 2016

M.H. Bilgin et al. (eds.), *Business Challenges in the Changing Economic Landscape - Vol. 1*, Eurasian Studies in Business and Economics 2/1,
DOI 10.1007/978-3-319-22596-8_27

education. This reciprocal positive relation between education and health contributes to a person's human capital accumulation. Increasing of a person's human capital accumulation affects economic growth, development, income distribution, economic activity, social welfare and many other factors. In addition to these, education reveals positive externalities on health through its contribution to the improvement of economic factors. In a similar way, health has also a positive effect on education. This reciprocal positive relation between education and health contributes to a person's human capital accumulation and this affect economic growth, development, income distribution, economic activity, social welfare and many other factors (Yardimcioglu 2013).

Feinstein et al. (2006) state that the effect that occurs on the attitudes and behaviors of people in health is one of the most powerful influences of education on health. Affecting an individual's health attitudes and behaviors in a positive sense, education has an influence on the individual's making better health-related choices about himself and his family. Increasing education expenditure cause behavior patterns change such as behavior changes of a person, healthy nutrition, doing regular sports activities, reducing smoking and alcohol consumption and it will direct one to exhibit more healthy behaviors (RWJF 2009).

In many studies in the literature, the results showing that there is a linear relationship between the level of education and healthy lifestyle choices have been emphasized. Education's contribution to people's choosing a better lifestyle by developing people's perspectives on the healthy lifestyles and results are shown as the most important reasons in the emergence of this result. Increasing information and education level of one's about health reduces the rate of using harmful substances such as drugs, smoking and drinking (Kenkel 1991; Johnston 2004).

Education also effective on individuals' healthy eating habits, contributes to the reduction of obesity risk (Yardimcioglu 2013). Obesity that affects the efficiency of the individual adversely can bring with it the individual's taking a smaller share of national income. An increase in obesity in a country may bring about adverse effects on the total factor productivity and income distribution. In many studies it is concluded that education has effects on the protection of physical health and on the reduction of the risk of obesity (Yardimcioglu 2012).

Another benefit of education is its contribution to a person's physical health as well as to the mental and spiritual (mental) health (Johnston 2004). Forming positive effects on health by reducing stress, education (Lochner 2011) affects the individual's productivity and therefore it constitutes positive effects on economic growth and income distribution in the context of total factor productivity.

Education is an important element in the increase of susceptibility to infectious diseases. Increasing of a person's susceptibility eliminates the risk of developing these diseases and it contributes to the fact that the economy and society benefit from a person's human capital accumulation more effectively. In many studies it is observed that (Yardimcioglu 2012) education contributes to the increasing of susceptibility to infectious diseases.

Another of the most important requirements of having a healthy life is that the person has a regular habit of doing sport (Yardimcioglu 2012). Kenkel (1991) indicates that an increase in the level of education also increases an individual's fitness habit. Physically less active people compared to physically active people spend more time in hospitals and benefit more from health services. Social costs of being not active are quite important for the health care system, economic growth and the distribution of income. The results of many empirical studies show that individuals who exercise regularly live a longer and a more healthy life (Yardimcioglu 2013).

The positive effects of education on the health can be considered as elements extending the average life expectancy of the individual. Considering the fact that an increase in the average life expectancy of the individual's paves way for the increasing of duration in benefitting from human capital accumulation, the importance of education on economic growth and income distribution (such as macroeconomic variables) come more to the fore (Yardimcioglu 2012).

The basic hypothesis of this study is to reveal that there is a long- term mutual relation between education and health. In this context, the aim of this study is to find out the relationship between education and health particular in Turkey and the size and direction of this relationship. The relation between education and health has been introduced after the conducted studies were summarized and the relationship between education and health for the period of 1980–2012 in Turkey was investigated by using the Maki Cointegration Test. Then coefficients of the relation between education and health were estimated by the method of FMOLS and finally causality relationship was determined by applying the method of VECM.

It has been observed that the Maki cointegration analysis used as one of the methods in the study has not been used before in the previous studies related to this field. From this point of view this study differs from earlier studies conducted especially in terms of the method used. In addition, the period examined differs from other studies in the literature in terms of the time period. Thus the results obtained are considered to contribute to the literature.

2 Literature Review

Many practical work indicate that education has a positive effect on health (Stacey 1998), the individual's education affect his/her health-related attitudes and behaviors and reveal positive externalities for the health (RWJF 2009). Education brings with it healthy individuals and at the same time healthy individuals can also get more training (Webber 2002; Stacey 1998). Surely unless an individual is healthy, he/she cannot study and cannot produce any benefit achieved with training (Stacey 1998). Education has positive effects on health associated with increasing the employment opportunities and raising the income levels of people (that is to say bringing about an improvement in economic factors) (RWJF 2009). Higher levels of education also bring health standards to be high, and high health standards (of an individual) are a factor that contributes to productivity growth. Because the productivity level of healthy people is higher (Weale 1992). Health has positive effects on the increase of a person's human capital accumulation, on economic growth in the context of total factor productivity, on income distribution in terms of increased personal productivity. In this context, education and health are important in terms of both micro as well as macro aspect. Reviewing the literature in the many practical work, the fact that education has positive effects on health through different channels has been concluded (Yardimcioglu 2013).

Lantz et al. (1998) state that smoking rate of people having a low level of income and education is much greater. Walque (2007) points out the fact that education affect people's smoking decisions; educated individuals tend to smoke less compared to untrained individuals and individuals who started to smoke tend to quit smoking more. Grimard and Parent (2007) tell the increase in the participation rate of education reduces smoking habits. Brunello et al. (2011) explain in their study carried out in the 12 EU countries that education reduces cigarette smoking, alcohol use attitudes and behaviors. Fagan et al. (2005) investigated the relationship between parents' education levels and these children's families' smoking rates in USA and they concluded that children of the families having low education levels (blue-collar) are more prone to smoke compared to children of the families having higher levels of education (white-collar). Although very few, there are also studies finding no relationship between education and smoking habits. Tenn et al. (2010) could not find any significant relationship between education and smoking behavior in their study made in the United States. A study carried out in Turkey shows that the more the level of education increases the more the rate of smoking among women increases. Similarly women having a high level of wealth smoke more compared to women having a low level of wealth (HU 2009).

Baum et al. (2010) found that individuals who have received a college education in every age group are less obese compared to the individuals who have a lower level of education. According to this study the possibilities of being obese among children grown alongside adults with higher levels of decrease compared to other children, while the incidence is higher among people with decreased level of education. In the study the incidence of obesity among children is associated with the education level of the family (Baum et al. 2010). Martin et al. (2008) indicate that obesity is associated with lower levels of education. Moreira and Padrao (2006) state in the same way in their study conducted in Portugal that an increase in the participation rates of education reduces the risk of becoming obese. Similarly, Lantz et al. (1998) report that persons with low education and income levels are more likely to smoke more as well as to be obese. As it can be concluded, the increasing level of education can be said to reduce the risk of obesity (Yardimcioglu 2012).

In many studies it is concluded that education has positive effects on the protection of mind and soul (mental) health. Parsons and Bynner (1998) state that 36 % of women whose literacy rate is low and 18 % of men have depression problems and these levels are in the order of 7 and a 6 % among individuals with high level of literacy (Feinstein et al. 2006). Dench and Regan in their research made in the UK state that education has positive effects on 80 % of people's psychological health/well-being (Feinstein 2002).

Vandemoortelei and Delamonica (2000) indicate in their work regarding 32 countries that almost one of both illiterate women ignored HIV/AIDS-related basic facts. The lacking level of knowledge among these women about AIDS are five times more than those who have received post-primary education. Also, beliefs among illiterate women that there is no possible prevention against AIDS are four times more than those educated. Moreover, uneducated women are three times more likely not to know that AIDS is infected from mother to child than those who educated. While in Malawi 27 % of uneducated women knew that the probability of HIV transmission decreases during pregnancy by taking medicines, the rate increases to 59 % among women having a high school and school education (UNESCO 2011). In a study carried out in Zambia, AIDS spread twice more rapidly among uneducated girls and the possibility of the spread and contamination of diseases such as malaria is noted to increase as the level of education gets lower (Vandemoortelei and Delamonica 2000). In a study conducted in Uganda it has been found out that with an annual increase in education of girls, these girls getting in touch with the HIV virus has been found to decrease by 6.7 % (Walque 2007).

Lantz et al. (1998) indicate that people with low levels of education and income give less importance to physical activity. Kenkel (1991) noted that highly educated people do more sport than people who have received less training and they pay more attention to their health. In a study conducted on England, it is noted that women and men with higher levels of education do regular and active sports and that halves the possibility of smoking and decreases the probability of being overweight by 20 % (Feinstein 2002). Leigh and Dhir (1997) found a strong relationship between sport and school enrollment rates. Tatar et al. (2009) concluded that women with higher levels of education do more sports in Turkey. Brunello et al. (2011) in their study made in indicate that education has a positive impact on the behaviors of an individual's making sports.

Sorlie et al. (1995) found a relationship between low levels of education, income levels and mortality rates excess. The authors state that mortality rate in both men and women is said to reduce as the level of education increases. According to the authors the fact that income and education level reduce the mortality rate may be associated with purchasing power of a person's health services, health-related habits and behaviors and an increase in awareness and knowledge that is provided by education. Results of the study suggest that poor individuals are the ones with low education, who need health care the most and in the need of being helped and protected (Sorlie et al. 1995). Lleras-Muney (2005) states that 1 year of additional education reduces the probability of the mortality rate of the next 10 years by 3.6 %. It is also added that a 1-year increase in compulsory education reduces the death rate by 3 % after the age of 35, while the level of life expectancy increase is said to be up to 1.7 years. Lantz et al. (1998) indicate that among people with low education and income levels, mortality rates are high. Oreopoulos (2003) show that 1 year increasing of the U.S. compulsory education level would reduce disability/handicap rate by 1.7 %, an increase in the rate of the 1-year enrollment would reduce the rate of being an unhealthy individual in the UK by 3.2 % would reduce and the rate of being healthy individuals is predicted to increase by 6 %.

Bour (2003) concluded that there is a relationship between the reduction of the child mortality with the increase of maternal education level and increase in child mortality rates with the decrease of maternal education level. Kravdal (2008) by using a data covering the years of 1980–2003 and Norwegian citizen women and men born in the years of 1950–1973 indicate that death rates among educated peers are less than the uneducated ones. Moreover, the author also indicates that there is an opposite relationship between families' education and child mortality rates. In sub-Saharan Africa in 2008 1.8 million children whose mothers have at least high school education are reported to have been rescued (UNESCO 2011). Very few studies state that there is no relationship between education and the mortality rates. Albouy and Lequien (2009) in their study conducted in France concluded that there no relationship between education and the mortality rates.

Education reveals positive externalities on the health through some economic channels. Higher levels of education increase the possibility of employment and finding a job with a higher income level (Feinstein 2002; RWJF 2009). Also by affecting to have better working conditions (RWJF 2009) affect health indirectly by uncovering improvements in economic factors (Feinstein 2002). In particular, income affected by education is said to be one of the key factors that influence health (Feinstein et al. 2006; Lochner 2011). Evaluated within context, because individuals with higher levels of education have also high revenues they can allocate more resources to health-related spending (Currie and Moretti 2003; Murray 2007; RWJF 2009; Lochner 2011). Individuals whose level of income increase can feed their families healthier and can live in better conditions. In addition, by buying a better health care for themselves and for their families whenever they want (Feinstein 2002; RWJF 2009: 7) they may live in an environment whose living conditions are more safely and properly and may experience less stress (RWJF 2009).

Education levels also affect a person's work environment. The majority of employees who have not received formal education work in worse situations than educated people in the sense of salary and working environment, as well as job security (risk of death and the possibility of injury). In addition to this, workers with low level of education work under stress in the psychological sense (RWJF 2009). Employees with low levels of education (parallel to their low income levels) can benefit less from opportunities such as sick pay, personal care, upgrading programs for workplace, child and adult care services, retirement-related allocations, and changes. Because employers pay less unemployment benefits for these people, they benefit less from other benefits related to social security and health (RWJF 2009). Considering all these factors collectively, an increase in the employment opportunities of people, an improvement in the work environment and being not under psychological stress in their work can be specified to give a positive contribution to personal productivity, and indirectly, to economic growth (Yardimcioglu 2012), and an increase in life expectancy rates.

As noted in detail above, there is a correlation between education and health. Investments in education increase the rate of return on investments in health care, while investments in health also increase the rate of return of investments in education. An individual's to be healthy is an important factor in the attending to school and learning process. As life expectancy of healthy people increases so does the effect of time for the investments in the training of these people. Having basic education is important in learning many health programs. Considering the training of health personnel, education investments increase return rates of health investment in a similar way (Sab and Smith 2001). Sab and Smith (2001) state that there is a tight relationship between investment in education and health and that there is an unconditional convergence between life expectancy and school enrollment rates and survival at birth. The authors also add that human capital accumulation effects life expectancy and a healthy child is more successful in school, and also an individual with higher levels pay more attention to health thanks to the available information obtained in the school. Peters et al. (2010) concluded that behaviors of people towards the protection of the health have parallels with the level of education. Individuals with higher levels of education exhibit more attention to their health.

Yardimcioglu (2013) examine the relationship between education expenditures and health (life expectancy level) over 25 OECD countries for the period of 1975–2008. It is concluded that both variables in the long run have a cointegration relationship. While in the short term a unidirectional causality from health to education expenditures exists, in the long term long-term a bidirectional causality exists between education expenditure and health. Yardimcioglu (2013) argue that there is a mutual relationship between the variables of education expenditures and health in the long term. In addition, as people with a higher level of education give more importance to the health, so does increase the rates of using health services provided them by the public economy (Yardimcioglu 2012). When all these positive externalities of education are considered together, it reveals that education increases a person's life expectancy. Similarly, healthy individuals will be able to benefit from educational services more effectively.

3 Econometric Analysis

In this section firstly information about the data used in the article will be given, then the econometric methods that have been used will be introduced and finally the results will be evaluated.

3.1 Dataset and Methods

In this study, *HEALTH* data sets, health expenditure to GNP and *EDUCATION* data set is the ratio of education index for the period of 1980–2012 have been used. *EDUCATION* data sets were obtained from the Human Development Report compiled by the United Nations, while *HEALTH* data sets were obtained from the OECD Statistics.

Firstly whether variables to be used in the study prior to econometric analysis contains will be tested and later a cointegration test will be applied in order to determine whether variables in the long term move together or not and a causality analysis will be performed to determine the presence and direction of causality between the variables. During the period of 1980–2012 when empirical application was discussed, new tests taking structural breaks in the analysis into account will be applied based on the fact that economic and political changes were experienced in this period.

3.2 Kapetanios Unit Root Test and Results

The basic hypothesis of Kapetanios (2005) is that the series contain a unit root, while the alternative hypothesis has developed a new unit root test in which the series are broken, but still static. In this test, unlike other structural break unit root tests, the determination of the refractive index in advance is not obligatory. In this test in which the refractive index is determined internally in accordance with this test, the total maximum refractive index will be identified and analyzed (Yilanci 2013). The model used in this test is as follows:

$$y_t = \mu_0 + \mu_1 t + \alpha y_{t-1} + \sum_{i=1}^{p} \delta_i \Delta y_{t-i} + \sum_{i=1}^{m} \phi_i DU_{i,t} + \sum_{i=1}^{m} \varphi_i DT_{i,t} + e_t \quad (1)$$

$$DU_{i,t}\begin{cases} 1 & \text{while } t \succ TB \\ 0 & \text{in other cases} \end{cases}$$

$$DT_{i,t}\begin{cases} t - TB & \text{while } t \succ TB \\ 0 & \text{in other cases} \end{cases}$$

The hypotheses of the tests are:
H_0: $\alpha = 1$
H_a: $\alpha \prec 1$ (Kapetanios 2005).
The operation of the test can be summarized as follows (Yilanci 2013):

- For a given refractive index the breaks for all samples is searched and t-statistics of H_0 hypothesis are obtained.
- The structural breaks date of the model in which residual sum of squares (RSS) is minimized is selected.
- A second structural breaks date between the remaining parts is sought by adding to the model he estimated date of the first break and the t-statistics for $\alpha = 1$ is calculated and the break date is determined again by finding the minimum RSS. This step is continued until the breaking index M is obtained.

- Appropriate refractive index is the breaking index, which gives the minimum t-statistic.

Residual sum of squares appropriate for the model is calculated in the following way (Kapetanios 2005):

$$KKT = \sum_{t=k+2}^{T} \left(y_t - \hat{\mu}_0 - \hat{\mu}_1 t + \hat{\alpha}\, y_{t-1} + \sum_{i=1}^{p} \hat{\delta}_i \Delta y_{t-i} + \hat{\phi}_1 DU_{1,t} + \hat{\varphi}_1 DT_{1,t} \right) \tag{2}$$

The maximum number of delay developed by Schwert (1989) in practice was determined using the formula $k = 12x(T/100)^{0.25}$. In this formula, k denotes the maximum length of the delay, while T denotes the number of observations. Kapetanios unit root test has been applied for the Model C/S (regime change) that takes into account fixed and gradient breaks. According to the results of Kapetanios unit root test of the minimum value of the t statistic gives the appropriate breaking index.

The suitable breaking number for *EDUCATION* series is five (t-static is where is minimum) and break dates are 1983, 1989, 1993, 2004 and 2008. As the test static at all levels is smaller than the critical values in the sense of absolute value the basic hypothesis of the series that expresses the series contain a unit root can not be rejected.

The proper number for the *HEALTH* series is designated as five and the break dates are 1986, 1990, 1994, 2000 and 2008. As the test static at all levels is smaller than the critical values in the sense of absolute value, the basic hypothesis of the series that expresses the series contain a unit root cannot be rejected.

Thus, according to the results of Table 1, *EDUCATION* and *HEALTH* series are stationary in the first differences. In addition, a breaking realized in both data sets resulting from the global financial crisis in 2008.

Table 1 Kapetanios unit root test results

	Education		Health	
Number of breaks	t-ist.	Breaking dates	t-ist.	Breaking dates
5	**−3.42**	**1983–1989–1993–2004–2008**	**−5.89**	**1986–1990–1994–2000–2008**
4	−3.78	1989–1993–2004–2008	−7.68	1986–1990–1994–2000
3	−3.83	1989–1993–2004	−7.63	1986–1990–2000
2	−5.05	1989–2004	−7.92	1990–2000
1	−4.82	2004	−6.33	21

Note: The critical values were obtained from Kapetanios (2005) according to the number of breaks. Maximum lag length is determined according to the Schwarz information criteria (SIC) The bold values are statistically significant.

3.3 Maki Cointegration Test and Results

Maki (2012) test the existence of cointegration between the series with the presence of a structural breaks up to five. In the test developed by Maki, structural breaking points are determined internally. Each period in tests is considered to be a possible breaking point; t statistics are calculated and the minimum points of the t statistic is considered to be a breaking point. As a result of the analysis of the data set obtained, the cointegration equation arising during the analysis with three or more structural breaks can be used as a test more superior than other cointegration (Maki 2012). Maki formulated four test models:

Model 0: where there is a refracture in the constant term, a model without trend;

$$y_t = \mu + \sum_{i=1}^{k} \mu_1 K_{i,t} + \beta x_t + u_t \tag{3}$$

Model 1: There is refracture in fixed term and in grade, a model without trend;

$$y_t = \mu + \sum_{i=1}^{k} \mu_1 K_{i,t} + \beta x_t + \sum_{i=1}^{k} \beta_i x_t K_{i,t} + u_t \tag{4}$$

Model 2: There is refracture in fixed term and in grade, a model with trend;

$$y_t = \mu + \sum_{i=1}^{k} \mu_i K_{i,t} + yt + \beta x_t + \sum_{i=1}^{k} \beta_i x_t K_{i,t} + u_t \tag{5}$$

Model 3: there is refracture in fixed term, in the grade and in the trend;

$$y_t = \mu + \sum_{i=1}^{k} \mu_i K_{i,t} + yt + \sum_{i=1}^{k} y_i t K_{i,t} + \beta x_t + \sum_{i=1}^{k} \beta_i x_t K_{i,t} + u_t \tag{6}$$

The hypotheses of the Maki test can be expressed as follows;

H_0: There is no cointegration under structural breaks.
H_1: There is cointegration under structural breaks.

The critical values needed to test the hypothesis have been calculated by using Monte Carlo simulations and Maki (2012) has also taken part in it. When the calculated value is larger than the critical value as absolute value, the hypothesis is rejected and that there is cointegration relationship between the series is considered (Maki 2012).

On the other hand, the test developed by Maki can be said to be a meaningful test for developing countries such as Turkey. Because these countries stand out as the countries where historically long-term political or economic stability cannot be

Table 2 The results of Maki cointegration test

Model 0	Model 1	Model 2	Model 3
−6.67[a] [−5.41]	−5.13 [−5.70]	−6.68[a] [−5.86]	−10.53[a] [−7.55]
Breaking dates			
Model 0	Model 1	Model 2	Model 3
1986–2008	1985–2003	1991–2005	1986–1993–2003–2007

Note: [] Values were taken from Maki (2012), Table 1, they are the critical values with a significance level of 1 %

[a]Represents that there is a cointegration at 1 % significance level among the variables

Table 3 Long-term coefficient estimates based on cointegration relationship

	FMOLS	t statistics	p-value
Education → Health	0.043915	10.29092	0.0000
Health → Education	20.52402	10.21507	0.0000

repeated, even some years a sudden shock or economic developments can be seen, thus statistically refractures occur.

Maki cointegration test, minimum test statistics and corresponding breaking dates are shown in Table 2 for their four models.

As seen from Table 2, a cointegration relationship between variables has been determined for all models except Model 1 as the test statistic is greater than the critical value. As the cointegration relationship between the variables as a result of Maki cointegration test has been identified the long-term coefficients were estimated by using the method of FMOLS.

In Table 3 the long-term prediction coefficients obtained by the method of FMOLS is shown. According to the findings, it has been concluded that a unit increase in health expenditure will increase the education volume index at 0.04 unit, while one-unit increase in education index will increase health expenditure by 20.52. In addition, as the t-statistic related to the estimated coefficient is significant, the coefficient estimates may give reliable results.

According to the results of cointegration coefficient estimates as the level of education increases so does the health expenditure along with the increasing importance given to health services. With the increase in health expenditure the level of education can be said to rise. Since a cointegration relationship between the variables is determined, a causality analysis based on the Vector Error Correction Model (VECM) has been performed and the results obtained are presented in Table 4.

According to the results of Causality Analysis VECM, the causality relationship between the variables at 5 % significance level is unidirectional from *EDUCATION* to *HEALTH*. In this context, in parallel with the cointegration test results, improvement in the educational level can be said to increase health expenditure.

Table 4 VECM causality test results

	Chi-sq	df	Prob
Education ↛ Health	5.471322	1	0.0193
Health ↛ Education	0.009640	1	0.9218

4 Conclusion

In this study, by using Causality Analysis based on the Kapetanios Unit Root Test taking structural breaks into account, the Maki Cointegration Test and Vector Error Correction Model, the mutual relations between the level of education and health expenditure for the period of 1980–2012 in Turkey were investigated.

Firstly, the Kapetanios unit root test was made and it was observed that the series are not stationary in levels, they are stationary in first differences [I (1)]. According to the Kapetanios unit root test in both data sets a refracture occurred resulting from the global financial crisis in 2008. In the second stage the Maki cointegration test has been applied. A cointegration relationship between variables for all other models except Model 1 has been determined as the test statistic is greater than the critical value.

As a result of the Maki cointegration test the cointegration relationship between the variables are identified and the long-term coefficients were estimated by using the method of FMOLS. According to the findings, it has been concluded that a unit increase in health expenditure will increase the education volume index at 0.04 unit, while one-unit increase in education index will increase health expenditure by 20.52. In addition, as the t-statistic related to the coefficient estimates is significant, the coefficient estimates may give reliable results.

As a cointegration relationship between the variables is determined, a causality analysis has been performed based on the Vector Error Correction Model (VECM) and the causality relationship between variables at significance level of 5 % from *EDUCATION* to *HEALTH* was found to be unidirectional. In this context, in parallel with the cointegration test results, improvement in the educational level can be said to increase health expenditure (level).

In conclusion, in the light of the findings obtained as the results of the econometric analysis in the period of 1980–2012 a long-term relationship between the level of health and the level of education for Turkey can be specified.

References

Albouy, V., & Lequien, L. (2009). Does compulsory education lower mortality? *Journal of Health Economics, 28*(1), 155–168.

Baum, S., Ma, J., & Kathleen, P. (2010). *Education pays 2010: The benefits of higher education for individuals and society*. Accessed April 15, 2015, from https://trends.collegeboard.org/sites/default/files/education-pays-2010-full-report.pdf

Bour, D. (2003). Mothers education and childhood mortality in Ghana. *Health Policy, 64*, 297–309.

Brunello, G., Margherita F., Nicole S., & Rudolf, W. (2011). *The casual effect of education on health: What is the role of health behaviors?* The Institute of Study of Labor (IZA) (Discussion Paper Series, 5944).

Currie, J., & Moretti, E. (2003). Mother's education and the intergenerational transmission of human capital: Evidence from college openings. *Quarterly Journal of Economics, 118*, 1495–1532.

Fagan, P., Brook, J. S., Rubenstone, E., & Zhang, C. (2005). Parental occupation, education, and smoking as predictors of offspring tobacco use in adulthood: A longitudinal study. *Addictive Behaviors, 30*, 517–529.

Feinstein, L. (2002). *Quantitative estimates of the social benefits of learning 2: Health (depression and obesity)* (Wider Benefits of Learning Research Report No. 6). Centre for Research on the Wider Benefits of Learning, Institute of Education, University of London.

Feinstein, L., Sabates, R., Anderson, T. M., Sorhaindo, A., & Hammod, C. (2006). What are the effects of education on health? *Measuring the effects of education on health and civic engagement: Proceedings of the Copenhagen Symposium, OECD* (pp. 173–354).

Grimard, F., & Parent, D. (2007). Education and smoking: Were Vietnam War draft avoiders also more likely to avoid smoking? *Journal of Health Economics, 26*, 896–926.

HU (Hacettepe University). (2009). *TurkiyeNufusveSaglikArastirmasi* [Demographic and Health Survey]. Hacettepe. Accessed March 10, 2014, from http://www.hips.hacettepe.edu.tr/tnsa/download.php

Johnston, G. (2004). *Healthy, wealthy and wise? A review of the wider benefits of education* (New Zealand Treasury working paper, 04/04).

Kapetanios, G. (2005). Unit-root testing against the alternative hypothesis of up to m structural breaks. *Journal of Time Series Analysis, 26*(1), 123–133.

Kenkel, D. S. (1991). Health behavior, health knowledge, and schooling. *Journal of Political Economy, 99*(2), 287–305.

Kravdal, O. (2008). A broader perspective on education and mortality: Are we influenced by other people's education? *Social Science and Medicine, 66*, 620–636.

Lantz, P. M., House, J. S., Lepkowski, J. M., Williams, D. R., Mero, R. P., & Chen, J. (1998). Socioeconomic factors, health behaviors, and mortality: Results from a nationally representative prospective study of US adults. *Journal of the American Medical Association, 279*(21), 1703–1708.

Leigh, J. P., & Dhir, R. (1997). Schooling and frailty among seniors. *Economics of Education Review, 16*(1), 45–57.

Lleras-Muney, A. (2005). The relationship between education and adult mortality in the United States. *Review of Economic Studies, 72*, 189–221.

Lochner, L. (2011). *Non-production benefits of education: Crime, health, and good citizenship* (NBER Working Paper, 16722).

Maki, D. (2012). Tests for cointegration allowing for an unknown number of breaks. *Economic Modelling, 29*(5), 2011–2015.

Martin, A. R., Nieto, J. M. M., Ruiz, J. P. N., & Jimenez, L. E. (2008). Overweight and obesity: The role of education, employment and income in Spanish adults. *Appetite, 51*, 266–272.

Moreira, P., & Padrao, P. (2006). Educational, economic and dietary determinants of obesity in Portuguese adults: A cross-sectional study. *Eating Behaviors, 7*(3), 220–228.

Murray, J. (2007). *The wider social benefits of education. A Research Report.* Centre for Integrated Sustainability Analysis, The University of Sydney. Accessed March 10, 2014, from http://www.isa.org.usyd.edu.au/publications/documents/ISA_Wider-SocialBenefits_Report.pdf

Oreopoulos, P. (2003). *Do dropouts drop out too soon? International evidence from changes in school-leaving laws* (NBER Working Paper, 10155).

Parsons, S., & Bynner, J. (1998). *Influences on adult basic skills.* London: The Basic Skills Agency.

Peters, E., Baker, D. P., Dieckmann, N. F., Leon, J., & Collins, J. (2010). Explaining the effect of education on health: A field study in Ghana. *Psychological Science, 21*(10), 1369–1376.

RWJF (Robert Wood Johnson Foundation). (2009). *Education matters for health* (Issue Brief 6: Education and Health).

Sab, R., & Smith, S. C. (2001). *Human capital convergence: International evidence* (IMF Working Paper, 32).

Schwert, G. (1989). Tests for Unit Roots: A Monte Carlo Investigation. *Journal of Business & Economic Statistics, 7*(2), 147–159.

Sorlie, P. D., Backlund, E., & Keller, J. B. (1995). US mortality by economic, demographic, and social characteristics: The national longitudinal mortality study. *American Journal of Public Health, 85*(7), 949–956.

Stacey, N. (1998). Social benefits of education. *The Annals of the American Academy of Political and Social Science, 559*, 54–63.

Tatar, G., Tozoglu, E., & ve Pehlivan, Z. (2009). 20–40 Yas Arasi Calisan Ve Calismayan Kadinlarin Spor Yapmalarini Etkileyen Bazi Faktorlerin Incelenmesi (Sivas Il Merkezi Ornegi) [The study of factors effecting doing sports of working and nonworking women aged between 20–40]. *Atabesbd, 11*(3), 28–41.

Tenn, D., Herman, A., & Wendling, B. (2010). The role of education in the production of health: An empirical analysis of smoking behavior. *Journal of Health Economics, 29*, 404–417.

UNESCO. (2011). *Education counts: Towards the millennium development goals.* Accessed March 18, 2014, from http://unesdoc.unesco.org/images/0019/001902/190214e.pdf

Vandemoortelei, J., & Delamonica, E. (2000). Education vaccine against HIV/AIDS. *Current Issues in Comparative Education, 3*(1), 6–13.

Walque, D. (2007). How does the impact of an HIV/AIDS information campaign vary with educational attainment? Evidence from rural Uganda. *Journal of Development Economics, 84*(2), 686–714.

Weale, M. (1992). *Education, externalities, fertility and economic growth* (Working Paper. Education and Employment, Population and Human Resources Department. The World Bank WPS, 1039).

Webber, D. (2002). Policies to stimulate growth: Should we invest in health or education? *Applied Economics, 34*, 1633–1643.

Yardimcioglu, F. (2012). *Egitim Harcamalari, Ekonomik Buyume ve Gelir Dagilimi Iliskisi*, Doktora Tezi [The Relationship Among Education Expenditures, Economic Growth And Income Distribution, Ph.D. Thesis]. Sakarya: T.C. Sakarya Universitesi Sosyal Bilimler Enstitusu.

Yardimcioglu, F. (2013). Egitim ve Saglikİlişkisi: Panel Esbutunlesmeve Panel Nedensellik Analizi [The relationship between education and health: Panel cointegration and panel causality analyses]. *Abant Izzet Baysal Universitesi Iktisadive Idari Bilimler Fakultesi Ekonomikve Sosyal Araştirmalar Dergisi, 9*(1), 49–74.

Yilanci, V. (2013). *Ekonometri Semineri Ders Notlari* [Lecture notes of econometrics seminar] (pp. 1–104). Sakarya Universitesi.

Part IV
Regional Studies

Soft Power Concept and Soft Power Indexes

Kiymet Yavuzaslan and Murat Cetin

Abstract Many state remains owned power supplies in the line of domestic and international level. Even though, both policies which are followed in this case primarily are based on the military and economic power, "Soft Power" item which was used for the first time by Joseph Nye (Bound to lead: The changing nature of American power. Basic Books, 1990), has become more important so as to keep pace with today's requirements and the world order. The soft power resources have a legitimizing effect on countries' policies that the others accept by their own free will. Many countries which realized the importance of the soft power, worked about to develop soft power resources. Besides the academic study, in order to measure and to compare the results obtained so far in many other countries, has been created various soft power indexes on basis of the elements of the soft power.

Keywords Power • Soft power • Soft power measurement • Soft power index

1 Introduction

To understand developments in the world, the politics based on the power in the international arena will be appropriate to follow. So, the concept of power is a phenomenon that forms the basis of the study area of the discipline of international relations and among the theories developed so far, "power" phenomenon is one of the key concepts. Each state wishes and desires to determine a power policy in accordance with their national interests. In addition, they should develop new policies in each field to prove their power. When we look at the historical process in a comprehensive manner, we see that the soft power sources have been used by many great empires so far. Yet, in the 1990s, corresponding to the end of the Cold War period, Joseph Nye's (1990) book "Bound to Lead: The Changing Nature of American Power" which was influential all around the world the concept of "soft power" was used for the first time and gained a conceptual quality.

K. Yavuzaslan (✉) • M. Cetin
Department of Economics, Istanbul University, Istanbul, Turkey
e-mail: kiymetyavuzaslan@gmail.com; muratcetin05@hotmail.com

© Springer International Publishing Switzerland 2016

M.H. Bilgin et al. (eds.), *Business Challenges in the Changing Economic Landscape - Vol. 1*, Eurasian Studies in Business and Economics 2/1,
DOI 10.1007/978-3-319-22596-8_28

The concept of soft power, bringing a different dimension to classic power sources, is kind of a handbook in forming a structure by legitimizing the use of force for all countries desiring to keep power in their hands. In this study, by conceptualizing soft power, the results obtained within the framework of the content and the indicators of soft power indexes formed by being supported with the quantitative data.

2 The Concept of Soft Power

Before defining the concept of soft power concept which was put forward academically and theoretically for the first time by a political science professor at Harvard University and the United States international security expert Joseph Nye (1990), it will be useful to explain the concept of "power". For example, before Nye (1990) explained the concept of soft power, he tried to clarify the concept of "power" by using the dictionary meaning of it. According to Nye, in the simplest terms, the power is the ability to influence the behavior of the opponent in order to achieve the desired results (Nye 2003).

Niccola Machiavelli who is author of the book "Prince", published in 1532, attaches top priority to power and the security of the state and draws attention of the all empires, and says the continuation and survival efforts of a state form the basis of all other purposes. According to "Machiavellism", which is a disgraceful term to some, what is important is to get power and it does not matter how it is won (Ari 2001).

In order to achieve the intended object, many states try to use their powers effectively. Considering the historical process, the power, the biggest tool for reaching the desired goal, has been subject to some changes over time from a conceptual perspective. The open-ended analysis of these changes made it difficult to determine the definition and demarcation of power at times. Consequently, power has been a gain in terms of many different factors and dimensions. As it was in the past, only with measured resources like land and a large population, it is not enough for a country to determine intensity of the power anymore (Lord 2006). Since the beginning of the Westphalia system, even before, the fact that how long the assessment of power, in terms of its physical properties, will take can never be predicted (Brown and Ainley 2007). So, under present conditions, it is clear that the optimism should be exported and new alliances and partnerships should be formed by leaving aside the fear strategy.

In terms of realism and liberalism which are important schools of the discipline of international relations, the power definitions have been attempted to be expressed in different ways. According to Morgenthau (1962) who is one of the major representatives of the realist school, the power means that a person has control over other people's ideas and actions. According to liberals, power can be specified as the ability of an actor to get things that others cannot do under normal circumstances done or to have control over the results (Keohane and Nye 1989). When examined more closely, although the power sources are differently perceived, it is seen that the definitions of the concept of power are in the same way for each discipline.

In short, when we look at the balance of power system until today it is intended to prevent war resulting from power combinations leading a country's own efforts to change the status quo (Polanyi 2009). Before, it was easier to appreciate international power sources. In international politics, super power meant "war power" (Taylor 1954). One of the most important criteria adopted about a state's power has been military power status.

The Armed Forces that constitute the military forces must be strong and ready for use even in peacetime because a country, both at national and international levels may have to engage military operations at any moment. Thus, having military power is the primary task of all administrators in the country.

However, when the phenomenon of power is examined in a more detailed manner, some classifications are seen. For example, in terms of power sources (concrete-abstract) and the style of power application (hard-soft), it can be classified under two main titles. If considered generally, the components of a state's power (resources) can be grouped under two headings (Gonlubol 2000). Concrete elements are Geographical location, Population and labor, Natural resources, Industrial and agricultural potential and level of development, and Number of Military personnel. Abstract elements are National morale, The quality of Diplomacy, and The quality of government.

It has become more evident that power sources constituting concrete items such as geographical location, population and labor force, natural resources, industrial and agricultural development, number of military personnel do not make sense all alone on the power scale of a country (Lord 2006). Beyond the elements of the concrete power, it is important to create the agenda in the world politics and attract foreign public opinion.

Nye (2005) basically gathered power elements under two headings although he classified power types as military, economic and soft power (Table 1). The elements of the power he called as "Hard power" are, in general, the military inventories in a

Table 1 Classification of power in the international order

Power types	Behaviors	Basic tools	Government policies
Military power	Coercion	Threat	Coercive diplomacy
	Deterrence	Force	War
	Protection		Alliance
Economic power	Encouragement	Money-making	Help
	Coercion	Investment	Bribery
	Admirableness	Values, culture	Public diplomacy
Soft power	Creating agenda	Policies	Bilateral and multilateral diplomacy
		Institutions	

Source: Nye (2005)

country. While economic power may be actually considered under the hard, it can be said that it is overlapped with soft power.

Nye (2005) proposed that soft power consists of a country's history, geography, cultural diversity, economic strength, social pattern, democratic development, civil society organizations' prevalence and impacts, science and technology infrastructure and values like art and sports which the social life produced in the intellectual sense. Nye (2005) defines the soft power as a country's power momentum that is created by all the possibilities and opportunities a country has apart from direct military force, but this power supports military forces if necessary and he has created the concept of soft power to explain the spiritual dimension of power. Ensuring that others desire the outcomes you desire attracts people without forcing them. In short, soft power relies on the ability to shape the preferences of others and it is a power which is attractive to other countries.

When a country determines the international world politics, she is able to get the results she wants by ensuring target country or countries pursue and admire her. This strategy is stronger than determining the agenda of world politics and influencing other countries by forcing them to change with the use of economic or military vehicles. As a government that frightens and oppresses people can never achieve and maintain a sustainable success, use of force that is based on consent is always more effective in the international order (Cox 2004).

The leaders in all countries should use their soft power resources "to exert their authorities" for the national and international policies. Because in the modern world order, not only using military force threat or using economic sanctions to force others to change, but also creating the agenda in world politics and to attract the other countries are important. This soft power, that is to say pretending that others want what you want, attracts people to you instead of forcing them (Nye 2005).

Recently, that the ideas and discussions that America's hegemony ended and her likely successor is China (Layne 1993) and that she places emphasis on soft power and engaged in activities (like Beijing Olympics, etc.) indicates that the concept of power is quite up-to-date and important (Uzer 2013).

Hence, after the Second World War and the Cold War the United States has proven herself as the sole superpower of the twentieth century and the use of soft power has brought a great deal of benefits to her in foreign affairs. With its soft power elements, The United States have managed to build a large foreign political culture. Such a power can be an effective tool to easily change the facts according to the time, so USA fulfills its task as the "Superman" that will be called to intervene in case of any problem taking place in the international arena (Sumer 2008).

3 Causes and Consequences of Use of Soft Power

Here, I will try to touch upon the use of soft power and since what time it has been used to determine the policies of the countries and for what reasons it is used. In fact, about 500 years ago, Machiavelli recommended the Italian princes that to be scared is more important than to be loved as he believes that any means which is used to reach a goal is allowable. In history, many states used their powers and applied their military forces to provide security against the dangers and to achieve the results they want; today policies in the same way continue to be used. Using economic strength is also a way of using power that often has short lasting impacts and is simple. However, although its way and duration of use is more troublesome, the results obtained with the use of soft power may be more enduring and positive.

After the Second World War, The United States and the Soviet Union entered in a competition to win dominance in economic and political area and the Cold War began. This bi-polar power struggle has ended with the disintegration of the Soviet Union in 1991 (Bromley 2008). After the Cold War, the spread of democracy, the media's excessive growth and development, and the development of global civil society protest movements have changed the nature of power and as conceptualized by Nye (1990) in that period, the policies based on more soft power have gained importance (Sancar 2012).

Although soft power has sometimes a direct impact on specific purposes, it has more effects on a country which is trying to reach general purposes. The use of hard power, in the environment of global economy, may adversely affect the country's economic goals. War may deter investors which control the flow of capital in the globalized economy (Friedman 1999). But soft power initiatives are the exact opposite of hard power initiatives. In addition, results show that soft power influenced the framework of the economic power of hard power elements. For example, the soft power has effect on the essence of economic structure such as production technology, corporate organization model, management science, brand strategy, innovation (Li et al. 2012). The resources forming the soft power and tools can sometimes be training activities, sometimes arts, sports or theater and sometimes can also be leaders and regimes. At this point, for the popular American culture and Hollywood films, in many countries of the World, it is very difficult to say that they do not create interest and curiosity.

The United States, thanks to the use of soft power in the Post-Cold War period, have become more attractive in terms of economy and politics among the available alternatives in the global sense. This has made the USA a model in which the iron curtain countries have envied (Demirtepe and Ozertem 2013). This can be seen clearly when a comparison between Warsaw Pact and NATO is made. When The Warsaw Pact disintegrated, becoming a member of the US-led NATO membership has become an important goal for many. These countries' race to be a member of NATO is not just for military force support, but also for it makes one close to U.S. image and be in line with a peaceful country. Here, too, we can see that the most important success of soft power is to make a country to adopt one's goals as if its own.

4 General Features and Dimensions of Soft Power

Nye (2010) has made an analogy about the power as; power means possessing royal flush in the international poker game. Of course, if you do not evaluate the cards as required or if you keep bluffing and cheating, you will lose again or you cannot get the results you want. Soft power is a form of passive power, he adds. Countries where the soft power is applied would like to follow the moral values, prosperity or culture of the country which holds the soft power. This is the second face of power and in some cases the country on which the soft power is applied does not recognize that such a force is applied to her. Soft power is not directly applied to the target countries, but countries are affected by this power voluntarily and change their behavior.

For the concept of power that is an important element in terms of international relations and political science, it is evident that it is not a one-dimensional character. Ability to achieve the desired results is mostly related to having certain resources. Thus, the power can, in short, be defined as having elements such as population, natural resources, land, military and economic force, and political stability. Apart from concrete items such as tanks, artillery, guns, number of aircrafts a country has, as mentioned earlier, a country has also abstract resources. However, it is not possible to examine all of them exactly in terms of numerical data. In other words, the phenomenon of power is a concept whose existence is known but some difficulties arise in measuring its exact size. Soft power may differ for each country and soft power is inherently relative. Something which is valid for a country may have an adverse impact for another one. In addition, each country has unique features such as belief system and values; these unique features create these countries' political culture. The political culture of a country may have an impact on the country's power as much as other elements of physical capacity (McClory 2010). In addition, the support of a community for the government's policy, or the opposite, becomes important elements when taking the power of a country into consideration.

That the country gives the impression of being divided or acting together about the issues of territorial integrity and sovereignty, the absence of deep social and economic divisions within the country, adopting the same ideology provide significant effect on the strength of the country.

When you talk about elements and tools of soft power, things that first come to mind are media, culture, art, science, sports, education, which are specific to a country (Nye 2005). In the current policy that is followed on a global scale countries' power of the elements determine the sustainability of these policies (Demirtepe and Ozertem 2013). There are some soft-power resources for each country and through these sources; each country develops her appropriate soft power strategies (Nye 2003).

To Nye (2005), soft power is based on three sources and in the order of importance the first one is the emphasis on culture, he says this because he suggests culture can be attractive to others. Second one is political values and the third one is foreign policy developments, he regards these as sources of soft power. The culture and political values that determine the soft power must be compatible to those living in the country and abroad as this integration will determine the greatness of the power. The use of soft power will have a positive impact on the target group, if foreign policy is evaluated as reasonable, legitimate and moral. How to use soft power and its elements are expressed in this way by Nye (2005).

During the literature review, many efforts about definitions of soft power and the elements of soft power were observed. In this article, we have discussed "soft power index" in accordance with the valuation criteria used in the calculations and the elements of soft power and resources will be discussed again.

5 Soft Power Index

The domestic and foreign policies of the countries with the ability to impose their preferences, cultural values and institutional structures enable them to earn an attractive character in which soft power is the most important factor (Nye 2005).

In general, the concept of power including soft power is actually relative and the explanations applied from the power of the elements or sources are often insufficient. When compared with other countries' capacities, it may become a meaningful concept. This comparison is easy in an environment where few actors exist, but in many state's complex relationships, to make this comparison is more difficult than expected. Especially, developing countries are now reducing their defense budget which is the most prominent feature of the elements of hard power and whether or not it is supported by the state, the elements of soft power requires more structured and intelligent application. Assessment of each country is different in terms of soft power because soft power sources are different from each other and while some countries are aware of these resources, some cannot use these resources appropriately. The soft power's frame is expressed consistently in the definitions made. However, during the implementation of soft power, the cost-benefit analysis rather than definition should be well done (Ozdermir 2008).

First of all, in terms of its impact, the soft power policy objectives must be global. When the cost of a global initiative to the state is more than the advantages it brings, it will lead to a waste of resources and will become time consuming rather than become effective (McClory 2010). As a result of political, economic and military analysis, it should be planned so as to ensure maximum impact. It should be implemented in different ways in different areas, and the results should be analyzed in the best way. In this regard, to see if the success is achieved or not, it is needed to express of the soft power in numerical values and soft power index calculations are being made by independent research institutions. The studies respectively conducted so far in 2010, 2011 and 2012 indicate that the soft power indexes were formed. Indexes conducted in 2010 and 2011, established in order to increase the effectiveness of "The Institute for Government" (IFG) under the leadership of the UK's independent charitable organization "The Institute for

Government" (IFG) aimed to increase the effectiveness of The British governments. Since the index in 2011 is an improved version of the index in 2010, IFG's soft power index report in 2011 will be considered in this study. Another soft power index discussed here is an index study conducted by the initiative of the US-based international independent auditing firm Ernst & Young (E & Y) in 2012.

5.1 The New Persuaders Soft Power Index

In the Soft Power index prepared by Jonathan McClory (2010) with the support of IFG, by examining 30 countries determined as the strategic partner of UK it was aimed to compare UK's soft power situation with the other 30 countries.

In "The New Persuaders I-II" entitled soft power indexes, it has not been tested how much soft power the countries have, it has been tested how effective they use their soft powers (McClory 2010). To determine this index, by taking the superiority of countries in many fields into consideration like membership to the international organizations such as NATO, UN; in many areas such as GDP on foreign aid rate, the country's non-governmental organizations (NGOs) number, signed environmental agreements, UNESCO World Heritage Site and number of Olympic medals, country's income distribution status, academic publications, the number of foreign correspondents certain rankings have been made. These areas are primarily classified under five main headings and then, the worldwide statistics and indices on this topic which were prepared by leading organizations have been employed.

Main titles and descriptions based on as soft power as indicator are summarized in the following four statements (McClory 2010):

As mentioned previously, in addition to these main categories (Tables 2, 3, 4 and 5) created by using a variety of statistics and indexes, the experts have rated a number of criteria from IFG and Monoclo magazine as for non-quantitative values under a separate heading.

These criteria determined as "Subjective Expert Panel Categories" are assessments of those countries' many aspects such as cultural outputs, soft power icons, cuisine, national airlines and airports, global leaders, foreign policy direction, trademarks (McClory 2011).

According to this index IFG published for the first time in 2010, Britain and France are on the first place. In Table 6 ranking on which the USA, Germany and Switzerland also take place and they constitute the top five countries in terms of soft power (IFG). Britain's most important TV channels, BBC's closure in many countries due to budget problems have deeply influenced her international image. Also, The British government's Arab Spring Strategies promote democracy for some countries while for some other countries they support dictators, this has led to a loss in the order for the calculation of the soft power in 2011. A new ranking appeared in 2011, because France failed to fight with the financial crisis in Europe due to the policies it followed, that caused France to face soft power drop.

Table 2 Soft power index indicators and descriptions prepared by IFG Index: Indicators considered under the heading "diplomacy"

Indicator	Description	Source
Foreign aid	Total overseas development assistance	OECD and United Nations Statistics
Visa freedom	It is compiled according to the pieces of his country visa-free travel of its citizens by Britain's Independent Consulting Company, "Henley And Partners"	Henley Visa Restrictions Index
National brand power	The ranking according to ANHOLT-GFK the National Brand Index	ANHOLT-GFK Brand Index
Number of cultural mission	Number of Special Cultural Mission made on Abroad	The number of Direct State or Embassy Employees
Online structure	Ministry of Foreign Affairs and Minister of Foreign Affairs of Total Number of Twitter Followers	www.twitter.com
Global diplomatic structure	Number of foreign embassies and consulates situated on abroad	Ministry of Foreign Affairs Web Sites and Other Resources
Diplomatic resources for multilateral organizations	Total number of multilateral organizations	Ministry of Foreign Affairs Web Sites and Other Resources
Global connectivity structure	The total number of international/multi-biased of organizations which a country that is a member	CIA World Fact Book[a]
Environmental awareness and actions	The number of total environmental agreements signed by country	CIA World Fact Book
Openness to refugees	The total number of refugees accepted to the country (Out of 1000)	The United Nations Refugee Agency Annual Statistics

[a]Even if partially it is updated every week, it is an official CIA website which is prepared for the needs of the United States Federal Government

While preparing the index, the chart was formed in accordance with criteria to be the best in the international arena; it included the calculation of each country's soft power elements, each country's own peculiar importance. As it is seen, generally, The European countries, particularly, The United States and Britain, are at the top in the ranking among the best ones as noted in Table 7. The Scandinavian countries taking part in the first three are noteworthy, this is another factor in the "Government" criteria in which the government policies of the countries have been evaluated.

Table 3 Soft power index indicators and descriptions prepared by IFG Index: Index indicators considered under the heading "Government"

Indicator	Description	Source
The united nations human development indicators	"Human Development" measurements are taken into account by economics, education, and health indices created by seeking on the results	The United Nations' Human Development Index
Government effectiveness	"The one" collected based on the countries to measure the quality of government by the world bank	World Bank "Good Government Index"
Individual freedom	Political and personal freedom index	Index prepared by Freedom House Organization
Democratic institutions	Democratic freedom and responsibility index	The Economist "Freedom Index"
Thought centers activities	Total number of think tanks in the country	"The Global Go-To Think Tanks"
Informal economy	The country's informal economy size	Forthcoming in International Tax and Public Finance
Social violence	Murder rate	United Nations "Murder Rate" Data
Government responsibility	An index that measures the responsibilities of the national mechanism	World Bank Report
Death penalty	The number of death penalty given in a year in the country	Various Resources
Government trust	A compound points people give to the government according to the trustiness	World Economic Forum Government Confidence Index
Income distribution	Gini coefficient	World Bank statistics

5.2 *Rapid-Growth Markets Soft Power Index*

Rapid-Growth Markets Soft Power Index was prepared and published by international independent auditing firm Ernst & Young (2012) whose center is in America in cooperation with Skolkovo Institute whose center is in Moscow. In this index prepared in 2012, 13 different variables were used and a numerical scoring was performed by giving certain coefficients to these variables.

While constructing the index of Ernst & Young (2012), the variables that describe soft power have been organized in three main categories including "Global Image", "Global Integrity" and "Global Integration".

The scoring results are evaluated according to the developing countries' soft power index criteria, the soft power seems to have a close relationship with GDP by looking at the ranking in 2010 (Table 8). The world closely follows BRIC (Brazil, Russia, India and China) countries, those countries are the rising economies and they are positioned in a special way, it is no surprise that these four countries are the

Table 4 Soft power index indicators and descriptions prepared by IFG Index: Index indicators considered under the heading "culture"

Indicator	Description	Source
Tourism	Annual total number of tourists	The United Nations World Tourism Organization
Tourism expenditures	Average spending by tourists (in dollar terms)	The United Nations World Tourism Organization
Foreign correspondents	Total foreign correspondents in the country	Press Association and Other Resources
Language	The Index demonstrating the global power of the native language	George Weber, "The World's Ten Most Influential Languages", Language Monthly, 3: 12–18, 1997
Olympic profile	The number of medals won in last summer and winter games	Data of the International Olympic Committee
Music	World sales list number of Albula in the first 50 coverage	The International Federation Datas
Art gallery	World's most visited 100 museum's annual cumulative visitors number	The Art Newspaper
World heritage	The number of UNESCO world heritage situated in the country	UNESCO World Heritage List Http://Whc.Unesco.Org/En/List
International football status	The country's FIFA world ranking	FIFA

Table 5 Soft power index indicators and descriptions prepared by IFG Index: Index indicators considered under the heading "business/innovation"

Indicator	Description	Source
International patents	International patent procurement of GDP ratio	World Wealth Organization Publications
Commercial competition	Competitiveness index of the world economic form	World Economic Forum
Level of corruption	International transparency association "corruption perceptions index" country rankings are taken into account	International Transparency Association "Corruption Perceptions Index"
Innovation	The innovation index by developed INSEAD and the world intellectual property organization	Dutta, S. (2011) "Global Innovation Index", INSEAD Business School
International investment	Foreign direct investment in gross fixed capital ratio	United Nations Trade and Development Statistics
Internet addiction	How many internet users per 100 inhabitants	CIA World Fact Book

Source: McClory (2011)

first four economies in terms of soft power among the developing economies. Although it is not included in the estimation of soft power index population size and the GDP size are among important sources increasing the soft power.

Table 6 Country soft power ranking calculated at IFG soft power index score (2011)

Line	Country	Score	Line	Country	Score
1	USA	7.41	16	Italy	4.28
2	United Kingdom	6.48	17	New Zealand	4.17
3	France	6.21	18	Austria	4.1
4	Germany	6.15	19	Belgium	3.8
5	Australia	5.65	20	China	3.74
6	Sweden	5.35	21	Brazil	3.55
7	Japan	5.08	22	Singapore	3.49
8	Swiss	5.07	23	Turkey	3.33
9	Canada	4.91	24	Chile	2.94
10	Netherlands	4.9	25	Portugal	2.81
11	Norway	4.82	26	Israel	2.67
12	Denmark	4.78	27	India	2.64
13	Spain	4.68	28	Russia	2.43
14	Korea	4.52	29	Czech Republic	2.36
15	Finland	4.45	30	Greece	2.35

Source: McClory (2011)

Table 7 IFG soft power index basic criteria for the top 10 country (2011)

Line	Government	Culture	Diplomacy	Education	Trade/Innovation
1	Sweden	USA	France	USA	Singapore
2	Norway	England	England	England	Switzerland
3	Denmark	France	Germany	Germany	Finland
4	Switzerland	Australia	USA	France	Switzerland
5	Finland	Spain	Sweden	Canada	Denmark
6	New Zealand	Germany	Norway	Australia	Netherlands
7	Netherlands	China	Netherlands	China	Germany
8	Australia	Italy	Canada	Japan	Belgium
9	Canada	Canada	Italy	Netherlands	Korea
10	Austria	Russia	Switzerland	Korea	Japan

Source: McClory (2011)

In addition, this study conducted in 30 selected developing countries, it has been determined that there is 75 % correlation between GDP and soft power status (Ernst & Young 2012). Furthermore, the research results reveal that the countries with strong "soft power" brand attract more direct foreign investment.

Table 8 Soft power index by Ernst & Young emerging economies soft power rankings

Line		2005	2006	2007	2008	2009	2010
1	China	31.1	32.2	32.2	32.2	33.7	30.7
2	India	22.6	21.5	21.9	26.7	22.6	20.4
3	Russia	22.9	18.4	22.9	21	23.5	18
4	Brazil	5.9	6	9.3	12.7	9.7	13.8
5	Turkey	10.3	12.5	11.4	14.4	10.3	12.9
6	Mexico	10	11.8	11.8	17.1	19.3	11.5
7	South Africa	13	10	8.5	12.6	11.8	10.3
8	Hungary	12.2	11.1	7.4	9.2	9.2	10
9	Czech Republic	8.5	9.2	9.2	9.2	10.7	9.6
10	Slovakia	7	7.4	6.6	6.6	7	9.2

Source: Ernst & Young (2012)

6 Conclusion

Many studies have been made so far on concept of "soft power" which occupies a considerable place in the literature of international relations. In particular, the disclosure and sustainability of American hegemony has been discussed within the concept of soft power, it is attempted to analyze the elements of soft power in terms of the balance of power and whether the countries are in competition with the USA, as in the case of China. For the elements of soft power which are important in explaining the international world order, the need of conducting various studies is very obvious beyond the conceptual definition. However, since the use of this concept for the first time 23 years ago, only two different soft power calculations have been seen to be carried out so far.

The basic mission in the soft power index published by two different institutions operating in the United Kingdom and the United States is to express the soft power numerically and to compare countries' soft power potentials. Some variables that are non-relative or evaluated with the scales in numerical parameters for the calculation of the index have been added to the analysis. These variables have provided a ranking of countries according to their soft power. The world's first official index of soft power, the New Convincing Soft Power Index, is an index created by IFG' which is an Independent think tank in the UK. As it focuses on England in particular in order to make specific assumptions and conclusions, the results obtained in this index have limited effect. Even the fact that the selection has been made in an objective manner to calculate the index of the countries participating in the analysis itself may be subject to criticism. In the report of "Rapidly Growing Market Soft Power Index" about the economic growth rate in terms of attention on emerging markets as a result of the recent global crisis prepared by America's independent auditing firm Ernst & Young, it shows that the analysis was not made on a global scale because not all countries are included in the selection. In this regard, it can be said that both indices do not contain a general view covering the whole world.

When the soft power indices and IFG which has been formed under the initiative of Ernst & Young and are compared, as IFG includes more countries and a limited number of variables (based on four main titles with 13 variables) is used for calculations by Ernst & Young (2012) index, it is seen that the IFG index includes more comprehensive analysis. However, while the soft power index prepared by IFG increases the number of variables and creates new variables through a committee of its members, it is very clear that the index results cannot pass through an objective decision-making process since it is based on the Britain's soft power potential. Likewise, when we look at the countries in the first ranking on the index table (Table 7) published by IFG, questions arise as it indicates that Britain is the second best country in the world in terms of soft power in the fields like "culture", "diplomacy", and "education." In the same way, the index prepared by Ernst & Young is designated to analyze the soft power situations of the developing countries makes a comparison between US and China and comes to the conclusion that China cannot be a rival to US in the way of becoming a superpower. IFG's soft power index is specially prepared for Britain and Ernst & Young, America's soft power index is specially prepared for USA and in short, it can be said that they analyze by taking side with the country which they work for.

Apart from all these aspects, while the soft power as a phenomenon appears to express the current global turmoil continuously, it is seen that soft power loses its conceptual quality and through indexes of tangible and quantitative data and it enables analysis based on the countries. For instance; in the "New Convincing Soft Power Index" prepared twice in 2010 and 2011, when we compare the previous index between Brazil and Turkey's soft power state, these two very different countries are seen that they surprisingly develop in the same fields. Indeed, in these two countries in 2013, almost at the same time, there have been social movements arising from domestic issues. As it will contribute to understanding of events in a better way that influence national and international order, it is an important matter that the soft power indexes previously prepared or those that will be prepared in the future with different evaluation processes and criteria are continuous.

References

Ari, T. (2001). *Uluslararası iliskiler ve dis politika* [International relations and foreign policy] (4th ed.). Istanbul: Alfa.

Bromley, S. (2008). *American power and the prospects for international order*. Cambridge: Polity Press.

Brown, C., & Ainley, K. (2007). *Uluslararası iliskileri anlamak* [Understanding international relations] (2nd ed.). Istanbul: Yayin Odasi.

Cox, R. W. (2004). Beyond empire and terror: Critical reflections on the political economy of world order. *New Political Economy, 9*(3), 18–25.

Demirtepe, M. T., & Ozertem, H. S. (2013). Yukselen tehdit algisi karsısında Cin'in yumusakguc siyaseti: Politikalar ve sinirliliklari [China's soft power politics against the increasing threat perception: Policies and limitations]. *Journal of Bilig, 65*(5), 96–105.

Ernst & Young. (2012). Rapid-growth markets soft power index: Spring 2012. *Ernst & Young Soft Power Index*. Accessed May 25, 2014, from http://www.ey.com/Publication/vwLUAssets/Rapid-growth_markets_soft_power_index:_Spring_2012/$FILE/softpowerindex.pdf

Friedman, T. L. (1999). *The Lexus and the olive tree: Understanding globalization* (1st ed.). New York: Farrar Status and Giroux.

Gonlubol, M. (2000). *Uluslararası politika* [International politics] (5th ed.). Istanbul: Siyasal Kitabevi.

IFG. (2011). *Foreign policy: Soft power and national security*. Institute for Government. Accessed June 10, 2014, from http://www.instituteforgovernment.org.uk/our-work/better-policy-making/foreign-policy-soft-power-and-national-security

Keohane, R. O., & Nye, J. S. (1989). *Power and interdependence: World politics in transition* (3rd ed.). Boston: Little-Brown.

Layne, C. (1993). The unipolar illusion: Why new great powers will rise. *International Security, 17*(4), 88–100.

Li, H., Liu, M., & Zhao, J. (2012). Construction of soft power of small and medium-sized enterprises. *Cross-Cultural Communication, 8*(5), 88–92.

Lord, C. (2006). *Losing hearts and minds, public diplomacy and strategic influence in the age of terror*. New York: Praeger Security.

McClory, J. (2010). *The new persuaders: An international ranking of softpower*. Institute for Government. Accessed May 18, 2014, from http://www.instituteforgovernment.org.uk/sites/default/files/publications/The%20new%20persuaders_0.pdf

McClory, J. (2011). *The new persuaders II: A 2011 global ranking of softpower*. Institute for Government. Accessed May 18, 2014, from http://www.instituteforgovernment.org.uk/sites/default/files/publications/The%20New%20PersuadersII.pdf

Morgenthau, H. J. (1962). *Politics among nations*. New York: Chicago Press.

Nye, J. S. (1990). *Bound to lead: The changing nature of American power* (1st ed.). New York: Basic Books.

Nye, J. S. (2003). *Amerikan gucunun paradoksu: Dunyatek süper gucu neden tek basina davranamaz* [The paradoox of American power: Why the World's superpower can't go it alone] (1st ed.). Istanbul: Literatur.

Nye, J. S. (2005). *Dunya siyasetinde basarinin yolu: Yumusak guc* [Soft power: The means to success in world politics] (1st ed.). Istanbul: Elips Kitap.

Nye, J. S. (2010). American and Chinese power after financial crisis. *The Washington Quarterly, 33*(4), 143–153.

Ozdermir, H. (2008). Uluslararası ilişkilerde guc: Cokboyutlu bir değerlendirme [Power in international relations: A multidimensional assessment]. *Journal of Ankara University SBF, 63*(3), 8–21.

Polanyi, K. (2009). *Buyukdonusum: Cagimizinsiyasal ve ekonomik kökenleri* [The great transformation: The political and economic origins of our time] (8th ed.). Istanbul: İletisim.

Sancar, G. A. (2012). *Kamu diplomasisi ve uluslararası halkla ilişkiler* [Public diplomacy and international public relations]. Istanbul: Beta.

Sumer, G. (2008). Amerikan dispolitikasinin kokenleri ve Amerikan dis politik kulturu [The origins of American foreign policy and the culture of American foreign policy]. *Journal of International Relations, 5*(19), 119–144.

Taylor, A.J.P. (1954). *The struggle for mastery in Europe, 1848–1918* (1st ed.). Oxford: University Press.

Uzer, U. (2013). 21. Yuzyildatek kutupluluk tartismalari [The discussions of uni-polarity in 21st century]. *Bilge Strateji, 1*(8), 18–36.

Enotourism: A New Profitable Business? Poland's Case

Katarzyna Jesiotr and Elzbieta Szymanska

Abstract The research problem considered in this paper is enotourism. The aim of this article is to assess and suggest the prospects for the development of enotourism in Poland. The following research hypothesis was verified: appropriate promotion is the most important factor contributing to the development of enotourism in Poland. In order to achieve this objective, the questionnaire survey method was used. The survey questionnaire was sent to all the vineyards available (those that had an e-mail address). The return rate was 23 %. The research was carried out in April 2014. As a result of the survey, the hypothesis posed earlier was verified positively. The research makes an important contribution to the economic practice of the wine-making business and tourism by recommending measures which would drive the development of this form of tourism. The most important ones include the need to amend the wine-making legislation in effect in Poland. Supportive actions on the part of local authorities (territorial self-government units) and measures to popularize the wine drinking culture are also necessary.

Keywords Tourism • Enotourism • Business • Poland

1 Introduction

The wine culture developed already in the ancient times. Known as "Enoturismo" in Spanish and "Enotourisme" in French, enotourism is, at its core, tourism focused on wine. Where other forms of tourism may be sitting at the beach, wandering amongst medieval ruins, or working for an NGO in another country, enotourism is all about enjoying the wine of a region and the people that make it.

Enotourism is also called wine tourism or enological tourism. This name comes from the term *enology*, which means a science related to broadly understood issues of wine-making (Wozniczko and Orlowski 2009). The definition of enotourism encompasses travels to places where grapevine is cultivated. Tourists visit vineyards and wine-making farms, and also participate in such events as wine

K. Jesiotr • E. Szymanska (✉)
Management Faculty, Bialystok University of Technology, Bialystok, Poland
e-mail: kasia2010x@wp.pl; e.szymanska@pb.edu.pl

© Springer International Publishing Switzerland 2016
M.H. Bilgin et al. (eds.), *Business Challenges in the Changing Economic Landscape - Vol. 1*, Eurasian Studies in Business and Economics 2/1,
DOI 10.1007/978-3-319-22596-8_29

festivals, presentations and tastings (Bosak 2008). Enotourism began to develop in the 1920s. It was then that the so-called *Weinstraßen* started to emerge in Germany. These were educational trails focused on grapevine cultivation, as well as wine production and consumption (Wozniczko and Orlowski 2009).

The point of departure for reflections on enotourism is culinary tourism, which is very often called *gastronomical tourism* (Kowalczyk 2008), the main purpose of which is to become acquainted with the cuisine of a given country or region. This includes both traditional recipes for making dishes and beverages, as well as places for having meals (Becker and Steinecke 1997), which represent the character of the region (Rohrscheidt 2008). In the opinion of the European Economic and Social Committee (2006) of the EU, culinary values have substantially gained in significance and attract increasingly large numbers of tourists.

The interest in the cuisine of individual regions and countries leads to the interest in the local culture (Wolf 2004; Kowalczyk 2008). Culinary travels involve not only consumption, but also e.g. tours of palaces, castles, churches, museums and regional restaurants, exhibitions on culinary issues and the participation in regional food fairs. Production plants are also visited, including milk and cheese dairies, vineyards, distilleries and breweries. Demonstrations accompanying production operations are an inseparable feature of culinary tourism (Rohrscheidt 2008). The activities related to culinary tourism are also based on socialising activities, consisting in joint consumption of dishes and savouring of drinks (Kowalczyk 2005). In connection with the development of culinary tourism, numerous thematic routes, called culinary trails, began to emerge (Rohrscheidt 2008).

Traditionally, the largest wine-makers include the European countries in the Mediterranean, the United States of America and, in recent years, certain South American countries. However, new producers appear on the market, including those from areas which are not associated with grapevine cultivation, e.g. those in Central and Eastern Europe. This group also includes Poland. Moreover, in addition to wine production, they can offer a new product related to tourism services. This gives rise to a new business, i.e. entourism, which is the research problem considered in this paper. Its purpose was to assess and identify the prospects for the development of enotourism in Poland. The following research hypothesis was verified: appropriate promotion is the most important factor contributing to the development of enotourism in Poland.

The questionnaire survey method was used in the research, in an attempt to reach all the vineyards operating in the research area (110 operators). Twenty percent of wine-making enterprises which had an e-mail address replied (84). As a result, the survey covered 19 operators. Its results indicate that as a wine producer Poland does not pose a danger to traditional wine-making regions, since the development of wine tourism in Poland has so far remained at a relatively low level. In contrast, a new tourism product which enotourism constitutes is characterised by a large growth rate; therefore, it can be assumed that the prospects of this form of tourism, particularly when addressed to Poland's inhabitants, are very promising. As a result of the research, the hypothesis posed earlier was verified positively, since the respondents recognised that the promotion of Polish wine-producing regions in the country would make the greatest contribution to intensification of enotourism. This was indicated by 84 % of the respondents.

2 Characteristics of Enotourism

The wine tourism is one of the fastest growing sectors of the global tourism industry. This is confirmed by the research done by Smogor (2012) and Wawro (2013).

Enotourism is characterised by Sharma (2005, p. 49) by the following distinguishing factors:

- It is a lifestyle experience (different from everyday life).
- Wine is perceived as one of important attractions of a given region.
- It shows linkages to the regional cuisine, as well as arts and crafts.
- It plays an educational function.
- In certain cases, it is part of a richer tourism offer.
- It provides the prospects for development for both wine-makers and the region.
- It enhances the economic, social and cultural values of the region.
- It shapes the national and international image of a given region, based on tourism values.

The industry around enotourism has grown significantly throughout the first decade of the twenty-first century (Hard 2014). The wine tourism is most widely disseminated in countries characterised by a high wine drinking culture (Wozniczko and Orlowski 2009). Two models of enotourism have been distinguished in the relevant literature. The first one is the European model which is related to cultural tourism, whereas the other is the American and Australian model which shows linkages to entertainment and trade (Kowalczyk 2003). In the United States 27 million travellers, or 17 % of American leisure travellers, are engaged in culinary or wine-related activities (Hard 2014). Wine travellers spend, on average, $973 per trip, with about one-fourth (23 % or $219) of their travel budget going towards wine-specific activities (Hard 2014). "California is the best example of the development of wine tourism" (Kruczek 2014, p. 5). It generates 80 % of wine produced in the entire United States. The Napa Valley is most often offered by tour operators. In the Valley, there are almost a 1000 vineyards, with several dozen of them offering comprehensive wine-related programmes. An organisation of guides and interpreters of the wine-making heritage has been founded and each wine-shop has its own museum which documents its wine-making traditions.

With its flagship regions of Champagne, Bordeaux, Burgundy and Cognac, France is also extremely strong in enotourism. In Italy, as informed Italy Magazine (2008), which is the second strongest in Europe, there are approximately five million travellers, generating 2.5 billion euros in revenue. The enotourism offer is also very well developed in the Iberian peninsula. The whole of South Spain is known for wine production (particularly Catalonia and Andalusia) (Kruczek 2014.

With its 1,180,000 ha dedicated for this purpose, Spain has the largest grapevine cultivation area in the world. However, it comes third in wine production, following Italy and France (periodical droughts in this country have an adverse effect on yields). The Province of La Rioja, situated on the banks of the Ebro River, is the best known wine-making region of Spain. Other well-known regions include Priorat near Tarragona, Penedès south Barcelona and Ribera del Duero on the Duero River.

Numerous wine-related associations are founded, including e.g. the Spanish Wine and Food Tourism Association (SW&FTA). The mission of this organisation is to position Spain as a leading destination for food and wine orientated tourism. In order to popularise enotourism and wine drinking culture, the second Sunday of November is officially the *Enotourism Day*. That means that this November 11th, it's time to tour some cellars, drink some wine, and see what the harvest dragged in around Germany, Austria, Slovenia, Spain, France, Greece, Hungary, Italy, and Portugal.

As indicated by statistics from different regions, 68–75 % tourists visiting wine-making farms buy on the site at least one bottle of the wine produced there (Kruczek 2014). In the literature, there is a classification which takes into account both tourists' interest in wine and their knowledge of wine. This classification distinguishes three groups of enotourists (Pearce, 2005 cited in Mazurkiewicz-Pizlo 2013, pp. 120–121): "wine lovers and connoisseurs, persons who show their interest in wine and persons called beginners".

In turn, Bosak (2008, p. 13) enumerates five major features which characterise those engaged in wine tourism: "...aged more than 25 years; however, with the range of 35–45 years dominating; higher education, revenues exceeding the average level, high professional skills, most often travelling in couples or men". With respect to enotourists' age (Pearce, 2005 cited in Mazurkiewicz-Pizlo 2013, pp. 122–123), identified "the age range of 35–50 years and indicated that they usually travelled with friends or persons whom they knew". In characterising enotourists, it should be emphasised that in many cases they demonstrate common preferences related to travels; specifically (Bosak 2008): their resignation from one longer trip in favour of several shorter ones, preferences for shorter sojourns and visiting several places in the course of one travel, spending nights at high-standard sites and an interest in the local cuisine and the cultural heritage of a given region.

It can be recognised, therefore, that enotourism falls within the scope of culinary and cultural tourism and that its participants are very desirable customers because of the frequency of their travels and financial standing.

3 Selection of a Research Sample and Research Methodology

It is difficult to find Poland on the world map of wine-related travels; still, "...we can find here offers related to this form of tourism, although it emerged here relatively recently" (Pearce, 2005 cited in Mazurkiewicz-Pizlo 2013, p. 123).

In order to identify the population, the websites of vintners associations operating in Poland were analysed. It was found that six wine associations grouped a total of 110 vineyards. A non-random selection was applied, since the research sample consisted of vineyards belonging to Polish vintners associations. In the light of this, an attempt was made to investigate the whole population, which was analysed in terms of two criteria. The first criterion was whether vineyards had a website, but this criterion had no effect on a change in the sample size. The other criterion was whether those vineyards had a valid e-mail address and this criterion had an effect on a change in the sample size, since, as the e-mail based technique was used, a valid e-mail address was indispensable to enable the research to be carried out.

The analysis indicated that 39 vineyards had their own website. These vineyards represented 35 % of all the vineyards belonging to vintners associations. 88 vineyards had their own e-mail address. These vineyards represented 80 % of all the vineyards belonging to vintners associations. The survey questionnaire was sent electronically to the 88 owners of these vineyards. The survey was carried out in April 2014. In the course of the survey, it turned out that four respondents had no valid e-mail address. Ultimately, the research sample to which the questionnaires were sent consisted of 84 units. Nineteen respondents, representing 23 % of the population surveyed, returned the questionnaire survey. The survey used the questionnaire method, consisting in written communication between the researcher and the respondent. Its main advantage is the ability to examine a large community in a short time (Hermaniuk 2005).

The operation periods of Polish vineyards are differentiated, varying between several and a few dozen years. The Golesz Vineyard has operated for the longest period, i.e. for 32 years. The Kombornia Manor Vineyard has been in operation for the shortest period, i.e. 2 years. The survey showed that vineyards with operation periods of 5–10 years dominated. Twelve vineyards, representing 63 % of all the vineyards, fell within this range.

Polish vineyards are differentiated in terms of their surface area. The Mierzęcin Palace Vineyards has the largest surface area, amounting to 6.75 ha. The Kombornia Manor Vineyard is the smallest, with its 0.05 ha only. The average surface area of the vineyards indicated in the figure is about 1.55 ha. The analysis of the survey performed also indicated that vineyards with a surface area of up to 1 ha dominated. Eleven vineyards, representing 58 % of all the vineyards, fell within this range.

In the division of Polish wine-making regions, two classifications are taken into account in 2008 by Meeting of Polish Vintners (MPV). The first one relates to the climate conditions occurring in given regions of the country. The other classification of wine-making regions was set out in the course of the third MPV in 2008, organized by the Polish Institute for Grapevine and Wine, the WINO (WINE) Magazine and the Marshall of Podkarpackie Province who was a co-organiser of the Meeting. The Meeting took place on 30 August 2008 in Jasło. The wine-making regions, established in the course of the third Meeting of Polish Vintners, were divided on the basis of the natural conditions occurring in given regions. Their administrative borders were also taken into account by the MPV (WinoKultura 2008).

The greatest concentration can be found in South-eastern Poland. The traditional areas where grapevine is cultivated also include those near Zielona Góra. An important issue which should be covered by considerations of Poland's potential to develop enotourism is the activity of organisations that associate vintners operating across the country. The four most important ones are: the Podkarpacie Winegrowers Association, the Zielona Góra Wine Association, the Vintners Association of the Vistula River Gorge in Little Poland and the Little Poland Wine Forum.

The largest vintners' organisation to operate in Poland is the Podkarpacie Winegrowers Association, which was founded in 2006 (Wawro 2013). Wawro claims that Podkarpacie was the first Polish region to have its own local wine growing tradition. It is exactly Podkarpacie that has made the greatest contribution to the flourishing of viniculture in the country and now constitutes the most interesting wine-making region of Poland. In this region, the first professional vineyard was set up in Poland in 1984. It was the Golesz Vineyard in Jasło, which initiated the revival of Polish wine-making. The wines of Podkarpacie have gained renown, as a result of which they attract wine lovers from Poland and abroad. Vineyard owners take efforts to continuously develop their operations. Among others, wine tourism was part of this development. Another association is the Zielona Góra Wine Association. It began its activity in 2006, as a result of the integration of two entities, i.e. the Lubuskie Vintners Association and the National Polish Association of Grapevine Growers and Wine Producers. In 2008, the Vintners Association of the Vistula River Gorge in Little Poland was founded. The main purpose of the activity of this Association is the development of vineyards situated in the region of the Vistula River Gorge in Little Poland and the areas round it. The fourth association of interest is the Tarnów Land Vintners Association (Wawro 2013). In 2011, the Silesian Vintners Association was established. The youngest wine-makers' association operating in the Polish territory is the Sandomierz Vintners Association, which was officially entered into the Register of Associations in 2013.

The enotourism offer of Polish vineyards is at the development stage. Most vineyards have their basic offer, including vineyard tours and wine tasting. However, some of them offer tourists a wider range of attractions, consisting, for example, of the regional cuisine, sightseeing in the environs, horse rides or different types of feasts.

In the reflections on Poland's potential to develop enotourism, consideration should be given to wine trails. According to Olszewski and Drozdz (2013, pp. 436–

440) the most important Polish wine trails include: the Lubuskie Wine and Mead Trail, the Podkarpackie Vineyards Trail, the Little Poland Wine Trail and the Sandomierz Wine Trail. The Lubuskie Wine and Mead Trail has the greatest potential to develop enotourism. This is primarily related to a large diversity of sites situated on the trail. It was established in 2006 (Wierzynski 2011), and its route encompasses, e.g., museums, including open-air ones, agri-tourism farms, bee-keeping farms and vineyards.

4 Prospects for the Development of Enotourism in Poland in the Light of Empirical Studies

The first research area was the development of enotourism to date in Poland. A second research area concerned the prospects for the development of enotourism in this country. Respondents assessed it from *very poor* to *very good*; they could choose one option from a 5-level scale patterned after the Likert scale (Fig. 1).

It follows from the surveys which were carried out that most respondents assessed the development of enotourism to date in Poland as poor. Such an answer was indicated by 10 respondents, who represented 53 % of all the respondents. Moreover, two respondents thought that the development was very poor; they represented 11 % of all the respondents. It follows from this that in the opinion of 64 % of the respondents the development of enotourism to date in Poland was at a poor or very poor level. According to one third of respondents, the development of enotourism in Poland was good or very good. Four respondents assessed the development of enotourism to date as good; they represented 21 % of all the respondents. In turn, two respondents assessed the development of enotourism to date as very good; they represented 11 % of all the respondents.

It follows from the surveys which were carried out that the largest number of respondents assessed the prospects for the development of enotourism in Poland as good. Such an answer was indicated by seven respondents, who represented 37 % of

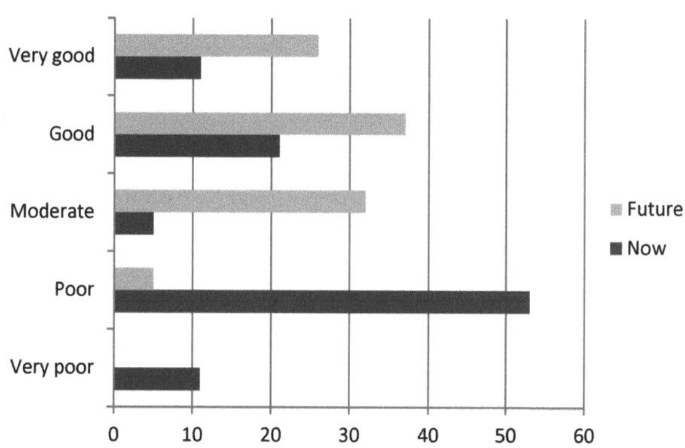

Fig. 1 Respondents' assessment of the development of enotourism to date and the prospects for the development of enotourism (%). *Source*: Own elaboration based on surveys

all the respondents. Moreover, five respondents assessed these prospects as very good; they represented 26 % of all the respondents. It follows from this that in the opinion of 63 % of respondents the prospects for the development of enotourism in Poland were good and very good. Six respondents assessed the prospects for the development of enotourism in Poland as moderate; they represented 32 % of all the respondents. It follows from the surveys which were carried out that a total of 95 % respondents assessed the prospects for the development of enotourism in Poland as at least moderate. In turn, one respondent assessed the prospects for the development of enotourism in Poland as poor.

Another research area consisted of measures contributing to the development of enotourism in Poland. The question provided for eight options of reply and had the nature of a half-open cafeteria-style checklist. The respondents could mark any number of options of reply and were also able to give their own suggestions. The results are given in Fig. 2.

It follows from the surveys which were carried out that the promotion of wine-making regions in Poland and the popularisation of the wine drinking culture would make the greatest contribution to the development of enotourism in Poland. These two answers were indicated by 16 respondents, who represented 84 % of the

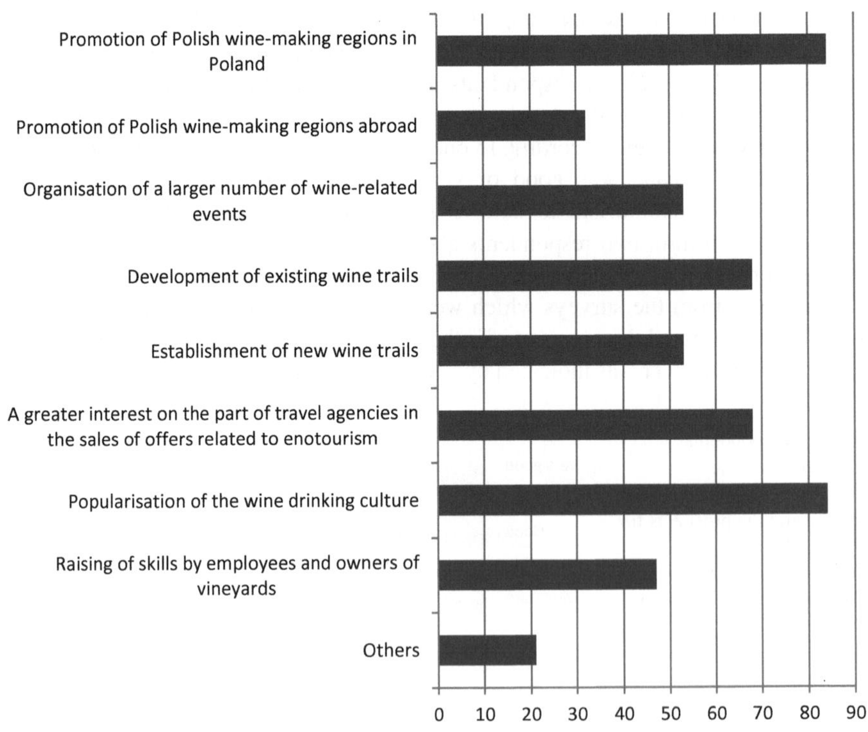

Fig. 2 Measures contributing to the development of enotourism in Poland, according to respondents (%). *Source*: Own elaboration based on surveys

research sample. The development of existing wine trails and a greater interest on the part of travel agencies in the sales of offers related to enotourism came next. These two answers were indicated by 13 respondents, who represented 68 % of all the respondents. Two factors came third with the same support. More than half (53 %) of respondents indicated that the development of enotourism would be boosted by the organisation of a larger number of wine-related events and the establishment of new wine trails.

In respect of the development of enotourism in Poland, an important issue is also the raising of skills by employees and owners of vineyards. Such an answer was given by 47 % of respondents. Four respondents gave their own examples of measures which, in their opinion, would play an important role in the development of enotourism in Poland; specifically: support from local and regional authorities, amendment (liberalisation) of wine-making law to align it with the EU legislation, the construction of state of the art wine-shops, co-financed from the state budget, and an enhanced interest of mass media, e.g. in morning and weekend broadcasts.

5 Conclusions and Recommendations

In Poland, the tourism market which provides services related to the broadly understood wine-making issues is at the development stage. According to *A Report on Enotourism* (Wydawnictwo Eurosystem 2012), enotourism continues to be considered a niche form of tourism. Despite this situation, the interest in this form of tourism can be seen to grow. This interest is demonstrated not only by tourists and entrepreneurs, but also by local authorities. In this respect, typical wine-making regions and wine trails, which are gaining in significance, are of substantial importance (Dudek-Mankowska and Duda-Gromada 2009).

It follows from the surveys which were carried out that enotourism in Poland is at an early development stage. In turn, the prospects of such tourism are relatively optimistic, since 63 % of respondents assess them as good or very good. None of the respondents considered them to be very poor and only one thought that they were poor.

The group of measures which would make the greatest contribution to intensification of the development of enotourism included the promotion of Polish wine-making regions in Poland and the popularisation of the wine drinking culture the country (84 % each). In this case, the hypothesis posed earlier concerning the promotion of Polish wine-making regions as a measure which would make the greatest contribution to the development of enotourism (the most frequently chosen answer) was positively verified. The importance of the development of existing wine trails and a greater interest on the part of travel agencies in the sales of offers related to enotourism came next (68 % of indications). The measures of importance for this form of tourism included the organisation of a larger number of wine-related events and the establishment of new wine trails, as indicated by 53 % of respondents. It can also be seen that the respondents associated the future of enotourism primarily with the domestic tourism movement (84 %) rather the tourism movement abroad (the promotion of Polish wine-making regions abroad—32 %).

If further research focused on the development of enotourism in Poland is undertaken, it needs to consider two important issues. Firstly, they include the provisions of wine-making law applicable to wine-makers in Poland. Secondly, they encompass the measures taken by local and regional authorities to develop wine-making and enotourism.

After a comprehensive assessment of all the indicated answers, it is impossible to indicate any specific measure which would strongly contribute to the development of enotourism in Poland, since its development is affected by a number of factors. In addition, it should be emphasised, as highlighted by the respondents themselves, that this research has been carried out for the first time in Poland. In the light of this, it is recommended that this research should be continued and expanded in order to identify specific measures fostering the development of enotourism in Poland and to indicate barriers which impede it. The research and discussion should contribute to better exploration of the problems of the enotourism activity, which turns out to be a new, dynamically developing business, not only in countries which are more suitable for it, but also in the regions which have so far not been associated with the wine culture.

References

Becker, C., & Steinecke, A. (1997). *Kulturtourismus: Strukturen und Entwicklungsperspektiven*. Hagen: Fern-Uniwersität.

Bosak, W. (2008, July/September 28–29). Wino i turystyka [Wine and tourism]. In *Winiarz Zielonogórski* [Zielona Góra Wine-maker] (pp. 13–16).

Dudek-Mankowska, S., & Duda-Gromada, K. (2009). The wine-making region of the Vistula River Gorge in Little Poland as a tourism product. In A. Stasiak (Ed.), *Kultura i turystyka. Wspólnie zyskać!* [Culture and Tourism. Gain Together!]. Łódź: School of Graduate Studies in Tourism and Hospitality Management in Łódź.

European Economic and Social Committee. (2006). Opinion of the European economic and social committee on tourism and culture: Two forces for growth. *Official Journal of the European Union, 49*, 1–8.

Hard, R. (2014). *Study: Food and wine travel increases in popularity*. Accessed August 20, 2014, from http://eventplanning.about.com/od/venueselection/a/travelstudy.htm

Hermaniuk, T. (2005). *Podstawy badań marketingowych* [Fundamentals of Marketing Surveys – in Polis]. Rzeszów: Publishing House of the University of Rzeszów.

ITALYMagazine. (2008, May 12). *Popularity of wine tourism grows*. Accessed August 20, 2014, from http://www.italymagazine.com/italy/food-drink/popularity-wine-tourism-grows

Kowalczyk, A. (2003). Szlaki winne – nowa forma aktywizacji turystycznej obszarów wiejskich [Wine trails – a new form of tourism-related activisation of rural areas]. *Prace i Studia Geograficzne, 32*, 69–98.

Kowalczyk, A. (2005). Turystyka kulinarna – ujęcie geograficzne [Culinary tourism – a geographical look – in Polish]. *Turyzm, 15*(1–2), 163–186.

Kowalczyk, A. (2008). Współczesna turystyka kulturowa – między tradycją a nowoczesnością [Contemporary cultural tourism – Between tradition and modernity]. In A. Kowalczyk (Ed.),

Turystyka kulturowa. Spojrzenie geograficzne [Cultural tourism – A geographical look]. Warsaw: Faculty of Geography and Regional Studies of Warsaw University.

Kruczek, Z. (2014). *Enoturystyka w Polsce i na świecie* [Enotourism in Poland and in the World]. Poland: Proksenia. Accessed August 20, 2014, from http://www.proksenia.pl/download/Enoturystyka_Wspolczesne_formy_turystyki_kulturowej.pdf

Mazurkiewicz-Pizlo, A. (2013). *Enoturystyka jako szansa rozwoju społeczno-ekonomicznego obszarów wiejskich* [Enotourism as an opportunity for the socio-economic development of rural areas – in Polish]. Warsaw-Toruń: Scientific Society for Organisation and Management "Organiser's House".

Olszewski, J., & Drozdz, R. (2013). Polska oferta w zakresie "enoturystyki" [The Polish offer in the scope of"enotourism"]. *Hygeia Public Health, 48*(4), 436–440.

Rohrscheidt, A. M. (2008). *Turystyka kulturowa. Fenomen, potencjał, perspektywy* [Cultural Tourism. The Phenomenon, Potential, Prospects]. Gniezno: Gniezno College of the Humanities and Management Millenium in Gniezno.

Sharma, K. K. (2005). *Tourism and development*. New Delhi: Sarup & Sons.

Smogor, J. (2012). Wpływ autostrady Warszawa-Berlin na rozwój enoturystyki w województwie lubuskim [The impact of the Warsaw-Berlin motorway on the development of enotourism in Lubuskie Province]. *Studia Periegetica, Scientific Papers of Wielkopolska College of Tourism and Management in Poznań, 7*, 121–130.

Wawro, E. (2013, May 9). *Stowarzyszenie Winiarzy Podkarpacia [The Podkarpacie Winegrowers Association]*. Accessed April 6, 2014, from http://www.winiarzepodkarpacia.pl/o-nas/stowarzyszenie

Wierzynski, W. (2011). *Klastering w branży turystycznej [Clustering in the tourism sector – in Polish]*. Accessed April 14, 2014, from http://www.pi.gov.pl/parp/chapter_86196.asp?soid=E565ED9AD2444DDA96C2D1D3021D8D7A

WinoKultura. (2008). *Regiony winiarskie w Polsce* [Wine-making regions in Poland]. Accessed March 23, 2014, from http://www.winokultura.pl/dokument,regiony-winiarskie-w-polsce.,23

Wolf, E. (2004). *Culinary tourism: A tasty economic proposition*. Portland: June Publishing House, International Culinary Tourism Association.

Wozniczko, M., & Orlowski, D. (2009). Winiarstwo jako narodowe dziedzictwo kultury i jego wykorzystanie w enoturystyce północnych Węgier [Wine-making as the national cultural heritage and its use in enotourism in northern Hungary]. In: A. Stasiak (Ed.), *Kultura i turystyka. Wspólnie zyskać!* [Culture and tourism. Gain together!]. Łódź: School of Graduate Studies in Tourism and Hospitality Management in Łódź.

Wydawnictwo Eurosystem. (2012, August 15). Raport Enoturystyka [A Report on Enotourism]. *Wiadomości Turystyczne [Tourist News]*. Accessed March 23, 2014, from http://www.wiadomosciturystyczne.pl/artykuly/artykul/646,0,47,0,raport_enoturystyka.html

The European Union Policy Towards the Post-Soviet Countries of Central Asia

Agnieszka Konopelko

The project is financed by founds of National Science Center based on the number of decision DEC-2011/03/B/HS4/05930.

Abstract The European Union develops multilateral and multidimensional international activities by the use of common long-term strategies and developmental programmes in political, economic, security and cultural spheres. The empirical study underlines that Central Asia is perceived by the EU as an outlying yet neighboring territory. On the other hand, the EU remains a marginal player in Central Asia. The EU is not a great power in the region and cannot compete with China, Russia or the US in hard power politics. However, the European Union has developed a common strategy towards the Central Asia region as a whole. In turn, bilateral relations are based on the Partnership and Cooperation Agreements where the strategy areas are outlined. The author indicates that the European Union strategy towards the region is based mainly on a political and security approach. The EU wants to play a normative role in its relations with external partners. Thus, economic development does not always reflect the political dimension, however, political initiatives can have a strong economic impact. Recently, the mutual relations of the EU with the post-Soviet republics of Central Asia have increased over the last years. Moreover, the EU has tried to increase its presence in the region, beyond simply a diplomatic dimension.

Keywords Central Asia • European Union • Post-Soviet countries

A. Konopelko (✉)
Faculty of Management, Bialystok University of Technology, Białystok, Poland
e-mail: agacon@tlen.pl

© Springer International Publishing Switzerland 2016

M.H. Bilgin et al. (eds.), *Business Challenges in the Changing Economic Landscape - Vol. 1*, Eurasian Studies in Business and Economics 2/1,
DOI 10.1007/978-3-319-22596-8_30

1 Introduction

The post-Soviet Central Asia (CA) region unites five former Soviet republics: Kazakhstan, Kyrgyzstan (Kyrgyz Republic), Tajikistan, Turkmenistan and Uzbekistan. Common features and specificity of the region are based on the Islamic religion and ethnic heterogeneity. All of the Central Asian countries are political successors of the former Soviet republics, the presidents were former communist leaders and the leader parties were former communist parties after transformation. With the collapse of the USSR the heads of the Central Asian states have strengthened their power and reduced political opposition, which means a lack of democratic regimes and development of the authoritarian tendencies.

Processes on the former Soviet Union area are hermeneutically placed in the context of the Soviet tradition. Thus, activities (policies, strategies) of the external partners towards the Central Asian region should consider this specific context. Taking into account the main determinants of the EU interests in Central Asia region, such as: the economic issues (natural resources and sales markets), energy issues, logistical issues (transport corridors), security issues (military, political, energetic, ecological), and relations with Russia and its integration initiatives, the European Union, as one of the many players in the region, seeks to find effective instruments to develop and enhance mutual relations.

The article analyzes and evaluates the scope and basis of the European Union policy towards the post-Soviet Central Asian countries and progress in its implementation. The main objectives of the paper concentrate on: identification and assessment of the main advantages and disadvantages in multilateral relations between the EU and the Central Asian states and the effectiveness of the EU policy towards Central Asia region.

The research study is developed through the empirical analysis and interpretation of data and documents of the EU, regional organizations, national agencies and the analytical theoretical research on the EU external policy.

2 The Bases of the Eu Policy Towards the Post-Soviet Central Asian Countries

The European Union develops multilateral and multidimensional international activities. The EU shapes its international activity by the use of common long-term strategies and developmental programmes in political, economic, security and cultural sphere. The EU has developed a common strategy and policy towards the Central Asia region as a whole. The EU launched its strategy in the Central Asia region to accomplish the fostering of relations through peaceful ties and prosperity. Bilateral relations are based on the Partnership and Cooperation Agreements (PCAs) where the strategy areas are outlined. The four countries of Central Asia concluded the Partnership and Cooperation Agreements in 1999—Kazakhstan,

Kyrgyzstan, Uzbekistan and in 2004—Tajikistan. The PCA's are based on three pillars: political dialogue, trade and economic relations and cooperation in a variety of sectors (European Community 2007). Turkmenistan remains a closed and isolated country. The European Parliament has blocked the enforcement of the PCA with Turkmenistan for the country's failure to meet human rights standards (Boonstra 2011).

Kazakhstan, Kyrgyzstan, Tajikistan, Turkmenistan and Uzbekistan are countries of priority within "The EU and Central Asia: Strategy for a New Partnership" (Council of the European Union 2007) signed by the European Council in 2007 and "European Community Regional Strategy Paper for Assistance to Central Asia during 2007–2013" (European Community 2007) adopted in 2007 by the European Commission. The strategy strengthens relations in all areas of cooperation, such as: EU-Central Asia political dialogue with regular meetings of EU and Central Asian Foreign Ministers, dialogue on human rights, cooperation in the areas of education, rule of law, energy and transportation, environment and water, common threats and challenges (including border management and combating drug trafficking), and trade and economic relations.

The European Union developed its strategy to gain access to Central Asia oil and gas resources, diversify its trade partners and supply routes, reduce dependence on Russian supplies and pipelines, develop regional trading corridors, exchange of know-how, and to create energy networks and systems (European Union External Action 2009).

The EU Members States and the European Commission have cooperated closely in the following areas: human rights, rule of law, good governance and democratization; youth and education; economic development, trade and investment; energy and transportation links; environmental sustainability and water; combating common threats and challenges and intercultural dialogue (European Community 2007).

The strategy puts an emphasis on three main areas of intensified policy dialogue and enhanced cooperation: Rule of Law, Education and Environment. The EU–Central Asia Rule of Law Initiative started in 2008 and supported for legal and judicial reforms and developed an intensified policy dialogue at all levels. The Initiative launched the EU-Central Asia Rule of Law Platform (with regular meetings at ministerial and regional levels) that provided services required for an efficient implementation of the Rule of Law Initiative, and promoting regional cooperation between the countries of Central Asia, in order to advance constitutional, legal and judicial reforms in the region (EU Rule of Law Initiative for Central Asia n.d.). The EU–Central Asia Education Initiative, established in 2007, concentrated on educational exchanges, education reform and vocational training. The initiative developed programmes at a regional level: Tempus (modernization in the higher education sector), Erasmus Mundus Partnerships (academic partnerships and mobility) and the Central Asia Research and Education Network (financing for high-speed information and communication networks). The European Union also supported the EU-Central Asia Education Platform to strengthen education reforms in the region (European Commission 2011). The

EU-Central Asia Environment and Water Initiative is led by Italy with the support of the European Commission, representatives from the Central Asian countries, and the OECD or the UN Economic Commission for Europe. The EU-Central Asia Join Expert Working Group established in 2008 aim at facilitating of regional cooperation in the fields of climate change, protection of the environment, rational use of water resources as well as land and forest management. The regional environmental programmes for Central Asia facilitate the development of the EU-Central Asia Environment and Water Cooperation Platform and focus on integrated water resource management, environmental protection measures, environmental governance and climate change (European Union External Action 2009).

The EU Strategy was supported by the European Community Regional Strategy Paper for Assistance to Central Asia during 2007–2013 (European Community 2007) adopted in 2007 by the European Commission. In 2007–2013 it allocated a total amount of €750 million including €635 million based on Development Cooperation Instrument (DCI). The "Central Asia Development Cooperation Instrument Indicative Programmes" 2007–2010 (European Commission 2006), 2011–2013 (European Commission 2010), were approved by the European Commission and replaced the "Technical Assistance to the Commonwealth of Independent States programme" (TACIS) (European Economic Community n.d.). The Central Asia DCI Programmes provided a multi-annual indicative programming, which in 2007–2010 amounted to €314 million and in 2011–2013 to €321 million (European Commission 2006, 2010).

In a newly proposed EU Partnership Instrument "First Multi-annual Indicative Programme during 2014–2017" the countries of Central Asia were recognized as one of the strategic partners of the European Union. The EU's interests will be mainly focused on trans-regional challenges, such as: illicit trafficking of human beings and substances, organized crime and terrorism. The programme is to be complementary to other EU external instruments (European Commission 2014).

Under the draft of the "New European Strategy Programme for Central Asia 2014–2020" (European Commission 2013), the European Union is ready to allocate 1€ billion during 2014–2020 to support the development of the Central Asian countries. In 2013 the former European Commissioner for Development Andris Piebalgs announced in Brussels that "For the next seven years we are ready to support measures to strengthen security, promote democracy and the rule of law in the amount of 1 billion euro". The financial assistance will be addressed mainly to Kyrgyz Republic (€184 million for security, energy, water, environment), Tajikistan (€251 million for education, health, rural development, local governments and civil society projects). Turkmenistan, Uzbekistan and Kazakhstan can also receive assistance on basis of regional and thematic programs of cooperation. Funding will be allocated to improve the regional management of natural resources, social and economic development as well as regional security (European Commission 2013).

3 Implementation of the Eu Policy Towards the Post-Soviet Central Asia Region

The European Union has focused its regional financial support on three flagship programmes in Central Asia: sustainable regional development (energy and environment initiatives), education initiative, and the rule of law and border management initiatives (see Table 1).

Table 2 demonstrates that a considerable share of the regional funds was committed to educational programmes-Erasmus and Tempus programmes (36 %) and the Investment Facility for Central Asia programme (29 %) (European Commission 2011).

Bilateral cooperation with the countries of Central Asia concentrated on: poverty reduction, improving living standards, good governance and economic reformation. As we can notice in Table 3, the main beneficiaries of the EU assistance—Kyrgyzstan and Tajikistan, the poorest countries in the region—were supposed to obtain almost half of total resources, especially for: social protection, health sector, agriculture development and education sector (European Commission 2011).

However, it should be emphasized that implementation of the EU strategy was rather slow. According to the European Court of Auditors, "The regional programmes did not achieve a genuine regional dimension; a significant share consisted merely of 'multi-country' facilities available to each partner country

Table 1 Regional cooperation to Central Asia (2007–2013) in € million

	2007–2010	2011–2013	2007–2013
Sustainable regional development (energy/environment/business cooperation networks)	49.60	51.00	100.60
Education, science	66.40	42.00	108.40
Rule of law, border management, customs and the fight against organized crime	21.00	12.00	33.00
Total regional cooperation	137.00	105.00	242.00

Source: European Commission 2011

Table 2 EU funding to Central Asia by main cooperating sectors (2007–2013) in € million

	2007–2013
Education/Higher education	159.80
Health and social protection	139.50
Governance	125.80
Environment/Energy/Climate	106.20
Agriculture/Rural development	55.20
Economy/Trade/Private sector	48.90
Cross-border/Security	23.00
Other	15.40

Source: European Commission 2011

Table 3 Bilateral cooperation to Central Asia (2007–2013) in € million

	2007–2010	2011–2013	2007–2013
Kazakhstan	44.00	30.00	74.00
Kyrgyzstan	55.20	51.00	106.20
Tajikistan	66.00	62.00	128.00
Turkmenistan	22.00	31.00	53.00
Uzbekistan	28.60	42.00	70.60
Total bilateral cooperation	215.80	216.00	431.80

Source: European Commission 2011

Table 4 Central Asia regional strategy 2007–2013. Development cooperation instrument–Asia implementation. Contracts and disbursements (31.12.2012)

	Total allocations 2007–2013 (€ million)	Contracted amounts 2007–2012 (in %)	Disbursed amounts 2007–2012 (in %)
Kazakhstan	74	60	28
Kyrgyzstan	106	73	45
Tajikistan	128	65	32
Turkmenistan	53	21	13
Uzbekistan	71	28	9
Region	242	42	26
Total	674	50	27

Source: European Court of Auditors 2013

individually". They recommend that the design of any future regional programmes are done so that they achieve a real regional dimension and concentrate on smaller number of sectors (maximum three in each country) and improve to design programmes considering administrative costs, anti-corruption mechanisms and changing circumstances (European Court of Auditors 2013, p. 7).

At the end of 2012, 50 % of overall planned commitments for the 2007–2012 period under the Development Cooperation Instrument–Asia had been contracted and only 27 % paid (Table 4). The auditors identified cases in which there were long delays in the implementation of programmes. For example, in Uzbekistan, it took, on average, 2 years to sign the financing agreement and 1 year to start the implementation of the programmes. In Turkmenistan and Uzbekistan the progress in strategy implementation had been slowed by differences in priorities and approaches to development cooperation between the both sides. In Kyrgyzstan and Tajikistan implementation was faster. This reflects an improvement in developmental cooperation between the EU and the two countries (European Court of Auditors 2013).

Nevertheless, it should be noted that the strategy intensified the mutual relations and the EU engagement in Central Asia, especially in political and human rights dialogue, democratic reforms, energy dialogue, education cooperation and diplomatic presence.

The European External Action Service and the European Commission services in their document entitled "Progress Report on the implementation of the EU Strategy for Central Asia" (European External Action Service 2012) underline their significant contribution to: political engagement and financial assistance in the crisis in the Kyrgyz Republic (2010), implementation of the rule of law initiative (under European Instrument for Democracy and Human Rights-EDHIR), Border Management Programme for Central Asia (BOMCA), and Central Asia Drug Action Programme (CADAP), development of SME's sector (by Central Asia Invest Programme and European Investment Bank loans and grants), regional energy cooperation (under Baku Initiative), pan-European corridor through the Black Sea and the Caspian Sea (INOGATE and TRACEA programmes) and water management production, promotion of the Central Asian countries' export to the EU (the EU Generalized System of Preferences-GSP), establishment of the EU Delegations in Central Asian countries, the EU Special Representative for Central Asia, and the High Level EU-Central Asia Security Dialogue and security cooperation on counter-terrorism (Council of the European Union 2012; European External Action Service 2012).

However, the European External Action Service and the European Commission perceive the challenges ahead of a new financial perspective. Within regional programs funding will be provided for regional sustainable development, security, and economic support, social and institutional reforms in Central Asia. Thus, it seems to be important to promote economic diversification, sustainable regional development and SME's development. More advanced WTO negotiations with Kazakhstan, Uzbekistan, Turkmenistan and their ultimate accession will foster modernization and development of these economies. The Trans-Caspian Pipeline System (Southern Gas Corridor) would enable diversified energy supplies and integrate the energy markets (European External Action Service 2012).

What is emphasized is an improvement of coordination of the existing EU programmes (Central Asia Research and Education Network, EU-Central Asia High Level Security Dialogue, EU regional Water and Environment Initiative) and sectorial cooperation in: promotion and protection of human rights, judicial independence, good governance, civil society development, rule of law (Rule of Law Platform is being established) and parliamentary dialogue (Parliamentary Cooperation Committees). However, most need mutual engagement by other international actors (OSCE, UN, GRECO) active in the region, mainly in: border management, promoting responsible, efficient and economic usage of water and energy resources, combating of drug trafficking and cross-border crime, regional cooperation in Afghanistan after withdrawal of ISAF troops in 2014—new phase of BOMCA ("Border Management in Central Asia"), CABSI ("Central Asia Border Security Initiative"), and CBRN (to counter a threat of spreading chemical, biological and nuclear materials) (European External Action Service 2012).

4 Evaluation of the European Union Relations with the Central Asian States

The European Union strategy towards the region is based mainly on a political and security approach. Thus, the economic development does not always reflect the political dimension. However, the mutual relations of the EU with five post-Soviet republics of the Central Asia have increased over the last years.

The European Union is one of the region's largest trading partner, accounting for nearly one-third of Central Asia's external trade (Table 5). We can observe worse conditions for the EU exporters in the post-Soviet area although a relatively high volume of trade between the Central Asian countries and the EU should be noted. Nonetheless, Central Asian exports to the EU is limited to a few commodities such as cotton, metals and crude oil. Similarly, the structure of the EU exports to the region, is based on machinery and transport equipment (European Commission Directorate-General for Trade 2014; Gast 2014).

Favorable access to the EU's internal market is possible through a Generalized System of Preferences (GSP 2006/2015) (EUR-Lex 2006). The GSP scheme is implemented by developed countries (like European Communities) under GATT (WTO) and UNCTAD arrangements to accord preferential tariff treatment to developing countries to improve development, financial or trade situations and to help them to reduce poverty and obtain international trade revenue (EUR-Lex 2006). The system remains an important tool to promote and diversify the export of Central Asian countries (especially the poorest countries in the region-Kyrgyzstan and Tajikistan).

Kazakhstan borders Russia and China, but the EU has become Kazakhstan's first trading partner (Table 6) and first foreign investor, representing over half of total FDI in Kazakhstan. In 2013, more than half of Kazakhstan's total trade with the EU reached around \$53.4 billion and in the first half of 2014—\$28.4 billion. More than half of gross foreign direct investment, nearly \$100 billion, has come from the EU countries (Nazarbayev 2014).

The Central Asian authorities and the European Union underline the importance of cooperation in transnational security threats such as: drug-trafficking, human trafficking, organized crime and terrorism (Sharshenova 2013). However, in the context of the NATO/ISAF troops withdrawal from Afghanistan the EU should pay particular attention to security issues especially under the BOMCA and CADAP Action Programmes.

Opening of the EU delegations in Central Asia countries and the establishment of the EU Special Representative in Central Asia has been perceived positively by both sides but the recent withdrawal of EU Special Representative and appointment of the EU Special Envoy for Central Asia raises some doubts about its status and competency in a genuine role in mutual relations. Doubled financial support for the region (DCI—2007–2013) is positively evaluated but in comparison to China's or Russia's offer—US \$10 billion anti-crisis fund, lower gas prices for Kyrgyzstan the EU assistance is still too limited in its funds.

Table 5 Main trading partners of post-Soviet Central Asia region in 2013 (in % of total)

	Export		Import		Total trade	
Partner	%	Partner	%	Partner	%	
1.	**European Union**	38.1	China	32.8	China	32.3
2.	China	31.8	Russia	21.3	**European Union**	28.1
3.	Russia	8.7	**European Union**	18.2	Russia	15.0
4.	Turkey	4.3	Turkey	6.0	Turkey	5.1
5.	Canada	3.3	South Korea	4.8	Ukraine	2.7
6.	USA	1.7	Ukraine	4.3	South Korea	2.6
7.	Switzerland	1.5	USA	2.6	USA	2.2
8.	Iran	1.4	Belarus	2.0	Canada	1.8
9.	Ukraine	1.1	Japan	1.4	Japan	1.1
10.	Serbia	1.0	U.A. Emirates	1.0	Belarus	1.1

Source: European Commission Directorate-General for Trade 2014

Table 6 Main trading partners of post-Soviet Central Asian countries in 2013

	Kazakhstan	Kyrgyzstan	Tajikistan	Turkmenistan	Uzbekistan
Export	EU	Kazakhstan	Turkey	China	China
	China	Uzbekistan	Iran	EU	Russia
	Russia	Russia	China	Turkey	Kazakhstan
	Canada	U.A. Emirates	EU	U.A. Emirates	Turkey
	Turkey	Afghanistan	Bangladesh	Afghanistan	Bangladesh
Import	China	China	China	Turkey	China
	EU	Russia	Russia	Russia	Russia
	Russia	Kazakhstan	Kazakhstan	EU	South Korea
	Ukraine	EU	Turkey	China	EU
	USA	Turkey	EU	U.A. Emirates	Kazakhstan
Total trade	EU	China	China	China	China
	China	Russia	Russia	Turkey	Russia
	Russia	Kazakhstan	Kazakhstan	EU	Kazakhstan
	Ukraine	EU	Turkey	Russia	South Korea
	Turkey	Uzbekistan	EU	U.A. Emirates	EU

Source: European Commission Directorate-General for Trade 2014

The EU policy towards Central Asia established legal and institutional frames of cooperation and an increased EU presence in the region but the first EU Strategy showed serious weaknesses: shortcomings in defining of the Europe's political interests and comparative advantages in the region (Melvin 2012) or setting unrealistic goals (too restrictive demands for the Central Asian regimes) and a prioritization of self-interest objectives (Boonstra 2011), a gap between the normative objectives and the implementation in the region, failure in a democratization area due to a little substantial progress on human rights, governance and civil society, too many beneficiary sectors and too complicated bureaucratic procedures (Peyrouse 2014).

Taking into account new conditions like economic slowdown, the situation in Afghanistan, possible comparative advantages and complementary role towards the engagement of the other external partners, the EU in the new Strategy should outline the real strategic objectives (Melvin 2012).

Undoubtedly, in a view of the Eurasian Economic Union creation and the European Neighbourhood Policy together with the Eastern Partnership an intensification of multilateral (interregional) cooperation in the region (beyond geographical approach) would be profitable for both sides. Therefore, what seems to be important is an opening of the EU Delegation to Turkmenistan, conclusion of the PCA Agreement with Turkmenistan, prolongation and clarification of the previous PCAs and intensification of WTO negotiations with Kazakhstan and Uzbekistan.

According to "Central Asia Development Cooperation Instrument Indicative Programme" 2011–2013, "The strong EU commitment towards its Eastern neighbors within the framework of the European Neighborhood Policy will also bring Europe and Central Asia closer to each other, in terms of both political cooperation and economic development" (European Commission 2010, p. 8).

One of the challenges ahead of the EU is a problem of the human rights, political and civil liberties in Central Asia. In spite of many EU instruments, such as: Development Cooperation Instrument (DCI), the European Instrument for Democracy and Human Rights (EIDHR), the Non-State Actors and Local Authorities in Development (NSA-LA), the Institution Building and Partnership Programme (IBPP), and the Instrument for Stability (IfS), human rights situation in Central Asia has not improved over the last decade (European Parliament 2014). Most of the Central Asian countries have noted a regular decline of democracy scores in Freedom House, Amnesty International and Human Rights Watch reports.

Table 7 demonstrates the Freedom House ratings on Democracy score, Freedom status, Civil liberties and Political rights. The ratings are based on a scale of 1–7, with 1 representing the highest level of democratic progress and 7 the lowest.

Only one of the post-Soviet Central Asia countries, Kyrgyzstan, was recognized as a partly free political system whereas the rest of the countries with the lowest scores represent "not free" freedom status (Freedom House 2014).

It is hard to disagree with Patricia Flor, the former EU Special Representative for Central Asia that "there cannot be stability, peace, prosperity, and social justice if you do not ensure rule of law and respect for human rights in a country" (Muckenhuber 2013).

5 Conclusions

Central Asia is perceived by the European Union as a distant neighboring territory. On the other hand, the Europe remains a marginal player in Central Asia. The EU cannot compete with China, Russia and US in a hard power politics (BOMCA programme can be exception). EU has increased its presence in the region, mainly in diplomatic dimension. Within the framework of the soft power, the UE needs to

Table 7 Freedom House ratings in the countries of Central Asia (2010–2014)

		2010	2011	2012	2013	2014
Kazakhstan	Democracy score	6.43	6.43	6.54	6.57	6.61
	Freedom status	Not free	Not free	No free	Not free	Not free
	Civil liberties	5	5	5	5	5
	Political rights	6	6	6	6	6
Kyrgyzstan	Democracy score	6.21	6.11	6.00	5.96	5.89
	Freedom status	Not free	Partly free	Partly free	Partly free	Partly free
	Civil liberties	5	5	5	5	5
	Political rights	6	5	5	5	5
Tajikistan	Democracy score	6.14	6.14	6.18	6.25	6.32
	Freedom status	Not free	Not free	Not free	Not free	Not free
	Civil liberties	5	5	5	6	6
	Political rights	6	6	6	6	6
Turkmenistan	Democracy score	6.93	6.93	6.93	6.93	6.93
	Freedom status	Not free	Not free	Not free	Not free	Not free
	Civil liberties	7	7	7	7	7
	Political rights	7	7	7	7	7
Uzbekistan	Democracy score	6.93	6.93	6.93	6.93	6.93
	Freedom status	Not free	Not free	Not free	Not free	Not free
	Civil liberties	7	7	7	7	7
	Political rights	7	7	7	7	7

Source: Freedom House 2014

create a positive vision of Central Asia and mutual relations and better understanding of the EU beyond traditional diplomacy.

One of the determinants that hinder development of an effective long-term EU strategy towards the Central Asia region has been the world financial crisis. It has influenced both the EU member countries and the countries of the "eastern neighbourhood". Another determinant lies in a traditional Russian strategy of reintegration of the Soviet influence zone and its natural comparative advantages in the post-Soviet area.

Although, almost all Central Asian countries note a higher volume of trade with the EU than with Russia, Russia offers the eastern partners concrete proposals, such as: liberalization of visa policy, possibility of legal work, supplies of cheaper energy resources, investments in infrastructure and energetic sector and advanced forms of integration like the Custom Union and the Eurasian Economic Union (hard power) (Popescu and Wilson 2010).

Another problem in the successful implementation of the EU policy is a specificity of the political systems and their leaders. Autocratic style of leadership, tribal linkages in the state and society (informal relations), high level of corruption and restrictions of political rights and civil liberties disable a full fulfillment of the main objectives of the EU strategy. Still, the European Union wants to play a normative role in the region.

However, the EU should develop not only the top-down policy (institutional cooperation at governmental level) but also the bottom-up relations with non-governmental organizations and people-to-people contacts (Boonstra 2011).

Recently, both sides have perceived the importance of interregional relations in Central Asian region. There is a mutual will of the EU and partner countries to enhance multilateral economic cooperation, including diversification of trade and investment promotion.

According to Jose Manuel Barroso, the former President of the European Commission it is important to deepen and develop interregional relations between EU and Custom Union (of Russia, Kazakhstan and Belarus). In turn, Nursultan Nazarbayev (2014), President of Kazakhstan underlined that the new PCA agreement signed in 2014 would help to strengthen already existing ties and build new ones.

References

Boonstra J. (2011). *The EU's interests in Central Asia: Integrating energy, security and values into coherent policy, EDC 2020 Working Paper*, 9, [online] Available at http://www.eadi.org. Accessed 20 Nov 2014.

Council of the European Union. (2007). *The EU and Central Asia: Strategy for a new partnership, 10113/07*. Brussels: European Union.

Council of the European Union. (2012, June 25). Council conclusions on Central Asia. *3179th Foreign Affairs Council Meeting*, Luxembourg.

EU Rule of Law Initiative for Central Asia. (n.d.). [online] Available at http://ruleoflaw.eu/about-us/eu-ca-strategy-for-a-new-partnership/eu-rule-of-law-initiative-central-asia. Accessed 27 Dec 2014.

EUR-Lex. (2006). *Scheme of preferences from 2006 to 2015–Guidelines*, [online] Available at http://eur-lex.europa.eu/legal-content/EN/TXT/?qid=1419844349615&uri=URISERV:r11016. Accessed 1 Oct 2014.

European Commission. (2006). *Central Asia development cooperation instrument indicative programme 2007–2010*, [online] Available at http://eeas.europa.eu/central_asia/rsp/nip_07_10_en.pdf. Accessed 5 Nov 2014.

European Commission. (2010). *Central Asia development cooperation instrument indicative programme 2011–2013*, [online] Available at http://www.eeas.europa.eu/central_asia/docs/2010_ca_mtr_en.pdf. Accessed 5 Nov 2014.

European Commission. (2011). *European Union-Central Asia development cooperation*, [online] Available at http://www.ec.europa.eu/europeaid/infopoint/publications/europeaid/documents/263a_en.pdf. Accessed 10 Dec 2014.

European Commission. (2013). *EU announces future commitments for development with Central Asia region*, [online] Available at http://ec.europa.eu/commission_2010-2014/piebalgs/index_en.htm. Accessed 12 Dec 2014.

European Commission. (2014). *First multi-annual indicative programme for the period 2014–2017*, [online] Available at http://ec.europa.eu/dgs/fpi/documents/pi_mip_annex_en.pdf. Accessed 29 Dec 2014.

European Commission Directorate-General for Trade. (2014). *European Union, trade in goods with Central Asia (5)*, [online] Available at http://trade.ec.europa.eu/doclib/docs/2013/november/tradoc_151896.pdf. Accessed 17 Dec 2014.
European Community. (2007). *Regional strategy paper for assistance to Central Asia for the period 2007–2013*, [online] Available at: http://www.eeas.europa.eu/central_asia/rsp/07_13_en.pdf. Accessed 5 Dec 2014.
European Court of Auditors. (2013). *EU development assistance to Central Asia* (European Court of Auditors, Special Report No. 13/2013). Luxembourg.
European Economic Community. (n.d.). *Technical assistance to the commonwealth of independent states programme* (TACIS), 2157/91 of 15 July 1991.
European External Action Service. (2012). *Progress report on the implementation of the EU strategy for Central Asia. Implementation review and outline for future orientations*, [online] Available at http://eeas.europa.eu/central_asia/docs/20120628_progress_report_en.pdf. Accessed 20 Nov 2014.
European Parliament. (2014). *Evaluation of the EU's human rights policies and engagement in Central Asia,* [online] Available at http://www.europarl.europa.eu/RegData/etudes/etudes/join/2014/433788/EXPO-DROI_ET%282014%29433788_EN.pdf. Accessed 9 Dec 2014.
European Union External Action. (2009). *The European Union and Central Asia: The new partnership in action*, [online] Available at http://eeas.europa.eu/central_asia/docs/2010_strategy_eu_centralasia_en.pdf. Accessed 10 Nov 2014.
Freedom House. (2014). *Freedom in the World 2010–2014*, [online] Available at https://freedomhouse.org. Accessed 28 Dec 2014.
Gast, A. S. (2014). *No European impact in Central Asia?,* [online] Available at http://carnegie.ru/eurasiaoutlook/?fa=54790. Accessed 12 Dec 2014.
Melvin, N. (2012). The EU needs a new values-based realism for its Central Asia strategy. *EUCAM Working Paper*, 28.
Muckenhuber, D. (2013, May 17). Interview with Patricia Flor, European Union special representative for Central Asia. *Global Observatory*, [online] Available at http://theglobalobservatory.org/interviews/499-interview-with-patricia-flor-european-union-special-representative-eusr-for-central-asia.html. Accessed 24 Nov 2014.
Nazarbayev, N. (2014). *The next chapter in Kazakhstan-EU relations*, [online] Available at http://www.eurodialogue.eu/The%20Next%20Chapter%20in%20Kazakhstan-EU%20Relations. Accessed 11 Nov 2014.
Peyrouse, S. (2014). How does Central Asia view the EU?. *EUCAM Working Paper*, 18.
Popescu, N., & Wilson, A. (2010). *Polityka Unii Europejskiej i Rosji wobec wspólnych sąsiadów* (pp. 15–16). London-Warsaw: Europejska Rada Spraw Zagranicznych, Fundacja im. StefanaBatorego
Sharshenova, A. (2013, September 2–4). The costs and benefits of the EU-Central Asian political cooperation. *UACES 43rd Conference*, Leeds, [online] Available at http://www.uaces.org. Accessed 23 Nov 2014.

Research of Cluster Structure in Regions of Russia (Case Study: St. Petersburg)

Tatiana Jurievna Kudryavtseva

Abstract The purpose of this study is to analyze the regional cluster structure of the Russian economy. To achieve this goal the following things were done. The cluster groups' kernels structure, which had been developed by the European cluster observatory, was adapted for the Russian economy. Statistical databases were created with the number of employees and number of companies for the regions of the Russian Federation over the period of 2008–2012. The geographical concentration of cluster groups was assessed. The cluster groups developed in the Russian regions, for example in St. Petersburg, were identified according to the European cluster observatory criteria. Detection of positive agglomerative effects of concentration or urbanization in advanced cluster groups of the region allows assessing the innovative potential of the region development. The results of the study can be used to substantiate actions following the regional cluster policy.

Keywords Regional economy of Russia • Cluster groups • Geographical concentration • Urbanization • Localization • Regional cluster policy

1 Introduction

Russian literature has been focusing a lot on examining clusters as specific forms of inter-organizational cooperation between economic agents (Andreev and Naumova 2012; Kharlamova 2012; Vorobyev and Lipatnikov 2012; Babkin et al. 2011). This growing interest of the Russian scientific community has been supported by governmental initiatives aimed at developing regional clusters as forms of industrial engineering that boost innovative activities.

After it was analyzed the cluster policy of St. Petersburg was characterized as sector, technological and innovative, focused on supporting the largest and advanced industrial sectors and, in addition, as tactic, aimed at funding the private sector or, in the context of federal special purpose programs with poor regional

T.J. Kudryavtseva (✉)
Engineering and Economic Institute, Saint-Petersburg State Polytechnical University, Saint Petersburg, Russia
e-mail: tankud28@mail.ru

© Springer International Publishing Switzerland 2016
M.H. Bilgin et al. (eds.), *Business Challenges in the Changing Economic Landscape - Vol. 1*, Eurasian Studies in Business and Economics 2/1,
DOI 10.1007/978-3-319-22596-8_31

financing, and concentrated on supporting the few strong and stable regional clusters. The analysis has revealed that an important element of efficiency of such a policy is to assess objectively how strong and stable are the clusters that the regional government bodies are developing through application of scientifically grounded methods and identification of the cluster groups in the region.

The purpose of this paper is to analyze the cluster structure of the federal subjects of Russia (regions of Russia), i.e., to identify regions, localization of different cluster groups and do comparative research of agglomeration externalities resulting from collocation of enterprises belonging to different clusters in the regions of Russia, for example St. Petersburg.

2 Methodology

A cluster is a specific form of agglomeration of enterprises which directly entails appearance of specific agglomeration externalities, i.e., proximity effects that are caused by collocation of enterprises. Agglomeration and agglomeration externalities are inter-influencing but at the same time independent phenomena.

High geographical concentration of enterprises in the same industry, which is also called localization, is a sign of industrial specialization of an area and can be defined by the degree of the employment non-uniformity in a certain industry by regions in comparison with, for example, the general number of population or working people. This type of concentration strengthens "Marshallian" proximity effects, i.e., concentration effects.

Uneven general agglomeration clearly shows intensity of economic activities in a region and is called urbanization. This type of concentration encourages "Jacobian" proximity effects, i.e., urbanization effects caused by concentration of any industrial companies in a certain area.

Geographical concentration localizes and increases proximity effects, such as, for example, labor resources mobility, efficient use of existing skills and development of new ones. Proximity effects, in their turn, boost and support geographical concentration and, thus, make areas where they are distributed economically attractive (Lindqvist 2009).

The cluster theory, developed by Porter (2005), is intermediate in between "Marshallian" and "Jacobian" proximity effects While "Marshallian" effects show result of geographical concentration of enterprises in the same industry and "Jacobian" effects reflect agglomeration externalities, related to co-localization of enterprises involved in different lines of business in a certain area, the concept of a cluster implies considering companies that operate in inter-related and complementary industries (Simmie 2013). The inter-industry nature of clusters is one of the key distinctions of this type of enterprises' agglomeration in comparison with other agglomeration forms.

The localization coefficient, which is used as the most common measurement of geographical concentration to identify and analyze cluster groups, does not help to make a judgment about factors causing collocation of enterprises. At the same time, decomposition of Ripley's K-function by concentration and urbanization indices, presented in Lindqvist (2009), allows selecting factors encouraging geographical concentration of clusters.

Concentration index (Conc) shows the degree of attraction to collocate for enterprises of a certain cluster group in comparison with the degree of attraction to co-localize for companies involved in all sorts of business. If the index value is more than 1, it signals that these enterprises are prone to collocation, which implies a positive economic effect from concentration for the enterprises in this cluster.

The urbanization index (Urb) demonstrates the degree of attraction between the enterprises of a certain cluster group to co-localize with enterprises involved in all sorts of business in comparison with the degree of attraction between enterprises involved in all sorts of business to collocate with each other. Thus, if the index degree is more than 1, it means that the enterprises in the cluster under examination have a tendency to be located in areas with high density of enterprises operating in all sorts of business, which, again, implies positive effects from urbanization for the enterprises in this cluster group.

Values of concentration and urbanization indices depend on the selected distance value in terms of which the trend for collocation of enterprises is studied. The distance in terms of which this trend is looked into can vary depending on the purpose of the analysis. The key issue of this paper is to define the proneness of cluster enterprises to collocate within the limits of one subject of the Russian Federation. A federal subject has been chosen as a unit of territorial division because a cluster is seen, first of all, as an innovation-oriented form of enterprises' agglomeration. Innovative policy is normally implemented at the regional level since distribution of non-formalized knowledge, which can only be obtained through social interaction and is, at the same time, a major factor contributing to innovation, is limited by a region, in accordance with empirical research (Lindqvist 2009; Gerben 2004). As a result, the transformed formulae have the following form:

$$Urb = \frac{\frac{1}{\sum_{j=1}^{N} n_{ij} \sum_{j=1}^{N} n_{xj}} \sum_{j=1}^{N} n_{ij} n_{xj}}{\frac{1}{\sum_{j=1}^{N} n_{xj} \left(\sum_{j=1}^{N} n_{xj} - 1 \right)} \sum_{j=1}^{N} n_{xj} (n_{xj} - 1)} \quad (1)$$

$$Conc = \frac{\frac{1}{\sum_{j=1}^{N} n_{ij} \left(\sum_{j=1}^{N} n_{ij} - 1 \right)} \sum_{j=1}^{N} n_{ij} (n_{ij} - 1)}{\frac{1}{\sum_{j=1}^{N} n_{ij} \sum_{j=1}^{N} n_{xj}} \sum_{j=1}^{N} n_{ij} n_{xj}} \quad (2)$$

where N—is the number of federal subjects; n_{ij}—is the number of enterprises belonging to i-cluster in j-federal subject; n_{xj}—is the number of enterprises engaged in all sorts of business in j-federal subject.

Depending on the presence of positive or negative proximity effects from collocation with enterprises of an analogous cluster group (*Conc* is more or less than 1), and, also, from collocation with enterprises engaged in all sorts of business (*Urb* is more or less than 1), all clusters can be classified as concentrated or scattered, and urban or rural (Lindqvist 2009).

In order to research proximity effects from collocation of enterprises, belonging to various cluster groups, on the basis of statistics about the average number of workers within the limits of regions and on the basis of 4-digit OKVED codes (Russian Classification of Economic Activities). 36 cluster groups have been formed. In 2012 the total number of people working for the enterprises belonging to the cluster groups was 1974.87 thousand people for the Russian Federation (41 % of the national employment). When defining the industry contents of the cluster groups, the ECO methodology was used and matching between NACE rev.1 and OKVED classifier codes was done. It has to be mentioned that so as to avoid dual accounting of the employed or companies that may arise due to overlapping cluster groups, the object of the analysis is cluster kernels exceptionally, which implies referring each type of business activities to a single cluster only (Porter 2003).

In order to determine the geographical limits of the clusters in Russia and the regions of their localization, relative indices have been calculated, which characterize significance or strength of a cluster in the region and assess presence and development of positive economic effects influencing the companies included in a cluster. Thus, the ECO methodology implies that a cluster group is important in the region in case there is correspondence to two or more of the following criteria:

1. Localization coefficient ≥ 2;
2. The region belongs to 10 % regions, leading by Size;
3. The region belongs to 10 % regions, leading by Focus.

Rating formulae of indices are given in Lindqvist (2009). The threshold value of the localization coefficient is variable. Thus, Porter (2005) defined the threshold value of the localization coefficient at the level of 8.0–1.0 (Porter 2005) whereas U.S. Department of Commerce sets the threshold value equal to 1.3. Because of its nature, the localization index evaluates non-uniformity of the size distribution in a certain area. It is obvious that differences in defining the limits of the index are caused, first of all, by varying geographical features of Europe and America: thus, the average density of population in Europe is 72 people per km^2, whereas it is 32 people per km^2 in America. Owing to a vast territory and relatively low density of population equal to 8.2 people per km^2, economic geography of Russia is more similar to America rather than to Europe, which is why we use the value 1.3 when identifying significant clusters of a region in our study. Moreover, a cluster group of a region cannot be recognized as significant if the total number of people working in this group is fewer than 1000 people.

The revealed complex of important clusters localized in a certain region forms the cluster structure of this region. The research results of St. Petersburg's cluster structure are presented below.

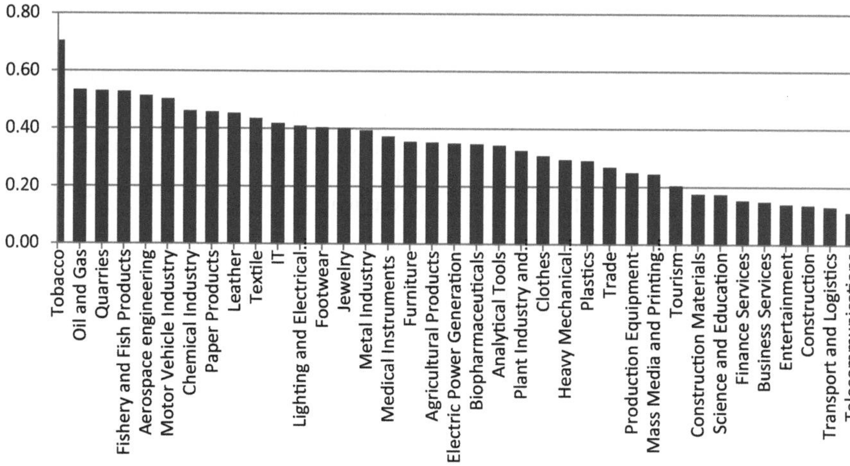

Fig. 1 Level of non-uniformity in distribution of the number of employees in clusters by federal subjects of Russia (agglomeration coefficient value) at the average in 2008–2012

3 Results

On the basis of the statistics about the number of enterprises and organizations by areas and types of economic activities in 2012, agglomeration, concentration and urbanization indices have been calculated for each cluster group (Fig. 1 and Table 1). With the analysis of the employment statistics by the ECO methodology, strong cluster groups of subjects of the Russian Federation have been discovered. The calculations have been worked out by the ECO methodology for all subjects of the Russian Federation for 2008–2012. Table 2 includes a fragment of the calculation results for the important clusters of St. Petersburg.

Analysis of the cluster structure of the St. Petersburg economy led to the following conclusions. As a result of defining the list of important clusters of the region and on the basis of the data on overlapping clusters by related industries set by M. Porter (2003), a map of overlapping for the important clusters of St. Petersburg has been created. Table 2 and Fig. 2 demonstrate that 8 important clusters of St. Petersburg have been identified: "Information Technology", "Science and Education", "Trade", "Biopharmaceuticals", "Lighting and Electrical Equipment", "Electric Power Generation and Transmission", "Finance Services", "Analytical Tools". These ones account for the cluster structure of St. Petersburg that is represented in Fig. 2.

A comparative analysis of the cluster structure of the St. Petersburg economy in comparison with other regions led to the following conclusions.

The region accommodates a majority of cluster groups with a high degree of urbanization and concentration, namely: Biopharmaceuticals, Information Technology, Science and Education, Finance Services, etc. (see Table 1). The enterprises of these clusters belong to concentrated cluster groups of the city and

Table 1 Concentration and urbanization of cluster groups in Russia in 2012

Cluster group	Conc	Urb	Cluster group	Conc	Urb
Information technology	2.02	1.81	Analytical tools	1.09	0.98
Science and education	1.92	1.74	Aerospace engineering	1.05	0.8
Entertainment	1.79	1.62	Lighting and electrical equipment	1.03	0.99
Mass media and printing industry	1.74	1.59	Construction	1.02	1.01
Finance services	1.68	1.53	Plastics	1.02	0.75
Oil and gas	1.61	0.76	Chemical industry	0.96	0.83
Fishery and fish products	1.61	0.35	Production equipment	0.95	0.89
Business services	1.55	1.47	Heavy mechanical engineering	0.92	0.9
Telecommunications	1.53	1.44	Paper products	0.92	0.81
Biopharmaceuticals	1.52	1.36	Metal industry	0.92	0.69
Medical instruments	1.4	1.34	Electric power generation and transmission	0.91	0.78
Trade	1.38	1.33	Tourism	0.9	0,85
Plant industry and animal production	1.37	0.28	Clothes	0.89	0.79
Quarries	1.33	0.44	Agricultural products	0.89	0.58
Textile	1.28	0.84	Construction materials	0.88	0.63
Jewelry	1.17	1.06	Footwear	0.86	0.65
Tobacco	1.13	0.79	Transport and logistics	0.84	0.76
Leather	1.11	1.05	Furniture	0.82	0.67
Motor vehicle industry	1.11	0.7			

experience considerable positive proximity effects due to being located so close both to each other and to the enterprises engaged in any other lines of business. These cluster groups have a high potential to develop in big cities or federal subjects with high density of population and significant economic activity.

So the cluster "Biopharmaceuticals" correspond to two and more strength criteria in St. Petersburg, Kursk Oblast, Moskow Oblast, Tula Oblast, Kurgan Oblast and Penza Oblast, Republic of Tatarstan. St. Petersburg ranks No. 3 in terms of the number of the employed in the cluster Biopharmaceuticals, falling behind only Moscow and Moscow Oblast. In 2010 there started a program of the governmental support of the St. Petersburg pharmaceutical cluster, which was later expanded to the pharmaceutical and medical industry cluster with the purpose to help create, produce and bring into use innovative medical products, generic drugs and medical equipment. Indirect evidence, proving efficiency of these measures, is the growing number of workers in this cluster in St. Petersburg, which has increased by 11 %, with the total number of people employed in this industry falling by 16 % countrywide.

The dynamically developing cluster "Information Technology" demonstrated the biggest value of the localization coefficient in Moscow. This region employed most people in this sector (35.6 % of the total number of the employed in the

Table 2 Results of identifying the cluster groups of St. Petersburg in 2008–2012

	Localization coefficient					Focus (rank)					Size (rank)				
	2008	2009	2010	2011	2012	2008	2009	2010	2011	2012	2008	2009	2010	2011	2012
Analytical tools	1.29	1.65	1.38	1.57	1.41	24	16	22	17	22	3	1	1	1	2
Biopharmaceuticals	1.49	1.40	2.09	1.65	1.86	13	13	9	12	12	3	3	3	3	3
Information technology	2.48	3.12	2.10	3.20	3.17	3	2	2	1	2	2	2	2	2	2
Science and education	1.96	1.98	1.93	2.02	2.01	1	1	1	1	1	2	2	2	2	2
Lighting and electrical equipment	1.48	1.48	1.77	1.77	2.22	18	16	15	16	10	3	3	2	1	1
Electric power generation and transmission	1.49	1.46	1.67	1.34	1.59	20	19	16	22	19	3	2	2	3	2
Trade	1.85	1.89	1.88	1.79	1.47	4	3	3	3	3	2	2	2	2	2
Finance services	1.15	1.10	1.06	1.08	1.09	4	5	5	4	4	2	2	2	2	2

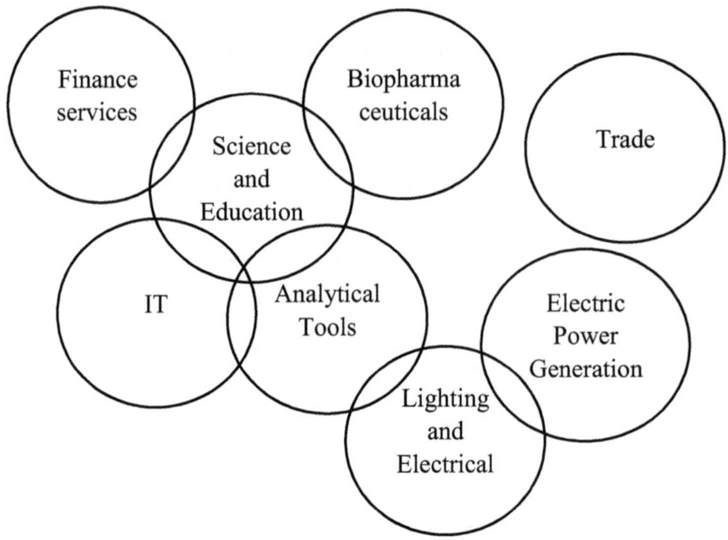

Fig. 2 Map of important overlapping clusters in St. Petersburg

Information Technology cluster all over Russia) in 2012. However, the growth dynamics of the St. Petersburg cluster is significantly bigger than that of the Moscow cluster both in absolute and relative indices. Thus, the number of workers in the cluster rose by 76 % in St. Petersburg while in Moscow it grew only by 5 % over 2007–2012.

St. Petersburg is one of the country leaders in terms of the total number of workers in the cluster group “Analytical Tools” giving way only to Moscow. It is worth specific mentioning that in 2006 a special economic zone of the technology implementation type was created, which is meant to encourage entrepreneurship by a number of businesses that include precision and analytical instrument industry and belong to the cluster “Analytical Tools”. Residents of this zone are provided with tax and customs incentives, and have opportunities to follow a simplified procedure so as to obtain a plot of land and have favorable rent conditions. In 2008 the St. Petersburg Association of Enterprises of Radioelectronics, Instrument Engineering, Means of Communication and Infotelecommunications was set up. It has been used as a basis of the St. Petersburg innovation territorial cluster of radioelectronics, instrument engineering, means of communication and infotelecommunication, which obtains governmental support through a number of federal grant programs. Undoubtedly this entails additional positive economic effects caused by the location of the enterprises belonging to the cluster industries in St. Petersburg.

The cluster “Science and Education” is one of the most common clusters in Russia and features an extremely high degree of concentration and urbanization with a rather low agglomeration value at the same time (see Table 1 and Fig. 1). The low value of the agglomeration coefficient means that enterprises of this industry are widely spread in Russia. The high urbanization level is confirmed with a clear strength of the cluster "Science and Education" in the densely populated federal subjects of Russia with high economic activity. Absolute leaders in terms of the importance of this cluster are Moscow, St. Petersburg and Moscow Oblast. Most people employed in the cluster "Science and Education" work in Moscow. However, in relative terms, the share of people working in this cluster from the total number of employed is higher in St. Petersburg than in Moscow (9.37 % and 8.75 % respectively). St. Petersburg is one of the biggest scientific and educational centers in Russia and has more than 350 scientific organizations including 70 organizations of the Academy of Sciences of the Russian Federation and other state academies, 56 public and 45 private institutions of higher education. Among them there are many leading universities that train specialists in natural, technical and humanitarian sciences. Revealingly, with general fall in the number of the cluster group in Russia by 7 %, the cluster "Science and Education" of St. Petersburg demonstrates a slight growth in employment.

It has to be said that in accordance with the overlapping defined by Porter (2003), the cluster "Science and Education" has the biggest influence on such cluster groups as "Biopharmaceuticals", "Analytical Tools", "Information Technology". Thus, the strength of the cluster group "Science and Education" considerably contributes to developing a number of other science-driven cluster groups in St. Petersburg.

Production of lighting and electrical equipment in Russia is represented by strong clusters in several federal subjects, including St. Petersburg, Smolensk Oblast, Tver Oblast, Tula Oblast, Chelyabinsk Oblast, Republics of Mordovia, Chuvashia and Mari El. The cluster "Lighting and Electrical Equipment" holds the leading countrywide position in St. Petersburg. Its number grew by almost a quarter over the period under review and was 9528 people in 2012.

The cluster "Electric Power Generation and Transmission" corresponds to 2 and more criteria of importance in a number of federal subjects, which include St. Petersburg, Pskovsk Oblast, Kursk Oblast, Kirovsk Oblast, Penza Oblast, Samara Oblast, Saratov Oblast and the Republic of Udmurtia. St. Petersburg holds the second position in Russia after Moscow in terms of the number of workers in the cluster" Electric Power Generation and Transmission", although the number of people working here fell by 9 % over the 5 year period. In St. Petersburg there are several key enterprises producing electrical machinery and equipment for thermal, nuclear, hydraulic and gas-turbine power plants. Moreover, a distinctive feature of some enterprises in St. Petersburg, belonging to the cluster "Electric Power Generation and Transmission", is the fact that they operate as research and production enterprises and associations.

The biggest share of the cluster group kernel "Trade" is taken by wholesale trade, since the core activities of retail business account for local industries. A distinctive feature of the Russian cluster "Trade" is its strong concentration in the capital city with relatively low presence in other regions. Thus, 26.73 % of all the workers in the cluster group were employed in Moscow in 2012. The second largest cluster group "Trade" is located in St. Petersburg. Nevertheless, its size is 4 times smaller than that of Moscow and takes 6.32 % of all the people working in the cluster group in all federal subjects. Although the size of the cluster group "Trade" is diminishing both in Moscow and in St. Petersburg, the rate of drawdown in St. Petersburg exceeds that of the cluster in the capital city.

The cluster group "Finance Services" is marked by a low agglomeration coefficient (0.15), (see Fig. 1) which says for quite a uniform distribution of the number of workers by federal subjects of Russia. Financial market of St. Petersburg is the second largest regional financial market of Russia. However, it is falling behind remarkably. Thus, the total number of people working in this cluster in St. Petersburg is 5 times smaller comparing to the same cluster in Moscow and takes just 4.71 % of the total number of those employed in the cluster group industries throughout Russia. Nevertheless, the development level of the city financial infrastructure is quite high: 45 commercial banks, more than 100 branches of banks from other regions and over 400 financial and brokerage companies are registered in St. Petersburg.

It has to be said that from 8 important cluster groups 7 ones, consistent with the "wide" definition of the cluster, overlap each other, according to M. Porter (Fig. 2). Since in this research cluster "kernels" are studied, it excludes any possibilities of direct influence of the overlapping cluster groups on the strength level of each other through inclusion of industries that belong to the kernels of other clusters and components of the overlapping groups. However, almost 90 % of the important cluster groups in St. Petersburg overlap each other. Correspondingly, it can be assumed that this is caused by positive proximity effects in this region.

Thus, it can be concluded that the economy of St. Petersburg has a unique cluster structure that is based on tight interaction between science and production. St. Petersburg is a centre of localization for science-driven and high-tech cluster groups that have high concentration and urbanization levels and, correspondingly, are prone to be located in big cities.

4 Discussion

Comparison of the research results of the cluster structure of St. Petersburg and the federal and regional industrial development programs has revealed that the following meaningful clusters in the region are actively supported by the government: "Information Technology", "Biopharmaceuticals", "Lighting and Electrical Equipment", "Electric Power Generation and Transmission", "Analytical Tools". At the same time there are no development programs for the following important cluster groups: Science and Education", "Trade", "Finance Services". However, the Committee on Industry and Innovation Development of St. Petersburg implements the development programs of car-making and ship-building clusters whose enterprises are weakly localized in the region.

Today the literature includes active debates about the degree and ability of government to affect the economy when applying the tools of industrial policy (Hospers et al. 2009; Kaplina 2013; Babkin et al. 2013). We agree with the idea that the ability of government to create and develop clusters of industrial enterprises is extremely limited. The major risk when implementing cluster policy is the wrongly chosen subject of research since there is information asymmetry, lack of statistic data and no effective tools for revealing clusters and their prototypes. Governmental policy focused on supporting the traditional and well-established enterprises in a certain region partly solves social problems of the regions, but at the same time makes worse the competitive environment, which is the basic factor for appearance and development of a cluster. On the other hand, when hi-tech industries are supported there are also risks caused by the lack of institutional infrastructure in the region which patterns after successful inter-related industries and enterprises of other regions. In this context, in St. Petersburg there is no program for developing the cluster "Science and Education", which is infrastructural for all the hi-tech clusters, such as: "Information Technology", "Biopharmaceuticals", "Analytical Tools". As a result there are problems related to personnel and the chain from development of a product to development of production equipment is broken. However, positive effects from development programs of the high-tech clusters in the region are also there since localization of such enterprises in St. Petersburg grew over years 2008–2012 (see Table 2).

5 Conclusion

As a result of seeing into the theories of Porter (2003, 2005) and Lindqvist (2009), one can conclude that a cluster is a specific form of agglomeration of enterprises, which, correspondingly, entails specific agglomeration externalities, including both concentration and urbanization effects. Identification of the regions where clusters localize, analysis of positive proximity effects from concentration and urbanization of a cluster group helps to evaluate a potential for development of a region and can be used to assess efficiency of measures of regional cluster policy.

These methods have made it possible to define the important clusters of St. Petersburg's economy. Thus, it can be concluded that the economy of St. Petersburg has a unique cluster structure that is based on tight interaction between science and production. St. Petersburg is a centre of localization for science-driven and high-tech cluster groups that have high concentration and urbanization levels and, correspondingly, are prone to be located in big cities.

The major target of the further research is in-depth study of the condition and dynamics of certain cluster groups developed in St. Petersburg so as to justify the need for regional cluster policy measures and increase the efficiency of state investments in the development of the cluster structure of the region.

Acknowledgements The article is prepared with the support of the Ministry of Science and Education of the Russian Federation (project No. 26.1303.2014/K).

References

Andreev, V., & Naumova, E. (2012). Approaches to the estimation of regional clusters' functioning. *Scientific Technical Journal of Saint Petersburg Technical Institute. Economical Sciences, 4*(151), 34–41.

Babkin, A., Kudryavtseva, T., & Bahmutskaya, A. (2011). Problems and directions of regional industrial politics formation (by the example of Saint Petersburg). *News of Saint Petersburg State University of Economics and Finance, 4*(70), 27–34.

Babkin, A., Kudryavtseva, T., & Utkina, S. (2013). Identification and analysis of industrial cluster structure. *World Applied Sciences Journal, 28*(10), 1408–1413.

Gerben, V. (2004). Agglomeration externalities: Marshall versus Jacobs. *Journal of Evolutionary Economies, 14*, 593–604.

Hospers, G., Sautet, F., & Desrochers, P. (2009). The next silicon valley? On the relationship between geographical clustering and public policy. *International Entrepreneurship and Management Journal, 5*(3), 285–299.

Kaplina, A. (2013). The analysis of the models of clusters structures formation in the system of regional economics: Managerial aspect. *The Journal of Rostov State Institute of Economics, 4* (44), 119–127.

Kharlamova, T. L. (2012). Innovative network form of development of clusters in Megapolis. *Nauchno-Tekhnicheskie Vedomosti of St. Petersburg Polytechnical University. Economic Science, 1*(139), 80–86.

Lindqvist, G. (2009). *Disentangling clusters. Agglomeration and proximity effects*. Ph. D., Stockholm School of Economics.

Porter, M. (2003). The economic performance of regions. *Regional Studies, 37*(6/7), 549–578.

Porter, M. (2005). *Competition* (N. Makarov, Trans.). Moscow: The Publishing House "Williams".

Simmie, J. (2013). *Innovations and clusters in global world economy* (E. S. Izotova, Trans.). Modern Production Forces, 2, 125–144.

Vorobyev, V., & Lipatnikov, V. (2012). Organizational principles of innovation industrial clusters formation. *Scientific Technical Journal of Saint Petersburg Technical Institute. Economical Sciences, 6*(161), 63–70.

International Integration: From a Dream to a Political Dogma

Aleksandrs Fedotovs and Oksana Sakalosh

Abstract The aim of the paper is to revise some widespread views on international economic integration with focus on successive enlargements of the EU. Authors propose to clearly distinguish between the terms globalization, integration, and cohesion. Globalization, integration, and cohesion are considered as three different aspects of modern economic development which do not necessarily go hand in hand. Although EU membership has been turned into a political dogma in the East European countries, it is argued in the article that enlargement of the EU is nowadays pushed ahead too hasty and beyond economic rationality—both in terms of spatial expansion and strengthening of internal unification. Research methodology is based on economic theory, study of economic literature, analysis of statistical data, and author's own calculations.

Keywords Globalization • Economic integration • Cohesion • European Union • EU enlargement • EU new member states

1 Introduction

Among the characteristic features of world development since 1990s there was a substantial growth in number of new states, in Eastern Europe in particular. By the beginning of the twenty-first century the number of states in Europe proved to be the biggest since the 1860s (Fig. 1).

On the other hand, the attained national sovereignty usually proved to be without delay sacrificed to the idea of international integration. Devotion to international integration manifests itself in East and South-East European countries as striving for membership in the European Union. Moreover, in these countries membership in the European Union is being imposed on public as a political dogma.

A. Fedotovs (✉)
Department of Economics and Finance, RISEBA University, Rīga, Latvia
e-mail: alexandrfedotov@yahoo.co.uk

O. Sakalosh
College of Business Administration, Rīga, Latvia
e-mail: oxanasf@mail.ru

© Springer International Publishing Switzerland 2016

M.H. Bilgin et al. (eds.), *Business Challenges in the Changing Economic Landscape - Vol. 1*, Eurasian Studies in Business and Economics 2/1,
DOI 10.1007/978-3-319-22596-8_32

Fig. 1 Number of sovereign states in Europe, 1860–2010. *Sources*: Berthold (1976), Muir (1982); authors' calculations

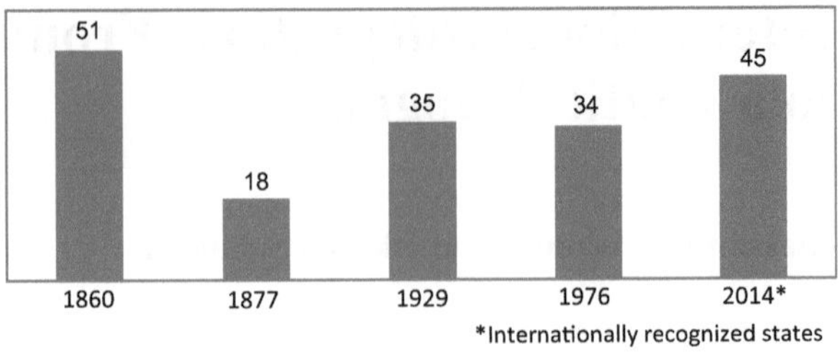

It has become a commonplace statement in the modern world that globalization and international economic integration are objective and inescapable processes. Let us therefore try to find out: what exactly is meant today by globalization and economic integration and what are corresponding implications in the context of the European Union?

2 Integration or Globalization?

Interpretations of the term "economic integration" have experienced substantial change during recent decades. Once upon a time, in the early 1990s, in definitions of economic integration it was sufficient to refer only to free trade conditions, e.g.,: "Economic integration occurs when two or more nations join to form a free-trade zone" (Case and Fair 1994, p. 888). Gradually definitions of integration were expanded to embrace a more broad range of characteristics. According to Rugman and Hodgetts (2003, p. 104), "economic integration is the establishment of trans-national rules and regulations that enhance economic trade and cooperation among countries". Daniels et al. (2007, p. 749) interpret economic integration as "abolition of economic discrimination between national economies".

As compared to integration, globalization is a relatively new term which has become popular in recent decades. Its interpretations also do not remain unchanged. In the early 2000s, Rugman and Hodgetts (2003, p. 432) meant by globalization "production and distribution of products and services of a homogeneous type and quality on a worldwide basis"; Hill (2003 p. 684) characterized globalization as merger of national markets, "a trend from distinct national economic units toward one huge world market". Daniels et al. (2007, p. 6) globalization is "the process of growing interdependence among countries". Mankiw et al. (2013, p. 536) point out financial aspect of the process: in their view, "the term *globalization* refers to the growth of interdependence amongst world economies usually seen as resulting from the removal of many international regulations affecting financial flows". It proves difficult, however, to discern difference between explanations of the two above-mentioned terms given in modern economic literature. Most often the two processes are described in actually the same words. In 2007, Hill (2007, p. 5) defines globalization as "shift toward a more integrated and interdependent world economy". The terms "integration" and "globalization" are often used interchangeably as synonyms—e.g., for Samuelson and Nordhaus (2005), globalization is just a popular term used to designate growing processes of economic integration of different countries. Sometimes one can find attempts to give a more comprehensive definition of globalization including broader range of features, e.g.,: "Entry of all countries—depending on scientific and technological, economic and social potential reached by each of them—into world economy, their integration and interaction, washing away of borders between national economic complexes, formation of global economic space" (Maksimova and Noskova 1995, p. 84). Again, no clear distinction between globalization and integration is suggested in such definitions.

We believe, first of all, that the content of globalization should not be reduced to just merger of markets (either goods markets or financial ones). What seems true in the existing definitions is the accent placed on the word "market": indeed, under globalization any area—economic life, politics, culture, and moral—becomes increasingly subdued by market forces. In our opinion, globalization implies a trend not just to a single world market and mutual dependence of national economies, but also to similar consumption habits, similar material culture and values all over the world—with all positive and negative consequences of such a process. However, globalization and integration are different phenomena which we should not confuse: one does not necessarily mean the other.

Let us remember that in its original meaning, the verb "integrate" is explained as "to complete (imperfect thing) by addition of parts" or "combine (parts) into a whole" (Seidl and McMordie 1982). The latter of the constructions seems to be the most appropriate in the case of international economic integration.

In our opinion, globalization is an objective, spontaneous process of intensification of international economic and cultural contacts, growing interdependence of all countries of the world. This process stems from technological progress, exchange in products and information, development of means of transportation and communication, migrations of population. However, the fact that jeans, Coca-Cola or McDonald's have spread all over the world does not imply by itself that the world has become more united. Integration, in its turn, is a deliberately planned, organized and promoted process of uniting countries in a single entity. It is carried out by political means assuming that economic preconditions have been matured. Integration is impossible without adequate economic basis, and economic integration in due course is followed by political integration.

Integration of nations is a dream cherished from ancient times, at least since Alexander the Great's idea of merging Greeks and Persians in a single nation of "Perso-Hellenes". During many centuries worldwide brotherhood of nations was advocated by philosophers and poets. World history has witnessed numerous attempts to integrate nations on different bases: military, dynastic, religious, ideological, and economic. Most often these attempts began with (more or less forcible) political unification supplemented afterwards with ideological or economic means. The Arab Caliphate or empire of Charles the Fifth can be mentioned as examples in the Middle Ages: the first strived for uniting the world under the religion of Islam while the latter claimed for the same under the aegis of Catholic faith. In more recent times the Soviet Union declared integration of "fraternal Soviet peoples" on the basis of Communist ideology. A concept of "new international community of people—the Soviet people"—was invented and propagated (to be fair, the concept denied assimilation or loss of national identity). All of the above-mentioned as well as many other endeavours have failed. It is worth reminding that many attempts of integration of sovereign states, especially among less developed countries in Africa and Latin America (like South American Community of Nations proclaimed in 2004) remained purely formal and lacking vital capacity because of insufficient economic basis.

The advantage of the European Union seems to be that the process of integration was started from creating economic foundation consistently supplemented with political superstructure. Nowadays, however, strengthening of political integration seems losing touch with economic and social preconditions.

3 Integration Is Not Convergence or Cohesion

For the post-Communist East European countries, globalization merged with integration into the European Union. These countries cherished exaggerated hopes for quick economic progress and equalization of living standards with Western Europe. The hopes, however, proved premature. Globalization, economic integration and convergence are three different aspects of modern economic development which do not necessarily go hand in hand.

The 13 new member states admitted to the EU since 2004 make up 26 % of the EU territory. Their share in the total population of the 28 EU countries is about 1/5; as seen in Fig. 2, this share has slightly decreased since 2004 because of unfavourable demographic trends. However, the share of the 13 new members in GDP of the EU-28 turns out extremely small (Fig. 3).

Along with enlargement of the European Union, its heterogeneity steadily increased, turning into one of the most acute problems. Each of the successive enlargements of the EU in 1973–2013, besides increase in number of member states, contributed to diversity of economic and social development levels within the united Europe. It is especially true for the EU enlargements from 2004 onwards since the new member states had appreciably lower development indices in all areas. Now the differences between the 28 member states of the EU are much greater than they were in the European Community consisting of 6, 9, or 15 countries. This obviously impedes the process of integration. As a result, need for such special terms as "convergence" and "cohesion" appeared in European political terminology.

Opposition of core to periphery (or centre to periphery), as well as that of the North to the South, is well known in literature dealing with the global economy. Now the European Union has acquired its own North and South. In the expanding EU, the separation into more developed core and less developed periphery started

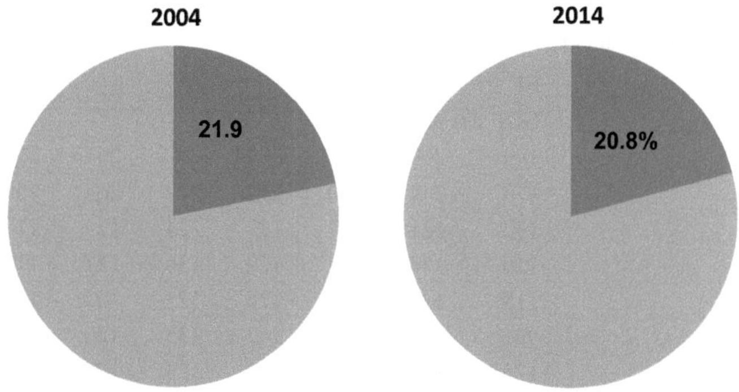

Fig. 2 Share of the 13 new member states in the EU-28 population. *Sources*: Eurostat (2014); authors' calculations

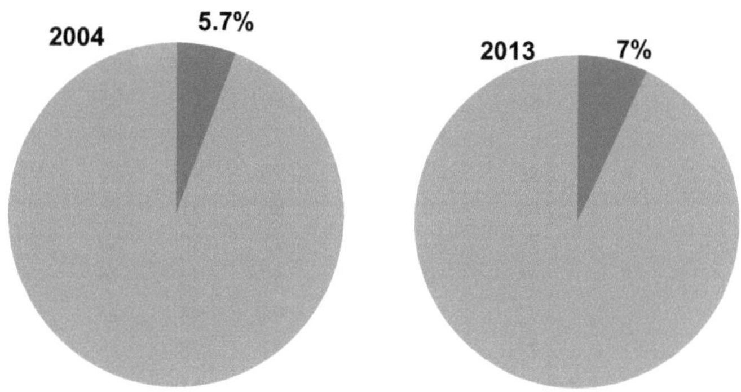

Fig. 3 Share of the 13 new member states in the EU-28 GDP. *Sources*: Eurostat (2014); authors' calculations

since the 1970s–1980s with admission of Ireland, Greece, Portugal, and Spain. The separation continued and became especially obvious in the 2000s.

After the enlargement of the EU in 2004, opinions were expressed by some experts that the new member states would need 15, 30, 40 or even more years to reach at least the average EU development level. No doubt, some degree of development levels' equalization among the EU countries is observed in the last two decades. This can be concluded from Table 1 containing data on GDP and AIC (actual individual consumption) per capita. The gap between the highest and the lowest GDP per capita (amplitude of Max/Min value), as well as standard deviation (σ) and coefficient of variation (k_v) calculated for GDP per capita, have obviously decreased since 2000 (although the Max/Min ratio in 2013 proves almost the same as in 1995). It is impossible, of course, to check whether the convergence in 2000–2013 had been achieved due to membership in the EU or it would also occur under other historical conditions. Similarly, it cannot be asserted that progress of the European Union had caused further polarization of economic development levels of countries in Europe as a whole. Furthermore, the process of equalisation is

Table 1 GDP per capita, 1995–2013, and actual individual consumption (AIC) per capita, 2011, in the EU-28 countries (at current market prices, PPS)

	EU-27=100						
	GDP per capita						AIC per capita
Country	1995*	2000	2002	2004	2008	2013	2011
Luxembourg	179	244	240	252	279	264	150
Austria	130	131	127	127	124	129	117
Netherlands	120	134	133	129	134	127	113
Sweden	118	127	122	126	123	127	115
Ireland	99	131	138	142	133	126	100
Denmark	125	131	128	125	123	125	113
Germany	120	118	114	116	116	124	119
Belgium	120	126	125	121	115	119	111
Finland	106	117	115	116	118	112	112
France	115	115	115	110	107	108	112
United Kingdom	111	119	121	123	115	106	118
Italy	116	117	112	106	104	98	102
Spain	88	97	100	101	103	95	94
Malta	:	83	82	77	79	87	83
Cyprus	86	89	89	90	97	86	95
Slovenia	68	80	82	86	91	83	81
Czech Republic	70	68	73	75	80	80	70
Slovakia	45	50	54	57	72	76	70
Greece	72	84	90	94	94	75	94
Portugal	73	81	80	77	78	75	82
Lithuania	34	39	45	50	61	74	66
Estonia	36	45	50	57	68	72	57
Poland	41	48	48	51	56	68	70
Hungary	50	55	61	63	64	67	61
Latvia	30	37	41	46	56	67	56
Croatia	38	43	54	49	63	61	56
Romania	:	26	30	34	47	54	47
Bulgaria	31	28	32	35	44	47	44
Max/Min value	6	9.4	8	7.4	6.3	5.6	3.4
Standard deviation (σ)	–	47.1	44.5	44.9	44.8	41.1	26.9
Coefficient of variation (k_v)	–	0.51	0.48	0.48	0.46	0.42	0.3

*EU-25 = 100

Sources: Eurostat (2014, 2012a, c, 2011, 2008, 2005, 2004); authors' calculations

fluctuating: being quite apparent initially, it gradually slows down or sometimes even makes a step backwards.

One of the crucial aspects in economic comparisons among countries is the level of labour productivity. Although demonstrating noticeable progress in this respect, most of the East European new EU member states still have relatively low levels of

Table 2 Labour productivity in the East European new EU member states, 2000–2012 (EU-27 = 100)

Country	Productivity per person employed			Productivity per hour worked		
	2000	2008	2012	2000	2008	2012
Slovakia	58	80	82	55	74	75
Slovenia	76	84	81	76	83	86
Croatia	62	78	81	:	:	:
Czech Republic	62	74	74	52	68	67
Hungary	58	71	71	49	59	62
Estonia	47	66	70	41	56	61
Poland	56	62	74	46	50	59
Lithuania	43	62	74	40	54	65
Latvia	40	55	66	31	46	56
Romania	24	49	51	22	44	44
Bulgaria	31	40	45	33	39	44

Sources: Eurostat (2014, 2012b)

productivity—with the same possibility that convergence with the EU average level may in some cases slow down or even stop (Table 2).

Huge differences exist between the EU member states in terms of such indices as Global Competitiveness Index, Gini index, Corruption Perceptions Index, Doing Business index, Innovation score etc. For instance, in 2013–2014 Global Competitiveness Index, Finland ranked the 3rd in the world while Greece was in the 91st place (World Economic Forum 2014). As concerns the East European EU members on the whole, their position in the index is not better than in 2006. Although ratings of Romania and Bulgaria have substantially improved, ranks of such countries as Slovenia, Hungary, Croatia and Slovakia worsened drastically; thus, the East European EU members still rank between the 29th and 77th places in the list (the 26th and 74th in 2006–2007) (Table 3).

History of the European Union demonstrates that the enlargement process of the EU is pushed ahead more rapidly than economic convergence of the member states can occur. A contradiction emerges between the development of integration "in breadth" (as embracing more and more of countries) and "in depth" (as cohesion of the countries). Experience of the EU and some other unions, including the former USSR, corroborates the conclusion that equalisation process in a heterogeneous group of nations uses to advance to a certain point but later may stop or even reverse (see data for Czech Republic, Spain, Cyprus, Slovenia, Greece, Portugal in Table 1). As concerns the EU new members, their lag from the most advanced EU countries is most likely to remain substantial in a foreseeable future, and equalisation with the richest countries seems to be a long-term and rather uncertain perspective.

Table 3 Ranks of the EU East European members in global competitiveness indexes, 2007–2014

Country	Rank in global competitiveness index						
	2006–2007	2007–2008	2008–2009	2009–2010	2012–2013	2013–2014	2014–2015
Estonia	26	27	32	35	34	32	29
Poland	45	51	53	46	41	42	43
Czech Republic	31	33	33	31	39	46	37
Lithuania	39	38	44	53	45	48	41
Latvia	44	45	54	68	55	52	42
Bulgaria	74	79	76	76	62	57	54
Slovenia	40	39	42	37	56	62	70
Hungary	38	47	62	58	60	63	60
Croatia	56	57	61	72	81	75	77
Romania	73	74	68	64	78	76	59
Slovakia	37	41	46	47	71	78	75

Source: World Economic Forum (2014)

4 On a Right Trail?

Putting aside general wording that the European Union is "a family of democratic European countries, committed to working together for peace and prosperity" (Mankiw et al. 2013, p. 524), we have to admit that in the modern world economic integration is used as a tool in international competition for resources and markets. Only few of the EU new member states proved prepared for that; some other seemed unable to successfully protect their economic interests in European structures.

In the East European countries, membership in the European Community was propagated to public since the last years of the Communist rule as an indisputable ultimate goal. Joining the EU was immediately put in the forefront of foreign policy after the change of political regimes in these countries. However, scepticism towards this political course always remained.

Integration is by no means a unanimously hailed process without opposition. As to recent history, one may remember that in the EU accession referendums carried out in 2003, substantial part of voters in the candidate states did not support joining the European Union. For instance, 46 % voted against in Malta, 33 % in Estonia and 32 % in Latvia (Fig. 4).

It is worth reminding also that, in the case of Estonia and Latvia, the voters eligible for participation in the referendum consisted only of population possessing citizen rights. In Latvia in particular, at the time of referendum the permanent residents deprived of voting rights (those officially called *non-citizens*) accounted for about 1/3 of total population. So, merely 2/3 of the country's population was given the opportunity to vote; out of them, only 71 % participated in referendum, and 67 % of the latter were in favour of joining the EU. It implies, in fact, that fate

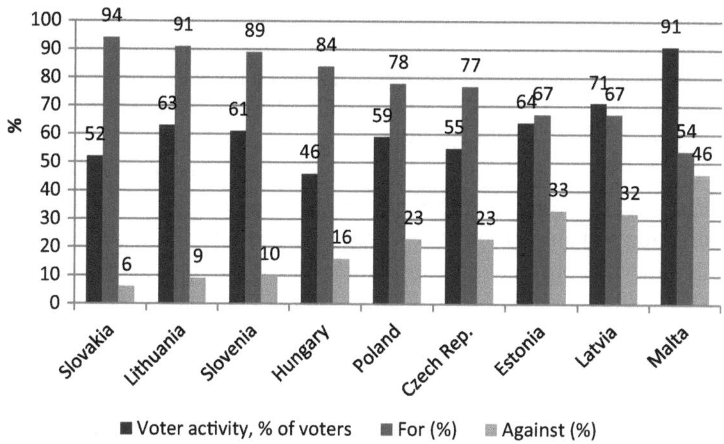

Fig. 4 Vote of the citizens of the EU accession countries in the EU accession referendums. *Source*: Republic of Latvia Ministry of Economics (2003)

of the nation's joining the European Union was decided by votes of hardly 1/3 of population. Number of "Eurosceptics" obviously grew all over the Europe during the years of global economic crisis. This was clearly demonstrated by results of the recent elections to European parliament. As concerns transition to single European currency, in Latvia, for instance, on the eve of introduction of euro on January 1, 2014, public opinion polls showed that opponents of euro outnumbered its supporters.

Further economic and political integration is being now actively promoted in Europe using full arsenal of political means. It can be argued, however, that integration process is carried out too hasty—both in terms of spatial expansion of the EU and strengthening of centralization. The process seems to be pushed ahead faster than the necessary economic and social preconditions have matured. The EU looks too aggressive in continuing its territorial expansion. One might interpret this as a search to remedy internal economic and social problems via territorial enlargement; but if it proves so, it is not a right trail. The point is reached at which there is almost no space for further expansion of the EU. Just several last remainders of former Yugoslavia and Soviet Union have left in the east and south-east of Europe. Hasty attempts to draw them into orbit of the EU will inevitably create new problems. Crisis in Ukraine has clearly proved that further peaceful expansion of the EU is hardly possible. Striving for new areas may face active resistance from both inside these areas and outside. Instead of acquiring new territories, more attention should be paid by the EU to solving problems of economic growth, employment and poverty.

Attempts of further political unification and centralization would also tend to face growing opposition. Struggle around approval of new European constitution and creation of post of the EU president not long ago, as well as strengthening protests against the austerity policy have already indicated this. Slogan of "the

United States of Europe" has at least a hundred-year history, but Europe can never be analogous to the USA. The point is that the United States of America from the very beginning was not made of sovereign nations having centuries of independent statehood tradition and heritage of national identity. Any project of a single European state does not look believable in foreseeable future.

Ideas of the EU reformation are gaining increasing popularity now. Possibly, at the attained level of economic development, an integration model with less degree of centralization and unification may work better and some other models (in Eurasia and North America) prove more appropriate for the dynamic modern world.

5 Conclusion

- Globalization, economic integration and cohesion are three different aspects of economic development which do not necessarily go hand in hand.
- It cannot be asserted that enlargement of the European Union had caused either equalization or greater polarization of economic development levels among European countries.
- A contradiction has emerged in the EU between the progress of integration "in breadth" (embracing new countries) and "in depth" (cohesion of the member states).
- Process of European integration is being pushed ahead too hasty and beyond economic rationality—in terms of both spatial expansion of the EU and strengthening of unification. If the EU tries to remedy internal economic and social problems via territorial enlargement, it is not on a right trail.
- Possibly, an integration model with less degree of centralization and unification may work better. The "United States of Europe" does not look attractive in visible perspective.

References

Berthold, L. (Ed.). (1976). *Atlas zur Geschichte*. Bd. 1. Gotha/Leipzig: Hermann Haack.

Case, K. E., & Fair, R. C. (1994). *Economics* (3rd ed.). Englewood Cliffs, NJ: Prentice Hall.

Daniels, J. D., Radebaugh, L. H., & Sullivan, D. P. (2007). *International business: Environments and operations* (11th ed.). Upper Saddle River, NJ: Pearson Prentice Hall.

Eurostat. (2004). *Eurostat yearbook 2004. The statistical guide to Europe*. Luxembourg: Office for Official Publications of the European Communities.

Eurostat. (2005). *Europe in figures—Eurostat yearbook 2005*, Available at http://epp.eurostat.ec.europa.eu/cache/. Accessed 25 Aug 2014.

Eurostat. (2008). *Europe in figures—Eurostat yearbook 2008*, Available at http://epp.eurostat.ec.europa.eu/cache/. Accessed 23 Aug 2014.

Eurostat. (2011). *Europe in figures—Eurostat yearbook 2011*, [online] Available at http://epp.eurostat.ec.europa.eu/cache/. Accessed 23 Aug 2014.

Eurostat. (2012a). *Compact guides. Basic figures on the EU.* Autumn 2012 edition, [online] Available at http://epp.eurostat.ec.europa.eu. Accessed 20 Aug 2014.

Eurostat. (2012b). *Europe in figures—Eurostat yearbook 2012*, [online] Available at http://epp.eurostat.ec.europa.eu/cache/. Accessed 22 Aug 2014.

Eurostat. (2012c). *GDP per capita in the member states ranged from 45 % to 274 % of the EU27 average in 2011. Eurostat news release 97/2012—20 June 2012,* Available at http://ec.europa.eu/eurostat. Accessed 12 Aug 2014.

Eurostat. (2014). *Europe in figures—Eurostat yearbook*, [online] Available at http://epp.eurostat.ec.europa.eu/statistics_explained/index.php/Europe_in_figures_-_Eurostat_yearbook. Accessed 22 Aug 2014.

Hill, C. W. (2003). *International business: Competing in the global marketplace* (4th ed.). Boston, MA: McGraw-Hill/Irwin.

Hill, C. W. (2007). *International business: Competing in the global marketplace* (6th ed.). Boston, MA: McGraw-Hill/Irwin.

Maksimova, L., & Noskova, I. (1995). *Mezhdunarodnie ekonomicheskie otnosheniia.* Moscow: UNITI.

Mankiw, N. G., Taylor, M. P., & Ashwin, A. (2013). *Business economics.* Clifton Park, NY: Cengage Learning.

Muir, R. (1982). *Muir's atlas of medieval and modern history.* London/Melbourne/Milwaukee: George Philip.

Republic of Latvia Ministry of Economic. (2003, December). *Economic development of Latvia: Report.* Riga: Ministry of Economics, Republic of Latvia.

Rugman, A. M., & Hodgetts, R. M. (2003). *International business* (3rd ed.). London/New York: Prentice Hall/Financial Times.

Samuelson, P. A., & Nordhaus, W. D. (2005). *Economics* (18th ed.). Boston, MA: McGraw-Hill/Irwin.

Seidl, J., & McMordie, W. (1982). *The concise Oxford dictionary* (7th ed.). Oxford: Oxford University Press.

World Economic Forum. (2014). *The global competitiveness report 2013–2014.* Full Data Edition, Available at http://www3.weforum.org/docs/WEF_GlobalCompetitivenessReport_2013-14.pdf. Accessed 25 Aug 2014.

Analysis of Agrarian Structure in Poland in 1921 and 2002 Based on the Example of Selected Districts

Damian Walczak and Michal B. Pietrzak

Abstract The objective of this article is to present the diversity of the agrarian structure in Poland based on the example of selected neighboring districts. The selected districts, which in the years 1795–1918 (the period when Poland's area was divided and occupied by three invaders) were located in two different annexed territories, and since 1918 have been the territory of one country—Poland. The analysis of the variation of the agrarian structure employed the Gini coefficient and the average size of farms in individual districts in 1921 and in 2002 was calculated. The obtained results allowed to conclude that the agrarian structure in Poland is considerably spatially differentiated. Undoubtedly one of the reasons is the complex history of Poland's borderlines. The agrarian structure for selected districts which belonged to the same annexed territory is not significantly different. However, in the case of districts belonging to different annexed territories (even for neighboring districts), the differentiation of the agrarian structure was substantial and it still remains so.

Keywords Agriculture • Agrarian structure • Poland • Gini coefficient • Long-term structure

1 Introduction

As indicated by Banski and Czapiewski (2007), Pietrzak and Walczak (2013, 2014), and Grancelli (2011) farming in Poland is significantly diversified in its agrarian structure. Agrarian structure is one of the most important determinants of a country's food security, since small farms produce far less per hectare than large ones (Helfand and Levine 2004; Reyes 2002). Also, large farms to a greater extent comply with the principles of Corporate Social Responsibility, due to their greater

D. Walczak (✉) • M.B. Pietrzak
Faculty of Economic Sciences and Management, Nicolaus Copernicus University in Torun, Toruń, Poland
e-mail: dwalczak@umk.pl; michal.pietrzak@umk.pl

© Springer International Publishing Switzerland 2016

M.H. Bilgin et al. (eds.), *Business Challenges in the Changing Economic Landscape - Vol. 1*, Eurasian Studies in Business and Economics 2/1,
DOI 10.1007/978-3-319-22596-8_33

financial possibilities (Genier et al. 2008)[1]. Undoubtedly, one of the causes of this diversification can be a complicated history of Poland' territory.

For the above reasons this work will present the agrarian structure of neighboring districts, which until 1795 were located within the Polish territory, and for 123 years as a result of the division and annexation of Poland (from 1795 to 1918) were located in separate countries—Russia, Prussia or Austro-Hungary. It was only after Poland regained its independence in 1918, when these areas were again included in the reborn Poland. In 1918 Poland introduced a three-level administrative division of the country, including districts. In Poland, a district as an administrative unit ceased to exist after World War II, but re-emerged in 1998 within the territory similar to that of 1921, which made it possible to present a credible analysis.

The aim of this article is to present the diversity of the agrarian structure in Poland based on the example of neighboring districts, which for 123 years were within the area of two different partitions. For the purpose of this study data from 1921 to 2002 respectively were taken into account. In this work the following hypothesis was verified (Braudel 1971; Klopot 2011): the agrarian structure is a long-term structure within the meaning of Braudel (1971). Among numerous definitions of the agrarian structure available, we define agrarian structure as the pattern of land distribution among landholders (Ludewigs et al. 2009; de Souza et al. 2013).

The presented analysis is based on a comparison of neighboring districts that were situated on different sides of the former Russian-Prussian and Russian-Austrian-Hungarian borders.

As regards the Russian-Prussian borderline, on the Russian 'side' there were districts with their authorities seated in the following towns: Mlawa, Zuromin, Sierpc[2], Rypin, Lipno, Aleksandrow Kujawski, Radziejow, Konin, Slupca, Kalisz, Wielun and Wieruszow (in 1921 Mlawa, Sierpc, Rypin, Nieszawa[3], Konin, Slupca, Kalisz, Wielun[4]). On the Prussian 'side' there were districts with their seats in Dzialdowo, Nowe Miasto Lubawskie[5], Brodnica, Inowroclaw Mogilno, Gniezno, Wrzesnia, Jarocin, Pleszew, Ostrow Wielkopolski, Ostrzeszow[6], Kepno (in 1921 Dzialdowo, Lubawa, Brodnica, Wabrzezno, Torun, Inowroclaw Mogilno Strzelno[7], Gniezno, Witkowo[8], Wrzesnia, Jarocin, Pleszew, Ostrow, Odolanow[9], Ostrzeszow, Kepno).

---

[1] Please see Dziawgo and Dziawgo (2010), Krupa (2012), and Manning (2013) for more about CSR.

[2] The Zuromin district was created out of the land of the Sierpc district.

[3] The Nieszawa district was divided into two separate districts: Aleksandrow Kujawski and Radziejow.

[4] The Wieruszow district was created out of the land of the Wielun district.

[5] In 1921 Nowe Miasto, the then Nowe Miasto Lubawskie, was part of the district seated in Lubawa.

[6] Some of the land (approximately 20 %) belonged to the Russian partition.

[7] At present the Mogilno district.

[8] At present the Gniezno district.

[9] At present the Ostrow Wielkopolski district.

The analysis excluded those districts whose territories cannot be assigned to any of the parts, because their present territories are composed of the lands of both the former Prussian and of the Russian partitions in comparable proportions—the Golub-Dobrzyn district (Fig. 2).

In the case of the borderline between the Russian and Austro-Hungarian partitions the following districts were examined:

1. Within the area of the Russian partition: Bedzin, Myszkow, Zawiercie, Dabrowa Gornicza, Sosnowiec, Olkusz, Miechow, Proszowice, Pinczow, Kazimierza Wielka, Busko Zdroj, Sandomierz, Staszow, Janow Lubelski, Krasnik, Bilgoraj, Tomaszow Lubelski (in 1921 Bedzin[10], Miechow, Pinczow, Stopnica, Sandomierz, Janow Lubelski, Bilgoraj, Tomaszow Lubelski).
2. Within the area of the Austro-Hungarian partition: Chrzanow, Jaworzno, Cracow, Wieliczka, Bochnia, Brzesko, Tarnow, Dabrowa Tarnowska, Mielec, Tarnobrzeg, Stalowa Wola, Nisko, Lancut, Lezajsk, Przeworsk, Jaroslaw, Lubaczow (in 1921 Chrzanow, Cracow, Wieliczka, Bochnia, Brzesko, Tarnow, Dabrowa Tarnowska, Mielec, Tarnobrzeg, Nisko, Lancut, Przeworsk, Jaroslaw, Cieszanow).
3. The study does not include the Czestochowa and Klobucki districts (the Russian partition) because there was nothing to compare their agrarian structures with. The neighbouring districts from the Prussian side currently are in Kluczbork, Olesno and Lubliniec. Kluczbork and Olesno became Polish cities only in 1945, and Lubliniec, admittedly on March 20, 1921 but it was not included in the statistics on which the article was based.

In the case of Konin, Kalisz, Torun, Cracow[11], and Tarnobrzeg for 2002 only landed districts (ones without towns in which there are also individual farms) were included. Due to the availability of data at the level of districts, which were changing their shapes for almost 100 years, or due to the quality of collected data, the data presented include some distortions. However, according to the authors, the data presented may provide a basis for the formulation of relevant and reliable conclusions.

2 Data and Methodology

The work is based on data taken from the general agricultural census from 1921 and from 2002 (GUS 1928, 2014)[12]. The study analyzed only farms with the area of more than 1 ha. All data were calculated for the following ranges (in hectares): 1–5; 5–10; 10–20; 20–50; 50-. The Gini coefficient, which is a commonly used measure

[10] The land of the Bedzin district in 1921 was formed of the land of the following districts: Bedzin, Myszkow, Zawiercie, Dabrowa Gornicza, Sosnowiec.

[11] In the case of Cracow also for 1921.

[12] The analysis included data from 2002, more recent data aggregation does not allow the comparison of them with data from 1921.

of the distribution of the variable (e.g., arable land in farms), was used in the analysis of the concentration of the agricultural area in order to determine uneven distribution of arable land (and in order to increase the comparability of data). The value of the Gini coefficient ranges from 0 to 1. It equals 0 if the distribution of the variable is equal (e.g., 50 % of arable land is possessed by 50 % of agricultural holdings), and it moves towards 1 together with an increase in the concentration of agricultural land (Pietrzak and Walczak 2012).

The Gini coefficient was calculated with the Brown Formula shown below (Ozdemir et al. 2011):

$$G = 1 - \sum\nolimits_{k=0}^{n-1} (X_{k+1} - X_k)(Y_{k+1} - Y_k) \quad (1)$$

where X is the cumulated share of the number of farms, and Y is the cumulated share of the area of arable land. We also calculated the average size of farms in individual districts in 1921 and in 2002.

3 The Outcome of the Research

The values contained in Tables 1, 2, 3, and 4 show the Gini coefficient and the average size of farms in the districts analyzed in 1921 and in 2002. Attention should be paid to small changes in this respect in particular districts, which were situated

Table 1 Basic characteristics of the agrarian structure for selected districts from the Russian partition

1921	2002	1921		2002	
		Gini coefficient	The average size of farms (in ha)	Gini coefficient	The average size of farms (in ha)
Total		0.53	9.8	0.46	9.2
District	District	Gini coefficient in district	The average size of farms in district (in ha)	Gini coefficient in district	The average size of farms in district (in ha)
Mlawa	Mlawa	0.56	12.9	0.44	13.7
Sierpc	Zuromin, Sierpc	0.52	13.2	0.41	12.0
Rypin	Rypin	0.58	10.2	0.41	13.5
Lipno	Lipno	0.59	12.4	0.44	10.6
Nieszawa	Aleksandrow Kujawski, Radziejow	0.58	13.4	0.47	11.3
Konin	Konin	0.47	8.7	0.46	7.5
Slupca	Slupca	0.56	10.5	0.51	10.9
Kalisz	Kalisz	0.51	8.7	0.41	7.5
Sieradz	Sieradz	0.42	6.7	0.39	7.6
Wielun	Wielun, Wieruszow	0.38	5.7	0.37	6.3

Table 2 Basic characteristics of the agrarian structure for selected districts from the Prussian partition

1921	2002	1921		2002	
		Gini coefficient	The average size of farms (in ha)	Gini coefficient	The average size of farms (in ha)
Total		0.66	17.3	0.58	13.9
District	District	Gini coef-ficient in district	The average size of farms in dis-trict (in ha)	Gini coef-ficient in district	The average size of farms in district (in ha)
Dzialdowo i Lubawa	Dzialdowo, Nowe Miasto Lubawskie	0.63	18.6	0.60	17.1
Brodnica	Brodnica	0.63	16.1	0.53	12.4
Wabrzezno	Wabrzezno	0.61	14.9	0.55	16.3
Torun	Torun	0.68	19.3	0.57	11.7
Inowroclaw	Inowroclaw	0.69	26.1	0.59	17.1
Mogilno i Strzelno	Mogilno	0.60	26.6	0.54	16.3
Gniezno oraz Witkowo	Gniezno	0.66	23.4	0.6	19.1
Wrzesnia	Wrzesnia	0.66	26.7	0.58	15.4
Jarocin	Jarocin	0.74	20.6	0.63	13.9
Pleszew	Pleszew	0.70	19.8	0.53	11.2
Ostrow i Odolanow	Ostrow Wielkopolski	0.58	9.4	0.52	8.7
Ostrzeszow	Ostrzeszow	0.51	9.3	0.45	8.3
Kepno	Kepno	0.66	12.6	0.53	11.1

within the area of the same partition as well as to the maintenance of the differences between neighboring districts from different partitions.

3.1 *The Outcome of the Research: The Prussia-Russia Borderline*

The average farm size in the border districts in the Russian zone in 1921 was 9.8 and dropped to 9.1 in 2002 (Table 1). For comparison, the average size of farms on the other side of the borderline fell from 17.3 to 13.9 (a comparable fall was noted in the Gini coefficient) (Table 2). In both parts of these values declined.

Table 3 Basic characteristics of the agrarian structure for selected districts from the Russian partition

1921	2002	1921		2002	
		Gini coefficient	The average size of farms (in ha)	Gini coefficient	The average size of farms (in ha)
Total		0.41	5.64	0.39	5.29
District	District	Gini coefficient in district	The average size of farms in district (in ha)	Gini coefficient in district	The average size of farms in district (in ha)
Bedzin	Bedzin, Myszkow, Zawiercie, Dabrowa Gornicza, Sosnowiec	0.32	4.0	0.47	3.0
Olkusz	Olkusz	0.31	4.6	0.25	3.2
Miechow	Miechow, Proszowice	0.45	6.2	0.36	5.6
Pinczow	Pinczow, Kazimierza Wielka	0.47	6.0	0.34	3.5
Stopnica	Busko Zdroj	0.38	5.3	0.36	5.4
Sandomierz	Sandomierz, Staszow	0.44	6.0	0.30	4.1
Janow Lubelski	Janow Lubelski, Krasnik	0.41	6.3	0.34	5.8
Bilgoraj	Bilgoraj	0.36	5.9	0.36	5.9
Tomaszow Lubelski	Tomaszow Lubelski	0.48	6.9	0.52	7.4

However, these figures still show the diversity and are closer to the size of the output data rather than to the size of the neighboring districts situated within the area of another partition. The best example of maintaining the differences from over 100 years ago are adjacent districts: the Slupca district (the Russian zone) and the Gniezno district (the former Prussian zone). In the Slupca district the average farm size changed but only symbolically—it increased from 10.5 ha to 10.9 ha (the Gini coefficient decreased from 0.56 to 0.51). However, in the Gniezno district the average size decreased from 23.4 to 19.1 ha (the Gini coefficient decreased from 0.66 to 0.60), but still farms in this district are much larger than those of the the Slupca district.

Figures 1 and 2 present the average size of farms in 1921 and in 2002 subsequently. As can be seen in the figures, the average farm size was and is lower on the eastern side of the partitions borderline (the Russian partition). The average size of a farm in the Prussian partition was and still is significantly different from that of

Table 4 Basic characteristics of the agrarian structure for selected districts from the Austrian-Hungarian partition

1921	2002	1921		2002	
		Gini coefficient	The average size of farms (in ha)	Gini coefficient	The average size of farms (in ha)
Total		0.34	3.8	0.30	3.5
District	District	Gini coefficient in district	The average size of farms in district (in ha)	Gini coefficient in district	The average size of farms in district (in ha)
Chrzanow	Chrzanow, Jaworzno	0.31	3.2	0.28	2.4
Cracow	Cracow	0.42	4.0	0.33	3.3
Wieliczka	Wieliczka	0.33	3.5	0.33	2.9
Bochnia	Bochnia	0.28	3.3	0.21	3.0
Brzesko	Brzesko	0.29	3.5	0.26	3.2
Tarnow	Tarnow	0.36	4.3	0.25	3.3
Dabrowa Tarnowska	Dabrowa Tarnowska	0.23	3.7	0.30	4.3
Mielec	Mielec	0.40	4.9	0.31	4.0
Tarnobrzeg	Tarnobrzeg, Stalowa Wola	0.43	4.1	0.18	3.0
Nisko	Nisko	0.32	4.3	0.26	3.8
Lancut	Lancut, Lezajsk	0.23	3.1	0.24	3.0
Przeworsk	Przeworsk	0.39	3.9	0.32	3.7
Jaroslaw	Jaroslaw	0.44	4.4	0.46	5.0
Cieszanow	Lubaczow	0.39	4.1	0.44	6.1

the Russian occupational zone. It should also be noted that in the districts situated in the southern part (at the bottom) of the borderline presented (Konin, Slupca, Kalisz, Sieradz, Wielun—the Russian partition; Ostrow, Ostrzeszow, Kepno—the Prussian partition) there were and there are smaller farms than those in the northern part (at the top) of the former Russian-Prussian border. Of course in this part farms from the Prussian zone were and are larger than those situated in the former Russian partition.

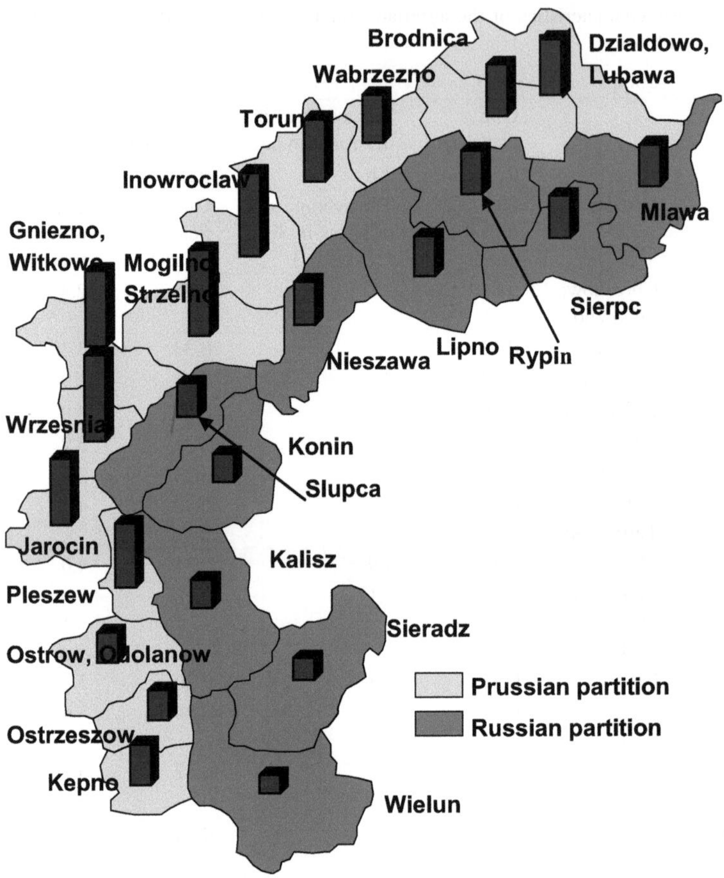

Fig. 1 The average size of farms in neighbouring districts from the Russian and Prussian partitions in 1921

3.2 The Outcome of the Research: The Austria-Hungary-Russia Borderline

The average farm size in the border zone districts in the Russian zone in 1921 was 5.64 and dropped to 5.29 in 2002. For comparison, the average size of farms located across the borderline in the districts of the former Austro-Hungarian partition fell from 3.8 to 3.5. In both parts, these values fell by about 6 %, which means that for almost 100 years the existing differences were not equalized but they were only changing at a comparable pace. The Gini coefficient also saw a comparative decrease: from 0.41 to 0.39 in the border zone districts of the Russian zone and

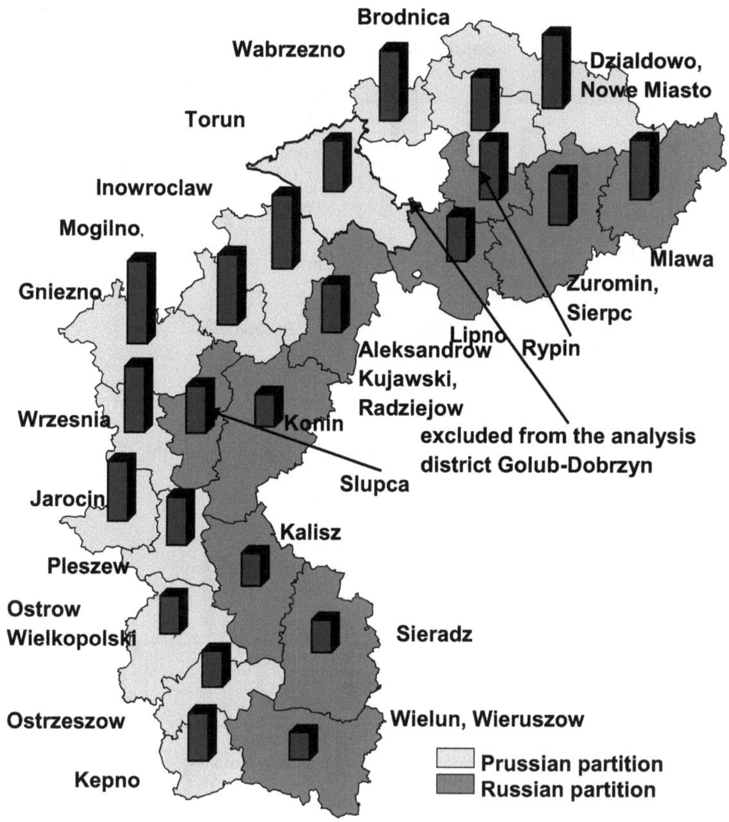

Fig. 2 The average size of farms in neighboring districts from the Russian and Prussian partitions in 2002

from 0.34 to 0.30 in the border zone districts in the Austria-Hungary partition. Also in this case the differences that existed in 1921 still occur today. It may also be indicated that, for example, the lowest Gini coefficient in the districts of the former Russian zone was and still can be seen in the Olkusz district (0.31; 0.25) and the highest value in the districts of the Austria-Hungarian partition was and is in the district of Jaroslaw (0.44; 0.46).

Figures 3 and 4 present the average size of farms in 1921 and in 2002 subsequently. As can be seen in the figures, the average size of farms was and is lower in the districts of the former Austro-Hungarian partition. The average size of a farm in the Russian partition was considerably different (and still differs) from that of the Austria-Hungarian partition.

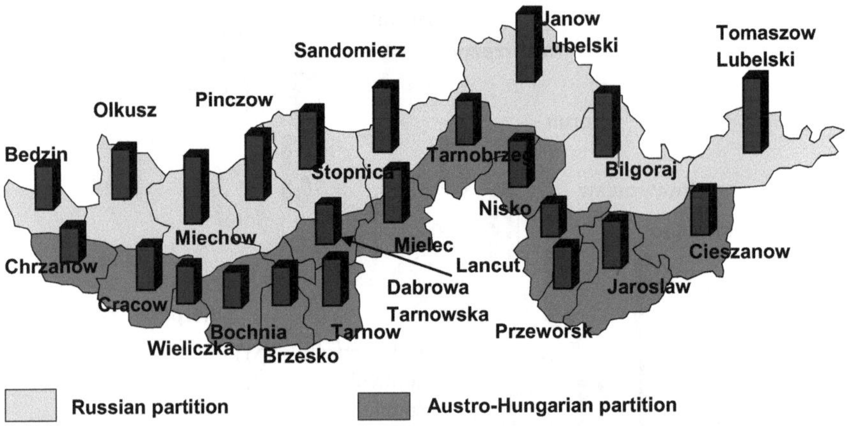

Fig. 3 The average size of farms in neighbouring districts from the Russian and Austria-Hungarian partitions in 1921

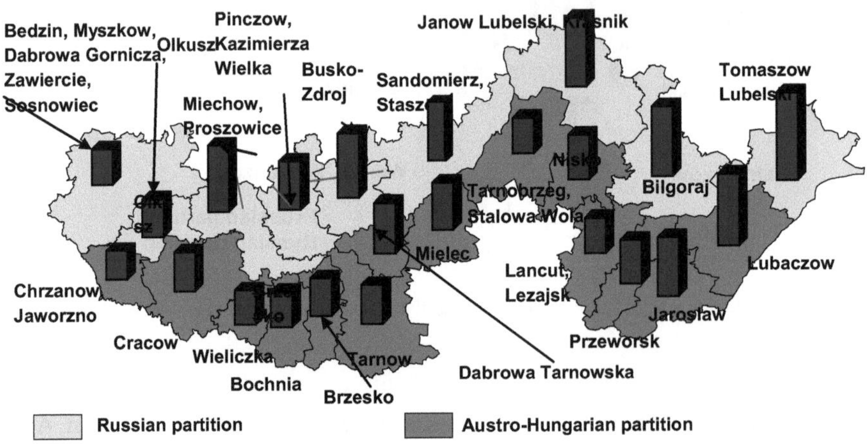

Fig. 4 The average size of farms in neighbouring districts from the Russian and Austria-Hungarian partitions in 2002

4 Conclusions

As shown in the work, the agrarian structure is different in various districts. For districts that were part of the same partition the differentiation is small, but in the context of the neighboring districts representing different partitions the differentiation is significant. This shows that historical factors are important, if not the most important factor in shaping today's agrarian structure of Polish agriculture.

To sum up, it may be stated that although farms were located within the same country and in the close neighborhood, in the time period 1921–2002 the major factor deciding about their structure was history. It must be emphasized that these farms were subject to uniform laws and economic and political factors over many years. In the period 1918–1939 the Second Republic of Poland had a capitalist system (until 1926 Poland was a fully functioning democratic state and later it was based on a presidential-autocratic system); in the time period 1939–1945 Poland was a scene of warfare; in the years 1945–1989 the Polish People's Republic was a communist state that after 1989 it again become a capitalist state and democracy. Despite that large farms of the Prussian partition remained large and those of the Russian zone remained considerably smaller, etc. That stems from the fact that the agrarian structure is a long-term structure within the meaning of Braudel.

It should be stressed that the implementation of all activities in the field of programmes aimed at changing the agrarian structure (e.g., enlarging the size of farms) can be difficult due to the durability of the structure as was shown in this article.

References

Banski, J., & Czapiewski, K. L. (2007). *Ekspertyza. Diagnoza zroznicowania wybranych elementow struktury przestrzennej oddzialujacych na gospodarke rolna w skali regionow [Expertise. Diagnosis differentiation of selected elements affecting the spatial structure of the economy as a scale agricultural regions]* (pp. 1–30). Warszawa: Instytut Ekonomiki Rolnictwa i Gospodarki Zywnosciowej—Panstwowy Instytut Badawczy.

Braudel, F. (1971). *Historia i trwanie* [History and duration]. Warszawa: Czytelnik.

de Souza, R. A., Miziara, F., & De Marco, J. P. (2013). Spatial variation of deforestation rates in the Brazilian Amazon: A complex theater for agrarian technology, agrarian structure and governance by surveillance. *Land Use Policy, 30*(1), 915–923.

Dziawgo, L., & Dziawgo, D. (2010). CSR i IR–nielatwe antidotum na toksyczna bankowosc [CSR and IR—Not easy antidote to the toxic banking]. *Bezpieczny Bank, 1*(40), 98–113.

Genier, C., Stamp, M., & Pfitzer, M. (2008). *Corporate social responsibility in the agrifood sector: Harnessing innovation for sustainable development draft for publication.* Geneva: Food & Agriculture Organization of the United Nations.

Grancelli, B. (2011). Local development in the rural regions of Eastern Europe: Post-socialist paradoxes of economic and social entrepreneurship. *Journal for East European Management Studies, 16*(1), 31–53.

GUS. (1928). *Pierwszy Powszechny Spis Rzeczypospolitej Polskiej z dnia 30 wrzesnia 1921 r* [The first general census in Poland from 30 September 1921]. Warszawa: Glowny Urzad Statystyczny.

GUS. (2014). *Local data bank.* Warszawa: Glowny Urzad Statystyczny.

Helfand, S. M., & Levine, E. S. (2004). Farm size and the determinants of productive efficiency in the Brazilian Center-West. *Agricultural Economics, 31*, 241–248.

Klopot, S. W. (2011). Struktura agrarna indywidualnego rolnictwa w latach 1945–2010 [Agrarian structure of individual agriculture in the years 1945–2010]. *Annales UMCS, SECTIO I Philosophia-Sociologia, 36*(2), 93–111.

Krupa, D. (2012). Fundusze inwestycyjne odpowiedzialne spolecznie [Socially responsible investment funds]. *Annales Universitatis Mariae Curie-Sklodowska. Sectio H. Oeconomia, 46*(1), 307–316.

Ludewigs, T., de Oliveira D'antona, A., Brondízio, E. S., & Hetrick, S. (2009). Agrarian structure and land-cover change along the lifespan of three colonization areas in the Brazilian Amazon. *World Development, 37*(8), 1348–1359.

Manning, L. (2013). Corporate and consumer social responsibility in the food supply chain. *British Food Journal, 115*(1), 9–29.

Ozdemir, P., Karabulut, E., & Mentes, T. (2011). Examination of inequality of life span by using the Gini coefficient in the Turkish population for the period 1990–2008. *Balkan Medical Journal, 28*(4), 420–423.

Pietrzak, M. B., & Walczak, D. (2012). The evaluation of the agrarian structure in the Pomerania and Kujawy regions in the years 1921 and 2002. *Roczniki Naukowe Stowarzyszenie Ekonomistow Rolnictwa i Agrobiznesu, 14*(6), 211–214.

Pietrzak, M. B., & Walczak, D. (2013). Changes in agrarian structure in Poland in 1921 and 2002 based on the example of selected provinces from three annexed territories. *Roczniki Naukowe Stowarzyszenie Ekonomistow Rolnictwa i Agrobiznesu, 15*(4), 333–335.

Pietrzak, M. B., & Walczak, D. (2014). The analysis of the agrarian structure in Poland with the special consideration of the years 1921 and 2002. *Bulgarian Journal of Agricultural Science, 20*(5), 1019–1039.

Reyes, C. M. (2002). *Impact of agrarian reform on poverty*. Manila: Philippine Institute for Development Studies Discussion Paper Series, 2002–02

The Eurasian Economic Union: Complimentary or Competitive Structure to the European Union

Katarzyna Czerewacz-Filipowicz

Abstract Regional integration between Russia, Belarus, and Kazakhstan appears to be the most effective integrational process in the post-Soviet area. In the very nearly future the Customs Union can evolve to the Eurasian Economic Union (the EEU)—a structure characterized by the features of common market. Geographical evolution is also taken into consideration. New members of the structure are going to be Armenia and Kyrgyzstan and maybe some other countries. From the point of view of the customs union theory this structure should enhance efficiency in production, increase production levels, improve positions of these countries in international division of labour and improve their level of integration with the world economy. But not all custom unions have been economic success. The particular integrational steps should be driving factors for their economies but sometimes they perpetuate economic backwardness. The EEU can be a formula of cooperation with the European Union. The main aim of this article is an answer to the questions how much economic integration in the framework of the EEU can be complementary to the processes in the EU, and how much it is rather a kind of competition model or even an alternative way of economic relations to the ties linking post-Soviet countries with the EU countries.

Keywords The Eurasian Economic Union (EEU) • Regional integration agreements (RIAs)

1 Introduction

The answer to the question of complementarity or competitiveness of the Eurasian Economic Union (EEU) in relation to the European Union (EU) is important from the perspective of both structures. The use of complementarity with European countries could become an important driving factor for the EEU countries and

K. Czerewacz-Filipowicz (✉)
Department of Economics and Social Sciences, Bialystok University of Technology, Białystok, Poland
e-mail: k.czerewacz@pb.edu.pl

© Springer International Publishing Switzerland 2016

M.H. Bilgin et al. (eds.), *Business Challenges in the Changing Economic Landscape - Vol. 1*, Eurasian Studies in Business and Economics 2/1,
DOI 10.1007/978-3-319-22596-8_34

their economies. On the other hand, the EU cares about friendly business relations with neighboring countries. In addition, internationally developed economic ties are a factor increasing the competitiveness of the economies, enable international specialization and improve their position in the international division of labor. The current political situation and the restrictions imposed in mutual economic relations by the EU and Russia are not conducive to economic development considerations based on the complementarity between the EEU and the EU. However, in the last quarter, we saw many unexpected turns in the policies of the researched countries, while a large part of economic relations remained stable.

The European Union is one of the world's most outward-oriented economies and this openness is a source of strength. The EU is the biggest trading partner for 59 countries (also for Russia and Kazakhstan) (European Commission 2014a).

Today, the Eurasian Economic Union is only the conception and song of the future but it is put on a very strong base. The foundations of this conception are the Eurasian Economic Community and the Customs Union which is going to transform firstly into the Single Economic Space, established in 2012, and secondly into the Eurasian Economic Union in 2015. After the collapse of USSR many different regional integration agreements (RIAs) were created in this area (e.g., CIS, SCO, GUAM, EurAsEC). Many reasons of this were connected with the situation that newly created states had to define their role and place both in the region and in the world. Politics of regional integration in many cases was an attempt to determine the path of economic and political development. The integration of post-Soviet area is considered in both political sciences and economics. The opinions concerning the causes and the results of RIAs in this region are diverse. Libman and Vinokurov (2012) and Vinokurov and Libman (2012) emphasize that it is a holding-together regionalism: the integration of countries which, until recently, were part of a single political entity. In this study, it should be noted that this is really about stopping disintegration and maintaining the former economic ties. On the other hand, some researchers (Trenin 2002) and politicians treat the integration initiatives in the post-Soviet area as a transitional political concept without a future.

There are also researchers taking a different perspective by which the integration of the post-Soviet area is only a part of Russia's policy of creating a multipolar world (Makarychev and Morozov 2011; Bieleń and Raś 2008). Some researchers would like to see integration in this region, not simply as bringing the member states together, but rather as a factor influencing their economic development in a positive way (Libman 2012). Such different approaches arose due to the fact that many of the signed RIAs were not realized. Mattli (1999b) emphasized that the singing of RIA does not establish integration. True integration is achieved through the implementation of this promise, which entails a lengthy process of establishing common rules, regulations and policies.

The Eurasian Economic Community was established on 10 October 2000 by Russia, Belarus, Kazakhstan, Kyrgyzstan and Tajikistan. The range of the EurAsEC also includes the establishment of the Customs Union on the EurAsEC territory by Belarus, Russia and Kazakhstan in 2010, and its subsequent transformation into the Single Economic Space in 2012 and into the Eurasian Economic Union in 2015.

The Customs Union has a major impact on the regulation of cross-border trade, both across its members and with third parties. The Single Economic Space and the Eurasian Economic Union have even more ambitious goals connected with services, capital and labor flow.

In the preamble to the agreement on the Eurasian Economic Union the main principles and values of the organization were singled out, among other things: respect for the constitution of the Member States emphasizing the validity of human rights, strengthening cooperation, solidarity and harmonization of interests of the organization with the interests of the Member States, strengthening the economy of the member states by building the economy of the community and economic progress as a result of joint actions, confirmation of efforts to build up cooperation between third countries and international. According to the assumptions, it could be a structure integrating its members into the global economy, including the European Union.

2 Theoretical Approach

From a theoretical point of view the processes of regional economic integration are the amalgamation of separate economies into larger free trading regions (Mattli 1999a). Regional economic integration is known as a very positive phenomenon in the contemporary world's economy, the phenomenon being set up mainly to make the economic development of member states more dynamic. Countries joining regional groups expect faster economic growth, a better position in the international division of labour, strengthening their position at the international scene.

In accordance with the opinion and theory of El-Agraa (1999), at the customs union (and free trade area) level, "*the possible sources of economic gain can be attributed to*

- *Enhanced efficiency in production made possible by increased specialization in accordance with the law of comparative advantage;*
- *Increased production levels due to better exploitation of economies of scale made possible by the increased size of the market;*
- *An improved international bargaining position, made possible by the larger size, leading to better terms trade;*
- *Enforced changes in economic efficiency brought about by enhanced competition, and;*
- *Changes affecting both the amount and quality of the factors of production due to technological advances.*" (El-Agraa 1999, p. 35)

If the level of economic integration is to proceed beyond the customs union level (and this is the example of the EEU), to the economic union level, "*then further sources of gain become possible due to:*

- *Factor mobility across the borders of member nations,*
- *The coordination of monetary and fiscal policies; and*
- *The goals of near full employment, higher rates of economic growth and better income distribution becoming unified targets.*" (El-Agraa 1999, p. 35)

The integration within the EEU (in accordance with the assumptions) could provide a significant boost to the member states. The realisation of the economic union (previously common market) could make the markets of the Member States attractive mainly from the EU countries perspective.

3 Assumptions and Data

International economic complementarity goes far beyond the issues of trade, but the analysis of the structure of trade can be a good measure of the degree and nature of complementarities. Since the Eurasian Economic Union is about to arise, presented data was prepared on the basis of the data concerning the EurAsEC countries. The main emphasis was placed on the states being a member of the Customs Union (as both the structures lay foundations of the Eurasian Economic Union).

The countries belonging to the EurAsEC (as well as the future EEU) differ in size, the level of economic development, the possession of natural resources, the structure of economies. In many areas the differences between them are significant. This disparity is reflected in the structure (patterns of trade relations) of business relationships of individual countries.

Analyzing the directions and structure in trade among individual countries of the EurAsEC over the last 20 years it can be told that a lot of changes have taken place in the volume of trade with individual partners. What had the impact on this were:

- The processes of integration and disintegration in the researched area,
- Changes in their economic conditions,
- Changes in global economy,
- China's economic explosion.

However we can find a pattern of trade relations of the Customs Union and generally the EurAsEC countries. Tables 1 and 2 present the share of the EurAsEC countries in the trade turnover of particular member states. The trade within the EurAsEC has dominated the foreign trade of Belarus and it is an abiding tendency. The trade with partners from the EurAsEC is also very important for Kyrgyzstan and Tajikistan, although in the case of these two small and poor countries, they are a place of the collision of influence of three powerful neighbors (Russia, China and Kazakhstan) changing the image of economic relations of these countries.

For Kazakhstan, the EurAsEC is an important direction of imports, in a smaller part of exports. From the perspective of Russia, the trade with the group makes approximately 8.5 % of the turnover. Since the EurAsEC countries are very diverse in terms of size, economic potential, raw materials and so on, it is not hard to guess

Table 1 The percentage of the EurAsEC in exports of the member states

Country	1995	2000	2007	2010	2011	2012	2013
Belarus	46.30	50.96	38.27	41.27	37.31	37.6	47.97
Kazakhstan	48.29	19.05	13.00	7.05	5.93	13.37	10.56
Kyrgyzstan	49.07	21.62	41.37	52.47	43.88	43.88	41.70
Rosja	7.59	7.71	8.76	6.43	3.94	8.18	8.03
Tajikistan	14.29	34.92	8.71	11.33	15.34	13.34	14.08

Source: International Monetary Fund

Table 2 The percentage of the EurAsEC in imports of the member states

Country	1995	2000	2007	2010	2011	2012	2013
Belarus	57.24	65.48	60.52	52.99	54.85	59.67	53.46
Kazakhstan	53.09	49.80	36.69	21.19	34.09	62.56	23.90
Kyrgyzstan	47.19	35.16	54.54	22.18	22.63	27.18	30.03
Russia	10.71	18.57	7.00	6.15	3.71	7.48	8.53
Tajikistan	20.62	18.26	48.39	45.55	26.36	30.01	29.52

Source: International Monetary Fund

that the ties with Russia are the majority of the business relationship of Belarus and Kazakhstan.

Analyzing the data in Tables 3 and 4 you can tell immediately that the trade within the Customs Union and the EurAsEC for Belarus is in fact the trade with Russia. It applies to Kazakhstan too—trade relations with Russia are most important. On the other hand, in the case of Kyrgyzstan and Tajikistan trade integration affects not only Russia but also Kazakhstan.

Tables 5 and 6 present the European Union's share in the trade of the EurAsEC countries. This shows how important direction of trade to Russia, Kazakhstan and Belarus are the European countries. Especially in the case of Russia, the degree of economic ties with the EU has grown rapidly over the last 20 years. First of all, for Russia but also for Kazakhstan trade relations with the countries of the European Union are more important than those in the framework of the EurAsEC (and the EEU).

Russia is also important to the EU. In 2013, it was the third most important EU trading partner with its 9.5 % of total trade turnover. 12.3 % of EU imports came from Russia, and 6.9 % of exports went on its market. Kazakhstan ranked at the 26th position among the EU trading partners with the participation of 0.9 %. Belarus took 44th position with its 0.4 % (European Commission 2014a).

The main problem for the future of the EEU countries is the structure of trade turnover with the European Union. The UE imports from Russia: mineral products 78.2 %, not classified products 9.4 %, base metals and articles thereof 4.0 %, while Russian imports from the EU are mainly: machinery and appliance 31.6 %, transport equipment 16.2 %, products of the chemical or allied industries 14.2 % (European Commission 2014b). In the case of Kazakhstan, its exports to the EU is even more focused on mineral products, which comprise 93.5 % of total exports.

Table 3 The percentage of the Russian Federation in exports of the member states

Country	1995	2000	2007	2010	2011	2012	2013
Belarus	44.43	50.60	36.57	39.39	35.03	35.43	45.29
Kazakhstan	45.07	17.73	8.99	5.25	4.68	11.75	8.30
Kyrgyzstan	23.60	12.92	20.69	33.58	22.31	16.36	11.10
Tajikistan	12.68	33.61	6.63	8.52	8.14	5.89	5.88

Source: International Monetary Fund

Table 4 The percentage of the Russian Federation in imports of the member states

Country	1995	2000	2007	2010	2011	2012	2013
Belarus	56.11	64.82	59.96	51.83	54.48	59.37	53.23
Kazakhstan	49.91	48.32	35.28	22.80	29.58	58.04	20.79
Kyrgyzstan	26.79	23.87	40.52	14.83	13.75	17.10	21.16
Tajikistan	16.79	15.67	30.85	32.25	16.46	15.91	15.90

Source: International Monetary Fund

Table 5 The percentage of the European Union in exports of the EurAsEC member states

Country	1995	2000	2007	2010	2011	2012	2013
Belarus	12.5	9.40	43.72	30.07	37.90	38.15	28.25
Kazakhstan	21.41	20.89	40.12	53.78	52.54	54.39	45.23
Kyrgyzstan	1.24	33.98	6.52	1.82	2.52	3.13	4.75
Russia	33.58	35.81	55.64	49.19	45.55	52.91	51.81
Tajikistan	46.33	51.74	43.16	3.71	8.27	8.26	6.94

Source: International Monetary Fund

Table 6 The percentage of the European Union in imports of the EurAsEC member states

Country	1995	2000	2007	2010	2011	2012	2013
Belarus	15.66	14.92	21.76	21.64	18.99	20.06	24.44
Kazakhstan	13.55	20.32	24.76	30.15	35.58	28.02	22.22
Kyrgyzstan	14.54	12	9.45	4.09	6.63	5.64	5.11
Russia	38.8	32.9	43.67	42.85	31.54	41.89	43.63
Tajikistan	25.93	4.03	9.50	9.80	4.23	4.70	5.49

Source: International Monetary Fund

Kazakhstan imports from the EU: machinery and appliance 33.5 %, transport equipment 17.7 %, products of the chemical or allied industries 17.2 % (European Commission 2014c). Belarus exports to the EU mineral products 37.5 %, products of the chemical or allied industries 16.6 %, and base metals and articles thereof 15.1 %. Belarussian imports from the EU are mainly: machinery and appliance 34.0 %, transport equipment 15.3 %, products of the chemical or allied industries 11.0 % (European Commission 2014d).

Russia and Kazakhstan are afraid of being only a raw material exporters. Oil and gas are strategic products but 1 day they can be replaced by other sources of energy. All the countries of the EEU are providers of low-processed products and recipients of highly processed ones. Over the last 20 years between the EU and the countries of the EEU have not developed any significant intra-relations. From the perspective of the EEU, it is not a favorable situation and it causes looking for other opportunities.

Although my work is on the EU—EurAsEC relationship, the change of China's role in the trade of the EurAsEC countries is also worth being taken into account, as Russia has repeatedly pointed to the possibility of replacing the economic ties with the European countries just by the ties with China.

China is today the most important economic partner for almost all Central Asian countries (in EurAsEC for Kyrgystan and Tajikistan). Kazakhstan, which increases the export of raw materials to China, has a quick chance to join this group of countries. But the growth of Chinese position as a trade, investment partner and a source of capital is so fast that is making those countries afraid about their future economic independence. In this case, integration with Russia and post-Soviet region is a kind of alternative and economic diversification of foreign relations (see Tables 7 and 8).

The attractiveness of the Russian market can be also demonstrated by its investment position. In 2013, Russia took the third place in the ranking of the most attractive countries, directions of foreign direct investment. It was overtaken only, although significantly, by the United States and China. The Latin American countries (Brazil), the Asian countries, (Hong Kong, Singapore), Canada, Australia were left behind. The European countries were left far behind. Although, it should

Table 7 The percentage of China in exports of the EurAsEC member states

Country	1995	2000	2007	2010	2011	2012	2013
Belarus	0.67	2.02	2.03	1.92	1.56	0.94	1.26
Kazakhstan	5.73	6.83	15.43	17.69	19.80	19.38	23.55
Kyrgyzstan	0.62	8.75	5.46	6.08	7.84	6.93	5.06
Russia	4.75	5.21	4.60	8.79	6.57	7.09	7.22
Tajikistan	0.80	0.44	0.57	37.41	6.60	9.38	8.48

Source: International Monetary Fund

Table 8 The percentage of China in imports of the EurAsEC member states

Country	1995	2000	2007	2010	2011	2012	2013
Belarus	0.40	0.57	2.85	4.84	4.80	5.12	6.59
Kazakhstan	1.05	3.01	21.89	16.52	23.39	28.03	31.32
Kyrgyzstan	6.89	6.65	14.72	62.35	59.29	55.05	51.77
Russia	2.06	2.81	12.29	17.99	15.61	16.33	17.09
Tajikistan	1.85	1.77	10.88	9.02	46.24	41.17	41.74

Source: International Monetary Fund

Table 9 FDI inflows: top 10 host economies, 2012 and 2013 (billions of dollars)

Country	2012	2013
United States	161	188
China	121	124
Russian Federation	51	79
Hong Kong, China	75	77
Brazil	65	64
Singapore	61	64
Canada	43	62
Australia	56	50
Spain	26	39
Mexico	18	38

Source: UNCTAD (2014)

Table 10 FDI outflows: top 10 home economies, 2012 and 2013 (billions of dollars)

Country	2012	2013
United States	367	338
Japan	123	136
China	88	101
Russian Federation	49	95
Hong Kong, China	88	92
Switzerland	45	60
Germany	80	80
Canada	55	43
Netherlands		33
Szwecja	29	32

Source: UNCTAD (2014)

be noted that the majority of these investments came precisely from the European Union (see Tables 9 and 10).

Russia, in 2013, was also the fourth largest foreign investor after the USA, Japan and China (see Table 10), but in the majority, the Russian investments go to the markets of the EurAsEC countries. In 2015, this position will probably not be maintained due to the deteriorating economic situation in Russia resulting from the drastic decline in oil prices. However, such a high ranking in terms of both FDI inflows and FDI outflows may be conducive to both integration within the EEU as well as with the EU.

4 Conclusions

The first unknown concerning the EEU is the question whether or not the countries that signed the Treaty establishing the EEU will be able to bring real economic integration. In other words, whether or not such large number of differences making these countries different can enter the freedoms of the common market. These concerns also stem from the bad experiences of other groups that the researched countries tried to create in the past.

Moreover, we have a unique situation here, because Russia has been integrating with the countries which are not today its main trading partners. The reasons for the directions of integration processes created by Russia may be the structure of the Russian turnover with particular countries and structures. The structure of Russian turnover with the EU is a kind of challenge and doesn't seem to be in accordance with the Russian vision of economic development and the Russian vision of the world's order. According to an official Russian strategy, the Russian President would like to see Russia as an economy based on knowledge, specializing in the latest technologies, and a superpower, of course.

On the other hand, Russian trade relations with the EEU countries are intrasectional in many sectors, Russian products are very competitive in the EEU countries, including highly processed products. It is essential, however, to answer the question whether or not it is possible to increase the exports of these products to the markets of the poor, flooded by cheap Chinese goods countries of the EEU? On the other hand, if the Russian market can increase demand for the goods of the poorer partners? Or rather, if all those countries lack the capital and technological support from outside? The Eurasian Economic Union can be a natural element of cooperation with the European Union of post-Soviet countries. There is a big potential in bilateral trade relations and generally economic potential. Relying on commercial ties a number of functional planes of bilateral cooperation such as international transport, direct investment, raw material linkages could also be indicated. On the basis of it, spill-over effects of mutual cooperation could be expected.

But one of the biggest traps of this conception is the danger that the integration in the framework of the Eurasian Economic Union will have more competition than cooperation features in the area of international relations with the EU. It is mainly political factors that can seal the attempts to reduce mutually beneficial economic dependence.

From the European Union perspective free trade is more important than ever for the economic growth and job creation. Two thirds of imports are raw materials, intermediary goods and components needed by EU manufacturers (European Commission 2014a).

The EEU regional economic integration processes should be complementary to the European integration (mainly the EU), Asian integration (e.g., ASEAN, APEC) and generally should improve the level of integration of these countries with the world's economy. If the model of integration at the post-Soviet area takes a form of competition with the rest of the world it will perpetuate the economic backwardness of this region and can deepen existing problems. Integration into the world economy is an important element of the strategy of economic development of a particular country.

Acknowledgement The project has been financed from the National Science Centre funds awarded on the basis of Decision DEC-2011/03/B/HS4/05/930.

References

Bieleń, S., & Raś, M. (2008). *Polityka zagraniczna Rosji* [Russian Foreign Policy]. Warsaw: Difin.

El-Agraa, A. M. (1999). *Regional integration. Experience, theory, and measurement.* New York: Palgrave Macmillan.

European Commission. (2014a). *The European Union explained: Trade.* European Union, 2014, [online] Available at http://europa.eu/pol/pdf/flipbook/en/trade_en.pdf. Accessed 5 Dec 2014.

European Commission. (2014b). *European Union, trade in goods with Russia,* [online] Available at http://trade.ec.europa.eu/doclib/docs/2006/September/tradoc_113440.pdf. Accessed 15 Sep 2014.

European Commission. (2014c). *European Union, trade in goods with Kazakhstan,* [online] Available at http://trade.ec.europa.eu/doclib/docs/2006/September/tradoc_113406.pdf. Accessed 15 Sep 2014.

European Commission. (2014d). *European Union, trade in goods with Belarus,* [online] Available at http://trade.ec.europa.eu/doclib/docs/2006/September/tradoc_113351.pdf. Accessed 15 Sep 2014.

Libman, A. (2012). *Studies of regional integration in the CIS and in Central Asia: A literature survey* (Report 2). Saint Petersburg: Eurasian Development Bank.

Libman, A., & Vinokurov, E. (2012). *Holding-together integration: 20 years of the post-soviet integration.* London: Palgrave Macmillan.

Makarychev, A., & Morozov, V. (2011). Multilateralism, multipolarity, and beyond: A menu of Russia's policy strategies. *Global Governance: A Review of Multilateralism and International Organizations., 17*(3), 353–373.

Mattli, W. (1999a). *The logic of regional integration. Europe and beyond.* Cambridge: Cambridge University Press.

Mattli, W. (1999b). Explaining regional integration outcomes. *Journal of European Public Policy, 6*(1), 1–27.

Trenin, D. (2002). *The end of Eurasia: Russia on the border between geopolitics and globalization.* Washington: Carnegie Center.

UNCTAD. (2014). *World Investment Report 2014 (WIR14),* [online] Available at http://unctad.org/en/PublicationsLibrary/wir2014_en.pdf. Accessed 15 Oct 2014.

Vinokurov, E., & Libman, A. (2012). *Eurasian integration: Challenges of transcontinental regionalism.* London: Palgrave Macmillan.

Fiscal Contractions in Eurozone in the Years 1995–2013: Can Non-Keynesian Effects Be Helpful in Future Deleverage Process?

Adam P. Balcerzak, Michał Bernard Pietrzak, and Elżbieta Rogalska

Abstract Last global financial crisis has led to massive fiscal stimulation actions in EU which resulted in significant increase of public debt. As a result, in near future EU countries will have to adopt much stricter long term fiscal policy that will be necessary for deleveraging process. In this context the aim of the research is to check whether one can find non-Keynesian effects of fiscal consolidations in Eurozone countries in last decade. If the answer is positive, then could these non-Keynesian effects be significant developing factor. The third scientific question concentrates on the ways the fiscal consolidations were implemented and the potential influence of consolidations strategies on short term growth. The research is based on European Commission and Eurostat fiscal and macroeconomic data for the years 1995–2013. The econometric dynamic panel model based on the concept of conditional convergence was applied. As a complementary method qualitative analysis of cases of significant contractions was used with the concentration on the differences between expansionary and conventional Keynesian cases of fiscal contractions. The research gives some arguments for existence of fiscal transitions channels leading to non-Keynesian effects of fiscal policy, which in the same time can be a factor of conditional convergence.

Keywords Fiscal policy • Fiscal consolidations • Non-Keynesian effects • Conditional convergence

A.P. Balcerzak (✉)
Department of Economics, Nicolaus Copernicus University, Toruń, Poland
e-mail: apb@umk.pl

M.B. Pietrzak
Department of Econometrics and Statistics, Nicolaus Copernicus University, Toruń, Poland
e-mail: michal.pietrzak@umk.pl

E. Rogalska
Department of Microeconomics, University of Warmia and Mazury, Olsztyn, Poland
e-mail: e.rogalska@interia.pl

© Springer International Publishing Switzerland 2016

M.H. Bilgin et al. (eds.), *Business Challenges in the Changing Economic Landscape - Vol. 1*, Eurasian Studies in Business and Economics 2/1,
DOI 10.1007/978-3-319-22596-8_35

1 Introduction

The end of twentieth century was a period when most academic economists and decision makers accepted the view that the anti-cyclical policy should be mostly based on the monetary tools. In that period many believed that principals of prudent fiscal policy should be concentrated on the middle and long term aims supporting long term growth. As it was stated by Martin Eichenbaum: "In sharp contrast to the views that prevailed in the early 1960s, there is now widespread agreement that countercyclical discretionally fiscal policy is neither desirable nor politically feasible. Practical debates around stabilization policy revolve almost exclusively around monetary policy" (Eichenbaum 1997, p. 236). In that time a wide research on the possibility of non-Keynesian effects of fiscal consolidations was started (see Giavazzi and Pagano 1990; Alesina and Ardagna 1998).

In the sphere of fiscal policy in European Union last decade of twentieth and the beginning of twenty-first century were influenced with the process of Eurozone creation and the efforts to fulfill Maastricht Treaty criteria. As a result in that period a significant decrease of government debt for countries that created euro area was obtained. The average level of government consolidated gross debt for first 11 members of the Eurozone decreased from the level of 69 % of their GDP in 1995 to 54 % in 2007.

However, global financial crisis that started in the year 2008, at least in the sphere of fiscal policy practice of developed countries, has led to a serious change in the approach to fiscal policy. Most European countries implemented massive fiscal policy stimulation programs that in Keynesian way were supposed to increase aggregate demand and bring short term anti-crisis effects. This resulted in significant increase of government debts in European Union that in longer term can become serious obstacle for growth. In case of mentioned 11 first members of euro area the average level of government consolidated gross debt rose from the mentioned 54 % in 2007 to 89.2 % in 2013. In case of the Eurozone (27 countries) this value rose from the average level of 58.9 % in 2007 to 87.4 % of GDP in 2013.

In this context three scientific questions are the base for that paper. First of all, the aim of the research is to check whether one can find non-Keynesian effects of fiscal consolidations in Eurozone countries in last two decades. If the answer is positive, then could these non-Keynesian effects be significant developing factor in case of Eurozone countries? The third scientific question concentrates on the ways the consolidations were implemented and the potential influence of consolidations strategies on short term growth.

In order to find the answer to the first two questions the hypothesis of conditional β-convergence for 11 countries that started euro area for the years 1995–2013 was tested. As the variables determining the output in the steady state the investments per capita and the government primary balance describing the fiscal policy were used. The verification of hypothesis of β-convergence process enables to identify the long term tendency of output per capita among analyzed countries. In the same time verification of the hypothesis enables to identify non-Keynesian effects of fiscal prudence as a positive influence of fiscal restrictive policy on the level of output per capita. The empirical part is based on the Eurostat database data. The data concerning primary balance was taken from European Commission report (2013).

The article consists of three parts. In the first one the theoretical background concerning the non-Keynesian effects is discussed. The second and third parts have strictly empirical nature. The second part is devoted to econometric analysis of consequences of fiscal prudence. Here the econometric dynamic panel model based on the concept of conditional convergence was applied. In the third part qualitative analysis of cases of significant consolidations was made with the concentration on the differences between expansionary thus non-Keynesian cases and conventional Keynesian cases of fiscal contractions.

2 Fiscal Consolidations as a Positive Supply Shock Supporting Convergence

Based on the basic textbook approach in the long term prudent (defined as rather restrictive) fiscal policy is considered as a factor supporting capital accumulation and productive investments. Thus, it is improving long term growth and can be a factor supporting economic convergence. On the other hand, form the short term Keynesian perspective fiscal consolidations tend to negatively influence aggregate demand and with multiplier effects dampen current growth, whereas fiscal expansions in spite of the possibility of crowding out effects (Balcerzak and Rogalska 2014) tend to support current activity of economy and short term growth.

However, the end of 1980s with the experiences of Denmark in the years 1983–1984 and Ireland in the years 1987–1989 showed the possibility of not standard short term effects of fiscal restrictions, where the improvement of government fiscal balance led to increase of aggregate demand and product. New research program concerning expansionary (non-Keynesian) effects of fiscal consolidations was started (Giavazzi and Pagano 1990).

The models explaining the transmission mechanisms of non-Keynesian effects of fiscal consolidations are usually classified to two groups. The first one attributes the non-Keynesian effects to the demand side of economy and the results of expectations change of private agents in the situation of uncertainty concerning their future tax burden (Rogalska 2012). This mechanism is based on the expectation of households that due to current fiscal consolidations the future tax burden will decrease, which is the source of wealth effect. As a result the households that tend to smooth their consumption during their lifespan can increase their current consumption, which under positive circumstances (for example determined by the relation between the agents maximizing their consumption during their whole lives and liquidity constrained agents depending on their current income) can offset the negative effects of decrease of government expenditures (Alesina and Ardagna

2009). In that context three factors tend to increase the possibility of non-Keynesian occurrence. First of all, the scale of consolidations must be big enough to convince the households that there is a real chance for lower tax burden in the future. The second condition is the credibility of fiscal authorities. The household must believe that the government is not going to change the prudent fiscal policy with the minor improvement of situations. In that context the third factor which is current budget situation can be also decisive. Some models predict that in case of very high and growing level of public debt when the household expect that the level of debt is not sustainable, it must result in inevitable and significant increase of taxes, the implementation of strict consolidations can be a reason for change of expectations (see Perotti 1999).

The second group of models concentrates on the supply side of economy and the positive influence of reducing government expenditures on the costs level and thus competitiveness of enterprises (Rzońca and Ciżkowicz 2005). In the literature there are many models concentrating on the supply side of economy and reactions of enterprises to fiscal adjustments. The most important determinant of results of fiscal consolidations is the composition of adjustment (Rzońca and Varoudakis 2007; Alesina et al. 1999; Lane and Perotti 2001; Alesina and Ardagna 1998, 2009). Alesina and Perotti (1997) were investigating supply side effects of fiscal adjustments in unionized economies with imperfect competition markets. In case of labor markets with strong unions, fiscal consolidations that were mainly based on income tax increases were resulting in increased pressure on wage rises, thus increasing costs of enterprises and diminishing their price competitiveness. In the end this can become additional negative supply shock that can threaten effectiveness of fiscal adjustment. On the other hand, the strategy based on public expenditures cuts in case of positive influence on enterprises price competitiveness can have offsite results. When the lower public expenditures are the result of wages cuts and lower employment in public sector, the lack of possibilities of earning and lower wages in public sector can decrease the wage pressure in private sector, which can influence positively enterprise profits and increase their investment capabilities. The final consequence of this mechanism can be higher international price competitiveness of enterprises and it can result in non-Keynesian results of fiscal consolidation (Alesina and Ardagna 2009). Of course, the whole mechanism is quite complex and it depends on many factors such as the influence of export channel on the national economy, the ratio of labor costs to global costs of enterprises, the speed and rate of influence of positive supply shock in the sphere of labor costs.

Concentrating on the problem of relation of short term fiscal policy and middle or long term growth, thus the chances for obtaining the convergence process, the effectiveness of transmission mechanisms of the supply side models is crucial. In this context from the perspective of supply side economy, the basic role of government should be decreasing the price rigidity on the product markets and increasing elasticity of labor markets. When the markets are characterized with sufficient elasticity the export channel can be a factor increasing the chances for successful fiscal consolidations. Based on that approach, in case of short term fiscal policy consolidation actions should rather concentrate on the effort to reduce government expenditures than the programs of tax and revenue increases (see more Alesina and Ardagna 2009).

3 Fiscal Prudence and Conditional Convergence: Econometric Analysis

In order to verify the hypothesis of the paper the convergence analysis for the first 11 euro zone members was done. The parameters of the dynamic panel model for 1995–2013 were estimated, which enable to identify conditional *β-convergence* process. The convergence analysis framework has been widely discussed in the literature. The problems of absolute convergence, conditional *β-convergence,* σ-convergence, club-convergence, stochastic convergence and application of panel models or tools of spatial econometric for the convergence analysis were discussed by Baumol (1986), Barro and Sala-i-Martin (1991, 1992, 1995), Bond et al. (2001), Caselli et al. (1996), Sala-I-Martin (1996a, b), Mankiw et al. (1992), Durlauf and Johnson (1995), Quah (1993a, b, 1996a, b), Bernard and Durlauf (1995), Evans and Karras (1996), Islam (1995), Rey and Montouri (1999), Le Gallo and Ertur (2003), Ciołek (2005), Arbia (2006).

The phenomena of β-convergence means that all the analyzed countries in the long term converge in terms of income per capita. In a given period that common income per capita is reached within the long term steady state. The convergence phenomena was enriched with conditional β-convergence where one assumes that every country tend to reach his own steady state. The income level in the steady state for every region is determined by economic process that characterize the fundamental conditions of economy such as the investment rate and depreciation, the demographic processes and population growth, the quality of human capital, and the technology (see Mankiw et al. 1992; Levine and Renelt 1992). In case of β-convergence the countries can reach the same income level but only provided that they are similar in terms of economic variables that determine the output in the steady state.

The hypothesis of conditional β-convergence was tested by estimation of parameters of dynamic panel model (Baltagi 1995) that is described with the Eq. (3). The dependent variable was GDP per capita in purchasing power standards. The independent variable was the real investment per capita and the primary balance defined as government net lending or net borrowing excluding interest, which is variable that characterize the fiscal policy approach. The positive value of that variable is equivalent to government surplus whereas negative means the government deficit. In the context of the theoretical background described in "Fiscal Consolidations as a Positive Supply Shock Supporting Convergence" of the paper that parameter α_1 should be positive and statistically significant.

$$\mathbf{Y}^*_{it} = \beta_0 - \beta_1 \ln\mathbf{Y}_{it-1} + \alpha_1\mathbf{X}_{1,it} + \alpha_2\ln\mathbf{X}_{2,it} + \boldsymbol{\eta}_i + \boldsymbol{\varepsilon}_{it}. \quad (1)$$

$$\mathbf{Y}^*_{it} = \ln(\mathbf{Y}_{it}/\mathbf{Y}_{it-1}) \quad (2)$$

$$\ln\mathbf{Y}_{it} = \beta_0 + \gamma\ln\mathbf{Y}_{it-1} + \alpha_1\mathbf{X}_{1,it} + \alpha_2\ln\mathbf{X}_{2,it} + \boldsymbol{\eta}_i + \boldsymbol{\varepsilon}_{it} \quad (3)$$

$$\gamma = (1 - \beta_1) \quad (4)$$

Where: $\mathbf{Y}_{it}$ is the vector of GDP per capita, $\mathbf{Y}^*_{it}$ is the vector of the rate of growth of GDP per capita, $\mathbf{X}_1$ is the vector of primary balance describing fiscal prudence, vector $\mathbf{X}_2$ describe the investment per capita, $\beta_0, \beta_1, \alpha_1, \alpha_2, \gamma$ are the structural parameters of the model $\boldsymbol{\eta}_i$ is the vector of individual effects of a panel model), a $\boldsymbol{\varepsilon}_{it}$ is the vector of disturbances. All the variables are determined for i-country in the period t. Variables X_1 and X_2 are the potential variables that determine the output in the steady state.

Obtaining the statistically significant value of parameter that is lower than 1[1] positively γ verifies the hypothesis of conditional β-convergence for the analyzed countries. The convergence process will occur provided that all the countries will be characterized with similar level of variables that determine the output in the steady state. The lower value of γ (higher positive value of parameter β1) the faster convergence process occur. The identification of convergence process enables to answer the question concerning the economic variables that determine the possibility of convergence process between a given group of countries. Additionally the estimated value of parameter γ enables to estimate average annual speed of convergence and the time that is needed for reaching the half the distance between the starting level of output and the output in the steady state (see Barro and Sala-i-Martin 1995; Ciołek 2005). The average speed of convergence[2] is described with the Eq. (5):

$$b = -\ln(\gamma)/T, \quad (5)$$

and the time that is needed for reaching the half way between the average starting level of GDP and the GDP in the steady state is given with Eq. (6):

$$\tau = -\ln(2)/\ln(\gamma). \quad (6)$$

In the model of convergence described with the Eq. (1) the growth rate of GDP per capita depends on the fiscal policy prudence which is understood as rather restrictive fiscal policy approach and the level of investments per capita. Obtaining the positive estimate of the parameter α_1 means that there is a positive influence of fiscal consolidations in a given period t on the rate of growth of GDP per capita during all the period of analysis. It can be interpreted as the occurrence of

[1] It means that the value of parameter β_1 is positive.

[2] T is the number of years, for which the rate of GDP growth is estimated. In case of panel models, where the period is 1 year, T equals to 1.

Table 1 The estimated conditional β-convergence model[a]

Parameter	Parameters estimation	p-value
γ	0.887992	≈0.000
α_1	0.00612837	≈0.000
α_2	0.134660	≈0.000
Testy statystyczne		
Sargan Test	10.3058	1
AR(1)	−2.60076	0.0093
AR(2)	−0.777938	0.4366

Source: Own estimation based on Eurostat data and European Commission (2013)

[a]The calculations were made with the application of the GRETL software (version 1.9.7)

non-Keynesian effects of fiscal policy for 11 analyzed countries of the European Union.

In order to estimate the parameters of model (3) the system GMM estimator was used (Blundell and Bond 1998), which is a development of first-difference GMM estimator (Holtz-Eakin et al. 1988; Arellano and Bond 1991; Ahn and Schmidt 1995). The idea of system GMM estimator is the estimation of both equations in first differences and equations in levels. The results of two-step estimation with asymptotic standard errors are presented in the Table 1.

The Sargant test enables testing of over-identifying restrictions (Blundell et al. 2000). The obtained statistic of the test equals 10.3058 and we reject the null hypothesis. All instruments were proper. Autocorrelation of the first-differenced of disturbances was tested too. The statistic of the test for first-order serial correlation equals −2.6007 and we reject the null hypothesis that there is no first-order serial correlation. The statistic of the test for second-order serial correlation equals −0.7779 and we does not reject the null hypothesis of no second-order serial correlation (Baltagi 1995). It means that the system GMM estimator was consistent and efficient.

The parameter γ is statistically significant. The estimate of the parameter γ which is below 1 enables to estimate the value of parameter β_1 equal to 0.1120 and verification of the hypothesis of convergence. The average annual speed of convergence is equal to 11.88 % of the distance provided similar level of investments and the degree of restrictiveness of fiscal policy for all the countries. It means that the time needed for reaching the half way between average starting output and the output in the steady state is 5.8 years.

Both parameters α_1 and α_2 are statistically significant. It means that variables X_1 and X_2 significantly determine the convergence process for 11 countries. The positive estimate of the parameter α_1 suggests positive influence of restrictive fiscal policy and it can be interpreted as a confirmation of non-Keynesian effects of fiscal consolidations. The positive estimate of the parameter α_2 means the same direction of changes between investment per capita and the rate of growth per capita which is consistent with basic macroeconomic theory. It should be remembered that the speed of convergence is only conditional. It means that only provided the unified fiscal policy for all the analyzed countries and similar level of investment per capita could result in the estimated convergence process. Thus, the question concerning the possibility of obtaining similar level of investment and unified fiscal policy is an important policy problem. When the answer to this question is negative the average speed of convergence equal to 11.88 % will not be reached.

4 Qualitative Analysis of Fiscal Consolidations

The aim of this part of the paper is to analyze the fiscal consolidations from the perspective of their Keynesian or non-Keynesian results and the question on the differences in the way both group of adjustments were implemented. The main question can be formed as follows: Were the expansive (non-Keynesian) consolidations mostly based on revenue increases or rather expenditure reductions?

Based on both demand and supply side theoretical models previously discussed one can point that the analysis should concentrate only on significantly big consolidations. Concentrating only on significantly big adjustments is also necessary as it is required to omit minor cyclical changes of budged balance and the influence of automatic stabilizers that are not the result of policy reaction. As a result for this research the significant fiscal consolidation is defined as the one when the general government primary balance improves more than 2.5 % point of GDP in 1 year or at least 3 % of GDP in 2 consecutive years. This definition is a little stricter than the one applied by Purfield in research of fiscal adjustment in transition countries, as she assumed 2 % pint of GDP improvement for 1 year (Purfield 2003).

The first step of the analysis was the classification of episodes on two groups: expansionary thus non-Keynesian episodes and Keynesian consolidations. The definition of expansionary (non-Keynesian) episode is the following: the consolidation episode is expansionary when the average GDP growth during the consolidation and 1 year after the consolidation is above the average growth rate of potential GDP (compare Purfield 2003). Based on that definition 14 non-Keynesian and 4 Keynesian episodes were selected, which are presented in Table 2.

Table 3 presents fundamental macroeconomic data for all analysed episodes of fiscal consolidations. First of all, for 15 analysed episodes only in case of two Portugal in 2011 and Spain in 2013 one could see negative GDP change, which can be attributed to difficult condition of both economies after global financial crisis from the year 2008. In case of composition of episodes, most of them have mixed character with some increases of revenues and cuts of expenditures. Only two episodes—Belgium in 2006 and Finland in 1996 an increase in expenditures and more than proportional increase in revenues could be seen. Three episodes Ireland in 2011, Austria in 1998–1999 and Finland in 1997–1998 were based on decrease in both revenues and expenditures.

Figure 1 presents average annual changes of government budget revenues and expenditures for the group of non-Keynesian and Keynesian episodes of fiscal consolidations. The average change of annual expenditures in case of

Table 2 Fiscal episodes fulfilling the criteria of significant consolidation

Non-Keynesian consolidations		Keynesian consolidations	
Belgium	2006	Germany	1996
Germany	1999–2000	Luxemburg	2006–2007
	2006–2007	Portugal	2011
	2011	Spain	2000
Ireland	2011		
	2012		
Austria	1998–1999		
	2007		
Luxemburg	1997		
	2000		
Portugal	2006–2007		
Finland	1996		
	1997–1998		
Spain	2013		

non-Keynesian consolidations was −2.67 % of GDP whereas for group of Keynesian episodes it was −3.5 %. However, a serious difference can be seen in case of annual change of revenues. For the group of expansionary episodes the average increase of revenues was three times lower than in the group of Keynesian consolidations, which can suggests that expansionary episodes were based on the tax increases to much lesser extent than the non-expansionary episodes. These results are conducive to the research of Alesina and Ardagna (2009) for OECD countries in the years 1970–2007.

First of all, in case of interpretation of the above presented results it must be remembered that this kind of qualitative analysis has serious methodological drawback. The main problem is the small number of examined consolidations; in that case especially the number of Keynesian episodes is not satisfactory. Then all the qualitative analyzes are quite sensitive to changes of definitions of significant and expansionary episodes. Thus these results can be only treated as a voice in the discussion, definitely not as prevailing argument.

5 Conclusion

The end of the twentieth and the beginning of the first decade of current century made a period of significant deleverage and public finance stabilization, which was in part the element of process of the Eurozone creation. That situation was changed with the global financial crisis of the year 2008 that resulted in the significant increase of government debt of highly developed countries.

The conducted econometric analysis gives significant arguments on the thesis that last decades in case of 11 analyzed countries made a period of conditional β-convergence where prudent fiscal policy was the significant convergence factor.

Table 3 Fundamental macroeconomic data for episodes for fiscal consolidations

	Belgium	Germany				Ireland		Luxemburg			Austria		Portugal		Finland			Spain
	2006	1996	1999–2000	2006–2007	2011	2011	2012	1997	2000	2006–2007	1998–1999	2007	2006–2007	2011	1996	1997–1998	2000	2013
Improvement of primary deficit during the episode	2.6	6.1	3.3	3.5	3.4	17.6	6.2	2.5	2.6	3.8	3.6	2.8	3.7	6.7	3	4.4	5.1	4.5
Annual percentage change of GDP during the episode	2.7	0.8	3.05	2.5	3.3	2.2	0.2	5.9	8.4	5.75	3.65	3.7	1.9	−1.3	3.6	5.6	5.3	−1.2
Annual percentage change of GDP 1 year after the episode	2.9	1.7	1.5	1.1	0.7	0.2	−0.3	6.5	2.5	−0.7	3.7	1.4	0	−3.2	6.2	3.9	2.3	–
Annual percentage change of GDP 2 years after the episode	1	1.9	0	−5.1	0.4	−0.3		8.4	4.1	−5.6	0.9	−3.8	−2.9	−1.4	5	5.3	1.8	–
Annual percentage change of potential GDP during the episode	1.7	1.5	1.65	1.4	1.3	−0.1	−0.8	4.2	5.2	3.65	2.7	2	0.85	−0.5	2.7	3.65	4	−1.4

Annual percentage change of potential GDP 1 year after the episode	1.8	1.4	1.5	1.2	1.4	−0.8	0	4.6	5	2.3	2.7	1.6	0.9	−1.6	3.4	4	3.9	−1.5
Annual percentage change of potential GDP 2 years the after episode	1.6	1.5	1.4	0.8	1.3	0	1.1	5.7	4.7	0.9	2.4	0.9	−0.2	−1.2	3.9	4	3.4	
Annual change of total revenues (% of GDP) during the episode	0.8	0.3	0.25	0.05	0.6	−0.9	0.5	2	1	−0.3	−0.25	1	0.5	3.4	1.3	−1.05	2	0.6
Annual change of total expenditures (% of GDP) during the episode	0.3	−5.8	−1.45	−0.9	−2.7	−18.4	−4.5	−0.4	−1.6	−2.6	−0.05	−0.5	−1.1	−2.2	0.5	−3.6	−3.4	−3

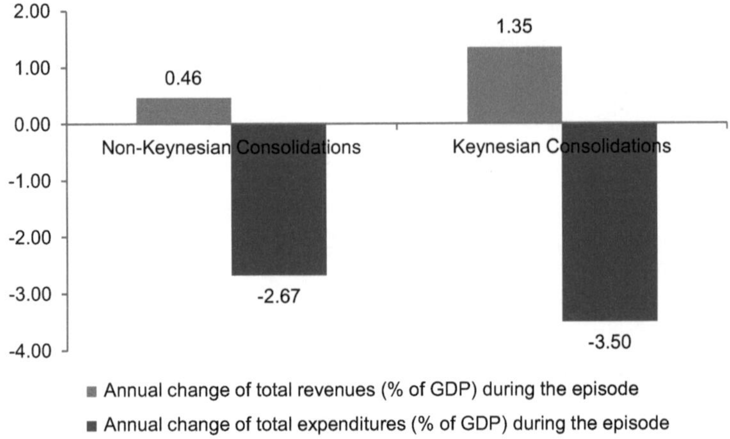

Fig. 1 Average annual changes of government budget revenues and expenditures for non-Keynesian and Keynesian episodes of fiscal consolidations

Thus, the analysis based on convergence framework can be interpreted as an argument supporting the thesis on the possibility of non-Keynesian effects in case of significant fiscal consolidations. In the same time the analysis can give some argument that the future deleverage process, which will be probably necessary for keeping long term growth perspective in Europe, in case of proper construction of consolidation programs does not have to be a short term growth obstacle. In spite of its serious methodological drawback, the qualitative analysis showed that in case of the group of expansionary episodes the increases of taxes and revenues were much lower than in case of typical Keynesian consolidations. This can be a factor to consider in the context of plans for future effort to deleverage and stabilize fiscal systems of European Countries.

The next steps concerning future research in the field should be coverage of wider group of countries such as examining whole countries of current euro area and in the end all countries of European Union. The next steps should be also more detailed concentration on the fiscal transitions mechanism that accompanied non-Keynesian and typical Keynesian consolidations in European Union.

References

Ahn, S. C., & Schmidt, P. (1995). Efficient estimation of models for dynamic panel data. *Journal of Econometrics, 68*(1), 5–27.

Alesina, A., & Ardagna, S. (1998). Tales, of Fiscal adjustment. *Economic Policy, 13*(27), 489–545.

Alesina, A., & Ardagna, S. (2009). *Large changes in Fiscal policy: Taxes versus spending*. NBER working paper series (Working paper No. 15438).

Alesina, A., Ardagna, S., Perotti, R., & Schiantarelli, F. (1999). *Fiscal policy, profits and investment*. NBER working papers (Working paper 7207).

Alesina, A., & Perotti, T. (1997). The welfare state and competitiveness. *American Economic Review, 87*(5), 921–939.

Arbia, G. (2006). *Spatial econometrics*. Berlin: Springer.

Arellano, M., & Bond, S. (1991). Some tests of specification for panel data: Monte Carlo evidence and an application to employment equation. *Review of Economic Studies, 58*(2), 277–297.

Balcerzak, A. P., & Rogalska, E. (2014). Crowding out and crowding in within Keynesian framework. Do we need any new empirical research concerning them? *Economics and Sociology*, *7*(2), 80–93.

Baltagi, B. H. (1995). *Econometric analysis of panel data*. Chichester: Wiley.

Barro, R. J., & Sala-I-Martin, X. (1991). Convergence across states and regions. *Brookings Papers on Economic Activity*, 100–182.

Barro, R. J., & Sala-I-Martin, X. (1992). Convergence. *Journal of Political Economy, 100*(2), 223–251.

Barro, R. J., & Sala-I-Martin, X. (1995). *Economic growth theory*. Boston: McGraw-Hill.

Baumol, W. J. (1986). Productivity growth, convergence and welfare: What the long run data show. *American Economic Review, 76*(5), 1072–1085.

Bernard, A. B., & Durlauf, S. N. (1995). Convergence in international output. *Journal of Applied Econometrics, 10*(2), 97–108.

Blundell, R., & Bond, S. (1998). Initial conditions and moment restrictions in dynamic panel data model. *Journal of Econometrics, 87*(1), 115–143.

Blundell, R., Bond, S., & Windmeijer, F. (2000). Estimation in dynamic panel data models: Improving on the performance of the standard GMM estimator. In B. Baltagi (Ed.), *Nonstationary panels, Panel cointegration and dynamic panels*. Amsterdam: Elsevier Science.

Bond, S., Hoeffler, H., & Temple, J. (2001). *GMM estimation of empirical growth models*. Discussion Paper no. 3048, Centre for Economic Policy Research.

Caselli, F., Esquivel, G., & Lefort, F. (1996). Reopening the convergence debate: A new look at cross-country growth empirics. *Journal of Economic Growth, 1*(3), 363–389.

Ciołek, D. (2005). *Konwergencja do Unii Europejskiej krajów w okresie transformacji*. Doctoral thesis, Uniwersytet Gdański, Gdańsk.

Durlauf, S. N., & Johnson, P. A. (1995). Multiple regimes and cross-country growth behaviour. *Journal of Applied Econometrics, 10*(4), 365–384.

Eichenbaum, M. (1997). Some thoughts on practical stabilization policy. *American Economic Review, 87*(2), 236–239.

European Commission. (2013, Spring). *General government data. General government revenue, expenditure, balances and gross debt, Part II: Tables by series.*

Evans, P., & Karras, G. (1996). Convergence revisited. *Journal of Monetary Economics, 37*(2), 249–265.

Giavazzi, F., & Pagano, M. (1990). Can severe Fiscal contractions be expansionary? Tales of two small European countries. In O. Blanchard & S. Fisher (Eds.), *Macroeconomics annual 1990* (pp. 75–122). Cambridge, MA: MIT Press.

Holtz-Eakin, D., Newwey, W., & Rosen, H. (1988). Estimating vector auto regressions with panel Data. *Econometrica, 56*(6), 1371–1395.

Islam, N. (1995). Growth empirics: A panel data approach. *Quarterly Journal of Economics, 110* (4), 1127–1170.

Lane, P. R., & Perotti, R. (2001). *The importance of composition of Fiscal policy: Evidence from different exchange rate regimes*. Trinity College Dublin, Department of Economics, Trinity Economics Papers, Number 200116.

Le Gallo, J., & Ertur, C. (2003). Exploratory spatial data analysis of the distribution of regional per Capita GDP in Europe, 1980-1995. *Papers in Regional Science, 82*(2), 175–201.

Levine, R., & Renelt, D. (1992). A sensitivity analysis of cross-country growth regressions. *American Economic Review, 82*(4), 942–963.

Mankiw, N. G., Romer, D., & Weil, D. N. (1992). A contribution to the empirics of economic growth. *Quarterly Journal of Economics, 107*, 407–437.

Perotti, R. (1999). Fiscal policy in good times and bad. *The Quarterly Journal of Economics, 114* (4), 1399–1436.
Purfield, C. (2003). *Fiscal adjustment in transition countries: Evidence from the 1990s*. IMF working paper, WP/03/36.
Quah, D. (1993a). Empirical cross-section dynamics in economic growth. *European Economic Review, 37*, 426–434.
Quah, D. (1993b). Galton's fallacy and tests of the convergence hypothesis. *Scandinavian Journal of Economics, 95*(4), 427–443.
Quah, D. (1996a). Empirics for economic growth and convergence. *European Economic Review, 40*(6), 1353–1375.
Quah, D. (1996b). Twin peaks: Growth and convergence in models of distribution dynamics. *Economic Journal, 106*, 1045–1055.
Rey, S. J., & Montouri, B. D. (1999). U.S. regional income convergence: A spatial econometric perspective. *Regional Studies, 33*(2), 143–156.
Rogalska, E. (2012). Efektywność stymulacyjnej polityki fiskalnej państwa w warunkach kryzysu zaufania budżetowego. *OeconomiaCopernicana, 4*, 5–22.
Rzońca, A., & Ciżkowicz, P. (2005). *Non-Keynesian effects of Fiscal contraction in new member states*. European Central Bank, Working Papers series, No. 519/September.
Rzońca, A., & Varoudakis, A. (2007). The quality of Fiscal adjustments in transition economies. *Bank i Kredyt, 7*, 7–28.
Sala-I-Martin, X. (1996a). Regional cohesion: Evidence and theories of regional growth and convergence. *European Economic Review, 40*(6), 1325–1352.
Sala-I-Martin, X. (1996b). The classical approach to convergence analysis. *Economic Journal, 106* (437), 1019–1036.

The Region of Southeast Europe: The Island of Missing Gas Connectivity and Its European Implications

Monika Moraliyska

Abstract The objective of the paper is to analyze how the region of Southeast Europe (SEE) performs in terms of natural gas supply and energy security, and how it completes the picture of Europe's overall energy security. For that purpose the import dependence of energy resources (overall and in terms of natural gas) of the EU and SEE is analyzed. The possible solutions for energy diversification are presented in the light of the projected gas pipeline projects linking the European continent with the Caspian and Asia Minor regions, passing through SEE region. EU's chances of obtaining energy security through self-sufficiency are low so new routes of gas pipelines are urgently needed. The region of SEE is even more problematic, as it is highly dependent on solid fuels and does not have the infrastructure to provide itself and to transit natural gas. On the other hand, it could be a part of the solution, as any energy diversification for Europe through the Caspian and Asia Minor is possible with transmission through SEE countries. The attraction of significant investments and the EU political will are crucial factors for the future energy security of the EU and its strategic energy and political influence in the region.

Keywords Energy • Security • European Union • Southeast Europe • Gas • Pipelines

1 Introduction

1.1 The Region of Southeast Europe or Just the Balkans?

Southeast Europe is a geographical and political region located on the Balkan Peninsula. Geographically it includes the following countries—Albania, Bosnia

M. Moraliyska (✉)
International Economic Relations and Business Department, University of National and World Economy, Sofia, Bulgaria
e-mail: monika_moraliyska@abv.bg

© Springer International Publishing Switzerland 2016

M.H. Bilgin et al. (eds.), *Business Challenges in the Changing Economic Landscape - Vol. 1*, Eurasian Studies in Business and Economics 2/1,
DOI 10.1007/978-3-319-22596-8_36

and Herzegovina, Bulgaria, Croatia, Cyprus, Greece, Kosovo, Macedonia, Moldova, Montenegro, Northern Cyprus, Romania, Serbia, Slovenia and Turkey.

There is no common or acknowledged understanding and scientific definition of the term "region". Different interpretations arise depending on the factors taken in mind—"geographic proximity", cultural factors, social and economic similarities between the countries, economic flows between them or their foreign policies. Most often, a "region" is defined as a group of countries, located in the same geographical area. The disadvantage of this approach is that it does not always give unanimous answers which geographic areas represent regions.

According to the geographical concept, the region of SEE is determined by the physical boundaries of the Balkan Peninsula, with the northern border being defined by the line drawn from the rivers Danube-Sava-Cup. Thus it includes only countries located entirely on the Balkans: Albania, Bosnia and Herzegovina, Bulgaria, Greece, Macedonia and Montenegro.

However, the geographical definition may include not only countries, which are largely located on the peninsula, like Croatia (49 %) and Serbia (60 %), but also some countries that are mainly outside of it, like Romania (6 %) and Turkey (3 %).

Nevertheless, these countries have more in common than simple geographical proximity. In theory the member countries of a region establish among themselves also cultural, economic, linguistic and/or political connections. Mansfield and Milner (1999) note that while there is no perfect definition (of a region), pragmatism supposes that definitions are based on continents and subdivided in accordance with their combination of cultural, linguistic, religious criteria and those related to their growth stage.

Numerous studies, however, define the region namely according to similar non-geographic criteria and pay relatively little attention to the countries' physical location. The so-called "social constructionists" even argue that countries that share a common identity are included in the region, regardless of their geographical location. Bechev (2012) define the common identity as a major factor in the formation of regions in general and in particular in the region of Southeastern Europe, where it has played a key role in shaping the "Balkan identity". He notes that although it is difficult to refute the role of material interdependence and the importance of external factors as powerful engines of cooperation on regional level, this shared identity played a major role for the different projects for regionalization that took place in Southeastern Europe in the last decades.

In a similar direction comes the reasoning of other researchers. Tsachevski (2010) analyzed the name of the region and the countries that are included in it, and concluded that the term "Southeast Europe" is necessary for two reasons—firstly, due to the expanding geographic scope of the European integration and secondly, because it means a wider format of multilateral cooperation with the participation of more countries, including those the geography of which is no reason for them to be unconditionally assigned to the region.

Among the scholars who define the region in non-geographical terms are those who focus on the preferential economic agreements concluded by geographically distant countries. In this case, the physical location of the parties involved is not relevant to the formation of the region and the relations, on which it is based, but is more on a contractual basis and with specific goals.

Chavdarova (2012) focuses on the existing institutionalized forms of regional cooperation and adopts the following definition of the "subregion" of South-Eastern Europe (Balkans): Albania, Bosnia and Herzegovina, Bulgaria, Croatia, Greece, Kosovo, Macedonia, Montenegro, Romania, Serbia, Slovenia and Turkey. Moldova is the only non-Balkan country that is a member of sub-regional forums and organizations to coordinate cooperation in Southeast Europe after 1999. Despite the facts that Slovenia is not considered a Balkan country, and 97 % of the territory of Turkey is in Asia, these countries are included in the South European (Balkan) subregion because of the political, economic, geostrategic, cultural and other factors of development. She notes that in the beginning of twenty-first century the USA renamed the region from 'Balkans' to 'Southeast Europe' in order to distinguish it from the negative effects of the "Balkanization", understood as unpredictable relationship of military threat, hostility and constant smoldering conflicts.

The signed in 1999 Stability Pact for Southeast Europe, main purpose of which was to preserve and maintain peace and stability in the region, includes the following countries from the region[1]: Albania, Bosnia and Herzegovina, Bulgaria, Croatia, Moldova, Montenegro, Romania, Serbia and the former Yugoslav Republic of Macedonia. In 2008 the Pact transformed into the Regional Cooperation Council, which preserved the same composition of Member States.

Modifying the Pact's form for the purposes of this study, the author defines the SEE region as including the following countries: Albania, Bosnia and Herzegovina, Montenegro, Serbia, Kosovo and Macedonia (the Western Balkan countries), together with the EU member states Bulgaria, Romania, Greece and Croatia.

1.2 *Europe's Natural Gas Import Dependence and Energy Supply Diversification Opportunities*

In general, the total demand for energy in the EU has been gradually falling since its all-time peak in 2006 (in 2012 it is around 1,750,000 ktoe in EU28, which is more than 8 % below its 2006 level), because of the economic crisis, the structural changes in the EU economy, as well as due to some efficiency improvements achieved in the last 10 years. Another important factor is the enormous increase of fossil fuel prices, most notably oil (European Commission 2014).

Despite this, a trend is evident of increasing EU import dependency of energy resources—by almost a quarter (10 percentage points) in the last 20 years. The main

[1] Apart from the countries in the region, the EU member states, European Commission, third countries, international organizations and financial institutions and others are also included in the Stability Pact.

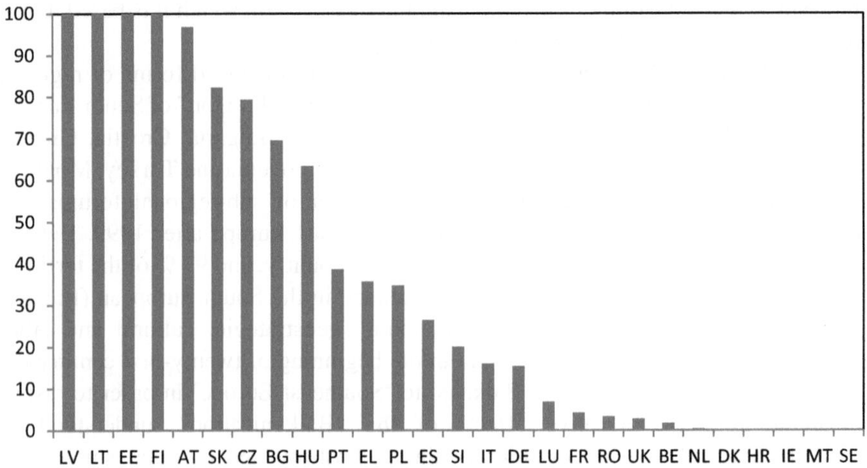

Fig. 1 Supplier concentration of natural gas in 2012. *Note*: The supplier concentration index takes into account both the diversity of suppliers and the exposure of a country to external suppliers: Large values indicate limited diversification with imports forming a large part of consumption. *Source*: http://ec.europa.eu/energy/sites/ener/files/documents/20140528_energy_security_study_0.pdf

reasons for that are, on one hand, the significant decline of EU production of oil, gas and coal, linked to a gradual depletion of EU reserves and the closure of uncompetitive sources, and on the other—the growing amounts of imported oil, gas, and coal to compensate for declining domestic production. In terms of gas, the import dependency of the EU is about 66 % (oil still constitutes the largest quantity of imports and its import dependency level is almost 90 %, hard coal's import dependency is at 62 %, renewable energy (chiefly biomass) is at 4 %). There are major differences among member states, but nearly all are heavily import dependent. Eighteen member States import more than 50 % of their energy. Some northern and eastern member states depend on a single supplier (the Baltic States, Finland, Slovakia and Bulgaria), and often on one supply route, for their entire natural gas consumption, while others have a more diversified portfolio of suppliers (Fig. 1).

Over 60 % of the natural gas that the EU consumes is imported. The problem is that almost two thirds of these imports are from countries outside of the European Economic Area. According to the COMEXT database of Eurostat, in 2013 the EU imported natural gas at the value of 87 billion euros. In it, from the countries outside the EEA, Russia has the biggest share of total imports in value terms (41 %), followed by Norway (32 %), Algeria (14 %) and Libya (7 %).

In 2013 the EU long-term contracts for pipeline natural gas provide for 17–30 % of its market demand, almost entirely from Russia. The import pipeline capacity of the Union is 8776 GWh/day, nearly comparable to the capacity of LNG terminals (6170 GWh/day). The scope for using of the LNG capacity differs among terminals and depends on their location and infrastructure. These opportunities are bigger on the Iberian Peninsula and smaller in Eastern Europe.

The European Network of Transmission System Operators of Gas analyzed the response of the gas infrastructure in the EU (in terms of pipelines, LNG, storages) in order to estimate the impact of a possible disruption crisis caused by disruption of gas supplies from Russia or transit from Ukraine (ENTSO-G 2014). As a result of it, the vulnerability of Member States in the South-East of the EU and the Balkans was confirmed. If disruptions of gas supply from Russia occur during daily peak demand in January, almost the whole European Union would be directly affected, except for the Iberian Peninsula and the southern France. The effects would be less severe in the case of disruption from Ukraine, but still Southeast Europe could face a situation where a very big part of the gas supply (60–80 %) would not be covered.

The disruption of gas supplies from Russia across season (June 2014–March 2015) would result in shortages in most East-European countries. In this case, the most affected would be Bulgaria and FYROM, which might face a disruption of 60–80 % of demand from September to March, as well as Lithuania and Poland. Latvia and Estonia could face problems from October to March with more than 80 % of demand not covered, while Finland could have similar problem from January to March. For the late 2014/early 2015 a 20–40 % disruption might also appear in Romania, Croatia, Serbia and Greece. Cross seasonal disruption to supplies that transit through Ukraine would also cause shortages in Southeast Europe, with Bulgaria and FYROM affected from September onwards.

Southeast Europe's natural gas consumption and import dependency are quite different from the EU average and these circumstances make the problems of the region even more serious. Natural gas occupies a small part of the region's final energy consumption but it needs to grow in order to decrease the existing in the region over-utilization of coal in both: electricity generation and industrial uses. The SEE region is almost totally dependent on Russian gas supply. It imports natural gas in Croatia, Serbia, and Bosnia and Herzegovina through one old pipeline passing through Hungary. Except for Croatia, which produces 60 % of its gas it needs, only Serbia has some gas reserves, although in a limited amount, not more than 7 % of its consumption. Bosnia and Herzegovina and FYROM also consume only Russian gas transited through Serbia, while Kosovo and Montenegro use no natural gas. Albania consumes negligible quantities of self-produced natural gas. In the entire region only Serbia and Croatia have a meaningful natural gas market, being followed by Serbia and Bosnia and Herzegovina.

The risk of over-dependence on a single supply source became reality in the SEE region in January 2009, when the Russian-Ukrainian gas crisis took place. It began when only 10 % of the normal gas exports flowed from Russia to Slovakia (the gas would thereafter flow through western Hungary and Slovenia to Croatia). On its behalf, Eastern Hungary, which represents the transit point to Serbia and Bosnia and Herzegovina, received 20 % of the normal volumes. The main consequence of this was that all commercial gas exports were stopped, which left the West Balkan consumers with no imports of gas. Of all affected countries only Croatia coped with the gas crisis by increasing its own production, as well as by importing some

German gas via Slovenia. Serbia also resorted to its gas storage capacity, but it was insufficient to compensate the missing Russian supply. Later Bosna and Herzegovina and the eastern parts of Serbia received some of Hungary's gas reserves, but it was insufficient again and Serbia had to resort to a utilization of lignite and fuel oil (CSIS and EKEM 2010).

It looks like despite the fact that Europe's dependence of natural gas supply has been articulated as a major challenge in the last decade, it still has not been addressed. Russia's rich natural gas reserves, geographic location, rapidly developing pipeline systems, technical skills and know-how make it the most significant energy partner of the European continent. However, the high dependence of a big number of European countries on Russian natural gas creates doubts on energy security. Impressions have been developing that Russia uses natural gas as a political weapon and this doubles worry about European energy security.

One of the reasons why Russian exports of natural gas flowing to Europe cannot be taken for granted anymore arise from the decline of production in the major gas-producing regions as West Siberia and Yamal peninsula where the three giant fields Yamburg, Urengoy and Medvezhye lie. Another reason is that Russia's domestic gas consumption is rising faster than the projected in the country's Energy Strategy (436 BcM in 2030). The Gazekonomika study estimate 654 BcM by 2030 and project that the amount of Russian gas replaced by Central Asian gas could total 24 BcM in 2014; 30 BcM in 2015; and reach 56 BcM by 2030 (Bilgin 2009).

Besides that China is relatively better placed to obtain Russian gas supplies as it can tap into western as well as eastern gas fields. This could happen through the Altai gas pipeline project from West Siberia to China, which could make Europe compete with China for the gas resources in the region. Europe should therefore not assume that gas reserves, even if Russia manages to increase its production and despite the fact the Europe has historically been the major consumer of Russian gas, will automatically flow to Europe (Spanjer 2007).

Some researchers also share that the risk associated with relying on Russian gas and Ukrainian transit routes is not the only threat to the European gas supply security, adding to it "the chronic lack of investment" in Russian gas industry that may not be in a position to meet the EU demand by 2020 (Erdogdu 2010).

The increasing Europe's gas imports dependence imposes the need for looking for urgent cost effective options that could diversify its supply mix. Different opportunities have been analyzed and discussed in the recent years in that direction, starting with increased gas imports from Northern Africa, mainly from Algeria with supply costs in the range of 32–55 h/1000 m^3.

Apart from Northern Africa, LNG imports from the Middle East, especially Iran with its large gas reserves, could be an acceptable LNG supply source for Europe (estimated costs of 67 h/1000 m^3), (Remme et al. 2008). Besides competition with Asian countries for these gas resources, recent political tensions in the relationship of Iran and the West, however, may be an obstacle to implement this.

There is still a shortage of studies on feasibility and possible effects of connecting Middle Eastern gas supply, including Iraqi and Egyptian gas, with the EU. Egypt emerges as a potential gas supplier. The latest discovery of new gas fields converted the country to a gas net exporter. Currently Egypt focuses mainly on shipping LNG to the Mediterranean energy markets. However, there are prospects for the extension of the Arab Gas Pipeline, allowing gas exports to Turkey and further to the EU (Mavrakis et al. 2006).

The main and most important alternative source remains the Caspian Region, which includes significant natural gas fields and the existing or planned pipeline systems which could supply the EU with adequate gas through the South energy corridor. The strategic goal for the Southern Gas Corridor[2] is to bring new gas sources to the EU and to diversify the concentrated markets in SEE. Its purpose is to directly link the EU gas market to large deposits of gas in the Caspian Region, the Middle East and the Eastern Mediterranean basin. The planned transit routes for these gas volumes are through Turkey, the Black Sea and the Eastern Mediterranean. The corridor's pipeline components will also be adopted to deliver substantial additional quantities of LNG to Europe, in particular from the Middle East (Persian Gulf and Egypt). Ultimately the Southern Gas Corridor should create an additional supply corridor, in addition to the existing ones from North Africa, Russia and Norway.

The fields of Shah Deniz in Azerbaijan (1.027 $/MBTU), Shatlyk in Turkmenistan, South Pars in Iran (1.109 $/MBTU) and Al–Anfal in Iraq (0.637 $/MBTU) have a total supply potential of 13.85 Tcm. Moreover, the Eastern Anatolia Natural Gas Transmission Pipeline, the under construction South Caucasus Pipeline (Shah Deniz Pipeline), the under negotiation Trans-Caspian Pipeline (a proposed submarine pipeline between Türkmenbaşy in Turkmenistan and Baku in Azerbaijan) and Iraq-Turkey pipelines outline a pipeline network for natural gas transportation to the West.

It can be concluded that Europe's increasing dependency on gas imports has increased the risks to security of supply. Assuming an increasing gas demand in Europe in the future and diminishing local gas resources, European gas supply will depend even more strongly on gas imports in the future. At present Russia is the main supplier of natural gas for Europe and probably it will remain among the most important ones. However, in the future the decline in gas production of the Russian fields Urengoy, Yamburg and Medvezhye, in combination with increasing domestic gas demand in the country, will require investments for the development of new and more costly Russian gas fields. In addition to that, the current complicated situation between the EU and Russia over the Ukraine crisis makes the question with energy supply even more dubious and unsure.

That's why it is crucial to improve the diversification of gas supplies of the EU, so that no member state would be dependent on one single supply source. Azerbaijan and Iran are the most attractive natural gas suppliers of the proposed

[2] Southern Gas Corridor ("SGC"): infrastructure for the transmission of gas from the Caspian Basin, Central Asia, the Middle East and the Eastern Mediterranean Basin to the Union, to enhance diversification of gas supply (European Parliament 2013).

south energy corridor. Both countries have significant reserves and existing or under construction export pipeline networks.

The EU internal market and its reverse flow and gas storage rules could also strengthen the Union's gas supply resilience and ensure bigger security of supply. Gas storage and reverse flows can mitigate the risk in cases of supply disruption. A well-functioning market would also help gas flows and increase storage volumes in events of restrictions to supply.

It is also important to significantly increase the gas system's flexibility and resilience in the short and medium term and be able to benefit from the recent developments in the LNG markets, biogas and unconventional resources. A well-integrated gas network is also the best guarantee to compensate for a possible failure of the largest gas infrastructure in any member state, an obligatory standard introduced by the gas security of supply regulation.[3]

2 Is Southeast Europe an Island Apart from the European Gas Infrastructure?

The region of SEE faces common challenges of increasing energy efficiency, reducing import dependency and expanding renewable energy sources, similarly to the EU as a whole, but the current state of affairs in the region, especially in the countries that are not EU members, is rather worse. The West Balkan countries are at differing positions along the path of European integration and they each hold varying energy and environmental standards and targets, even though they have started the process of their harmonization with the EU legislation. However, this process, especially at the current level of electricity/gas market liberalization and interconnectivity and regulatory/market transformations, seems long and slow.

In 2010 the Western Balkans countries (Albania, Bosna and Herzegovina, Kosovo, Macedonia, Montenegro and Serbia), along with the EU member states Poland, Bulgaria, Estonia and the Czech Republic, are the only European countries where coal still occupies a bigger share of TPES[4] than oil, something that has changed in Europe since the 1950s and 1960s when massive imports of Middle Eastern oil put an end of Europe's dependence on domestic coal (CSIS and EKEM 2010). In Serbia coal accounts for approximately 40 % of the energy demand and coal/lignite accounts for over 60 % of energy production. Coal nearly completely dominates the electricity generation mix in Kosovo (100 %) and FYROM (80 %), and it accounts for 20 % of the electricity supply of Croatia and Montenegro. Coal is accountable also to almost 60 % of the electricity generation in Bosna and Herzegovina, so that only Albania is coal-free, because it generates all of its electricity via three old hydroelectric plants. As a result, the region has still to

[3] N-1 standard, see Regulation (EU) No 994/2010, OJ L 295, 12.11.2010, pp. 1–22.

[4] Total Primary Energy Supply.

make the transition to a non-lignite based economy by substituting its lignite sources with natural gas and renewables.

Apart from the traditional sources of energy production, the problem seems even more serious with the regional gas infrastructure. It became clear in the previous part that the development of markets and gas infrastructure (interconnectors, reverse flows and storage) are of significant importance for each individual state, as well as for the whole EU. Scientific and practical evidence shows that a reliable, transparent and interconnected market has the potential to mitigate the risks of insecurity of the gas supply. The flexibility of transport infrastructure in terms of location, number and available capacity of pipelines and LNG terminals, underground storage and the way infrastructure is operated all play an important role in shaping the resilience of a national and the European gas sector. Besides that, the potential to operate pipelines in two directions increases the resilience in case of a supply disruption. That's why investments in physical reverse flows are extremely important.

It is obvious however, that often this is not the case. Below is shown the underground gas storage infrastructure in Southeast Europe.

Figure 2 shows that in 2013 the natural gas storage capacity in Southeast Europe was very low or missing. Little of it is planned or under construction, either, which cannot be satisfactory, despite the still low natural gas consumption in the region.

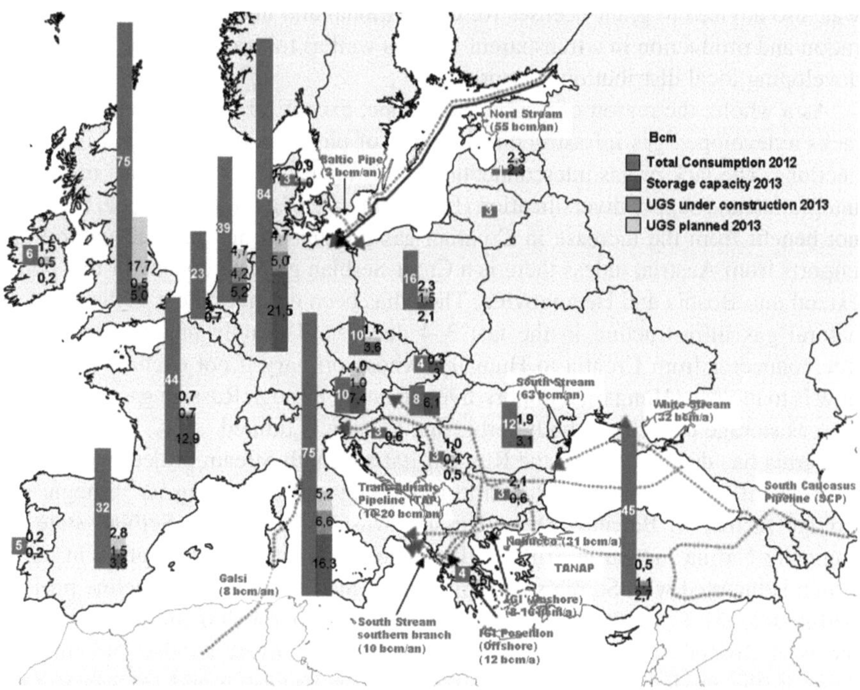

Fig. 2 Underground gas storage facilities in Europe. *Source*: CEDIGAZ, the international association for natural gas

Bulgaria has a central geographic position in SEE and it is of crucial importance for itself and the region, to have a national-wide transit network and sufficient natural gas storage infrastructure. The country is totally dependent on gas imports from Russia to satisfy its domestic demand. All gas imports flow via the Ukrainian-Western Balkan pipeline. In addition to this, the limited storage capacity of the country makes it very vulnerable in terms of gas supply security. Meanwhile, Bulgaria is an important transit country of Russian gas to the Balkan countries, among which Greece, FYROM and Turkey. In order to diversify gas supply some investments were made in the country, including the better connecting and expanding of the Chiren gas storage facility. Still a lot more needs to be done, among which further expansion of underground storage capacity and interruptible contracts. Another direction for improvement are the ongoing interconnector projects to connect Bulgaria's gas transmission systems with Romania, Serbia, Greece and Turkey. However, reverse-flow capacity at the borders with Romania and Greece is still quite limited (Fig. 4).

In 2013 the European Commission issued some recommendations concerning the gas infrastructure in the country, stressing that Bulgaria needs to continue to develop gas transmission, distribution and storage infrastructure, as well as to promote competition in the gas market. It also expects the country to continue to support gas international pipeline projects and ensure a physical connection between existing pipelines and the national transmission network. The country was also advised to grant licenses for conventional and unconventional gas exploration and production in a transparent way, as well as to examine the possibility of developing local distribution networks.

As a whole, the region of Southeast Europe, except for the EU member states, lacks a developed gas infrastructure in terms of pipelines, networks and interconnections. The lack of gas interconnections is a major hinder to the goals of market integration and supply diversification (Fig. 3). In case of a future crisis, Serbia could not benefit from the increase in Croatian gas production or increased natural gas imports from Austria, unless there is a Croat-Serbian gas interconnector that could extend into Bosnia and Herzegovina. There has been no investment in the region's natural gas infrastructure in the last 3–4 decades. The only new pipeline is an interconnector from Croatia to Hungary, whose primary if not exclusive purpose now is to increase Hungarian import diversification through Russian gas. Moreover, the gas storage capacity in both Serbia and Croatia is limited.

Serbia has decided to join the Russian-Italian South Stream project with which to secure its future gas imports while rebuilding and expanding its strategic gas storage facility in Banatski Dvor. Russia owns 56.5 % of the Serbian state oil company Naftna Industrija Srbije (NIS) under contract for privatization in 2008, which is bundled with Serbia's commitment to South Stream gas pipeline project. Serbia sold 51 % of the shares of NIS to Gazprom for 400 million euros and received Russia's commitment as well that it will invest another 500 million euros in the modernization of the oil refinery in Panchevo and the gas storage facility in Banatski Dvor. It is considered that this Serbian-Russian alliance was

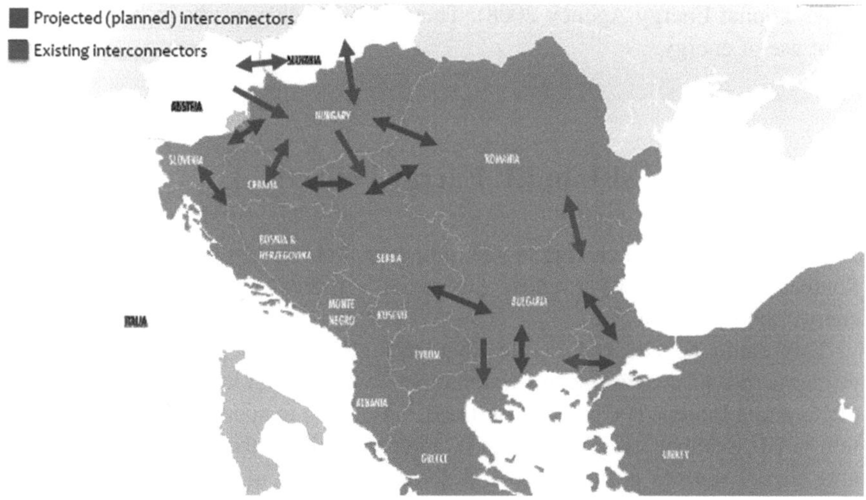

Fig. 3 Existing and projected natural gas interconnectors in SEE. *Source*: http://www.iene.eu/ienes-8th-se-europe-energy-dialogue-top-professionals-from-the-region-and-beyond-analyzed-the-new-energy-mix-p725.html

heavily influenced by the diplomatic isolation of Serbia from the West over the Kosovo issue.

After the failure of the Nabucco pipeline to the West Balkan countries, the countries rely on the South Stream project is a viable undertaking that could positively affect the region's energy security. The alternative regional pipeline project hopefully would be the Trans-Adriatic Pipeline/Ionian-Adriatic Pipeline (TAP/IAP), because the idea for establishing of the so-called West Balkans Natural Gas pipeline, originally promoted by Turkey's Botas and Greece's DEPA in 2003, has been abandoned in view of Greek and Turkish participation in the other gas projects.

TAP is a project that primarily seeks to export gas to Italy, not to the Western Balkans. The vital variant is if the TAP pipeline expands through the Western Balkan markets through the Ionian Adriatic Pipeline (IAP). In any case the IAP could not have been implemented soon, having in mind that first the TAP pipeline needs to be constructed that will transit Caspian gas to Italy after crossing Turkey, Greece, and Albania, which will not happen before 2016 (see projected pipelines in "European Gas Pipeline Projects and Their Implications on Southeast Europe").

In addition to the problem with security, the problem of energy poverty in the Western Balkans must also be addressed. Energy poverty is connected with inadequate access to energy supplies, which leads to insufficient and unreliable access to electricity of a big part of the country's population that deprives them of the ability to service basic household needs. The lack of reliable electricity supply is a key barrier for economic development and investment in the Western Balkan region, the effect being particularly pronounced in Albania and Kosovo

(International Energy Agency 2008). This condition also results in grossly inefficient use of energy.

3 The Place of SEE in EU Energy Policy

Is the EU playing hard enough to gain influence and relevant place in the region of Southeast Europe? Does it realize this region's strategic significance for its own energy supply security?

This could be checked in the long-term vision for a pan-European energy infrastructure of the European Commission from 2011. In it a first set of Projects of Common Interest (PCIs) were outlined, which aim to support the better integration of EU member states' networks in order to facilitate the integration of renewable energy sources in the Union and diversify sources of gas supply by opening new gas corridors. This would be particularly important for member states, which are dependent on a single source of oil or gas supply.

The PCI list contains 250 projects in electricity and gas transmission storage and LNG, as well as in smart grids and in oil, whose goal is to make sure that the remaining energy islands are integrated as soon as possible (European Commission 2013a). It is envisaged also that the European neighboring countries are effectively integrated with the Union through adequate infrastructure networks and regulatory frameworks in line with the strategy outlined in the Communication on security of energy supply and international cooperation (European Commission 2013b).

Among the projects of common interest in the gas field the Southern Gas Corridor through the Trans-Adriatic Pipeline is included as an important milestone. It must be complemented in 2018, by timely implementation of the other projects identified, notably the Trans-Anatolian Pipeline. Its goal is to enhance the security of supply throughout the region and further diversify it by tapping on the gas resources in the Eastern Mediterranean region.

Eurogas, the association representing the European gas wholesale, retail and distribution sectors, outlines the steps the EU needs to make up to 2035 (Eurogas 2013a). The traditional aims outlined include guarantying future security of supply, support development of new technologies for exploration and exploitation, creation of stable and competitive fiscal and regulatory regimes and improvement of infrastructure, including new supply routes to Europe and LNG terminals. However, the association emphasis on the need for long-term relations of cooperation, including with third countries outside the Union, stating that even if overall the future of gas supply to the European Union is rather positive and there are no big concerns about the availability of future sources, the European gas industry recognizes the importance of fostering long-term relationships with major suppliers, transit countries and key EU partners (Eurogas 2013b).

The EU regulation on guidelines for trans-European energy infrastructure[5] includes the following component elements needed for the gas infrastructure: transmission pipelines for the transport of natural gas and bio gas that form part of a network, which mainly contains high-pressure pipelines, excluding high-pressure pipelines used for upstream or local distribution of natural gas; underground storage facilities connected to the above-mentioned high-pressure gas pipelines; reception, storage and regasification or decompression facilities for liquefied natural gas (LNG) or compressed natural gas (CNG).

The projects of common interest need to involve at least two member states, either by directly crossing the border of one or more member states or by being located on the territory of one member state and having a significant cross-border impact.

Among the identified trans-European energy infrastructure priority corridors are:

- the North-South gas interconnections in Central Eastern and South Eastern Europe ("NSI East Gas"): regional gas connections between the Baltic Sea region, the Adriatic and Aegean Seas and the Black Sea, notably to enhance diversification and security of gas supply, with member States concerned: Austria, Bulgaria, Cyprus, Czech Republic, Germany, Greece, Hungary, Italy, Poland, Romania, Slovakia and Slovenia;
- Southern Gas Corridor ("SGC"): transmission of gas from the Caspian Basin, Central Asia, the Middle East and the Eastern Mediterranean Basin to the Union to enhance diversification of gas supply, with member states concerned: Austria, Bulgaria, Czech Republic, Cyprus, France, Germany, Hungary, Greece, Italy, Poland, Romania, Slovakia and Slovenia.

The European Energy Security Strategy is closely linked to the 2030 policy framework on climate and energy. It concludes that the development of competitive and well-integrated markets in the Baltic States and Southeast Europe lags behind, depriving those regions of the related security of supply advantages. That's why the development of critical infrastructure, as well as the establishment of regional gas hubs in these regions is needed.

Twenty-seven projects in the field of natural gas have been identified in the strategy as critical for EU's energy security in the short and medium terms because their implementation is expected to enhance diversification of supply possibilities and solidarity in the most vulnerable parts of Europe. A great deal of them is located in Eastern Europe (Table 1).

Even though the region of Southeast Europe is well represented in the list of PCIs, it is obvious that these projects cover mainly the EU member states. Besides that the large scale projects, except for the LNG terminals and storage projects, are complex and prone to delays, and the possibilities to speed up their implementation

[5] The regulation of the European Parliament and of the Council on guidelines for trans-European energy infrastructure and repealing Decision No 1364/2006/EC, Brussels, 19.10.2011, COM (2011) 658 final.

Table 1 Key security of supply infrastructure projects in Southeast Europe, as outlined by the European Commission

#	Name of project	Details	Finished by
Short-term projects 2014–2016			
1.	EL-BG interconnector	New interconnector to support diversification and deliver Shah Deniz gas in Bulgaria. Status: permitting, EIA (2 years delay)	2016
2.	EL-BG reverse flow	Permanent reverse flow on the existing interconnector (alternative/complement to IGB). Status: pre-feasibility	2014
3.	BG: storage upgrade	Increase storage capacity in Chiren; Status: pre-feasibility	2017
4.	HU-HR reverse flow	Reverse flow enabling gas flows from Croatia to Hungary. Status: feasibility studies.	2015
5.	HU-RO reverse flow	Project to enable gas flows from Romania to Hungary. Status: feasibility studies	2016
6.	BG-RS interconnector	New interconnector supporting SoS in Bulgaria and Serbia. Status: EIA, routing, financing (issued with Srbijagas unbundling to access finance)	2016
Medium-term projects 2017–2020			
7.	TANAP (TR-EL)	Trans-Anatolian Natural Gas Pipe bringing Caspian gas to the EU via Turkey and opening the Southern Gas Corridor. Status: feasibility/final investment decision	2019
8.	TAP (EL-AL-IT)	Intra-EU section of the Southern Gas Corridor. Direct connection to TANAP. Status: permitting	2019
9.	IAP (AL-ME-HR)	New interconnector part of the Balkan Gas Ring and connected to TAP. Status: feasibility/FEED	2020
10.	HR—LNG terminal	New LNG terminal in Krk supporting SoS and diversification in the Region. Status: feasibility/FEED (financing issues)	2019
11.	BG: internal system	Rehabilitation and expansion of transport system needed for regional integration. Status: feasibility/FEED	2017 (tbc)
12.	RO: internal sys-tem and reverse flow to UA	Integration of the Romanian transit and transmission system and reverse flow to Ukraine. Status: feasibility study (regulatory issues with reverse flow)	Tbd
13.	EL: compressor station	Compressor station at Kipi to enable TANAP and TAP connection. Status: permitting.	2019
14.	EL: Alexandroupolis LNG terminal	New LNG terminal in Northern Greece. Status: permitting	2016–2017
15.	EL: Aegean LNG Terminal	New LNG floating terminal at Bay of Kavala. Status: feasibility/FEED, permitting	2016

Source: Annex 2: Status of Key Security of Supply Infrastructure Projects, European Energy Security Strategy

require more than just early support from the Connecting Europe Facility (CEF), which is the financial instrument, supporting PCIs. It is clear also, that the smaller and interconnector projects are also envisaged only in EU member states, except for the Bulgaria-Serbia interconnector. Fortunately the TAP project, which includes Albania, could become a strategic milestone in SEE gas infrastructure provided that it is followed by the development of the IAP, which would lead to the establishment of a regional gas network (see explanation of projects in "See Natural Gas Interconnectors").

In June 2014 the European Council welcomed the Commission's European Energy Security Strategy and called for increased efforts to reduce Europe's high energy dependency and immediate implementation of a set of most urgent measures to strengthen Europe's resilience and increase its energy security in before the winter of 2014/2015 (European Council 2014). In addition to that, in view of enhancing the EU's energy security, it insisted that energy infrastructure investments, including those involving third countries (which are in full respect of all the EU's internal market and competition rules) be consistently enforced. The European Council stated that the EU will engage with its international partners to reduce the risk of disruption of energy supplies, while the Energy Community, which aims to expand the EU's energy acquis to enlargement and neighbourhood countries, should be reinforced so as to ensure the application of the acquis in those countries. This means that the development of the gas sector in the SEE is still seen by the EU only as compliance with the EU sector rules and not with building infrastructure.

It can be concluded that the EU membership is an insurmountable factor for the Union's support for energy infrastructure development. Though it seems quite logical, however, it is not reasonable to believe that the EU non-members in SEE region would find on their own the necessary expertise, know-how, financing and political will to initiate and develop an acceptable gas infrastructure, complying with the needs of their countries and the EU in the region. It seems that the growing awareness among EU officials of the SEE's region importance appears only on paper. Hopefully, the events in Crimea and the deepening of the Ukraine crisis could be a turning point and provoke the EU to start to slowly change its position towards the region and realize the Western Balkans' strategic importance not only for the continent's stability, but also for its energy supply security, because otherwise it could very quickly fall under the growing non-European Eastern influence.

4 The Attitude of SEE Countries Towards Energy Policy and Regional Cooperation

As part of the EU Romania, Bulgaria and Greece stick to the Union's sector legislation and regulation, even though sometimes the process of harmonization is hard and slow. In 2013–2014 some doubts have been raised whether Bulgaria's activities connected with the planned South Stream Project are in full compliance with the European energy regulations, in particular with the Third package. The rest of the SEE countries, at present EU non-members, are indispensably connected with the European legislation via their membership in the Energy Community.

There are different evaluations of the role and efficiency of the Energy Community in the region of Southeast Europe. The objective of securing energy in "wider Europe" in a stable, sustainable and competitive manner lies at the heart of the Treaty establishing the Energy Community, signed in October 2005. By extending the internal energy market beyond the boundaries of the European Union, the Energy Community carries forward the success story of European integration in the crucial sector of energy (High Level Reflection Group of the Energy Community 2014).

The Energy Community defines itself is a "win-win instrument", as on the one hand, it contributes to ensuring energy security and affordable energy prices (which is an advantage for the EU), and on the other, it aims at increasing efficiency and transparency through reforms, attracting investment and reaching economic and social stability (which, if achieved, would be an advantage for the non-EU states).

However, despite progress made by many of the EU non-members, the adoption of the acquis remains a significant challenge. The main difficulties are connected with the energy market reform that the countries need to implement, i.e. the opening of energy markets and the launch of cross-border cooperation. In addition to that, the investment environment is not still attractive enough for private investors, mainly due to relatively low credibility of the local judicial systems.

Researchers and experts evaluate positively the development of the SEE regional energy market in the framework of the Energy Community. Despite the many remaining open issues before its effective functioning and integration with the other REMs in Europe, many steps and great reforms have been undertaken in the electricity markets of the SEE countries at national but also at cross-border level.

Another remarkable thing about the Energy Community is that while the other regional initiatives covered some of the previous regional integrations established by the market players and NRAs' in different parts of Europe, the idea for the SEE REM was born solely by external actors. The third legislative energy package also underlined the importance of establishing REMs as transitional steps towards a truly integrated internal energy market.

However, the European Union is strongly criticized and accused of applying a uniformed approach to regions inside and outside it, despite their differences. Namely the European Commission's motto is claimed to be "our size fits all" (Bicchi 2006), due to the so called inherent eurocentrism, as well as deep belief of the European Union that its model can be applied to solve policy problems elsewhere in the same manner as within the Union itself.

The Energy Community is a prototype of the European Union in Southeast Europe, where it exports its rules and regulations. External governance is the process of applying domestic solutions to political problems beyond the border (Karova 2011). This is how the EU intends to create a zone of extended governance around its borders and thus, export its legislation to European countries, which are not members of it. In Southeast Europe this intention has realized through common institutions in the energy field and commitment of all parties to implement the acquis in energy, environment, renewables and competition. The goal of the EU's energy policy is to build up a wide network of countries around it, which act on the basis of the Union's rules and principles. Thus, the export of its own regulatory rules in energy is an explicit external strategy of the European Union, which is a rule exporter in energy policy.

The reasons why this policy is quite acceptable for the Western Balkan countries are several. The first one is connected with the distant perspective for them to become EU members, and adopting the EU legislation is a requirement for that and for further approximation within the Stabilization and Association Process. On the other hand, the harmonization with European sector legislation is needed to create a favorable climate for investments in energy production and transit and thus contributes to the security of energy supply in SEE.

However, it may be argued whether this method of regional integration was the best possible. Even though regional cooperation in SEE is sometimes considered as identical to the European integration, there is a fundamental difference between the two. The idea of a Coal and Steel Community was developed by one of the six founders of the European Communities, while the idea to create an Energy Community in Southeast Europe was an initiative of the European Commission. Its institutional structures were "consciously modelled" on those of the EU (Karova 2011). Moreover, the countries of Southeast Europe did not create their own rules for the regulation of their energy sectors within these institutions but committed themselves to adopt the relevant EU legislation. The EU "reproduced itself" in Southeast Europe and projected internal solutions to its external relations. In the Energy Community the EU was a rule exporter and europeanized the countries by copying internal structures to the region of Southeast Europe.

Similarly to the EU, the SEE non-EU countries have also realized the need for EU financial and technical support for the construction of the gas infrastructure they need. Something more—they have realized the need to work in cooperation to achieve this. In 2010 the V4+ Energy Security Summit was held, where the SEE countries reaffirmed that common energy challenges could be better dealt with on the basis of regional cooperation as well as in the EU framework, and underlined the importance of promoting the European Union's external relations with new alternative suppliers of energy, as well as boosting the energy dialogue of the Union with the existing supply-and transit countries.

The countries recognize the lack of adequate interconnections and limited possibilities of reverse flow among the countries of the region and stress that joint planning and development of infrastructure for the transport and for the storage of natural gas and crude oil as well as the proper functioning of the EU internal energy market is necessary in order to enable solidarity reaction in case of crisis. They also reaffirm their support to develop the Southern Energy Corridor facilitating the access of countries of Central-, East- and Southeast-Europe to gas and oil supplies from the Caspian Sea region and the Middle East and approve the EU approach to guarantee its security of energy supply through infrastructure projects within and outside the Union.

The Western Balkans countries have even started to coordinate their short and long-term goals in the energy sector. In 2013 they adopted Strategy SEE 2020, which has a significant contribution to that. It identifies the key actions and measures in the energy field, which need to be implemented in order to increase the efficient use of energy in the region (Regional Cooperation Council 2014). This includes the achieving of a minimum 9 % energy saving target by 2018 (in line with the Energy Services Directive), as well as measures to achieve national share of renewable energy in final energy consumption by 2020 (through the Renewable Energy Directive). The countries also agree to develop instruments to create an investment friendly climate and stimulate energy infrastructure development, as well as to complement the ongoing regional energy cooperation. However, the Western Balkan countries themselves admit that the growth prospects of the region have deteriorated over the last years (2010–2013), which limit their fiscal abilities to make and expand the much needed infrastructure investments, including those in the energy sector.

Strategy SEE 2020 also foresees some other relevant regional energy cooperation activities like sustainable energy development through implementation of Sustainable Energy Development Regional Initiative (SEDRI). The main goals of this initiative are the improvement of legislative, institutional and regulatory frameworks in the energy sector; construction of small-scale sustainable energy facilities in each of the member countries and strengthening of a framework for regional cooperation in the field of sustainable energy development, including awareness raising, education, research and scientific cooperation.

The Danube Strategy[6] has also contributed to rising of the awareness among the Western Balkan countries of their necessity to follow the European path. The challenges in the energy field that it highlights are high energy prices in the region (in relative terms), as a result of fragmented markets that lead to higher costs and reduced competition and reliance on too few external suppliers, which increases vulnerability.

The strategy states that the quality of infrastructure, security of supply, market organization, unsustainable demand, energy efficiency, and use of renewables are often problematic in the countries concerned, and that the modernizing and extending energy networks, especially in terms of interconnectors, is essential.[7] The focus in this strategy is on the efforts necessary to improve energy efficiency, including energy saving and more renewable sources, although the strategic goal to

[6] Geographically the strategy covers Germany (Baden-Württemberg and Bavaria), Austria, the Slovak Republic, the Czech Republic, Hungary, Slovenia, Romania and Bulgaria, Croatia, Serbia, Bosnia and Herzegovina, Montenegro, the Republic of Moldova and Ukraine (the regions along the Danube).

[7] Communication from the Commission to the European parliament, the Council, the European economic and social committee and Committee of the Regions, European Union Strategy for Danube Region, COM(2010) 715 final, Brussels, 8.12.2010, p. 7.

diversify the supply through interconnections and achieve genuine regional markets that will increase energy security, is also clearly articulated.

It can be concluded that SEE countries, as signatories of the Energy Community Treaty, have embarked on a path of energy market reforms and regional integration. However, it could be argued still, whether this could happen in a different way, leaving the countries with certain autonomy or giving them the chance to speak as a specific region, which has its common characteristics and views about its own future.

Another conclusion with European implication is that the region is in an urgent need of financial and technical resources (different from their own) in order to develop a sustainable and reliable energy infrastructure that the region and the EU as a whole need. This is where the EU should substantially reconsider its goals and positions and prioritize Western Balkans' energy infrastructure in its long-term plans and commitments.

5 European Gas Pipeline Projects and Their Implications on Southeast Europe

It became clear that the resource-rich states of the Middle East and the Caspian Region are considered as main potential alternative sources for Europe for it to achieve energy diversification and security of supply. By 2013 the two rival gas projects were Nabucco and the South Stream, the latter not being a real diversification alternative as it would also be supplied by Russian gas. The major EU-supported Nabucco pipeline was projected to transport Caspian gas through Turkey across Bulgaria, Romania and Hungary into Austria.

The Blue Stream has to be a trans-Black Sea pipeline constructed by Gazprom (Russia) and ENI (Italy) to transport gas from Russia to Turkey. The same two companies are now involved in the South Stream pipeline project that would transport gas from the Russian coast of the Black Sea to Bulgaria, Greece and from there on a south-western route into southern Italy and on a north-western route into Serbia and Hungary, continuing on to Austria or northern Italy (Fig. 4).

In these circumstances, the Southeast European countries are of a crucial importance due to the fact that some of the biggest gas pipeline routes would pass through the territory of the region to be a link for transit deliveries of gas from Russia, the Middle East and the Caspian Sea to the countries in Central and Western Europe.

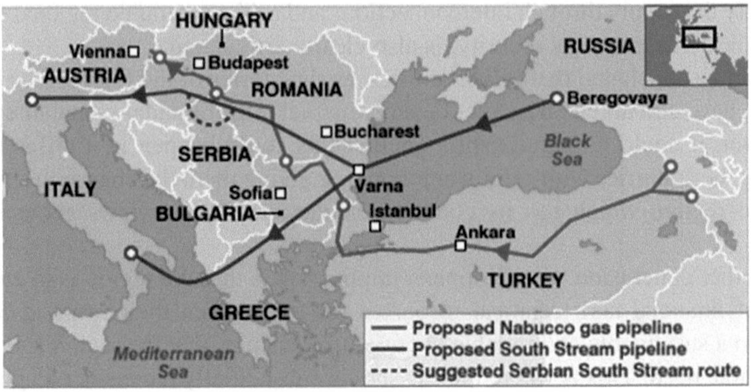

Fig. 4 Competing European (Nabucco) and Russian (South Stream) pipeline projects for a Eurasian gas corridor. *Source*: http://www.caspianresources.com/?q=node/12

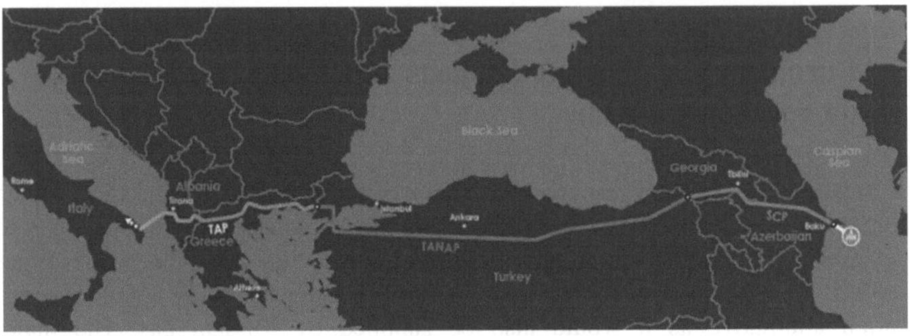

Fig. 5 The routes of TANAP and TAP pipeline projects. *Source*: http://www.tap-ag.com/the-pipeline

5.1 Nabucco

Nabucco was a project pipeline fully-supported by the EU and the USA for transporting natural gas from the Turkish-Georgian border or Turkish-Iraqi border to Baumgarten, Austria (Fig. 5). Participants in the project were the Bulgarian Energy Holding (BEH), BOTAS, Hungarian MOL, Austrian OMV Gas & Power, German RWE and Romanian Transgaz.

The annual transportation capacity of the gas pipeline was expected at around 31 billion cubic meters of natural gas. Within the early stages of the project the supplies were estimated at 16–17 billion cubic meters. It was expected that the full capacity of 31 billion cubic meters would be reached in 2020. The preliminary estimates of the project costs exceeded 10 billion euros.

The biggest challenge before the project was the provision of sufficient amounts of natural gas. Nabucco relied on the development of the Shah Deniz gas fields. However, other gas projects were also expected to feed Azeri gas from Shah Deniz into their pipes, which would strengthen competition. It was not unlikely that gas is negotiated from several places, the options being Kazakhstan, Turkmenistan, Northern Iraq and Iran.

The EU strongly supported the project that underlies the Southern Gas Corridor concept. The European Commission was even considering granting 250 million euros to enhance Nabucco. In early August 2010 all parties participating in the project gathered in Ankara to sign an agreement in support of Nabucco.

In July 2010, Bulgaria also demonstrated its support for the project by showing willingness to construct a gas connection with Turkey that will be the first operating section of the Nabucco pipeline. The implementation of this gas connection would provide Bulgaria and the EU an access to the gas resources of the Caspian Region and the Middle East.

However, in July 2013 the Nabucco pipeline project was annulled. The failure of the Nabucco project was due to a combination of geopolitical factors and business considerations. The Shah-Deniz II consortium, which runs the largest gas field in Azerbaijan, awarded the contract for the transportation of gas to the Trans Adriatic Pipeline (TAP), which runs through Greece and Albania and under the Adriatic Sea to Southern Italy.

The effect of the failure of the Nabucco project on SEE countries is considered significant and has negative implications on the region, except for Greece. It was positive for Greece, as it was replaced by the TAP project, which will run over Greek territory. While the country currently obtains the majority of its gas from Russia, it will likely soon become one of the largest importers of gas from Azerbaijan. Greek Prime Minister Antonis Samaras hailed TAP in a statement as "the most important and most positive development in the last ten years" for Greece, which would put the country on the international energy map (World Socialist Web site 2013).

For Bulgaria and Hungary, being involved in both projects, an end to Nabucco West was an end to the balancing act they had been performing with Russia and EU. For the past 2 years, Hungary and Bulgaria have benefited from competition between the two pipeline consortia. Russia gave Bulgaria and Hungary several incentives, including contract discounts, for their support of the South Stream pipeline at the expense of Nabucco West. The incentives notwithstanding, these two countries now find themselves nearly wholly dependent on Russian natural gas imports in the near future.

A big negative effect the failure on the project has on Romania, which finds itself without an EU-backed intercontinental pipeline project, which could also have helped the country economically through infrastructure investment and transit tariffs. It also prompted Romania to intensive the development of its own energy resources, namely the large hydrocarbon reserves. Romania still has vast untapped unconventional gas plays (shale in particular) and significant offshore deposits that have recently been exploited. However, the country lacks the money and the technology to pursue offshore and unconventional deposits by itself and needs to attract foreign investors. Western and Russian firms already are competing in the region, where Western firms hope to turn a profit from Romania and Russian firms want to mitigate the threat Romania poses as a potential rival to its energy dominance in the region. It seems like Romania is only one component of a much larger competition between the West and Russia for primacy in Central Europe (Nova Srpska Politichka Misao 2013).

Despite the project failure, the ability and possibility of Iran to supply the "Nabucco" pipeline has been repeatedly discussed lately on high level between Iran and uncited EU countries representatives. The condition for the project to be renewed with Iranian gas is agreement to be reached on the country's nuclear program. Moreover, Iran has reconfirmed its potential to deliver gas to Europe in the form of LNG (Mediapool.bg 2014).

5.2 TANAP and TAP

The Trans Anatolia Natural Gas Pipeline (TANAP) will provide the transportation of natural gas produced in Shah Deniz 2 field and other fields of Azerbaijan (and other possible neighboring countries) through Turkey to Europe. Memorandum of Understanding was signed between the governments of Turkey and Azerbaijan in December 2011. The companies appointed upon a joint consortium constituting of the State Oil Company of Azerbaijan (SOCAR), and Petroleum Pipeline Corporation of Turkey (BOTAS) and/or Turkish Petroleum Corporation (TPAO).

The project starts from the Georgia-Turkey border and crosses the whole country (Fig. 5).

The planned capacity of the pipeline will be 16 billion cubic meters per year at the initial stage reaching 60 billion cubic meters at the final stage. The pipeline will not be built under the direction of the EU (like Nabucco would be), but instead primarily under the control of Turkey and Azerbaijan. The laying of the TANAP and TAP pipelines will increase the geopolitical importance of these two countries as EU energy partners. The Trans Adriatic Pipeline (TAP) will transport Caspian natural gas to Europe (Fig. 6). Connecting with the TANAP at the Greek-Turkish border, TAP will cross Northern Greece, Albania and the Adriatic Sea before coming ashore in Southern Italy to connect to the Italian natural gas network.[8] The project is in implementation phase, preparing for construction, which will start in 2016.

It is expected that the TAP will be a direct and cost-effective transportation route opening up the vital Southern Gas Corridor, a 3500-km long pipeline from the Caspian Sea to Europe. Since it will enhance energy security and diversify gas supplies for several European markets, the TAP project is supported by the EU and seen as a "*Project of Common Interest*" and a part of the Southern Gas Corridor.

[8] When the feasibility study was concluded in March 2006, two route options were investigated: a northern route through Bulgaria, FYROM and Albania, and a southern route through Greece and Albania, which finally was considered to be more feasible.

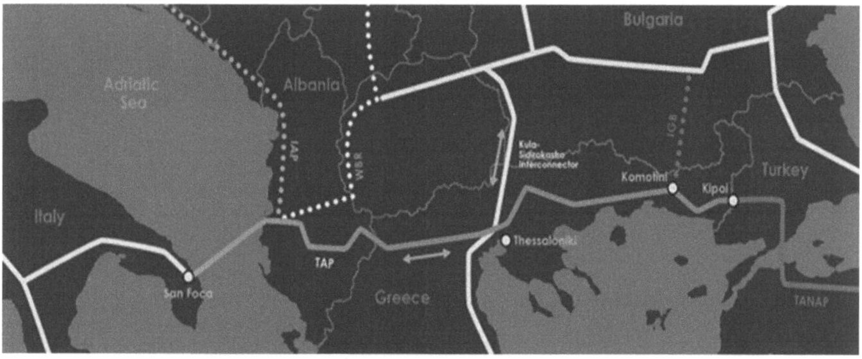

Fig. 6 The route of TAP pipeline project. *Source*: http://www.tap-ag.com/the-pipeline

On 28 September 2012, Albania, Greece and Italy confirmed their political support for the pipeline by signing a memorandum of understanding. In February 2013, Greece, Italy and Albania signed an intergovernmental agreement.

The project is supported by the EU that aims at decreasing its energy dependence on Russia and diversifying gas supplies. The European Parliament and the Council of Europe recognize TAP as per the guidelines of the Trans-European Energy Network (TEN-E). TAP has officially been acknowledged as the connecting pipeline of the EU between Greece, Albania and Italy.

EU Commissioner for Energy Oettinger stated in May 2010 that TAP is an interesting project that would supplement Nabucco, and as it could be implemented fast, it counted on the Union's support (Oettinger 2010). He thinks that Europe needs to tap into enormous gas resources in the Caspian region, in particular the second stage of the Shah Deniz gas field in Azerbaijan, and not leave them to be developed for China, Russia and Iran. It's also his words that despite the current global oversupply in natural gas, various pipeline projects need to be built to secure energy supply for decades to come.

TAP has positive implications on the region of Southeast Europe. It will supply gas to SEE countries, contributing to their energy supply and diversification. The Shah Deniz Consortium signed gas sales agreements in September 2013 with buyers in Europe, including energy companies in Greece and Bulgaria.

Acknowledging the boost this would give to their economic and social development, the governments of Albania, Bosnia and Herzegovina, Croatia, and Montenegro signed a Memorandum of Understanding (MoU) in support of TAP in May 2013. The same countries also agreed to support the proposed Ionian Adriatic Pipeline, which is planned to connect with TAP in Albania, making that country the gateway for Caspian gas to enter the West Balkans. Other energy markets in the region, such as Bulgaria, Slovenia, Hungary, Serbia and FYROM, could also benefit from TAP.

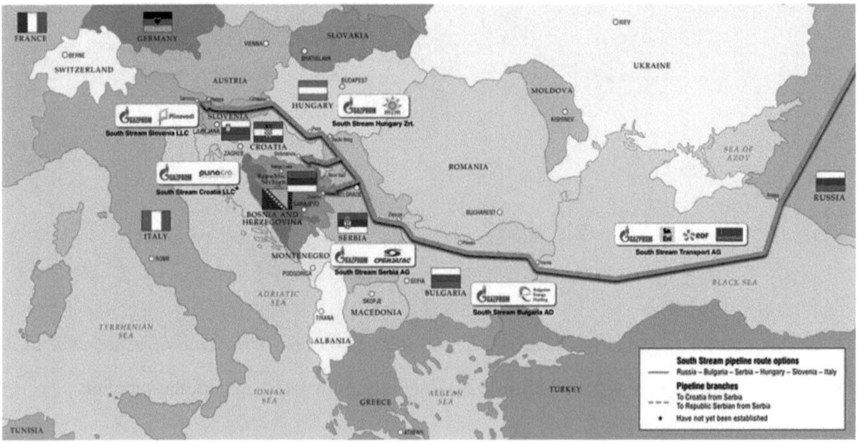

Fig. 7 The route of South Stream pipeline project. *Source*: http://www.south-stream.info/

5.3 South Stream Pipeline

Responding to Nabucco, Russia built the North Stream pipeline, which has been exporting gas from Russia under the Baltic Sea to Germany since 2011. In this way, it has bypassed transit countries such as Ukraine and Belarus. In addition, Russia took on the South Stream project (Fig. 7) in 2007, which has to be completed by 2018.

Intergovernmental agreements were signed with Bulgaria, Serbia, Hungary, Greece, Slovenia, Austria and Croatia in order to implement the onshore gas pipeline section. These agreements stipulate preparation of the feasibility study for South Stream construction in the project host countries, as well as creation of joint ventures between Gazprom and national energy companies authorized for the gas pipeline construction.

The total length of the gas transmission system will account for 2446 km. The execution period is from September 2010 to December 2019, whereas Eni (Italy), Wintershall Holding (Germany) and EDF (France) are Gazprom's partners for the offshore part.

On Russian land, the pipeline passes through eight federation constituents. There are several options of the South Stream route across the Black Sea. At the moment, the route passing through the exclusive economic zones of Russia, Turkey and Bulgaria is being worked out as primary. There were two optional routes for the onshore gas pipeline section: either to the northwest or southwest of Bulgaria. The northwest includes the pipeline passing through Pleven (Bulgaria), then deviating to Romania, crossing Serbia, passing through Hungary and/or Slovenia and reaching Austria. The southwest included the pipeline deviating in Pleven towards Thessaloniki where, passing through the Ionian Sea, it reaches the Italian coast at Otranto.

It is said that the South Stream project is aimed at strengthening the European energy security, and that it is a key project in the diversification strategy for gas supply routes to the EU. However, the diversification of EU gas supply with this project is not certain, because, after all, its source remains Russia. Even worse—it would probably increase Russian influence in the region of SEE. President Putin used to consider the launch of the project to lay the South Stream gas pipeline across Serbia as an event of major importance for Serbia and the Balkan countries, and for the whole of Europe (Voice of Russia 2013). He stated that South Stream will connect Russia's rich gas fields to the main markets in Southeast Europe, guaranteeing reliable gas shipments to the European consumers without transit risks and that this is expected to strongly consolidate international energy security. He also expected that the "unprecedented in scope" project construction will help to attract large investments in Serbia and other Balkan countries, creating employment and promoting socioeconomic development, and it will also turn Serbia into a "key energy center" in Europe after its gas transportation system is broadened and modernized.

Currently South Stream is in danger following the Crimea crisis, and the decision of EU leaders at their summit on 20–21 March 2014 to come up with a plan for decreasing energy dependence, primarily from Russia.

EU Energy Commissioner Oettinger's spokesperson said on 10 March 2014 that the EU executive had to take into account broader political developments, including the Crimea crisis. South Stream is facing problems, as the Italian oil major ENI, one of the key shareholders in South Stream, has expressed second thoughts about the project. With the deepening of the EU-Russia crisis over Ukraine, the project's implementation is temporarily under question, being stopped politically by the European Commission under doubts of incompliance of the Bulgarian contractors of the project.

5.4 *Ionian Adriatic Pipeline*

The Ionian Adriatic Pipeline (IAP) is a proposed natural gas pipeline in the Western Balkans.

It would run from Fier in Albania through Montenegro and Bosnia and Herzegovina to Split in Croatia. In Fier, IAP would be connected with the planned Trans Adriatic Pipeline. In Split the pipeline would be connected with the existing gas transmission system of Croatia (Fig. 8).

The ministerial declaration on the IAP project was signed on 25 September 2007 in the framework of the Energy Community. Trans Adriatic Pipeline AG has signed memorandums with understanding with developers of the IAP project, including Plinacro (Croatia), BH-Gas (Bosnia and Herzegovina), and governments of Montenegro and Albania. Croatia, Montenegro and Bosnia and Herzegovina joined Albania in backing TAP because they want it to build the Ionian-Adriatic Pipeline from TAP's possible landing point in Albania to supply them with gas and diversify

Fig. 8 The route of Ionian Adriatic pipeline project. *Source*: http://www.naturalgaseurope.com/tap-plan-start-pipeline-construction-2016

it, since they are also dependent on Russian natural gas imports. However, the project could not start before the completion of the TAP pipeline, which is in initial phase and would not be ready before 2016.

6 SEE Natural Gas Interconnectors

There are several important gas interconnector projects in Southeast Europe, which are on different stages of implementation. On first place, these are the interconnectors of Bulgaria with four of its five neighboring countries (all except for FYROM)—Romania, Serbia, Greece and Turkey. These projects are of extreme importance for the European single gas market, but even more they are urgently needed for Bulgaria's fast and efficient gas supply security, as well as diversification.

Even though the construction of the gas interconnections between Bulgaria and its neighboring countries has slowed significantly since the crisis of January 2009, when the dispute between Ukraine and Russia cut supplies to Bulgaria, the perspectives are good. By the end of 2014 the interconnection Bulgaria—Romania is expected to be launched. The delay was caused by improperly implemented preliminary geological surveys on the bottom of the Danube River. By the end of the year, the pipe must be able to supply natural from Romania with capacity of 1.5 billion cubic meters per year, which is slightly less than half of the total gas consumption in Bulgaria. In this situation, even if the pressure between Ukraine and Russia escalates and leads to stoppage of supply, it would not be so hard for

Bulgaria as in 2009. Romania can also import gas from Austria, through its reverse link where besides Russian, reaches also Norwegian gas.

The interconnection Bulgaria—Greece, which will link the gas stations in Komotini and Stara Zagora, is with planned capacity of 1.5 billion cubic meters per year. This, together with the possible imports from Romania, even exceeds the total consumption in Bulgaria. At the end of 2016 the project must be completed, and there is a plan also, which will be clarified whether a terminal for import of LNG will be built in Greece.

Relations with Turkey and Serbia develop more slowly, probably as they are not EU member states. This makes the projects' procedures and funding slow and difficult.

Another major SEE interconnector is the Italy-Greece gas connection (IGI Poseidon). It is a joint project of the Greek state-owned gas company DEPA (50 %) and the Italian private company Edison (50 %). The project is part of a bigger gas connection between Italy, Greece and Turkey—Italy-Greece-Turkey Interconnector (ITGI). The ITGI is a natural gas transportation project proposed in the framework of the Southern Gas Corridor. It was proposed for the transportation of natural gas from Azerbaijan's Shah Deniz gas field Phase II to markets in Europe via Greece and Italy. The Turkey–Greece pipeline was completed in 2007 while the future of the Greece–Italy pipeline project is unclear due to the competing Trans Adriatic Pipeline. If implemented, the pipeline would be the first link with the Caspian area.

The Serbia-Croatia interconnection is another planned gas project, which would have a positive effect not only on the EU, but also for Serbia, one of the few Western Balkan countries, which will receive the Union's support for its gas infrastructure.

7 Conclusion

The EU countries and institutions reasonably have grown increasingly concerned with energy security. The cut-off of gas supplies to Ukraine by Gazprom in 2005 opened the eyes of the Union. In addition to that, despite the decreasing gas demand, the import dependency of the EU on natural gas increases. The region of SEE is even more problematic, adding to the high natural gas import dependence, the lack of developed gas infrastructure that could bring to the region economic benefits and bigger security of supply. That is why, the European Commission was assigned to find alternative routes and projects to guarantee the Union's sustainable energy supply. The projects it has prioritized concern mainly or almost exclusively the EU member states, even though the major pipeline projects (mainly from the Caspian Sea) cross the region of SEE in countries outside the Union. Besides that, in the context of EU-Russian energy relations, the EU as a body has recognized Turkey's potential value as a relatively secure and independent route for importing non-Russian energy supplies.

The Western Balkan countries are expected to meet the opportunities and challenges of accession, as well as to respond and comply with the EU energy regulation as a requirement to receive the Union's support in the energy field. However, the process of this sector's harmonization in these countries is hard and slow, and the expected by them European financial support for energy infrastructure—uncertain and limited.

The hypothesis that the region of Southeast Europe is an island of missing connectivity in the European gas infrastructure proves true. The prospects seem bright only for the EU members states, which either will host the big gas pipeline projects (Greece), or which will benefit from the interconnectors established with neighboring countries (Bulgaria). The investment in member states gas infrastructure will contribute to the creation of real single energy market in the EU, but excluding the countries outside of the Union. The TAP project could bring gas to the region, provided that after its construction, the IAP is constructed and linked to it. At the present moment, what is left for the EU non-members is to continue the efforts towards compliance with the EU sector regulation and legislation, under the auspices of the Energy Community, as only under these circumstances they could continue to receive any EU support for their natural gas projects. However, this is insufficient having in mind the need of the region for investment in strategic gas infrastructure, and will have even bigger negative consequences for the European Union in middle and long-term in terms of lost physical and political positions in the region, on the contrary of the growing Eastern and non-European influence.

References

Bechev, D. (2012). Dynamics and achievements of regional cooperation. In P. Stubbs & C. Solioz (Eds.), *Towards open regionalism in South East Europe* (pp. 71–89). Baden-Baden: Nomos.

Bicchi, F. (2006). 'Our size fits all': Normative power Europe and the Mediterranean. *Journal of European Public Policy, 13*(2), 202, Special Issue: What kind of power? European Foreign Policy in Perspective.

Bilgin, M. (2009). Geopolitics of European natural gas demand: Supplies from Russia, Caspian and the Middle East. *Energy Policy, 37*(11), 4482–4492.

Chavdarova, M. (2012). *Interesi i vazmojnosti za satrudnichestvo mejdu darjavite ot Yugoiztochna Evropa [Interests and opportunities for cooperation between the Southeastern countries]*. Sofia: UNWE.

CSIS, & EKEM. (2010). *Re-linking the Western Balkans: The energy dimension.* CSIS-EKEM Policy Report. CSIS and EKEM. Retrieved September 20, 2014, from http://csis.org/files/publication/100921_CSIS-EKEM_PolicyReport3.pdf

ENTSO-G. (2014). *Summer supply outlook 2014*. ENTSOG. Retrieved June 14, 2014, from http://www.entsog.eu/public/uploads/files/publications/Outlooks%20&%20Reviews/2014/SO007_140423_SO2014_SR2013.pdf

Erdogdu, E. (2010). Bypassing Russia: Nabucco project and its implications for the European gas security. *Renewable and Sustainable Energy Reviews, 14*, 2936–2945.

Eurogas. (2013a). *Long term outlook for gas to 2035*. Eurogas. http://www.eurogas.org/uploads/media/Eurogas_Brochure_Long-Term_Outlook_for_gas_to_2035.pdf

Eurogas. (2013b). *Long-term outlook for gas demand and supply 2007–2030*. Eurogas. http://www.eurogas.org/uploads/media/Statistics_Eurogas_LT_Outlook_2007-2030_Final_25.11.10.pdf

European Commission. (2013a). Commission delegated regulation of 14 October 2013 (C(2013) 6766 final) amending Regulation (EU) No 347/2013 of the European Parliament and of the Council on guidelines for trans-European energy infrastructure as regards the Union list of projects of common interest.

European Commission. (2013b). Commission communication to the European Parliament, the Council, the European Economic and Social Committee and the Committee of Regions of 7 September 2011 on security of energy supply and international cooperation COM(2011) 539 final, The EU energy policy: Engaging with partners beyond our borders.

European Commission. (2014). Commission In-depth study of European Energy Security COM (2014) 330 final of 2 July 2014. Accompanying the document communication from the Commission to the Council and the European Parliament: European energy security strategy.

European Council. (2014). Council conclusions of the European Council on 26/27 June 2014, EUCO 79/14.

European Parliament. (2013). Regulation (EU) No 1316/2013 of the European Parliament and the Council of 11 December 2011 establishing the Connecting Europe Facility, amending Regulation (EU) No 913/2010 and repealing Regulations (EC) No 680/2007 and (EC) No 67/2010.

High Level Reflection Group of the Energy Community. (2014). *An energy community for the future*. High Level Reflection Group of the Energy Community. Retrieved May 19, 2014, from https://www.energy-community.org/portal/page/portal/ENC_HOME/DOCS/3178024/Energy_Community_HLGR_Report_FINAL_WEB.pdf

International Energy Agency. (2008). *Energy in the Western Balkans: The path to reform and reconstruction*. Paris: United Nations Development Programme.

Karova, R. (2011). Regional electricity markets in Europe: Focus on the energy community. *Utilities Policy, 19*(2), 80–86.

Mansfield, E., & Milner, H. (1999). The new wave of regionalism. *International Organization, 53*(3), 589–627.

Mavrakis, D., Thomaidis, F., & Ntroukas, I. (2006). An assessment of the natural gas supply potential of the south energy corridor from the Caspian Region to the EU. *Energy Policy, 34*(13), 1671–1680.

Mediapool.bg. (2014, August 11). *Iran ready to give gas for the stopped Nabucco project. Mediapool.bg*. [online]. Retrieved August 12, 2014, from http://www.mediapool.bg/iran-gotov-da-dade-gaz-za-spryaniya-proekt-nabuko-news223581.html

Nova Srpska Politichka Misao. (2013, July 13). *The Nabucco West Project comes to an end*. Nova Srpska Politichka Misao. Retrieved July 13, 2013, from http://www.nspm.rs/nspm-in-english/the-nabucco-west-project-comes-to-an-end.html

Oettinger, G. (2010, May 31). *EU Energy Commissioner Guenther Oettinger on TAP, TAP internet site*. Retrieved May 31, 2014, from http://www.tap-ag.com/news-and-events/2010/05/31/eu-energy-commissioner-guenther-oettinger-on-tap

Regional Cooperation Council. (2014). *South East Europe 2020 Strategy—Jobs and prosperity in a European perspective*. Retrieved April 20, 2014, from http://www.rcc.int/files/user/docs/SEE%202020%20Strategy%20Document%20-%20Draft%201.pdf

Remme, U., Blesl, M., & Fahl, U. (2008). Future European gas supply in the resource triangle of the Former Soviet Union, the Middle East and Northern Africa. *Energy Policy, 36*(5), 1622–1641.

Spanjer, A. (2007). Russian gas price reform and the EU-Russia gas relationship: Incentives, consequences and European security of supply. *Energy Policy, 35*(5), 2889–2898.

Tsachevski, V. (2010). *Bulgaria i Balkanite. Evropeizaciata ne e zavarshila [Bulgaria and the Balkans. The Europeanization has not finished]*. Sofia: Iztok-Zapad Publishing House.

Voice of Russia. (2013, November 24). *Putin: South stream will turn Serbia into key European energy center*. Voice of Russia. Retrieved March 15, 2014, http://voiceofrussia.com/news/2013_11_24/South-Stream-will-turn-Serbia-into-key-European-energy-center-Putin-3729/

World Socialist Web site. (2013, July 13). *European Union's Nabucco pipeline project aborted*. World Socialist Web site. Retrieved March 10, 2014, from http://www.wsws.org/en/articles/2013/07/13/nabu-j13.html

MIX
Papier aus verantwortungsvollen Quellen
Paper from responsible sources
FSC® C105338

If you have any concerns about our products,
you can contact us on
ProductSafety@springernature.com

In case Publisher is established outside the EU,
the EU authorized representative is:
Springer Nature Customer Service Center GmbH
Europaplatz 3, 69115 Heidelberg, Germany

Printed by Libri Plureos GmbH
in Hamburg, Germany